T0324136

Corporate Strategy and Sustainability

Corporate Strategy and Sustainability is a substantially updated, detailed overview of sustainability issues for business and economics students. Built to teach the evolution of the history of sustainability practices, this edition has expanded coverage of social sustainability issues, non-Western perspectives and sustainable supply chains. Rich in cases, these too have been updated to demonstrate best practice and the practical application of theory. Extensive discussions of tools show how to incorporate sustainability issues into strategic decision making. The book accentuates the value and importance of a strong sustainability approach in an age of climate change emergency. This textbook is an ideal companion to instructors and students of sustainability in business, economics, and management.

Peter N. Nemetz received a PhD in Economics from Harvard University and is Professor Emeritus of Strategy and Business Economics in the Sauder School of Business at the University of British Columbia, Canada. For twenty-nine years he held a visiting research position in the Department of Health Sciences Research at Mayo Clinic in Rochester, Minnesota. He has published more than one hundred books, academic articles, and consulting reports in the areas of natural disaster economics, natural resource and environmental economics and policy, international business, sustainability, and epidemiology. His most recent works include: *The Economics and Business of Sustainability* (Routledge 2022) and *Unsustainable World: Are We Losing the Battle to Save our Planet?* (Routledge Earthscan 2022).

Corporate Strategy and Sustainability

from Excellence to Fraud

Peter N. Nemetz

Routledge
Taylor & Francis Group

LONDON AND NEW YORK

Designed cover image: [COVER PHOTOGRAPH BY AUTHOR: PUFFIN COLONY, ISLE OF MAY, NORTH SEA OFF OF SCOTLAND]

First published 2025
by Routledge
4 Park Square, Milton Park, Abingdon, Oxon OX14 4RN

and by Routledge
605 Third Avenue, New York, NY 10158

Routledge is an imprint of the Taylor & Francis Group, an informa business

British Library Cataloguing-in-Publication Data
A catalogue record for this book is available from the British Library

ISBN: 978-0-367-77313-7 (hbk)
ISBN: 978-0-367-77312-0 (pbk)
ISBN: 978-1-003-17075-4 (ebk)

DOI: 10.4324/9781003170754

Typeset in Sabon
by Apex CoVantage, LLC

To my parents, Nathan and Bel, and my dearest wife, Roma, and our daughter, Fiona, who are the rock-solid foundation on which I have built my life's work.

Contents

List of Tables

List of Figures

Preface

This book is the third in a trilogy of works by the author devoted to the subject of sustainability, arguably the defining issue of this and future generations. The first work, entitled: *The Economics and Business of Sustainability* (2021) provides an overview of the interlinked economic and ecological concepts central to the new discipline of Ecological Economics. The theoretical discussion is supplemented with an array of real-world supporting data from Asia, Europe, and North America. The second work, *Unsustainable World: Are we losing the battle to save our planet* (2022) uses a cross-disciplinary, science- and economics-based approach to provide a sobering and comprehensive assessment of the multifaceted barriers to achieving sustainability at a global level. The volume outlines the sustainability challenges faced in transportation, manufacturing and agriculture, and then in turn addresses the solutions, conditional solutions and nonsolutions to these challenges. These include electric and autonomous automobiles, nuclear power, renewable energy, geoengineering, and carbon capture and storage.

The rationale for undertaking the daunting task of producing these books arose after many years of teaching courses in environmental policy, energy economics and, more recently, sustainability and business. The subject matter of sustainable development is, by definition, multidisciplinary and this presents numerous challenges to the amassing of its diverse subject matter within the covers of any one book. It is a tribute to the power of the modern concept of sustainability that so many books are now available on this subject. However, instructors tasked with distilling this material within a classroom setting whether for junior and senior level undergraduates or Masters students in business schools, economics departments and schools of public policy and government, must grapple with relatively few comprehensive treatments of the subject. The large array of books on the subject tend to fall into one of two general categories: (a) highly specialized, uni-disciplinary studies in such areas as marketing and accounting, or (b) broad and generally exhortatory works on sustainability and corporate strategy.

I suspect that most instructors in the area of sustainability and business, like myself, have been forced to cobble together a broad range of snippets from articles and books rather than being able to rely to some degree on a single work as a core source of material. This textbook and the two books immediately preceding it are an attempt to fill part of this gap. As such, the work included has, out of necessity, omitted certain business sub-disciplines such as sustainable marketing which are addressed in much greater detail in textbooks devoted solely to their analysis. This textbook focuses primarily on the inter-related areas of science, policy, economics, ecology, and corporate strategy.

The underlying message is that active buy-in by the business community to the concept and practice of sustainability is an absolutely necessary, although not sufficient, prerequisite for attaining global sustainability – necessary because the lion's share of economic activity is provided by commercial actors; not sufficient in and by itself because, despite the best of intentions, corporations need a level playing field and clear rules of the game, supplemented by regulations and economic incentives, which can only be provided by government.

The production of this work has been a labor of love, driven by many hundreds of hours of lively classroom interaction with students with inquiring and open minds from the United States, Canada and a broad range of countries in Latin America, Europe and Asia. It is because of them that I undertook this task which, in retrospect, was much more work than I ever realized. In addition to the many students who have inspired me to continue teaching in this field for almost four decades, I owe a deep debt of gratitude to numerous individuals who have contributed in one way or another to this book. To name but a few: the late Bert Allsopp, the late Ray Anderson, Ken Baker, Dyhia Belhabib, Harald Bergsteiner, John Blatherwick, Mark Bodnar, David Brand, Bill Cafferata, Jim Caudle, Linda Coady, Rand Cowell, Mikhail Davis, Timothy A. Dignam, Duncan Dow, Samantha Du Plessis, Ian Gill, Karin Goodison, Bettina von Hagen, Buddy Hay, Lauren Dekleva Haynes, Oyvind Jorgensen, Shona Kelly, John Lampman, Michelle Laurie, Todd Litman, Kim McGrail, Chris Milly, Gideon Mordecai, Jane Pan, Amelie Pelletier, Cassie Phillips, Rob Prins, Juan Reyero, Howard Rohm, Andrew Simms, Michael Vitt, Benedikt Wittmann, and Donovan Woolard. I also owe thanks to academic colleagues, Alan Abramson, Werner Antweiler, Joel Bakan, the late John Grace, Charlie Krebs, Daniel Pauly, Sue Pollock, Jerome Robles, Jordan Samaha, the late David Shindler, Rashid Sumaila, Peter Timmer, Peter Tyedmers, and Scott Valentine. Finally, I wish to single out several former students in particular who have been of immense help in this undertaking: Jana Hanova, Simon Bager, Patrick Dore, Cristina Infante, Jane Lister, Judy Feng and Rebecca Gu. It goes without saying that all of these individuals must be absolved of any responsibility for any oversights or errors that I may have committed. I also am very grateful to four anonymous reviewers whose detailed comments have significantly improved this work.

Finally, I owe my deepest gratitude to two people in particular: my daughter, Dr. Fiona Danks, who brought her scientific expertise to the task of reviewing several chapters for errors in science; and especially to my dearly beloved wife, Roma, who stoically endured the many evenings when I barricaded myself in our home office until all hours feverishly engaged in continuous revisions of these three books.

A Brief Note on the Origin of this Volume

An earlier book by this author (*Business and the Sustainability Challenge. An Integrated Perspective*, 2013) provided an integrated view of ecological and economic/business issues in sustainability. Much has changed since that date and the publisher requested an updated version in light of feedback from academics in several American business schools. Providing a comprehensive update to the 2013 textbook would have led to an unduly long revised volume, so the publisher requested that the book by revised and reissued as two separate volumes. Part One of this update was published in 2021 under the title: *The Economics and Business of Sustainability*. This second volume represents the final part of the original textbook devoted to corporate strategy and sustainability. It has been revised, updated, and expanded to include new material on the current and evolving ecological global situation and financial environment, current corporate initiatives (including ESG, net zero and carbon neutrality), two major new case studies (chapter 11 on aquaculture and chapter 15 on automobiles), and five new short cases (chapter 16).

Writing a book on sustainability presents an unusual challenge as the field is advancing rapidly, both theoretically and empirically. During manuscript preparation, it has been necessary to revise each chapter on a near-weekly basis. This experience brings to mind the words of Lewis Carroll's Red Queen in *Through the Looking Glass*: "It takes all the running you can do, to keep in the same place" (Carroll 1945, p. 42). Facing this challenge requires a certain degree of caution about making predictions about future prospects, for fear that future events – both near and midterm – will render them irrelevant. The author hopes that the reader will bear this caveat in mind given the inevitable delay between submission of the final manuscript to the publisher and the time the book reaches the reader.

Peter N. Nemetz
Vancouver, B.C.
October 2024

References

Carroll, Lewis (1945). *Through the Looking Glass and what Alice Found There*. The MacMillan Company.
Nemetz, Peter N. (2013). *Business and the Sustainability Challenge*. Routledge.
Nemetz, Peter N. (2021). *The Economics and Business of Sustainability*. Routledge.
Nemetz, Peter N. (2022). *Unsustainable World: Are we Losing the Battle to Save Our Planet?* Routledge.

A Brief Note on Case Study Analysis

Ask yourself:

1. Where does the company lie on Valentine's scale of corporate sustainability (Table 1.1)?
2. Is the corporation sustainable? If so, what criteria are you using? If not, what would it take to become sustainable?
3. What are the corporation's strategic options and prospects?
4. If you are an investor, would you buy, hold or sell the company's stock? How would this vary depending on what type of investor you are (Figure 19.1)?

Other Books by the Author

Editor, *Energy Policy: The Global Challenge*, Butterworth & Co. (Canada) Ltd., Montreal, 1979.

Editor, *Resource Policy: International Perspectives*, Montreal, 1980.

Editor, *Energy Crisis—Policy Response*, Montreal, 1981.

Economic Incentives for Energy Conservation, New York, 1984 (with Marilyn Hankey).

Editor, *The Pacific Rim: Investment, Development and Trade*, 1987.

Editor, *The Pacific Rim: Investment, Development and Trade*, 2nd revised edition, 1990.

Editor, *Emerging Issues in Forest Policy*, 1992.

Editor, *The Vancouver Institute: An Experiment in Public Education*, 1998.

Editor, *Bringing Business On Board: Sustainable Development and the B-School Curriculum*, 2002, co-sponsored by the National Round Table for the Environment and the Economy.

Editor, *Sustainable Resource Management: Reality or Illusion?*, 2007.

Business and the Sustainability Challenge, Routledge, 2013.

Co-editor, *Reflections of Canada. Illuminating our Opportunities and Challenges at 150+ years*, 2017 (with Philippe Tortell and Margot Young).

The Economics and Business of Sustainability, Routledge, 2021.

Unsustainable World: Are we losing the battle to save our planet? Routledge, 2022.

Part 1

Introductory Material

1 Introduction and Context

Sustainability is arguably the most critical issue facing humankind in history. Driven principally by climate change, the challenges of sustainability affect directly and indirectly virtually all aspects of global economics, society, ecology, and human health. What poses the greatest challenge is the apparent acceleration of climate change. This exponential phenomenon is driven by a series of positive feedback loops as illustrated in Figure 1.1

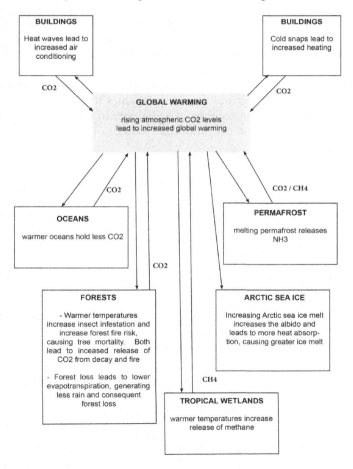

Figure 1.1 Some Major Positive Feedback Loops

DOI: 10.4324/9781003170754-2

(see Nemetz 2022). Corporations must be cognizant of this phenomenon in the form of increased number and intensity of storms, floods, fires, drought, and heatwaves as they may affect their supply chains, production, distribution, and ultimate use of their products. Appendix One provides a summary of exponential growth. This book focusses on the central role that business must play in addressing this overarching challenge.

Given its central role in our economic system, business and its production of goods and services is a key player in any attempt to achieve sustainability. The word *sustainability* has entered the lexicon of the modern corporation as most of the largest companies in North America and Europe have incorporated the concept into either their annual reports or stand-alone reports devoted exclusively to a discussion of sustainability. Corporate acceptance of this concept can be mapped on a continuum all the way from full-throttled embrace to begrudging and mere token reference. In an insightful analysis, Scott Valentine (2006) created a typology of corporate environmental governance coupled with an empirical metric for signalling the level of commitment based on qualitative and quantitative content of annual corporate reporting documents. Table 1.1 defines the five levels of corporate buy-in. Level 1 – the most committed – are deemed as leaders who are companies that have embraced the thrust of Michael Porter and Claas van der Linde's landmark *Harvard Business Review* article of 1995. In this seminal work, Porter discards the traditional false dichotomy between pollution control and corporate profitability. His thesis is that corporate strategy that recognizes, addresses, and incorporates issues of sustainability can yield significant and sustainable competitive advantage.

At the other end of Valentine's spectrum is Level 5 – avoiders – who make passing reference to the concept or avoid mentioning it all together. In fact, a sixth category can be added to this typology: a select number of companies that have consciously and illegally engaged in activity that compromises sustainability in the pursuit of profit. It can be argued that this pursuit of short-term profitability is not only counterproductive from a

Table 1.1 Corporate Levels of Sustainability Buy-In

Level	Are Defined As:	Which Appears in Environmental Reports As:
Level 1 – Leaders	Firms committed to setting quantitative benchmarks in environmental initiatives	Quantitative progress indicators related to environmental issues
Level 2 – Contenders	Firms that have adopted externally accredited environmental management systems	Specific reference made to ISO14000 or EMAS accreditation
Level 3 – Talkers	Firms that are currently experimenting with the effectiveness of environmental management initiatives	Qualitative stand-alone environmental reports
Level 4 – Pretenders	Firms that understand the threat posed by poor environmental governance and therefore endeavor to demonstrate that they meet all binding regulations	Qualitative environmental disclosure of over 50 words in Annual Reports or on websites
Level 5 – Avoiders	Firms that obey environmental regulations because they must but do not see a need to strategically address any environmental issues	Empty space: firms classified as Avoiders do not disclose any information on environmental issues

Valentine (2006, p. 76 [reproduced with permission of the author])

societal perspective, but also from that of the corporation itself if it wishes to ultimately prosper in the rapidly changing environment.

On balance, the evidence would seem to suggest that the distribution of firms along this response spectrum has shifted somewhat towards Level 1. However, this shift is not monotonic. Some companies wear their commitment to sustainability very lightly and can change course opportunistically. A case in point is the American agricultural corporation Cargill, which received praise for agreeing to a moratorium on buying soybeans from deforested lands in the Amazon. Since then, the company has refused to agree to a similar moratorium in another major soy producing area in Brazil (*New York Times* July 29, 2019). This prompted one ENGO to issue a scathing report entitled "The Worst Company in the World" (Mighty Earth 2019), calling out the company for its chequered record on pollution control and meat contamination as well as deforestation.

There are a multitude of factors and actors that influence corporate policy on sustainability. Included among these are, most obviously, government regulatory agencies, but also, to no less degree, suppliers, customers, competitors, banks, insurance agencies, nongovernmental organizations, financial markets, and the court of public opinion reflected in the formal and informal media.

There are several critical issues that lie at the heart of assessing the extent of sustainability within the corporate sector and these include: how the concept is defined, measured, and incorporated into corporate decision making. Each of these issues is discussed in this book in several bellwether case studies that summarize the track record of sustainability initiatives in the recent past, current activity, and future prospects. These case studies are supplemented with a range of tools that can be used by corporations to advance this agenda as well as a discussion of the rapidly changing financial environment which plays an essential role on business activity and success.

One word of caution is warranted: If one were to seek a definition of sustainability by utilizing a computer-based search, one would find literally dozens of definitions. The phrase has passed into common currency and is now ubiquitous. In an Orwellian twist, this descriptor is now considered an essential ingredient in any corporate mission statement and has been used by some corporations whose practices are the antithesis of sustainability. In some cases, these corporations have been included in one or more of the numerous indexes of sustainable businesses. As Farley and Smith (2013) have stated, when a term such as sustainability is used so widely it can mean anything, and in essence ends up meaning nothing. As such, this book attempts to provide a sober and realistic assessment of corporate sustainability absent spin and terminological obfuscation.

The Context

There is now irrefutable evidence that the earth is experiencing anthropogenic global warming, and it is accelerating with continued increases in global greenhouse gas emissions and positive ecological feedback loops. Several major recent reports have emphasized the gravity of the situation and the challenges facing government, the business sector, and the general public.

The first of these reports is the Sixth Synthesis report of the Intergovernmental Panel on Climate Change (IPCC) issued in March 2023. There are at least five major takeaways from the report *Huff Post* (March 21. 2023):

- Climate change has already wreaked havoc on the planet
- Every bit of warming matters

- The impacts of climate change are and will continue to be severe
- The warmer the world, the more animal species are at serious risk
- There is a window to act, but it is small and getting smaller.

Appendix Two summarizes the report's key findings. What is extraordinary about this document is that all 18 of the key findings are viewed with high confidence even though the process requires consensus among all the national participants, a process that occasionally in the past forced a weakening of the conclusions.

The findings of the IPCC have been corroborated by the State of the Global Climate report (WMO 2022) (see Appendix 3 to this chapter) and the Global Annual to Decadal Climate Update, also published by the World Meteorological Organization (WMO 2023). In the latter report, the WMO is predicting that the earth is likely to break the 1.5 degrees Celsius limit for the first time by 2027. Part of the reason for this impending event is the reinforcing effect of El Nino-Southern Oscillation (ENSO) that shapes extreme weather globally and can have a massive impact on the global economy. One estimate – subject to stochastic variation – of median cumulative losses over the period 2020–2099 is calculated to be $84 trillion (Callahan & Mankin 2023).

Of ultimate concern to both government and the business community are the economic consequences associated with climate change. The answers to these questions are provided by two other reports: the Economic Report of the President of March 2023 and the accompanying White Paper from the Council of Economic Advisors and the Office of Management and Budget (entitled "Methodologies and Considerations for Integrating the Physical and Transition Risks of Climate Change in Macroeconomic Forecasting for the President's Budget").

Several key messages distilled from the President's report include (*New York Times* March 20, 2023): a warning that a warming planet posed severe economic challenges for the US, which would require the federal government to reassess its spending priorities and how it influenced behavior; that climate change has upended the concept of risk in all corners of the American economy, distorting markets in ways that companies, people and policymakers have not fully

kept up with; and that home buyers and corporate investors appear to be underestimating climate-related risks in their markets, which could lead to a financial crisis.

The most detailed consideration of the explicit risks generated by climate change and a required energy transition away from fossil fuels have been presented in the CEA-OMB report (2023) and are summarized in Tables 1.2 and 1.3. The IPCC has repeatedly warned that any additional global warming in excess of 1.5–2.0 degrees Celsius will lead to major and potentially irreversible ecological changes. Figure 1.2 identifies the effects of various degrees of global temperature increase affecting sea levels, agricultural output, loss of biodiversity, and a range of natural disasters (Stern 2006, p. 294).

With any of these effects there are serious economic repercussions. Figure 1.3, which summarizes the essence of the ecological-economic nexus, is based on the emerging field of Ecological Economics that differs in many important respects from traditional Environmental Economics. In essence, the ecological economics model makes three major modifications to the environmental economics model: (1) waste products generated by both consumers and producers have a feedback loop, which means that such products have the capacity to negatively impact the production system from which they are generated; (2) there is a specific inclusion of certain natural resources as inputs such as clean

Table 1.2 CEA-OMB Risks from Climate Change

Broad Pathway	Specific Climate Pathway	Discussion
Labor	Migration	Climate change, including displacement from sea-level rise, could affect the propensity to migrate to and from the United States in complex ways, as well as the distribution of population within the United States
	Workweek	Changes in extreme temperatures alter hours worked, particularly in more exposed industries (e.g., construction, agriculture)
	Population Growth - Fertility	There is some suggestion climate change may affect fertility decisions, though magnitudes may be small for a services-led economy with high air conditioner penetration like the United States
	Population Growth - Mortality	Substantial evidence that temperature extremes lead to premature mortality, though effect sizes are smaller for prime work-force ages. Other mortality effects operate through changes in disease and extreme weather events
Capital Services	Destruction	Climate-change-related extreme events could destroy capital investments. Resources required for recovery may be diverted from productive investments.
	Uncertainty	Additional uncertainty from climate-change-related weather extremes raises risk premia on certain assets and financing costs for related investments. Climate uncertainty could limit availability or increase costs of disaster insurance in certain markets, slowing recovery.
Factor Productivity	Labor	Extreme hot temperatures lower labor productivity in highly exposed industries
	Capital Services	Changing climate may alter the productivity of climate-sensitive capital such as dams, electricity transmission and generation, and roads.
	Land	Higher temperatures and CO_2 concentrations affect agricultural yields and forest productivity

air, clean water, and assimilative capacity; and (3) most importantly, there is an ecological system that includes at least 17 *ecological services,* as described by Costanza et al. (1997). The fundamental premise of this major conceptual revision is that the economic system is embedded in the ecological system, cannot function without it, and is ultimately subject to the same laws and constraints that apply to natural systems.

Central to the preservation of a healthy and functioning ecosystem – that sustains our global economy – is the preservation of biodiversity. This poses the second and interrelated problem facing human society today as the loss of biodiversity is accelerating both locally and globally. The latest report on Global Risks from the World Economic Forum (WEF 2024) lists the top four risks over the next decade as (1) extreme weather events, (2) critical change to Earth systems, (3) biodiversity loss and ecosystem collapse, and

Table 1.3 CEA-OMB Required Energy Transition

Broad Pathway	Specific Energy-Transition Pathway	Discussion
Labor	Skill and Geographic Mismatch	The energy transition will decrease labor requirements in some industries while increasing them in others. Differences in the skill requirements and locationof growing compared with shrinking sectors, combined with labor market frictions, could lead to localized unemployment or labor shortages
Capital Services	Investment	A rapid energy transition requires large investments in new energy infrastructure. Macroeconomic effects of this investment might result from diversion of investment from other productive uses and economic stimulus undercertain circumstances. Capital adjustment frictions could lead macroeconomic costs to increase with the speed of the transition.
	Policy Uncertainty	Energy infrastructure investments are forward-looking and depend on investor expectations regarding future returns. Policy uncertainty around the speed and nature of the energy transition could lead to higher financing costs and under-investment in energy generally, with implications for energy prices and volatility.
Factor Productivity	Energy and Energy-Intensive Infrastructure	Rapidly changing policy conditions could lead energy infrastructure to under-perform relative to expectations. Capital in downstream, energy-intensive industries may also be rendered prematurely obsolete or less productive as energy markets and technology change.
Energy	Price Levels	Energy prices can affect macroeconomic conditions. For instance, oil prices are astandard factor in macroeconomic forecasting (Figure 3). The energy transition may change energy prices in the near-term, particularly if it is disorderly. The longer-term effects on energy prices are unclear, as they depend on future technological evolution and policy that could lead to either decreases or increases inenergy prices.
	Price Volatility	Volatile energy prices increase uncertainty for producers and consumers, potentially with macroeconomic implications. A disorderly transition could increase energy price volatility in the short- to medium-term. In the longer-run, the declining share of fossil fuels in the energy mix could lower price volatility.

(4) natural resource shortages. In addition, one of the remaining top ten risks is also related to climate change: involuntary migration.

While much of corporate strategy has shifted towards a recognition of the risks of global warming, much less attention has been paid to biodiversity as a form of natural capital essential for economic prosperity. A survey by Influence Map (2022) of industry

Projected Impacts of Climate Change

Global temperature change (relative to pre-industrial)

| 0°C | 1°C | 2°C | 3°C | 4°C | 5°C |

Food — Falling crop yields in many areas, particularly developing regions

Possible rising yields in some high latitude regions

Falling yields in many developed regions

Water — Small mountain glaciers disappear – water supplies threatened in several areas

Significant decreases in water availability in many areas, including Mediterranean and Southern Africa

Sea level rise threatens major cities

Ecosystems

Extensive Damage to Coral Reefs

Rising number of species face extinction

Extreme Weather Events

Rising intensity of storms, forest fires, droughts, flooding and heat waves

Risk of Abrupt and Major Irreversible Changes

Increasing risk of dangerous feedbacks and abrupt, large-scale shifts in the climate system

Figure 1.2 Projected Impacts of Climate Change

Source: Stern 2006, p. 294

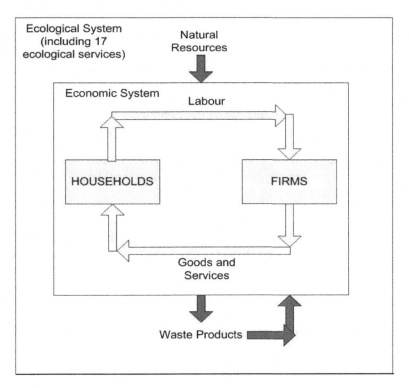

Figure 1.3 Economic-Ecological Model

associations' attitude towards biodiversity policy found only 5% positive, 6% mixed or unclear, and 89% negative. To quote their findings (p. 3):

> Industry associations representing key sectors and some of the largest companies in the world are lobbying to delay, dilute and rollback critically needed policy aimed at preventing and reversing biodiversity loss in the EU and US.
>
> Despite this apparent indifference, recent research has accentuated the absolutely vital role of biodiversity in ecosystem health while reporting an "unprecedented and accelerating decline in species extinction rates" (IPBES 2019).

This volume explores the track record of a board range of companies in tackling the issue of sustainability and reviews several methodologies and analytical techniques available to guide this assessment. As described in the Preface and outlined in chapter 2, the corporate responses lie on a broad spectrum that ranges from exemplary practice to dubious and occasion fraudulent responses. One industry stands out as posing the greatest challenge to halting the rapid progression of global warming. Energy is the essence of a modern industrial society and since the industrial revolution, energy has been largely produced by a progression of fossil fuels: coal, petroleum, and natural gas. It is essential to transition away from fossil fuels to renewables, such as wind and solar, but projected increases in demand for energy over the next few decades make this an exceedingly difficult challenge despite the inherent cost advantages of renewables.

There are several major challenges to such a massive transformation of energy systems. The first is technological. Smil (2010, 2014) has pointed out that historical energy transformations – from wood to coal to oil – have all taken 50–60 years, and he posits that a move to renewables would take no less a period of time, particularly in light of the magnitude of global energy supply and demand (cf. Temple 2018 and *New York Times* November 7, 2017). The percentage of fossil fuel in total global energy use has remained relatively constant at approximately 80% since the 1970s (IEA 2021; REN21 2023). The increased use of renewables has apparently been matched by comparable increases in the use of fossil fuels. Many countries of the developing world still rely on coal for a major proportion of their electricity production for two principal reasons: ubiquity and low cost (IEA 2022). China presents an excellent example of this conundrum. Despite the country's efforts to expand the use of renewable energy sources, China still relies on coal for most of its electricity production and continues to build coal-fired power stations to keep up with rapidly expanding demand (BBC September 26, 2018; *E&T* March 28, 2019).

Considering the inherent inertia of the global energy system, it is problematic that the fossil fuel industry plans to spend $932 billion on 425 new oil and gas developments over the next few decades, creating what have been termed "*carbon bombs.*" These developments will ultimately guarantee an increase in global temperature well over the 1.5–2.0 degrees target (*The Guardian* May 11 and June 17, 2022; Kuhne et al. 2022; Global Witness April 12, 2022). One recent study (Grasso & Heede 2023) has estimated the financial impact of the emissions over the period 2025–2050 of the largest 21 fossil fuel companies on drought, wildfires, sea level rise, and melting glaciers of $70 trillion.

The second major challenge to the energy transition is financial. Two recent reports from the International Renewable Energy Agency (IRENA) elaborate on this problem (IRENA 2023a, 2023b). They conclude that:

The energy transition is off-track. . . . Current pledges and plans fall well short of IRENA's 1.5°C pathway and will result in an emissions gap of 16 gigatonnes (Gt) in 2050. . . . Although global investment across all energy transition technologies reached a record high of USD 1.3 trillion in 2022, annual investment must more than quadruple to remain on the 1.5°C pathway. . . . Cumulative investments between now and 2030 need to total USD 44 trillion, with energy transition technologies represent-ing 80% of the investment, or USD 35 trillion" (IRENA 2023a).

To realize this daunting goal, IRENA (2023b) deems it absolutely essential that low-cost finance for the energy transition is available for both emerging and advanced market economies. To quote their findings:

> Crucially, enabling innovative frameworks that reduce the transaction costs of tech-nology transfers and facilitate foreign direct investments have played a key role in accelerating the deployment of new and critical low-carbon technologies in emerging markets. . . . The majority of the funds required for the energy transition will have to come from the private sector. . . . As a result, the public sector is a critical catalyst in engaging and attracting private sector investors and project developers under condi-tions that ensure low costs of capital. . . . Innovation is vital if governments are to scale up new and critical energy transition technologies. Along with economies of scale as markets grow, innovation is one of the main levers available to reduce technology costs, accelerate market penetration and unlock required financial resources.

Clearly there is both a responsibility and opportunity for both the corporate and gov-ernment sectors acting in concert to achieve this goal of energy transition. Invariably, there are at least two radically divergent definitions of how to achieve this goal. As the *New York Times* observes (March 19, 2022):

> According to the scientific consensus, the energy transition requires a rapid phasing out of fossil fuels and the immediate scaling up of cleaner energy sources like wind, solar and nuclear. But many in the oil and gas business say the energy transition simply means a continued use of fossil fuels, with a greater reliance on natural gas rather than coal, and a hope that new technologies such as carbon capture and sequestration can contain or reduce the amount of greenhouse gasses they produce.

There are several issues with the transition to natural gas as a replacement for coal. First, is the fact that, although natural gas has less carbon than coal, it is still a fossil fuel and can therefore not be considered as a permanent solution to global warming. Second, however, recent research (Gordon et al. 2023) has calculated that under certain circum-stances, the GHG emissions from natural gas are comparable to those of coal. This is because natural gas production, transportation, and utilization can leak methane, a GHG with a global warming potential 28–36 times that of coal. The authors calculate that a gas system leakage is on par with coal. They conclude:

> Recent aerial measurement surveys of US oil and gas production basins find wide-ranging natural gas leak rates 0.65% to 66.2%, with similar leakage rates detected worldwide. These numerous super-emitting gas systems being detected globally underscore the

need to accelerate methane emissions detection, accounting, and management practices to certify that gas assets are less emissions intensive than coal.

In a message to those who doubt the economic feasibility of transition toa low-carbon future, CITI Bank (2015) had an upbeat message in a report entitled: *Energy Darwinism II – Why a Low Carbon Future Doesn't Have to Cost the Earth*. They concluded that: "The incremental costs of following a low carbon path are in context limited and seem affordable, the 'return' on that investment is acceptable and moreover the likely avoided liabilities are enormous" (p. 1). Their estimates of the negative effects of climate change range from $20–72 trillion as global average temperature increases beyond the goal of 1.5 degrees Celsius, and the estimated costs of inaction exceed those of action by almost $2 trillion. They conclude with a list of methods and instruments through that financial markets, financial institutions, regulators, and policy makers can enable the capital to flow to address this critical issue. These suggestions include the use of green bonds, YieldCos, covered bonds, and securitization and are discussed further in chapter 18 on the role of financial markets in achieving a sustainable future.

The US government has moved a major step closer to addressing climate change and facilitating the energy transition with the Inflation Reduction Act (IRA) of August 2022. Among its principal goals, the act directs:

new federal spending toward reducing carbon emissions, to cut Americans' energy costs whilst creating new jobs and to aid US efforts in addressing climate change. The act directs $393.7 billion funding to climate efforts through tax incentives, grants and loans; including energy ($250.6 billion), manufacturing ($47.7 billion) and environment ($46.4 billion)" (Reuters 2023).

In its goal to revitalize American manufacturing, the act aims to "Build American clean energy supply chains, by incentivizing domestic production in clean energy technologies like solar, wind, carbon capture, and clean hydrogen" (US White House 2022a,b and 2023).

Two important developments have occurred in the attitudes and behaviour of the business sector. First, Gina McCarthy, the former national climate advisor and administrator of the US EPA, has concluded that business no longer sees climate action as driving job losses (*New York Times* September 19, 2022). And second, considering this shift in attitudes, the corporate sector has enthusiastically embraced the goal of the act because of the extensive climate-related tax breaks that incentivize more investment in American manufacturing. This is especially applicable to green technology in the form of such things as new battery factories, wind turbines, wind and solar farms, and electric vehicle plants (*New York Times* May 3, 2023).

Finally, the challenge of accelerating change for government, business and society, has been emphasized by the release of several media reports, scientific papers, and government documents in the fall of 2023 before and during the controversial COP28 conference in Dubai. All these publications stress the urgency of the problem where delay and half-hearted measures are no longer an option. A brief list of these items is presented in Appendix 4.

Chapter 2 reviews the steady shift in of corporate attitudes towards sustainability over the past few decades and outlines some of the most prominent current initiatives within the business community.

References

Anthony, Katey M. Walter, et al. (2012) "Geologic methane seeps along boundaries of Arctic permafrost thaw and melting glaciers," *Nature Geoscience*, May 20.

BBC News (2018) "China relies on coal to keep up with demand," September 26.

BBC News (2019) "Faster pace of climate change is 'scary', former chief scientist says," September 16.

Callahan, Christopher W., & Justin S. Mankin (2023) "Persistent effect of El Nino on global economic growth," *Science*, May 18.

Carney, Mark (2021) *Values(s): Building a Better World for All*. Signal.

Chadburn, S. E., et al. (2017) "An observation-based constraint on permafrost loss as a function of global warming," *Nature Climate Change*, May, pp. 340–344.

CITI Bank (2015) *Energy Darwinism II: Why a Low Carbon Future Doesn't Have to Cost the Earth*.

Colville, Robert (2017) *The Great Acceleration: How the World Is Getting Faster, Faster*. Bloomsbury.

Costanza, Robert, et al. (1997) "The value of the world's ecosystem services and natural capital," *Nature*, May 15.

Dorling, Danny (2020) *Slowdown: The End of the Great Acceleration – and Why It's Good for the Planet, the Economy, and Our Lives*. Yale University Press.

Dummett, Cassie, & Arthur Blundell (2021) "Illicit harvest, complicit goods: the state of illegal deforestation for agriculture," *Forest Trends*, May.

Etminan, M., et al. (2016) "Radiative forcing of carbon dioxide, methane, and nitrous oxide, a significant revision of the methane radiative forcing," *Geophysical Research Letters*, December 27.

Farley, Heather M. & Zachery A. Smith (2013) *Sustainability: If it's Everything, Is It Nothing?* Routledge.

Friedman, Thomas (2016) *Thank You for Being Late: An Optimist's Guide to Thriving in the Age of Accelerations*. Farrar, Straus and Giroux.

Gleick, James (2000) *Faster: The Acceleration of Just about Everything*. Vintage.

Global Witness (2022). "IPCC clarion call puts spotlight on fossil fuel industry's hypocrisy," April 12.

Gordon, Deborah, et al. (2023) "Evaluating life-cycle greenhouse gas emissions intensities from gas and coal at varying methane leakage rates," *Environmental Research Letters*, July 17.

Grasso, Marco & Richard Heede (2023) "Time to pay the piper: fossil fuel companies' reparations for climate damages," *One Earth*, May 19.

The Guardian (2022) "Revealed: the 'carbon bombs' set to trigger catastrophic climate breakdown," May 11.

The Guardian (2022) "Fossil fuel firms 'have humanity by the throat," says UN head in blistering attack," June 17.

Herndon, Elizabeth M. (2018) "Permafrost slowly exhales methane," *Nature Climate Change*, April 8.

Heubl, B. (2019) "Is China returning to coal-fired power?" *Engineering & Technology*, May, pp. 20–23.

HuffPost (2023) "5 takeaways from the dire IPCC climate report," March 21.

InfluenceMap (2022) "Big Oil's real agenda on climate change: An InfluenceMap report," September.

Intergovernmental Panel on Climate Change (IPCC) (2014a) *Climate Change Synthesis Report*.

Intergovernmental Panel on Climate Change (IPCC) (2014b) *Fifth Assessment Report*. AR5 Reports.

Intergovernmental Panel on Climate Change (IPCC) (2018). "Summary for policymakers of IPCC Special Report on Global Warming of 1.5°C approved by governments," https://www.ipcc.ch/2018/10/08/summary-for-policymakers-of-ipcc-special-report-on-global-warming-of-1-5c-approved-by-governments/

Intergovernmental Panel on Climate Change (IPCC) (2019) *Special Report: The Ocean and Cryosphere in a Changing Climate – Summary for Policymakers*, September.

Intergovernmental Panel on Climate Change (IPCC) (2023) *Sixth Synthesis Report*, March.

Intergovernmental Science-Policy Platform on Biodiversity and Ecosystem Services (IPBES) (2019) Media release: "Nature's dangerous decline 'unprecedented'; species extinction rates 'accelerating,'" May 6.

International Energy Agency (IEA) (2021). "Total primary energy supply by fuel, 1971 and 2019," August 6.

International Energy Agency (IEA) (2022) *Coal 2022: Analysis and Forecast to 2025.*

International Renewable Energy Agency (IRENA) (2023a) *World energy transition outlook 2023: Key messages.*

International Renewable Energy Agency (IRENA) (2023b) *Low-cost finance for the energy transition.*

Kuhne, Kjell, et al. (2022) "Carbon Bombs – Mapping key fossil fuel projects," *Energy Policy*, May 12.

Martens, Jannik, et al. (2020) "Remobilization of dormant carbon from Siberian-Arctic permafrost during the three past warming events," *Science Advances*, October 16.

McNeill, J. R. & Peter Engelke (2016) *The Great Acceleration: An Environmental History of the Anthropocene.* Belknap Press.

Mighty Earth (2019). "Cargill: The worst company in the world," https://stories.mightyearth.org/cargill-worst-company-in-the-world/

NASA (2018). "Ramp-up in Antarctic ice loss speeds sea level rise," June 13, https://www.nasa.gov/news-release/ramp-up-in-antarctic-ice-loss-speeds-sea-level-rise/.

Natali, Susan M., et al. (2019) "Large loss of VO2 in winter observed across the northern permafrost region," *Nature Climate Change*, October 21.

Nemetz, Peter N. (2022) *Unsustainable World: Are we Losing the Battle to Save Our Planet?* Routledge/Earthscan.

New York Times (2017) "Wind and solar power advance, but carbon refuse to retreat," November 7.

New York Times (2019). "From environmental leader to 'worst company in the world,'" July 29.

New York Times (2021) "This glacier in Alaska is moving 100 times faster than normal," April 13.

New York Times (2022) "There's a messaging battle right now over America's energy future," March 19.

New York Times (2023) "Biden warns that climate change could upend federal spending programs," March 20.

New York Times (2023) "Companies flock to Biden's climate tax breaks, driving up cost," May 3.

NOAA (2018) *Arctic Report Card – Executive Summary*, https://arctic.noaa.gov/report-card/report-card-2018/executive-summary-5/

Piel, Gerard, (1972) *The Acceleration of History.* Knopf.

Pistone, Kristina, et al. (2014) "Observational determination of albedo decrease caused by vanishing Arctic sea ice," *PNAS*, March 4.

Porter, Michael and Claas van der Linde (1995) "Green and competitive," *Harvard Business Review*, September–October.

REN21 (2023) *Renewables 2023: Global Status Report.*

Reuters (2023) *ESG Investment: North American Market Outlook.*

Smil, Vaclav (2010) *Energy Transitions: History, Requirements, Prospects.* Santa Barbara: Praeger.

Smil, Vaclav (2014) "The Long slow rise of solar and wind," *Scientific American*, January, pp. 52–57.

Steffen, Will, et al. (2015a) "The trajectory of the Anthropocene – the great acceleration," *Anthropocene Review*, 2(1), 81–98.

Steffen, Will, et al. (2015b) "Planetary boundaries," *Science*, February 13.

Stern, Nicholas (2006) *Stern Review Final Report (The Economics of Climate Change).* The National Archives, HM Treasury. United Kingdom, October 30.

Temple, James (2018) "At this rate, it's going to take nearly 400 years to transform the energy system," *MIT Technology Review*, March 14.

Turetsky, Merritt R., et al. (2020) "Carbon release through abrupt permafrost thaw," *Nature Geoscience*, February.

US Council of Economic Advisors & Office of Management and Budget (CEA-OMB) (2023) "Methodologies and considerations for Integrating the Physical and Transition risks of climate change int macroeconomic forecasting for the President's Budget," March.

US White House (2022a) *Economic Report of the President*, March.

US White House (2022b) "Fact sheet: The Inflation Reduction Act supports workers and families," August 19.

US White House (2023) *A Guidebook to the Inflation Reduction Act: Investments in Clean Energy and Climate Action*, January.

Valentine, Scott (2006) *An Empirical Test of the Corporate Environmental Governance-Financial Performance Relationship*. PhD dissertation, National University of Singapore.

Wagner, Gernot & Martin L. Weitzman (2015) *Shock: The Economic Consequences of a Hotter Planet*. Princeton University Press.

Wang, Taihua, et al. (2020) "Permafrost thawing puts the frozen carbon at risk on the Tibetan Plateau," *Science Advances*, May 6.

Wilkinson, S. L., et al. (2020) "Shallow peat is most vulnerable to high peat burn severity during wildfire." *Environmental Research Letters*, 15:104032.

World Economic Forum (WEF) (2024) *The Global Risks Report 2024*.

World Meteorological Organization (WMO) (2019) *The Global Climate in 2015–2019*.

World Meteorological Organization (WMO) (2020) *State of the Global Climate 2020*.

World Meteorological Organization (WMO) (2022) *State of the Global Climate 2022*.

World Meteorological Organization (WMO) (2023) "WMO Global Annual to Decadal Climate Update," May.

Zhang, Rudong, et al. (2019) "Unraveling driving forces explaining significant reduction in satellite-inferred Arctic surface albedo since the 1980s," *PNAS*, November 11.

Appendix One: A Brief Summary of Exponential Change

A central challenge to addressing the issue of climate change is the recognition of non-linear change in human and ecological systems. This poses a particularly difficult challenge for the human mind conditioned by millennia of relatively incremental change. For most of human history, at the moment of an individual's death, the earth and its society looked very much the same as it did at his/her birth. This has been the conditioning that has infused our social and economic institutions and worldviews until relatively recent times. One of the first works recognizing the phenomenon of nonlinear change was published by the late editor of the *Scientific American*, Gerard Piel, in his 1972 work entitled *The Acceleration of History*. More recent explications of this concept include Gleick's *Faster: The Acceleration of Just About Everything* (2000); Steffen et al. "The Trajectory of the Anthropocene: The Great Acceleration" (2015a); McNeill and Engelke's *The Great Acceleration: An Environmental History of the Anthropocene* (2016); Friedman's *Thank You for Being Late: An Optimist's Guide to Thriving in the Age of Accelerations* (2016): and Colville's *The Great Acceleration: How the World is Getting Faster, Faster* (2017).

While some have posited the beginning of the great acceleration during England's Industrial Revolution, McNeill and Engelke (2016) present a compelling case for its birth in the immediate postwar period. The following quote from their book supports this hypothesis:

> Within the last three human generations, three-quarters of the human-caused loading of the atmosphere with carbon dioxide took place. The number of motor vehicles on Earth increased from 40 million to 850 million. The number of people nearly tripled, and the number of city dwellers rose from about 700 million to 3.7 billion. In 1950 the world produced about 1 million tons of plastics but by 2015 that rose to nearly 300 million tons. In the same time span, the quantities of nitrogen synthesized (mainly for fertilizers) climbed from under 4 million tons to more than 85 million tons (p. 4).

The authors' hypothesis is given further credence by the graphical analysis of almost two dozen socioeconomic and earth system variables from 1750 to 2010 in Steffen et al. (2015a,b). Mark Carney (2021, p. 263–265), the former Governor of the Bank of England, provides several examples to illustrate the nature of this acceleration. To quote:

> Our oceans have become 30 percent more acidic since the Industrial Revolution. Sea levels have risen 20 centimetres over the past century, with the rate doubling in the past two decades. The pace of ice loss in the Arctic and Antarctic has tripled in the last decade. . . . Current extinction rates are around a hundred times higher than average over the past several million years. Since I was born, there has been a 70 per cent decline in the population of mammals, birds, fish, reptiles and amphibians. . . . It took 250 years to burn the first half-trillion tons of carbon. On current trends, the next half-trillion will be released into our atmosphere in less than forty years.

It should be noted, however, that not all observers feel that this acceleration will continue. Professor Danny Dorling (2020) of Oxford University has posited a slowdown and even end of the Great Acceleration. The author has presented evidence that suggests that many recent rapid changes are decelerating. However, the author candidly admits that one exception to his findings is the continued rapid rise in global temperatures, yet this is clearly the area that matters most; all other areas are secondary. As such, increased concerns over the critical issue of accelerating climate change remain front and centre among the challenges facing humanity.

Recent reports of the World Meteorological Organization (2019, 2020, 2022, 2023) confirm the findings that global warming is accelerating. (See also BBC September 16, 2019). Nowhere more apparent is this phenomenon of rapid change than in the Arctic which in many respects is the canary in the coal mine; a part of the globe that provide a premonition of the rest of the earth on fast forward (NOAA 2018; see also *New York Times* April 13, 2021 for an example of the speed of transition). Two particularly insidious forms of positive feedback in the Arctic are provided by the melting of both sea ice and permafrost: the former reducing the albedo of the Arctic Ocean, thereby absorbing more heat rather than reflecting it back into space; the latter by releasing entrained methane, a greenhouse gas approximately twenty-eight times as powerful as carbon dioxide, thereby further accelerating the process of global warming (Anthony et al. 2012; Pistone et al. 2014; Herndon 2018; IPCC 2014a,b; Etminan et al. 2016; Chadburn et al. 2017; Natali et al. 2019; Martens et al. 2020; Turetsky et al. 2020; Zhang et al. 2019). A similar threat of methane release from permafrost also appears to originate in the high-latitude/altitude Northern Hemisphere, such as the Tibetan Plateau (Wang et al. 2020). Another major Arctic and subarctic sink for carbon is peat in Northern Canada. Wilkinson et al. (2020) report that peat deposits, particularly those no deeper than 0.66 m, where water tables have fallen, are particularly vulnerable to wildfires, posing the threat of significant releases of carbon in light of the fact that peatlands store almost one-third of global organic soil carbon.

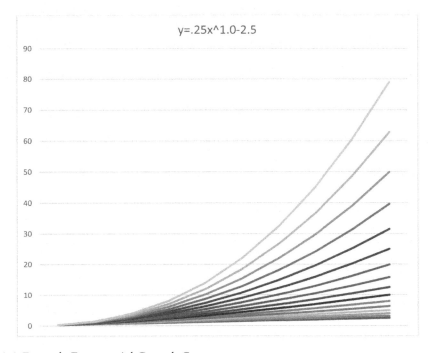

Figure 1.4 Example Exponential Growth Curves

There is continued surprise among the scientific community attending each new finding of the rapidity of global climate change. This could possibly be attributed to a misinterpretation of the data. As stated above, much of history can be characterized by either little or slow incremental change, captured by a simple linear extrapolation of past trends. Such projections can be misleading in the presence of exponential change driven by a multitude of positive feedback loops. Figure 1.4 represents a simple linear projection of past trends and several possible exponential growth curves. The problem of early identification of exponential change is that the first phases of this growth are difficult to distinguish from linear change. Even when the existence of nonlinear change is recognized, errors in projection may occur when the exponent of the exponential function is underestimated.

Appendix Two: IPCC AR6 Key Findings—March 2023

Current Status and Trends: Observed Warming and its Causes

A.1 Human activities, principally through emissions of greenhouse gases, have unequivocally caused global warming, with global surface temperature reaching 1.1°C above 1850–1900 in 2011–2020. Global greenhouse gas emissions have continued to increase, with unequal historical and ongoing contributions arising from unsustainable energy use, land use and land-use change, lifestyles and patterns of consumption and production across regions, between and within countries, and among individuals (high confidence).

A.2 Widespread and rapid changes in the atmosphere, ocean, cryosphere and biosphere have occurred. Human-caused climate change is already affecting many weather and climate extremes in every region across the globe. This has led to widespread adverse impacts and related losses and damages to nature and people (high confidence). Vulnerable communities who have historically contributed the least to current climate change are disproportionately affected (high confidence).

A.3 Adaptation planning and implementation has progressed across all sectors and regions, with documented benefits and varying effectiveness. Despite progress, adaptation gaps exist, and will continue to grow at current rates of implementation. Hard and soft limits to adaptation have been reached in some ecosystems and regions. Maladaptation is happening in some sectors and regions. Current global financial flows for adaptation are insufficient for, and constrain implementation of, adaptation options, especially in developing countries (high confidence).

A.4 Policies and laws addressing mitigation have consistently expanded since AR5. Global GHG emissions in 2030 implied by nationally determined contributions (NDCs) announced by October 2021 make it likely that warming will exceed 1.5°C during the 21st century and make it harder to limit warming below 2°C. There are gaps between projected emissions from implemented policies and those from NDCs and finance flows fall short of the levels needed to meet climate goals across all sectors and regions. (high confidence)

Future Climate change, risks, and long-term responses

B.1 Continued greenhouse gas emissions will lead to increasing global warming, with the best estimate of reaching 1.5°C in the near term in considered scenarios and modelled pathways. Every increment of global warming will intensify multiple and concurrent hazards (high confidence). Deep, rapid, and sustained reductions in greenhouse gas emissions would lead to a discernible slowdown in global warming within around two decades, and also to discernible changes in atmospheric composition within a few years (high confidence).

B.2 For any given future warming level, many climate-related risks are higher than assessed in AR5, and projected long-term impacts are up to multiple times higher than currently observed (high confidence). Risks and projected adverse impacts and related losses and damages from climate change escalate with every increment of global warming (very high confidence). Climatic and non-climatic risks will increasingly interact, creating compound and cascading risks that are more complex and difficult to manage (high confidence).

B.3 Some future changes are unavoidable and/or irreversible but can be limited by deep, rapid and sustained global greenhouse gas emissions reduction. The likelihood of abrupt and/or irreversible changes increases with higher global warming levels. Similarly, the probability of low-likelihood outcomes associated with potentially very large adverse impacts increases with higher global warming levels. (high confidence)

B.4 Adaptation options that are feasible and effective today will become constrained and less effective with increasing global warming. With increasing global warming, losses and damages will increase and additional human and natural systems will reach adaptation limits. Maladaptation can be avoided by flexible, multi-sectoral, inclusive, long-term planning and implementation of adaptation actions, with co-benefits to many sectors and systems. (high confidence)

B.5 Limiting human-caused global warming requires net zero CO_2 emissions. Cumulative carbon emissions until the time of reaching net-zero CO_2 emissions and the level of greenhouse gas emission reductions this decade largely determine whether warming can be limited to 1.5°C or 2°C (high confidence). Projected CO_2 emissions from existing fossil fuel infrastructure without additional abatement would exceed the remaining carbon budget for 1.5°C (50%) (high confidence).

B.6 All global modelled pathways that limit warming to 1.5°C (>50%) with no or limited overshoot, and those that limit warming to 2°C (>67%), involve rapid and deep and, in most cases, immediate greenhouse gas emissions reductions in all sectors this decade. Global net zero CO_2 emissions are reached for these pathway categories, in the early 2050s and around the early 2070s, respectively. (high confidence)

B.7 If warming exceeds a specified level such as 1.5°C, it could gradually be reduced again by achieving and sustaining net negative global CO_2 emissions. This would require additional deployment of carbon dioxide removal, compared to pathways without overshoot, leading to greater feasibility and sustainability concerns. Overshoot entails adverse impacts, some irreversible, and additional risks for human and natural systems, all growing with the magnitude and duration of overshoot. (high confidence)

Urgency of Near-Term Integrated Climate Action

C.1 Climate change is a threat to human well-being and planetary health (very high confidence). There is a rapidly closing window of opportunity to secure a liveable and sustainable future for all (very high confidence). Climate resilient development integrates adaptation and mitigation to advance sustainable development for all, and is enabled by increased international cooperation including improved access to adequate financial resources, particularly for vulnerable regions, sectors and groups, and inclusive governance and coordinated policies (high confidence). The choices and actions implemented in this decade will have impacts now and for thousands of years (high confidence).

C.2 Deep, rapid and sustained mitigation and accelerated implementation of adaptation actions in this decade would reduce projected losses and damages for humans and ecosystems (very high confidence), and deliver many co-benefits, especially for air quality and health (high confidence). Delayed mitigation and adaptation action would lock-in high-emissions infrastructure, raise risks of stranded assets and cost-escalation, reduce feasibility, and increase losses and damages (high confidence). Near-term actions involve high up-front investments and potentially disruptive changes that can be lessened by a range of enabling policies (high confidence).

C.3 Rapid and far-reaching transitions across all sectors and systems are necessary to achieve deep and sustained emissions reductions and secure a liveable and sustainable future for all. These system transitions involve a significant upscaling of a wide portfolio of mitigation and adaptation options. Feasible, effective, and low-cost options for mitigation and adaptation are already available, with differences across systems and regions. (high confidence)

C.4 Accelerated and equitable action in mitigating and adapting to climate change impacts is critical to sustainable development. Mitigation and adaptation actions have more synergies than trade-offs with Sustainable Development Goals. Synergies and trade-offs depend on context and scale of implementation. (high confidence)

C.5 Prioritising equity, climate justice, social justice, inclusion and just transition processes can enable adaptation and ambitious mitigation actions and climate resilient development. Adaptation outcomes are enhanced by increased support to regions and people with the highest vulnerability to climatic hazards. Integrating climate adaptation into social protection programs improves resilience. Many options are available for reducing emission-intensive consumption, including through behavioural and lifestyle changes, with co-benefits for societal well-being. (high confidence)

C.6 Effective climate action is enabled by political commitment, well-aligned multilevel governance, institutional frameworks, laws, policies and strategies and enhanced access to finance and technology. Clear goals, coordination across multiple policy domains, and inclusive governance processes facilitate effective climate action. Regulatory and economic instruments can support deep emissions reductions and climate resilience if scaled up and applied widely. Climate resilient development benefits from drawing on diverse knowledge. (high confidence)

C.7 Finance, technology and international cooperation are critical enablers for accelerated climate action. If climate goals are to be achieved, both adaptation and mitigation financing would need to increase many-fold. There is sufficient global capital to close the global investment gaps but there are barriers to redirect capital to climate action. Enhancing technology innovation systems is key to accelerate the widespread adoption of technologies and practices. Enhancing international cooperation is possible through multiple channels. (high confidence)

Appendix Three: WMO (2023) State of the Climate 2022 Key Messages

The global mean temperature in 2022 was 1.15 [1.02–1.28] °C above the 1850–1900 average. The years 2015 to 2022 were the eight warmest in the 173-year instrumental record. The year 2022 was the fifth or sixth warmest year on record, despite ongoing La Niña conditions.

The year 2022 marked the third consecutive year of La Niña conditions, a duration that has only occurred three times in the past 50 years.

Concentrations of the three main greenhouse gases – carbon dioxide, methane and nitrous oxide – reached record highs in 2021, the latest year for which consolidated global values are available (1984–2021). The annual increase in methane concentration from 2020 to 2021 was the highest on record. Real-time data from specific locations show that levels of the three greenhouse gases continued to increase in 2022.

Around 90% of the energy trapped in the climate system by greenhouse gases goes into the ocean. Ocean heat content, which measures this gain in energy, reached a new observed record high in 2022.

Despite continuing La Niña conditions, 58% of the ocean surface experienced at least one marine heatwave during 2022. In contrast, only 25% of the ocean surface experienced a marine cold spell.

Global mean sea level continued to rise in 2022, reaching a new record high for the satellite altimeter record (1993–2022). The rate of global mean sea level rise has doubled between the first decade of the satellite record (1993–2002, 2.27 mm per year) and the last (2013–2022, 4.62 mm per year).

In the hydrological year 2021/2022, a set of reference glaciers with long-term observations experienced an average mass balance of –1.18 metres water equivalent (m w.e.). This loss is much larger than the average over the last decade. Six of the ten most negative mass balance years on record (1950–2022) occurred since 2015. The cumulative mass balance since 1970 amounts to more than –26 m.w.e.

In East Africa, rainfall has been below average in five consecutive wet seasons, the longest such sequence in 40 years. As of August 2022, an estimated 37 million people faced acute food insecurity across the region, under the effects of the drought and other shocks.

Record-breaking rain in July and August led to extensive flooding in Pakistan. There were at least 1700 deaths, and 33 million people were affected, while almost 8 million people were displaced. Total damage and economic losses were assessed at US$ 30 billion.

Record-breaking heatwaves affected China and Europe during the summer. In some areas, extreme heat was coupled with exceptionally dry conditions. Excess deaths associated with the heat in Europe exceeded 15000 in total across Spain, Germany, the United Kingdom, France and Portugal.

Appendix Four: Recent Warnings In 2023–2024 about Climate Change

Date	Title	Source
2023		
Jan.14	No place in the US is safe from the climate crisis, but a new report shows where it's most severe	CNN
May 22	Global heating will push billions outside 'human climate niche'	*The Guardian*
May 31	Earth's health failing in seven out of eight key measures say scientists	*The Guardian*
July 20	Long-lost Greenland ice cores suggests potential for disastrous sea level rise	CNN
July 25	Gulf stream could collapse as early as 2025, study suggests	*The Guardian*
Aug. 21	Our forests have reached a tipping point	*Canada's National Observer*
Sept. 12	Record number of billion-dollar disasters shows the limits of American's defenses	*New York Times*
Sept. 13	Earth beyond six of nine planetary boundaries	Katherine Richardson et al. in *Science Advances*
Sept. 16	Antarctic sea ice at 'mind-blowing' low alarms experts	BBC
Sept. 21	Climate change could mean 'hundreds of billions' at risk in US housing market	*Globe and Mail*
Oct. 5	Gobsmackingly bananas': scientists stunned by planet's record September heat	*The Guardian*
Oct. 23	Rapid melt in west Antarctica now inevitable, research shows	*The Guardian*
Oct. 24	The state of the climate report: entering uncharted territory	William J. Ripple in *BioScience*
Oct. 24	Earth's latest 'vital signs' show the planet is in crisis	Meghan Bartels in *Scientific American*
Oct. 24	EU must cut carbon emissions three times faster to meet targets, report says	*The Guardian*
Oct. 25	Earth close to 'risk tipping points' that will damage our ability to deal with climate crisis, warns UN	*The Guardian*
Nov. 2	Action to protects against climate crisis 'woefully inadequate', UN warns	*The Guardian*
Nov. 9	Two studies on Greenland reveal ominous signs for sea level rise	*The New York Times*
Nov. 14	World behind on almost every policy required to cut carbon emissions, research finds	*The Guardian*
Nov. 14	The 2023 report of the Lancet Countdown in health and climate change; the imperative for a health-centred response in a world facing irreversible harm	*The Lancet*
Nov. 14	In a report card on global warming, nations get a very poor grade	*New York Times*
Nov. 14	Health risks linked to climate change are getting worse, experts warn	*New York Times*
Nov. 15	Scientists warn of 'dangerous future' if global emissions aren't cut	CBC
Nov. 20	World facing 'hellish' 3C of climate heating UN warns before COP28	*The Guardian*

(Continued)

Date	Title	Source
Dec. 4	Global carbon emissions from fossil fuels to hit record high	*The Guardian*
Dec. 6	Earth on verge of five catastrophic climate tipping points, scientists warn	*The Guardian*
Dec. 11	Countries most at risk call proposed climate agreement a 'death warrant'	*New York Times*
Dec. 11	A quarter of freshwater fish are at risk of extinction, a new assessment finds	*New York Times*
2024		
Jan. 6	Extreme heat is pushing India to the brink of 'survivability.' One obvious solution is also a big part of the problem	CNN
Jan. 11	Drought touches a quarter of Humanity, U.N. Says, Disrupting Lives Globally	*New York Times*
Feb. 8	World's first year-long breach of key 1.5C warming limit	BBC
Feb. 9	Atlantic Ocean circulation nearing 'devastating tipping point', study says	*The Guardian*
Feb. 27	Scientists are freaking out about ocean temperatures	*New York Times*
March 28	Copernicus online portal offers terrifying view of climate emergency	Paul Brown, Weatherwatch
April 5	Australia should prepare for 20-year megadroughts as the climate crisis worsens, study finds	*The Guardian*
April 6	'Simply mind-boggling': world record temperature jump in Antarctica raises fears of catastrophe	*The Guardian*
May 8	'I could not feel greater despair.' World's top climate scientists expect global heating to blast past 1.5C target	*The Guardian*
May 9	'The stakes could not be higher': world is on edge of climate abyss, UN warns	*The Guardian*
May 29	Antarctica's 'Doomsday Glacier' is Melting Even Faster than Scientists Thought	*Scientific American*
May 29	Oceans face 'triple threat' of extreme heat, oxygen loss and acidification	American Geophysical Union
June 11	'It's unbearable': in ever-hotter US cities, air conditioning is no longer enough	*The Guardian*
June 20	Fossil fuel use reaches global record despite clean energy growth	*The Guardian*

2 A Brief History of Corporate Response to Sustainability Issues and Their Current Status

In many respects, the beginning of the modern environmental movement began with the publication of Rachel Carson's *Silent Spring* (1962). The following decade was characterized not only by increased public awareness of the issues, but also by extensive and bipartisan governmental legislative initiatives. Environmental legislation passed under President Lyndon Johnson included: Clean Air, Water Quality, and Clean Water Restoration Acts and Amendments; Wilderness Act of 1964; Endangered Species Preservation Act of 1966; National Trails System Act of 1968, Wild and Scenic Rivers Act of 1968, Land and Water Conservation Act of 1965; Solid Waste Disposal Act of 1965; Motor Vehicle Air Pollution Control Act of 1965; National Historic Preservation Act of 1966; Aircraft Noise Abatement Act of 1968; and the National Environmental Policy Act of 1969. Johnson's successor, President Richard Nixon, implemented even more wide-ranging legislation, such as the Clean Air Act of 1970, and amendments to the Federal Water Pollution Control act in 1972, as well as establishing the Environmental Protection Agency (EPA), the Occupational Safety and Health Administration (OSHA), the Council on Environmental Quality, and the Consumer Product Safety Commission.

The decades following Rachel Carson's monumental work (1962) were also marked by numerous landmark events in the postwar environmental context of business: a major industrial accident in Seveso, Italy in 1976, marked by the extensive release of dioxin, a recognized carcinogen; the shipwreck of the tanker Amoco Cadiz off the shores of Brittany in 1978, spilling 1.6 million barrels of oil, the largest marine disaster of its kind; a serious civilian nuclear plant accident with the partial meltdown of the Three Mile Island nuclear reactor in Pennsylvania on March 28, 1979; the release of the toxic chemical methyl isocyanate at Union Carbide's chemical plant in Bhopal, India on December 2, 1984, leading to the death of thousands of residents in the immediate area, as well as serious injury to tens of thousands of others; the world's worst nuclear power accident at Chernobyl on April 26, 1986; the loss of 250,000 barrels of crude oil in the pristine waters of Prince William Sound, Alaska when the Exxon Valdez was grounded on March 24, 1989; the loss of approximately one half million barrels of crude from the sinking of the tanker, Prestige, off the coast of Spain on November 13, 2002; the Deepwater Horizon massive oil spill in the Gulf of Mexico in 2010 from a drilling platform owned by British Petroleum; and the 2011 Fukushima nuclear power plant disaster in Japan.

Many of the physical effects of these accidents remain to this day but the psychological impact on the conduct of business has been unprecedented. In his landmark study entitled "Corporate Strategy: the Avalanche of Change since Bhopal," Bruce Piasecki (1995) argues that the toxic release of gas from the Union Carbide mill was a watershed

DOI: 10.4324/9781003170754-3

in corporate attitudes toward environmental risk and the need to create new strategic initiatives for addressing such risks. In this case, the risks were substantial – not only the immense human tragedy, but also the threat to corporate license to operate as Union Carbide. The owner of the plant no longer exists as a corporate entity. There was a subsequent arrest warrant in India for the company's CEO, and in 2010 India renewed its request for the extradition of the chief executive, which was subsequently denied (*The Guardian* December 8, 2019). The US government also felt the necessity to react. In 1986, the US Congress enacted EPCRA (the Emergency Planning and Community Right to Know Act), which required most major industrial facilities to gather and publicize their emissions to land, air, and water. The resulting Toxic Release Inventory created a major impetus to the reduction in industrial pollution in the United States.

One of the most serious environmental disasters was not the result of a single industrial accident, but the continued production in the postwar period of a new class of chemicals called perfluoroalkyl and polyfluoroakyl substances (PFAS). These chemicals with a chain of linked carbon and fluorine atoms have come into widespread use in a broad range of industrial and consumer products because of their unique characteristics. PFAS are found in drinking water, waste sites, fire extinguisher foam, multiple manufacturing processes, consumer products (e.g., nonstick cooking wear and stain-resistant clothing), carpets, food packaging, biosolids, and food. Because of their strong chemical bonds, they do not tend to degrade in the environment and can be found in animals, water, food, soil, air, and human blood. In fact, it has been determined that 97% of Americans have blood-borne PFAS (US EPA n.d. and US NIH n.d.). Aside from their environmental persistence, concern has been raised about the health effects of the roughly 15,000 chemicals classed as PFAS and PFOS. According to the EPA, studies have shown that exposure to PFAS may lead to cancer, increased cholesterol and weight, reduced immune function, low birth weight, accelerated puberty, bone variations, and behavioral changes, as well as reproductive effects, such as reduced fertility and increased high blood pressure in pregnant women. The principal manufacturers of these chemicals (Chemours, DuPont. and 3M) have been the subject of ongoing litigation with mixed results (Bilott 2019; CNN June 4, 2023; Reuters November 28, 2023).

The controversy over PFAS and other potentially toxic chemicals raises the contentious and unresolved issue of onus of responsibility for testing new chemicals before being introduced into production and the marketplace. As detailed in Nemetz (2021), there has been a historical difference in the approaches adopted by the US Toxic Substances Chemical Act (TSCA) and Europe's REACH (Registration Evaluation and Authorization of Chemicals).

In contrasting the two disparate approaches to chemical regulation, the US GAO (2007, p. 2) concluded that:

TSCA places the burden of proof on EPA to demonstrate that a chemical poses a risk to human health or the environment before EPA can regulate its production or use, while REACH generally places a burden on chemical companies to ensure that chemicals do not pose such risks or that measures are identified for handling chemicals safely.

Fortunately, this disparity between the two regulatory systems has been blurred in recent years.

Clearly, much has changed from the halcyon days of the immediate postwar years. The business environment in which firms operate has been transformed significantly in the last few decades. The factors that have contributed most strongly to this new context are: globalization, economic crises, the continuing geopolitical problem of global poverty, increased global environmental degradation, and the emergence of environmental awareness among the general public, increasing attention to climate change at all levels of government, from municipal to federal.

Fischer and Schot (1993) characterized the history of corporate response to environmental pressures into two periods: 1970–85, and post-1985. According to the authors, the first period was characterized largely by fighting or reluctantly adapting to external pressure for environmental control. Three different sub-strategies were evinced: (1) crisis-oriented environmental management, which was ad hoc and reactive in nature; (2) cost-orientated management, characterized by the common view that environmental control was a cost to be minimized and a drag on corporate profitability; and (3) early environmental enlightenment, where a small number of corporations were beginning to perceive that environmental issues might be successfully and profitably addressed in new corporate strategic initiatives. In general, however, this era was characterized by a lack of willingness to internalize environmental problems and a reliance on cost-centred, end-of-pipe pollution control rather than fundamental changes in process and products, which could potentially enhance profitability.

The second era identified by Fischer and Schot, following 1985, represents the first glimmerings of strategic adjustments, most notably by a handful of large corporations and multinationals. Willams, et al. (1993) identified the following drivers of this corporate response: (1) increasingly stringent environmental legislation and enforcement; (2) increasing costs associated with pollution control, solid waste and effluent disposal; (3) increasing commercial pressure from the supply, consumption, and disposal of both intermediate and final products; (4) increasing awareness on the part of investors of companies' environmental performance in view of the cost implications associated with liability and the *polluter pays principle* (OECD 1975); (5) increasing training and personnel and information requirements; and (6) increasing expectations on the part of the local community and the workforce of the environmental performance of firms and their impact on the environment. Each of these factors set the stage for Porter's and van der Linde's landmark publication in the *Harvard Business Review* (1995) entitled "Green and Competitive: Ending the Stalemate," which represented a conceptual leap promising to transform these potential costs into sustainable competitive advantage.

A similar, but somewhat more disaggregated, analysis of the transformation in corporate attitudes relating to the environment was presented in Hoffman's (2001) work, entitled *From Heresy to Dogma, An Institutional History of Corporate Environmentalism.* To Hoffman, the transformation occurred over four periods: (1) 1960–1970, a period of "industrial environmentalism" where industry considered these issues largely peripheral to its business and had the latitude to handle pollution problems itself, largely without government interference; (2) 1970–1982, a period of "regulatory environmentalism", marked by the establishment of the US EPA and new federal environmental regulation and technical compliance by industry; (3) 1982–1988, a period of "environmentalism as social responsibility" where industry became more proactively involved in the public debate and rule setting processes addressing environmental degradation. Hoffman describes a change from technical compliance to managerial compliance where more corporate institutional processes and structures were established to deal with environmental matters; and (4) 1988–1993, a period "strategic environmentalism" that elevated environmental issues to the level of corporate strategy and the recognition of the explicit role of major stakeholders such as investors, insurers and competitors in environmental issues.

This last period represented the birth of a major change which has radically altered the strategic calculus of corporate decision-making – namely, the emergence of *stakeholders* as key players in the corporate environment, replacing the sole reliance on *shareholders* as the ultimate focus of corporate decision making. The OECD *Principles of Corporate Governance* endorsed by OECD Ministers in 1999 stated that "[i]n all OECD countries, the rights of stakeholders are established by law (e.g., labour, business, commercial and insolvency laws) or by contractual relations" (OECD 2010; see also du Plessis et al. 2011). This diverse range of additional players, who both constrain and empower corporate action, include bondholders, debtors, creditors, insurers, employees, suppliers, customers, regulators, and the general public. All combine to both enrich and increase the complexity of the corporate environment in which both short-term and long-term decisions must be made. Figure 2.1 summarizes the driving forces acting on corporations to improve environmental performance.

The critical question is how this process of transformation in corporate strategy impacted corporate value. This issue was specifically addressed by Dunphy (2007), who identified six specific evolutionary phases in strategy and linked them directly to a value

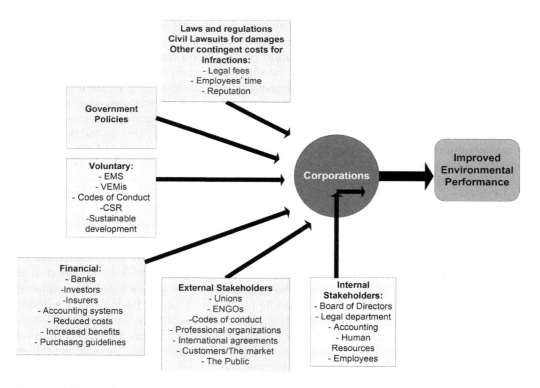

Figure 2.1 Forces Acting on Corporations to Empower Environmental Performance

Adapted from Thompson 2002

continuum that ranges from value destruction to value creation and sustainability (see Table 2.1). It is important to bear in mind that none of the rubrics of corporate environmental strategy suggest a mechanical progression of every firm through stages of increased engagement with sustainability issues. Rather, they are intended to reflect differing corporate attitudes which may characterize some, but certainly not all, firms in several distinctive periods in the last half of the twenty-first century. In one of the modern classics of environmentalism and business, entitled *Cannibals With Forks*, John Elkington (1997) identified seven revolutions that have been transforming corporate attitudes and behaviour in the realm of sustainable business: (1) increased domestic and international competition; (2) a global shift in human and societal values to include concern for social and ecological issues in addition to economic matters; (3) growing pressures for transparency; (4) the increasing adoption of lifecycle technology and measurement; (5) the emergence of new forms of partnerships, especially among NGOs and corporations; (6) the increasing need to take a longer view with respect to the impact of business decisions; and (7) dramatic changes in the philosophy of corporate governance. Elkington (1997) concluded his book with an extensive list of 39 steps required to shift business toward sustainability based on the seven revolutions he has identified (see Table 2.2).

Table 2.1 Typology of Evolutionary Phases in Strategy

Wave	Phase	Characterization	Effect on Corporate Value
1st	Opposition	Rejection	Value destroyers
	Ignorance	Non-responsiveness	Value limiters
2nd	Risk	Compliance	Value conservers
	Cost	Efficiency	Value creators
	Competitive Advantage	Strategic Proactivity	
3rd	Transformation	Sustaining corporation	Sustainable business

Derived from Dunphyet al. (2007, p. 17)

Table 2.2 Elkington's 39 Steps to Shift Business to Sustainability

#	Rubric	Old paradigm	New paradigm
1	Governance	financial bottom line	triple bottom line
2		physical and financial capital	economic, human, social, natural
3		tangible, owned assets	intangible, borrowed assets
4		downsizing	innovation
5		exclusive governance	inclusive governance
6		shareholders	stakeholders
7	Time	wider	longer
8		extraction	restoration
9		tactics	strategy
10		plans	scenarios
11		time bandits	time guardians
12	Partners	deregulation	reregulation
13		enemies	complementors
14		subversion	symbiosis
15		unconditional loyalty	conditional loyalty

(Continued)

Table 2.2 (Continued)

#	Rubric	Old paradigm	New paradigm
16		rights	responsibilities
17		green business networks	sustainability keiretsu
18	Life-cycle technology	responsibility to factory gate	stewardship throughout life cycle
19		sales	lifetime customer value
20		product and waste	co-products
21		environmental LCAs	triple bottom line LCAs
22		product	function
23		trial and error	biometrics
24	Transparency	closed, except financial reports	open, triple bottom line reports
25		need to know	right to know
26		facts and science	emotions and perceptions
27		one-way, passive communication	multiway, active dialogue
28		promises	targets
29	Values	careless, uncaring	careful, caring
30		control	stewardship
31		me	we
32		monocultures	diversity
33		growth	sustainability
34	Markets	externalization of costs	internalization of costs
35		compliance	competitive advantage
36		country-by-country standards	global consistency
37		adding volume	adding value
38		production growth	sustainable consumption
39		disruptive NGO campaigns	disruption as commercial strategy

Derived from Elkington (1997, chapter 12)

The Current Situation

Much has changed in the last two decades in attitudes towards sustainability among government, the public, corporations, and the financial sector. Indeed, it is hard to find a company whose corporate mission statement, annual reports, or public statements that do not make reference to sustainability. Public attention, driven by the media, however, tends to be focussed on the two diametrically opposed ends of the spectrum of corporate responses – from exemplary to dubious, or indeed fraudulent. By way of example, Table 2.3 lists the top companies deemed the most sustainable in several recent high-profile reports, while Table 2.4 lists the leading companies deemed to be the worst. Not surprisingly, most of these companies are in the energy sector, specifically fossil fuel producers or users.

From the perspective of private costs and benefits, there is little incentive for fossil fuel companies to abandon a business model that has generated – and continues to generate – significant profits. The problems is the lack of congruence of such private costs and benefits with social costs and benefits, especially when the potential costs include significant medium- to long-term harm to the environment, and ultimately to the economy as a whole. While some fossil fuel companies publicly stress the positive aspects of their production, the conduct of their business and lobbying activity are usually at odds with

Table 2.3 The Most Sustainable Companies

Source	Barron's (2023)	Financial Times (2023)	GlobeScan (2022)	Sustainable Business Forum (2023)	Corporate Knights (2024)	Earth.Org (2022)	S&P Global (2022)	S&P Dow Jones (2023)	Business Insider (2009)	WSJ 2020
Coverage:	USA	Europe	Global	Global	Global	Global	Global	Global	Mostly USA	Global
	Clorox	Tele (Sweden)	Unilever (UK)	Chr. Hansen (Denmark)	Sims Ltd (Australia)	Vesta Wind Systems A/S (Denmark)	ANA Holdings Inc. (Japan)	Microsoft Corp. (USA)	Hewlett-Packard (USA)	Sony (Japan)
	Intel	Telia Company (Sweden)	Patagonia (USA)	McCormick & Company (USA)	Brambles Ltd. (Australia)	Chr. Hansen Holding A/S (Denmark)	Hindalco Industries Ltd. (India)	Alphabet Inc. (USA)	Dell (USA)	Philips (Netherlands)
	Kimberley-Clark	Deutsche Telekom (Germany)	Natura & Co. (Brazil)	Cisco (USA)	Vestas Wind Systems A/S (Denmark)	Autodesk Inc (USA)	Leonardo S.p.a. (Italy)	Unitedhealth Group Inc. (USA)	Johnson & Johnson (USA)	Cisco Systems (USA)
	CBRE Group	Indra Sistemas (Spain)	IKEA (Sweden)		Taiwan High Speed Rail Corp. (Taiwan)	Schneider Electric SE (France)	Hankook Tire & Technology Co., Ltd. (Korea)	Tawian Semiconductor Manufacturing Co. Ltd. (Taiwan)	Intel (USA)	Merck KGaA (Germany)
	Waters	Porsche (Germany)	Microsoft (USA)		Nordex SE (Germany)	City Development Ltd. (Singapore)	Pirelli & C.S.p.A. (Italy)	AbbVie Inc. (USA)	IBM (USA)	Iberdrola (Spain)
	Jones Lang LaSalle	Inditex (Spain)	Interface (USA)		Banco do Brasil SA (Brazil)	American Water Works Company Inc. (USA)	Hyundai Motor Co. (Korea)	ASML Holding NV (Netherlands)	State Street (USA)	LG Electronics (South Korea)
	Best Buy	Intermediate Capital Group (UK)	Orsted (Denmark)		Schneider Electric SE (France)	Orsted A/S (Denmark)	GM Co. (USA)	Novartis AG Reg (Switzweland)	Nike (USA)	Melia Hotels International (Spain)
	Carrier Global	Kering (France)	Tesla (USA)		Chr Hansen Holding A/S (Denmark)	Atlantica Sustainable Infrastructure PLC (UK)	Ownes Corning (USA)	AstraZeneca Plc (UK)	Bristol-Myers Squibb (USA)	HP (USA)
	Ecolab	Nykredit (Denmark)	Danone (Canada)		Stantec Inc (Canada)	Dassault Systemes SE (France)	KB Financial Group Inc. (Korea)	Roche Hldgs AG PrgGenus (Switzerland)	Applied Materials (USA)	Georg Fischer (Switzerland)
	Hasbro	WPP (UK)	Google (USA)		SMA Solar Technology AG (Germany)	Branbles Ltd. (Australia)	Banco Bilbao Vizcaya Amentaria, S.A. (Spain)	Salesforce Inc. (USA)	Starbucks (USA)	Sekisui Chemical (Japan)
	Applied Materials	Elisa (Finland)	Nestle (Switzerland)		Autodesk Inc (USA)	Sims Ltd. (Australia)	Kasikornbank Public Company Ltd. (Thailand)		Johnson Controls (Ireland)	
	Proctor & Gamble		Suzano (Brazil)		WSP Global Inc (Canada)	Johnson Controls International PLC (Ireland)	Biogen Inc. (USA)		Cisco Systems (USA)	

Table 2.4 Major Companies Deemed Least Sustainable

Source:	Influence Map (2022)	Inside Climate News (2022)	Sustainable Business Forum (2024)	Ethical Consumer (2022)	Business Insider (2009)	The Guardian (2021)	MSCI (2023)
Coverage:	Global	USA	Global	Global	USA	USA	Global
Rank:	by impact	by pollutant					by carbon footprint
	Chevron (USA)	CO_2 - The Southern Company	Amazon (USA)	Nestle (Switzerland)	Peabody Energy (USA)	Chevron	Saudi Arabian Oil Company (Saudi Arabia)
	ExxonMobil (USA)	CH_4 - Consol Energy	Nestle (Switzerland)	Monsanto (USA)	NRG Energy (USA)	Exxon	Coal India Ltd. (India)
	BASF (Germany)	N_2O - Ascend Performance Materials	Peabody Energy (USA)	Amazon (USA)	Allegheny Energy (USA)	Chase Bank	PetroChina Company Limited (China)
	ConocoPhillips (USA)	HFC-23 -Chemours Co.		Shell (UK)	ConAgra Foods (USA)	BlackRock	Exxon Mobil Corporation (USA)
	Sempra Energy (USA)	SF_6 - American Electric Power		Tesco (UK)	Consol Energy (USA)	Koch Industries	BHP Group Limited (Australia)
	American Electric Power (USA)	CH_4 from landfill - GFL Environmental Holdings		Barclays (UK)	Ameren (USA)	Facebook	SAIC Motor Cororation Limited (China)
	Southern Company (USA)	CH_4 from underground gas storage - Boardwalk Pipeline Partners		Exxon (USA)	American Electric Power (USA)	News Corp	Vale S.A. (Brazil)
	Nipon Steel Corporation (Japan)			Wal Mart (USA) - former owner of ASDA (UK)	Bunge (USA)	Cargill	China Shenhua Energy Company Limited (China)
	Gazprom (Russia)			Coca Cola (USA)	Southern (USA)	Edelman PR	Shwell PLC (UK)
	Toyota Motor (Japan)				FirstEnergy (USA)		
	CenterPoint Energy (USA)			Primark (Ireland)	Duke Energy (USA)	Gibson Dunn LLP	Rio Tinto PLC (UK)
	Marathon Petroleum (USA)				Progress Energy (USA)		

Table 2.5 Major Companies Engaging in Greenwashing

Volkswagen (see chapter 15)
BP
ExxonMobil
Nestle
Coca-Cola
Starbucks
IKEA
Plastic Bottle Water Companies (e.g., Poland Spring, Evian, and Deer Park)
Major Banks (e.g., JP Morgan, Citibank, Bank of America, Wells Fargo,
    Barclays, Bank of China, HSBC, Goldman Sachs, and Deutsche Bank)
Fast Fashion Brands (e.g, H&M, Zara, and Uniqlo)

Source: Earth.org (2022)

facts on the ground, as the industry has engaged in extensive programs of climate denial and disinformation, or *greenwashing* (ISD and CASM Technology 2023). As Lobbymap (2022) finds: "Companies appear to 'cherry-pick' positive high-level statements from their industry associations when analyzing alignment, overlooking sometimes substantial evidence of detailed negative lobbying on climate-related policy" (p. 18). A Google Cloud Sustainability Survey of 2023 reinforces these findings by observing that: "Without measurement, corporate greenwashing and green hypocrisy remained pervasive concerns among this year's respondents, with many executives admitting to overstating — or inaccurately representing — their sustainability activities" (p. 2). Table 2.5 lists the most prominent companies engaging in extensive programs of greenwashing (Earth.org 2022 and Rainforest Action Network 2021).

While it is relatively easy to identify those companies with the worst sustainability records based on their emissions and related activities, the identification of best companies presents several challenges:

1. There should be arms-length third party verification of corporate claims to sustainability and/or standards that the corporation can publicly report (e.g., GRI, LEED, ISO 14001, B CORP, Green Business Bureau, Forest Stewardship [FSC], Marine Stewardship [MSC], Rainforest Alliance, and Verra). The reliability of some certifiers, such as the Marine Stewardship Council, has been called into question in the past (*The Guardian* January 6, 2011). More recently, the CEO of Verra was forced to resign after reports that the company had certified offsets for Chevron which were deemed worthless or did not cover 90% of emissions (*The Guardian* May 23 and 24, 2023; Corporate Accountability 2023; Climate & Capitalism May 24, 2023). In fact, Chevron is not alone among fossil fuel firms in making contestable environmental claims. An in-depth study of corporate net zero claims and achievements has found that, while an increasing number of these companies have pledged net zero targets, most do not cover Scope 3 emissions, which represent the largest component of their total emissions, rendering these claims "largely meaningless" (Net Zero Tracker 2023, p. 25).
2. The activities claimed to be sustainable must include most of the core business activities of a firm rather than just peripheral activities and investments (see chapter 14). For

example, at least one company (Nestle) appears on both good and bad lists, suggesting an insufficient appraisal of entire corporate activities.

3. Any sustainability index that includes sustainable companies must assign significant weighting to actual performance measures rather than stated goals and other less relevant variables. For example, an earlier version of the Dow Jones Sustainability Index devoted only a relatively small part of the scoring to actual environmental performance, as opposed to policy, management, reporting, and social issues. Despite the theoretical equivalence of the three pillars of sustainability ecology, economy, and society, it can be argued that the environment is paramount, since without a healthy ecological system, both the economy and society cannot function effectively. An archetypal example of this relationship is the extensive drought that has been afflicting Northeast Africa, with resulting starvation, migration, and death (WFP 2023). More recently, however, the DJSI has been significantly restructured and is built on reports and feedback from media and stakeholders, as well as the risks associated with corporate environmental, social, and governance (ESG) activities, including carbon emissions and carbon intensity (S&P 2023a; S&P 2023b).

4. The output of rating agency constructing lists or indexes of sustainability must be deemed to be reputable and meet stakeholder's needs. By way of example, the Sustainability Institute produces period reports on *Rating the Raters* (SI 2023a; SI 2023b), based on surveys of investors and corporations concerning the quality and usefulness of ESG ratings providers. The percentage of respondents rating *high quality* or *usefulness* ranged from a high of 80% for CDP and 65% for ISS-ESG to a low of 6% for JUST Capital and Sustainable Fitch and 3% for Refinitiv.

What is frequently lost in the dichotomy of best and worst is the broad range of companies in between the two extremes that are trying – with varying degrees of success – to incorporate sustainability into corporate strategy. GlobeScan's (2022) recent sustainability survey concludes that "almost all sectors are viewed by experts as performing poorly overall on transitioning to sustainability" with a percentage of 27% rating poor and 26% excellent in life sciences/biotechnology, and 75% poor and only 6% excellent in oil and gas. Bertrand and Parnaudeau (2019) conclude that "warm or cold weather impacts almost every industry as 70% of businesses are exposed to unexpected variations that influence demand for goods and services" (p. 391). There is clear need for corporations to adjust their strategy to recognize the new realities that will ultimately affect their profitability or even survival. A sole focus on cost is short-sighted as there are enormous economic opportunities for revised or new strategies that focus on new product and service markets, including adaptation to future climate change. By way of example, the World Economic Forum (2022) has estimated that adaptation could be a $2 trillion market by 2026.

To address the challenge of sustainability, several critical concepts have entered the lexicon of many corporations and the financial sector. The most prominent of these include *ESG* (environmental, social, governance), *net zero, carbon neutral*, and *net positive*.

ESG

Traditionally, the principal responsibility of the corporation has been to its *shareholders*. However, there is a broader group of *stakeholders* to which corporations have had an implicit or explicit responsibility to report concerning the financial status of the company. This group has included suppliers, banks, insurers. employees, government agencies and rating agencies. This responsibility has been largely met through the mechanism of financial reporting for which strict national and international rules have been developed.

However, with the advent of increased awareness and concern over environmental and social issues associated with the operation of business, a new emphasis has developed focusing on these additional issues, as well as governance, under the general rubric of ESG reporting.

> The goal is to capture all the nonfinancial risks and opportunities inherent to a company's day to day activities. . . . More and more investors are incorporating ESG elements into their investment decisions making process, making ESG increasingly important from the perspective of securing capital, both debt and equity (Deloitte 2021).

The Harvard Law School Forum on Corporate Governance (Bergman et al. 2020) details the components of each of the the three principal foci:

- "E" captures energy efficiencies, carbon footprints, greenhouse gas emissions, deforestation, biodiversity, climate change and pollution mitigation, waste management and water usage.
- The "S" covers labor standards, wages and benefits, workplace and board diversity, racial justice, pay equity, human rights, talent management, community relations, privacy and data protection, health and safety, supply-chain management and other human capital and social justice issues.
- The "G" covers the governing of the "E" and the "S" categories—corporate board composition and structure, strategic sustainability oversight and compliance, executive compensation, political contributions and lobbying, and bribery and corruption.

While the term *ESG* has appeared in only the last two decades or so, with its first documented use in a report by the United Nations entitled *Who Cares Wins* (2004), Byrne (2022) makes the case that many of the principles have existed for some time, including concern over worker rights, apartheid, and corporate governance codes. The problem facing the corporation today, either willing or required to adhere to standards of ESG reporting, is that a multitude of such standards have emerged from government and other organizations, including: the Sustainability Accounting Standards Board (SASB), Global Reporting Initiative (GRI), Carbon Disclosure Project (CDP), CDSB Framework Application Guidance, IIRC, UN SDGs, TCFD, ISSB, Taskforce on Climate-related Financial Disclosure (TCFD), the EU's European Sustainability Reporting Standards (ESRS) and US SEC (Fasken 2023; Lawton 2023; Sustainability Institute 2022b; Pointb 2023).

In order to overcome the problem posed by this "Alphabet soup" of ESG, on June 26, 2023, the International Sustainability Standards Board (ISSB) issued its inaugural global sustainability disclosure standards, initially in two parts: 1) IFRS S1 General Requirements for Disclosure of Sustainably-related financial Information, and 2) IFRS S2 Climate-related Disclosures (IFRS June 26, 2023b). This is an attempt to bring clarity and consistency to the current complex and confusing array of existing standards. To quote: "for the first time, the Standards create a common language for disclosing the effect of climate-related risks and opportunities on a company's prospects." Implementation of requirements for Scope 3 reporting have been delayed for a year, despite their importance for investors and bankers, to assess the transition risk exposure of their portfolio companies. The delay is mandated in recognition of the challenge facing companies "because of the need to map their overall value chain (Emmanuel quoted in Harrison [2023]). Faber, the ISSB Chair, has stated that several research projects are currently underway that may develop into specific rules in the future. These include biodiversity, ecosystems and ecosystem services, human capital, and human rights.

The Sustainability Institute has published periodic reports entitled *Rate the Raters*. Its latest report is entitled *ESG Rating at a Crossroads* (2023), an attempt to provide a state-of-the-art assessment of the current situation and the views of stakeholders concerning the reliability and usefulness of many ratings. They arrived at six general conclusions:

- Investor demand for ESG ratings is strong and growing
- Discontent among investor and companies is brewing over the shortcomings of ESG ratings
- Investor's growing use of in-house ratings diminishes the value of ESG raters
- Rating leaders stay on top through waves of consolidation
- Regulation has increasing influence, especially in the US and EU
- There is a clear choice for raters: evolve or erode.

Despite these reservations, there is clear evidence that adoption levels are increasing and will continue to do so despite certain corporate and political pushback. The Harvard Law School Forum on Corporate Governance (Ground 2022) reported on adoption rates and reasons for doing so in a study of European, North American, and Asia-Pacific jurisdictions (see Table 2.6).

The issue of adoption is coupled to reporting trends which have tended to vary by time, location and industry. For example, The Governance & Accountability Institute (G&A) publishes periodic reports on the extent of sustainability reporting, including ESG. Their 2022 study examined trends of companies on the S& P 500 and the Russell 1000. They found that,

> since our first research report covering corporate sustainability reporting trends in 2010, the number of companies publishing sustainability reports has increased each year. In this research report, which covers the 2021 publication year, G&A finds that sustainability reporting reached record highs among the largest US publicly traded companies, as represented in the Russell 1000 Index. The percentage of companies in the Russell 1000 publishing a sustainability report increased by 16% to an all-time high of 81%. The number of companies in the top half of the Russell 1000 (which comprise the S&P 500 Index) rose 4% to an all-time high of 96%.
>
> Most significant: G&A researchers determined that the largest increase was among companies in the bottom half of the Russell 1000, where the sustainability reporting percentage increased to 68% in 2021 from 49% in 2020. These trends

clearly demonstrate that annual sustainability reporting has become a best practice for leading US publicly traded companies.

Their report also includes a list of nonreporters among US corporates in the Russell 1000 Index. The percentage of nonreporters by industry varies from a high of 44% in communications to a low of 0% among utilities (see Table 2.7). The percentages of nonreporters has been decreasing steadily over the past several years in light of the rapidly evolving change in attitudes and requirements relating to sustainability reporting in general, and ESG in particular.

Table 2.6 Adoption Rate of ESG By Region (%)

		Europe		North America		Asia-Pacific	
		2021	*2022*	*2021*	*2022*	*2021*	*2022*
Esg Users	Conviction: ESG investing is central to our investment approach	36	31	16	18	22	22
	Acceptance: we apply ESG investing in our investment approach	32	36	34	30	32	34
	Compliance: we consider ESG issues in our investment approach	19	26	30	31	27	32
Non-Users	On the sidelines: we are yet to be convinced about ESG	10	6	18	20	16	10
	Non-adoption	2	0	3	2	3	1

Source: Adapted from Ground June 17, 2022

Table 2.7 Non-Reporting Companies in US Russell 1000 Index (2021)

Sector	*# companies*	*% non-reporting*
Communications	43	44%
Health Care	121	31%
IT	184	29%
Consumer discretionary	127	19%
Financials	144	15%
Industrials	153	11%
Real Estate	68	10%
Consumer staples	53	9%
Energy	31	6%
Materials	58	5%
Utilities	39	0%

Adapted from G&A (2022)

Several reports have outlined themes and related considerations that will influence ESG adoption and reporting in the near future: ISS ESG (2023) identifies several global trends that responsible investors will likely be focusing on through 2023 (see Box 2.1), and Harvard's Law School Forum on Corporate Governance (Romito et al. 2022) has identified 15 anticipated ESG-related considerations that will influence strategy in 2023 (see Box 2.2).

BOX 2.1: Global trends that responsible investors will likely be focusing on through 2023 (ISS ESG 2023)

- As many investors continue to move towards net zero, obtaining transparent, reliable, and standardized data on portfolio companies' emissions, targets, and reduction strategies will be in sharp focus in 2023.
- Heightened awareness of the environmental impact of specific industries, such as food and energy, will influence investment decisions, but investors will need to be creative as well as pragmatic in making these decisions.
- With growth volatility likely to be high in 2023, financial opportunities may be realized through nonconventional stock picking frameworks, such as a combination of EVA and ESG Performance Scores from ISS ESG.
- To keep pace with investors' demand for disclosures, global sustainability standards are in 2023 expected to broaden in Scope. Although regulations to promote reporting requirements are generally welcomed, ISS ESG finds that companies with the greatest transparency are not necessarily the best ESG performers.
- Certain industries' relationships with regulation also present contrasting situations to investors. For example, while the future performance of web-based businesses may be affected by increased regulatory measures meant to counter anticompetitive practices, seeking out regulation to protect consumers may become a required catalyst to restore confidence in the crypto sector.
- Finally, ongoing crises such as the COVID-19 pandemic and Russia's invasion of Ukraine are likely to remain destabilizing forces that will continue to shape the ESG investing landscape in 2023. The pandemic's toll on worker health will continue to create challenges for companies, while economic sanctions on Russia are expected to persist, short of a cessation of hostilities and reaching of a settlement.

Box 2.2: Harvard's 15 anticipated ESG-related considerations that will influence strategy in 2023 (Romito et al. 2022)

1. Blackrock's voting "democratization" will gain popularity & eventual adoption by State Street & Vanguard, thereby adding yet another drain on management's investor engagement resources.
2. GPs will be required to provide specific ESG-related quantitative data not only to proactively convey material differentiators but just to keep fundraising efforts alive.

3. Shareholder proposals will become even more focused on ESG data.
4. Public companies will strongly pressure their private company partners for ESG data points and policies.
5. Water metrics will quickly become an incredibly close second to emissions-related disclosures.
6. Scope 3 will not be included in the SEC climate disclosure mandate but will also not go away.
7. The advancement of the carbon markets, particularly offsets, will aggressively continue.
8. An "emissions avoided" metric will grow in popularity and utility.
9. ESG scores will increase in influence but will remain inherently flawed.
10. Europe's Sustainable Finance Disclosure Regulation will quickly trickle into the SEC's policy on greenwashing.
11. Quantitative climate-focused metrics will permanently revise credit underwriting due diligence processes.
12. The SEC will attempt to pass through additional incremental human capital management disclosures.
13. Cybersecurity disclosure expectations and mandates will also increase in 2023.
14. The Carbon Disclosure Project ("CDP") survey will grow in utility among global investors.
15. Capital markets participants will rethink the utility and pragmatism of net zero commitments.

Operationalizing ESG: the Development and Use of ESG Metrics

In choosing to engage in ESG reporting, the corporation has the option of reporting on dozens or even hundreds of variables. This process does not, in and by itself, usually produce useful information that can be easily digested by an investor. That is the job of rating agencies, whose function is to distill all the relevant information – from the company and public sources – into a small number of summary indicators or even a single value that attempts to capture the essence of a business' operation. The process is simple conceptually but can be complicated in its application. There are three foci of ESG ratings: materiality, data harvesting, and scoring (Makower 2022a). A common methodology is to assign a numerical score to a variable (e.g., out of 10) and then weigh all the variable to generate an overall letter grade or single number (GreenBiz 2022, Kerner 2023). There are at least five major rating agencies (ISS ESG, Moodys, MSCI, S&P Global, and Sustainalytics) as well as several others (Bloomberg ESG, Fitch, FTSE and CDP). There are several major issues that arise in the generation and interpretation of their resulting scores.

1. Rating agencies treat their methodology – specifically the scoring and weighting – as proprietary. There is no overall standard and accepted methodology. As a result, different ratings agencies may generate different numbers for the same companies and there is no clear way to differentiate among them (Brackley et al 2022). One study (SSGA 2019) found a correlation value of only 0.38 among top four raters' scores in contrast to a 0.99 correlation of credit ratings between the conventional financial risk

ratings of Moody's and Standard and Poor. Another study found the average correlation among prominent ESG ratings was only 0.54 (MIT Sloan 2023). Mayor (2019) has identified at least three source of divergence among ratings: Scope divergence, weight divergence and measurement divergence.

2. The rating apply to intraindustry comparisons only and cannot be used to compare firms across industries.

3. But perhaps, most importantly, there is disagreement over the degree to which these scores actually represent the sustainability goals implied therein. Some experts claim (Makower 2022b) that the sole purpose of the scores is to signal the risks associated with the financial activities of the company and nothing more. There are a number of examples which illustrate this conundrum. One example, in particular, cited in the literature, relates to the operation of the McDonald's restaurant chain. Ratings of this company by MSCI, for example, generally paint a very positive image of the company based on a narrow definition of its environmental practices inter alia (Simpson et al. 2021). On concluding that climate change does not pose a risk to McDonald's bottom line, the assessment clearly misses the prominent role that the company's supply chain plays in environmental despoliation in such places as Brazil's Amazonia region where the company sources a significant proportion of its beef (Bloomberg January 21, 2022).

This major disconnection between ESG scores and corporate sustainability does not, however, render the measure irrelevant. First, stakeholders still have the option of viewing and assessing the data generated by the corporation itself. Second, there are certain benefits associated with ESG reporting in addition to meeting requirements of government regulation and capital markets.

There are two general types of assessments of the value of ESG ratings: economic/business and ideological. While the former are, on balance, positive with some contradictory evidence, the latter are uniformly negative.

From the economics and business side, the positive assessments include the following:

- The ESG ratings are a complement to traditional financial ratings that do not cover the full range of modern risks faced by corporations. In the case where ESG ratings can identify important externalities, many of these could become tomorrow's financial risks. And ESG ratings can socialize and educate the financial and business to a range of topics with which they were not familiar (Makover 2022b).

- There is a valuable relationship between stock returns and ESG scores which is frequently drowned out by noise in the data which may represent up to 60% of the final score (Stackpole 2023). Berg et al. (2023a) correct for the noise using an instrumental variable approach in a multiple regression framework and confirm that the ESG ratings are indeed valuable since there is a statistically significant relationship between ESG scores and stock returns.

- Berg et al. (2023b) have also conducted an analysis of the returns of ESG investing and conclude that aggregate ESG ratings improve portfolio performance and therefore are very useful in portfolio construction.

- Other advantages for corporations stemming from the generation of ESG scores include brand building, (Makower 2022b), valuation of ESG-related activities, peer comparisons, benchmarking, managing progress, investor attraction and risk management (Kerner 2023).

- Perez et al. (2022) of McKinsey argue that while "valid questions have been raised about ESG, the need for companies to understand and address their externalities is likely to become essential to maintaining their social licence."
- Butler (2018) found that 68% of millennials bought a product with a social or environmental benefit in the past 12 months.
- 87% of consumers will have a more positive image of a company that supports social or environmental issues. 88% will be more loyal to a company that supports social or environmental issues. 87% would buy a product with a social and environmental benefit if given the opportunity. 92% will be more likely to trust a company that supports social or environmental issues.
- Some research suggests that there is a positive relationship between ESG performance scores and two valuation ratios, Market Value Added (MVA) and Future Growth Reliance Insights (Insights 2023a). The research has found that this relationship varies across sectors with communication services and energy the highest (Insights 2023b).
- An Australian study (Hoffman 2022) concluded that there seemed to be a "reasonable positive correlation between total shareholder returns (TSR) and improvement in ESG scores over a three-year horizon." It also found that improvements in ESG scores correlate positively with improvements in valuation multiples such as EV/EBITDA, EV/revenue and P/E over the same three-year horizon.
- A survey by Intelex (2022) of 700 EHS and ESG professionals in ten European countries found that "almost three-quarters of respondents are worried that failing to improve ESG performance will negatively impact their organisation's brand and reputation."
- A study by the management consultant Bain & Company (Seeman 2023) found that sustainability measures correlate with financial performance and that such connections were manifested in the areas of sustainable supply chains, renewable energy, employee satisfaction and DEI.
- A broad survey (Whelan et al. 2021) of over 1,000 studies published between 2015 and 2020 found a "positive relationship between ESG and financial performance for 58% of the corporate studies focused on operational metrics such as ROE, ROA, or stock price with 13% showing neutral impact, 21% mixed results and only 8% showing a negative relationship."
- A report by the Center for Audit Quality (Reuters 2022) concluded that "if a company is not looking at environmental and social factors, it is not well governed."
- A report by Intelex (2023) advanced the argument that ESG inspires technological innovation.

As stated above, however, not all economic assessments of ESG ratings are necessarily positive. King & Pucker (2022), for example, conclude that "managers create false hope, oversell performance and contribute to the delay of long past-due regulatory action." They find logic problems in four principal purported advantages of ESG ratings: (1) they deliver higher profits, (2) they signal higher future stock returns, (3) they lower the cost of capital, and (4) they lead to benefits from capital flows.

In an opinion piece in the *Economist*, Tariq Fancy (2021), former chief investment officer for sustainable investing at BlackRock, concludes that:

corporate ESG efforts have negligible impact. Worse, its saintly narratives distract the public from seeing the need for aggressive, systemic reforms that only governments have the ability and legitimacy to pursue. . . . In practice, ESG information has limited use in most investment processes. This is due to a combination of ambiguous data and inconsistent standards, short time-horizons for most investment strategies and the uncomfortable reality that being responsible usually isn't profitable. . . . Unfortunately, the utopian storyline around ESG actually undermines the case for government to play a role. Misleading public-relations activities foist the idea that sustainable investing, stakeholder capitalism and voluntary compliance are the answers.

In another opinion piece in the *Wall Street Journal* by Terrence Keeley (2022), a former senior executive at BlackRock, reported that:

Over the past five years, global ESG funds have underperformed the broader market by more than 250 basis points per year, an average 6.3% return compared with a 8.9% return. . . . Composite ESG scores—which attempt to summarize all material ESG risks into a single number or grade—convey little actionable investment information."

In a guest essay for the *New York Times*, Hans Taparia (2022), a clinical associate professor at the New York University Stern School of Business, expressed major reservations about criteria for inclusion of companies in ratings, particularly by MSCI. In citing the contentious inclusion of McDonalds, he continues:

This is hardly an isolated case. According to a recent Bloomberg analysis of 155 rating upgrades, only one cited a cut in emissions as a factor. Given this lenient rating system, it's not difficult for a company to be deemed environmentally or socially responsible. Indeed, 90 percent of stocks in the S&P 500 can be found in an E.S.G. fund built with MSCI ratings. Most technology stocks, including Alphabet and Meta, are part of E.S.G. funds, despite concerns about their role in facilitating the spread of misinformation and hate speech. Coca-Cola and Pepsi have gotten very high E.S.G. scores and find themselves in most big E.S.G. funds, despite manufacturing products that are a major cause of diabetes, obesity and early mortality and despite being the world's largest contributors to plastic pollution. Perhaps most egregiously, BP and Exxon get respectable ratings from MSCI.

While there continues to be a robust debate in the business and economic communities about the present and future value of ESG ratios, there is no such divergence of opinion when it comes to ideological views of ESG. The interpretation of ideological criticisms of ESG have been rendered more complex by the politicalizing of the topic in the American election cycle. There do, in fact, seem to be several principal lines of argument which have been presented (*New York Times* May 11, 2022; May 27, 2022; August 5, 2022; March 4, 2023; March 5, 2023; GreenBiz 2023a; G&A 2023a; G&A 2023b).

First, ESG represents an unwarranted intrusion on the affairs of business by government – this even though the business community itself and capital markets in particular appear to have a major role in driving the process.

Second, a focus on environmental and social issues in particular run counter to Milton Friedman's classic argument (1970) that the social responsibility of business of is to make a profit. There is certainly no doubt that current thinking on the role of business has changed markedly since Freidman wrote his classic essay over 50 years ago – and that is the point. Changing attitudes reflect the profound changes that have occurred in the economic, social, and ecological environment since that time – necessitating a much more complex and nuanced view of the role of business. Paul Polman, former CEO of Unilever (Polman & Winston 2021) has declared that "Milton Friedman is dead." He argues that:

> given the state and urgency of climate change, the moral imperative of tackling inequality and the changing nature of financial markets, the quarterly-focussed, shareholder-first mantra is widely unfit for today's world and is ultimately self-defeating (p.8; see also *New York Times* January 30, 2023).

Third, some politicians have gone so far as to characterize ESG as part of a *radical* attack on business itself. This line of argument seems particularly problematic, since it essentially calls into question a fundamental bedrock component of modern economic theory – that negative externalities exist and must be corrected to ultimately create a more efficient allocation of capital and maximize economic welfare. This is certainly not a radical concept and the use of this type of hyperbole only serves to distort what should be a rational assessment of ESG.

Much of the controversy over ESG ratings may disappear over time as it is likely that such ratings will ultimately be folded into a new and more comprehensive measure of corporate risk and corporate impact on the social, ecological and economic environment, combining traditional elements of financial risk assessment and current ESG components.

Net Zero and Carbon Neutral

Net zero and *carbon neutral* are related, but not identical terms, which describe the goal of balancing the emissions of greenhouse gases (GHG) with their removal. While net zero includes all GHGs, carbon neutral removal refers to only one (although most arguably the most important) – GHG. For a company aiming to become carbon neutral, for example, there are several steps required. The first, is the reduction in carbon output through changes in total production, switching to renewable (i.e. green energy), altering product mix and/or inputs, such as components or final products for resale. In most cases, these steps will not be enough to eliminate the output of GHGs, necessitating a second step: engaging in some form of offsetting where funds are used to fund removal and sequestration through technological means such as carbon capture and storage (CCS) or natural climate solutions such reforestation (see Appendix One).

The question remains as to whether carbon offsets are a necessary ingredient of any corporate attempts to achieve net zero. One of Australia's richest men, Andrew Forrest, has vowed to make his iron ore company, Fortescue Metals Group, truly carbon neutral by using solar and wind power, electric vehicles, hydrogen, and hydropower with pumped storage to eliminate the necessity for carbon credits (*The Guardian* September 29, 2022). Illustrative of this approach is the greenhouse gas mitigation hierarchy (Columbia University n.d.) that includes, in order of preference: avoid, reduce, replace, compensate (offsets), and neutralize (remove). In other words, offsets are essentially an option of last resort. Recent reports are supportive of this assessment, suggesting that "Carbon credit speculators could lose billions as offsets deemed worthless'" (*The Guardian* May 19, 2023; Jones & Lewis 2023). Ecosystem Marketplace

(2023) reported that "Average voluntary carbon markets (VCM) credit prices in 2022 were higher than they have been in 15 years, while overall trade volumes dropped from a 2021 peak. While the volume of VCM credits traded dropped by 51%, the average price per credit skyrocketed, rising by 82% from $4.04 per ton in 2021 to $7.37 per ton in 2022. This price hike allowed the overall value of the VCM to hold relatively steady in 2022, at just under $2 billion. To date in 2023, the average credit price is down slightly from 2022, to $6.97 per ton."

Reuters (September 1, 2023) has reported that "Voluntary carbon markets have shrunk for the first time in at least seven years, as companies including food giant Nestle and fashion house Gucci reduced buying and studies found several forest protection projects did not deliver promised emissions savings."

A recent United Nations Report (2021) makes several specific recommendations concerning claims concerning net zero:

- Nonstate actors cannot claim to be net zero while continuing to build or invest in new fossil fuel supply. Coal, oil, and gas account for over 75% of global greenhouse gas emissions. Net zero is entirely incompatible with continued investment in fossil fuels.
- Nonstate actors cannot buy cheap credits that often lack integrity instead of immediately cutting their own emissions across their value chain.
- Nonstate actors cannot focus on reducing the intensity of their emissions rather than their absolute emissions or tackling only a part of their emissions rather than their full value chain (Scopes 1, 2 and 3).

In gauging a firm's ultimate success, it is critical to understand the relative role of the three *Scopes* of the production process:

Scope 1 includes direct company owned or controlled emission occurring at source.
Scope 2 includes emissions associated with the production energy consumed by the company.
Scope 3 indirect emissions associated with company activities from sources not owned or controlled by a company, including both upstream and downstream activities.

It is frequently the case that the largest emissions flow from either energy consumption – depending on its source – and the activities of other entities that supply inputs to the final production process or use its output. Carnegie-Mellon University, for one, developed an extensive combined life-cycle, input-output database (called *EIOLCA*), which helped in identifying all the sources associated with any one product. For example, Table 2.8 reproduces sample data from the Ferrous Metal Foundries sector. Unfortunately, the database has been recently removed from the university's website because of lack of maintenance. Nevertheless, there are over fifty publicly available databases that can assist companies to identify all or part of their Scope 3 emissions (see Appendix Two).

MSCI (2023) has produced a database of 2011 companies and their GHG end targets. Table 2.9 lists the terminology gleaned from annual reports and other corporate statements. Clearly, the terminology varies but, in many cases, the meanings are identical and have been grouped together in the table. For those companies, stating a goal of emissions reduction, the values range from 1% to 100% with an average of 37%. For those companies stating an emissions intensity reduction target, the values range from 3% to 75%

Table 2.8 EIOLCA Analysis of Ferrous Metals Foundries, Sector 335510

GHG Emissions

		GWP MT CO2e	%
TOTAL EMISSIONS	FOR ALL SECTORS	914.17	100%
DIRECT EMISSIONS	Ferrous metal foundries	81.87	9.0%
INDIRECT EMISSIONS			
221100	Power generation and supply	388.08	42.5%
484000	Truck transportation	66.43	7.3%
562000	Waste management and remediation services	49.73	5.4%
331111	Iron and steel mills	43.49	4.8%
331112	Ferroalloy and related product manufacturing	37.31	4.1%
331419	Primary nonferrous metal, except copper and aluminum	30.87	3.4%
331312	Primary aluminum production	21.98	2.4%
212100	Coal mining	19.97	2.2%
S00202	State and local government electric utilities	17.00	1.9%
211000	Oil and gas extraction	14.73	1.6%
486000	Pipeline transportation	11.98	1.3%
327410	Lime manufacturing	10.66	1.2%
482000	Rail transportation	8.54	0.9%
481000	Air transportation	8.51	0.9%
324110	Petroleum refineries	7.37	0.8%
212230	Copper, nickel, lead, and zinc mining	6.87	0.8%
221200	Natural gas distribution	6.19	0.7%
420000	Wholesale trade	6.13	0.7%
212320	Sand, gravel, clay, and refractory mining	5.60	0.6%
	Other	70.86	7.8%

Source: www.eiolca.net no longer on line

with an average of 34%. It should be noted however, that these data are problematic as emission intensity reduction can be offset by increases in production and, inevitably, the most important value is the total output of GHGs (see chapter 14). One category, the term *science-based targets* specifically means reducing emissions in line with the goals of the Paris Agreement to limit global temperature rise to 1.5 degrees C. This entails implementing a full net zero profile (across all 3 Scopes) by 2050. Extensive guidance is proved to corporations on how to measure and achieve these results (See: SBTi 2022; SBTi 2023a; SBTi 2023b; SBTi 2023c).

One category, in particular, stands out from Table 2.9: *carbon negative* and *carbon positive* are used in the same sense and represent a marked difference from the

Table 2.9 Corporate Terminology for GHG Targets

Terminology	# companies
Carbon negative	8
Climate positive	5
Carbon neutrality	208
Zero carbon	9
Climate neutral	42
GHG neutrality	1
Net zero	565
zero emissions	11
1.5 degrees Celsius target	7
Absolute emissions target	2
Emissions reduction target	191
Emissions intensity target	31
Other	73
Science-based target	29
No target	829
TOTAL	2011

Source: Adapted from Net Zero Tracker 2023

other categories. To quote Paul Polman, the former CEO of Unilever and his coauthor Andrew Winston (2021):

> The net positive company will operate differently from what's normal today. It will, for example, eliminate more carbon than it produces; use only renewable energy and renewably sourced materials; create no waste and build everything for full circularity; and replenish and male cleaner all the water it draws (p. 9).

This is a herculean challenge, but several companies have achieved it with respect to selected products. An example is given in the chapter on Interface in this volume.

The paramount question is how far how companies are progressing in achieving the stated goal of net zero with respect to either carbon or total GHG emissions. At this stage, the results are mixed. Several recent reports suggest only modest increments to date.

- In a report on 24 major global companies, the New Climate Institute (2023) finds that "net-zero pledges break down to only moderate emission reductions alongside offsetting and Scope exclusions."
- The NGO *As You Sow* (2023) reported on the progress of 55 of the largest US corporations in reducing GHG emissions and found only three companies received an overall "A" grade across three pillars for an overall net zero grade (climate related disclosures, GHG reduction targets, and GHG reductions): Microsoft, Pepsico, an d Ecolab Inc.

- Researchers from Yale University's Center for Business and the Environment (Edmunds et al. 2020) reported on the progress of the S&P 100 companies and found that four had no emissions reporting and 18 reported only Scope 1+2 results and none for Scope 3. Financial Services had the highest number of firms with stated net zero goal (7/18) while Real Estate and Industrials had none (0/2 and 0/12, respectively). For those with stated net zero goals, the target dates range from 2034 to 2050 for Scope 1 and 2 emissions. The exception was Apple, which has achieved this goal already for its global corporate operations and has made a commitment for every device sold to be net zero by 2030 (Apple 2022; Team Consequence 2023).
- MSCI (2023) has produced an extensive summary of progress by the world's listed companies toward curbing climate risk. They conclude on a cautionary note:

> Listed companies are making progress toward net-zero. That includes mapping out and committing to decarbonization targets, and publishing greenhouse gas emissions across their value chains. A significant gap remains, however, between companies' collective climate ambition and the amount of greenhouse gases that they are continuing to emit into the atmosphere. The window to limit global temperature rise to 1.5 degrees C is "rapidly narrowing," as the IPCC noted in March. The emissions of listed companies, meanwhile, are on a trajectory to warm the planet by 2.7 degrees celsius this century. . . . The climate transition is gaining traction but is nowhere near where it needs to be if society is to avoid the most disruptive warming. Carbon emissions hover near all time highs, and the end of this critical decade for cutting emissions is approaching. The clock is ticking.

Another major study by the World Wildlife Fund (2021) provides a progress report of the *Fortune 500's Transition to a Net Zero Economy*. There has been a steady growth in corporate climate cation. They conclude that:

> 60% of Fortune 500 companies (2020) have set a climate or energy-related commitment. This represents a 12-percentage-point increase since Power Forward 3.0, published in 2017. Science-based target setting has grown significantly, with 63 Fortune 500 companies (13%) having set targets approved by the Science Based Targets initiative, six times the number of companies that had done so in 2017. The exciting and growing trend among companies is setting net-zero, carbon-neutral, or related commitments, with 83 (17%) of the Fortune 500 possessing such targets. Ninety-four companies have set a goal to buy or invest in renewable energy, up from the 53 that had done so in Power Forward 3.0. Fifty-eight of the 94 companies possess 100% renewable energy targets. . . . Additionally, the report highlights that despite significant growth in voluntary target setting, gaps in corporate climate action remain: 40% of the Fortune 500 do not have any type of public climate or energy-related target. 400 companies (80%) of the Fortune 500 have neither set, nor officially committed to set, science-based targets through the Science Based Targets initiative. Less than one in five Fortune 500 companies has a climate goal that covers Scope 3. The quality and credibility of certain net-zero or related claims remains uncertain. Adoption of targets varies widely across industry sectors.

One principal corporate mechanism towards addressing sustainability goals is to use offsets, defined as investing in greenhouse reducing activities generally off-site, to "offset" their own emissions. There are four major types of offsets: direct air carbon capture, forest carbon offsets, blue/marine carbon offsets, and soil carbon offsets (NCX 2022, p.9). This is an increasingly controversial practice that has encountered a significant amount of concern over their validity.

There are several conceptual and logistical issues raised by offsets (Nemetz 2022). First, it may be difficult to generate an accurate estimate of how much carbon is produced by engaging in a particular activity or how much carbon will be removed by any one project, especially if it is unconventional. Second, a carbon reduction project may look good on paper, but it is necessary to determine that it satisfies the condition of *additivity* (i.e., it will have an incremental effect over what would have occurred anyway). Third, it is important to ensure that the effect will be permanent and not transitory, and fourth, that the activity will not lead to displacement, where that activity simply moves to another location rather than replaces the activity that generates more net carbon. In the case of tree planting, it is essential to ascertain that the trees survive, thrive after planting, are not harvested, and that compensatory woodcutting for heating and cooking does not occur in another locale. But fifth, perhaps the most serious issue is that in the pursuit of carbon neutrality, offsets allow the individual or corporation to continue with business as usual. This is inconsistent with any serious attempt to tackle global warming and has been described as the equivalent of the medieval sale of indulgences as a means of atoning for one's sins (see also UNEP 2020).

One of the most egregious misuses of carbon offsets is the case of the certifier, Verra, and its customer Chevron, as described in the text above. One of the most forceful indictments of the use of bogus offsets was produced by Bloomberg and Company in November 2023, under the headline: "Junk carbon offsets are what make these big companies 'Carbon Neutral.'" One of the most common forms of offsetting, representing 40% of all offsets, involves investments in renewable energy. As Bloomburg (November 20, 2022) states:

> Purchasing credits tied to support of solar or wind projects sounds good for the climate. But experts consider these offsets largely bogus. The issue is timing: many renewable offsets came into being just as solar and wind power established themselves as the cheapest source of energy in most countries. Selling offsets for small sums as a way to support the economics of renewables doesn't provide any real benefit if it's already cheaper than building new coal or gas power plants.

Bloomberg examined 190 million tons of carbon offsets purchased in more than 50,000 transactions in 2021. One company stood out as the most egregious misrepresentation of carbon neutrality through renewable-energy offsetting of 13.5 M tons. To quote:

> Delta Air Lines Inc., which runs more than 4,000 flights every day, has for over two years claimed to be carbon neutral. That means it has wiped away in its own accounts millions of tons of CO_2 from burning all that jet fuel, which it has used to launch an advertising blitz aimed at guilt-ridden travelers. "Our customers shouldn't have to choose between seeing the world and saving the world," said Delta's managing director for sustainability Amelia DeLuca in a statement. "We're balancing our emissions with investments to remove carbon across our global operations." A closer look shows otherwise. The more stringent category of removal

offsets comprised just 6% of its 27 million tons of Delta's carbon credit purchases last year. Half the offsets Delta used to make that claim came from renewables, mostly wind and solar projects in India. An expert review of Delta's largest single source of renewable offsets, the Los Cocos II wind farm in the Dominican Republic, determined that it almost certainly didn't need additional support.

In the face of criticism, many companies have engaged in what is referred to as *greenwashing*. In its most benign form, this practice involves corporations overstating their sustainability achievements. However, a more extreme form represents a total misrepresentation of corporate activities, in some cases bordering on – or are actual – fraud (see chapter 15).

Greenwashing

There are three areas of common corporate greenwashing: net zero commitments, corporate climate change disclosures, and voluntary carbon markets (Fasken 2023). There are several typologies of greenwashing. Planet Tracker (Willis 2023) has described 6 distinct categories:

1. *Greencrowding* is built on the belief that you can hide in a crowd to avoid discovery; it relies on safety in numbers. If sustainability policies are being developed, it is likely that the group will move at the speed of the slowest.
2. *Greenlighting* occurs when company communications (including advertisements) spotlight a particularly green feature of its operations or products, however small, to draw attention away from environmentally damaging activities being conducted elsewhere.
3. *Greenshifting* is when companies imply that the consumer is at fault and shift the blame on to them.
4. *Greenlabelling* is a practice where marketers call something green or sustainable, but a closer examination reveals that their words are misleading.
5. *Greenrinsing* refers to when a company regularly changes its ESG targets before they are achieved.
6. *Greenhushing* refers to the act of corporate management teams under-reporting or hiding their sustainability credentials to evade investor scrutiny.

Reuters (December 4, 2023) adds yet another term to the lexicon of greenwashing: *greenbleaching*. In another study at Harvard University, Supran et al. (2022) conducted a textual and visual context analysis of 2325 organic social media posts by 22 major European Union-based companies in three industries: fossil fuel producers, car manufacturers, and airlines. They identified five types of activities:

- **Climate silence:** During a summer of unprecedented European heatwaves, droughts, and wildfires, only a negligible handful of posts made any explicit reference to climate change or global heating.
- **Greenwashing:** Two-thirds of oil and gas (72%), auto (60%), and airline (60%) companies' social media posts paint a 'Green Innovation' narrative sheen on their 'Business-as-usual' operations, which are given less airtime. This ratio of green-to-dirty

in each industry's public communications (3-to-1, 4-to-1, and 1.2-to-1, respectively) misrepresents their contemporary commitments to decarbonization, implying that at least some of their social media content constitutes greenwashing. We interpret greenwashing by the fossil fuel industry to be most blatant, whereas that by airlines is notably subtle.

- **Misdirection:** One-in-five oil and gas (23%), auto (22%), and airline (15%) company posts feature sports, social causes, and/or fashion. The overarching theme of this narrative of misdirection is to focus the audience's attention on engaging topics unrelated to companies' core business operations. This can variously: (1) legitimize fossil fuel interests' social license to operate; (2) distract attention away from firms' core business roles, responsibilities, and contributions to the climate crisis; and (3) market brands as exclusive, desirable, and relevant.
- **Nature-rinsing (formally termed "executional greenwashing"):** Statistical analysis reveals fossil fuel interests' systematic use of nature-evoking imagery to enhance the "greenness" of their brand image on social media. To our knowledge, this subtle intentionality to fossil fuel interests' green messaging has never previously been quantified.
- **Demographic greening and misdirection:** Statistical tests show that companies (particularly car manufacturers) variously leverage not just the imagery of nature, but also of female-presenting people, nonbinary-presenting people, non-Caucasian-presenting people, young people, experts, sports people, and celebrities to reinforce their messages of green innovation and/or misdirection.

The effects of greenwashing are not limited to misleading the consumer. In a recent article in the *Harvard Business Review*, Ioannou et al. (2022) report that 42% of green claims in Europe were "exaggerated, false, or deceptive, which points to greenwashing on an industrial scale." They concluded that:

> greenwashing not only has a negative impact on customer satisfaction but, by extension, it also harms brand, reputation, and brand loyalty, as well as customers' purchase intentions and repeat purchases. Greenwashing also poses a regulatory and legal risk in some countries while regulatory oversight globally is on the rise."

Professor George Georgiev, an academic expert on securities law at Emory University observed that "climate-related financial information is demanded by investors, not by environmentalists" (*The Guardian* August 19, 2022).

This last point is critical, as Emmanuel Faber, group chair of ISSB, has been quoted as stating that:

> Climate change will redefine competitive advantages in supply chains, in value chains, in finance, for the foreseeable future. And there is a clear need by investors that is expressed by having a language that allows them to measure, to count, things like climate change (Globe & Mail February 19, 2023).

Realizing the critical importance of climate change and the material risks it presents, several governments have already instituted a range of new regulations to make corporate-based climate risks more transparent to guarantee the continued efficiency and resilience of international capital markets. These initiatives have already been undertaken by the US, UK, and the European Union and include targeting greenwashing among a range of other disclosure and reporting requirements (SEC 2022, *National Law Review* 2022, UK 2023a, EU 2023; see also JTC 2022, Reuters October 21 2022 and February 16 2023, Weil 2022, IFRS 2023a, b; Duane Morris LLP 2023; GreenBiz 2023c; UK 2023b, 2023c).

A recent focus among regulatory bodies has been the inclusion of Scope 3 emissions in corporate disclosure of climate footprint. Scope 3 data is difficult to capture and manage, which leads to many companies not reporting, and those that do report relying on off-the-shelf software tools such as MSExcel. In fact, in March 2024, facing increased pushback from a range of companies and industries including fossil fuel producers, the SEC backed off requiring reporting emissions for corporate supply chains as well as abandoning a number of other critical reporting requirements (*New York Times*, March 6, 2024).

Ms. Allison Herren Lee, former acting chair and commissioner of the SEC has commented that: "if you don't have Scope 3 as a requirement, then what you have effectively done is cut out most of the emissions from the top-emitting Industries" (*The Guardian* August 19, 2022).

While much of the literature on greenwashing has been devoted to ecological issues (see for example, RepRisk 2022), a recent report by RepRisk (2023) has extended this analysis to *social washing* on an issue and sector-specific basis. In a review of 1116 cases over the period September 2018 to September 2023, social washing issues fell into ten categories: poor employment conditions (24%), human rights abuses and corporate complicity (23%), occupational health and safety issues (13%), impacts on communities (12%), discrimination in employment (7%), freedom of association and collective bargaining (7%), social discrimination (5%), local participation issues (4%), forced labour (4%), and child labour (25%). These entailed selective disclosure, empty claims and policies, misleading narratives and discourse and dubious certifications and labels. The economy was broken down into six major sectors: extractives, financial, food and beverage, retail, technology and utilities. The number of risk incidents leading to misleading communication (856) fell into two general categories: community relations and employee relations. The extractives industry had the highest number (208) for community relations and food and beverages and retail had the highest number of employee relations incidents with 63 and 60, respectively. As the authors conclude:

The drivers of greenwashing and social washing include increased demand for sustainable products and companies, as well as the expectation of competitive advantage derived from an image of sustainability. A lack of standardization and accountability around a rapidly evolving landscape of corporate sustainability are also contributing factors. Despite this, in recent years symbolic sustainability has backfired for many as media, regulators, and civil society have challenged unfounded claims. Emerging regulations have begun to tackle the issue by defining what constitutes sustainability and addressing the drivers of misleading communication. . . . The data shows that misleading communication on ESG issues and attention to the trend are on the rise. Beyond greenwashing, deceptive social responsibility tactics are also in the spotlight and frequently more severe.

The Way Forward

McKinsey (2021) has laid out nine requirements for a more orderly transition to net zero under three general categories. These are:

- *Physical building blocks*: technological innovation, ability to create at-scale supply chains and supporting infrastructure, and availability of necessary resources
- *Economic and societal adjustments*: effective capital reallocation and financing structures, management of demand shifts and near-term unit cost increase, and compensating mechanisms to address socioeconomic impacts
- *Governance, institution, and commitment*: governing standards, tracking and market mechanisms, and effective institutions; commitment by and collaboration among public-, private-, and social-sector leaders globally; and support from citizens and consumers.

Considering the increasing attention to issues of sustainability and their impact on corporate strategy, the question arises as to where this process is heading. Several reports have highlighted the top trends and issues as of 2023. The Network for Business Sustainability (2023) polled sustainability professionals about the top sustainability issues they were most curious about in 2023. The top ten of these topics were:

1. how to adopt sustainable innovation
2. how to tailor sustainable innovation to specific contexts
3. how to integrate circularity across a company
4. tips for reducing carbon emissions
5. measuring companies' climate footprints
6. how to integrate sustainability into business schools
7. how to strengthen employee commitment to sustainability
8. ways to uphold human rights
9. how to empower marginalized voices in climate decisions
10. paths to fund the transition sustainably

In the second report, by The Sustainability Institute (2023c), the top ten trends in the evolution if sustainable business included:

1. integrating ESG
2. valuing human capital
3. responding to climate change
4. safeguarding natural systems
5. building sustainable and resilient supply chains
6. enabling sustainable consumption and production
7. applying technology to sustainability
8. respecting fundamental rights
9. shaping policy, regulations, and norms
10. moving toward stakeholder capitalism.

Many of these topics are also addressed in greater depth in the following chapters on methodology and case studies that cover the range of corporate responses to the sustainability challenge and their relative degrees of success.

Appendix One: Carbon Capture and Storage and Natural Climate Solutions

Carbon capture and storage

One potential technology that has received a great deal of international attention is carbon capture and storage (CCS), also referred to as CCUS (carbon capture, utilization and storage) (IPCC 2005; Carbonbrief 2014; IEA 2020; Conniff 2020; Biniek et al. 2020; McKinsey 2020; *New York Times* March 8, 2021; *Science* March 26, 2021). There are two general approaches: recovery of CO_2 from flue gasses or directly from the atmosphere. Several flue gas recovery projects are currently in operation worldwide, associated with power plants, fertilizer, and steel production, as well as oil sands and biofuel (*New York Times* July 22, 2014; Carbonbrief, 2014; CCSA n.d.). In the energy sector, carbon dioxide is generally injected into underground fossil fuel reservoirs to promote recovery of oil and natural gas. In other industrial sectors, the carbon is captured at the point of emission and then injected into the earth where the goal is to isolate the gas indefinitely. Dowell et al. (2017, p. 243) argue that carbon utilization in industries outside of the oil and gas industry is a "costly distraction, financially and politically, from the real task of mitigation, since this potential market for the chemical conversion of CO_2 would account for no more than 1 percent of the mitigation challenge."

Several critical criteria must be met before flue-gas recovery can be considered a viable solution at the global level. First, the technology would only be useful for large single-point emission sources and inappropriate for distributed or fugitive sources. Second, there must be reasonably proximate favorable geological formations for carbon dioxide injection. Third, the costs must be a relatively small proportion of the total cost of energy production. And, finally, there must be some assurance that the geological formations designed to contain the injected CO_2 are stable and able to hold the gas indefinitely.

One report (Thomson 2009, p. 46) concluded that "by one estimate the United States would have to construct 300,000 injection wells at a cost of $3 trillion by 2030 just to keep emissions at 2005 levels." Smil (2010) has calculated that governments will have to construct CO_2 infrastructure about twice the size of the world's crude oil industry just to bury 25% of the world's emissions. These scale-up issues pose among the most imposing challenges to this technology, even if other scientific questions were to be resolved satisfactorily.

A fundamental uncertainty remains about the ultimate effectiveness and safety of such a system. It is not known with any certainty how long the CO_2 would stay underground and, if it were to escape, the consequence could be an environmental crisis of potentially greater magnitude than the original problem. This type of risk is an archetypal example of revenge theory (Tenner 1996). A US EPA study (2008) stressed the multitude of scientific uncertainties associated with CCS, focusing on the vulnerability of the geological system to unanticipated migration, leakage, undesirable pressure changes, and the possible negative consequences of system failure on human, plant, and animal life (see Figure 2.2).

While research continues into the scientific and economic feasibility of this technology, fewer than two dozen commercial-scale facilities are in operation, and several high-profile projects in the United States, Britain, and Canada have been cancelled (*New Scientist* 2011; *Globe and Mail* 2012; *The Guardian* 2011; *New York Times* July 13, 15 and 31, 2011; May 19, 2012) but proposals from the oil and gas sector continue to be advanced (*Vancouver Sun* July 13, 2021). While this technology may prove viable in the future,

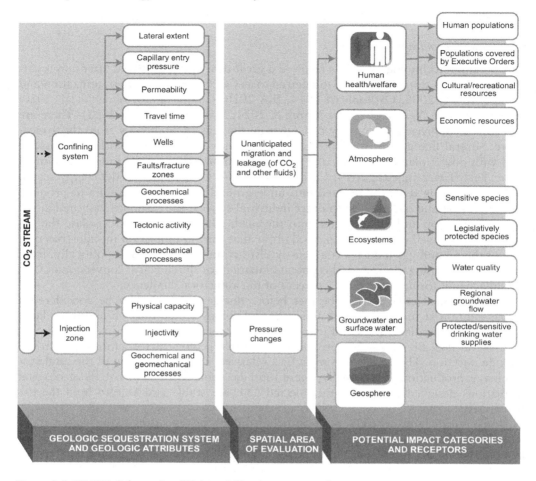

Figure 2.2 US EPA Schematic of Vulnerability Assessment of CCS

its recent track record and current level of uncertainty suggest that any corporate or governmental plans to rely extensively on this technology for carbon dioxide control entails an unacceptable risk (Kirchsteiger 2008; Wilday et al. 2011; Rochon et al. 2008; Smil 2010). A report from the National Academy of Sciences (2019, p. 4) cautions that:

> negative emissions technologies are best viewed as a component of the mitigation portfolio, rather than a way to decrease atmospheric concentrations of carbon dioxide only after anthropogenic emissions have been eliminated. . . . The committee recognizes that there is a possibility that large negative emissions in the future could result in a moral hazard, by reducing humanity's will to cut emissions in the near term. Reducing emissions is vital to addressing the climate problem.

This view is echoed by Anderson and Peters (2016, p. 183) who concluded that reliance on negative-emission concepts locks in humankind's carbon addiction. To quote:

"negative-emission technologies are not an insurance policy, but rather an unjust and high-stakes gamble."

Other studies reinforce ongoing concerns by focussing on direct costs (Biello 2016), air pollution and total social costs including intergenerational ethical issues (Lenzi et al 2018; Jacobson 2019), possible obstruction of mitigation (Lenzi 2018), and the incentive to maintain "dangerous habits" by allowing industry to continue business as usual (CBC 2019b; Plumer & Flavelle 2021).

In light of the economic and technological challenges facing the direct recovery of CO_2 from combustion sources, a second major approach has been proposed: the direct removal of carbon dioxide from the atmosphere. A major step toward the achievement of viable direct air capture and storage (DACS) (Mulligan et al. 2018) has been achieved by several demonstration projects (BBC News, June 7, 2018 and April 3, 2019; Keith et al. 2018). However, this potential solution must still overcome some of the fundamental challenges which face flue gas recovery: scale-up, number of global units required to achieve significant levels of atmospheric CO_2 reduction, energy inputs required, cost, and the issue of carbon dioxide disposition. Broecker and Kunzig (2008, p. 211) conclude that "we cannot solve the CO_2 problem without tacking small and mobile sources. Right now, Lackner and Wright's invention [scrubbing the gas directly from the air] offers the only hope." However, James Hansen et al. (2016, p. 577–578) concluded that:

> continued high fossil fuel emissions today place a burden on young people to undertake massive technological CO_2 extraction if they are to limit climate change and its consequences. Proposed methods of extraction such as bioenergy with carbon capture and storage (BECCS) or air capture of CO_2 have minimal estimated costs of USD 89–535 trillion this century and also have large risks and uncertain feasibility. Continued high fossil fuel emissions unarguably sentences young people to either a massive, implausible cleanup or growing deleterious climate impacts or both.

Natural Climate Solutions (NCS)

In contrast to these high-tech solutions with their attendant risks, *natural climate solutions* can increase carbon storage and/or avoid greenhouse gas emissions through conservation, restoration, and improved management practices across global forests, wetlands, grasslands, and agricultural lands (see, for example, Drever et al. 2021). Griscom et al. (2017) studied 20 possible natural climate solutions and concluded (p. 11645):

> We show that NCS can provide over one-third of the cost-effective climate mitigation needed between now and 2030 to stabilize warming to below 2 °C. Alongside aggressive fossil fuel emissions reductions, NCS offer a powerful set of options for nations to deliver on the Paris Climate Agreement while improving soil productivity, cleaning our air and water, and maintaining biodiversity.

A major and common natural climate solution is reforestation (Bastin et al. 2019). Along with oceans and soils, forests are among the principal global sinks for carbon which prevent the concentration of greenhouse gases in the atmosphere from becoming even

higher. While this undertaking can, in theory, make a difference, there are several qualifications to the extent of its potential success.

1. It has been estimated that foresting enough area to seriously address climate change
   would require land areas significantly more than what are available. In fact, if
   implemented as a global solution to climate change, the area would probably eliminate virtually all natural ecosystems. To quote one research report on the limits
   to global-warming mitigation by terrestrial carbon removal (Boysen et al. 2017,
   p. 463):

   Our results show that those tCDR measures are unable to counteract business-as-usual
   emissions without eliminating virtually all natural ecosystems. Even if considerable
   (Representative Concentration Pathway 4.5 [RCP4.5]) emissions reductions are
   assumed, tCDR with 50% storage efficiency requires >1.1 Gha of the most productive agricultural areas or the elimination of >50% of natural forests. In addition,
   >100 MtN/yr fertilizers would be needed to remove the roughly 320 GtC foreseen in
   these scenarios. Such interventions would severely compromise food production and/
   or biosphere functioning. Second, we reanalyze the requirements for achieving the
   160–190 GtC tCDR that would complement strong mitigation action (RCP2.6) to
   avoid 2 degrees C overshoot anytime. We find that a combination of high irrigation
   water input and/or more efficient conversion to stored carbon is necessary. In the face
   of severe trade-offs with society and the biosphere, we conclude that large-scale tCDR
   is not a viable alternative to aggressive emissions reduction.

2. Planting the billions of trees required would require an extensive effort to continuously monitor the seedling to guarantee that they received enough water and nutrients
   to survive and thrive and escape any human predation for domestic, commercial, or
   industrial purposes.

3. If carbon dioxide emissions continue unabated, there will be an ongoing requirement
   to plant more trees, regardless of whether the land for such expansion is available or
   even exists.

4. A prerequisite to this massive an undertaking is the stabilization of the current stock
   of forests being removed annually by human activity.

5. Climate change is already contributing to the loss of forest cover by insect predation,
   drought and forest fire and this also requires immediate remediation as some large
   global forests have been converted from carbon sinks into carbon sources (Natural
   Resources Canada 2007; Baccini et al. 2017; Sierra Club of BC 2019; CBC 2019a).
   The interaction of climate change and forests has become another in the list of
   threatening positive feedback loops which can accelerate global warming.

6. Even if forests which remain standing, climate change is affecting the quality of growth
   and the capacity to absorb carbon (Matricardi et al. 2020).

7. The expansion of forest land should not come at the expense of other crucial land
   uses, most notably for agriculture.

One study has found that as many as 58.9 million hectares of natural forest have
grown back since 2000 with little or no intervention (Force of Nature 2021). However,
global data reveal that this has been more than offset by global levels of deforestation. To counter this overall trend, several countries have embarked on major efforts
of reforestation. Most notable among these has been China's efforts to reverse the
pronounced negative economic and ecological effects of deforestation by undertaking

a massive program of reforestation, beginning in 1978 following the passage of the Natural Forest Conservation Program (NDCP) (Vina et al. 2016; NASA 2019). As a result of this effort, China has sought to compensate for its loss of forests for domestic use and export by increasing the importation of both lumber and round wood from global sources, including Russia, South America, Africa, and Southeast Asia (Katsigris et al. 2004; Hoang & Kanemoto 2021). These imports have been both legal and illegal (Mir and Fraser 2003; Johnson 2003; Global Witness 2015; Siriwat & Nijman 2018; EIA 2019; *New York Times* April 9, 2019). For example, a report by Chatham House (Hoare 2015) concluded that "half of all the trade in illegal wood-based products is now destined for China (p. viii)." They report that most of this illegal timber comes from Indonesia, Brazil and Malaysia, but that while some other countries produce less timber overall, they have a much higher share of illegal timber in their production. For example, this proportion in the Democratic Republic of Congo represents virtually 100% of their total production.

A systems analysis of China's overall success in addressing global warming and its own ecological requirements requires an accounting of the loss of other forests sacrificed for the Chinese market to determine if there has been any net gain at the global level. At issue is not only the total loss of forest cover but also the loss of biodiversity as highly-productive forests are replaced with less biodiversity in exporting countries. However, consideration of biodiversity and other vital ecological functions is not confined to exporters. Hua et al. (2018) reported on the results of China's new forest policy:

> We found that while the region's gross tree cover grew by 32%, this increase was entirely due to the conversion of croplands to tree plantations, particularly monocultures. Native forests, in turn, suffered a net loss of 6.6%. Thus, instead of truly recovering forested landscapes and generating concomitant environmental benefits, the region's apparent forest recovery has effectively displaced native forests, including those that could have naturally regenerated on land freed up from agriculture (p. 493).

Another archetypal example of problematic reforestation efforts is provided by the UK's efforts to reach net zero by planting conifer forests in Scotland. As Smyth (2023) observes, this effort is counterproductive as the trees are being planted on peat bogs which, when disturbed emit larger quantities of carbon dioxide than absorbed in new tree growth. In essence, this turns the goal of carbon positive forests into net sources.

None of these qualifications should deter efforts to use as many natural ecological processes as possible to stabilize or even reduce global warming. However, what should be apparent for the previous discussion of both technological and natural systems for removing carbon from the atmosphere is that there is absolutely no substitute for the decarbonization of the global economy. That must be the singular and principal focus of both national and international efforts.

Appendix Two: Third-Party Databases to Assist in Collecting Data for Product Life Cycle and Corporate Value Chain (Scope 3) GHG Inventories

---

3EID
Athena Institute
Australian National Life Cycle Inventory Database (AusLCI)
Bath Inventory of Carbon and Energy (ICE)
Bilan Carbone
Biomass Environmental Assessment Tool (BEAT)
Building Research Establishment
BUWAL
Canadian Raw Materials Database
Carbon Calculations over the Life Cycle of Industrial Activities (CCaLC)
Carnegie Mellon
Centre for Environmental Assessment of Product and Material Systems (CPM) Chalmers
Chinese Life Cycle Database (CLCD)
CEDA
Defra
E3IOT
Ecoinvent
Ecoinvent Wastewater Tool
EIME (Environmental Improvement Made Easy)
ELCD
Environmental Products Declarations (EPD)
ESU-services
European Aluminium Association (EAA)
European Container Glass Association (CGA)
European Copper Institute (ECI)
European Federation of Corrugated Board Manufacturers (FEFCO)
Footprint Expert
Franklin US LCI
GaBi Databases
Global Emission Model for Integrated Systems (GEMIS)
Global LCA Data Access (GLAD)
Greenhouse Gas Protocol
Greenhouse gases, Regulated Emissions, and Energy use in Transportation (GREET)
iLCA2010+
International Energy Agency (IEA) GHG Programme
International Iron and Steel Institute (IISI)
International Stainless Steel Federation (ISSF)
International Tin Research Institute (ITRI)
International Zinc Association (IZA)
Inventory Database for Environmental Analysis (IDEA)
IPCC Emissions Factor Database
LCI Calculation Tool for Crop Production
LCI Calculation Tools for Regionalised Waste Treatment
National Renewable Energy Laboratory (NREL) Life Cycle Inventory (LCI)
Nexus
OPEN IO
Plastics Europe
ProBas (Prozessorientierte Basisdaten furUmweltmanagement-Instrumente)
SICV Brazil
Sustainable Recycling Industries – Life cycle inventories project datasets and tools
Swiss Agricultural Life Cycle Assessment (SALCA)
SRI Global Refinery Model
US EPA Supply Chain Greenhouse Gas Emission Factors for US Commodities and Industries

---

Source: World Resources Institute and World Business Council for Sustainable Development – Greenhouse Gas Protocol

References

Anderson, Kevin & Glen Peters (2016) "The trouble with negative emissions," *Science*, October 14.

Angelova, Kamelia (2009) "The 15 best companies for the planet," *Business Insider*, September 23.

Apple, Inc. (2022) *Environmental Social Governance Report*. Investor Relations. https://s2.q4cdn.com/470004039/files/doc_downloads/2022/08/2022_Apple_ESG_Report.pdf

As You Sow (2023) "Road to Zero emissions." https://static1.squarespace.com/static/59a706d4f5e2319b70240ef9/t/654173fbfb360c7445aa3d0c/1698788352229/AsYouSow2023_RoadToZero_v5_FIN_20231031.pdf

Baccini, Alessandro, et al. (2017) "Tropical forests are a net carbon source based on aboveground measurements of gain and loss," *Science*, October 13.

Barron's (2023) "Barron's 100 most sustainable US companies," March 6.

Bastin, Jean-Francois, et al. (2019) "The global tree restoration potential," *Science*, July 5.

BBC News (2018) "Key 'step forward' in cutting cost of removing CO_2 from air," June 7.

BBC News (2019) "Climate change: 'Magic Bullet' carbon solution takes big step," April 3.

Berg, Florian, et al. (2023a) "The signal and the noise." *EconPol Forum*, 24(1): 23–27.

Berg, Florian, et al. (2023b) "Quantifying the returns of E.S.G. investing: an empirical analysis with six ESG metrics." MIT Sloan research paper, number 6930–23.

Bergman, Mark S., et al. (2020) "Introduction to E.S.G." *Harvard Law School Forum on Corporate Governance*, August 1. https://corpgov.law.harvard.edu/2020/08/01/introduction-to-esg/

Bertrand, Jean-Louis, & Mela Parnaudeau (2019) "Understanding economic effects of abnormal weather to mitigate the risk of business failures," *Journal of Business Research*, May.

Biello, David (2016) "Carbon capture may be too expensive to combat climate change," *Scientific American*, January 1.

Bilott, Robert (2019) *Exposure. Poisoned water, corporate greed, and one lawyer's twenty-year battel against DuPont*. Atria Books.

Biniek, Krysta, et al. (2020) "Driving CO2 emissions to zero (and beyond) with carbon capture, use, and storage," *McKinsey Quarterly*, June.

Bloomberg (2022) "How big beef is fueling the Amazon's destruction," January 21.

Bloomberg (2023) "Junk carbon offsets are what make these big companies 'carbon neutral,'" November 20.

Boysen, Lena R., et al. (2017) "The limits to global-warming mitigation by terrestrial carbon removal," *Earth's Future*, May 17.

Brackley, Aiste, et al. (2022) "Rating the Raters yet again: six challenges for E.S.G. ratings," October 5.

Broecker, Wallace S., & Robert Kunzig (2008) *Fixing Climate*. Hill and Wang.

Butler, Adam (2018) "Do customers really care about your environmental impact?" *Forbes*, November 21.

Byrne, Dan (2022) "What is the history of E.S.G.?" *The Corporate Governance Institute*.

Carbon Capture & Storage Association (CCSA) (n.d.), "International CCS Projects."

Carbonbrief (2014) "Around the world in 22 carbon capture projects," October 7.

Carson, Rachel (1962) *Silent Spring*, Houghton Mifflin.

CBC (2019a) "Canada's forests actually emit more carbon than they absorb – despite what you've heard on Facebook," February 1.

CBC (2019b) "Carbon capture and storage: Hasn't Alberta learned its lesson," November 29.

Climate & Capitalism (2023) "The net zero hoax: chevron's fraudulent climate, plan exposed," May 24.

CNN (2023). "Three companies agree to pay more than $1 billion to settle 'forever chemical' claims" June 4.

Columbia University (n.d.) "Greenhouse Gas Mitigation Hierarchy," Sustainable Columbia.

Conniff, Richard (2020). "The Last resort. Can we remove enough CO2 from the atmosphere to slow or even reverse climate change? *Scientific American*, Summer.

Corporate Accountability (2023). "Destruction is at the heart of everything we do: Chevron's junk climate action agenda and how it intensifies global harm," Corporateaccountability.org. https://corporateaccountability.org/wp-content/uploads/2023/05/Chevron-expose_English_FINAL.pdf

Corporate Knights (2023a). "Carbon neutral and net zero claims face global Greenwash crackdown," May 17.

Corporate Knights (2023b). "100 most sustainable companies of 2023 still flourishing in tumultuous times," Winter.

Corporate Knights (2024). "The Global 100 list: How the world's most sustainable corporations are driving the green transition," Winter.

Deloitte (2021). "#1 What is the ESG?: ESG explained, Article series exploring E.S.G. from the very basics." https://www2.deloitte.com/hu/en/pages/energy-and-resources/articles/esg-explained-1-what-is-esg.html

Dowell, Niall Mac, et al. (2017). "The role of CO2 capture and utilization in mitigating climate change," *Nature Climate Change*, April.

Drever, C. Ronnie, et al. (2021). "Natural Climate solutions for Canada," *Science Advances*, June 4.

du Plessis, Jean Jacques, Anil Hargovan and Mirko Bagaric (2011). *Principles of Contemporary Corporate Governance*, Cambridge: Cambridge University Press.

Duane Morris LLP (2023). "The SEC and continued focus and enforcement of greenwashing by Alek Smolij," April 17.

Dunphy, Dexter (2007). *Organizational Change for Corporate Sustainability*. Routledge.

Earth.org (2022). "The world's 50 most sustainable companies in 2022." https://earth.org/worlds-most-sustainable-companies-in-2022/

Ecosystem Marketplace (2023). "Paying for Quality. State of the Voluntary Carbon Markets 2023."

Elkington, John (1997). *Cannibals With Forks: The Triple Bottom Line of 21st Century Business*, John Wiley & Sons, Ltd.

Environmental Investigative Agency (EIA) (2019). *Ban-Boozled. How corruption and collusion fuel illegal rosewood trade in Ghana*. https://us.eia.org/wp-content/uploads/2019/07/BAN_Boozled_Rosewood_Ghana.pdf

Ethical Consumer (2022) "Five unethical companies." https://www.ethicalconsumer.org/retailers/five-unethical-companies

European Parliament (2023) "Parliament backs new rules for sustainable, durable products and no greenwashing." https://www.europarl.europa.eu/pdfs/news/expert/2023/5/press_release/20230505IPR85011/20230505IPR85011_en.pdf

Fancy, Tariq (2021) "Tariq Fancy on the failure of Green investing," *The Economist*, November 4.

Fasken (2023) "New ISSB standards – Is this the end of the 'alphabet soup' for EST disclosure retirement and how will Canada position itself?" Fasken.com. https://www.fasken.com/en/knowledge/2023/06/new-issb-standards

Fasken (2022) "'Climate-washing' risks and how to mitigate them," Fasken.com. https://www.fasken.com/en/knowledge/2022/02/28-climate-washing-risks-and-how-to-mitigate-them

Financial Times (2023) "FT – Europe's climate leaders 2023." https://www.ft.com/climate-leaders-europe-2023

Fischer Kurt and Johan Schot (1993). *Environmental Strategies for Industry: International Perspectives on Research Needs and Policy Implications*. Island Press.

Force of Nature (2021) "Mapping forest regeneration hotspots."

Friedman, Milton (1970) "The social responsibility of business is to increase its profits," *New York Times*, September 13.

Gardella, John, (2023) "SEC anti-greenwashing rules approved hearing," *The National Law Review*, May 26.

GlobalReporting.org (2021) *GRI standards: A short introduction to the GRI standards*. https://www.globalreporting.org/media/wtaf14tw/a-short-introduction-to-the-gri-standards.pdf

Global Witness (2015) *The cost of luxury: Cambodia's illegal trade in precious wood with China*. https://www.globalwitness.org/documents/17788/the_cost_of_luxury_1.pdf

Global Witness (2022) "IPCC clarion call puts spotlight on fossil fuel industry's hypocrisy," GlobalWitness.org (April 12). https://www.globalwitness.org/en/campaigns/fossil-gas/ipcc-clarion-call-puts-spotlight-on-fossil-fuel-industrys-hypocrisy/

Globe and Mail (2012) "Alberta's Carbon Capture Efforts Set Back," April 26.

Globe and Mail (2023) "New global climate accounting standards take aim at greenwashing," February 19.

GlobeScan (2022) *SustainAbility Survey: Sustainability Leaders 2022*. https://globescan.wpenginepowered.com/wp-content/uploads/2022/06/GlobeScan-SustainAbility-Leaders-Survey-2022-Report.pdf

Google Cloud (2023) "Google Cloud Sustainability Survey 2023." https://cloud.google.com/blog/transform/2023-google-cloud-sustainability-survey

Governance and Accountability Institute (G&A) (2022) *Sustainability Reporting in Focus: Examining 2021 Trends of Companies on the S&P 500+ Russell 1000*. https://www.ga-institute.com/research/ga-research-directory/sustainability-reporting-trends/2021-sustainability-reporting-in-focus.html

Governance and Accountability Institute (G&A) (2023a) "Is ESG a threat to humanity? Opponents think so, and are pushing back on climate crisis actions." https://www.ga-institute.com/nc/news/newsletter/press-release/article/is-esg-a-threat-to-humanity-opponents-think-so-are-pushing-back-on-climate-crisis-actions.html

Governance and Accountability Institute (G&A) (2023b) "Anti-ESG attacks continue at state and federal government levels." https://www.ga-institute.com/news/newsletter/press-release/article/anti-esg-attacks-continue-at-state-federal-government-levels.html

Grasso, Marco & Richard Heede (2023) "Time to pay the piper: fossil fuel companies' reparations for climate damages," *One Earth*. https://doi.org/10.1016/j.oneear.2023.04.012

GreenBiz (2022) "The secret life of EST ratings: part one," May 9. https://www.greenbiz.com/article/secret-life-esg-ratings

GreenBiz (2023a) "The first rule of ESG.: don't talk about ESG," March 13. https://www.greenbiz.com/article/first-rule-esg-dont-talk-about-esg

GreenBiz Group (2023b) *State of Green Business, 2023*. https://www.greenbiz.com/report/state-green-business-2023

GreenBiz (2023c) "CSRD, CSDDD, ESRS and more: A cheat sheet of EU sustainability regulations," June 12. https://www.greenbiz.com/article/csrd-csddd-esrs-and-more-cheat-sheet-eu-sustainability-regulations

Griscom, Bronson W., et al. (2017) "Natural Climate Solutions," *PNAS*, October 31.

Ground, Jessica (2022). "ESG global study 2022" Harvard Law School Forum on Corporate Governance, June 17. https://corpgov.law.harvard.edu/2022/06/17/esg-global-study-2022/

The Guardian (2011) "Sustainable fish customers, duped by marine stewardship Council," January 6.

The Guardian (2011) "Longannet Carbon Capture Project Cancelled," October 19.

The Guardian (2019) "'Bhopal's tragedy has not stopped': the urban disaster still claiming lives 35 years on," December 8.

The Guardian (2021) "The dirty dozen: meet America's top climate villains," October 27.

The Guardian (2022) "Revealed: the carbon bombs set to trigger catastrophic climate breakdown," May 11.

The Guardian (2022) "Fossil fuel firms, have humanity by the throat, says UN head in blistering attack," June 17.

The Guardian (2022) "How top US business lobby, promised climate action – but worked to block effort," August 19.

The Guardian (2022) "Companies using carbon credits to cover their tracks, says iron ore billionaire," September 29.

The Guardian (2023) "Fossil fuel firms, owe climate reparations of $209bn a year says study," May 19.

The Guardian (2023) "CEO of biggest carbon credit certifier to resign after claims offset worthless," May 23.

The Guardian (2023) "Worthless: Chevron's carbon offsets are mostly junk and some may harm, research says," May 24.

The Guardian (2023) "Carbon credit speculators could lose billions as offsets deemed 'worthless,'" August 24.

Hansen, James (2017) "Young people's burden: requirement of negative CO2 emissions." *Earth System Dynamics*, 8:577–616.

Harrison, Grant (2023). "The first ISSB reporting standards are here – what that means for investors." GreenBiz, June 26.

The Harvard Crimson (2022) "Fossil fuel companies are talking green, but acting dirty Harvard researchers find," October 3.

The Hill (2023) "DeSantis prohibits Florida state-run fund managers from considering E.S.G. factors," January 17.

Hoang, Nguyen Tien & Kelichiro Kanemoto (2021) "Mapping the deforestation footprint of nations reveals growing threat to tropical forests," *Nature Ecology & Evolution*, March.

Hoare, Alison (2015) *Tackling Illegal Logging and the Related Trade. What Progress and Where Next?* Chatham House.

Hoffman, Andre J. (2001) *From Heresy to Dogma, An Institutional History of Corporate Environmentalism,* Stanford: Stanford Business Books.

Hoffman, Rochel (2022) "Does E.S.G. impact company valuations? An Australian perspective," Deloitte, April 15.

Holland and Knight LLP (2023) "DOE loan programs office: 2023 updates, overview and key insights." https://www.hklaw.com/en/insights/publications/2023/02/doe-loan-programs-office-2023-updates-overview-and-key-insights

Hua, Fangyuan, et al. (2018) "Tree plantations displacing native forests - the nature and drivers of apparent forest recovery on former croplands in Southwestern China from 2000 to 2015," *Biological Conservation,* 222:113–124.

HuffPost (2023) "Five key takeaways from the dire IPCC climate report," March 21.

InfluenceMap (2022a) "Corporate climate policy footprint. The 25 most influential companies blocking climate policy action globally."

InfluenceMap (2022b) "Industry influence on biodiversity policy," October.

InfluenceMap (2022c) "Big oil's real agenda on climate change 2022," September.

Inside Climate News (2022) "Who were the worst climate polluters in the US in 2021?" November 21.

Insights (2023a) "ESG performance and enterprise value: do firms with stronger E.S.G. performance have higher valuation ratios?" January 20.

Insights (2023b). "ESG performance and enterprise value: in which sectors does E.S.G. performance matter the most for a company valuation?" May 9.

Intelex (2022). "Engaging workers, growing business, protecting the planet. How improving EHS and ESG performance can drive competitive advantage."

Intelex (2023). "Better, smarter, cleaner: how ESG inspires technology innovation," Insight report.

Intergovernmental Panel on Climate Change (IPCC) (2005). *Carbon Dioxide Capture and Storage.*

Intergovernmental Panel on Climate Change (IPCC) (2023). *Synthesis report of the IPCC Sixth Assessment Report (AR6): Summary for Policymakers,* March 19.

Intergovernmental Science-Policy Platform on Biodiversity and Ecosystem Services (IPBES) (2019). "Nature's dangerous decline. Unprecedented species extension rates accelerating," May 5.

International Energy Agency (IEA) (2020). *Energy Technology Perspectives 2020 – Special Report on Carbon Capture Utilisation and Storage: CCUS in Clean Energy Transitions.*

International Financial Reporting Standards (IFRS) (2023a). "Climate-related disclosures."

International Financial Reporting Standards (IFRS) (2023b). "ISSB issues inaugural global sustainability disclosure standards," June 26, Press Release.

International Financial Reporting Standards (IFRS) (2023c). "ISSB decides to prioritise climate-related disclosures to support initial application," April 23.

International Financial Reporting Standards (IFRS) (2023d). "ISSB decides to prioritize climate-related disclosures to support initial application."

International Renewable Energy Agency (IRENA) (2023a). "Low cost finance for the energy transition."

International Renewable Energy Agency (IRENA) (2023b) *World energy transitions outlook 2023. 1.5°C pathway. Preview.*

Ioannou, Ioannis, et al. (2022). "How greenwashing affects the bottom line," *Harvard Business Review,* July 21.

ISD and CASM Technology (2023). *Deny, Deceive, Delay. Documenting and Responding to Climate Disinformation at COP26 and Beyond.*

ISS ESG (2023). "Actionable insights. Top ESG themes in 2023: Global edition."

Jacobson, Mark Z. (2019). "The health and climate impacts of carbon capture and direct air capture," *Energy & Environmental Science,* 12: 3567–3574.

Johnson, S. (2003). "Estimating the extent of illegal trade of tropical forest products," *International Forestry Review,* 5(3): 247–252.

Jones, Julia P. G. & Simon L. Lewis (2023). "Forest carbon credits are failing," *Science,* August 24.

JTC Group (2022). "ESG, the SEC, and the war on greenwashing in 2022," September 8.

Katsigris, E., et al. (2004). "The China forest products trade: overview of Asia-Pacific supplying countries, impacts and implications," *International Forestry Review,* 6 (3–4).

Keeley, Terrence R. (2022). "HD E.S.G. does neither much good nor very well," *The Wall Street Journal* (September 13).

Keith, David W., et al. (2018) "A process for capturing CO2 from the atmosphere," *Joule*, 2:1573–1594.

Kerner, Sean Michael (2023) "ESG score" *TechTarget Network*, March.

King, Andrew, A, & Kenneth P Pucker (2022). "ESG and alpha: sales or substance?" *Institutional Investor*, February 25.

King, Jenniet, et al. (2022) *Deny, Deceive, Delay: Documenting and Responding to Climate Disinformation at COP26 and Beyond*. Institute for Strategic Dialogue.

Kirchsteiger C. (2008) "Carbon capture and storage-desirability from a risk management point of view," *Safety Science*, 46: 1149–1154.

Kuhne, Kjell, et al. (2022) "Carbon bombs – mapping key fossil fuel projects," *Energy Policy*, 166: 112950.

Lawton, George (2023) "A timeline and history of E.S.G. investing, rules and practices," *Techtarget Network*, April 7.

Lenzi, Dominic (2018) "The ethics of negative emissions," *Global Sustainability*, May 8.

Lenzi, Dominic, et al. (2018) "Weigh the ethics of plans to mop up carbon dioxide," *Nature*, September 20.

LobbyMap (2022) "The CA100+ target companies: scoring and analysis of climate lobbying."

Makower, Joel (2022a) "How ESG ratings are built," GreenBiz, May 11.

Makower, Joel (2022b) "Are ESG ratings really necessary?" GreenBiz, May 16.

Matricardi, Eraldo Aparaecido Trondoli, et al. (2020) "Long-term forest degradation surpasses deforestation in the Brazilian Amazon," *Science*, September 11.

Mayor, Tracy (2019) "Why ESG ratings vary so widely (and what you can do about it), MIT Sloan School, August 26.

McCarthy, Gina (2022) "What I saw as the country's first national climate advisor," guest essay, *New York Times* (September 19).

Mckinsey & Co. (2021) "Solving the net-zero equation: nine requirements for a more orderly transition," October 27.

McKinsey Quarterly (2020) "Driving CO2 emissions to zero (and beyond) with carbon, capture, use and storage," June.

Mir, J. & A. Fraser (2003) "Illegal logging in the Asia-Pacific region: an ADB perspective, *International Forestry Review*, 5(3): 278–281.

MIT Sloan Sustainability Initiative (2023) "The aggregate confusion project."

MSCI (2023) *The MSCI Net-Zero Tracker: A Periodic Report on progress by the World's Listed Companies toward Curbing Climate Risk*, May.

Mulligan, James, et al. (2018) "Technological Carbon Removal in the United States," World Resources Institute, working paper, September.

NASA Earth Observatory (2017) "China and India lead the way in Greening."

National Academy of Sciences (2019) *Negative Emissions Technologies and Reliable Sequestration: A Research Agenda.*

National Law Review (2022) "SEC Anti-Greenwashing Rules Approved at Hearing," May 26. https://natlawreview.com/article/sec-anti-greenwashing-rules-approved-hearing

Natural Capital Exchange (NCX) (2022) "Charting the path. A survey of sustainability leaders' priorities," May.

Natural Resources Canada (2007) "Is Canada's forest a carbon sink or source?" October.

Nemetz, Peter N. (2021) *The Economics and Business of Sustainability*, Routledge.

Nemetz, Peter N. (2022) *Unsustainable World: Are we losing the battle to save our planet?* Routledge.

Net Zero Tracker (2023) *Net Zero Stocktake 2023: Assessing the Status and Trends of Net Zero Target Setting across Countries, Sub-National Governments and Companies.* https://zerotracker.net/analysis/net-zero-stocktake-2023

Network for Business Sustainability (2023). "Top business sustainability issues of 2023," April 11.

New Climate Institute (2023) "Corporate climate responsibility monitor 2023. Assessing the transparency and integrity of companies' emission reduction and net-zero targets," February.

New Scientist (2011) "UK's carbon-capture failure is part of a global trend," October 24.

New York Times (2011) "Utility Shelves Ambitious Plan to Limit Carbon," July 13.

New York Times (2011) "AEP Move to Stop Carbon Capture and Sequestration Project Shocks Utilities, Miners," July 15.

New York Times (2011) "Obstacles to Capturing Carbon Gas," July 31.

New York Times (2012) "Growing Doubts in Europe on Future of Carbon Storage," January 16.

New York Times (2012) "With Natural Gas Plentiful and Cheap, Carbon Capture Projects Stumble," May 19.

New York Times (2014) "Corralling Carbon Before It Belches From Stack," July 22.

New York Times (2019) "China's Voracious Appetite for Timber Stokes Fury in Russia and Beyond," April 9.

New York Times (2021) "Oil giants prepare to put carbon back in the ground," March 8.

New York Times (2022) "There's a messaging battle right now over America's energy future," March 19.

New York Times (2022) "The pushback on E.S.G. investing," May 11.

New York Times (2022) "How an organized Republican effort punishes companies for climate action," May 27.

New York Times (2022) "How Republicans are 'weaponizing' public office against climate action," August 5.

New York Times (2023) "Politicians want to keep money out of E.S.G. funds. Could it backfire?" January 30.

New York Times (2023) "On Wall St., 'socially responsible' is common sense. In Congress. It's political," March 4.

New York Times (2023) "The week in business: the escalating battle over E.S.G." March 5.

New York Times (2023) "Biden warns the climate change could upend federal spending, March 20.

New York Times (2023) "Companies flock to Biden's climate tax breaks, driving up cost," May 3.

New York Times (2023) "To counter China, G7 countries borrow economic playbook," May 19.

New York Times (2024) "S.E.C. approves new climate rules far weaker than originally proposed," March 6.

Organization for Economic Co-operation and Development (OECD) (1975) *The Polluter Pays Principle*, Paris.

Organization for Economic Co-operation and Development (OECD) (2010) *Principles of Corporate Governance*. Paris.

Paul, Meredith (2020) "The future of E.S.G.?" December 22. https://www.esg.org/the-future-of-esg

Perez, Lucy, et al. (2022) "Does ESG really matter – and why?" *McKinsey Quarterly*, August.

Piasecki, Bruce (1995) *Corporate environmental strategy: An avalanche of corporate change since Bhopal*. John Wiley & Sons.

Pike, Oliver (2023) "How is scope three affecting sustainability reporting?" Reuters Events, February 23.

Plumer, Brad & Christopher Flavelle (2021) "Businesses aim to pull greenhouse gases from the air. It's a gamble," *New York Times*, June 18.

PointB (2023) "ESG reporting frameworks & regulations. What applies to me?" February. https://insights.pointb.com/reporting-frameworks-and-regulations

Polman, Paul, and Andrew Winston, (2021) *Net positive: How Courageous Companies Thrive by Giving More than They Take*. Harvard Business Review Press.

Porter, Michael and Claas van der Linde (1995) "Green and Competitive: Ending the Stalemate," *Harvard Business Review*, September-October.

Rainforest Action Network (2021) *Banking on Climate Chaos, Fossil Fuel Finance Report 2021*. https://www.ran.org/wp-content/uploads/2023/04/BOCC_2023_vF.pdf

Reuters (2022) "ESG investment. North American market outlook." Centre for Audit Quality.

Reuters (2022) "Global climate disclosures to cover, full gamut of carbon emissions," October 21.

Reuters (2023) "Legislations directories: insights on all major sustainability legislations," 2023 edition.

Reuters (2023) "G20-back standards body approves first global company sustainability rules," February 16.

Reuters (2023) "How is scope 3 affecting sustainability reporting?" February 23.

Reuters (2023) "Despite mounting climate, disasters, companies slow to heed, U.N. call to fund adaptation," April 26

Reuters (2023) "Carbon credit market confidence ebbs as big names retreat," September 1.

Reuters (2023) "3M. DuPont defeat massive class action over forever chemicals," November 28.

Robinson, Deena (2022) "10 companies called out for greenwashing," Earth.org. https://earth.org/greenwashing-companies-corporations/

Rochon, Emily (2008) *False hope. Why carbon capture and storage won't save the climate,* Greenpeace.

Romito, Dan (2022) "The top 15 anticipated ESG – related considerations will influence strategy in 2023," Harvard Law School Forum on Corporate Governance, December 31.

S&P Dow Jones Indices, (DJSI) (2023a) "Dow Jones sustainability indices methodology," January. https://www.spglobal.com/spdji/en/methodology/article/dow-jones-sustainability-indices-methodology/

S&P Dow Jones Indices, (DJSI) (2023b) "Dow Jones sustainability world index." https://www.spglobal.com/spdji/en/indices/sustainability/dow-jones-sustainability-world-index/#overview

Science (2021) "Carbon capture marches toward practical use," March 26.

Science Based Targets (2022) *Science-Based Net-Zero: Scaling Urgent Corporate Climate Action Worldwide,* June. https://sciencebasedtargets.org/resources/files/SBTiProgressReport2021.pdf

Science Based Targets (2023a) SBTi Corporate Net-Zeros Standard Criteria, Version 1.1, April. https://sciencebasedtargets.org/resources/files/Legacy_Net-Zero-Standard_v1.1.pdf

Science Based Targets (2023b) SBTi Criteria and Recommendations for Near-Term Targets, Version 5.1, April. https://sciencebasedtargets.org/resources/files/SBTi-criteria-v5.1.pdf

Science Based Targets (no date) "The Corporate Net-Zero Standard." https://sciencebasedtargets.org/net-zero

Securities and Exchange Commission (SEC) (2022) "SEC proposes rules to enhance and standardize climate related disclosures for investors." press release, March 21.

Seemann, Axel, et al. (2023) "Do E.S.G. efforts create value?" Bain & Company.

Sierra Club of BC (2019) "Hidden, ignored and growing: B.C.'s forest carbon emissions," January.

Simpson, Cam, et al. (2021) "The E.S.G., Mirage," *Business Week*, December 10.

Siriwat, Pewnthai & Vincent Nijman (2018) "Using online media-sourced seizure data to assess the illegal wildlife trade in Siamese rosewood," *Environmental Conservation*, January 13.

Smil, Vaclav (2010) *Energy Myths and Reality: Bringing Science to the Energy Policy Debate,* AEI Press.

Smyth, Mary-Ann (2023) "Plantation forestry: carbon and clime impacts," *Land Use Policy*, April 17.

Source Material (2023) "The worlds, biggest companies, from Netflix to Ben & Jerry's, or pouring billions into an offsetting industry, whose climate claims appear increasingly at odds with reality," January 18.

Stackpole, Beth (2023) "ESG ratings: don't throw the baby out with the bathwater," MIT Sloan School, February 23.

State Street Global Advisors (SSGA) (2019) "Into the mainstream: ESG at the tipping point," research report, November.

Supran, Geoffrey er al. (2022) "Three shades of green(washing): Content analysis of social media, discourse by European oil, car, and airline companies," Algorithmic Transparency Institute and Harvard University, September.

Sustainable Business Forum (2024) "The 3 most and least sustainable businesses of 2024."

Sustainable Columbia (n.d.) "Greenhouse Gas Mitigation Hierarchy," Columbia University. https://sustainable.columbia.edu/content/greenhouse-gas-mitigation-hierarchy

The Sustainability Institute (SI) (2022a) "Sustainability leaders 2022," GlobeScan-Sustainability Survey.

The Sustainability Institute (SI) (2022b) "The evolution of sustainability disclosure. Comparing the 2022 SEC, ESRS, and the ISSB proposals."

The Sustainability Institute (SI) (2023a) "Rate the Raters 2023. E.S.G. ratings at a crossroads."

The Sustainability Institute (SI) (2023b) "Rate the Raters 2023. Factsheet."

The Sustainability Institute (SI) (2023c) "The ongoing evolution of sustainable business. 2023 trends report."

The Sustainability Institute (SI) (2023d) "Rate the Raters 2023. ESG ratings at a crossroads."

The Sustainability Yearbook (SI) (2022) *The Sustainability Yearbook – 2022 Rankings.*

Taparia, Hans (2022) "One of the hottest trends in the world of investing is a sham," *New York Times*, September 29.

Team Consequence (2023) "Case Study: Apple's approach to net zero." Consequence.world. https://www.consequence.world/blog/case-study-apples-approach-to-net-zero

Tenner, Edward (1996) *Why things bite back. Technology and the Revenge of Unintended Consequences*, Knopf.

Thompson, Dixon (2005) *Tools for Environmental Management. A Practical Introduction and Guide*. Published by the author.

Thompson, Dixon (2002) *Tools for Environmental Management*. New Society Publishers.

Thomson, Graham (2009). "Burying carbon dioxide in underground saline aquifers: Political folly or climate change fix?" Munk Centre for International Studies.

United Kingdom (2023a). "Misleading environmental claims," January 26, GOV.UK.

UK (2023b) "Greenwashing: CMA puts businesses on notice," press release, September 20. https://www.gov.uk/government/news/greenwashing-cma-puts-businesses-on-notice

United Kingdom (2023c) "UK Sustainability Disclosure Standards," August 2.

United Nations (2004). "Who cares wins. Connecting financial markets to a changing world," The Global Compact.

United Nations (2021). "Integrity Matters: Net Zero Commitments by businesses, financial institutions, cities and regions." Report from the United Nations' high-level expert group on the net zero emissions commitments of nonstate entities.

United Nations Environment Programme (UNEP) (2020). *Emissions Gap Report 2020*.

US Council of Economic Advisors and Office of Management and Budget (2023a) White paper. "Methodologies and considerations for integrating the physical and transition risks of climate change into a macro economic forecasting for the President's budget," March 13.

US Council of Economic Advisors and Office of Management and Budget (2023b). *2023 Economic report of the President*. The White House. https://www.whitehouse.gov/wp-content/uploads/2023/03/ERP-2023.pdf

US Environmental Protection Agency (EPA) (2008) "Vulnerability Evaluation Framework for Geologic Sequestration of Carbon Dioxide," July 10, Washington, D.C.

US Environmental Protection Agency (EPA) (n.d.) "PFAS Explained."

US General Accountability Office (GAO) (2007). Chemical Regulation Comparison of US and Recently Enacted European Union Approaches to Protect Against the Risks of Toxic Chemicals, Washington, DC: US GAO.

US National Institute of Environmental Health Sciences (NIH) (n.d.) "Perfluoroalkyl and Polyfluoralkyl Sustances (PFAS)."

US The White House (2022) "Fact sheet: the Inflation Reduction Act supports workers and families," August 19.

US The White House (2023) "Building a clean energy economy: a guidebook to the Inflation Reduction Act's investments in clean energy and climate action." https://www.whitehouse.gov/wp-content/uploads/2022/12/Inflation-Reduction-Act-Guidebook.pdf

Vancouver Sun (2021) "Shell Alberta refinery carbon capture plan part of net-zero goal," July 13.

Vina, Andres, et al. (2016) "Effects of conservation policy on China's forest recovery." *Science Advances*, March 18.

Wall Street Journal (WSJ) (2020) "These are the World's 10 most sustainably managed companies," October 13.

Weil, Gotshal & Manges LLP (2022) "SEC targets greenwashing by investment funds: more proposals on the SCCESG agenda. Implications for funds and public companies." *Government & Securities Alert*, June 21. https://www.weil.com/-/media/mailings/2022/q2/sec-targets-greenwashing-by-investment-funds—more-proposals-on-the-sec-esg-agenda-220621.pdf

Whelan, Tensie, et al. (2021) "ESG and financial performance: Uncovering the relationship by aggregating evidence for 1000 plus studies published between 2015–2020." Rockefeller Asset Management and NYU Stern Center for Sustainable Business.

Wilday, Jill, et al. (2011) "Hazards from carbon dioxide capture, transport and storage." *Process Safety and Environmental Protection*, 89: 482–491.

Williams, Hugh E., James Medhurst & Kirstine Drew (1993). "Corporate Strategies for a Sustainable Future." In Kurt Fisher & Johan Schot (Eds.), *Environmental Strategies for Industry: International Perspectives on Research Needs and Policy Implications*. 117–146. Island Press.

Willis, John, et al. (2023) "Greenwashing Hydra." *Planet Tracker*, January.

World Economic Forum (2022) "Climate adaptation: the $2 trillion market the private sector cannot ignore." November 1.

World Economic Forum (2023) *The Global Risks Report 2023.*

World Food Programme (WFP) (2023) "Drought in the horn of Africa, Situation Update." July.

World Meteorological Organization (WMO) (2022). *State of the Global Climate 2022.* WMO, No. 1316.

World Meteorological Organization (WMO) (2023). "WMO global annual to decadal climate update."

World Wildlife Fund (WWF) (2021). *Power Forward 4.0: A Progress Report of the Fortune 500's Transition to a Net-Zero Economy.* https://wwfint.awsassets.panda.org/downloads/power_forward_4_0.pdf

Yarow, Jay (2009). "The 15 worst companies for the planet." *Business Insider*, September 23.

Part 2

Some Key Concepts and Methodology

3 Eco-Efficiency and Other Paradigms

In the pursuit of any major corporate goal, it is essential to have performance measures (or metrics) against which one can measure progress. This has proven particularly challenging for sustainability. Considerable research is underway to generate appropriate metrics for measuring and evaluating both corporate strategic initiatives and public policy undertakings that attempt to address issues related to sustainability. This and the chapters immediately following will examine some of the most prominent tools either proposed or currently in use by the business sector.

The Circular Economy

The concept of the *Circular Economy*, has been championed by the Ellen MacArthur Foundation. According to Stahel (2016, p. 435):

> A 'circular economy' would turn goods that are at the end of their service life into resources for others, closing loops in industrial ecosystems and minimizing waste. It would change economic logic because it replaces production with sufficiency: reuse what you can, recycle what cannot be reused, repair what is broken, remanufacture what cannot be repaired. A study of seven European nations found that a shift to a circular economy would reduce each nation's greenhouse gas emissions by up to 70% and grow its workforce by about 4%! – the ultimate low-carbon economy.

According to the Ellen MacArthur Foundation (2021), several factors indicate that the traditional linear model of production (i.e., "cradle to-cradle") is being challenged: economic losses and structural waste, price risks, supply risk, natural systems degradation, regulatory trends, advances in technology, acceptance of alternative business models, and urbanization.

But despite the emerging recognition of this imperative by both governments and many corporations, a 2018 report (de Wit et al. 2018) found that the world economy was only 9.1% circular. A major reason for this shortfall has been resource extraction, which has increased twelve-fold between 1900 and 2015. To quote:

> increased and accelerated material use is to a large extent driven by rising prosperity levels globally. Whilst elevating people out of poverty is a desirable, even essential outcome, the associated material use is not. The circular economy has a

DOI: 10.4324/9781003170754-5

key role to play in decoupling growth from material extraction, thereby creating the conditions for sustainable development to deliver more prosperity for a larger population, but with diminishing use of primary resources.

(de Wit et al., p. 11)

Unfortunately, an updated version of this report (Fraser et al. 2024) concluded that global circularity had fallen to 7.2%, continuing to be driven by rising material extraction and use.

In support of its goal of promoting the circular economy, the Ellen MacArthur Foundation has published almost three dozen studies on the subject. These include:

1. Three region-specific studies of China, India, and the European Union. The Foundation estimated savings/benefits in these areas of applying circular economy principles of 1.8 trillion Euros in Europe by 2030; 624 billion USD in India in 2050; and 5.1 trillion USD in China in 2030 (MacArthur 2023a, 2023b, 2023c).
2. Several industry and commodity studies on subjects as diverse as food, plastics, textiles, fashion, smart appliances, aluminum, steel, cement, packaging, consumer electronics, fashion, and consumer goods in general.
3. Several more narrowly focussed studies on biodiversity climate change, finance, global supply chains, urban biocycles, COVID-19, systems theory and artificial intelligence. The Foundation makes a case that AI could usher in a major transformation in the global economy with resulting ecological and economic benefits. To quote:

> Its principles are to design out waste and pollution, keep products and materials in use, and regenerate natural systems. The advantages of such an approach are substantial . . . addressing mounting resource-related challenges, creating jobs, spurring innovation, and generating substantial environmental benefits. . . . New technologies, including faster and more agile learning processes with iterative cycles of designing, prototyping, and gathering feedback, are needed for the complex task of redesigning key aspects of our economy. Artificial intelligence (AI) can play an important role in enabling this systemic shift. AI is a subset of the technologies enabling the emergent 'Fourth Industrial Revolution' era. . . . AI can complement people's skills and expand their capabilities. It allows humans to learn faster from feedback, deal more effectively with complexity, and make better sense of abundant data. . . . AI can enhance and enable circular economy innovation across industries in three main ways: (1) *Design circular products, components, and materials.* AI can enhance and accelerate the development of new products, components, and materials fit for a circular economy through iterative machine-learning-assisted design processes that allow for rapid prototyping and testing. (2) *Operate circular business models.* AI can magnify the competitive strength of circular economy business models, such as product-as-a-service and leasing. By combining real-time and historical data from products and users, AI can help increase product circulation and asset utilisation through pricing and demand prediction, predictive maintenance, and smart inventory management. (3) *Optimise circular infrastructure.* AI can help build and improve the reverse logistics infrastructure required to 'close the loop' on products and materials by improving the processes to sort and disassemble products, remanufacture components, and recycle materials. . . . The opportunities for AI to unlock value

in a circular economy are not industry specific. Combining the power of AI with a vision for a circular economy represents a significant, and as yet largely untapped, opportunity to harness one of the great technological developments of our time to support efforts to fundamentally reshape the economy into one that is regenerative, resilient, and fit for the long term.

(MacArthur 2023d)

Of course, the impact of AI on society in the form of employment opportunities remains the subject of intense debate (Talmage-Rostron 2023; Builtin 2023; IMF 2024).

4. Several general analytical pieces and guidance manuals for governments and industry (MacArthur 2023e).

Eco-Efficiency

One of the more commonly used metrics is called eco-efficiency. Developed in 1992 by the World Business Council on Sustainable Development (WBCSD) (2005a, 2005b, 2006), it brings together the essential ingredients – more efficient use of resources and lower emissions – that are necessary for increased economic prosperity. This framework can be used by any business to measure progress toward economic and environmental sustainability. The methodology provides a common set of definitions, principles and indicators, and is represented by the ratio:

(product or service value) / (environmental influence)

The generally applicable indicators for product/service value are quantity of goods or services produced or provided to customers, and net sales, while those relating to the environmental influence in product/service creation include energy consumption, materials consumption, water consumption, greenhouse gas emissions, and ozone depleting substance emissions. Figure 3.1 demonstrates – for a hypothetical company – how an eco-efficiency ratio is derived. The first graph presents the numerator data that focuses on some service value (such as net sales in dollars) or total product output mass; the second

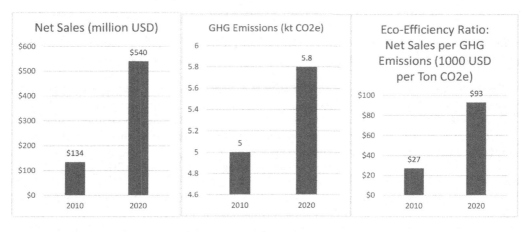

Figure 3.1 Derivation of Eco-Efficiency Ratio

graph represents the denominator, which could be GHG emissions or energy consumption; and, finally, the third graphic example calculates the eco-efficiency ratio as net sales per GHG emissions (or mass of product per GHG emissions). Alternatively, the numerator and denominator values can be interchanged to produce a ratio of GHG emissions per product mass or value. This is the more common type of eco-efficiency ratio used by industry.

These types of eco-efficiency ratios have been used by Interface Inc. in conveying their degree of success in pursuit of sustainability. In this respect, it is critical to present a time series to create a de facto benchmark. Interface Inc. has been able to do this since they have been tracking these data for over a decade (see chapter 10). The principal advantage of this type of metric is threefold: (1) it is relatively easy to compute; (2) it permits not only temporal trend analysis, but also cross-plant and cross-company comparisons; and (3) perhaps most importantly, the measure is independent of level of output. For example, a company's total greenhouse gas (GHG) output might decrease solely because the plant has reduced the level of production. The eco-efficiency ratio will signal whether this decrease in product output has been accompanied by relative reductions, increases, or no change at all in GHG.

Alternative Paradigms

There are two principal criticisms of the eco-efficiency measure. The first is the mirror image of advantage (3) in the list above. A firm may be achieving an improved eco-efficiency metric by lowering its GHG per unit of output but, if output is increasing sufficiently, the total level of GHG emissions will rise. Ultimately, from the perspective of society and the ecosystem, it is the total output that matters. This is a nontrivial distinction that lies at the heart of the third major case study in this volume, which is centered on the oil sands in chapter 14. The second critique is even more substantive and lies at the philosophical heart of how we design our modern industrial system. This critique is based on the work of William McDonough and Michael Braungart.

McDonough, an architect and planner, and Braungart, a chemical engineer, first laid out their radical proposals for a total redesign of our modern industrial system of production in an article in the October 1998 edition of *Atlantic Monthly*, entitled "The Next Industrial Revolution." This was followed by an in-depth elaboration of their proposal in a book published in 2002 called *Cradle-to-Cradle: Remaking the Way We Make Things*. They propose a transformation away from our current linear, once-through "cradle-to-grave" production system that is profoundly inefficient and generates massive amounts of waste. To quote:

> Cradle-to-grave designs dominate modern manufacturing. . . . Many products are designed with 'built-in obsolescence,' to last only for a certain period of time. . . . Also, what most people see in their garbage cans is just the tip of the material iceberg; the product itself contains on average only 5 percent of the raw materials involved in the process of making and delivering it.
>
> (McDonough and Braungart 2002, p. 27–28)

The fundamental thrust of the innovation proposed by McDonough and Braungart is to redesign our production systems so they mimic nature where there is no waste per se, where virtually all byproducts of natural production – with the exception of energy – are recycled into nutrients for the production of other organisms. The industrial challenge is

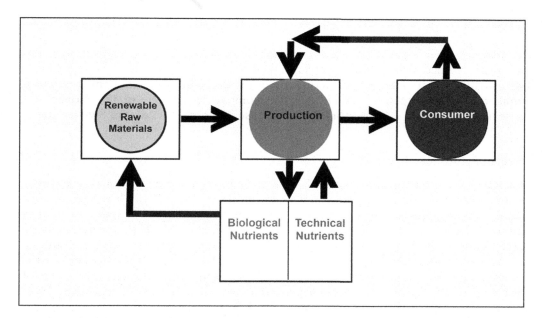

Figure 3.2 McDonough-Braungard Model

to alter the design process of modern industrial products so that their waste products can be recycled into two streams: what the authors call "biological nutrients" and "technical nutrients" as illustrated in Figure 3.2. There is a key distinction between these two waste streams: the first can re-enter the ecosystem without synthetic or toxic components and are thus able to be recycled without altering or contaminating natural cycles; the second, in contrast, are recycled in closed loop systems so that no toxins are released into the environment. This is the essence of the "cradle-to-cradle" system.

The basic critique advanced by McDonough and Braungart of current sustainability efforts is that eco-efficiency is focused on reducing the negative environmental impacts of industrial production but does not induce producers to change the basic design of the production process or the products themselves. In the words of the authors, "efficient is not sufficient." Improved technologies that reduce the flow of energy and materials in the cradle-to-grave system do not ultimately eliminate the wastes and toxic products. The approach proposed by McDonough and Braungart is twofold: to replace *eco-efficiency* with *eco-effectiveness and* change *downcycling* to *upcycling* – a step that Shaw Industries and some other companies, such as Honeywell have already undertaken (McDonough & Braungart 2004) (see chapter 10). The authors (1998) observe that "in our next Industrial Revolution, regulations can be seen as signals of design failure."

In a reconceptualization similar in spirit to Interface's partial substitution of a service for a good (see chapter 10), McDonough and Braungart (1998, p. 90) state:

> Imagine what would happen if a chemical company sold intelligence instead of pesticides—that is, if farmers or agro-businesses paid pesticide manufacturers to protect their crops against loss from pests instead of buying dangerous regulated chemicals to use at their own discretion.

To advance their agenda of transforming industrial production, McDonough and Braungart formed a consulting company called McDonough Braungart Design Chemistry (MBDC) that offered their services worldwide. While the company has had a number of both successes and failures (Fastcompany.com), one of the earliest and most important early success stories was the case of Rohner Textiles in Switzerland.

Case Study: Rohner Textil AG

A small textile company in Switzerland, Rohner Textil faced many of the similar environmental problems of other companies in the same industry (IEHN 2010). It was under regulatory economic pressure because of the necessity to treat its wastewater and the need to dispose of carpet trimmings deemed toxic by regulatory authorities. The impetus for change came from a textile designer in the US who requested that the company consider producing a completely biodegradable commercial fabric for office furniture. MBDC was employed as a consultant to the project to transform Rohner's production technology and the nature of the final product. The project was challenging as it involved not only finding new raw material for the textile itself – wool from pasture-bred sheep replaced cotton – but also by the much more imposing task of finding environmentally benign dyes. Only one major chemical company, Ciba-Geigy, was prepared to share its industrial secrets with the company, resulting in the identification of 16 environmentally benign chemicals out of a total of 8000.

The result of this re-engineering process was remarkable, as formerly toxic carpet waste could now be recovered and sold to local farmers as mulch. Toxic wastewater was eliminated and costs were reduced by the elimination of filtering of dyes and chemicals. The new product, called Climatex Lifecycle™ became a major contributor to the company's bottom line. This is a classic example of Michael Porter's thesis that sustainability and profitability can be one and the same. Table 3.1 compares Rohner's achievements with the pure model of sustainability posited for handwoven carpets. In this case, many of the basic ingredients

Table 3.1 Rohner's Achievements vs. Handwoven Carpets

Characteristic	Hand-woven	Rohner
fibre	natural (wool)	natural (wool)
source of fibre	pasture-bred sheep	pasture-bred sheep
type of dyes	natural	natural
major inputs	labor-intensive	capital and energy-intensive
looms	wooden	metal
toxic wastes	none	none

of sustainability have been successfully transferred into a modern, high-volume commercial product capable of meeting the large demands of the international market.

The Natural Step

Formulated by two Europeans, Dr. Karl-Henrik Robert and Dr. John Holmberg, The Natural Step principle was introduced into North America by Paul Hawken (Nattrass et al. 1999; Nattrass and Altomore 2002a, 2002b; Robert 2008). It was the goal of Dr. Robert to translate ecological principles into a form that could be implemented throughout a corporation with knowledge and participation at all levels. The Natural Step includes several core processes:

1. perceiving the nature of the unsustainable direction of business and society and the self-interest implicit in shifting to a sustainable direction
2. strategic visioning through backcasting (in contrast to forecasting, which starts from the present state and attempts to predict the consequences of current policies), which establishes a desirable future goal or state and then attempts to determine the best course of action to achieve that goal
3. applying four system conditions for sustainability, which are: preventing the accumulation in the environment of such things as nonrenewable materials extracted from the earth; similarly preventing the accumulation of man-made chemicals; preventing the overharvesting of resources and other forms of deleterious intervention in ecosystems; and requiring that resources are used fairly and efficiently in order to meet basic human needs worldwide.

Some major companies or organizations that have adopted the Natural Step include IKEA, Scandic Hotels, Interface, Inc., Collins Pine Company, Electrolux, Nike, Starbucks, and CH2M Hill. Figure 3.3 illustrates the implementation of The Natural Step at IKEA, the

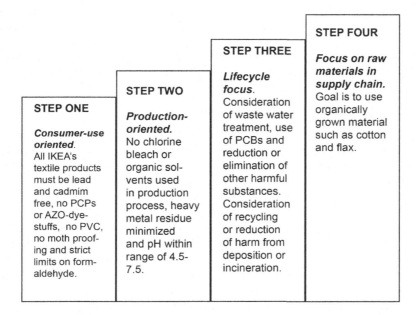

Figure 3.3 Natural Step at IKEA

Adapted from Nattras and Altomore 2002

world's largest retailer of furniture (Nattrass & Altomore 2002b). In some cases, the confluence of sustainability and profit is obvious and simple to achieve. One need only think of the request to guests by major hotel chains to consider using towels more than once or changing bedding every second day. Both the hotel and its guests have made a small contribution to achieving a more sustainable economy while saving the hotel on laundry bills.

A Brief Note on Forces Driving the Diffusion of Sustainability within the Corporate Sector

There is a clear role for government in facilitating the diffusion of sustainable technology, policy, and practices throughout the economy by providing a level playing field that allows these initiatives to compete freely with existing alternative technologies and strategies. Prime examples of this approach can be found in the area of renewable energy sources and demand-side management. However, an equally important phenomenon is the diffusion of sustainability within the corporate sector itself. While much of the popular literature on business and sustainability encourages all companies to incorporate sustainability considerations into their corporate strategy and adopt new and more sustainable production processes and products, this is rarely how new ideas are spread through economies. Figure 3.4 presents three models of diffusion that may be applied to the challenge of moving the industrial system closer to the goal of sustainability: Model A represents horizontal diffusion; Model B1 represents vertical diffusion, up the supply chain; Model B2 portrays vertical diffusion down the supply chain; and Model C represents vertical diffusion both up and down the supply chain. Each is briefly described in turn below.

Model A – Horizontal Diffusion

There are several ways in which sustainability innovation and policy can be transferred either directly or indirectly among competitors. The first, illustrated by the case of Interface Inc. and Shaw Industries (see chapter 10) is where one company sets the standard and forces other companies to respond. The second case represents the direct transfer of technology either through licensing for a fee or without charge. In the case of Rohner Textil, for example, the company offered to share its new nonpolluting technology with other companies in the same industry.

Model B1 – Vertical Diffusion: Up the Supply Chain

In some respects, this model potentially represents the most successful model of diffusion for sustainable production technology and strategy. As stated above, it is not realistic to expect all companies to adopt sustainable practices into their business models, especially when they are operating in highly competitive, low profit margin industries. Suggestions that these firms should adopt new practices that might, on balance, cost many of them lost profits in the short run is not a viable suggestion. In fact, it is counterproductive since it lowers the credibility of sustainability advocates within the business community.

However, this environment can change radically when a major corporation at the bottom of the supply chain mandates that its suppliers must meet sustainability criteria to continue to receive orders for their products. Once this greening of the supply chain (Sarkis 2010) occurs, the vast array of suppliers who previously might not be able to afford sustainability initiatives, cannot afford not to do so. The prime example of this phenomenon is Wal-Mart, which has moved aggressively in this area to

Model A -- Horizontal Diffusion

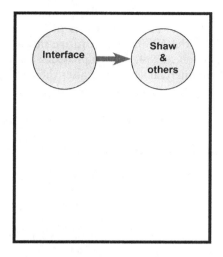

Model B1 -- Vertical Diffusion: UP

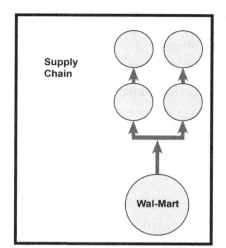

Model B2 -- Vertical Diffusion: DOWN

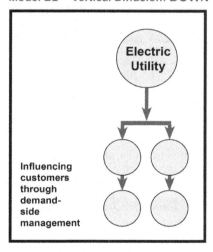

Model C -- Chained Vertical Diffusion

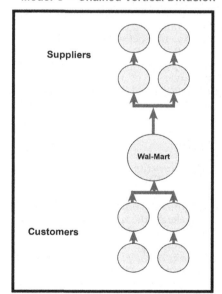

Figure 3.4 Three Models of Sustainability Diffusion

demand more ecologically friendly products from its approximately 100,000 suppliers. Consequently, Wal-Mart has been termed a "private regulator," achieving within the business sector what government might be unwilling or unable to attempt. This model represents one of the critical keys to the diffusion of sustainability throughout the economic system as Wal-Mart has come to realize that sustainable business is the key to sustainable profits (Humes, 2011) (see further discussion of the Wal-Mart case in chapter 16).

Model B2 – Vertical Diffusion Down the Supply Chain

In this model, corporations sitting atop or amidst a supply chain adopt practices and policies that induce their customers to follow suit. One example of this phenomenon is the adoption by electric power utilities as early as the 1980s of innovative rate structures, such as marginal cost pricing (Nemetz & Hankey, 1984), which provides a strong incentive to customers within the industrial and commercial sectors to alter their energy use – and perhaps input or product mix – in a more sustainable direction.

Model C – Chained vertical diffusion

This model combines the diffusion of sustainability both up and down the supply chain as portrayed in Models B1 and B2.

References

Builtin (2023) "AI taking over jobs: what to know about the future of jobs," September 12.

De Wit, Marc, et al. (2018) *The Circularity Gap Report: An Analysis of The Circular State of the Global Economy*. Circle Economy. https://assets-global.website-files.com/5e185aa4d27bcf3484 00ed82/650d963e13ca754672ab06d4_The%20Circularity%20Gap%20Report%202018%20 -%20Report_compressed.pdf

De Wit, Marc, et al. (2020) *The Circularity Gap Report 2020: When Circularity Goes from Bad to Worse; The Power of Countries to Change the Game*. Circle Economy. https://assets-global.website-files. com/5e185aa4d27bcf348400ed82/5e26ead616b6d1d157ff4293_20200120%20-%20CGR%20 Global%20-%20Report%20web%20single%20page%20-%2021 0x297mm%20-%20 compressed.pdf

DeSimone, Livio D. & Frank Popoff (1997). *Eco-Efficiency. The Business Link to Sustainable Development*. World Business Council on Sustainable Development, Switzerland.

Ellen MacArthur Foundation (2021) "Completing the picture: how the circular economy, tackles climate change."

Ellen MacArthur Foundation (2023a) "Growth within a circular economy. Vision for a competitive Europe."

Ellen MacArthur Foundation (2023b) "Circular economy in India: Rethinking growth for long-term prosperity."

Ellen MacArthur Foundation (2023c) "The circular economy. Opportunity for urban & industrial innovation in China."

Ellen MacArthur Foundation (2023d) "Artificial Intelligence and the Circular Economy. AI as a tool to accelerate the transition."

Ellen MacArthur Foundation (2023e) List of publications.

Fraser, Malcolm, et al. (2024) *The circularity gap report 2024. A circular economy to live within the safe limits of the planet*. Circle Economy.

Hawken, Paul (1993) *The Ecology of Commerce. A Declaration of Sustainability*. Harper Collins.

Humes, Edward (2011) *Force of Nature. The Unlikely Story of Wal-Mart's Green Revolution*. Harper Business.

International Monetary Fund (IMF) (2024) "AI will transform the global economy. Let's make sure it benefits humanity," January 14. https://www.imf.org/en/Blogs/Articles/2024/01/14/ ai-will-transform-the-global-economy-lets-make-sure-it-benefits-humanity

Investor Environmental Health Network (IEHN) (2010) Case Study. "Rohner Textiles: Cradle-to-Cradle Innovation and Sustainability."

McDonough, William & Michael Braungart (1998) "The next industrial revolution." *Atlantic Monthly* (October): 82–92.

McDonough, William & Michael Braungart (2002) *Cradle to Cradle: Remaking the Way We Make Things*. North Point Press.

McDonough, William & Michael Braungart (2004) "The Cradle-to-Cradle Alternative," in Brian Halweil and Lisa Masty (project directors) *State of the World 2004*, Worldwatch Institute, pp.104–105.

Nattrass, Brian & Mary Altomore (1999) *The Natural Step for Business*. New Society Publishers.

Nattrass, Brian & Mary Altomore (2002a) *Dancing with the tiger: Learning sustainability step by natural step*. New Society Publishers.

Nattrass, Brian & Mary Altomore (2002b) "IKEA: Nothing is Impossible." In Peter N. Nemetz (Ed.), *Bringing Business on Board: Sustainable Development and the B-School Curriculum*. JBA Press, pp. 429–458.

Nemetz, Peter N. & Marilyn Hankey (1984). *Economic Incentives for Energy Conservation*. John Wiley & Sons.

Talmage-Rostron, Mark (2023) "How Will Artificial Intelligence Affect Jobs 2023–2030," Nexford University, September 11.

Robert, Karl-Henrik (2008) *The Natural Step Story. Seeding a Quiet Revolution*. New Society Publishers.

Sarkis, Joseph (2010) *Greening the Supply Chain eco-efficiency*. Springer.

Seiler-Hausmann, Jan-Dirk, Christa Liedtke & Ernst Ulricj von Weizsacker (Eds.) (2004). *Ecoefficiency and Beyond. Towards the Sustainable Enterprise*. Greanleaf.

Stahel, Walter R. (2016) "Circular Economy." *Nature*, March 24.

World Business Council on Sustainable Development (WBCSD) (2005a) *Eco-Efficiency: Creating More Value with Less Impact*.

World Business Council on Sustainable Development (WBCSD) (2005b) *Measuring ecoefficiency. A Guide to Reporting Company Performance*.

World Business Council on Sustainable Development (WBCSD) (2006) *Eco-efficiency. Learning Module*, August 24, Geneva.

4   Closing the Loop

Mimicking Nature – Biomimicry and Industrial Ecology

This chapter provides a brief overview of two other concepts and related methodologies currently being used or deployed to incorporate closed-loop principles of nature into industrial production. The first is industrial ecology (IE), the second is biomimicry.

Industrial Ecology (IE)

Smith (2007, pp. 304–341) summarizes the field of industrial ecology as follows:

> Using nature as a model, industrial ecology views the industrial plant or system as an integrated set of cyclical processes in which the consumption of energy and materials is optimized, waste generation is minimized, and wastes from one process serve as feedstock for other production processes. Industrial ecology views industrial production as a "metabolic" process. It attempts to close the "open materials cycle" characteristic of industrial society, whereby materials and energy are lost to economic use, and harmful toxic substances are released to the environment. Industrial ecology tries to "close the loop" in two ways: (1) by eliminating waste from production processes, and (2) by redesigning wastes as useful byproducts that can be used in other processes.

An extensive literature exists on the subject and there have been numerous applications of its basic principles (Ayres and Ayres 1996; Graedel & Allenby 2010) This book reviews some of the key concepts of IE such as eco-efficiency (chapter 3), industrial metabolism (chapter 5), and Life Cycle Analysis (chapter 6). One of the most advanced applications of the principles of industrial ecology, termed industrial symbiosis, can be found in eco-industrial parks (EIPs) – a grouping of systems-based diverse and complementary industrial plants where wastes, byproducts, and energy are exchanged among plants (UNIDO 2023). Several examples of operating or proposed parks are drawn from experiences in three countries: Kalundborg, Denmark; Scotsford, Alberta; and Tampico, Mexico UN.

Perrucci et al. (2022) conducted an extensive study of the successes and failures of EIPs globally. Table 4.1 summarizes some of their findings. The US stands out for its relative lack of success in establishing success EIPs. The authors ascribe this problem to three factors: (1) missing trust among potential participants who might be reluctant to describe their production processes and waste streams; (2) supply uncertainty, such as over-reliance on one firm and vulnerability to its level of production; and (3) governance, specifically the optimal level of government involvement, which can be either too high or too low. It is useful to have a government presence which establishes an environment

DOI: 10.4324/9781003170754-6

Table 4.1 Eco-Industrial Parks Successes and Failures

Country	Successes	Failures
USA	4	12
Netherlands	13	0
Italy	3	3
Sweden	3	3
Canada	0	1
China	2	0
Australia	2	0

Adapted from Perrucci et al. 2022

facilitating the development of an EIP without overregulating and interfering with the initiatives of participating companies. To quote Perrucci et al. (2022: 10):

> Although there should be governmental support, the initiative for the eco-industrial park project should be taken by the involved companies themselves. In a past study, the comparative success between US and Dutch EIPs was conducted. The Dutch EIPs were concluded to be more successful with the main attribution to the success being that the Dutch EIPs were initiated by stakeholders, while the US mainly originated through different levels of the government. Nonetheless, without the correct policies and actions by the government eco-industrial parks would struggle for success.

Kalundborg, Denmark

The world's first eco-industrial park has been in full operation as a complex interdependent system for over two decades and is located on the coast, 75 miles west of the capital city, Copenhagen. Figure 4.1 presents a schematic of the park which shows the interchange of at least 17 flows among 8 large industrial operations in fields as diverse as coal-fired power, oil refining, pharmaceutical and enzyme manufacturing, and plasterboard. It is noteworthy that it was not the original intention of the participants to create a symbiotic industrial complex. The industrial plants had all been established in relative close proximity, but evolved to the current high level of interconnectedness over time as they sought means to reduce waste streams and garner revenue from byproduct production (Ehrenfeld & Gertler 1997). The complex has since been expanded to include district heating, conventional agriculture as well as fish farming, and the use of fly ash as supplement to concrete for roads (Chertow 2007).

Scotsford, Alberta

In some respects, the origins of eco-industrial parks lie in the longstanding practice of petrochemical companies to create industrial parks that interchange feedstocks and utilities. With the principal goal of reducing costs by increasing the utilization of byproducts, the fortunate side effect is the reduction of wastes from an otherwise very pollutant-intensive industry. Figure 4.2 illustrates the layout of a major industrial park in Alberta that includes a mixture of oil refineries and chemical plants (McCann 2002). It should be

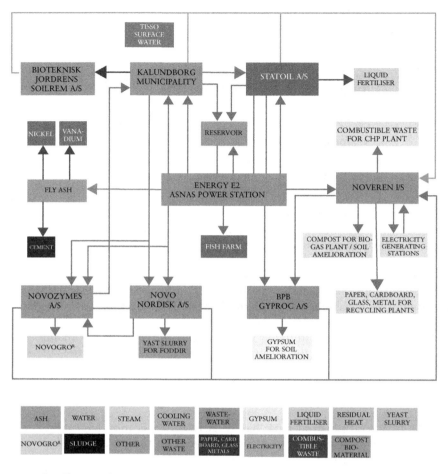

Figure 4.1 Kalundburg Industrial Park Schematic
Source: http://www.kalundborg.dk

noted, however, that such agglomerations of petrochemical-related industrial operations pose a disaster risk that would not be present if the plants were not in close proximity. One way that this risk can be reduced is to increase the physical separation among the plants and interconnect them with pipelines, in those cases where it is possible to move product by pipeline and sustain the chemical or physical characteristics of the product. This is a viable option and less risky as long as such an undertaking is not so expensive as to offset cost reductions from byproduct interchange. Another more likely risk is created by the potential dependence of one plant on the output of another. If one industrial operation were to temporarily cease operation due to accidents or other causes, there is a risk of a cascading impact on all other companies in the park.

Tampico, Mexico

The first North American effort to create an eco-industrial park based on the concept of byproduct synergy was initiated in Mexico with the support of the World Business

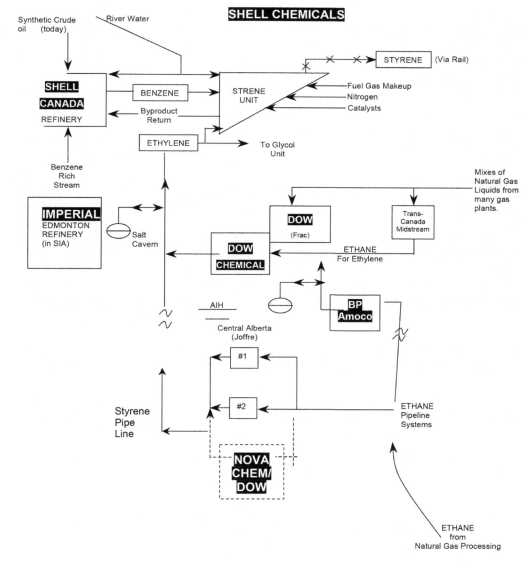

Figure 4.2 Alberta Industrial Park
Adapted from McCann 2002

Council on Sustainable Development. A diverse range of 21 different companies were encouraged to plan an integrated site and several small demonstration projects were undertaken. Table 4.2 lists the companies and their products, while Figure 4.3 summarizes the anticipated interplant flows of the critical byproducts (Young et al. 2002). A primer on byproduct synergy (Mangan 1997) clearly enunciated the challenges facing the establishment of an eco-industrial park, and most of these caveats remain in force today. They include the following:

- *Technical*: Is conversion of the byproduct technically feasible?
- *Economic*: Is it economically feasible?

- *Business*: Is it competing against other investment opportunities?
- *Corporate practice*: Is the company's decision-making process hindering investment?
- *Regulatory*: Are there government-created barriers to synergy?
- *Risk*: Could the use of or transportation of what might be considered a waste product lead to increased liability and, if so, who is responsible?
- *Geographic*: Can the byproduct by economically transported from its generator to its consumer?
- *Trust*: Are companies comfortable working together?
- *Time*: Is byproduct synergy a low or high priority to the company?

In light of this comprehensive list of challenges to the formation of successfully function-ing eco-industrial parks (EIPs), it is not surprising that development has been careful and deliberate and that many parks are quite modest, encompassing a relatively small number of plants. Peerrucci et al. (2022, pp. 7–8) provide a summary of seventeen past American Eco-industrial park implementations since 1998. In his synthesis of industrial symbiosis, Chertow (2007) concludes that de novo attempts to create eco-industrial parks from scratch have generally been failures; more successful results have evolved from corpora-tions recognizing the potential for synergies with industrial operations that are already in existence. The author identifies three policies which can facilitate the recognition of these opportunities: "(1) forming reconnaissance teams to identify industrial areas likely to

Table 4.2 Tampico Industrial Park Companies

Company	Product
Plastics	
Indelpro S.A. de C.CV.	PCC
G.E> Plastics	ABS
Grupo Primex	PVC resin and dust, phtalic anhydride
Policyd	PVC resin and dust, phtalic anhydride
Polioles	Polustyrene
Pecten Poliesters	Polyethylene
Industrial Minerals	
PPG	purse silica
Dupont	TiO2 pigment
Chemical / Petrochemical	
Novaquim	chemicals for rubber industry, herbicides
NHUMO	synthetic rubber
INSA-Emulsion	rubber products (tires, hoes)
INSA-Solucion	rubber products (roads, shoes)
Pemex	petroleum refinery products
Petrocel-DMT	dimthyl terephtalate
Petrocel-PTA	phteraphtalic acid
Metallurgical	
Sulfamex	manganese sulfate
MineraAutlan	ferromanganese, silicomanganese
Miscellaneous	
Cryoinfra	industrial gases
Grupo Tampico	Coca-cola bottler
Johns Manville	impermeable membranes
Enertek	electric power

Source: Young et al. 2002, p. 473 (2022)

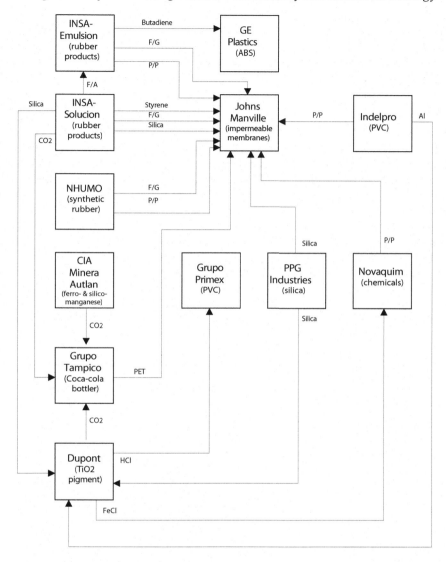

Figure 4.3 Tampico Industrial Flows
Adapted from Young et al. 2002, p. 473

have a baseline of exchanges and mapping their flows accordingly, (2) offering technical or financial assistance to increase the number of interactions once some kernels are found to be in place, inspired by managers with a symbiotic mindset, and (3) pursuing locations where common symbiotic precursors already exist, such as co-generation, landfill gas mining, and waste water reuse, often as one-off activities, to determine whether they may be likely candidates for technical or financial assistance as bridges to more extensive symbiosis (p. 26)." The most common challenges to the widespread adoption of this type of industrial organization are the issues of location, proximity and complementarity, but a more cogent problem from a sustainability perspective is that eco-industrial parks can, by their nature, mimic only part of natural closed cycles. There will still be significant industrial waste associated with these undertakings and, as such, they are vulnerable to the critique of eco-efficiency advanced by McDonough and Braungart. Are there other technologies or technological systems which more closely approximate the sustainable model inherent in natural processes? One approach is biomimicry.

Biomimicry

Derived from the Greek words *bios* (life) and *mimesis* (imitation), biomimicry is a relatively new set of scientific and engineering principles focused on transferring natural designs and processes into production processes and products (Benyus 1997). One biomimicry website (www.brainz.org/15-coolest-cases-biomimicry/) cites numerous modern inventions based on mimicking nature. These are listed in Table 4.3. (see also www.natrualedgeproject.net)

One of the most prominent emerging applications of biomimicry is architecture in a subfield designated "ecotecture" (*New York Times Magazine* May 20, 2007). Some common examples include rooftop gardens or grass roofs, and vertical gardens or "green walls." Figure 4.4 illustrates the maintenance of a grass roof on a commercial building in Coombs, BC. One of the most intriguing and visually attractive applications of ecotecture is in use of innovative exterior cladding or fabrics on commercial and other buildings. An archetypal example is the outside walls of the Institut du Monde Arabe in Paris

Table 4.3 Examples of Biomimicry

Area of innovation	Insired by:	Product name
Air conditioning	termites	
Economic cluster	rainforest	
Value-added business	nutrient cycling	
Bacterial control	red algae	
Building Material from CO2	mollusks	
Fog harvesting	a desert beetle	
Economic cluster	the mangrove forest	
Vaccines without refrigeration	resurrection plant	
Fiber manufacture	golden orb weaver spiders	
Water purification	the marsh ecosystem	
C02 capture	algae	
Pacemaker replacement	humpback whales	
Fire retardant	animal cells	
Plastics from CO2	plants	
Self-assembling glass	sea sponges	
Wound healing	flies	
Solar cells	leaves	
Friction-free fans	nautilus	
Bacterial control	barberry	
Self-cleaning surfaces	lotus plant	
Optical brighteners	Cyphochilus beetle	
Adhesion without glue	geckos	Gecko Tape ®
Adhesive fabrics	cockleburs	Velcor ®
Farics with passive humidy control	stomata	Stomatex ®

Adapted from www.brainz.org/15-coolest-cases-biomimicry

(see Figure 4.5). The exterior wall is composed of 1600 "irises" designed to replicate the workings of the human eye. More detailed pictures of individual components viewed from both outside and inside the building are reproduced in Figures 4.6 and 4.7. Each mechanical iris opens and shuts depending on the balance of interior and exterior temperatures to let more or less light and heat into the building. In this way, the biomimicry can reduce the cost of both heating and cooling.

Biomimicry is not a totally new concept in the area of building design as some ancient buildings incorporated natural processes of cooling by air and water into their architectural design. An archetypal example of this historical phenomenon is provided by the great Alhambra hilltop palace, built between 1238 and 1358 by the Moors in Granada, Spain. Despite outside temperatures in excess of 100 degrees Fahrenheit, the inside of the palace remains relatively cool because of extensive still and running water and open courtyards and breezeways. This example is suggestive of a broader principle: many ancient civilizations had knowledge that could be of use to us today in the pursuit of sustainability, but many of these historical precedents from such countries as diverse as Ancient Greece, Rome, and China remain ignored or forgotten today (Temple 2007; Needham 1981; Jordan & Perlin 1979; Butti & Perlin 1980). The following chapters describe in greater detail several other major examples of industrial ecology with special application to sustainable industrial production, including mass balances, industrial metabolism, and lifecycle analysis.

Figure 4.4 Coombs, BC

Figure 4.5 Institut du Monde Arab – Outside Wall

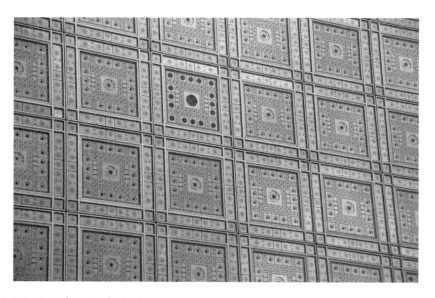

Figure 4.6 Institut du Monde Arab – Outside Wall Close-Up

Figure 4.7 Institut du Monde Arab – Inside Wall Close-Up

References

Ayres, Robert U. & Leslie W. Ayres (1996) *Industrial Ecology. Towards Closing the Materials Cycle.* Edward Elgar.

Benyus, Janine (1997) *Biomimicry: Innovation Inspired by Nature.* Harper Collins.

Butti, Ken & John Perlin (1980) *A Golden Thread: 2500 Years of Solar Architecture and Technology.* Cheshire Books.

Chertow, Marian R. (2007) "'Uncovering' industrial symbiosis." *Journal of Industrial Ecology,* 11(1): 11–30.

Ehrenfeld, John & Nicholas Gertler (1997) "Industrial ecology in practice: The evolution of interdependence at Kalundborg." *Journal of Industrial Ecology,* 1(1): 67–79.

Graedel, T. E. & B. R. Allenby (2002) *Industrial Ecology.* Prentice Hall.

Graedel, T. E. & B. R. Allenby (2010) *Industrial Ecology and Sustainable Engineering.* Prentice Hall.

Jordan, Borimir & John Perlin (1979) "Solar energy use and litigation in ancient times." *Solar Law Reporter,* 1(3): 583–594.

Lowe, Ernest A. (2001) *Eco-Industrial Park Handbook for Asian Developing Countries: Report to the Asian Development Bank.* http://www.indigodev.com/ADBHBdownloads.html

Lyons, Donald I. (2007) "A spatial analysis of loop closing among recycling, remanufacturing, and waste treatment firms in Texas." *Journal of Industrial Ecology,* 11(1): 43–54.

Mangan, Andy (1997) *Byproduct Synergy: A Strategy for Sustainable Development.* World Business Council for Sustainable Development. https://www.environmental-expert.com/articles/byproduct-synergy-a-strategy-for-sustainable-development-1451

McCann, T. J. (2002) "Chemical industry integration." In Peter N. Nemetz (Ed.), *Bringing Business on Board: Sustainable Development and the B-School Curriculum.* 475–492. JBA Press.

The Natural Edge Project. www.naturaledgeproject.net

Needham, Joseph (1981) *Science in Traditional China.* Harvard University Press.

New York Times Magazine (2007) "Eco-tecture," May 20.

Perrucci, Daniel V., et al. (2022) "A review of international eco-industrial parks for implementation success in the United States." *City and Environment Interactions*, August 30.

Smith, W. G. B. (2007) "Accounting for the environment: can industrial ecology pay double dividends for business?" In Peter N. Nemetz (ed.) *Sustainable Resource Management: Reality or Illusion?* 304–341. Edward Elgar.

Temple, Robert (2007) *The Genius of China*. Inner Traditions.

United Nations Industrial Development Organization (2023). *Eco-Industrial Parks: Achievements and Key Insights from the Global RECP Programme 2012–2018.* https://www.unido.org/sites/default/files/files/2019-02/UNIDO_EIP_Achievements_Publication_Final.pdf

Van Beers, Dick, et al. (2007) "Industrial symbiosis in the Australian minerals industry." *Journal of Industrial Ecology*, 11(1): 55–72.

Young, Rebekah, et al. (2002) "Byproduct synergy: Mexico." In Peter N. Nemetz (Ed.), *Bringing Business on Board: Sustainable Development and the B-School Curriculum*. 459–474. JBA Press.

Zhu, Qinghua, et al. (2007) "Industrial symbiosis in China: Case study of the Guitang Group." *Journal of Industrial Ecology*, 11(1): 31–42.

5   Thinking Systemically (I)
Mass Balances and Industrial Metabolism

The process of thinking systemically brings a powerful analytical approach to both corporate strategy and government policy with respect to sustainability. In this chapter, we review the basic principles of mass balances and metabolic analysis, providing examples to illustrate their application.

Mass Balances

The quantification of the total amount of all materials into and out of a process is referred to as mass balance. This type of analysis provides confirmation that all materials have been fully accounted for and no streams are missing. The fundamental concept is that the total mass flowing into a process should equal total mass flowing out (See Figure 5.1). In practice, it is a useful way to identify previously hidden waste streams: if the mass coming out of a process is less than the combined mass of the inputs, then some other

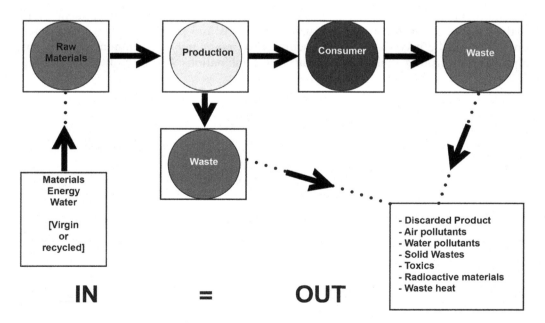

Figure 5.1 Mass Balances Schematic

DOI: 10.4324/9781003170754-7

stream – most likely waste – must be leaving the process too. This is a particularly important tool considering the maxim that "waste is lost profit."

Table 5.1 presents a highly simplified example of mass balance analysis using the drying yield of potatoes (Earle n.d.). In this case, the 1000 kg of total mass in the form of raw potatoes and their constituents is balanced by 1000 kg of total mass out in the form of dried product and losses. Clearly, a much more complex production process would require an equally complex mass balance analysis.

This type of methodology can be very useful in two specific areas of concern to the corporation: (1) finding a least-cost solution to pollution release regulatory requirements in the form of standards or economic incentives, and (2) determining if waste streams could be profitably recovered as marketable byproduct. Examples of each of these circumstances are presented in Case Study 1 below. Case Study 2 examines a similar problem of total waste cost minimization faced by a local government, such as a municipality.

Case study 1 – Mass balance analysis to assist corporate strategy

This case concerns the output of wastes as distinct from the inputs and examines a small rural township with several industrial plants: an abattoir, plywood/sawmill plant and dairy (Figure 5.2). The case focuses on the reduction of five-day biochemical oxygen demand (BOD5) – a pollutant whose municipal discharge is dominated by the waste stream from the dairy. Table 5.2 is a simplified and truncated mass balance for the township listing the load into and out of the municipal sewage treatment plant (STP) as well as direct discharges from the three industrial operations.

Abattoir

Pollution control in the modeled abattoir presents the richest choice of treatment alternatives among the three major industrial operations and provides a convincing demonstration of the necessity for, and usefulness of, computer programming in arraying and choosing from a multitude of treatment combinations. From the literature, three

Table 5.1 Mass Balance of Potatoes

Mass In		Mass Out	
Raw Potatoes:		*Dried Product:*	
Potato solids	140 kg	Potato solids	129 kg
Water	860 kg	Associated water	10 kg
		Total product	139 kg
		Losses	
		Peelings	
		solids	11 kg
		water	69 kg
		Water evaporated	781 kg
		Total losses	861 kg
Total	1000 kg	Total	1000 kg

Adapted from www.nzifst.org.nz/unitoperations.matlenerg2.htm

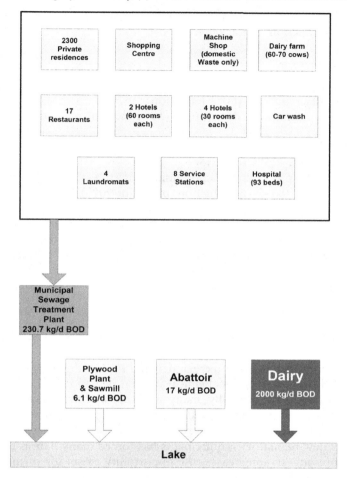

Figure 5.2 Mass Balance of Small, Rural Town

Table 5.2 Mass Balance of Small Rural Township

	Flow in L/d	*BOD in mg/L*	*Total BOD in Kg/d*
STP in	2,247,392	165	371
STP out	2,247,392[a]	22	48
Dairy	37,854	44,000	1,666
Abattoir	11,356	1,250	14
Plywood 1	3,153	860	3
Plywood 2	59,052	40	2
Plywood combined	62,205	82	5

[a] estimated, exclusive of evaporative losses

subprocess changes have been identified as well as three add-on alternatives listed as follows (with BOD5 reduction in brackets):

(I) Subprocess changes

    A. Add evaporator to wet rendering system (50% reduction)
    B. Change to dry rendering (60% reduction)
    C. Precede wet cleanup wet dry cleanup (10 reduction)

(II) Add-on Treatment

    D. Catch basin only (25% reduction)
    E. Trickling Filter (65–95% reduction, midpoint 80%)
    F. Activated sludge (85–95% reduction, midpoint 90%)

Some of these alternatives are substitutes, while others are complements. In addition, when computing overall plant BOD5 removal, it is important to recognize the process ordering of specific pollutant reduction technologies. There are, in total, 23 alternative process/treatment combinations that require examination. Eight of these involve total flow reduction as well as BOD5 abatement because of the lower water use inherent in option B.

Dairy

In cheese manufacturing, Chemical oxygen demand (COD) dominates the waste stream (with 20,559 mg/l) followed by biochemical oxygen demand (BOD) (with 5312 mg/l) (Ryan and Walsh 2016). Traditionally, many small dairies have found it simplest to discharge their high COD and BOD organic waste in the form of whey (the portion of the milk remaining after cheese curd is removed) directly to receiving waters. The removal of this option by new regulatory requirements has forced many dairies to consider their waste disposal options. In some cases, the opportunity exists for turning these wastes into profits. Within the last several decades, whey has been transformed from an undesirable waste product into a high value food additive in baking, candy, sports drinks, animal feed and calf-milk replacements (USDA 2008). The North American whey protein market size equaled $3.73 billion in 2021 and is expected to continue growing (Fortune Business Insights 2022) Whey's wholesale price has varied considerably with a high of 48.95 cents per pound in September 2022, and a recent value of 24.69 cents per pound in August 2023 (USDA 2022, 2023). Table 5.3 illustrates the type of cost calculation that the dairy farm might conduct in assessing the potential profitability of redirecting its whey from the waste stream to a marketable product. While the incremental value of the recovered whey is not high, this is a relatively small dairy/cheese operation, and the total value of the whey must be combined with the avoided costs of either treating the waste or paying for its discharge to the municipal sewage system.

    The plywood plant and sawmill have not been included in this analysis as their relatively low-level waste can be accommodated by a simple hookup to the STP with little additional cost.

    The critical importance of corporate-level mass or material balances is demonstrated in chapter 17, which discusses the use of activity-base costing to allocate a corporation's environmentally-related costs in a manner that can reduce costs and increase profit potential.

Table 5.3 Dairy Farm Whey Economics

#cows	65
lbs of milk per cow	20,000
total lbs of milk	1,300,000
percent going to cheese	50%
milk to cheese	650,000
dry whey%	5.8%
whey butter%	0.27%
total dry whey in lbs	37,700
total whey buttter in lbs	1,755
September 2022	
Price of dry whey/lb Sept. 2022	$ 0.49
price of whey butter/ lb Sept 2022 (approx 1.5 x dry whey)	$ 0.73
total value of dry whey Sep. 2022	$ 18,454.15
total value of whey butter Sep. 2022	$ 1,288.61
TOTAL VALUE OF WHEY Sep. 2022	**$ 19,742.76**
August 2023	
Price of dry whey/lb Aug. 2023	$ 0.25
price of whey butter/ lb Aug. 2023 (approx 1.5 x dry whey)	$ 0.37
total value of dry whey August 2023	$ 9,308.13
total value of whey butter Aug. 2023	$ 649.96
TOTAL VALUE OF WHEY Aug. 2023	**$ 9,958.09**

Case study 2 Mass balance analysis to assist government policy

Studies of municipal waste treatment cannot be confined to an examination of treatment provided by urban government alone but must address the larger issue of treatment on a system-wide basis that identifies all major waterborne pollutant dischargers within an urban environment and then determines the most efficient combination of treatment installations.

There are basically three steps in the analysis. The first step is to construct a systems materials balance of a few critical parameters, such as suspended solids and five-day biochemical oxygen demand (BOD5). The second step involves an assessment of alternative capital and operating costs of treatment at both municipal treatment plants and sites of industrial pollution generation. The third and final step is the identification of the optimal treatment solution – that is, the least-cost solution subject to the constraint of maximum permissible effluent discharge to the environment. The list of alternatives should not be restricted to conventional end-of-pipe waste treatment processes. Industrial process changes or other methods of pollution abatement may be cheaper than conventional end-of-pipe treatment and, consequently, must be included in this analysis. Also, multiple discharge sites, transportation cost savings, and damage changes (increases or decreases) should be considered.

A municipality with a population of approximately 4000 people has been chosen for this study because of the relative ease of model formulation and solution. Table 5.4 presents a simplified representation of the municipal sewer system with major waste load contributors by type and number.

Table 5.4 Materials Balance of Municipal Sewer System

Source	Flow (avg.)	BOD5 (avg.)		Suspended Solids (avg.)	
	IGPD [a]	lb / day	ppm	lb / day	ppm
Residential [b,e]	304,367	613.1	231	719.6	271
Commercial and government [c,e]	46,429	202.0	498	236.0	582
Industry					
Brewery [d]	316,985	2,520.0	911	3,155.0	1,140
Sawmill [d]	35,000	105.0	344	64.5	211
Infiltration [e,f]	658	1.0	174	1.0	174
Total estimated sewage treatment plant influent	703,439	3,441.1	561	4,176.1	680
Measured sewage treatment plant influent [d]	721,520	3,138.0	498	4,289.0	681
Percentage error [g]	-2.6%	8.8%		-2.7%	
Measured sewage treatment plant effluent [d]	720,000	75.0	75	950.0	130

The least-cost solution on a systemwide basis is found by solving the following two equations:

$$(1)\ dC_R/dQ_R = dC_C/dQ_C = dC_{IA}/dQ_{IA} = dC_{IB}/dQ_{IB} = dC_{STP}/dQ_{STP}$$

$$(2)\ Q_R + Q_C + Q_{IA} + Q_{IB} + Q_{STP} = X$$

where:

C = cost of pollutant removal
Q = quantity of pollutant removed
X = total system-wide reduction of pollutant desired
and subscripts
R = residential sector
C = commercial sector
IA = industry A
IB = industry B
STP = municipal sewage treatment plant

In other words, the least cost solution requires that the marginal cost of abatement for all waste treaters be equal, and the summation of all pollutant reductions equals the total desired level of system pollutant removal. There are several problems facing the town chosen as an example, the most important being a planned major increase in brewery production. A revised materials balance reflecting this proposed increase in capacity is presented in Table 5.5.

The economic systems analysis concludes that the least cost solution to effluent abatement in this municipality entails a division of responsibility for effluent abatement between the town and its principal industrial discharger, the brewery. Clearly, each town or city represents a unique situation with a potentially stronger or weaker argument for industrial pretreatment. What this study demonstrates, however, is that a systems analysis

Table 5.5 Revised Material Balance for Example Municipality

Source	Average Flow	Average BOD5		Average Suspended Solids	
	(IGPD)	lb / day	ppm	lb / day	ppm
Brewery	1,000,000	7,950	911	9,950	11,140
Other sources	400,000	985	282	1,107	317
S.T.P. influent	1,400,000	8,935	731	11,057	905

based on mass balances and cost data are critical ingredients in the determination of least cost solutions to urban wastewater control. Specifically, least cost solutions cannot be achieved by an examination of alternative treatment installations by the municipality alone but can be realized only by a broader system perspective that also incorporates treatment alternatives and process changes available to the major dischargers within the urban environment.

An analysis of total system costs is particularly appropriate considering current water pollution control policies where (i) municipalities are required to charge industrial users of the municipal system for the full costs they impose, and (ii) state agencies pressure many existing sources to connect to existing municipal systems rather than discharge directly to surface waters. The adoption of a comprehensive systems analysis of the urban wastewater treatment problem in North America would be a significant step toward reducing the costs associated with implementation of modern water pollution control policy.

Metabolic Analysis

Metabolic analysis as used in sustainability studies is the sum of all physical and chemical processes taking place at various levels of geographic scale. One of the most useful applications of this type of mass balances is at the urban, regional or national levels where flows of energy, materials and pollutants can be tracked through cites and across national boundaries. Two brief case studies are presented of urban metabolism and the international transport of persistent organic pollutant (POPS).

Case study: Urban metabolism

Urban metabolic studies usually focus on several principal flows: water, materials, energy, nutrients and toxics. The rationale for these studies is to provide a systematic tracking of the total environmental health of a conurbation, as increasing metabolism implies more traffic and pollution as well as a potential displacement or loss of farms, forests, and wildlife. Notable studies have been conducted in such major global cites as Brussels, Tokyo, Hong Kong, Sydney, Toronto, Vienna, London, and Capetown (for example, Newcombe1978; Warren-Rhodes et al. 2001; Sahely et al. 2003). Figure 5.3 is a particularly data-rich summary of urban metabolism drawn from an early study of Brussels (Lachmund 2017: 149). In 2002, the City of London commissioned an extensive resource flow and ecological footprint analysis of its urban area with the assistance of five NGOs and professional institutes (CIWM 2002) (see Figure 5.4).Without this type of

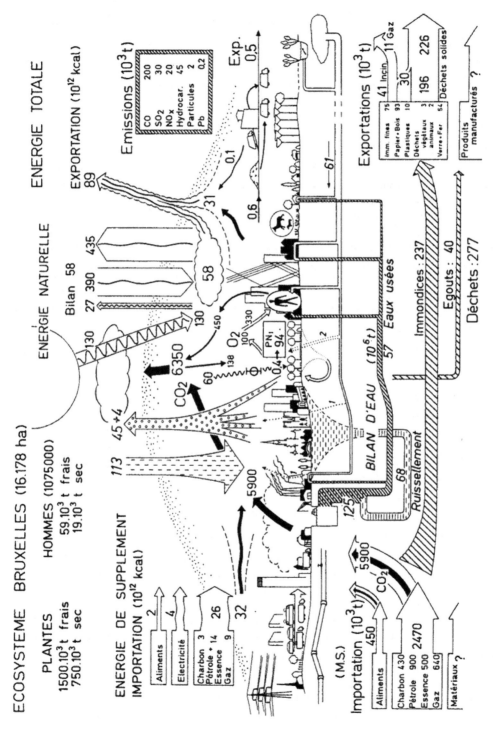

Figure 5.3 Brussels Urban Metabolism Schematic

Source: Lachmund 2017, p. 149

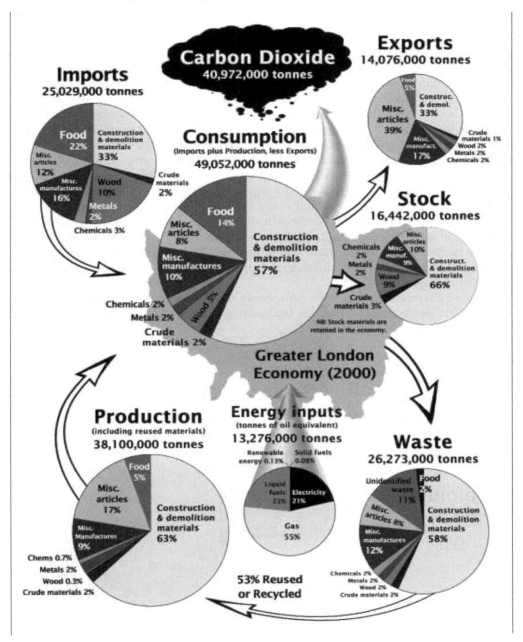

Figure 5.4 City of London Resource Flows

Source: Best Foot Forward. Reproduced with permission.

comprehensive systems analysis, it is extremely difficult for a government to identify the major sources of environmental stresses and design appropriate ameliorative measures.

Case Study: International Transport of Persistent Organic Pollutants (POPs)

In 2005, the European Community with the assistance of a Russian research center published a complex mass balance report which tracked the transport of selected POPs across Europe (Gusev et al. 2005). The following figures relate to the transport of benzo[a] pyrene, a highly carcinogenic product of certain industrial processes, incomplete fossil fuel combustion, and transportation, especially diesel engines. Figure 5.5 shows the origin by country of external sources of B[a]P depositions in Germany, while Figure 5.6 shows the effect of German sources on neighboring countries. More disaggregated data are available that detail the deposition by region within both Germany and its immediate neighbors. These data are essential to the analysis of the effects of various regulatory regimes – whether command and control or economic incentives – on the actual level of deposition in any one geographic area (see also NRC 2009). This information suggests that any unilateral control measures would probably be ineffective. What is required is a system-wide and integrated multilateral system of controls which lowers deposition levels and eliminates hot spots.

The next chapter describes what is probably the most important and useful tool for the corporate and government sectors in the assessment of the environmental impact of production processes: lifecycle analysis.

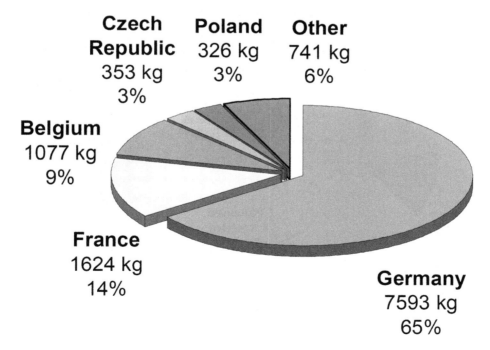

Figure 5.5 External Sources of B[a]P Deposition in Germany
Source: Gusev et al. 2005

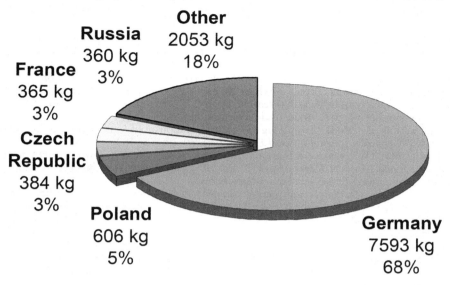

Figure 5.6 Germany B[a]P Deposition in Europe

Source: Gusav et al. 2005

References

Chartered Institute of Wastes Management (CIWM) (2002) *City Limits: A Resource Flow and Ecological Footprint Analysis of Greater London*, commissioned report, CIWM Environmental Body, Marefair, Northampton.

Decker, E. H., Elliott, S. M., Smith, F. A., Blake, D. R., & Rowland, F. S. (2000) "Energy and material flow through the urban ecosystem," *Annual Review of Energy and Environment*, 25: 685–740.

Douglas, Ian, et al. (2002) "Industry, environment and health through 200 years in Manchester," *Ecological Economics*, 41: 235–255.

Earle, R. L. (n.d.) "Material and Energy Balances," in R. L. Earle (Ed.) *Unit Operations in Food Processing*, The New Zealand Institute of Food Science & Technology Inc.

Fortune Business Insights (2022) "Whey protein market size, Share & COVID-19 impact analysis, by type (isolates, concentrates, other), application (Food & Beverages, Animal fee, and others), and regional forecast, 2022–2029," Report ID: FBI106555. https://www.fortunebusinessinsights.com/whey-protein-market-106555

Gusev, A., et al. (2005) *EMEP Regional Multicompartment Model MSCE-POP*, Meteorological Synthesizing Centre – East, Moscow.

Hendriks, C. et al. (2000) "Material flow analysis: A tool to support environmental policy decision making. Case studies on the city of Vienna and the Swiss lowlands," *Local Environment* 5: 311–328.

Huang, S. (1998) "Urban ecosystems, energetic hierarchies, and ecological economics of Taipei metropolis," *Journal of Environmental Management* 52: 39–51.

Huppes, Gjalt, et al. (2006) "Environmental impacts of consumption in the European Union: High-resolution input-output tables with detailed environmental extensions," *Journal of Industrial Ecology*, 10(3): 129–146.

Lachmund, J. (2017) "The city as ecosystem: Paul Duvigneaud and the ecological study of Brussels," in R. de Bont & J. Lachmund (eds.), *Spatializing the history of ecology: Sites, journeys, mapping*. 141–161. Routledge.

Moll, Stephan & Jose Acosta (2006) "Environmental implications of resource use. Environmental input-output analyses for Germany," *Journal of Industrial Ecology*, 10(3): 25–40.

Newcombe, Ken, et al. (1978) "The metabolism of a city: The case of Hong Kong," *Ambio*, 7(1): 3–15.

Newman, Peter W. G. & Jeffrey R. Kenworthy (1989) "Gasoline consumption and cities. A comparison of U.S. cities with a global survey," *Journal of American Planning Association*, Winter, 55(1): 24–37.

Ryan, Michael P. & Gary Walsh (2016) "The characterization of dairy waste and the potential of whey for industrial fermentation," US EPA Research Report 2012-WRM-MS-9. https://www.epa.ie/publications/research/waste/research-report-173---the-characterisation-of-dairy-waste-and-the-potential-of-whey-for-industrial-fermentation.php

Sahely, Halla R., et al. (2003) "Estimating the urban metabolism of Canadian cities: Toronto area case study," *Canadian Journal of Civil Engineering*, 30(2): 468–483.

Toasa, Jose (2008) "Whey, once a marginal byproduct, comes into its own," USDA Economic Research Service. *Amber Waves*, April 1. https://www.ers.usda.gov/amber-waves/2008/april/whey-once-a-marginal-byproduct-comes-into-its-own/

USDA (2021) "Livestock, dairy, and poultry outlook: Retail prices for eggs, chicken, pork, and beef," USDA Economic Research Service. https://www.ers.usda.gov/webdocs/outlooks/102168/ldp-m-327.pdf?v=2678.5

USDA (2023) "Livestock, dairy, and poultry outlook: First-half 2023 year-over-year changes in animal product export volumes reflect industry-specific conditions," August 17. https://downloads.usda.library.cornell.edu/usda-esmis/files/g445cd121/sq87d961p/fx71c409c/LDP-M-350.pdf

Warren-Rhodes, Kimberley & Albert Koenig (2001) "Escalating trends in the urban metabolism of Hong Kong: 1971–1997," *Ambio*, 30(7): 429–438.

Zucchetto, James (1975) "Energy-economic theory and mathematical models for combining the systems of man and nature, case study: the urban region of Miami, Florida," *Ecological Modelling*, 1: 241–268.

6 Thinking Systematically (II)
Lifecycle Analysis

Figure 6.1 is an archetypal application of Michael Porter's theory of corporate profit-ability from sustainability. In 2009, Apple ran an advertisement embodying a major corporate initiative to seize a competitive advantage based on sustainability. Apple was chafing from ratings (*Newsweek* 2009) that placed its principal rivals Dell and HP as the first and second greenest companies in the United States.

Business Week (September 24, 2009) published an article entitled "Apple Launches Major Green Effort," which reported that Apple had launched a major attack on the underpinnings of the green comparative ranking scheme. To quote:

> Apple's real goal is to change the terms of the debate. Company executives say that most existing green rankings are flawed in several respects. They count the promises companies make about green plans rather than actual achievements. And most focus on the environmental impact of a company's operations, but exclude that of its products. HP and Dell put their carbon emissions at 8.4 million tons and 471,000 tons respectively, though both are larger than Apple in terms of revenue. Their numbers exclude product use and at least some manufacturing. The companies have said that including those factors would boost their carbon totals several fold.

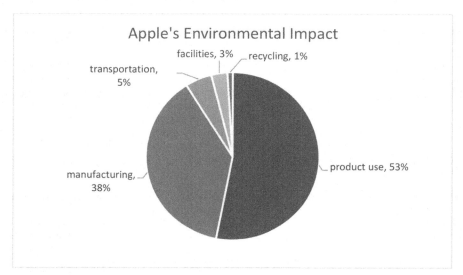

Figure 6.1 Adapted from Apple Website Ad in 2009

DOI: 10.4324/9781003170754-8

The essence of Apple's counterattack was a methodology that has become an essential ingredient in corporate strategy and government policy with respect to sustainability: lifecycle analysis (LCA). Figure 6.1 reports Apple's conclusion that product use accounted for 53% of the total lifecycle emissions of greenhouse gases, a source of emissions ignored by their competitors. In their latest Environmental Report (2023), Apple reported on their goals and progress to date, with a particular emphasis on reducing their Scope 3 footprint (see Table 6.1).

The relative significance of product use in total GHG emissions from cradle-to -grave is often not intuitively obvious. Early research on this subject dates to pioneering work conducted by R. Stephen Berry and colleagues in the Department of Chemistry at the University of Chicago. In their exhaustive analysis of lifecycle energy consumption of an automobile, Berry and Fels (1972 and 1973) found that during each year of operation, a typical American car used as much energy as was consumed in its production (i.e., a ratio of 1:1). The largest single contributor to this energy profile (38%) was attributable to the cold rolling of steel from iron ore. The GHG profile can be derived directly from the total energy utilization. Since the date of these early studies, there have been significant changes in the fuel economy, size and distance travelled of automobiles as well as changes in their production. The modern automobile, for example, uses significantly more aluminum and plastic than its predecessor – both energy-intensive products (see, for example, Wards MVF&F 2019, p. 57). More recent research based on information from the United Kingdom reported the following data (UNESCO 2002):

Average distance travelled each year: 16,000 km
Energy content of fuel: 40 million joules (MJ) per litre
Average fuel consumption: litres per10 km of travel
Energy required to make and assemble a car: 20,000 million joules (MJ)

A simple arithmetic calculation of energy use based on these data suggest an annual usage/production ratio of 3.2, a figure that is significantly different from that of Berry and

Table 6.1 Apple Goals and Progress to 2022

Goal	Progress
Become carbon neutral for our corporate operations.	Achieved carbon neutrality since April 2020 by implementing energy efficiency initiatives, sourcing 100 percent renewable electricity for Apple facilities, and securing carbon offsets for the remaining corporate emissions.
Achieve carbon neutrality for our entire carbon footprint, including products, by 2030, reducing related emissions by 75 percent compared with 2015.	Over 45 percent emissions reduction since 2015 across our value chain.
Transition our entire product value chain, including manufacturing and product use, to 100 percent clean electricity by 2030	As of March 2023, over 250 suppliers have committed to transitioning to 100 percent renewable electricity for their Apple production, with over 85 percent of Apple's direct spend for materials, manufacturing, and assembly of our products worldwide included in those commitments.

Adapted from Apple Environment Report (2023)

Fels. A study by Maclean and Lave (1998) from Carnegie-Mellon found a ratio of 7.3:1 for lifetime automotive energy use compared to manufacture. The authors also found that the use phase dominates the production process for a wide range of toxic pollutants.

From a more modern perspective, it is useful to examine the GHG emissions of both ICE and EVS for manufacturing and use. The IEA (2021) reports the following estimates of GHG emissions in tCO_2e per vehicle lifetime: ICE Manufacturing: 6.0, Use: 35.9 vs EV Manufacturing 8.0, Use 11.7. The totals are then 41.9 ICE vs. 19.7 EV, indicating a clear advantage for EVs.

The importance of energy use (and hence GHG production) from the normal operation of modern information and communication technologies (ICT) as well as consumer electronic devices (CE) has only recently become apparent. For example, a major study by the International Energy Agency (2009) found that ICT and CE accounted for approximately 15% of world residential electricity use, and the IEA projected an increase in their energy use by a factor of three within the following two decades. In fact, it was projected that ICT and CE could become the largest end-use category in any countries before 2020 (IEA 2009: 237). More recent projections estimate that the electricity demand of networks, production of ICT, consumer devices and data centers could account for 20.9% of projected electricity demand in 2030 (Jones (2018).

Figure 6.2 presents a schematic representation of the range of LCA coverage of the production cycle, extending all the way from the production of raw material to the

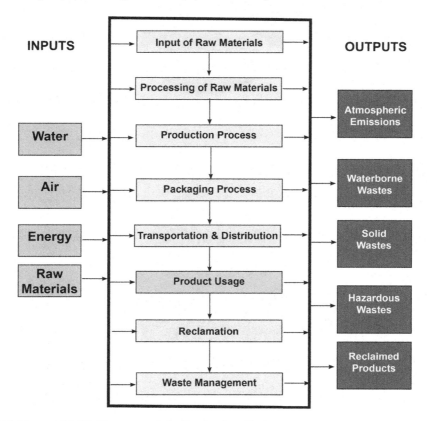

Figure 6.2 Range of LCA Coverage of the Production Cycle

product's final disposal. As displayed here, LCA represents a cradle-to-grave analysis. There is no reason, however, why it could not be enlarged to accommodate the cradle-to-cradle philosophy of McDonough and Braungart. [see chapter 3] According to Graedel and Allenby (1995, 2010), LCA serves three principal purposes: (1) to provide a comprehensive picture of the environmental impact of any product; (2) to assist in identifying reasonable trade-offs in product and process selection; and (3) to help to develop baselines against that future decisions can be made about modifying a product.

In 2009, the *Wall Street Journal* used LCA to measure the total GHG emissions of several well-known consumer products. Four of these are displayed in Figure 6.3: the Toyota

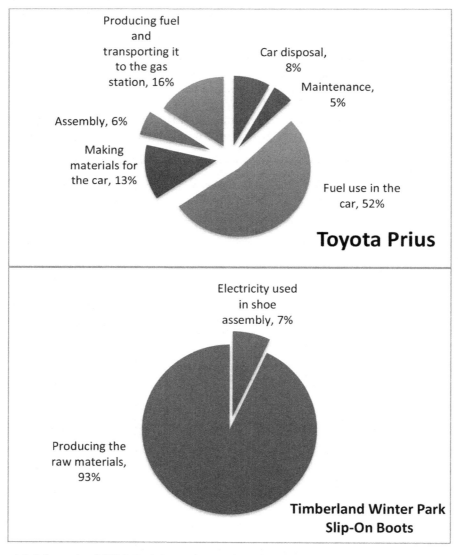

Figure 6.3 Schematic of GHG Emissions of Several Products
Adapted from WSJ March 1, 2009

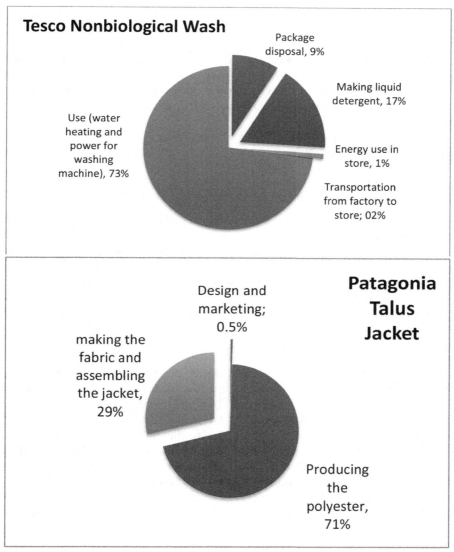

Figure 6.3 (Continued)

Prius, a pair of Timberland boots, Tesco washing liquid, and a Patagonia jacket. One of the most remarkable results of this type of analysis is that both consumers and producers can be surprised by the results that are often counterintuitive. Consider the *Wall Street Journal*'s report (March 1, 2009) on Timberland's analysis of its shoe line:

> By far the biggest contributor [to GHG] is the shoe's raw material. Leather drives the score. The average dairy cow produces, every year, greenhouse gas equivalent to four tons of carbon dioxide. Most of that comes not from carbon dioxide, in fact, but from a more-potent greenhouse gas: methane. Timberland's leather suppliers argue

that the carbon hit from a cow should fall not on their ledger, but on the ledger of beef producers. The leather producers reason that cows are grown mainly for meat, with leather as a byproduct, so that growing leather doesn't yield any emissions beyond those that would have occurred anyway. But Timberland has determined that 7% of the financial value of a cow lies in its leather. And lifecycle-analysis guidelines used by Timberland say the company should apply that percentage to compute the share of a cow's total emissions attributable to the leather.

This chapter will use a series of case studies to explore the complexities of LCAs and their sometimes counterintuitive results.

Case Study 1: A LCA comparison of an American and Finnish Office Building

While LCA can in theory track all major environmental impacts of the production cycle, it is frequently used to measure energy consumption and the associated production of carbon dioxide, sulfur dioxide, nitrogen oxides and particulates. The IEA (2023) estimates that the operations of buildings account for 30% of global final energy consumption and 26% of global energy-related emissions. 8% are direct emission in buildings and 18% indirect emission from the production of electricity and heat used in buildings. This case study summarizes the results of a more comprehensive, energy-related LCA of two buildings: one in Finland, the other in Minnesota (Junnila et al. 2006). Table 6.2 presents simple comparative data on the two buildings and Table 6.3 presents the results of the LCA on energy use, CO_2, SO_2, NO_x and PM_{10}.

There are three striking conclusions that can be drawn from this comparison. First, the use phase dominates energy consumption (70%) and all the pollutant emissions except for PM_{10}. Second, overall, the Finnish building performs much better since it uses a third less energy, and emits half the CO_2, a third of NO_x, and a fifth of PM_{10} associated with the US building's life cycle mainly due to the differences in the use phase. And third, the energy used for the operation of the Finnish building is only one-half of the US building, and the emission profiles of energy carriers in Finland are less intensive due to combined heat and power production. Part of the explanation for the variation in pollutant output is due to the different energy source mix in Finland and Minnesota: the former relied on natural gas for 67% and coal for 32% of its supply; the latter relying on a mix of natural gas (22%), coal (21%) and petroleum (40%). From the perspective of GHG and other combustion products, natural gas is considered the best fossil fuel and coal the worst.

Table 6.2 US and Finnish Office Buildings – Comparative Data

Country	Finland	USA
# Floors	4	5
Floor Area (sq m)	4,400	4,400
Volume (Cubic m)	17,300	16,400
Structural Frame	steel-reinforced concrete beam and column system	steel-reinforced concrete beam and column system with sheer walls at the core
Mass of materials (kg/sq m)	1,190	1,290

Adapted from Junnila et al. (2006)

Table 6.3 US and Finnish Office Buildings: LCA of Selected Air Pollutants

	Finland					Minnesota, USA				
	Energy	CO_2	SO_2	NO_x	PM10	Energy	CO_2	SO_2	NO_x	PM10
	GJ	Mg	kg	kg	kg	GJ	Mg	kg	kg	kg
PHASE										
Materials	15,000	1,300	2,300	4,000	2,100	31,100	2,000	9,300	8,000	2,700
Construction	4,800	200	500	1,800	400	5,500	400	800	8,300	700
Use	204,000	11,000	9,900	20,000	3,700	297,600	22,200	82,700	48,500	3,400
Maintenance	9,500	700	2,300	2,500	1,100	21,600	1,300	5,200	5,000	2,100
End of Life	800	60	50	700	90	3,300	200	400	5,800	400
TOTAL	234,100	13,260	15,050	29,000	7,390	359,100	26,100	98,400	75,600	9,300
PERCENTAGE										
Materials	6%	10%	15%	14%	28%	9%	8%	9%	11%	29%
Construction	2%	2%	3%	6%	5%	2%	2%	1%	11%	8%
Use	87%	83%	66%	69%	50%	83%	85%	84%	64%	37%
Maintenance	4%	5%	15%	9%	15%	6%	5%	5%	7%	23%
End of Life	0.3%	0.5%	0.3%	2%	1%	1%	1%	0.4%	8%	4%
TOTAL	100%	100%	100%	100%	100%	100%	100%	100%	100%	100%

Adapted from Derived from Junnila et al. (2006)

Case Study 2: Comparing Electric and Internal Combustion Powered Automobiles

The principal rationale for the introduction of electric-powered vehicles is to reduce energy use and related GHG emissions. While the market has been dominated by electric hybrids until recently, most notably Toyota's Prius, several major companies have moved one step further with the introduction of plug-in hybrids, (the Chevrolet Volt) or pure electric cars (e.g., a modified Prius, Nissan, Tesla, Volkswagen, Hyundai, SAIC Motor, and BYD). An essential ingredient in this new technology is the construction of an integrated electricity supply system that can back out internal combustion engines (ICEs) and support all-electric vehicles. In the pursuit of this strategy, relatively little publicity has been given to a lifecycle analysis of this alternative to conventional powered automobiles. Such a systems-based analysis can cast a crucial light on the choice of alternatives in pursuing a strategy of phasing out ICEs.

Figure 6.4 is a simple schematic of a lifecycle of alternative energy sources from origin to final automobile. The critical question in attempting to compare these radically

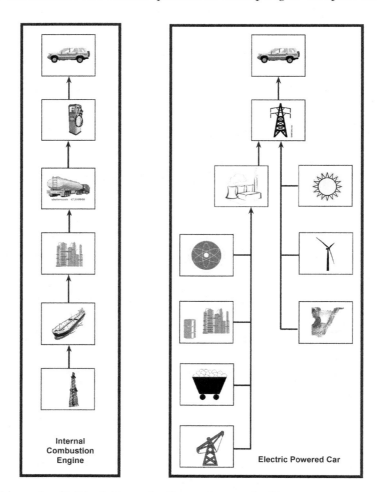

Figure 6.4 Schematic of LCA of Alternative Energy Sources for Cars

different automotive systems is the choice of performance measure. Three possible categories come immediately to mind: (1) emissions of the US EPA's five criteria air pollutants: CO, NO_x, HC, SO_2, and PM; (2) total energy use: and (3) greenhouse gas emissions. Table 6.4 drawn from an early study by Graedel and Allenby (1995) compares the two systems on the five criteria air pollutants. The results are mixed, neither propulsion system scoring consistently better than the other. Figure 6.5 is drawn from a study by the Argonne National Laboratory (2022) that presents a cradle-to-grave lifecycle analysis of US Light-Duty vehicle-fuel pathways. The results appear to unambiguously favor the hybrid electric vehicle. Modern data from the IEA on GHG emissions from BEVs and ICEs from 2021 suggest that the balance in favour of EVs is still unambiguously positive.

Systems analysis is critical in arriving at realistic estimates of relative pollutant emissions. First, comparisons will be influenced by the choice of system boundary. If the focus is solely on emissions from the automobile itself, then the electric vehicle is overwhelmingly favored, as it produces no emissions whatsoever. However, a comprehensive LCA adopts a systems' perspective by including emissions from power plants that produce the electricity required to power the electric cars. With this inclusion in the analysis, the source of fuel that powers the electric utility's power plant becomes critical as well as the timing of the power draw. The mix of energy sources for the US electric power sector in 2022 was composed of natural gas (39.8%), renewables (21.5%), coal

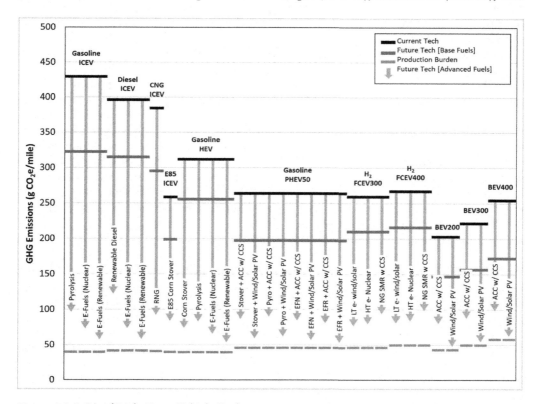

Figure 6.5 LCA of Light Duty Vehicle Fuels
Source: Argonne National Lab 2022

Table 6.4 LCA of Two Types of Automobiles

Pollutant	Electric	Internal-Combustion
CO		WORSE
NO$_x$		
Non-methane HC		WORSE
SO$_x$	WORSE	
PM	WORSE	

Derived from Graedel & Allenby (1995)

(19.5%), and nuclear (18.2%) (US EIA 2023). The figure for coals has fallen consistently over the last few years as this fuel has been backed out by a mix of other fuels, especially natural gas.

The use of an overall average can be misleading, however, when evaluating the environmental impact of electric vehicles at the regional level. The mix of fuel sources varies considerably by geographic region in the US. For example, the Pacific Northwest derives much of its power from hydroelectric sources, a relatively clean source of energy. A systems analysis of any initiative by Washington or Oregon, for example, to adopt electric vehicles would be misleading if it focused solely on hydropower as a fuel source for electric cars. The relevant source of electricity is neither the dominant regional source nor average mix, but the marginal generating capacity necessary to meet the incremental demand. If the Pacific Northwest sources this incremental power from the interconnected electric grid, then it is necessary to determine what fuel source is providing this additional power. If it were fossil-fueled, then the environmental impact would be considerably larger than hydropower.

There are three other factors relating to a LCA that must be considered in comparing ICE vs. electric systems of automobile motive power. First, a comprehensive LCA would also consider the emissions and environmental impacts of the vehicles themselves: their materials, their manufacture, and their eventual recycling. Second, the relative environmental impact of the different emissions must be addressed. For example, carbon monoxide emissions are generally considered a problem only in the immediate vicinity of high-volume traffic, while some of the other pollutants such as SO_2 and NO_x have much more significant effects both locally and regionally. And finally, a comprehensive LCA would have to include the environmental significance of difference battery types in electric vehicles, including lead-acid, nickel-cadmium, lithium ion, and others under development. Each of these has their own distinctive risks. Lithium has recently been the material of choice but has issues of safely and sourcing.

One of the most comprehensive analyses of the relative CO_2 life cycle of internal combustion and hybrid and all-electric vehicles was published by the Low Carbon Vehicle Partnership in the United Kingdom (Patterson et al. 2011). This report also stressed the critical importance of expanding any comparative analysis beyond a mere focus on tailpipe emissions to include the entire lifecycle of alternative vehicular technologies. Electric and hybrid cars have a lower carbon footprint than their fossil-fuel counterparts. Most of the carbon emissions in ICE vehicles are associated with driving, but fully 46% of the carbon footprint of electric vehicles is generated in the production process. This type of analysis clearly identifies areas in all the technical options where the most profitable research can be conducted to reduce systemwide carbon dioxide emissions.

One of the most persuasive pieces of data on the comparison of ICEs and EVs is a simple comparison of miles per gallon equivalent. In its latest report on conversion to an electric economy, Tesla (2023) summarizes the difference for passenger cars: ICE vehicle average: 24.2 MPG vs. Tesla's fleet of EVs: 115 MPGe (292 Wh.mi) representing an efficiency ratio of 4.8x.

Case Study 3: Paper vs. Plastic Cups

Most major food chains have, in the interest of sustainability, replaced their use of plastic cups with the paper equivalent. Is this really the most sustainable solution? LCA can cast some light on this issue. In a LCA study published in *Science* magazine (1991), Hocking conducted an extensive comparison of the two alternatives on the basis of twenty-five environmentally related variables. Somewhat surprisingly, on 21 of the 25 variables, the paper product fared less well than the plastic product. On only four variables did plastic come out the loser: the quantity of cooling water, the emissions of metal salts, the release of pentanes and the extent of biodegradability. Somewhat similar anomalous results emerge from comparisons of paper and plastic shopping bags, despite the frequently successful efforts of some cities and supermarkets to discourage the use of plastic bags. It is estimated that in the US, more than 100 billion plastic bags are used per year, requiring an estimated 12 million barrels of oil to produce (Center for Biological Diversity accessed 2023). The comparable figure worldwide is 500 billion plastic bags annually (Plastic Oceans, n.d.)

Figure 6.6 presents a simple schematic of the life cycle of a shopping bag (Sustainability Victoria 2007). This LCA conducted in Australia found that assumptions about end-of-life treatment (such as recycling) have a major impact on the comparative results. The critical point missed in a simple comparison of paper and plastic bags is that this is an incomplete and misleading dichotomy. It appears that neither product is desirable from a sustainability perspective, hence the increasing use of more environmentally benign reusable fabric and nonwoven polypropylene "green bags" (Sustainability Victoria 2007), commonly used in the Europe and North America.

A comprehensive LCA can be a time-consuming and resource-intensive exercise. Fortunately, several research groups around the world have already conducted extensive analysis for many products, and their results are available online either for free or a fee. Foremost among these is the Ecoinvent database produced by the Swiss Centre for Life Cycle Inventories (Frischknecht et al. 2007) that includes approximately 4,000 datasets for products, services and processes used in many LCA studies.

One of the principal impediments to the use of LCA as a definitive arbiter of total environmental impacts of specific products is the absence of some common metric to compare the relative importance of diverse environmental effects. This challenge is apparent above in the comparison of electric and ICE cars based on the US EPA's five criteria air pollutants, as well as Hocking's comparison of plastic and paper bags. Considering the methodology of monetizing environmental effects, it is tempting to consider converting all the disparate effects into dollar equivalents. Unfortunately, this is a daunting task and open to criticism on the unresolved issues emerging from monetization and discounting. Two analytical techniques currently in use are full-cost accounting and lifecycle cost analysis. While in theory, these methodologies might be applicable, in practice their use has largely been restricted to easily quantifiable financial costs for nonenvironmental effects. The next chapter considers another variant on systems analysis, namely carbon accounting (or carbon footprinting). The following chapter revisits the controversial question of the system boundaries of the typical LCA.

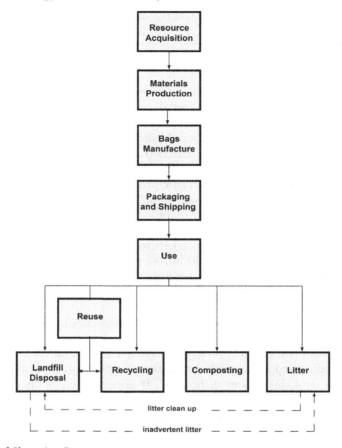

Figure 6.6 LCA of Shopping Bag

A Brief Note on Social Life Cycle Assessment

All the discussion above pertains to the environmental effects of products and services and has been labeled E-LCA by the United Nations Environment Programme (UNEP) to differentiate it from a companion measure known as Social Life Cycle Assessment S-LCA (UNEP 2009). Developed more recently, the S-LCA tool parallels the framework and analysis of the E-LCA except that its focus is on social and socio-economic impacts of products and services throughout their entire lifecycle from cradle to grave. There are five stakeholder categories who are the focus of these studies (workers, local community, society, consumers, and value chain actors), and six impact categories (human rights, working conditions, health and safety, cultural heritage, governance and socio-economic repercussions). A brief examination of these impact categories suggests why S-LCA is more difficult to perform than a conventional E-LCA where effects may be more obvious and measurable. UNEP listed several limitations that affect S-LCA today but that have been the subject of ongoing research (UNEP 2009, pp. 76–79): novelty of the technique, difficulty in accessing the data, difficulty of quantification and aggregation, ignorance of causal chain relations, skill deficiencies among practitioners, frequent inadequate input from stakeholders, difficult assessment of the product use phase, and inadequate transparency in the communication of results. Despite these limitations, not all of which are specific to S-LCA, the UNEP emphasized the need for the continued development and refinement of this tool.

References

Apple (2023) *Environmental Progress Report for 2022.*

Argonne National Laboratory (2022) *Cradle-to-Grave Lifecycle Analysis of US Light-Duty Vehicle-Fuel Pathways: A Greenhouse Gas Emissions and Economic Assessment of Current (2020) and Future (2030–2035) Technologies*, ANL-22/27.

Berry, R. Stephen & Margaret F. Fels (1972) *The Production and Consumption of Automobiles. An Energy Analysis of the Manufacture, Discard and Reuse of the Automobile and its Component Materials.* Illinois Institute for Environmental Quality.

Berry, R. Stephen and Margaret F. Fels (1973) "The energy cost of automobiles," *Science and Public Affairs* 29(10): 11–60.

Esty, Daniel & Andrew Winston (2009) *Green to Gold.* John Wiley & Sons.

Frischknecht, Rolf, et al. (2007) *Implementation of Life Cycle Impact Assessment Methods*, Swiss Centre for Life Cycle Inventories, St-Gallen, Switzerland.

Graedel, T. E. & B. R. Allenby (1995) *Industrial Ecology.* Prentice Hall.

Graedel, T. E. & B. R. Allenby (2010) *Industrial Ecology and Sustainable Engineering.* Prentice Hall.

Hocking, Martin B. (1991) "Paper versus polystyrene: A complex choice," *Science* 251, February 1: 504–505.

International Energy Agency (2009) *Gadgets and Gigawatts. Policies for Energy Efficient Electronics*, Paris.

International Energy Agency (2021) "Comparative lifecycle greenhouse gas emissions of a midsize BEV and ICE vehicle," May 5.

International Organization for Standardization (ISO) (2006a) *ISO 14040 Environmental management – Life Cycle Assessment – Principles and Framework*, Geneva.

International Organization for Standardization (ISO) (2006b) *ISO 14044 Environmental management – Life Cycle Assessment – Requirements and Guidelines*, Geneva.

Jones, Nicola (2018) "The information factories," *Nature*, September 13.

Junnila, Seppo, et al. (2006) "Lifecycle assessment of office buildings in Europe and the United States," *Journal of Infrastructure Systems*, March, pp. 10–17.

Maclean, Heather L. & Lester B. Lave (1998) "A lifecycle model of an automobile," *Environmental Science and Technology*, July 1: 322–330.

Newsweek (2009) "Apple and the environment."

Parks K., et al. (2007) *Costs and Emissions Associated with Plug-In Hybrid Electric Vehicle Charging in the Xcel Energy Colorado Service Territory*, National Renewable Energy Laboratory (NREL), Golden, CO.

Patterson, Jane, et al. (2011) "Preparing for a life cycle CO_2 measure," Low Carbon Vehicle Partnership, London.

Plastic Ocean (n.d.) "Plastic pollution facts."

Royte, Elizabeth (2007) "Why the bag backlash?" *Huffington Post*, April 8.

Sustainability Victoria (2007) *Comparison of Existing Life Cycle Analysis of Shopping Bag Alternatives*, report No. 1. Victoria, Australia.

Swiss Centre for Life Cycle Inventories. *EcoInvent Reports, Master Plan Part 3.* www.ecoinvent.org/documentaiton/reports/

Tesla (2023) *Master Plan Part 3.* https://www.tesla.com/blog/master-plan-part-3

UK Environment Agency (2005) *Life Cycle Assessment of Disposable and Reusable Nappies in the UK.*

United Nations Environment Programme (UNEP) (2009) *Guidelines for Social Life Cycle Assessment of Products.*

UN Educational, Scientific and Cultural Organization (UNESCO) (2002) *Module 1: Cars and Energy.* http://portal.unesco.org/education/en/file_download.php/a01355752c9e869a63cc5651084cfa 30Cars+and+energy.pdf]

US Energy Information Administration (EIA) (2023) "Electricity explained. electricity in the United States."

Wall Street Journal (2009) "Six products, six carbon footprints," March 1.

Wards Automotive Group (2019), *Motor Vehicle Facts & Figures (MVF&F).*

7 Thinking Systemically (III)

A Brief Note on Carbon Accounting

With the advent of the European Trading System (ETS) for greenhouse gases (EC 2008), European corporations have been faced with the necessity of generating accurate estimates of their output of carbon dioxide. A new series of metrics and methodologies emerged to measure the carbon footprint of business. Several major regulatory agencies have recently introduced guidelines or rules for reporting GHG emissions (see chapter 2).

Carbon accounting, or carbon footprinting, is a hybrid of lifecycle analysis and the ecological footprint that measures the total quantity of greenhouse gases emitted by an entity – whether it be an individual, plant, firm, or geographic entity. As well as scholarly and professional publications on this subject (Pandey et al. 2011; CFI 2023), numerous books and articles have been written on this subject for the public, including, inter alia, *How Bad Are Bananas? The Carbon Footprint of Everything* by Mike Berners-Lee (2011), and the "The Cheeseburger Footprint" by Jamais Cascio (2007). This latter study uses detailed data on energy use in the food sector codeveloped by Stockholm University and the Swiss Federal Institute of Technology (Carlsson-Kanyama & Faist, n.d.) to construct an approximate picture of the magnitude of the greenhouse gases associated with this ubiquitous American product. The results are startling, as the author concludes that "the greenhouse gas emissions arising every year from the production and consumption of cheeseburgers is roughly the amount emitted by 6.5 million to 19.6 million SUVs." There are now approximately 35 million SUV's currently on the road in the US.

Carbon accounting has become a common metric in the corporate sector for both internal and external use. The giant British food chain, Tesco has adopted carbon labelling on many of their products. There are at least five reasons why companies would be willing to calculate their carbon footprint in an environment even where such an exercised is not legally mandated. According to the Carbon Trust (2008b), measuring the carbon footprint of products across their full lifecycle is a powerful way for companies to collect the information they need to reduce GHG emissions; identify cost savings opportunities; incorporate emissions impact into decision making on suppliers, materials, product design and manufacturing processes; demonstrate environmental/corporate responsibility leadership; meet customer demands for information on product carbon footprints; and differentiate and meet demands from green consumers.

Added to this list is a new and powerful incentive in finance. The US Securities and Exchange Commission has encouraged corporations to add environmental issues to the list of material risks that they report every year in their reports to the SEC (see chapter 2)

DOI: 10.4324/9781003170754-9

The reporting of such risks has already become mandatory in that bank and insurance companies are increasingly loath to fund or insure corporations with unclear potential liabilities emerging from a company's products, processes and waste management practices. As Repetto stated (2007b):

> For corporations in environmentally sensitive industries the message is clear. Shareholders are demanding and governments are requiring more transparency regarding the ways in that environmental costs, risks and liabilities are affecting their financial conditions and prospects. There is no reason to believe that these demands will weaken. Well-managed companies will realize that they can benefit from this trend because financial markets clearly reward good corporate governance, and public trust is a valuable business asset.

As early as 2009, Trucost Ltd. estimated the exposure to carbon costs among large corporations in a report entitled "Carbon Risks and Opportunities in the S&P 500." In their words, "carbon intensity indicates financial risk." They concluded that:

> carbon liabilities could equate to 2% to 17% of EBITDA for Utilities companies in the S&P 500. Because of its reliance on fossil fuels, the utility sector is the most vulnerable sector, while insurance, banks and other service industries have the least exposure.

These analyses have been updated listing the exposure to various sectors of the US economy by S&P Index (S&P Global 2022) (see Table 7.1) They conclude that:

> Almost 60% of companies in the S&P 500® (market capitalization of $18.0 trillion) and more than 40% of companies in the S&P Global 1200 (market capitalization $27.3 trillion) hold assets at high risk of physical climate change impacts. Wildfires, water stress, heatwaves and hurricane (or typhoons) linked to increasing global average temperatures represent the greatest drivers of physical risk.

Detailed data at the corporate level are available thorough subscription.

Table 7.1 Corporate Assets and Risk Due to Climate Change

Index constituents with assets at high physical risk by index. Moderate climate change scenario2050. High physical riskis defined asscores greater than 75 out of 100 in the Trucost Climate Change Physcial Risk dataset. (Trucost Analysis as at 13 November 2019).

	# Companies with assets at high physical risk on at least one indicator	*Market cap of companies with assets at high risk ($US Trillion)*	*Reveunue of companies with assets at high risk ($US Trillion)*
S&P/TOPIX 150	40 (27%)	$1.3 (42%)	$2.1 (55%)
S&P/ASX 200	88 (44%)	$0.9 (89%)	$0.4 (82%)
S&P Globl 1200	521 (43%)	$27.3 (66%)	$16.6 (66%)
S&P Europe 350	101 (29%)	$4.3 (52%)	$3.2 (48%)
S&P 500	297 (59%)	$18.0 (72%)	$9.0 (74%)

Adapted from S&P Global (2022)

Several international standards have been created to assist corporations in constructing a carbon footprint. Foremost among these are the International Organization for Standardization's ISO 14064 for greenhouse accounting and verification (Weng and Boehmer 2006 and ISO 14065 International Organization for Standardization (2020).

Carbon accounting methodology has also been made readily available by such key players as The Carbon Trust, an independent company established in 2001 under the aegis of the government of the United Kingdom. With the mandate to facilitate the transition to a less carbon intensive economy, the trust consulted broadly with corporations and NGOs to develop a set of standard protocols. American partners in this process included Coca-Cola, Coors, Kimberley-Clarke, and Pepsico. The principal product from this work has been the development of PAS 2050 (Carbon Trust 2008c) (where PAS = publicly available specification). PAS 2050 describes five steps to calculating a carbon footprint: (1) building a process map of a product's lifecycle, from raw materials to disposal, including all material, energy and waste flows; (2) confirming the boundaries of the analysis (i.e,. how many suppliers, processes and inputs to include) and performing a high-level footprint calculation to help prioritize efforts; (3) collecting data on material amounts, activities and emission factors across all lifecycle stages; (4) calculating the product carbon footprint; and (5) assessing the precision of the footprint analysis. Table 7.2 lists five stages of the cradle-to-grave production process and the data requirements associated with each.

Figure 7.1 presents a simplified schematic of a PAS 2050 process map for croissant production (Carbon Trust 2008b). Table 7.3 lists the six steps from raw material acquisition to waste disposal, the subcategories of data that are required to compute the overall footprint, and the component results. Figure 7.2 focuses on only one part of the production chain to provide some idea of the nature of the calculations. Commensurate with PWC's focus on the importance of the supply chain, these data reveal that almost half of the carbon footprint of croissant production is due to the nature of raw material production, followed by the manufacturing process itself, which accounts for less than one-third of the carbon footprint (disposal is 14.4%; consumer use is 3.6%; and distribution and retail is only 0.5%).

With a clearer understanding of where the challenges lie – and the opportunities for cost reduction and profit increments – a corporation has several generic emission reduction opportunities (Carbon Trust 2008c):

- *Energy use*. Change fuels (e.g., from electricity to gas); increase the proportion of energy produced by renewables
- *Production*. Decrease waste volumes by process changes or byproduct recovery for resale; increase the size of manufacturing operations to capitalize on opportunities for economies of scale; decrease the amount of processing; change manufacturing practices and improve efficiency.
- *Distribution*. Decrease the degree of energy-intensive heating and/or cooling in storage and transportation; decrease the distances traveled by relocating production and/or distribution facilities.
- *General*. Include energy/carbon criteria in purchasing/supplier choices; include energy/carbon criteria in product design, configuration and/or materials; change technology to more energy efficient processes; and improve inventory management.

Table 7.2 Five Stages of Cradle-to-Grave Production Process

Raw Materials	Manufacture	Distribution/Retail	Consumer Use	Disposal/Recycling
All inputs used at any stage in the life cycle	All activities from collection of raw material to distribution: all production processes, transport/storage related to production, packaging, site-related emissions, e.g., lighting, ventilation, temperature	All steps in transport and related storage	Energy required during use phase: storage, preparation, application, maintenance and repair	All steps in disposal: transport, storage, processing
Include processes related to raw materials: mining/extraction of minerals, farming, forestry, pre-processing, packaging, storage, transport	All materials produced: product, waste, co-products (useful byproducts), direct emissions	Retail storage and display		Energy required in disposal/recycling process
Account for impact of raw materials: fertilizer production, transport and application, and land use changes				Direct emissions due to disposal/recycling: carbon decay, methane release, incineration

Based on Carbon Trust (2008c, p. 14)

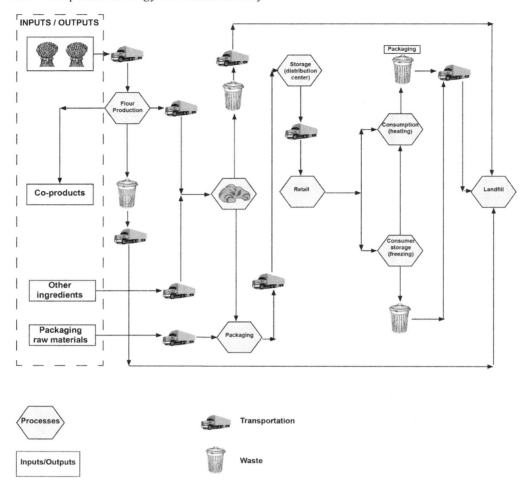

Figure 7.1 PAS 2050 Process Map for Croissants

Adapted from Carbon Trust 2008

One of the most important findings of this type of analysis is that for many products the greatest reduction in their systemwide carbon footprint lies not within their own operation, but among its suppliers, thereby suggesting that a corporation might more profitably direct its attention to reconstructing or modifying its supply chain (PWC 2009; Humes 2011). In addition to providing a metric for calculating carbon footprints, the Carbon Trust also consulted services available for corporations willing to respond to this initiative. There is a long list of case studies, based largely on UK companies, where significant efficiencies and cost savings have been achieved (Carbon Trust n.d.). For example, at two plants in the UK, Heinz Ltd. was able to lower their CO_2 emissions by 17,600 metric tons over four years with a resulting saving of 13% in their energy budget and a credit of 700,000 UKP on an enhanced capital allowance scheme in one year.

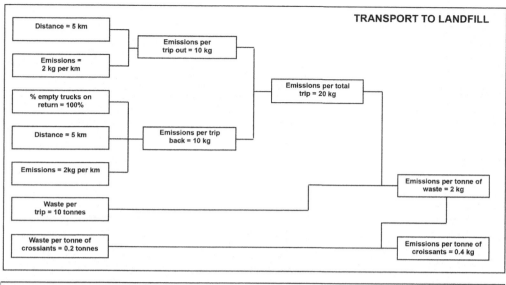

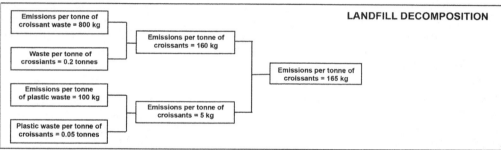

Figure 7.2 One Segment of Production Chain for Croissants

Adapted from Carbon Trust 2008

Table 7.3 Carbon Accounting for Croissant Production

Raw material cultivation and transport - wheat	1a	Farming	450
	1b	Wheat transport	9
Raw material production - wheat	2a	Flour production - milling	45
	2b	Flour transport	7
	2c	Waste transport	1.4
		Waste disposal	54
Croissant production	3a	Baking	300
	3b	Packaging	40
	3c	Waste transport	2
		Waste disposal	30

(*Continued*)

Table 7.3 (Continued)

Distribution and retail	4a	Transport to distribution centre	30
	4b	Storage	0.5
	4c	Transport to store	5
	4d	Retail	20
Consumer use	5a	Storage - freezing	5
	5b	Consumption - heating	36
Disposal	6a	Transport to landfill	0.4
	6b	Landfill decomposition	165
Total per tonne of croissants (Kg CO2e)			1200
Total per 12-croissant package			1.2

Derived from Carbon Trust 2008b

PriceWaterhouseCoopers (Hawksworth 2006) has devoted significant effort to examining the carbon-related issue of supply chain management and has concluded that the benefits are substantial and include short and long-term cost reductions, improved supplier loyalty, risk management and maintaining or developing competitive advantage.

The following chapter presents a critique of both LCA and Carbon Footprinting and suggests a hybrid methodology using Input-Output analysis that can overcome some of their deficiencies.

References

AXA Investment Managers and Trucost (2010) "Taking Carbon Risk into Account."

Berners-Lee, Mike (2011) *How Bad Are Bananas? The Carbon Footprint of Everything*. Greystone Books.

Carbon Trust (n.d.) http:www.carbontrust.co.uk/abut-carbon-trust/what-we-do/casestudies/Pages/casestudies.aspx

Carbon Trust (2008a) *Product Carbon Footprinting: The New Business Opportunity*. https://www.carbontrust.com/our-work-and-impact/guides-reports-and-tools/product-carbon-footprinting-the-new-business-opportunity

Carbon Trust (2008b) *Guide to PAS 2050*.

Carbon Trust (2008c) *PAS 2050:2008 Specification of the Assessment of the Lifecycle Greenhouse Gas Emissions of Goods and Service*.

Carbon Trust (2010) *Carbon Footprinting*.

Carbon Trust (2011) *Green Your Business for Growth*.

Carlsson-Kanyama, Annika & Mireille Faist (n.d.) "Energy use in the food sector: A data survey." Department of Systems Ecology, Stockholm University, Department of Civil and Environmental Engineering, Swiss Federal Institute of Technology (ETH Zurich).

Cascio, Jamais (2007) "The cheeseburger footprint." The Open Future., http://www.openthefuture.com/cheeseburger_CF.html

Corporate Finance Institute (CFI) (2023) "Carbon accounting."

European Commission (EC) (2008) "EU action against climate change: The EU emissions trading scheme."

GreenBiz Group (2011) *State of Green Business 2011*.

Hawksworth, John (2006) "The world in 2050: implications of global growth for carbon emissions and climate change policy," PriceWaterhouseCoopers (PWC).

Humes, Edward (2011) *Force of Nature. The Unlikely Story of Wal-Mart's Green Revolution*, Harper Business.

International Organization for Standardization (ISO) (2020) "ISO 14065:2020(en) General Principles and requirements for bodies verifying environmental information."

Pandey, Divya, et al. (2011) "Carbon footprint: current methods of estimation," *Environmental Monitoring and Assessment* 178: 135–160.

PriceWaterhouseCoopers (PWC) (2008) "How your company can prepare to manage carbon as an asset."

PriceWaterhouseCoopers (PWC) (2009) *Carbon Disclosure Project Supply Chain Report 2009.*

Repetto, Robert (2007a) "Better financial disclosure protects investors and the environment," in Trucost (2009) *Carbon Risks and Opportunities in the S&P 500.*

Repetto, Robert (2007b) "Better financial disclosure protects investors and the environment," in Peter N. Nemetz (ed.) (2007) *Sustainable Resource Management: Reality or Illusion?* 342–375. Edward Elgar.

S&P Global (2022) "Understanding climate risk at the asset level: the interplay of transition and physical risks."

UK Environment Agency (2011) "Environmental disclosures. the third major review of environmental reporting in the annual report & accounts of the FTSE all-share companies."

US Securities and Exchange Commission (SEC) (2010) "SEC issues interpretive guidance on disclosure related to business or legal developments regarding climate change." www.tesco.com/climatechange/carbonfootprint.asp

Weng, Chan Kook & Kevin Boehmer (2006) "Launching of ISO 14064 for greenhouse gas accounting and verification," *ISO Insider*, March–April.

8   Thinking Systemically (IV)

LCA, Carbon Footprinting, and Input-Output Analysis

While lifecycle analysis and its subset, carbon footprinting, are powerful tools for tracking the environmental impact of a product, there are certain inherent theoretical drawbacks to these methodologies (Lave et al. 1995). Perhaps the most important of the limitations to this type of engineering, process-based analysis is the somewhat arbitrary definition of the system boundary. The analysis is usually limited, by necessity, to what are perceived to be the most important negative environmental impacts from the chain of production. This presents a classic systems problem, as it is not always clear how much of the total impact has been captured within the defined boundaries of the analysis. By way of example, Lester Lave of Carnegie-Mellon University's Department of Engineering developed a methodology for expanding the analysis to include, in theory, all the possible impacts of any given pollutant release throughout the entire chain of production. The essence of this analytical approach, called *EIOLCA*, rested on Input-Output (I-O) analysis that had the capacity to track the multitude of direct and indirect relationships among all sectors of a national economy (see chapter 2 for a discussion of other databases that have replaced the EIOLCA).

By way of example, Lave revisited the analysis by Hocking (see chapter 6) of the comparative lifecycle analyses of paper and polystyrene cups (Lave et al. 1995). The task faced by Hocking – and anyone else attempting a process analysis of this type – is immense because of the vast array of direct and indirect suppliers and inputs associated with every level of the production chain, from raw materials to final product. Figure 8.1 is a representation of the narrow boundaries of Hockings' analysis as determined by Lave. This restricted analysis focused on a limited set of direct suppliers. In contrast, once input-output analysis is brought to this problem, the boundary is significantly wider and is represented in Figure 8.2. Lave's conclusions were twofold: (1) while the toxic discharges from all direct suppliers were substantial, indirect suppliers have more than twice the toxic discharges of direct suppliers; and (2) while on a per dollar, or per pound, of output, plastic generates greater toxic discharges than paperboard, on a per cup basis paperboard generates more toxic waste than plastic. To make this comparison, Lave totaled all toxic releases to air water, underground and land in pounds.

While this is an important step in generating a commensurable metric, there is one major problem that is finessed by this analysis – the lack of comparability among pollutants. To generate a meaningful overall value in pounds of pollutant release, it is necessary to assume that one pound of pollutant x has an equivalent health or environmental effect as one pound of pollutant y. This is a tenuous assumption. There are two partial solutions to this problem: first, to use the US EPA system of toxicity equivalence values,

DOI: 10.4324/9781003170754-10

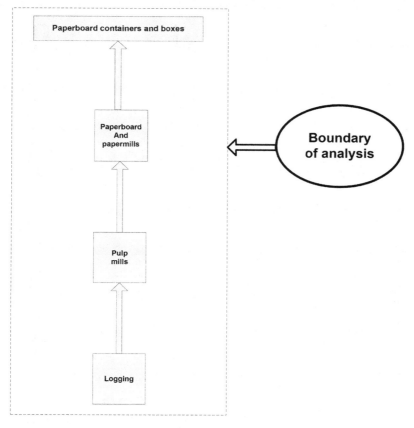

Figure 8.1 Hocking's Boundaries for His Analysis of Paper vs. Plastic Cups

although this pertains principally to human health effects (US EPA 2023). Second is to convert major impacts to monetized value. Although, conceptually, this second approach is much more comprehensive, it is extremely difficult to implement in practice.

As mentioned above, Carnegie-Mellon University established an extensive, publicly accessible website that facilitated the application of I-O analysis to the study of any major production process (Sussman and Clewlow n.d.). There were six types of industry-specific data available on this EIO-LCA database: (1) economic activity; (2) conventional air pollutants, such as SO_2, CO, NOx, volatile organic compounds (VOC), lead (Pb), and particulate matter (PM_{10}); (3) greenhouse gases, such as CO_2, CH_4, N_2O, CFCs, all converted to their global warming potential (GWP);[1] (4) energy by fuel type; (5) toxic releases to air, water, land, underground, both on-site and off-site; and (6) employment data. Another comprehensive database is available from the Ecoinvent Centre, the Swiss Centre for Life Cycle Inventories). This dataset covers nearly 4,000 industrial processes and, although a charge is levied for use, the website contains several dozen freely downloadable published studies that focus on specific industries and chemicals. Table 2.8 provided data from the now outdated Carnegie-Mellon database on the GHG emissions of one example industry, ferrous metal foundries. The key distinction is between direct and indirect emissions.

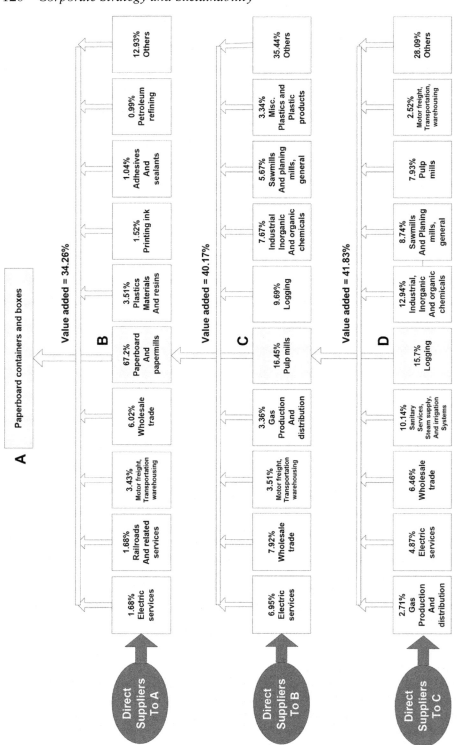

Figure 8.2 Lave's Wider Boundaries of Paper vs. Plastic Cups

In this case, direct emissions account for only 9% of the total of all emissions attributable to this industry. A brief comparison of both process-based LCA and EIO-LCA is provided in Table 8.1 by Hendrickson et al. (2006).

A similar type of in-depth analysis applied to carbon footprinting was reported in a special issue of *Economic Systems Research* in 2009. Six papers addressed the theoretical issues and presented case studies covering land use accounting, corporate footprints, national examples from Australia and Japan, and multiregional analysis. A paper by Huang et al. (2009) paralleled in many respects the analysis of Lave with respect to the potential contributions of I-O analysis to LCA. The authors identified the same problem of arbitrary cut-offs thresholds in LCA that can lead to a serious underestimate of the total environmental impact of a production chain.

Huang et al. observed that to be as complete as possible, many engineering process LCAs adopt a cut-off of 95–99% % (i.e., they attempt to include within the boundary of analysis all inputs that have at least a 1% or 5% contribution to the total environmental release of carbon). But, as the authors pointed out, it is logically impossible to determine if such a coverage has been achieved if the total impact is unknown. The true aggregate impact can only be determined using input-output analysis. Huang et al. presented

Table 8.1 Comparison of EIO-LCA with Process-Based Models

	Process-Based LCA	*EIO-LCA*
Advantages	results are detailed, process specific allows for specific product comparisons identifies areas for process improvements, weak point analysis provides for future product development assessments	results are economy-wide, comprehensive assessments allows for systems-level comparisons uses publicly available, reproducible results provides for future product development assessments provides information on every commodity in the economy
Disadvantages	setting system boundary is subjective tend to be time intensive and costly difficult to apply to new process design use proprietary data cannot be replicated if confidential data are used uncertainty in data	product assessments contain aggregate data process assessments difficult must link monetary values with physical units imports treated as products created within economic boundaries availability of data for complete environmental effects difficult to apply to an open economy (with substantial non-comparable imports) uncertainty in data

Source: Hendrickson et al. (2006, reproduced by permission of Taylor and Francis Group)

several industry-level empirical calculations from Australia and the US to demonstrate their point, and their results were quite startling. For example, in the US newspaper publishing sector, the top contributor of carbon in the supply chain was electricity used by the publishers themselves with 5% of total contributory emissions. The authors observed that if only items that represented at least 5% or more of total emissions were included, then clearly 95% of total emissions would be missed. The comparable missed total for a 1% cutoff was 72%.

One of the more amusing discoveries yielded by the total systems analysis provided by I-O came from a totally unanticipated source of carbon. To quote:

> In an upstream scope-3 calculation, supply chains start with an emitting upstream sector, and end with the purchasing industry sector under investigation. The meaning of upstream chain is best explained using an example. Consider the supply chain Beef cattle -> Meat processing -> Restaurant. The emissions associated with this supply chain are caused, for example, by land clearing or enteric fermentation in animals slaughtered for meat that is supplied to a restaurant's kitchen. Another way of expressing this is to say that emissions from beef-cattle farming become 'embodied' in the restaurant meal (Huang et al. 2009).[2]

In sum, lifecycle analysis and carbon footprinting both have a serious deficiency – the lack of appropriate system analysis. This obstacle can be largely overcome using I-O analysis that encompasses an entire national economy. There are, however, several drawbacks to a sole reliance on I-O analysis (Huang et al. 2009). These include firstly the degree of sectoral aggregation. I-O tables can range in size from very small to very large, depending on how finely each sector is defined. For example, the North American Industrial Classification System (NAICS) drills down to the six-digit level of industries, and the greater the disaggregation, the larger the data requirements (Statistics Canada). Conversely, the lower the level of disaggregation, the greater the simplifications and possible distortions.

Secondly, many models are generally based on single geographic-political areas and do not account for interregional flows where regions can be subnational or transnational. If, for example, a significant proportion of inputs comes from an offshore supplier and no comparable I-O-based pollutant data are available, the result can be seriously incomplete. Within a national context, however, regional models can be linked more easily. Thirdly, I-O analysis is essentially static and usually relies on data collected several years before the analysis can be completed. Fourthly, the lack of price data is problematic since changes in prices clearly influence how an economic system will respond to changes in inputs due to such factors as regulations or economic incentives. Fifthly, a simplifying assumption in this type of I-O analysis is one of a fixed, or linear, relationship between physical output and resulting pollution.

And, finally, the underlying system of industry classification used in the construction of I-O tables must deal with the sometimes complex problem of primary versus secondary products generated by establishments. While establishments are classified to industries based on their primary products or services, many establishments create other products or services that may be produced or used differently from their primary products. This can produce challenges to the process of classification. In the construction of I-O tables, the US Bureau of Economic Analysis (2009: 4–5) addresses this problem through the creation of two sets of "make" and "use" tables called standard tables and supplementary tables. To quote:

> The standard tables closely follow NAICS and are consistent with other economic accounts and industry statistics. The supplementary tables are derived from the standard tables by reassigning some secondary products to the industry in which they are the primary products. In most cases, the reassignment decisions are based on comparisons of the production processes for the two industries.

As a result of the limitations of a sole reliance on I-O analysis, it is the measured opinion of Lave, Huang and others that a hybrid model is appropriate, where both an engineering, process-based LCA and I-O regional model are used to inform the decision-making process.

Notes

1 The global warming potential (GWP) of major greenhouse gases (GHGs) is usually cast in terms of carbon dioxide equivalent (CO_2e). The GWPs for the major GHGs are defined in Table 8.2 (http://unfccc.int/ghg_data/items/3825.php).

Table 8.2 GWP of Major GHGs

SPECIES	Chemical Formula	Lifetime (yrs)	Global Warming Potential		
			20 years	100 years	500 years
CO2	CO_2	variable [a]	1	1	1
Methane [b]	CH_4	12+/-3	56	21	6.5
Nitrous oxide	N_2O	120	280	310	170
HFC-23	CHF3	264	9,100	11,700	9,800
HFC-32	CH2F2	5.6	2,100	650	200
HFC-41	CH3F	3.7	490	150	45
HFC-43-10mee	C5H2F10	17.1	3,000	1,300	400
HFC-125	C2F5	32.6	4,600	2,800	920
HFC-134	C2H2F4	10.6	2,900	1,000	310
HFC-134a	CH2FCF3	14.6	3,400	1,300	420
HFC-152a	C2H4F2	1.5	460	140	42
HFC-143	C2H3F3	3.8	1,000	300	94
HFC-143a	C2H3F3	48.3	5,000	3,800	1,400
HFC-227ea	C3HF7	36.5	4,300	2,900	950
HFC-236fa	C3H2F6	209	5,100	6,300	4,700
HFC-245ca	C3H3F5	6.6	1,800	560	170
Sulfur hexafluoride	SF6	3,200	16,300	23,900	34,900
Perfluoromethane	CF4	50,000	4,400	6,500	10,000
Perfluoroethane	C2F6	10,000	6,200	9,200	14,000
Perfluoropropane	C3F8	2,600	4,800	7,000	10,100
Perfluorobutane	C4F10	2,600	4,800	7,000	10,100
Perfluorocyclobutane	c-C4F8	3,200	6,000	8,700	12,700
Perfluoropentane	C5F12	4,100	5,100	7,500	11,000
Perfluorohexane	C6F14	3,200	5,000	7,400	10,700

[a] derived from the Bern carbon cycle model
[b] The GWP for methane includes indirect effects of tropospheric ozone production and stratospheric water vapor production

Source: http://unfccc.int/ghg_data/items/3825/php

2 Scope is a boundary concept associated with the Greenhouse Gas Protocol, a joint initiative of the World Resources Institute and the World Business Council for Sustainable Development. To quote its website (www.ghgprotocol.org):

> The GHG Protocol is the most widely used international accounting tool for government and business leaders to understand, quantify, and manage greenhouse gas emissions. The GHG Protocol is working with businesses, governments, and environmental groups around the world to build a new generation of credible and effective programs for tackling climate change. It provides the accounting framework for nearly every GHG standard and program in the world - from the International Standards Organization to The Climate Registry - as well as hundreds of GHG inventories prepared by individual companies. The GHG Protocol also offers developing countries an internationally accepted management tool to help their businesses to compete in the global marketplace and their governments to make informed decisions about climate change.

With respect to scope, the Protocol defines direct and indirect emissions as follows:

> Direct GHG emissions are emissions from sources that are owned or controlled by the reporting entity. Indirect GHG emissions are emissions that are a consequence of the activities of the reporting entity, but occur at sources owned or controlled by another entity. The GHG Protocol further categorizes these direct and indirect emissions into three broad scopes: Scope 1: All direct GHG emissions. Scope 2: Indirect GHG emissions from consumption of purchased electricity, heat or steam. Scope 3: Other indirect emissions, such as the extraction and production of purchased materials and fuels, transport-related activities in vehicles not owned or controlled by the reporting entity, electricity-related activities (e.g. T&D losses) not covered in Scope 2, outsourced activities, waste disposal, etc.

References

Hendrickson, Chris T., et al. (2006) *Environmental Life Cycle Assessment of Goods and Services: An Input-Output Approach*. Resources for the Future Press.

Huang, Y. Anny, et al. (2009) "The role of input-output analysis for the screening of corporate carbon footprints," *Economic Systems Research* 21(3): 217–242.

Lave, Lester, et al. (1995) "Using input-output analysis to estimate economy-wide discharges," *Environmental Science & Technology*, September, 29(9): 420A–426A.

Statistics Canada (n.d.) *The North American Industrial Classification System*.

Sussman, Professor Joseph & Regina Clewlow (n.d.) "EIO/LCA method tutorial & stakeholder & policy analysis, Recitation 9."

US Environmental Protection Agency (EPA) (2023) "Provisional peer-reviewed toxicity values (PPRTVs)."

Part 3
Case Studies

9   Waste to Profits

The Case of Consolidated Mining and Smelting Ltd.

Porter and van der Linde's seminal *Harvard Business Review* article of 1995 made a powerful argument about the false dichotomy between environmental control and profitability. As evidenced by recent corporate annual reports, numerous large corporations are beginning to appreciate this argument and are starting to make significant modifications to their corporate strategies to simultaneously advance the cause of corporate profitability and sustainability. It is interesting to note, however, that there is at least one example of a major international company that arrived at this conclusion over half a century ago and adjusted its strategy accordingly driven by a powerful force of circumstance that threatened its very existence. The essence of this strategic response is the environmental economics dictum "waste is lost profits."

The Consolidated Mining and Smelting Company (renamed Cominco in 1966 and acquired by the Teck Corporation in 2001) was formed in 1906 and four years later bought the Sullivan Mine, the world's largest silver-lead-zinc ore body, located at Kimberley in the southeast corner of the Canadian province of British Columbia, which borders on the American states of Washington, Idaho and Montana. The complex sulfite ore was shipped to the company's newly acquired and redesigned smelter in Trail, BC, some 160 km to the southwest in the Columbia River valley. As the lead and zinc concentrates contained from 17–33% sulfur, their smelting produced significant quantities of sulfur dioxide as a waste product that was off-gassed from a 409-foot-tall stack. By 1930, these releases had reached a high of 651 tons per day of SO_2 (or 325.5 tons as sulfur).

The topography of the Trail region presented some unusual challenges and problems, as

> the Trail Smelter lies in a deep gorge cut out by the Columbia River. The region is decidedly rugged and the Columbia is flanked on either side by mountains sufficiently high to preclude a diffusion of smoke fumes to east or west (Howes and Miller, 1929:6).

The net result of this topographical configuration was a funneling of SO_2 waste gases 11 miles down the Columbia River valley into northeast Washington State (Trail Smelter Arbitration Tribunal, 1935: 8). In 1926, citizens of the town of Northport in Stevens County, Washington complained that the toxic fumes were destroying crops, killing their cattle, corroding their barbed wire fences and galvanized roofs and peeling building paint. The US government complained to Canada and both countries agreed to take the case to arbitration under the International Joint Commission (IJC), marking the first time that an issue of air pollution came before an international tribunal.

DOI: 10.4324/9781003170754-12

The IJC found against the smelter in 1931, recommending that financial compensation of $350,000 be paid and that the company be required to reduce the massive amounts of SO_2 released into the atmosphere. The US government rejected the Commission's recommendations as inadequate, and the issue was not finally settled until March 1941, when a special panel (the Trail Smelter Arbitration Tribunal), established in 1936, issued its "Final Decision." Well before the date of settlement, the Consolidated Mining & Smelting Company had hit upon an answer to the problem and had installed several new industrial processes at their site in Trail. The solution was to extract sulfur from the gaseous emissions and produce sulfuric acid (H_2SO_4) that could then be used to manufacture fertilizer.

On the face of it, being forced to expend large sums of money on the control of waste products, estimated at more than $20 million, posed a significant financial challenge to the smelting company. Fortuitously, the system designed to use sulfur dioxide to produce fertilizer addressed a number of critical issues facing the company at the time: (1) most importantly, the new control procedures essentially removed a threat to the continued operation of the smelter; (2) it provided a more diversified product base that allowed the company to weather falling metal prices in the Great Depression; and (3) it allowed the company to capitalize on an emerging market for synthetic fertilizers, both nationally and internationally.

The production of fertilizer was largely based on the conversion of SO_2 to H_2SO_4 that was used, in turn, to produce fertilizers such as ammonium sulfate, ammonium phosphate and superphosphate. Figure 9.1 presents a simplified schematic representation of part of the company's extensive industrial complex in the immediate post-WWII period. Not shown here are separate components devoted to the production of nitric acid (and subsequently, ammonium nitrate), a chlor-alkali plant and facilities for iron and steel production.

On a volume basis, Cominco's historical metal production has been largely dominated by lead and zinc (Figure 9.2) and this has also been reflected in corporate metal-based revenues (Figure 9.3). Metal prices are notoriously erratic, and the effects of price declines in the Great Depression (Figure 9.4) are evidenced in Cominco's revenues.

The unusual set of circumstances that forced the smelter to undertake extensive and costly pollution control led to a transformation in the strategic direction of the company. Once fertilizer production was underway in 1930, it continued an almost steady increase until the mid-1960s (see Figure 9.5). Figure 9.6 details the extraordinary changes in sulfur emissions and feed that occurred at the Trail smelter over the period from 1900 to 1999. Figure 9.7 summarizes the contribution of fertilizer production to company finances. These contributions peaked in 1944 with fertilizer revenue as a percentage of total revenue at 31.7%, and the comparable percentage for profit at 42.7%.

As Figure 9.6 illustrated, the release of Sulfur Dioxide from Cominco's operations at Trial has declined steadily since the company instituted waste gas recovery in the late 1920s. Despite the enormous reductions in SO_2 emissions, the nature of the ore and smelting technology precluded the total elimination of this pollutant. As a result, Cominco instituted a unique system of air pollutant monitors located downwind of the smelter to provide telemetric feedback on ambient SO_2 levels that vary by season and time of day, depending on temperature, winds, and other atmospheric conditions. Any levels of SO_2 deemed excessive led to a temporary curtailment of smelting operations.

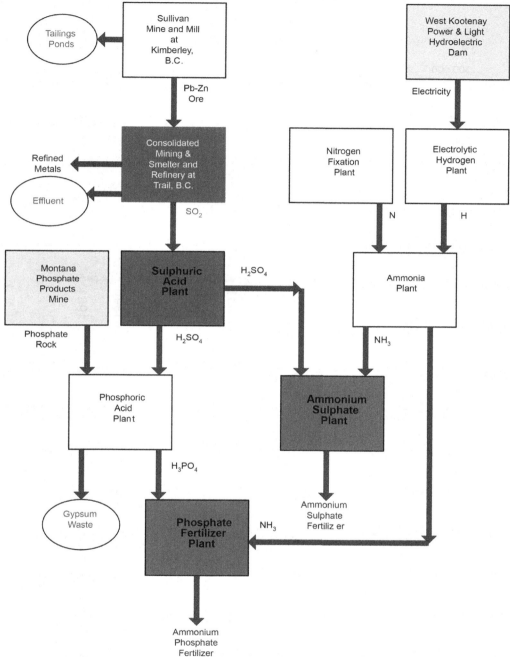

Figure 9.1 Schematic of Cominco's Industrial Complex

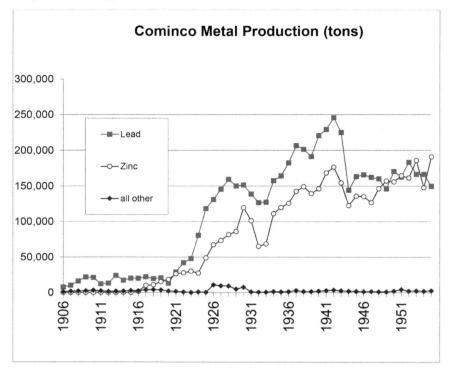

Figure 9.2 Cominco's Pb-Zn Historical Production

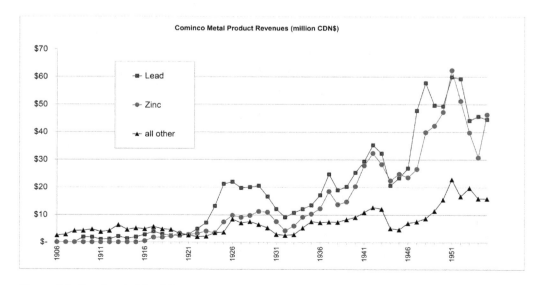

Figure 9.3 Cominco's Metal Revenues

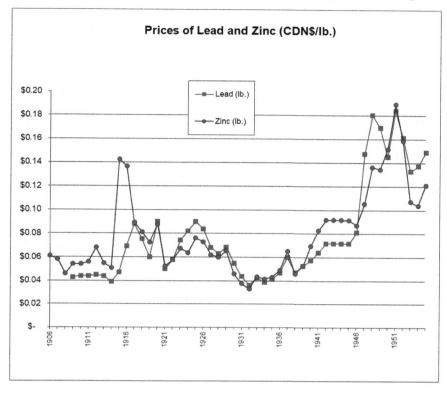

Figure 9.4 Prices of Lead and Zinc

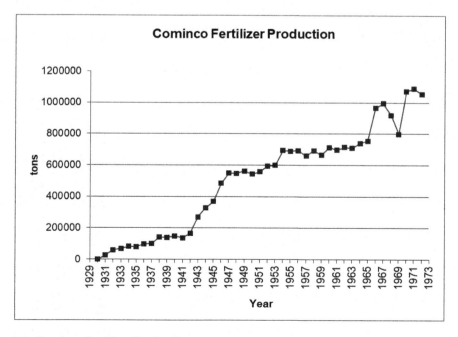

Figure 9.5 Cominco Fertilizer Production

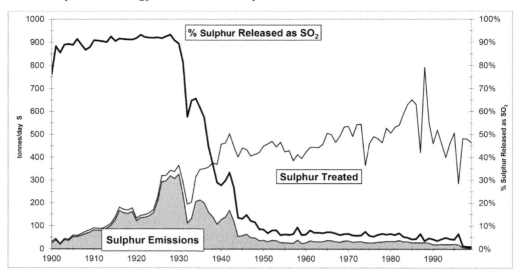

Figure 9.6 Cominco's Sulphur Emissions over Time

Reproduced with permission

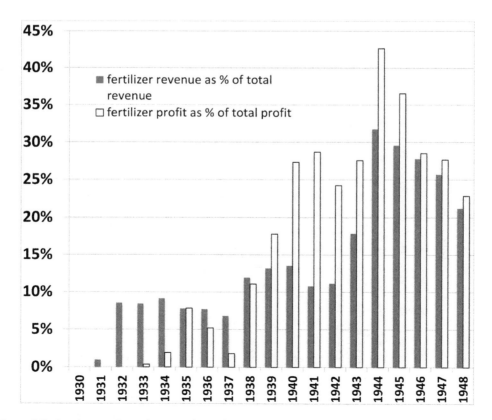

Figure 9.7 Cominco – Contribution of Fertilizer to Corporate Finances

While numerous examples have been produced of recent efforts by companies in a broad range of industrial activities to convert waste to profits, less attention has been paid to Cominco's pioneering experience from seven decades ago. This unusual historical example provides a cogent argument for reconceptualizing the opportunities that may lie hidden in ostensible threats to corporate profitability and survival. It seems clear that even if waste product recovery had not contributed to profit at the company, pollution control would still have been justified, since it essentially eliminated the threat of plant closure and permitted the continued operation of all other corporate activities.

The recognition that waste is lost profit is a concept that is slowly being manifested in corporate strategy among several sectors of the economy. Of particular note in this regard is the petrochemical industry. The conversion of waste to usable intermediate or final product can be conducted at the plant level, but is sometimes facilitated by what are called *industrial parks*, where manufacturing plants either within one industry or across industries situate in close proximity to each other. Under these circumstances, waste streams previously considered cost centers can be sold to each other as essential inputs, thereby yielding a source of revenue, as well as reducing environmental discharges. This concept is described in greater detail in chapter 4 under the rubric of *industrial ecology*.

While Cominco and numerous petrochemical companies have been able to convert major waste streams to profit, it is not realistic to expect that all companies will have such extraordinary opportunities. Key ingredients include, inter alia, technological complementarities and a favorable market environment. Chapter 3 describes the circumstances under that a radical transformation in the market environment can open up a range of opportunities to adopt sustainable business practices among large numbers of small to medium-sized businesses.

Addendum and Caveat

Metal smelters pose complex challenges for corporate owners and regulatory agencies because of numerous environmental pollutants released into multiple media (e.g., air, land, and water, depending on the complexity of the ore and the technology used). For example, Tables 9.1 and 9.2 summarize the latest data on air and water discharges from the Trail smelter (Canada NPRI 2021).

Table 9.1 Latest Data on Air Discharges from Trail Smelter

		Air
Ammonia (total)	tonnes	101.75
Anthracene	kg	0.001
Antimony (and its compounds)	tonnes	0.138
Arsenic (and its compounds)	kg	253.25
Asbestos (friable form only)	tonnes	-
Cadmium (and its compounds)	kg	203.33
Carbon monoxide	tonnes	81.03
Chlorine	tonnes	-
Chromium (and its compounds)	tonnes	1.36
Cobalt (and its compounds)	kg	0.4232
Copper (and its compounds)	tonnes	0.0676

(*Continued*)

Table 9.1 (Continued)

		Air
Dioxins and furans - total	g TEQ	0
Hexachlorobenzene	grams	0
Lead (and its compounds)	kg	669.25
Manganese (and its compounds)	tonnes	0.19
Mercury (and its compounds)	kg	31.0689
Methanol	tonnes	9.48
n-Hexane	tonnes	1.113
Naphthalene	tonnes	6.3
Nitrate ion in solution at pH >= 6.0	tonnes	-
Nitrogen oxides (expressed as nitrogen dioxide)	tonnes	498.17
Phenanthrene	kg	329.68
PM10 - Particulate Matter <= 10 Micrometers	tonnes	72.61
PM2.5 - Particulate Matter <= 2.5 Micrometers	tonnes	48.94
Selenium (and its compounds)	kg	0.003
Silver (and its compounds)	tonnes	0.0155
Sulphur dioxide	tonnes	3,077.93
Sulphuric acid	tonnes	22
Thallium (and its compounds)	kg	84.29
Total particulate matter	tonnes	78.43
Volatile Organic Compounds (VOCs)	tonnes	17.642
Zinc (and its compounds)	tonnes	87.8

Source: NPRI 2021

Table 9.2 Latest Data on Water Discharges from Trail Smelter

Substance releases 2021	Units	Water
Ammonia (total)	tonnes	50.03
Antimony (and its compounds)	tonnes	1.836
Arsenic (and its compounds)	kg	346.9
Cadmium (and its compounds)	kg	118.8
Copper (and its compounds)	tonnes	0.233
Lead (and its compounds)	kg	639.4
Manganese (and its compounds)	tonnes	2.288
Mercury (and its compounds)	kg	3.58
Nitrate ion in solution at pH >= 6.0	tonnes	6.33
Selenium (and its compounds)	kg	1815
Thallium (and its compounds)	kg	549.4
Zinc (and its compounds)	tonnes	4.53

Source: NPRI 2021

One of the archetypal examples of smelter-related environmental despoliation was the former Inco and Falconbridge nickel-copper smelters in Sudbury, Ontario. The sulphur dioxide emission denuded the local landscape to such an extent that NASA used this area as a training ground for its astronauts practicing in a mock moon-like landscape. The smelter has since instituted elaborate controls on air emissions and undertaken a massive landscape restoration effort notable for its success (Llana 2020).

This type of problem, accompanied by more stringent regulation, as well as increased metal recycling and labor costs, is the principal reason why most North American smelters have been closed and or relocated to developing nations (Doe Run Company 2013; Western Washington University 2021). The Doe-Run smelter in Missouri was the last primary lead smelter in the US to close in 2013, leaving only Teck's Trail operations and Penoles' Torreon in northern Mexico as the last two primary lead smelters in North America.

The Problem of Lead in Soil

Cominco's smelter in Trail, BC treated a Lead-Zinc ore with a high sulphur content and, over the years, air emissions of lead built up in Trail and adjacent areas. Lead has been produced for the past 5500 years (Settle and Patterson 1980; Nriagu 1996; Hong et al. 1994; Fischetti & Bremer 2020) and was widely used in Roman times for cooking utensils, water pipes, and as a sweetener addition to wines in the form of "sugar of lead." In modern times, lead has been widely used in lead-acid batteries, paints, solder, alloys, cosmetics, ammunition, roofing, and as a gasoline octane enhancer in the form of tetraethyl lead. Some of these uses have been curtailed or discontinued because of the diverse and serious impacts on human health. Included among these effects are hypertension, coronary heart disease, atherothrombotic brain infarctions, initial cardiovascular accident, reduced IQ, and subsequent criminal behaviour, as well as suspected cancer (Needleman et al. 1979; Baghurst et al. 1992; US EPA 1997; Canfield et al. 2003; IARC 2006; Nevin 2007; Reyes 2007; Flora et al. 2012; Lee et al. 2022). Since its introduction in 1923 as a gasoline additive, tetraethyl lead was the largest contributor to airborne lead pollution over the following decades (NAS 1980; US EPA 2000; Dignam et al. 2019). In 1973, the US government began a phase out of leaded gasoline under the terms of the new Clean Air Act and it was finally abolished in 1996 for on-road vehicles. As tetraethyl lead was phased out, there was a corresponding decrease in average air lead concentrations in the United States [r=0.92] (Dignam et al. 2019). Canada had banned its use in 1990.

In its first study of the benefits and costs of the Clean Air Act over the period 1970–1990, the USEPA (1997, Table ES-4) estimated that the present value of benefits (discounted at 5%) of the Clean Air Act, due to reductions in mortality, loss of IQ, hypertension, and hospital admissions attributed to lead could exceed $4 trillion in 1990 dollars. The adverse effects of lead were not included in a follow-up study covering the period of 1990 to 2010 (USEPA 1999, fn. 2:5) "since airborne emissions of lead were virtually eliminated by pre-1990 Clean Air Act programs."

An epidemiological study conducted in Trail in the late 1970s (Neri et al. 1978) found blood lead levels in younger children as high as 22 ug/dl: "While there is no safe lead threshold, blood lead levels as low as 1–2 ug/dl are associated with adverse health outcomes particularly in children" (BC Interior Health 2021). From the late 1970s, Cominco undertook a series of measure in order the reduce lead emissions. It was not until a major epidemiological study was undertaken in Trail in 1989, however, that a more intensive effort was undertaken to address this serious problem. The average blood lead level was 13.8 micrograms per decilitre with a range of 4–30. The highest readings were in proximity to the smelter and local gasoline stations. Significantly elevated levels were determined to be derived principally from exposure to lead levels in soil and secondarily from household dust (Hertzman et al. 1990, 1991; Kelly et al. 1994).

A multiparticipant taskforce was established in the mid 1990s to continue monitoring of blood lead levels on an annual basis and explore alternative methods of lowering this burden on the local population (Hilts 1996). Figure 9.8 shows annual output of lead from the Trail smelter over the period 1956 to 2021 (a continuation of earlier data in Figure 9.2). Figure 9.9 shows the levels of lead emissions from the smelter over the period 1993–2021. Figure 9.10 presents ambient levels of lead from 1992–2021. Figure 9.11 presents geometric averages of children's blood lead levels in Trail and its environs from a high of 13.6 ug/dl in 1991 to 2.5 ug/dl in 2021 (BC Interior Health 2021). As expected, these results are congruent with the causal chain of reduced emissions to ambient levels to blood lead levels. Table 9.3 presents the correlation matrix among the four variables. The change in readings from 1991 to 2021 represents a

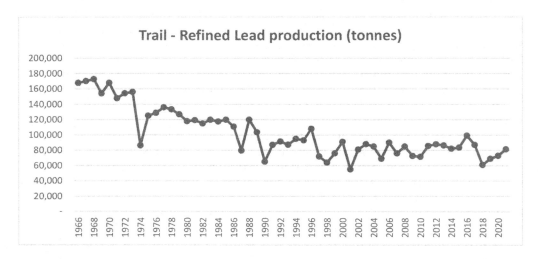

Figure 9.8 Cominco's Annual Pb Output from Trail Smelter

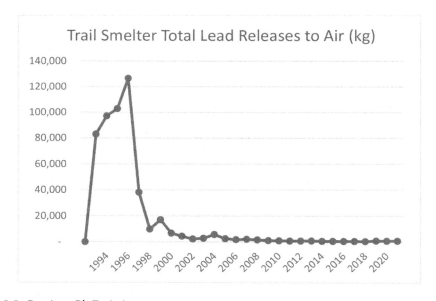

Figure 9.9 Cominco Pb Emissions

Source: NPRI

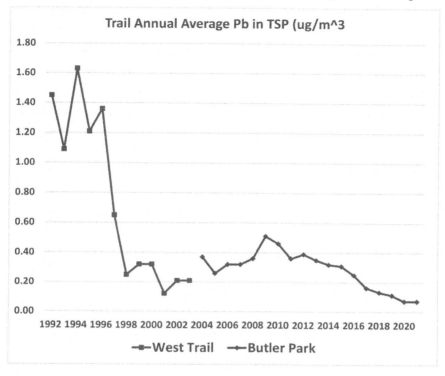

Figure 9.10 Ambient Pb Levels in Trail
Source: BC Interior Health 2021

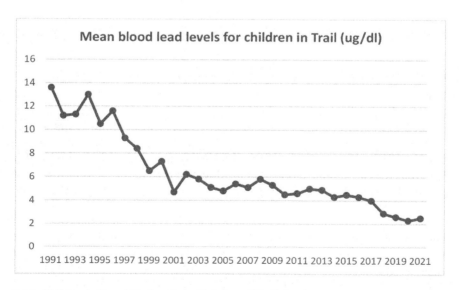

Figure 9.11 Children's Blood Pb Levels in Vicinity of Trail Smelter
Source: BC Interior Health 2021

Table 9.3 Correlation Matrix of Pb Pollution in Trail, BC

	Production	Emissions	Ambient levels	Blood levels
Production	1			
Emissions	0.49246246	1		
Ambient levels	0.53361081	0.93622401	1	
Blood levels	0.43730059	0.87593143	0.895967317	1

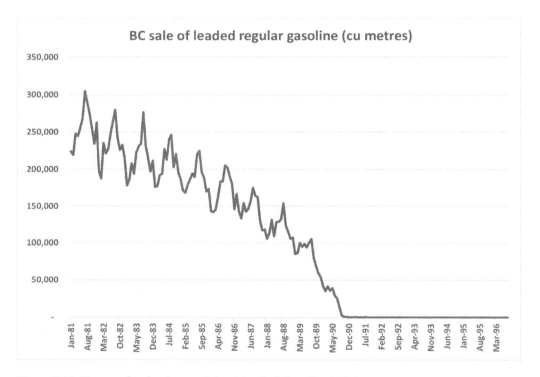

Figure 9.12 Temporal reduction on Sale of Leaded Gasoline in BC

Source: Statistics Canada

significant reduction although, clearly, more work needs to be done as the full range of blood lead levels in Trail reached as high as 13.1 ug/dl in 2021. As context, the geometric mean of blood lead levels in Canadian children ages 3–5 over the period 2018–2019 was 0.5 ug/dl (Health Canada 2021). The problem of lead clean-up is particularly challenging as lead is generally not biodegradable and can remain in the environment for an extended period.

While the dramatic reduction in blood lead levels can be attributed to the change in smelter emissions, the period from 1970 to 1990 was also marked by the phase out of leaded gasoline in Canada. Figure 9.12 shows the temporal reduction in the sale of regular grade leaded gasoline in BC from 1981–1990. During this time, sampling from one of the principal monitoring sites in Trail decreased from 1.43 ug/m3 to 0.86 ug/m3. While the reduction in leaded gasoline use can be expected to have a salutary impact on blood lead levels in Trail, it is unlikely that this effect would be significant as the estimated lead emissions from gasoline consumption represented only a tiny fraction of the smelter-produced airborne lead releases (Shelton et al. 1982) provides estimates of the lead content of gasoline in the United States over this period.

Teck, the current owner of the smelter summarized the history of efforts at remediation (personal communication, November 2022):

> Since the late 1970's, over $1.7 billion has been invested in a modernization program to improve operational and environmental performance at Teck Trail Operations. We realized our largest improvements in the 1990s through the introduction of the KIVCET smelter [also known as the Oxygen Flash Cyclone Electro Thermal Process]. Environmental improvements over the past 25 years have reduced emissions by over 95%. Major investments include:
>
> **Stack Emissions Management**: Since the replacement of Lead Smelter blast furnaces with the KIVCET lead furnace in 1997 and subsequent operations improvement, there has been a 99.5% reduction in stack lead emissions, and a 75% reduction in stack sulphur dioxide (SO_2) emissions. KIVCET has also had a significant carbon emissions benefit.
>
> **Fugitive Dust Management**: In recent years, major investments and operational improvements have been made to reduce fugitive dust including:
>
> construction of the $35 million Smelter Recycle Building, close to the size of two Canadian football fields, in 2016 to enclose mixing and storage of process feed materials; installation of a $1.9 million, ten-metre high wind fence reducing dusting where feed materials are mixed; installation of wheel washes and truck washes onsite help reduce tracking of materials onto roads; onsite street cleaning, via street sweepers and water trucks, provide a year-round program of roadway sweeping and flushing; and, identification and reduction of fugitive dust sources from work activities inside operating plants. In addition, two new acid plants [2014 and 2019] have been constructed, resulting in improved operational reliability and environmental performance.

As a recent annual report from the local health authority (BC Interior Health 2021) states: "while these levels have generally decreased steadily since the institution of remedial measures at the smelter and in local homes and the environment, . . . recent studies have suggested that intellectual impairment can occur at levels as low as 1 ug/dl (see for example Canfield et al. 2003). In sum, while challenges remain, the response to this problem is an outstanding example of the joint recognition and response of multiple key actors, including local government, civil society and the smelter company.

The problem of contaminated waste streams

Unfortunately, the challenges facing the smelter have not been restricted to the aforementioned cases of airborne sulphur dioxide and soil-contaminated by lead.

As illustrated in Tables 9.1 and 9.2 above, there are numerous potentially toxic waste emissions associated with the normal operation of a lead-zinc smelter.

In 2011, a lawsuit was filed against Teck by members of the Confederated Tribes of the Colville Reservation in Washington State, under CERCLA (the US Comprehensive Environmental Response, Compensation and Liability Act). The suit claimed that Teck and its predecessor, Cominco, over the course of its history had discharged millions of tons of slag containing toxic metals into the Columbia River that subsequently flowed into Washington State (Seattle PI March 16, 2011; US Court of Appeals for the Ninth Circuit No. 08–35951, D.C. No. 2:04-cv-00256-LRS).

Nevertheless, in the three decades since the Canadian government started collecting pollutant release data from industrial operations under its National Pollutant Release Inventory system (NPRI), except for selenium, the smelter has made significant progress in reducing discharges of most of these pollutants into the Columbia River (see Table 9.4).

Parenthetically, it should be noted that selenium discharges have been a continuing source of contention between the American Northwest states of Montana and Idaho and a major coal mining operation owned by Teck in Southeast BC. This issue remains unresolved and is the subject of litigation. In 2021, Teck was fined $50 million under the Canadian Fisheries Act for the unlawful release of selenium into the Fording River that ultimately ends up in the US (*New York Times* July 11, 2023). Teck Resources has stated that selenium clean-up costs could equal $1.9 billion. However, a recent consulting report suggested that this amount could amount to $6.4 billion (CBC March 19, 2024).

One of the major initiatives undertaken by the smelter at Trail, BC was the elimination of slag discharges in 1995. To quote a consulting report commissioned by Cominco (G3 Consulting Ltd. 2001):

> Prior to this, up to 145,000 tonnes of slag had been discharged annually, which moved downstream to settle out in slower flowing, sandy areas. The environmental effects of slag discharge to the river included both chemical and physical components. Chemical effects included increased loads of heavy metals and potential bioaccumulation and toxicity problems in river organisms. Physical effects included scouring of plant and animal life from river substrates, damage to gills and soft tissues of aquatic insects and fish, and smothering of habitat and food sources.

The report did note that "since mid-1995, a slag product has been provided to the concrete industry as part of the reduction process." This process continues to this day, providing another instructive example of the potential conversion of waste into

Table 9.4 Trail Smelter Wastewater Discharges 1993 vs. 2021

	2021 value vs. original NPRI value	*time range*
Ammonia (total)	9%	1994–2021
Antimony (and its compounds)	26%	1993–2021
Arsenic (and its compounds)	2%	1993–2021
Cadmium (and its compounds)	2%	1993–2021
Copper (and its compounds)	0.04%	1993–2021
Lead (and its compounds)	0.4%	1993–2021
Manganese (and its compounds)	46%	1993–2021
Mercury (and its compounds)	1%	1993–2021
Nitrate ion in solution at pH >= 6.0	6%	2000–2021
Selenium (and its compounds)	181%	2009–2021
Thallium (and its compounds)	89%	2014–2021
Zinc (and its compounds)	0.2%	1995–2021

Source: NPRI

revenue, although on a smaller scale than the case of sulphur dioxide capture described earlier in this chapter.

In its submission to the court, Teck admitted that it had in fact discharged the material as claimed in the lawsuit but has argued that it is exempt from US law since the source of this pollution is located in a foreign country and that the statute of limitations had expired (*Global Mining* September 28–29, 2022). On September 22, 2022 an American court rejected Teck's bid to block the CRECLA lawsuit (US EPA 2022) and, as of the writing of this chapter, the issue remains outstanding.

In sum, it should be clear from these results that success in addressing one pollutant in one medium is clearly insufficient in gauging the overall environmental impact of a major industrial plant. Several other case studies are presented in this book of successful utilization of waste products for profitability in two different industries such as dairy and carpet manufacturing. However, despite the fact that not all waste streams can be turned to profit, the principal advantage is frequent reduction of corporate exposure to financial liability from regulatory action by government, law suits by civil actors and, and negative responses from multiple institutions in the financial sector including banks, insurance companies and shareholders.

References

Agent for the Government of Canada (1936) "Statement of facts submitted by the agent for the government of Canada, May 3, 1936," in *Trail Smelter Question*, Government of Canada, King's Printer, Ottawa.

Anon (1948) "Producing of chemical fertilizers by The Consolidated Mining and Smelting Company of Canada Limited."

Baghurst, Peter A., et al. (1992) "Environmental exposure to lead and children's intelligence at the age of seven years – The Port Pirie cohort study," *New England Journal of Medicine* (October 29).

BC Interior Health (2021) "Blood lead levels in Trail Fall 2021," November.

BC Ministry of Environment, Lands and Parks and Environment Canada (1993) *State of the Environment Report for British Columbia*.

Canada National Pollutant Release Inventory (NPRI) (2021).

Canfield, Richard L., et al. (2003) "Intellectual impairment of children with blood lead concentration below 10ug per deciliter," *New England Journal of Medicine*, April 17: 1517–1526.

CBC (2024) "$6.4B needed to clean toxic selenium from bc coal mines: report," March 19.

Dignam, Timothy, et al. (2019) "Control of lead sources in the United States, 1970–2017; Public health progress and current challenges to eliminating lead exposure," *Journal of Public Health Management and Practice*, May 16 (Supplement 1):1–16.

Doe Run Company (2013) "The doe run company provides update on closure of last primary lead smelter in us," https://doerun.com/media/news/the-doe-run-company-provides-update-on-clo sure-of-last-primary-lead-smelter-in-us/

Fischetti, Mark & Nadieh Bremer (2020) "Heavy metal history: Abrupt changes in lead pollution highlight dramatic world events," *Scientific American*, October: 84.

Flora, Gagan, et al. (2012) "Toxicology of lead; A review with recent updates," *Interdisciplinary Toxicology*, June 5(2): 47–58.

G3 Consulting Ltd. (2001) "Cominco Ltd. trail operations: Environmental performance review of the new KIVCET lead smelter and elimination of slag discharge," Assessment of Columbia River Receiving Waters, June.

Global Mining (2012) "Teck confesses to a century of US river pollution," September 11.

Health Canada (2021) *Sixth Report on Human Biomonitoring of Environmental Chemicals in Canada*, December.

Hertzman, Clyde, et al. (1991) "Childhood lead exposure in trail revisited," *Canadian Journal of Public Health*, 82 (November/December): 395–391.

Hertzman, Clyde, et al. (1990) *Trail Lead Study Report: Submitted to BC Ministries of Health and Environment*. University of British Columbia, Centre for Health Sciences and Policy Research, June 7.

Hilts, Steven R. (1996) "A co-operative approach to risk management in an active lead/zinc smelter community," *Environmental Geochemistry and Health*, 18: 17–24.

Hong, Sungmin, et al. (1994) "Greenland ice evidence of hemispheric lead pollution two millennia ago by Greek and Roman civilizations," *Science*, September 23.

Howes, Dean E.A. and Dean F. G. Miller (1929) "Trail smelter question, appendix a1, the deans' report: Final report to the international joint commission," King's Printer, Ottawa.

International Agency for Research on Cancer (2006) *IARC Monographs on the Evaluation of Carcinogenic Risk to Humans, Volume 87: Inorganic and Organic lead compounds*, World Health Organization.

International Joint Commission (IJC) (1931) "Report of the international joint commission, signed at Toronto, 28th February, 1931," Appendix A3, *Trail Smelter Question*, Government of Canada, King's Printer, Ottawa, 1936.

Kelly, Shona J., et al. (1994) "Trace element analysis of soils collected near a lead/zinc smelter, environmental policy as social policy?: The impact of childhood lead exposure on crime," *Canadian Journal of Public Health*, 85(3): 156–157.

Lee, Haena, et al. (2022) "Childhood lead exposure is associated with lower cognitive functioning at older ages," *Science Advances*, November 9.

Llana, Sara Miller (2020) "The Sudbury model: how one of the world's major polluters went green," *Christian Science Monitor*, September 24.

Murray, Keith A. (1972) "The Trail Smelter case: international air pollution in the Columbia Valley," *BC Studies*, 15(Autumn): 68–85.

National Academy of Sciences (1980) *Lead in the Human Environment*. A Report prepared by the Committee on lead in the human environment, Environmental Studies Board, Commission on Natural Resources, National Research Council.

Needleman, Herbert L., et al. (1979) "Deficits in psychologic and classroom performance of children with elevated dentine lead levels," *New England Journal of Medicine*, March 29.

Neri, L.C., et al. (1978) "Blood lead levels in children in two British Columbia communities," in Delbert D. Hemphill (Ed.) *Trace Substances in Environmental Health. Proceedings of University of Missouri's 12th Annual Conference on Trace Substances in Environmental Health*: 403–408.

Nevin, Rick (2007) "Understanding international crime trends: the legacy of preschool lead exposure," *Environmental Research*, 104: 315–336.

New York Times (2023) "Tracing Mining's Threat to US Waters," July 11.

Nriagu, Jerome O. (1996) "A history of global metal pollution," *Science*, April 12.

Porter, Michael and Claas van der Linde (1995) "Green and competitive: Ending the stalemate," *Harvard Business Review*, 73(5): 120–134.

Read, John E. (1963) "The Trail Smelter dispute," in Charles B. Bourne (Ed.) *The Canadian Yearbook of International Law*, 1: 213–229.

Reyes, Jessica Wolpaw (2007) "Environmental Policy as social policy? The impact of childhood lead exposure on crime," *Contributions in Economic Analysis and Policy*, 7(1).

RWD (1938) "Memorandum to Mr. S.G. Blaylock, Vice-President & General Manager," Consolidated Mining and Smelting Company, March 14, V.F. No. 661.12.

Seattle Post Intelligencer (2011) "Teck Cominco seeks dismissal of suit over pollution in Lake Roosevelt," March 16.

Settle, Dorothy M. and Clair C. Patterson (1980) "Lead in albacore: Guide to lead pollution in Americans," *Science*, March 14.

Shelton, Ella Mae at al. (1982) *Trends in Motor Gasolines: 1942–1981*. United States Department of Energy, DOE/BETC/RI-82/4, June.

Trail Smelter Arbitration Tribunal (1941) "Decision reported on March 11, 1941 to the Government of the United States of America and to the Government of the Dominion of Canada by the Trail Smelter Arbitration Tribunal, under the convention signed April 15, 1935."

US Court of Appeals for the Ninth Circuit No. 08–35951, D.C. No. 2:04-cv-00256-LRS. Joseph A. Pakootas, an individual and enrolled member of the Confederated Tribes of the Colville Reservation and Donald R. Michel, an individual and enrolled member of the Confederated

Tribes of the Coville Reservation, Plaintiffs-Appellants, No. 08–35951; STATE OF WASHINGTON, Petitioner-Intervenor-Appellant, D.C. No.2:04-cv-00256-LRS And CONFEDERATED TRIBES OF THE COLVILLE RESERVATION, Plaintiff, v. TECK COMINCO METALS, LTD., a Canadian corporation, Defendant-Appellee.

US EPA (1997) *The Benefits and Costs of the Clean Air Act 1970–1990.*

US EPA (1999) *The Benefits and Costs of the Clean Air Act 1990–2010.*

US EPA (2000) *National Pollutant emission trends 1900–1998.*

US EPA (2022) "Teck loses latest bid to block CERCLA Suit over cross-border pollution," InsideEPA.com, September 22.

Western Washington University (2021) "ASARCO smelter: Tacoma's industrial legacy," Washington State Department of Ecology, May 20.

10 Designing the Corporation of the 21st Century

Case Study of Interface Inc.

The archetypal example of the attempted application of the circular model is Interface Inc. the world's largest producer of modular carpets for the commercial sector. The critical individual in Interface was the late Ray Anderson who founded the company in 1973. Anderson has written several books and articles (Anderson 1999, 2007, 2009) explaining his radical conversion to the cause of sustainability when he realized that he and his company were a "plunderer of the earth." They "were part of the endemic process that is going on at a frightening, accelerating rate worldwide to rob our children and all their descendants of their futures" (Anderson 2007: 91). Anderson described this revelation as tantamount to a "spear through the heart" and he undertook to convert his company into the world's most sustainable enterprise. Anderson identified seven fronts on which serious change must be achieved for sustainability: zero waste; benign emissions; renewable energy; closed loop recycling; resource efficient transportation; a "sensitivity hookup," which includes service to the community and closer relations with employees, suppliers and customers; and a redesign of commerce itself that entails:

> the acceptance of entirely new notions of economics, especially prices that reflect full costs. To us, it means shifting emphasis from simply selling products to providing services; thus, our commitment to downstream distribution, installation, maintenance and recycling. These are all aimed at forming cradle-to-cradle relationships with customers and suppliers, relationships based on delivering, via the Evergreen Service Agreement™, the services our products provide, in lieu of the products themselves" (2007, pp. 104–105).

In sum, Anderson's conceptualization of the Prototypical company of the twenty-first century is that it is "strongly service-oriented, resource-efficient, wasting nothing, solar-driven, cyclical (no longer take–make–waste linear), and strongly connected to our constituencies – our communities (building social equity), our customers, and our suppliers – and to one other (p. 105)." Figures 10.1 and 10.2 illustrate Anderson's conception of the typical company of the twentieth century and his view how modern corporations should be redesigned for sustainability. Figure 10.3 is the traditional model of industrial production, typically referred to as "once through" or "linear" that relies on virgin raw materials and generates waste in both production and consumption. Figure 10.4 portrays Interface's modular carpet take-back system and its improvements

DOI: 10.4324/9781003170754-13

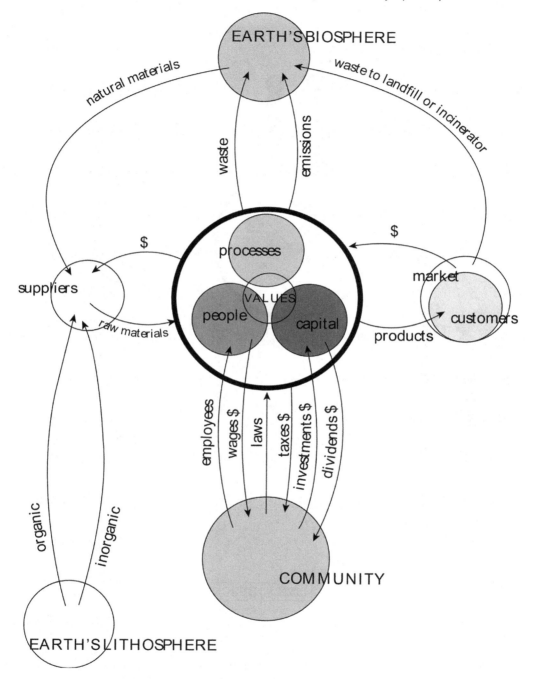

Figure 10.1 Anderson's Conception of the Typical 20th Century Company

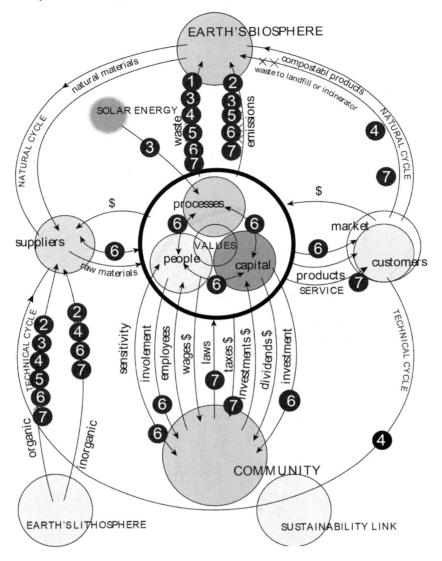

LINK #	DESCRIPTION
1	Zero waste
2	Benign Emissions
3	Renewable energy
4	Closing the loop
5	Resource-efficient transportation
6	Sensitivity hookup - service to community, closer relations among stakeholders
7	Redesign of commerce itself

Figure 10.2 Anderson's Model of Corporate Sustainability

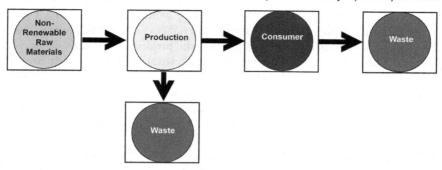

Figure 10.3 Traditional Model of Industrial Production

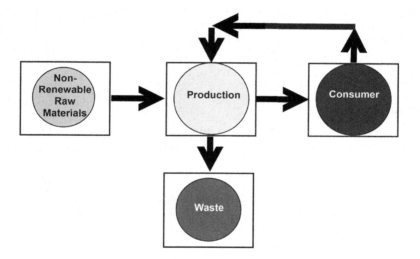

Figure 10.4 Schematic of Interface's Modular Carpet Production System

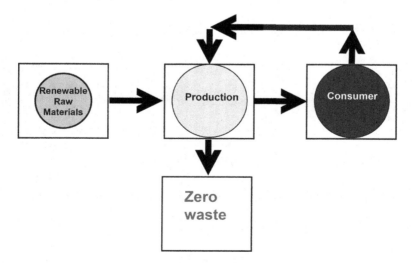

Figure 10.5 Interface's Sustainability Goals

in energy efficiency, material throughput and waste generation. Figure 10.5 represents the goal that Interface is pursuing: a modern industrial corporation relying exclusively on renewable inputs (both material and energy) and the production of zero waste.

Two central parts to operationalizing Interface's sustainability strategy are: first the adoption of a leasing system (called an *Evergreen Lease*) where the carpet is not owned by the customer but by Interface instead; and, second, the use of carpet tiles. When a carpet starts to show signs of fading, wear or damage, individual tiles are removed – rather than the entire carpet – and returned to Interface for recycling into new carpet. This is a type of *reverse logistics* is defined by Sarkis (2010, p. 19) as a system "for the recovery of products or packaging from the consumer, or supply chain member." This process is formalized in Interface's Clause 6 of its Evergreen Lease that reads (Anderson and White 2009, p. 288):

> During the lease term [7 years], nothing contained herein shall give to Customer any right, title or interest in or to the Carpet except as a lessee. At all times, legal title to the Carpet shall remain with Interface, and the Carpet shall not be considered a fixture for any purpose regardless of the degree of its installation in or affixation to real property [see Appendix One for the company's recent financial data].

Interface's Achievements

On their corporate website (Interface.com), Interface presents an annual update of their progress towards their goal of zero total ecological impact. The company was ranked

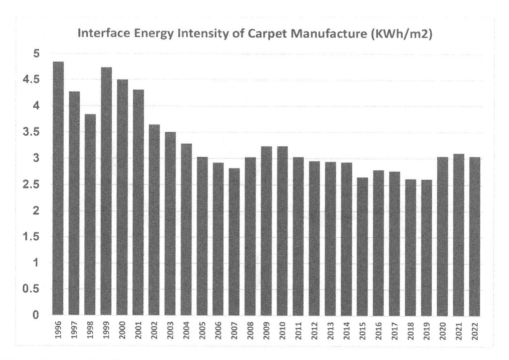

Figure 10.6 Interface Total Energy Use Per Unit Production 1996–2022

Reproduced with permission

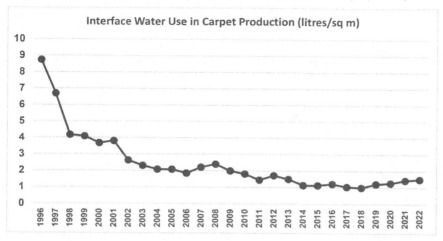

Figure 10.7 Interface Water Use 1996–2022

Source: Interface 2022 Impact Report

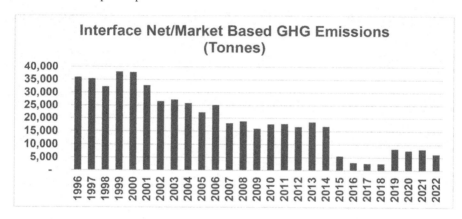

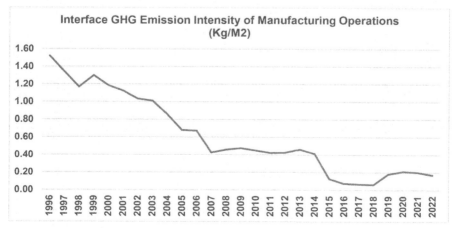

Figure 10.8 Interface Total GHG Emissions and GHG Per Sq M of Product 2008–2022

Source: Interface 2022 Impact Report

sixth (after Patagonia, Unilever, IKEA, Natura & Co., and Microsoft) in the Globescan 2023 Sustainability Survey. Figures 10.6–10.10 and Table 10.1 summarize recent trends in Interface's efforts to achieve sustainability. Other sustainability achievements by Interface are presented in Appendix Two. The recent uptick in several of these metrics

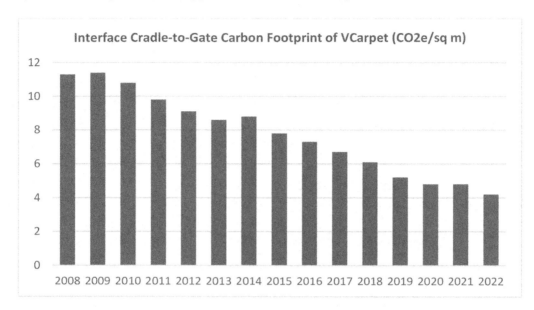

Figure 10.9 Interface Cradle-to-Gate Footprint of Carpet 2008–2022
Source: Interface 2022 Impact Report

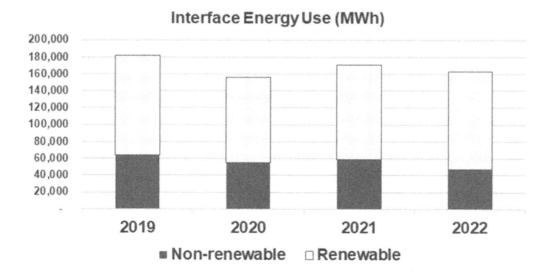

Figure 10.10 Interface Energy Uses 2022
Source: Interface 2022 Impact Report

appears to be an anomaly, which can be ascribed to two factors: (1) efficiency of the carpet manufacturing process has not yet recovered from COVID-related disruptions to staffing, process changes, supply chain changes, and lower volume; and (2) Interface had to reset some baselines for 2018–2019 data since they acquired nora rubber flooring in Germany (that changes the operational metrics baseline) and started outsourcing some other resilient (hard surface) flooring from South Korea.

It is particularly noteworthy that Interface has gone to great lengths to identify and quantify its Scope 3 GHG emissions. This is a goal which still has eluded most companies so far because of its complexity. Not surprisingly l, Scope 3 emissions dwarf those for Scopes 1 and 2 (see Table 10.2].

Table 10.1 Interface Life Cycle Footprint of Products (avg. kg CO2 per sqm)

	Raw Materials	Manufacturing	Delivery, Installation & Use	End of Life	Total
Carpet Tile	5.8	0.3	3.3	0.7	10.1
LVT	10.4	1.6	4.4	0.5	16.9

Interface (2021)

Table 10.2 Interface 2021 Global GHG emissions (MT CO2e)

SCOPE 1		PERCENTAGE
Direct emissions	5,923	1.2%
SCOPE 2		
Indirect emissions	8,178	1.7%
SCOPE 3		
Purchased goods & services	233,000	47.9%
Capital goods	19,900	4.1%
Fuel & energy-related activities	10,400	2.1%
Waste generated in operations	4,880	1.0%
Upstream transportation & distribution	6,650	1.4%
Business travel	470	0.1%
Employee commuting	6,290	1.3%
Upstream leased assets (included in scopes 1 & 2 above)		
Downstream transportation & distribution	17,210	3.5%
Processing of sold products	4,300	0.9%
Use of sold products	147,300	30.3%
End of life treatment of sold products	22,360	4.6%
TOTAL	486,861	100.0%

Source: Interface 2021 Environmental, Social, and Governance (ESG) Report

Anderson's Reconceptualization of the Modern Corporation

Re-engineering a major industrial corporation and reconceptualizing its strategic mission is a daunting undertaking, but Ray Anderson adopted a radical approach to business and economics. The standard economic model subdivides the products of a modern industrial economy into two categories: goods and services. Anderson was among the first to realize that this categorization represents a false dichotomy. With the exception of purchases partially motivated by concerns over appearance and personal prestige, such as some automobiles, consumers do not buy goods for their physical presence; they buy them for the services they provide. Does one buy a refrigerator, for example, because one likes a large colored metal box in one's kitchen? The answer is no. This good is bought because of the service it provides in the form of refrigeration of food.

By adopting this insightful new and unified view of goods and services, it is possible to focus on the nature of the service provided rather than the physical good itself. Instead of selling carpet per se, Interface made the conceptual jump to selling services. To Interface, the key carpet services that the consumers were buying included color, design, texture, warmth, acoustics, comfort under foot, cleanliness, and improved indoor air quality. The customer benefits in several ways: a smaller amount of carpet is replaced, there is no requirement for waste disposal by the customer, and the carpet can be expensed rather than capitalized. By reclaiming and recycling carpet tiles, Interface can lower its material costs, reduce its environmental impact, and lock customers into a longer-term leasing relationship with the vendor rather than a one-off sale.

Anderson envisaged the emergence of the truly sustainable corporation, a modern industrial corporation relying exclusively on renewable inputs (both material and energy) and the production of zero waste.

The Competitive Environment

A crucial question is whether a company such as Interface that adopts a radically different business model can survive and prosper in a highly competitive marketplace. The answer depends on the nature and direction of the competitive environment. If the market is moving toward more sustainable products and Interface has a leadership role in this area, then the assessment of the company's prospects is more positive. This is congruent with Porter and van der Linde's thesis that a sustainability strategy is an important route to building a strong competitive advantage.

Two of the most significant competitors to Interface are Mohawk Industries and Shaw Industries – the former a public company, the latter a private entity. The critical question is whether either of these firms has an equally strong sustainability strategy which can threaten Interface's potential competitive advantage.

Mohawk Industries

Mohawk Industries is the world's largest flooring company with net sales of $11.737 billion in 2022 compared with Interface's $1.298 billion. Mohawk's first sustainability report in 2009 (Mohawk 2009) laid out the company's goals in four key areas: reductions in energy use, water use, greenhouse gas emissions, and waste to landfill. The stated intention was to improve upon the performance in each area by 25% by 2020. This was in marked contrast to Interface's "Mission Zero," which aimed for a zero environmental impact by 2020. In their report for 2016, Mohawk listed eight metrics used to measure their progress toward sustainability: pounds of recycled waste, water consumption reduction, GHG intensity reduction, energy intensity reduction, water intensity reduction, number of products containing recyclable material, number of plastic bottles recycled annually, and pounds of tires recycled into doormats. The interpretation of these data was somewhat problematic since, in some cases, there was no denominator or baseline with which to measure the degree of progress. Four graphs, however, did provide historical data from 2010 for comparative purposes: energy intensity, GHG intensity, water intensity, and waste to landfill intensity.

Its most recent environmental report of 2023 Mohawk provided updated data with baseline 2010 comparative purposes for two major variables: total Scope 1 & 2 GHG emissions and total waste to landfill. These and other reported variables with numerical data are listed in Table 10.3.

Table 10.3 Mohawk Environmental Indicators

Variable	Units	value in 2010	value in 2019	value in 2021	value in 2022	goal 2025
Total scope 1 & 2 GHG emissions	tonnes CO2/ Rev CC	0.280			0.374	0.2800
Direct GHG emissions	metric tonnes CO2e		1,785,392	1,826,592		
Idirect GHG emissions	metric tonnes CO2e		1,140,548	924,610		
Energy consumption	MWh		12,963,066	12,468,860		
renewable energy	percentage				11%	
Other renewable sources (Thermal reclaim, CHP generation, solar, wind, etc.)	MWh		335,302	491,015		
Total waste recycled/ reused	metric tonnes		1,593,281	1,337,842		
Total waste disposal	metric tonnes		105,730	244,268		
Total waste to landfill	Tons/Rev CC	0.0118			0.0250	0.0175
Total water consumption	million cubic meters		15.85	14.24		
% of product that meets applicable product certification VOC standards	percentage				100%	
End-of-life material recovered	Tons				361	
% of recovered material recycled and/or reused	percentage				47%	
% of wood products from 3rd party-validated sources	percentage				87%	
% of wood products are FSC/PEFC certifed or controlled	percentage				76%	

Adapted from Mohawk (2023)

Shaw Industries

With sales estimated at more than $6 billion annually, the fact that this company is privately held by Berkshire Hathaway poses a challenge to access of all relevant financial information. However, the company has published sustainability reports for over a decade and these reports provide a glimpse of the company's achievements in this area. Table 10.4 summarizes these data from the company's latest sustainability report of 2022. Shaw has established a goal of being totally net zero by 2030 but states that its commercial carpet operations worldwide have been carbon neutral since 2018 (Shaw ESG Report 2022).

Shaw achieved carbon neutrality across its commercial carpet operations by first reducing its energy consumption, then switching to cleaner fuels; producing renewable energy at its own facilities; and incentivizing additional renewable energy development and usage through the purchase of renewable energy credits. These efforts include installing a 1 MW solar array atop its carpet tile manufacturing facility in Cartersville, Ga. in 2013 (Sustainablebrands.com 2018).

Table 10.5 summarizes basic financial data for Interface and Mohawk, its other publicly held competitor. Shaw and Engineered Carpets are both privately held. Shaw dominates the industry.

Table 10.4 Shaw Carpets Sustainabilty Indicators

Variable	Units	Value
Products cradle-to-cradle certified	percentage	90%
Outlet identified for additional manufaturing waste	million pounds	2
Reduction in Scope 1 & 2 carbon footprint from 2010	percentage	60%
Recycled plastic bottles turned into flooring	billion	2.7
Reclamined and recyled carpets since 2006	billion pounds	1
Reduction in water use per pound of finished product compared to 2010	percentage	43%

Adapted from Shaw ESG Report (2022)

Table 10.5 Basic Financial Data of Interface's Major Competitors

Basic Financial Data for Interface vs. Mohawk and Shaw (2022)

in millions	Interface	Mohawk	Shaw	U.S. Carpet Market
Net Sales	$1,297.9	$ 11,737	$4,500 (e)	$33,290 (e)
Operating Income	$75.4	$ 244.2	n.a.	
Net Income	$19.6	$ 25.8	n.a.	
# Employees	3,671	40,900	30,000	
Status	Public	Public	Private	

Sources: Interface, Mohawk, Hoover's and World Market Intelligence

One additional very important piece of information is available which bears upon a corporation's commitment to, and movement towards, sustainable production. For reasons of cost, many companies in this and numerous other industries rely to a certain degree on recycled rather than virgin material. An excellent example is provided by the pulp and paper industry where recycled paper products are part of a profitable international market. The principal trade-off is in the nature of the recycling process itself where the fibers tend to degrade with each recycling loop. As such, it is always necessary to make up for this deficiency by supplementing the production process with virgin feedstock. This phenomenon, referred to as *downcycling*, appears somewhat related to the laws of thermodynamics and has appeared to impose a major constraint on industrial processes.

Recent technological advances have led to the emergence of *upcycling* where waste products are converted into higher value products. Shaw Industries was an early adopter of upcycling, using old carpet fiber to produce new carpet material with no loss of quality. While Interface has only recently been undertaking upcycling, Shaw Industries may have achieved sustainable competitive advantage with this technological advance. In a case study of Shaw Industries, the Investor Environmental Health Network (IEHN) claimed that Shaw Industries was prompted to pursue its intensive research into technological innovations to pursue sustainability by the very public commitment to this cause by Ray Anderson and Interface.

It is instructive to ask if it is possible to conceive of an existing carpet manufacturing process which meets Anderson's criteria for true sustainability. Somewhat tongue-in-cheek, one possible answer would be a carpet which relies for its raw material on pasture-bred sheep, natural organic dyes, human labor, wooden looms and produces biodegradable waste. In fact, such carpets have been produced – and continue to be produced – in countries such as Turkey, Iran, Pakistan and India. On reflection, this model still suggests two possible problems with achieving sustainability: (1) the output is limited, although a major ramping up of production for the global market might go a long way toward solving the endemic problem of unemployment and underemployment in the developing world; and (2) the carpets must be shipped from their locus of production to global markets by modern and energy-intensive transport. Since the products' delivery is not time dependent, one solution might be the adoption of wind-driven, sea transport or novel hybrid versions thereof recently demonstrated in the shipment of wine. Of course, wine tends to mature with age, so extra time on the high seas might not be an unfavorable economic issue (see, for example, Gardner 2020; *New York Times* June 28, 2021, October 3, 2023, October 30, 2023).

Assessing Interface's Current and Future Competitive and Sustainability Situation

There are at least two critical issue to consider when attempting to answer this question: (1) the existence and sustainability of Interface's competitive advantage, and (2) the prospects that the company will achieve its sustainably goals in the immediate future. A useful concept to use in conducting this analysis was developed by Hamel and Valikangas (2003) called *strategic decay*. The authors outline four metrics to assess a firm's performance using this concept: (1) *Replication* (Is the company's strategy losing its distinctiveness?) (2) *Supplantation* (Is the company's strategy in danger of being superceded?) (3) *Exhaustion* (Is the company's strategy reaching the point of exhaustion?); and (4) *Evisceration* (Is increasing customer power eviscerating the company's margins?)

Firstly, it appears that Interface may be facing strategic decay risk on replication through increased adoption of sustainability initiatives by its principal competitors. And second, the problem of potential exhaustion can be manifested if the pace of improvement in key performance metrics is slowing down. A hint of this issue was indicated by some of Interface's graphed eco-efficiency metrics in its previous reports (Nemetz 2013). Some of these metrics displayed initially rapid technological achievements followed by a levelling off. These included metrics for waste to landfills from manufacturing sites and energy use per unit of finished product, although this latter problem is tempered by the increasing use of renewable energy. More revealing, however, is the trend of metrics for which historical trends are no longer displayed, including water intake for both modular and broadloom carpet. Interestingly, a similar mixed pattern in historical trends of some eco-efficiency metrics was characteristic of some of Mohawk's results as well, including water intensity and waste to landfill intensity in their Mohawk 2016 CSR report. What this seems to suggest is that for some aspects of production, what has been termed low-hanging fruit, have already been picked and that further advance will require a change in or modification of technology. Interface and its competitors have clearly made remarkable strides towards remoulding their corporate strategies and technology toward greater sustainability. The issue, instead, revolves round the prospects of making significant new strides in the immediate future.

There is one additional factor which must be considered in assessing sustainability, and this focuses on a systemwide assessment as opposed to a singular focus on the production process *per se*. In making an assessment, it is useful not only to closely examine the financial statements of the company, but also to consult filings by the corporation required by the US Securities and Exchange Commission (SEC). Of these filing requirements, the 10-K form is frequently the most informative as it requires the corporation to disclose, among other things, all major current and anticipated risks. It is important to bear in mind, however, that a corporation may be inclined to include or overstate risks solely for the purpose of avoiding any future legal challenges that they have not disclosed all material facts. In spite of this caveat, however, the 10-K provides critical information on the state of the corporation. Among the most significant entries in a recent 10-K section on risk for Interface (US SEC 2023) are as follows:

Item 1A. Risk Factors

Large increases in the cost of our raw materials, shipping costs, duties or tariffs could adversely affect us if we are unable to pass these cost increases through to our customers.

Petroleum-based products (including yarn) comprise the predominant portion of the cost of raw materials that we use in manufacturing carpet. Synthetic rubber uses petroleum-based products as feedstock as well.

Unanticipated termination or interruption of any of our arrangements with our primary third-party suppliers of synthetic fiber or our primary third-party supplier for luxury vinyl tile ("LVT") or other key raw materials could have a material adverse effect on us.

We depend on a small number of third-party suppliers of synthetic fiber and are largely dependent upon two primary suppliers for our LVT products. The unanticipated termination or interruption of any of our supply arrangements with our current suppliers of synthetic fiber (nylon), our primary suppliers of LVT, or other key raw material suppliers, including failure by any third party supplier to meet our product specifications, could have a material adverse effect on us because we do not have the capability to manufacture our own fiber for use in our carpet products or our own LVT.

Clearly, a reliance on fossil-based synthetics represents an additional obstacle to achieving the corporate goal of long-term zero impact. Table 10.6 lists the energy consumption of alterative textiles fibres (BSR 2009). The report makes three observations with respect to these data: first, energy data are used as a proxy for the relative contribution of fibre production to GHG because direct estimates of GHG emissions can be confounded by the fuel used in textile production; second, these data exclude the potential methane production from enteric fermentation in sheep. When these estimates are added, it appears that wool may have the highest contribution to global warming, nevertheless sheep are also used for meat production as well as wool and some of these emissions must be credited to meat rather than wool production; and third, the energy content of fossil fuel feedstocks used to produce synthetic fibers are included in the data despite the fact that these fuels do not create GHG emissions in the production process because they are not combusted. However, they may generate GHG if they are incinerated after disposal. As an additional note it is important to remember than GHGs will be produced in the production of fossil fuel feedstocks.

Interface has recently achieved a remarkable advance in the GHG profile of one of its products: it is carbon negative. As Interface reports in describing the creation of a carbon negative product (Interface 2023a):

First-Ever Carbon Negative Carpet Tile In 2020: Interface launched the first ever carbon negative carpet tile, a first for Interface and a first for the industry. By using recycled content and bio-based materials in an innovative way we created carpet tiles using materials that store carbon, preventing its release into the atmosphere. These products achieved a negative carbon footprint measured cradle-to-gate, without the use of carbon credits. Our carbon negative carpet tile is well-positioned to meet the world's growing interest in decarbonization and low carbon products, especially as more than 90% of our top customers have publicly declared commitments to reduce their carbon footprints. Many of our global customers are specifying Interface products with carbon negative backings or carbon negative carpet tile to support their own climate ambitions. The architecture, engineering, and construction industry is also taking similar steps to reduce its environmental impact by putting low-carbon products into

Table 10.6 Energy Consumption of Textile Fibers

Fabric	MJ/kg
acrylic	158
nylon	138.5
polyester	109.5
cotton	49.5
wool	41
viscose	36
linen	24

Adapted from BSR (2009)

specifications and considering carbon in procurement decisions to achieve sustainability goals. This innovation has helped us make progress to reduce the virgin raw materials used in the backing of our carpet tile products and replaced them with recycled and bio-based materials.

Interface explained how it is possible for products to have negative embodied carbon (Interface n.d.):

> Some materials are made from atmospheric carbon either through photosynthesis or direct air capture of CO_2 and other GHGs, so they remove carbon from the atmosphere. If the emissions of carbon from the handling, transport, and processing the material are less than the carbon they have removed from the atmosphere, the result is net negative Embodied Carbon. When we say negative carbon backings, we mean the material used in our CQuest™ backings (measured on a stand-alone basis) are net carbon negative. Not every carpet made with CQuest ™ backing is carbon negative. It is only when CQuest™BioX backing is paired with specialty yarns and tufting processes that the result is a cradle to gate carbon negative carpet tile.

While Interface is one of the leaders in the creation of net carbon negative products, there is an emerging industry to produce similar products. As reported in the *New York Times Magazine* (Payne & Gertner 2021):

> Interface is far from the only company trying to "embed" large amounts of carbon within commercial merchandise. For the past few years, several start-ups have begun developing products that aim to fold in carbon dioxide captured from smokestacks and other sources of pollution, in an attempt to reach a new level of environmentally friendly manufacturing: one in which greenhouse-gas molecules are not only kept out of the atmosphere but also repurposed. This undertaking, usually characterized as carbon utilization, goes well beyond flooring — to plastics, jet fuels, diesel, chemicals, building materials, diamonds, even fish food. Advocates of carbon utilization, or *carbontech*, as it's also known, want to remake many of the things we commonly use today. But with one crucial difference: No emissions would have been added to the environment through their fabrication.

Siegel (2018, p. 2) has categorized the companies making up the carbon-negative supply chain into three groups:

> The first group is focused on direct air carbon capture (as opposed to capture from exhaust streams, which can be carbon neutral at best). The second is focused on using captured CO_2 to create raw materials. And the third is focused on creating products directly from captured CO_2.

This is clearly one of the principal pathways to a sustainable industrial future.

Interface takeaway lessons

There are several lessons which emerge from the analysis of Interface's revolutionary approach. First, is the absolutely essential buy-in from senior management. Without Ray

Anderson's leadership, it is unlikely that Interface would have pursued its current course of action but, notably since his death, senior management has continued, if not accelerated, his commitment. Second, is the importance of intercorporate transferability of technology, whether through sharing or competitive pressure. Mohawk and Shaw Industries have been clearly motivated to respond to some of Interface's past initiatives.

Considering Interface's achievements, it has been approached by numerous companies for advice. To address this issue, Interface established a program called InterfaceRAISE. To quote one report (InterfaceRaise 2007, p. 3):

> InterfaceRAISE was created in response to repeated visits and questions from companies taking or exploring their own mid-course correction and curious about the lessons learned by Anderson and Interface. . . . Providing executive education and organizational inspiration, the InterfaceRAISE team consists of senior executives and global sustainable development experts who know how to increase business value through sustainability education, cultural transformation and innovation.

One of Interface's most successful adherents has been Wal-Mart (InterfaceRaise 2007, p. 3), a collaboration which began with Ray Anderson's friendship with the former Walmart CEO, Lee Scott.

Third, is the underlying challenge of technological barriers which take a firm only so far on the road to total sustainability and then require a concerted research effort to move to the next stage. And, finally, this case study highlights the importance of the contribution of a firm's supply chain to the total greenhouse gas releases associated with its products. In many cases, the supply chain contributions far exceed those of the firm's own operations. An excellent data source for tracking these system data on an industry-by-industry basis has been the now outdated EIO-LCA (Environmental Input-Output: Life Cycle Analysis) database produced by Carnegie Mellon University. While a corporation such as Interface has made significant strides in reducing their own carbon footprint, these data highlight the need to identify and attempt to reduce the supply chain contributions of suppliers across all industries. These approaches are described briefly in the case studies on Wal-Mart and Puma (see chapter 16).

Table 10.7 compares Interface's and Rohner's achievements with the pure model of sustainability posited earlier for handwoven carpets. In the case of Rohner Textil (see chapter 3), many of the basic ingredients of sustainability have been successfully transferred into a modern, high-volume commercial product capable of meeting the large demands of the international market.

Table 10.7 Interface vs. Rohner vs. Handwoven Carpets Inputs

Characteristic	Interface	Rohner	Hand-Woven
fibre	nylon	natural (wool)	natural (wool)
source of fibre	fossil fuels	pasture-bred sheep	pasture-bred sheep
type of dyes	synthetic	natural	natural
major inputs	capital and energy-intensive	capital and energy-intensive	labor-intensive
energy source	renewable	renewable	labor
looms	metal	metal	wooden
toxic wastes	some	none	none

The Path Forward

Interface recently published a document entitled "Lessons for the Future" that summarizes their achievements to date and their plans for the future. The company has declared victory on "Mission Zero" established in 1994 with most of their original goals achieved (see Appendix Table 10.12) and decided to adopt a much more ambitious agenda entitled "Climate Take Back." This involves moving beyond a principal focus on their own company and an increased emphasis on changing the company's environment, specifically an increased focus on their supply chain, their competitors, and other industries. There are four areas of this strategy: (1) *Live Zero* (aiming for zero negative impact on the environment); (2) *Let Nature Cool* (support the biosphere's ability to regulate the environment); (3) *Love Carbon* (stop seeing carbon as the enemy and start using it as a resource; and (4) *Lead the Industrial Revolution* (Transform industry into a force for the future we want). One of the most ambitious components of this strategy is switching the mindset from limiting the damage done by climate change to thinking about reversing it. One example of this is the company's new carbon negative carpet and underfelt. Clearly, much of these four components are aspirational at this time, but given Interface's exemplary record in achieving its Mission Zero, there appears to be a significant chance that the company will realize these challenging goals over time.

Addendum

Over the period 2016–2018, several reports were published by an NGO questioning the commitment of the US carpet industry as a whole to sustainability. The reports focussed on toxic chemicals in carpets, lack of transparency in data provided by the companies, and lobbing efforts by the industry to foretell more stringent government regulation (GAI & Changing Market 2016, 2017a, 2017b, 2017c; Changing Markets Foundation 2018). The problem is the age of these publications, since no update has been provided to determine if any of these criticisms are still valid.

Research Questions

1. As an investor, would you consider investing in Interface as opposed to its competitors?
2. How will the company fare in the future considering the Hamel and Valikangas' concept of strategic decay?
3. How important is Interface's supply chain exposure to GHG and does that affect their role as a sustainable corporation?
4. How important are embodied fossil fuels in synthetic fibres for Interface's GHG profile?
5. How important are the risk factors mentioned in the text above?
6. How can Interface compete with its two largest competitors, Mohawk and Shaw Carpets?

References

Anderson, Ray (1999) *Mid-Course Correction: Toward a Sustainable Enterprise: The Interface Model*, Atlanta: Peregrinzilla Press.
Anderson, Ray (2007) "Mid-Course Correction: Toward a Sustainable Enterprise" in Peter N. Nemetz (ed.) *Sustainable Resource Management: Reality or Illusion?* Cheltenham: Edward Elgar: 88–114.

Anderson, Ray & Robin White (2009) *Confessions of a Radical Industrialist: Profits, People, Purpose – Doing Business by Respecting the Earth.* (Reissued in 2011 in paperback as *Business Lessons from a Radical Industrialist.*) Toronto: McClelland & Stewart.

Anderson, Ray et al. (2010) "Changing Business Cultures from Within," Worldwatch Institute, State of the *World 2010. Transforming Cultures. From Consumerism to Sustainability,* Washington, D.C.: 96–102.

Business for Social Responsibility (BSR) (2009) "Apparel Industry Life Cycle Carbon Mapping," June.

Gardner, Nic (2020) "Brief guide to sail-assisted cargo ships web.mit.edu," Thetius.

Global Alliance for Incinerator Alternatives (GAIA) (2016) *Swept under the Carpet: Exposing the Greenwash of the US Carpet Industry.*

Global Alliance for Incinerator Alternatives (GAIA) (2017a) "The CAREless Carpet Industry: A critique of the California Carpet Stewardship Programs Reliance on Incineration."

Global Alliance for Incinerator Alternatives (GAIA) (2017b) Letter to CEO Mohawk Industries Incorporated, January 31.

Global Alliance for Incinerator Alternatives (GAIA) (2017c) Letter to CEO Shaw Industries Group Incorporated, January 17.

Globescan (2023) *Sustainability Survey 2020,* June.

Interface (n.d.) "A Look Back/ Interface's Sustainability Journey." https://www.interface.com.cn/page/interfacestory?lang=en

Interface (n.d.) "Mission Zero/ Measuring Our Progress."

Interface (n.d.) "Carbon FAQs." https://interfaceinc.scene7.com/is/content/InterfaceInc/Interface/Americas/WebsiteContentAssets/Documents/Sustainability%20Carbon%20Negative%20FAQ/wc_am-carbonnegativefaqfinal.pdf?ref=csofutures.com

Interface (n.d.) "Lessons for the Future. The Interface guide for changing your business to change the world," https://prd-sites.interface.com/content/dam/interfaceinc/interface/sustainability/emea/25th-anniversary-report/Interface_MissionZeroCel_Booklet_EN.pdf

Interface (2020) "From carbon neutral to carbon negative."

Interface (2023a) *Annual Report 2022.* https://s22.q4cdn.com/139673446/files/doc_financials/2022/ar/tile-20230101_ar_v1-bm.pdf

Interface (2023b) *Design with Purpose. 2021 Environmental, Social, and Governance (ESG) Report.*

Interface (2023c) 10-K, United States Securities and Exchange Commission Report.

InterfaceRaise (2007) "InterfaceRAISE & Walmart: mentoring the world's largest retailer."

Investor Environmental Health Network (IEHN) (2010) Case Study. "Rohner Textiles: Cradle-to-Cradle Innovation and Sustainability" (www.iehn.org/publications.case.rohner.php).

Mohawk (2023) *Sustainability Report and Data Center.*

Mohawk Industries, Inc. (2009) *2009 Sustainability Report.*

New York Times (2021) "Can massive cargo ships use wind to go green?" June 28.

New York Times (2023) 'In shipping, a push to slash emissions by harnessing the wind," October 3.

New York Times (2023) "Shipping contributes heavily to climate change. Are green ships the solution? October 30.

Payne, Christopher and Jon Gertner (2021) "Has the Carbon tech revolution begun?" *New York Times Magazine,* June 23.

Sarkis, Joseph (2010) *Greening the Supply Chain eco-efficiency,* London: Springer.

Shaw (2022) *Sustainability Report 2022.*

Siegel, B.P. (2018) "Manufacturing goes carbon negative," *Energy & Sustainability,* May 7, Summer, Issue 81.

Sustainablebrands.com (2018) "Shaw Industries achieves carbon neutrality in its commercial carpet manufacturing operations."

Appendix One – Interface's Recent Financial Data

Interface's Historical Revenue and Profit
  P&L (Statement of Operations)
  Balance Sheet
  Cash Flows

Table 10.8 Interface Historical Revenue and Profit (in million $)

	revenue	profit
1982	$ 57.1	$ 4.6
1983	$ 80.1	$ 6.1
1984	$ 107.3	$ 4.9
1985	$ 123.4	$ 8.0
1986	$ 137.4	$ 8.6
1987	$ 267.0	$ 13.7
1988	$ 396.7	$ 20.2
1989	$ 581.8	$ 24.5
1990	$ 623.5	$ 23.6
1991	$ 581.8	$ 8.9
1992	$ 594.1	$ 12.3
1993	$ 625.1	$ 13.8
1994	$ 725.3	$ 16.5
1995	$ 802.1	$ 16.8
1996	$ 1,002.1	$ 26.4
1997	$ 1,135.3	$ 37.5
1998	$ 1,281.1	$ 29.8
1999	$ 1,228.2	$ 23.5
2000	$ 1,283.9	$ 17.3
2001	$ 1,103.9	$ (36.3)
2002	$ 924.1	$ (87.7)
2003	$ 923.5	$ (33.3)
2004	$ 881.7	$ (55.4)
2005	$ 985.8	$ 1.2
2006	$ 1,075.8	$ 10.0
2007	$ 1,081.3	$ (10.8)
2008	$ 946.8	$ (40.9)
2009	$ 765.3	$ 10.9
2010	$ 862.3	$ 8.3
2011	$ 953.0	$ 38.7
2012	$ 932.0	$ 5.9
2013	$ 960.0	$ 48.3
2014	$ 1,003.9	$ 24.8
2015	$ 1,001.9	$ 72.4
2016	$ 958.6	$ 54.2
2017	$ 996.4	$ 53.2
2018	$ 1,179.6	$ 50.3
2019	$ 1,343.0	$ 79.2
2020	$ 1,103.3	$ (71.9)
2021	$ 1,200.4	$ 55.2
2022	$ 1,297.9	$ 19.6

Interface Annual Reports (2022)

Table 10.9 Interface P&L

Interface, Inc. And Subsidiaries Consolidated Statements Of Operations
(in thousands, except per share data)

	Fiscal Year		
	2022	2021	2020
Net sales	$ 1,297,919	$ 1,200,398$s	1,103,262
Cost of sales	860,186	767,665	692,688
Gross profit	437,733	432,733	410,574
Selling, general and administrative expenses	324,190	324,315	333,229
Restructuring, asset impairment and other charges	1,965	3,621	(4,626)
Goodwill and intangible asset impairment charge	36,180	—	121,258
Operating income (loss)	75,398	104,797	(39,287)
Interest expense	29,929	29,681	29,244
Other expense, net	3,552	2,483	10,889
Income (loss) before income tax expense	41,917	72,633	(79,420)
Income tax expense (benefit)	22,357	17,399	(7,491)
Net income (loss) $	$ 19,560	$55,234$	(71,929)
Earnings (loss) per share – basic	$ 0.33	$ 0.94 $	(1.23)
Earnings (loss) per share – diluted $	$ 0.33	$ 0.94 $	(1.23)
Common shares outstanding – basic	58,865	58,971	58,547
Common shares outstanding – diluted	58,865	58,971	58,547
Net income (loss)	$ 19,560	$ 55,234 $	(71,929)
Other comprehensive income (loss), after tax:			
Foreign currency translation adjustment	(38,334)	(40,110)	52,808
Cash flow hedge gain (loss)	1,973	3,468	(2,027)
Pension liability adjustment	26,340	15,400	(12,588)
Other comprehensive income (loss)	(10,021)	(21,242)	38,193
Comprehensive income (loss)	$ 9,539	$ 33,992 $	(33,736)

Interface Annual Reports (2022)

Table 10.10 Interface Balance Sheet

Interface, Inc. And Subsidiaries Consolidated Balance Sheets(in thousands, except par values)

	End Of Fiscal Year	
	2022	2021
ASSETS	$	$
Current assets		
Cash and cash equivalents	97,564	97,252
Accounts receivable, net	182,807	171.676
Inventories, net	306,327	265,092
Prepaid expenses and other current assets	30,339	38,320
Total current assets	617,037	572,340
Property, plant and equipment, net	297,976	329,801
Operating lease right-of-use assets	81,644	90,561
Deferred tax asset	17,767	23,994
Goodwill and intangibles, net	162,195	223,204
Other assets	89.884	90,157
Total assets	$ 1,266,503	$ 1,330,057
LIABILITIES AND SHAREHOLDERS' EQUITY	.. $	$
Current liabilities		
Accounts payable	78,264	85,924
Accrued expenses	120,138	146,298
Current portion of operating lease liabilities	11,857	14,588
Current portion of long-term debt	10,211	15,002
Total current liabilities	220,470	261,812
Long-term debt	510,003	503,056
Operating lease liabilities	72,305	77,905
Deferred income taxes	38,662	36,723
Other long-term liabilities	63,526	87,163
Total liabilities	904,966	966,659
Commitments and contingencies		
Shareholders' equity		
Preferred stock, par value $1.00 per share; 5.000 shares authorized; none issued or outstanding at January 1, 2023 and January 2, 2022		
Common stock, par value $0.10 per share: 120.000 shares authorized: 58,106 and 59.055 shares issued and outstanding at January 1, 2023 and January 2, 2022, respectively	5,811	5,905
Additional paid-in capital	244,159	253,110
Retained earnings	278,639	261,434
Accumulated other comprehensive loss — foreign currency translation	(138,775)	(100,441)
Accumulated other comprehensive loss — cash flow hedge	(749)	(2,722)
Accumulated other comprehensive loss — pension liability	(27,548)	(53,888)
Total shareholders' equity	361,537	363,398
Total liabilities and shareholder's' equity	1,266,503	$ 1,330,057

Interface Annual Reports (2022)

Table 10.11 Interface Cash Flows

Interface, Inc. And Subsidiaries Consolidated Statements Of Cash Flows (in thousands)

| | Fiscal Year | | |
	2022	2021	2020
OPERATING ACTIVITIES:			
Net income (loss) $	19,560	$ 55,234 $	(71,929)
Adjustments to reconcile net income (loss) to cash provided by operating activities:			
Depreciation and amortization	40,337	46,345	45,920
Stock compensation amortization expense (benefit)	8,527	5,467	(502)
Loss on disposal of fixed assets	4,319	4,427	4,996
Bad debt expense	26	(263)	3,843
Deferred income taxes and other	13,414	(16,379)	(20,794)
Amortization of acquired intangible assets	5,038	5,636	5,457
Goodwill and intangible asset impairment	36,180	—	121,258
Working capital changes:			
Accounts receivable	(17,489)	(36,096)	40,090
Inventories	(49,651)	(47,074)	38,667
Prepaid expenses and other current assets	7,020	(4,800)	12,967
Accounts payable and accrued expenses	(24,220)	74,192	(60,903)
Cash provided by operating activities	43,061	86,689	119,070
INVESTING ACTIVITIES:			
Capital expenditures	(18,437)	(28,071)	(62,949)
Other	—	—	1,260
Cash used in investing activities	(18,437)	(28,071)	(61,689)
FINANCING ACTIVITIES:			
Revolving loan borrowing	206,031	76,000	110,000
Revolving loan repayments	(189,281)	(71,500)	(131,024)
Term loan repayments	(13,191)	(60,485)	(304,425)
Proceeds from issuance of Senior Notes due 2028	—	—	300,000
Repurchase of common stock	(17,171)	—	—
Dividends paid	(2,355)	(2,362)	(5,565)
Tax withholding payments for share-based compensation	(402)	(193)	(1,511)
Debt issuance costs	(1,032)	(36)	(7,896)
Payments for debt extinguishment costs	—	—	(660)
Proceeds from issuance of common stock	—	—	93
Finance lease payments	(2,089)	(2,282)	(1,727)
Cash used in financing activities	(19,490)	(60,858)	(42,715)
Net cash provided by (used in) operating, investing and			
financing activities	5,134	(2,240)	14,666
Effect of exchange rate changes on cash	(4,822)	(3,561)	7,086
CASH AND CASH EQUIVALENTS:			
Net increase (decrease)	312	(5,801)	21,752
Balance, beginning of year	97,252	103,053	81,301
Balance, end of year $	97,564	$ 97,252 $	103,053

Interface Annual Reports (2022)

Appendix Two: Interface' Latest Sustainability Metrics

Table 10.12 Interface Sustainabiltiy mMetrics

Ref ESG Report 2021				
1996 to 2021 changes	1996 Actual	2009 Actual	2021 Calculated	units
96% fewer GHG emissions	95.0	38.0	3.8	000 MT CO2e
86% less water used to make products				
85% less waste sent to landfills	15.0	3.3	2.2	million lbs
76% renewable energy used at global manufacturing sites				
76% reduced carbon footprint of carpet tile products				

RESULTS SINCE 2003

Sold more than 551 million square yards of carbon neutral flooring products

Retired 6.1 million metric tonnes of verified emission reduction credits

2021 RESULTS

Sold 50 million square yards of carbon neutral flooring products

Retired 442 thousand metric tonnes of verified emission reduction credits

2021 GHG Emissions update

Scope 1: reduction of 13%
Scope 2: reduction of 2%
Scope 3: Category 1 (purchased goods and services) reduction of 24%
Scope 3: Category 6 (Business Travel): reduction of 90%
Scope 3: (Category 7): employee commuting: no change

2021 Operational metrics

Energy consumed: 530,763 GJ of energy consumed from all manufacturing sites				
Renewable energy: 76% of energy used at manufacturing sites is from renewables	1.5%	30.1%	76.0%	percentage
Water: 14.1 million gallons of water intake from all manufacturing sites				
Waste: 19.2 million pounds of waste discarded from all manufacturing sites				
Electricity: 100% of all electricity usage at our manufacturing sites is sourced from renewable sources				

(Continued)

Table 10.12 (Continued)

Ref ESG Report 2021				
1996 to 2021 changes	*1996 Actual*	*2009 Actual*	*2021 Calculated*	*units*

Global Product Carbon Footprint

Carpet 4.8 kg CO2e/m2 - down 76% since its baseline year of 1996

Rubber flooring 8.5 kg CO2e/m2- down 21% since its baseline year of 2019

LVT & Other resilient 9.1 kg CO2e/m2 - down 24% since its baseline year of 2018

Recycled Materials

	1996 Actual	2009 Actual	2021 Calculated	units
64% of all of the materials used to make our carpet tiles are from recycled or bio-based sources	0.7%	36.4%	64.0%	percentage

39% of all the materials used to make LVT and other resilient flooring are from recycled or bio-based sources with the use of recycled fibers. This is the highest amount of recycled content in this category within the industry

8% of all the materials used to make our rubber flooring are from recycled or bio-based sources with natural rubber and recycled fillers contributing the most.

Circular Economy ReEntry Metrics Results since 2017

Collected 53 million pounds of post-consumer carpet

70% of post-consumer carpet given a second life through reprocessing internally or recycled through one of our ReEntry partners

The other 30% was sent to a waste-to-entry site because it was unusable

2021 Results

Collected 6.1 million pounds of post-consumer carpet

4.0 million pounds recycled; 1.2 million pounds reused; 0.9 million pounds waste-to-energy

50% of the raw materials used to make our products came from recycled or bio-based sources

Source: Interface ESG Report (2021)

11 MOWI – World Leader in Aquaculture

A Questionable Solution

Fish have historically been a critical part of the global ecosystem, and fishing provides a significant proportion of food resources for almost half of the world's population, representing 34% of global animal protein consumption (Mowi 2022), as well as making a significant contribution to economic and social systems worldwide. According to the FAO (Globefish n.d.), the nutritional benefits are unique: "Increased attention is given to fish as a source of essential nutrients in our diets, not only high value proteins, but more importantly also as a unique source of micronutrients and long chain omega-3 fatty acids."

Figure 11.1 presents global fisheries capture for the period 1950–2021 (FAO 2023). Total fish capture increased steadily until the late 1980s and has stabilized since then. Fisheries researchers have concluded that we are approaching or have reached the limits

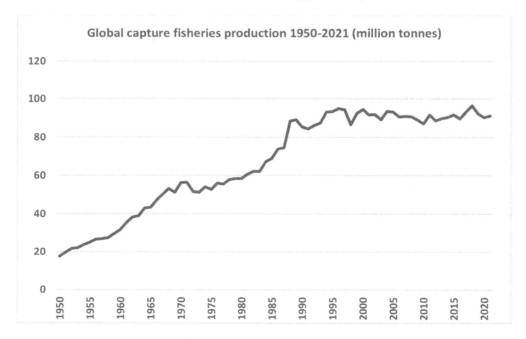

Figure 11.1 Global Fisheries Capture 1950–2021
Source: FAO 2023

DOI: 10.4324/9781003170754-14

of exploitable capacity (Pauly 2010). This poses a serious problem for world food supply as global population continues to increase and there is a pressing need to move away from the consumption of red meat because of this sector's substantial contribution to global warming. The carbon footprint of fish is 5.1 kg CO_2 per kg edible meat compared to 8.4 for poultry, 12.2 for pork and 39.0 for beef (Mowi 2022). In another comprehensive study of the contribution of various food sources to global mean surface air temperature, Ivanovich et al. (2023) found that seafood in general contributed only 3% compared to ruminant meat's 33%. Up until recently, it was assumed that the state of global fisheries was both well-known and reasonably stable, but research has cast serious doubt on these conclusions and suggests that there is a crisis in global fisheries that threatens its very sustainability despite the fact that per capita fish consumption is expected to continue increasing over the next decade (OECD-FAO 2021).

The fisheries crisis is multifaceted. Watson and Pauly (2001, p. 534) reported an important issue with respect to national reporting of fisheries catches: the United Nations' Food and Agriculture Organization (FAO) "must generally rely on the statistics provided by member countries, even if it is doubtful that these correspond to reality." While extensive research undertaken by Pauly and Zeller (2016) concluded that global catch data is underreported, there is incontrovertible evidence that it is in decline.

Second, there is no way of determining if the current catch levels are sustainable. One methodology that may shed light on this issue is the concept of Catch per Unit Effort (CPUE), which measures the temporal trends in total catch with effort adjusted for increases in technology, specifically changes in fishing vessel efficiency. This is a very important factor as the last few decades has been marked by a major shift among fishing fleets to larger and more powerful boats with more advanced technology for finding and catching fish. Figure 11.2, based on the doctoral research of Ahmed Abda Gelchu (2006) demonstrates a trend of temporally declining CPUE. This provides initial evidence of the increasing pressure on global fish stocks and the unsustainability of the current path of exploitation.

Third, the question of sustainability is complicated further by the inability to generate an accurate measure of global fish stocks. The only observable variable is fish catch, and inferences must be made from these data as to the magnitude and characteristics of the stock from which they are drawn. There is a complex relationship between catch volume and stocks. *In extremis*, raw catch data could be consistent with increasing stocks, stable stocks, declining stocks, or crashing stocks. The nature of this problem can be illustrated by borrowing simple concepts from financial analysis. In the world of finance, a known quantity of capital yields a given return, or income, in the form of interest payments. There is no confusing the distinction between the two quantities. No rational or honest business person would use up capital and claim that is income. The conceptual basis of fisheries is identical, with an important distinction: with no way of directly measuring the total stock of fish (i.e., natural capital), there is no way of determining whether the fish catch is all "interest" or "interest + capital." This inability to determine what is an appropriate level of sustainable catch has led to a number of catastrophic stock failures and continues to put pressure on remaining global fisheries resources. In a real world of complex ecological processes, the determination of the dynamic path of fish stocks is made exceedingly difficult by the range of biological, physical, chemical, atmospheric and oceanographic factors which influence stock dynamics. It will be argued later, however, that even if such perfect knowledge of fish stocks and their temporal path were

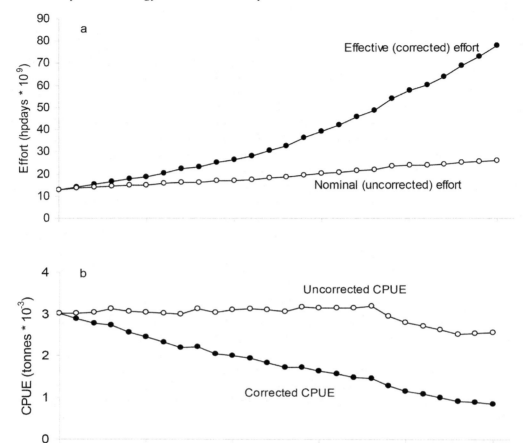

Figure 11.2 Trends in CPUE

Source: Gelchu (2006) Reproduced with Permission

available, the institutional structure and economic incentives in place would still lead to an unsustainable fishery.

Fourth, and perhaps most importantly, the apparently positive appearance of the historical data with rising and recently stabilized catches has been challenged by important new theoretical and empirical research which focuses on the changing composition of fish stocks at the global level. This critical advance in knowledge is called "fishing down the food web" and has been pioneered by Professor Daniel Pauly of the University of British Columbia (Pauly et al. 1998; Pauly 2010). Pauly and Chuenpagdee (2007, p. 175) have essentially cast the status of global fishing in an entirely new and more pessimistic light:

> a fishery starts by catching abundant large fish high in the food web, then gradually shifts to smaller fish, lower in the food web, as the former resource becomes less abundant. This process, which occurs in virtually all fisheries of the world, usually

goes along with habitat destruction, typified by the gradual disappearance of the bottom structure created by bottom organisms.

There are two principal effects of fishing down the food web: (1) the depletion of the number of the larger fish which provide humanity with much of its seafood, and (2) the foreclosure of opportunities to rebuilding these stocks at the top trophic levels because, as fishing proceeds down the food chain, the food supply is depleted at the next lowest tropic level. The net result of this ongoing depletion of predators atop the food chain has been a radical transformation of an entire marine ecosystem in many parts of the global oceans over the past few decades (Jackson et al. 2001).

In addition to the critical concept of fishing down the food web, Pauly and his colleagues have made another ground-breaking contribution to the science of fisheries by creating several elaborate ecosystem models which help to open the black box of fisheries dynamics and help to advance our knowledge of the state and direction of fish populations. Three linked modeling systems have been developed, entitled, *Ecosim, Ecopath* and *Ecospace* (Christensen & Pauly 1992; Pauly et al. 2000; Christensen et al. 2000; Christensen & Walters 2004). All have been made publicly available for use by scientists worldwide. *Ecopath* is a static, mass-balanced snapshot of the system; *Ecosim* (a time dynamic simulation module for policy exploration) and *Ecospace* (a spatial and temporal dynamic module primarily designed for exploring the impact and placement of protected areas [Walters et al, 1997, 2000; Sumaila & Charles 2002]). The Ecopath software package can be used to address ecological questions, evaluate ecosystem effects of fishing, explore management policy options, analyze impact and placement of marine protected areas, predict movement and accumulation of contaminants and tracers, and model effect of environmental changes. The usefulness of these models can be illustrated with a case study of the Atlantic cod, once one of the world's most important sources of marine food.

Case Study: The Atlantic Cod

Cod has played an important role in the history of Western Europe and North America, providing a large supply of easily accessible food not only for early American settlers and aboriginals, but also acting as an attractant for European fisherman from the times of the Vikings in 800 AD. Mark Kurlansky, in his 1998 book *Cod: A History of the Fish that Changed the World,* quotes a letter from Raimondo di Soncino, Milan's envoy in London to the Duke of Milan on December 18, 1497, reporting on John Cabot's return on August 6 of that year. The letter stated, in part, "*The Sea was swarming with fish which can be taken not only with the net but in baskets let down with a stone, so that it sinks in the water*" (Kurlansky 1998: 48). This bountiful marine harvest continued for centuries to feed peoples of both sides of the Atlantic until the early 1990s. Figure 11.3 presents the temporal trend in Atlantic cod catch since 1950 (FAO FISHSTAT). The catch peaked in 1968, fell almost continuously after that until stabilizing in the 1980s and then collapsed in the 1990s. The catastrophe of the 1990s represents a potential ecological tipping point for the Atlantic cod as the stock has faced major obstacles to rebuilding itself despite fisheries closures and other remedial interventions.

The reasons for the decline and collapse are multifold but are principally due to overfishing and inadequate understanding of the ecological dynamics of fisheries that drove misguided policy on allowable catch by the Canadian government's department

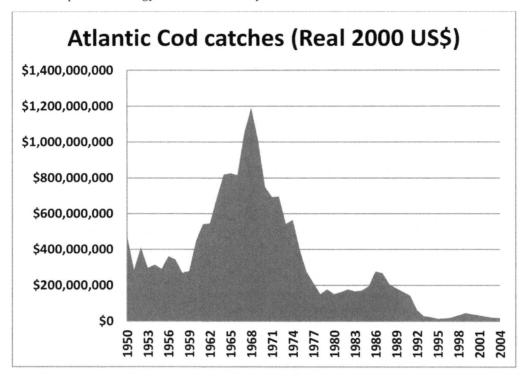

Figure 11.3 Temporal Trend in Catch of Atlantic Cod
Source: FAO FISHSTAT

responsible for fisheries (Rose 2008). Pilkey and Pilkey-Jarvis (2007:9) term the government's actions as "one of the most important and far-reaching scientific blunders of the age." In general, the inability of fish stocks to recover can be due to a mix of diverse factors, including continued fishing pressure, a density of fish population so low that it makes it impossible for the existing fish stock to find sufficient mates to rebuild the population, and the loss of the species' *ecological niche* to other species.

While the cod dominated the catch from the Grand Banks in the 1980s, it was not the only species to face collapse. As illustrated in Figure 11.4, a process of serial collapses included redfish, American plaice, capelin, Greenland halibut, haddock and yellowtail flounder. The aggregation of species losses is very strong evidence of Pauly's theory of fishing down the food chain (Pauly 2001). Kleisner et al. (2012) present a graphical analysis of the current state of global fisheries in Figure 11.5. The authors used global catch data to construct this chart, which divided fish population into four categories: collapsed, overfished, fully exploited, developing, and undeveloped. It is noteworthy that both developing and undeveloped fisheries have virtually disappeared, demonstrating the extreme pressure on current fishery resources. In a landmark research paper that preceded Kleisner by a decade, Myers and Worm (2003) found that intensive industrial fishing had led to the loss of 90% of large predatory fishes globally.

The marketing response to extensive overfishing and loss of premium species at the global level has been to harvest fish formerly considered undesirable for human

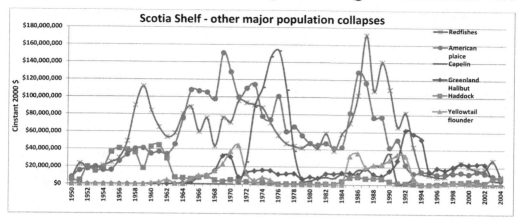

Figure 11.4 Serial Collapse of Fish Stocks in Grand Banks
Source: Canada Fisheries Statistics Yearbooks

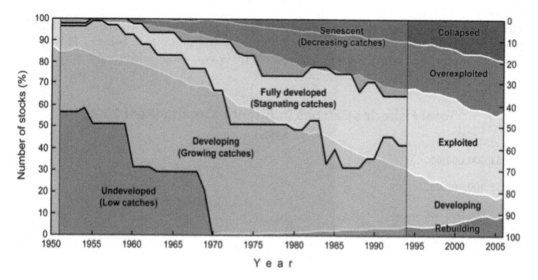

Figure 11.5 Current State of Global Fisheries
Source: Kleisner et al. (2012) Reproduced with permission

consumption. Many of these so-called *junk fish* have now made it onto the platters of Americans and other diners through a process of rebranding or mislabeling. Jacquet and Pauly (2008a,b) conducted an in-depth analysis of changing patterns of fish availability and concluded that fully 40% of all fish sold in the US is misbranded. These findings have been corroborated by other research work (Oceana 2016; Cawthorn et al. 2018; *The Guardian* March 15, 2021). In addition, many other species have received new and more acceptable names. One of the most graphic examples of this marketing initiative has been the introduction of "rock salmon," a fish that now has a name synonymous with one of the most highly valued global species. In fact, the rock salmon is just a rebranded spiny dogfish, long considered as unworthy of catching. There are numerous other examples, such as the rebranding of Patagonian toothfish as Chilean seabass, slimehead as orange roughy, witch as Torbay sole, oilfish as blue cod, Malabar blood snapper as scarlet snapper, and sablefish as black cod (Jacquet 2009, p. 123; see also Stiles et al. 2011; *Consumer Reports*, 2011; *The Guardian* March 5, 2021). Jacquet and Pauly (2008a,b) described the unfortunate results of both renaming and mislabeling: consumer losses, subversion of ecomarketing, further degradation of fisheries resources and potential adverse effects on human health.

The recent development of ecosystem modeling in a marine environment has gone a long way to explain the underlying reasons for fisheries population collapse, especially the Atlantic cod. In particular, this type of modeling demonstrates how economic signals from the fisheries sector may seriously mislead efforts to understand the nature and extent of the problem of fisheries collapse. By way of example, Figure 11.6 presents the timeline of economic value derived from the Atlantic Canada fisheries over the period 1950 to 2004. The loss of economic value from the collapse of the cod fishery has been compensated for with the advent of other fisheries. But this diagram is essentially a black box version of this transition. The Ecosim and related models allow us not only to look inside this black box, but also to determine their underlying dynamics and significance. Figure 11.7 presents a disaggregation of the historical catch data by principal species. This figure demonstrates that the inflation-adjusted value of just two species – shrimp/prawn and crab – now equal or exceed the former cod-dominated fishery. This emergence of a new and larger market focused on these two large crustaceans appears, in

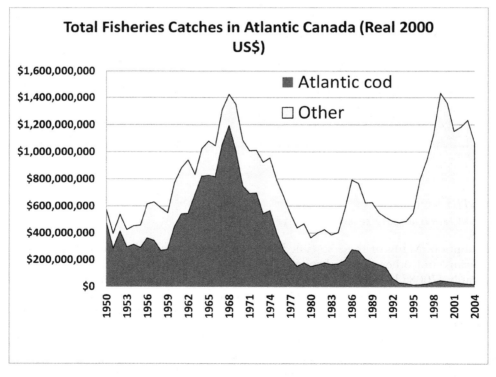

Figure 11.6 Timeline of Economic Value from Atlantic Canada Fisheries 1950–2020

Source: Canada Fisheries Statistics Yearbooks

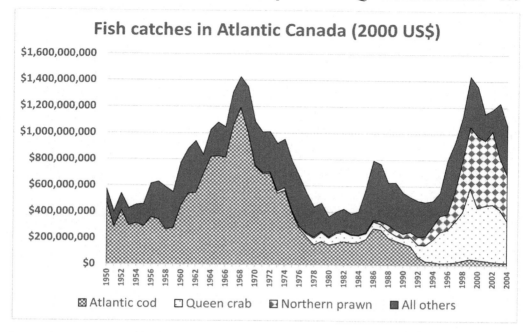

Figure 11.7 Disaggregation of Historical Catch Data

Source: Canada Fisheries Statistics Yearbooks

some respects, to be more attractive than what it replaced, but in fact is a result of fishing down the food web.

The collapse of the cod fishery has led to a radical restructuring of the marine eco-system (called a *trophic cascade* [see Frank et al. 2005; Bundy & Fanning 2005]) where creatures formerly the primary prey of fish from higher trophic levels have now come to assume a much more important place in an ecosystem that has been rendered much less complex due to the loss of larger predatory fish. In simple terms, cod have lost their "ecological niche" with the new dominance of lower-trophic level species, and the system has lost resilience through the marked decrease in biological diversity.

Pauly and others make very clear the potential result of this type of transitioning of global fisheries, using as an example the rapid growth of jellyfish populations in several global locations (see also Richardson et al. 2009). Lynam et al. (2006) and Belhabib (2015) describe the profound ecosystem change that has occurred in the once highly productive Atlantic Ocean off Namibia as traditional fish stocks have entered a period of precipitous decline (see Figure 11.8). There has been a virtual explosion in the number of jellyfish where their biomass (estimated at 12.2 MT) now far exceeds that of other spe-cies. The authors describe this transition as a "trophic dead end," since jellyfish – aside from having little value in the human food chain – have few natural predators. Once this transition to a jellyfish-dominated ecosystem has occurred, it may be very difficult or impossible to reverse by attempting to rebuild the stocks of higher level pelagic fish for several reasons: first, jellyfish feed on fish eggs and larvae, and are strong competitors for fish food; and, second, the concomitant overfishing of sardines off the coast of Namibia, which feed on plankton, has led to a bloom of plankton that, when dying, fall to the sea bottom. This produces an anoxic condition where low levels of oxygen lead to anaerobic

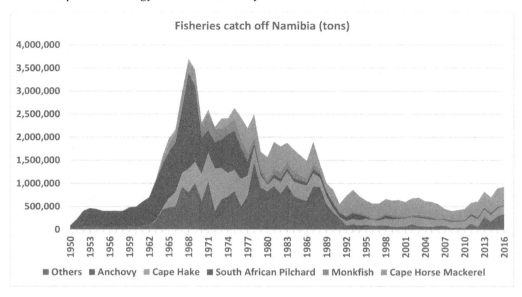

Figure 11.8 Namibia's Fisheries Trends

Source: Belhabib (2015) Reproduced with permission

decay, with the resulting production of methane and hydrogen sulfide. This environment is highly unfavorable to most fish species. There are strong indications that a similar transition to a jellyfish dominated ecosystem may also be occurring in other major fishing grounds, such as the North Sea (Lynam et al 2005; *New York Times* April 30, 2017; Sommer et al. 2002).

Namibia is not the only country experiencing increasing pressure on dwindling fish stocks. In light of depletion of stocks in other oceans, foreign fishing fleets have capitalized on the availability of rich fishing grounds either through illegal intrusion into African and Pacific coastal waters or through controversial intergovernmental agreements for access to the fisheries (AllAfrica.com 2012; Greenpeace 2015; *New York Times* April 30, 2017; Doumbouya et al. 2017; *The Guardian* August 25 and September 17, 2020; Sumaila et al. 2020). Sumaila et al. (2020; see also Daniels et al. 2022; Belhabib & Le Billon 2020, 2022; Welch et al. 2022; Park et al. 2023) conclude:

> Globally, between 8 and 14 million metric tons of unreported catches are potentially traded illicitly yearly, suggesting gross revenues of US$9 to US$17 billion associated with these catches. Estimated loss in annual economic impact due to the diversion of fish from the legitimate trade system is US$26 to US$50 billion, while losses to countries' tax revenues are between US$2 and US$4 billion.

The United Nations (2024) has also estimated the magnitude of related losses, recognizing the uncertainty associated with these estimates. They conclude that "illegal, unreported and upregulated fishing activities are responsible for the loss of 11–26 million tonnes of fish each year, which is estimated to have an economic value of US$10–23 billion.

Compounding the problem of loss of fish to foreign fishing fleets, marine high temperature extremes amplify the impacts of climate change on fish and fisheries where 77% of exploited fishes can experience a loss in biomass (Cheung et al 2021). In addition, nations in the tropics and subtropics are facing the loss of species that are forced to move northward to more hospitable habitat in cooler waters as a result of global warming (Cheung et al. 2009, 2013; Goldfarb 2017; Morley et al. 2018; *New York Times* November 29, 2019 and April 4, 2023). While more northerly fishing nations will have to make the adjustment to a change in species catches, it is unclear what fish will be able to survive in the less hospitable waters nearer the equator. This shift in species' location cannot continue indefinitely, as several studies have forecasted that continued global warming – if unabated – threatens the existence of ocean mass extinctions, including but not limited to fish life (Pinsky & Fredston 2022; Penn & Deutsch 2022).

Adding to the problems of overfishing and climate change have been two additional issues: bottom trawling and the discarding of *bycatch* by industrial, large-scale fisheries. Bottom trawling accounts for more than a quarter of all global catch but has serious environmental effects: overfishing bycatch and seabed damage due to scouring of the seabed (Steadman et al. 2021). Bycatch is defined as marketable fish and other marine organisms that are caught although they were not targeted. Zeller et al. (2018) estimate that the current extent of global bycatch has represented as much as 10–20% of all catches. The loci of most bycatch have shifted over time, from the northern Atlantic in the period 1950s to 1980s, to the West Coast of Africa and, more recently, the Northwest Pacific and Western Central Pacific.

Behind the Current Crisis in Global Fisheries

Two critical questions emerge from this picture of global fisheries decline: what factors are responsible and what are the options available in search of a viable solution? In one of the seminal articles of modern economics, Garrett Hardin (1968) enunciated the principle of the "tragedy of the commons" based on the historical experiences of the English Commons. The inevitable degradation of resources on the commons resulted from unrestricted access. This model has been used to explain the continuing overexploitation of global fisheries resources.

Despite the critique that Hardin had confounded the issue of commons and open access resources, the issue of unlimited access still looms large as a major contributor to the depletion of global fisheries stocks. There is another major factor, however, and that is the chronic overcapitalization of the fisheries industry. As Greboval and Munro (1998:2) state,

> Over the two decades, 1970–1990, world industrial fisheries harvesting capacity grew at a rate eight times greater than the rate of growth of landings from world capture fisheries. One clear indication that something is seriously wrong with the state of harvesting capacity in world fisheries is the fact that the world fishing fleet has continued to expand while accruing significant annual losses for quite some years. Losses of this magnitude are sustainable only because of extensive government subsidy programs. While the estimates of the magnitude of these subsidies differ greatly, it is revealing that the *lowest* estimate puts the subsidies at not less than US$ 8–10 billion per annum.

In fact, Sumaila et al. (2019 and 2022) provided updated estimates of these subsidies ranging as high as $35.4 billion in 2018.

Overcapitalization and concomitant overfishing are also the result of misguided governmental policies which have attempted to control the overexploitation of the fishery resource through such regulatory mechanisms as restricting the number of fishing boat licenses and narrowing of time windows for allowable commercial fishing. Each of these initiatives creates a perverse incentive to overcapitalize. Even in the absence of such governmental intervention, however, a process of overcapitalization and increased application of more sophisticated technology could be expected as a response to the diminished density of fish, leading in turn to smaller total catches and a lower CPUE.

The Future of Global Fisheries

In sum, global fisheries are facing an unprecedented threat to their continued viability with the confluence of several major factors, including increased human population and its demand for marine-based protein, increased per capita consumption of fish, the increased use of wild fisheries stocks devoted to feedstock for the livestock sector, and an increasingly hostile environment driven by climate change and the rising burden of conventional pollutants.

With projected declines in the wild ocean fishery, several major solutions have been advanced which vary in their scope, feasibility and potential effectiveness; most prominent among these is the increased reliance on aquaculture.

Aquaculture

Defined as the artificial and controlled rearing of marine or riverine fish and other waterborne species, aquaculture has emerged as a major contributor to global food supply, with the highest growth rate among food production sectors for the past half century (Hall et al. 2011). Figure 11.9 presents the history of aquaculture in the context of total fisheries production from 1950–2020 (FAO 2022b). Table 11.1 lists the major species currently being produced at the global level (FAO 2022c). The FAO (2022b) has predicted that total output of aquaculture could reach as high as 160 million metric tonnes by 2050, exceeding capture fisheries under all major scenarios (business as usual, low-road and high-road). The largest producer of farmed seafood products is China which has accounted for 58% of global production (FAO 2022b). China has been engaged in aquaculture for millennia (IDRC 1973, Fagan 2017), which involved the use of small ponds on agricultural land that mixed fish, animal manure, and plants in an integrated system (IDRC 1973, Singh et al. 2011) (see Figure 11.10).

Fish farming remains a highly diverse industry in China and is influenced by a variety of government directives and policies. More than 100 freshwater and 60 marine fish species are raised in habitats and infrastructures that include ponds, cages in lakes and coastal waters, and raft and bottom-sowing systems in shallow seas and mud flats. Carps in polyculture, tilapia in monoculture and polyculture, and penaeid shrimp in monoculture are three of the largest subsectors, constituting over half of China's total aquaculture production by volume. In 2012, China produced >90% of the world's carp, 50% of global penaeid shrimp, and 40% of global tilapia (Cao et al. 2015).

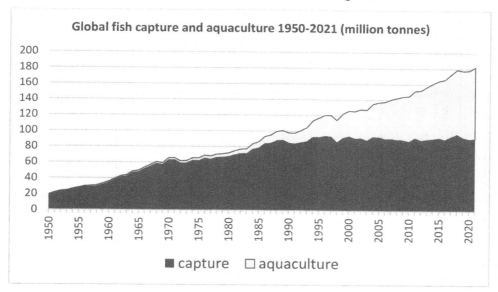

Figure 11.9 Aquaculture History 1950–2021
Source: FAO 2023

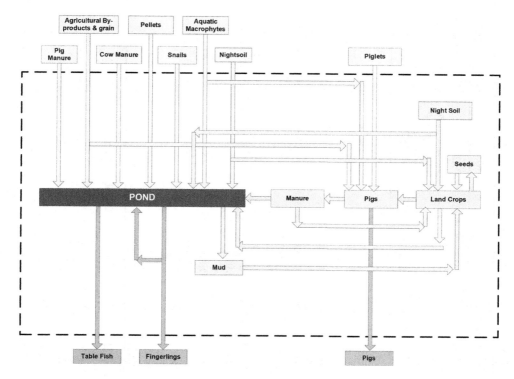

Figure 11.10 Chinese Integrated Fish Farm Schematic
Adapted from IDRC 1972

Table 11.1 Major Aquaculture Species

World aquaculture production, 2020

Top 10 species groups

Species group	ISSCAAP division	Number of ASFIS species items in the group farmed in world aquaculture	Number of countries farming the species group	World production Quantity of the species group (live weight; tonnes)	Share of world production value of all species (%)	Vaue in 2019 US$ million	% of total value
1. Carps, barbels and other cyprinids	Freshwater fishes	42	95	30,568,763	24.94%	$ 63,234	24.4%
2. Red seaweeds	Algae	11	34	18,123,262	14.78%		
3. Brown seaweeds	Algae	9	13	16,841,615	13.74%	$ 40,674	15.7%
4. Marine shrimps and prawns	Crustaceans	15	63	6,863,413	5.60%		
5. Oysters	Molluscs	13	46	6,260,194	5.11%	$ 7,243	2.8%
6. Tilapians and other cichlids	Freshwater species	17	124	6,104,312	4.98%	$ 12,347	4.8%
7. Catfishes	Freshwater species	34	91	6,019,881	4.91%		
8. Clams, cockles, arkshells	Molluscs	25	24	5,742,807	4.68%	$ 9,667	3.7%
9. *Salmons, trouts, smelts*	*Diadromous fishes*	23	81	4,035,973	3.29%	$ 23,219	8.9%
10. Freshwater fishes nei	Freshwater fishes	1	71	2,854,069	2.33%		
Other species		258	n.a.	19,165,898	15.64%		
ALL SPECIES		448	197	122,580,187	100.00%	$ 259,547	100.0%

Source: FAO (2022a) Top 10 species groups in global aquaculture 2020

A modern terminology for this type of production is "Integrated Multitrophic Aquaculture," which has several distinct advantages over single species production: "IMTA uses coculture of organisms of different trophic levels (TLs) to reduce nutrient concentrations to a point that they do not cause ecological damage, such as eutrophication, harmful algal blooms, or green tides. In IMTA systems, various plant and filter-feeding organisms convert waste from fed aquaculture into growth" (Klinger and Naylor 2012, p. 254).

On-land pool-based production remains the most common form of global aquaculture, especially in Asia. While such fishponds are still common in many agricultural areas in China, the country is beginning to adopt larger scale and what are deemed to be more *economically efficient* production practices associated with open net marine-based aquaculture for some species with attendant ecological consequences (Chen et al. 2007; Mayer 2018; *South China Morning Post* May 5, 2018).

In addition to China, numerous jurisdictions around the world (such as Norway, Chile, the United Kingdom and British Columba) have now moved to significant production of farmed fish, particularly Atlantic Salmon. While salmon account for only 3.3% of total global aquaculture production, their value is 8.9%, particularly because this fish is considered a premium product among western consumers. Salmon farming is the fastest growing sector of the seafood industry and its production now represents almost three-quarters of all global salmon production (both wild and farmed) (WWF n.d.; FAO 2017). A significant proportion of the production of salmon, along with shrimp and tilapia, is traded internationally. In contrast, carp, the aquaculture product accounting for the largest share of industry production, is largely farmed and consumed domestically in China (Intrafish 2020b). Rising global population, urbanization and income are shifting food demand toward animal protein, and fish, particularly. Of special note is that salmon has a particularly high resource-efficient production ratio of 56 kg of edible meat per 100 kg of feed, in comparison with 39 for poultry, 19 for pork, and 7 for beef (Mowi 2022).

Mowi ASA

While there are numerous companies involved in salmon aquaculture at the global level, the Norwegian firm, Mowi, has emerged as the world's largest with more than double the production of the second largest producer (Intrafish 2020b). In 2018, its predecessor, Marine Harvest, changed its name back to to Mowi, in honour of its founder Thor Mowinckel (Frantz and Collins 2022). Mowi is a vertically integrated producer including feed production, salmon raising and an increasing presence in consumer-ready products under a Mowi-branded label. Table 11.2 lists the location of Mowi's ocean-based fish farms; Figure 11.11 shows historical production volume; Tables 11.3a-c list current financials; Figure 11.12 summarizes the last 12 years of revenue and profit (Mowi annual reports multiple years); and Figure 11.13 displays Mowi's stock price over the period 2008–2023. (Note: over that period, the USD to NOK exchange rate dropped from 5.1 to 10.6). The company's fortunes are inexorably tied to the price of salmon. The historical price for this fish is shown in Figure 11.14 and the relationship between this price and Mowi's profitability is shown in Figure 11.15 (F=19.119 p. = 0.0014; t statistic = 4.3726, p=0.0014). This is clearly the reason why the stated ultimate goal of the company is to decommoditize the salmon market over time by expanding into new global markets for its final products.

In its 2021 annual report, Mowi reported that it had been "recognized as the world's most sustainable animal protein producer for the third year running." The company's

Table 11.2 **Locations of Mowi production**

	2023	
Country	*GWT*	*%*
Norway	294,501	62%
Chile	69,199	15%
Scotland	54,950	12%
Canada	28,575	6%
Iceland	11,878	3%
Faroes	11,027	2%
Ireland	4,534	1%
TOTAL	474,664	100%

Source: Mowi Annual Report (2022)

Table 11.3 Mowi Financial Statements

Mowi Group *(EUR million)*	2023	2022
Revenue	5 478.3	4 907.3
Other income	27.5	33.5
Revenue and other income	**5 505.7**	**4 940.8**
Cost of materials	-2 738,1	-2 283.1
Net fair value adjustment biornass	37.4	113.7
Salary and personnel expenses	-647.9	-612.6
Other operating expenses	-696.5	-671.6
Depreciation and amortisation	-403.8	-386.6
Onerous contracts provision	-18.3	-8.3
Restructuring costs and other provisions	-4.9	-13.7
License/production fees	-40.7	-22.5
Other non-operational items	-16.6	-2.1
Income/loss from associated companies and joint ventures	28.4	59.2
Impairment losses & write-downs	-23.5	-59.5
Earnings before financial items (EBIT)	**981.0**	**1 053.8**
Interest expenses	-113.1	-52.6
Net currency effects	35.9	1.4
Other financial items	-5.1	-1.8
Earnings before taxes	**898.7**	**1 000.9**
Income taxes	**-459.2**	**-215.5**
Profit or loss for the year	**439.5**	**785.4**
Other comprehensive income		
Currency translation differences	-41.1	-19.2
Total items to be reclassified to profit or loss in subsequent periods	**-41.1**	**-19.2**
Actuarial gains (losses) on defined benefit plans net of tax	-5.8	-7.9
Total items not to be reclassified to profit or loss	**-5.8**	**-7.9**
Total other comprehensive income	**-46.9**	**-27.0**

(*Continued*)

Table 11.3 (Continued)

Mowi Group (EUR million)	2023	2022
Comprehensive income for the year	**392.6**	**758.3**
Profit or loss for the year attributable to		
Non-controlling interests	-4.9	3.0
Owners of Mowi ASA	444.4	782.4
Comprehensive income for the year attributable to		
Non-controlling interests	-17.4	3.0
Owners of Mowi ASA	410.0	755.3
Earnings per share - basic and diluted (EUR)	0.86	1.51
Earnings per share for continuing operations - basic and diluted (EUR)	0.86	1.51
ASSETS		
Non-current assets		
Licenses	1 213.9	1 194.2
Goodwill	368.1	371.4
Deferred tax assets	76.0	69.1
Other intangible assets	32.5	29.8
Total intangible assets	**1 690.4**	**1 664.5**
Property, plant and equipment	1 883.9	1 711.0
Right-of-use assets	470.1	452.1
Investments in associated companies and joint ventures	211.7	211.7
Other non-current financial assets	2.7	2.7
Other non-current assets	0.6	0.6
Total non-current assets	**4 259.5**	**4 042.6**
Current assets		
Inventory	605.1	603.9
Biological assets	2 143.6	1 912.5
Trade receivables	654.3	600.1
Other receivables	253.7	183.7
Other current financial assets	19.9	10.0
Restricted cash	14.5	7.6
Cash in bank	288.4	170.9
Total current assets	**3 979.5**	**3 488.7**
Total assets	**8 239.0**	**7 531.3**
EQUITY AND LIABILITIES		
Equity		
Share capital and reserves attributable to owners of Mowi ASA	3 593.3	3 507.5
Non-controlling interests	161.4	179.7
Total equity	**3 754.7**	**3 687.1**
Non-current liabilities		
Deferred tax liabilities	820.4	332.4
Non-current interest-bearing debt	2 093.0	1 725.8
Non-current leasing liabilities	299.3	239.4
Other non-current liabilities	6.6	8.2

(Continued)

Table 11.3 (Continued)

Mowi Group (EUR million)	2023	2022
Total non-current liabilities	**3 219.3**	**2 355.7**
Current liabilities		
Current tax liabilities	184.4	377.4
Current interest-bearing debt	0.1	211.6
Current leasing liabilities	174.5	173.5
Trade payables	560.7	437.0
Other current financial liabilities	6.3	11.9
Provisions	44.8	33.7
Other current liabilities	293.9	243.3
Total current liabilities	**1264.8**	**1 488.4**
Total equity and liabilities	**8 239.0**	**7 531.3**
Cash flow from operations		
Earnings before taxes	898.7	1 000.9
Interest expenses	113.1	52.6
Net currency effects	-35.9	-1.4
Other financial items	5.1	1.8
Impairment losses, depreciation and amortisation	427.4	446.1
Net fair value adjustment on biological assets and onerous contracts	-20.3	-105.5
Income from associated companies and joint ventures	-28.4	-59.2
Taxes paid	-219.6	118.3
Change in inventory, trade payables and trade receivables	-173.5	-491.4
Restructuring and other provisions	-2.6	-48.3
Other adjustments	28.2	-32.3
Cash flow from operations	**992.2**	**644.8**
Cash flow from investments		
Sale of fixed assets	7.9	9.3
Purchase of fixed assets and additions to intangible assets	-396.3	-335.2
Proceeds and dividend from associates and other investments	18.7	59.1
Purchase of shares and other investments	-43.9	-202.6
Cash flow from investments	**-413.6**	**-469.4**
Cash flow from financing		
Proceeds (payments of) interest-bearing debt (current and non-current)	158.9	499.9
Down payment leasing debt	-196.2	-199.6
Interest received	6.4	2.0
Interest paid	-110.0	-51.1
Realised currency effects	8.8	29.4
Dividend	-326.1	-380.6
Cash flow from financing	**-458.2**	**-99.9**
Currency effects on cash	-2.8	0.5
Net change in cash in period	**117.6**	**75.9**
Cash - opening balance	170.8	94.9
Cash - closing balance total	**288.4**	**170.8**

Source: MOWI Annual Report (2022)

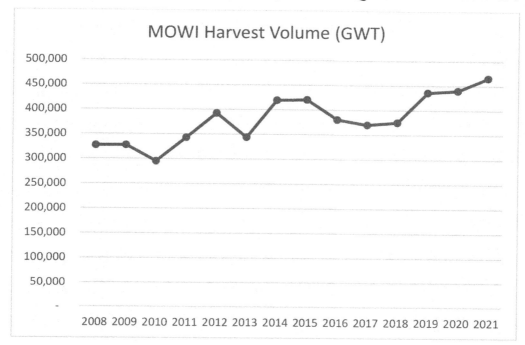

Figure 11.11 Mowi Historical Production Volume

Source: Mowi Annual Reports

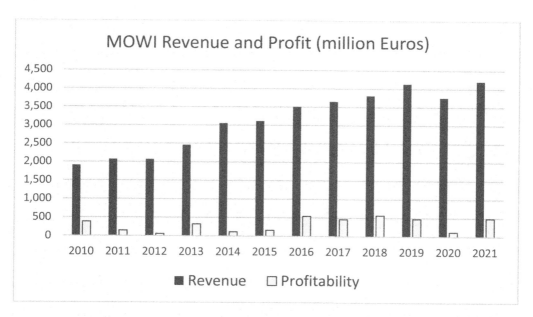

Figure 11.12 Mowi Recent Trends in Revenue and Profit

Source: Mowi Annual Reports

Figure 11.13 Mowi Stock Price 2008–2023
Source: Yahoo Finance

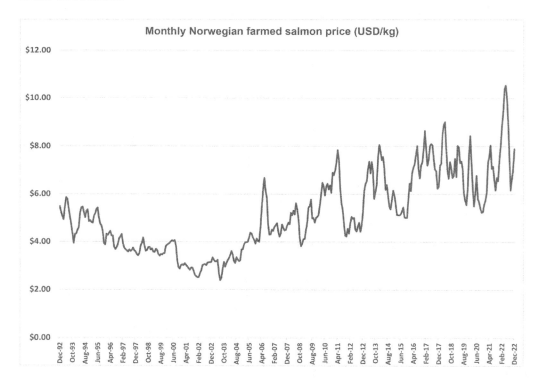

Figure 11.14 Historical Prices for Salmon
Source: Index Mundi based on IMF data

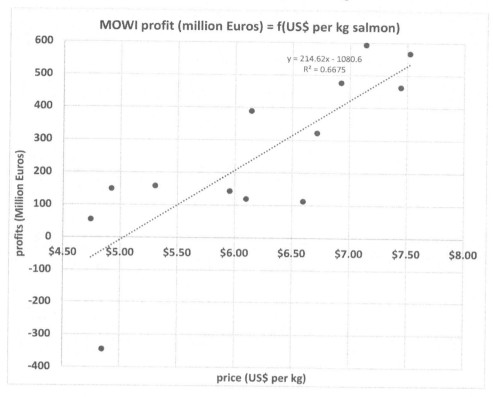

Figure 11.15 Relationship Between Salmon Prices and Mowi Profitability

stated goal is to lead "The Blue Revolution" by raising in a sustainable fashion the share of ocean-sourced foods globally from its current level of only 2%. Figure 11.16 reproduces a table from the company's latest annual report, which lists its sustainability ratings, awards, and framework. Table 11.4 summarizes key ecological indicators for the company. Note that *Fish-in Fish-out* (FIFO) is defined as the ratio of wild fish caught used to produce 1 kg of farm-raised salmon. To quote the 2021 annual report:

In 2021, Mowi Farming used 0.8 kg of wild caught fish to produce 1 kg of farm-raised salmon – comparatively in 2020 we used 0.68 kg. We sourced a high proportion of marine ingredients from the northern hemisphere in 2021, much in line with the situation in 2020. The increase of FIFO in 2021 is related with disruption of the supply of fish feed ingredients. In particular, the market for vegetable feed raw materials such as wheat gluten and pea protein concentrate was highly disrupted when the European ports were unable to both trans ship cargos of Asian-origin materials or indeed, distribute the European-made equivalent products. As a result of these supply chain disruptions and in order not to compromise the nutritional integrity of our feeds, it was necessary for Mowi to default to the use of fishmeal which, due to its proximity to our facilities, remained available to buy and receive at relatively short notice. Despite increasing the amount of fishmeal consumed, we were able to achieve this increase without compromising the sustainability of our sources. The value of FIFO of 0.8 is further reduced to 0.68 (recapture FIFO, rFIFO) if one takes into account the recapture marine raw materials, i.e. the fact that the salmon byproducts after processing are used to produce fish meal and oil used for other aquaculture (non-salmon) species and pet food.

Figure 11.16 Mowi's Ratings and Awards

Source: Mowi Annual Report 2021, p. 23

Table 11.4 Mowi Key Ecological Indicators

MOWI Annual Report (2021, p. 50)				
	sustainability certification (% of sites certified)	*Fish in fish out (FIFO)*	*GHG emissions (tonnes CO_2e) - scope 1 and 2*	*GHG emissions (tonnes CO_2e) - scope 3*
2010	na	na	na	na
2011	na	na	na	na
2012	na	na	81,018	na
2013	na	0.8	83,912	na
2014	4%	0.8	105,509	na
2015	24%	0.74	159,757	na
2016	26%	0.77	200,483	na
2017	31%	0.73	294,251	na
2018	34%	0.75	325,359	1,950,541
2019	37%	0.66	356,762	1,979,211
2020	45%	0.68	322,836	1,941,085
2021	50%	0.8	269,020	1,992,528
2022	47%	0.76	244,930	1,936,197
2023	55%	0.78	233,663	2,135,209

Ref 2023 Mowi annual report, p. 323

The Ecological Complexities of Ocean-Based Farmed Salmon Production

While aquaculture has been portrayed as the ultimate solution to the inability of the wild fisheries to feed a growing and more affluent global population, there are a number of significant issues that are associated with the use of marine-based open net systems which emerge from the application of systems theory (Pew Oceans Commission 2003). The first is the presence of environmental externalities associated with the common method of marine farming (Naylor et al. 1998). These include the release of greenhouse gases from the supply chain for fish farms (especially the production of feed) (Intrafish 2020a; FAO 2017), the impact of concentrated releases of fish-related waste, such as ammonium, phosphorus, fecal matter, and excess feed, into the immediate environment, as well as the indirect impact of penned salmon rearing on wild salmon stocks and human health (see, for example, *New York Times* November 6, 2017; Nyland et al. 2019; and Mordecai et al. 2021). Attention has been focused, in particular, on the decrease in wild stocks near fish farms, and empirical evidence that lice have been spreading from farmed to wild salmon populations (Krkosek et al. 2007; *New York Times*, November 6, 2017; Urbina 2021). Intrafish (2019) has reported that the annual losses to Chile's salmon-farming industry due to lice has run as high as $350 million, while Solheim and Trovatn (2019) report Norwegian losses in excess of NOK 15 billion over the period 2016–2019. Veterinaerinstituttet (2018, p. 5) has reported that the "injurious effect of salmon lice remains the major health-related problem in Norwegian Aquaculture." (see also Just Economics 2021).

WatershedWatch (2024) has described the negative impacts of fish farming on multiple species in addition to wild salmon, including humpback whales, orca whales, seals and sea lions, birds, sharks and other types of wild fish.

There is also and indirect impact on human health related to the use of antibiotics in fish farming in a manner like that found in animal feedlots (UVic GAPI 2010; FAO/WHO/OIE 2007). The use of antibiotics has been mandated by the high density of the penned stock. These drugs are required to counteract natural forces (i.e., disease), which act to reduce the number of animals in a highly crowded environment. Epidemiological models of diseases (Anderson & May 1979; May & Anderson 1979) identify density as one of the critical determining factors in the development of epidemics, their spread and endurance. There is strong, if not conclusive, evidence that one of the major causes of emerging bacterial resistance to antibiotics is overuse of pharmaceuticals in both fish and livestock (FAO 2007, 2018a). Through a process of Darwinian selection, the overuse and misuse of antimicrobials inadvertently breeds stronger and more resistant bacteria, thereby threatening the continued usefulness of antibiotic therapy. In recognition of this systemic problem, Norway and several other countries such as the UK, Ireland and Canada have employed vaccines to effectively combat bacterial infections although Chile and Vietnam still rely heavily on antibiotics (Naylor et al. 2021; Vererinaerinstituttet 2021; Henriksson et al. 2018).

These advances against bacteria, however, do not prevent the infection of farmed fish by viruses, and the nature of confined rearing has led to massive losses of stock in both Chile and Norway and viruses remain an endemic problem (Thorud & Djupvik 1988; Kongtorp et al. 2014; *New York Times* March 27, 2008 and July 27 2011; OECD 2009; Vererinaerinstituttet 2021). Several jurisdictions, such as British Columbia, have been able to trace outbreaks of viruses to fish farms in Norway (The Canadian Press 2021). The fundamental issue is one of private versus social costs. In this case, short-term and narrowly defined concepts of economic efficiency give the appearance of a cost-effective system for fish production only because it excludes major negative externalities.

The fisheries economist, Professor Rashid Sumaila, has coined the term "Infinity Fish" (Sumaila 2022), which refers to natural systems (such as wild fisheries) that generate an infinite and essentially self-sustaining stream of benefits at essentially zero or minimal cost. Modern aquaculture replaces this natural system by an anthropogenic process that requires an annual infusion of time, money, and effort in order to generate product. If this effort is interrupted at any point, the future stream is jeopardized, if not destroyed. Again, the fundamental trade-off is one of short-term economic *efficiency* versus long-term system *resilience* (i.e., the capacity to recover from shocks). Table 11.5 summarizes the principal differences between farmed and wild fisheries. The human-constructed systems are much more vulnerable to shocks which can reduce or eliminate their stock in a very short period of time. This is truly a Faustian bargain that fails the test of sustainability.

In addition to the issue of interspecies transfer of parasites, there is another potential threat to natural stocks. There is documented evidence from such important fish farming areas as Scotland and Norway that, in the presence of fish farms, wild salmon completely disappear from many local rivers with traditional salmon runs. It is unclear at this point whether this is due to the fact that escaped stocks of farmed salmon are outcompeting local wild salmon or are crossbreeding and producing a hybrid which is less suited to survival in local ecosystems (see for example Moreau et al. 2011). It has been reported that over the decade 2010–2020, over 2 million fish escaped from Norwegian fish farms (Intrafish 2020D).

The final, and perhaps most critical issue with respect to much of farmed fish is found in the application of systems analysis. Some of the species now widely reared commercially, such as salmon, are carnivorous and rely on a significant input of fish-based products for food. Table 11.6 lists some of the major farmed species and two measures of the ratio of wild fish input to farmed fish output (Naylor et al. 2000, 2021). There are herbivorous fish whose ratio of wild fish to farmed fish use/production is less than 1.0, raising the prospect of a positive net output of fish food. A more exhaustive systems-based analysis of the production of farmed fish is made possible using lifecycle analysis (Ayer

Table 11.5 Farmed vs. wild fisheries

Characteristic	Wild fish	Farmed Fish
Time horizon	infinite	approx. one year
Reproduction	natural	human-assisted
Food Source	natural	human supplied
Food cost	free	costly
Rearing	natural	human-assisted
Resilience	high	low
Resistance to pathogens	high	low
Annual human intervention required for survival	NO	YES
Net gain in biomass (carniverous species)	YES	NO
Negative externalities	NO	YES

& Tyedmers 2009; Pelletier et al. 2009) or by a methodology called *fishprinting*, which represents the application of ecological footprinting to a marine environment. This incorporates a broad range of factors including biological inputs (e.g., fish meal, agricultural crops, and livestock byproducts used as feed), labor, fossil fuel, and electricity use (Talberth et al. 2006).

As in most sustainability issues, systems analysis is the gold standard for assessing ecological viability. One recent paper (Hilborn et al. 2018) conducted a comprehensive literature review of research studies, which focussed on animal source food production for livestock, aquaculture, and capture fisheries. They measured energy use, greenhouse-gas emissions, release of nutrients, acidifying compounds, freshwater demand, pesticide use, and antibiotic use. The authors found up to 100-fold differences in impacts between specific products and, in some cases, for the same product, depending on the production method being used. The lowest impact production methods were small pelagic fisheries and mollusk aquaculture, whereas the highest impact production methods were beef production and catfish aquaculture, suggesting that even some forms of herbivorous aquaculture are not without problems. As stated, in those cases where this ratio exceeds 1.0, there is a net loss of total fish mass available for consumption. Clearly, this cannot be a solution to the increasing demand for fish as food. It has been estimated that currently aquaculture accounts for approximately 70% of total annual consumption of fish meal and fish oil (Intrafish 2020c). Recognition of the inherent limits to this form of feed has led the industry to explore alternatives, including insects, algae, plant-based ingredients, and gas fermentation of nitrogen, methane, and ethanol to produce food protein (Intrafish 2020c). Any increased demand for crop-based feeds will increase competition with food crops destined for human consumption. An additional concern derived from lifecycle analysis of the systemic effects of feed is that this crucial input accounts for more than 90% of the environmental impact from aquacultural production (Little et al. 2017; Newton & Little 2018).

Table 11.6 Major Farmed Species inputs

Farmed Fish	Naylor 2000 Ratio of wild fish to fed farmed*	Naylor et al. 2021 FIFO in 2017
Marine finfish	5.16	1.25
Eel	4.69	2.98
Marine Shrimp	2.81	0.82
Salmon	3.16	1.87
Trout	2.46	1.82
Tilapia	1.41	0.03
Milkfish	0.94	0.07
Catfish	0.84	0.02
Carp: Fed	0.75	0.02

* = ratio of wild fish used for fishmeal to farmed production using compound feeds.
** = wild fish inputs to fed fish output
Sources: Naylor 2000, 2009, 2021 [See also FAO 2022a,b,c]

Mowi is conscious of many of these drawbacks and this recognition is reflected in their analysis of potential risk factors listed in their 2021 annual report. These include:

- Risks related to the sale and supply of our products
- Risks related to governmental regulations
- Risks related to our fish farm operations
- Risks related to our supply of fish feed and our feed operations
- Risks related to our industry
- Risks related to our business
- Risks related to our financing arrangements
- Risks related to tax and legal matters
- Risks related to climate change
- Risks related to cyber security and technological innovation
- Risks related to our strategy – acquisitions and expansions
- Risks related to reporting
- Risks related to other legal matters

While many of these risks are generic to business, many apply to the fish farming industry and Mowi in particular. A full description of each of these risks and their components

Table 11.7 Summary of Mowi's Sustainability Strategy

Category	Goals/Targets
Climate change	Achieve science-based targets: Reduce our total (Scope 1,2 and 3) GHG emissions by 35% until 2030 and 72% until 2050
Plastics	By 2025, 100% of our plastic packaging will be reusable, recyclable or compostable
	By 2025 at least 25% of plastic packaging will come from recycled plastic content
	By 2023, all plastic farming equipment (nets, ropes, feeding pipes) is reused or recycled
Waste	By 2025, Zero waste to landfill at our processing plants
Freshwater Use	By 2025, achieve a reduction of 10% on water intensity at our processing plants located in medium-high water scarcity risk* (using 2018 as reference year)
Sustainability certifications	100% of harvest volumes sustainably certified by a GSSI-recognised standard
	100% of farming sites with minimum benthic impact (as defined per national regulations)
Sustainable feed	100% traceability of feed raw materials
	100% of marine raw materials are certified (Marin Trust or equivalent)
	• 100% of soy is certified (ProTerra or equivalent)
	• Towards lower FCR
	Towards lower carbon footprint of feed raw materials
Fish health & welfare	By 2025, 99.5% survival in sea (average month)*
	• Reduction in antibiotic use from 2015
	By 2023 minimum 50% of our stock with real time welfare monitoring
Sea lice	0% of sites above national limit (monthly average)
Escapes	Positive trend towards zero-escapes
	100% of site personnel trained on Mowi's
	Farming Excellence Program – Zero escapes

Source: Mowi (2022)

is presented in the appendix to this chapter. It is particularly noteworthy that climate change also poses a threat to both wild fish and fish farms in their current manifestation as increased temperature will lead to increased stress, lower production and mortality (for example, see *The Guardian* May 26, 2022).

Mowi is being proactive with respect to many of these risks and Table 11.7 lists summarizes the components and goals of their sustainability strategy.

Despite these efforts, Mowi has encountered several significant problems with respect to their operations. As reported in the general and industry press, these include:

- April 22, 2019 "Kerry Fish Farm Licence Discontinued After Probe," *Irish Examiner*
- May 20, 2019 "Fish farms under investigation for allegedly breaking environmental rules," *The Ferret.*
- May 20 2019 "Salmon farming giant Mowi probed over chemical use," *BBC.*
- August 12, 2019 "Proposed salmon farm raises environmental concerns in Hebrides," *The Guardian.*
- August 22, 2019 "Mowi pledge to tackle smell and noise issues at Kyleakin fishfeed plant," *West Highland Free Press.*
- October 30, 2019 "Mowi's strong growth in Norway offset by major problems in Canada," *Salmonbusiness.com*
- November 10, 2019 "Salmon company Moiw rapped over fish welfare after 700,000 deaths," *The National* (Scotland)
- August 17, 2020 "ISA suspected at troubled Mowi salmon farming operation in Canada," *Intrafish.*
- August 26, 2020 "Scotland problems force Mowi to cut harvest target," *Fishfarmingexpert.*
- August 31, 2020 "Mowi forced to empty cage as ISA confirmed at Canada farm site," *Atlantic Salmon Foundation.*
- April 2, 2021 "Mowi USA Ducktrap Salmon Class Action settlement updates 2021 – $25 for each class member from $1.3 million . . .," *Considertheconsumer.com.*
- May 11, 2021 "North wind gives Mowi hope of salvaging crop after Bantry Bay die-off," *Fishfarmingexpert.*
- October 26, 2021 "Mowi exploring impact of micro-jellyfish on salmon health Mowi exploring impact of micro-jellyfish on salmon health," *Seafoodsource.com.*
- November 11, 2021 "Mowi pauses NL expansion after near $8M hit on salmon problems," *Atlantic Salmon Federation.*
- November 12, 2021 "Mowi Scotland profits hit by poor fish health and price deflation," *The Grocer.*
- December 19, 2021 'State body concerned over Mowi Ireland plans for Connemara fish farm," *Afloat.ie*

Perhaps the most significant incident – one particularly relevant to fish farming as recently practiced – was the aforementioned Chilean fish farm disaster that affected Marine Harvest, Mowi's former corporate name. Millions of salmon were lost to a virus called infectious salmon anemia (or ISA) Several problems were identified with these Chilean operations, including high stocking levels associated with fish pens in too close proximity to each other, and excessive use of antibiotics, colorants, and fungicides (OECD 2009). An additional concern is the threat of algae to farmed salmon. While algae can pose a problem in tank-based systems, the marine environment presents a much more hospitable medium for their growth. Diaz et al. (2019) reported that a major algae bloom in Chile in 2016 led to the loss of 40,000 tonnes of farmed salmon at a cost of $800 million USD. A similar bloom in 2018 killed 250,000 salmon at two fish farms in British Columbia (*Vancouver Sun* June 12, 2018). Climate change can contribute to the increasing frequency and severity of such blooms, posing a significant threat to marine-based aquaculture.

All these factors lead to significant concerns about the long-term viability of much of modern aquacultural practices: and whether the strategy pursued by Mowi, in particular, is ultimately sustainable. This is particularly the case because several jurisdictions have recently brought in regulation banning the installation and operation of fish farms in tidal waters. These include: Alaska, Washington, and California, and British Columbia is considering following suit with similar bans on all open-net-pen salmon farms after the Canadian federal government ordered their phase out in selected areas on the BC coast (Canada 2020; Owens 2022; Times Colonist 2022; Vancouver Sun November 23 2022; Associated Press 2022; CBC February 17 2023; Intrafish 2023). In addition, both Norway and Chile have instituted more restrictions on new licenses (Mowi 2022). Ultimately, biological constraints, seawater temperature requirements and other natural constraints limit the geographic availability of suitable sits for marine-based aquaculture to certain coast lines within a small number of countries such as Norway, Chile, Scotland, the Faroe Islands, Iceland, Canada, USA, Tasmania, and New Zealand (Mowi 2022).

One recent study (Just Economics 2021) concluded that since 2013, pollution, spread of disease, pests and high mortality rates in ocean-based systems in Chile, Norway, Canada, and Scotland incurred costs of $47 billion, composed of $28.1 billion economic costs, $14.5 billion in environmental costs, and $4.7 billion in social costs.

On-Land, Closed-Circuit Technology

If this reconceptualization of the risks of fish farms become more widespread, the profound change in the operation environment have led some fish farmers to seek alternative methods to raise fish for the global market. One of the most recent innovations being adopted by several companies is to use on-land closed-circuit pens which eliminate many, but not all, of the negative environmental externalities associated with current industry practice (*New York Times* October 17, 2023). Intrafish (2019) lists 73 land-based salmon projects in the following countries with estimated annual production ranging from 90–220,000 metric tonnes:

Norway	25
USA	11
Canada	4
China	3
Sweden	3
France	3
Japan	3
Denmark	3
Iceland	2
Russia	2
UAE	2

Poland	2
Chile	1
Belgium	1
Spain	1
Brunei	1
Finland	1
Germany	1
Switzerland	1
Lesotho	1
S. Africa	1

Solheim and Trovatn (2019) had reported 809,450 MT planned production capacity equal to 32.3% of global production in 2018. One of the principal barriers to the adoption of this new technology is cost. Clearly, any transition to land-based, closed containment systems will involve both capital and operating costs associated with the construction of holding tanks and buildings, electricity, ventilation, water temperature, and chemical balance control, filters, and specialized feed requirements in addition to those relevant to current in-water systems, such as disease control. (see, for example, Bjorndal and Tusvik 2019; Canada 2020). Table 11.8 summarizes some of the differences between these two systems.

Table 11.8 Some Major Differences between open-net and closed Salmon Aquaculture Systems

	Open-net	*Closed systems*
Sea Lice	yes	no
Negative Interaction with wild species	yes	no
Detrimental discharges to the environment	yes	no
Capital investments	modest	significant
Feed costs	major	major
Feed storage costs	yes	lower
Threat of closure or bans	yes	no
High FIFO ratio	yes	yes
Vulnerability to disease from high density stocking	yes	yes
vulnerability to increased ambient temperature, marine water quality, storms, and strong currents	yes	no
vulerabiity to predators	yes	no
vulnerability to hydrozoans	yes	no
Competition with commercial fisheriess and recreation	yes	no
vulerability to toxic algae blooms	yes	no
potential early maturation of Atlantic Salmon	no	yes
can be locad near major markets	with difficulty	easily
limited locations for further development	yes	no
potential for off-taste problems	no	yes
Carbon footprint in CO_2e per kg at producer gate* [Liu et al. 2016]	3.75–15.22	4.14–7.41

* depending on mode of transport and form of energy used

Early estimates of the transition costs from open-net to closed systems were gross overestimates. More recent data suggest a more modest cost premium. Estimates by the Norwegian University of Science and Technology (Bjorndal & Tusvik 2017) suggest a land-based cost of 38.7 NOK/kg vs. 28.54–29.88 NOK/kg for traditional methods depending on the grow out of 100-g vs 410 g smolts. Estimates from the Norwegian Directorate of Fisheries as reported by Bjorndal and Tusvik (2018) suggest that traditional open-pen farming has costs 30.5% lower than land-based facilities, while Liu et al. (2016) suggest only a 10% premium. An additional degree of uncertainty in the cost estimates of sea-based production is associated with the uncertainty related to lice-related costs The comparative cost estimates are likely to shift as sea-based systems face a more stringent regulatory environment. Despite this apparent current cost disadvantage for on-land systems, there are several important conclusions: first, numerous companies have conducted their own risk analysis and clearly determined that investment in land-based systems are worth the investment; second, the price of salmon has trended upward for the last several decades (see Figure 11.14) and this trend is expected to continue, creating a more favourable environment for the introduction of new technologies; and third, there are certain inherent advantages associated with land-based systems which tend to favour them over open-net sea-based production. To quote Liu et al. (2016):

> Land-based, closed containment water recirculating aquaculture systems technology offers the ability to fully control the rearing environment and provides flexibility in locating a production facility close to the market and on sites where cost of land and power are competitive. This flexibility offers distinct advantages over Atlantic salmon produced in open net pen systems, which is dependent on access to suitable coastal waters and a relatively long transport distance to supply the US market.

Despite the inherent attractiveness of land-based closed containment systems, the finances remain a challenge, and numerous start-ups have succumbed to bankruptcy. Intrafish (2019) has identified at least twenty such corporations which lost the battle to survive from 1991 to 2015. While land-based systems will probably be the dominant systems for salmon aquaculture in the medium to long-term, there are numerous concerns and issues which are relevant to current production systems. Naylor et al. (2021:558) state that "Recirculating aquaculture systems [RAS] have lower direct land and water requirements than conventional aquaculture and enable higher stocking densities but are constrained by large energy requirements, high production costs, waste disposal challenges, and risk of catastrophic disease failure."

In addition, two recent surveys elaborate on the challenges and research needs of the sector. In a 2012 survey focussed on the main issues on management and future challenges for RAS systems, Badiola et al. (2012) identified at least six crucial information and research needs: engineering, management, construction, viability, financial, and cultured species biology. The second survey conducted in 2018 (Badiola et al. 2018) identified five major issues: energy use-environmental impacts, decrease of feed conversion ratio (FCR), animal welfare enhancement, fish meal alternatives, and chemical usage decrease.

Despite the apparent trade-offs inherent in moving from marine, open-pen systems to land-based closed containment, there is one factor which tilts the balance markedly in favour of the latter, namely the impact of continuing and accelerating climate change. The effects of climate change are multifaceted and include extreme weather, precipitation and surge-based flooding, water stress, ocean acidification, sea-level rise, saltwater intrusion, changes to temperatures, salinity, dissolved oxygen, toxic algae blooms, hypoxia and the occurrence and virulence, growth rates, intensity of host, and infectious diseases and parasites (Barange et al. 2018; Reid et al. 2019). "While infectious diseases are common in marine environments . . . land-based management of quarantining, culling and vaccination are not successful in the ocean" (Burge et al. 2014).

As stated, within the last few years many land-based proposals have been advanced and numerous companies have been established. It is the consensus among industry experts however, that many of these will fall by the wayside for lack of expertise and inability to find adequate capital. One company, in particular, has become the bell-wether for the prospects of future industry success. Founded in 2010, Atlantic Sapphire, owner by Norwegian investors has a relatively small operation in in Denmark but a substantial operation in Florida due to its location in the leading national market for salmon (Mowi 2022). The company goal is to produce 220,000 tonnes of fish by 2030 and was able to begin actual production in 2020. Actual production was 2400 tons in 2021. Their road so far has not been without challenges. In three separate incidents in Denmark and Florida, the company sustained massive die-offs of their fish stocks due to a number of diverse causes: for example, in March 2020 they lost 227,000 fish in 30 hours and in 2021 lost 500,000 (Seafood Source March 24, 2021; Fishfarmingexpert September 16, 2021).

Atlantic Sapphire has a market capitalization in $1.1 billion in 2023 (Yahoo Finance), despite minimal revenues and significant annual losses (Atlantic Sapphire n.d.) (see Table 11.9). Figures 11.17a and 11.17b display recent stock price and volume.

Attempting to diversify their product offerings, the company has entered into a joint venture to produce byproduct salmon oil, proteins and calcium products for feed and pet and human consumption (Intrafish 2020a).

Finally, and perhaps most importantly, the current cost premium for land-based production internalizes the economic externalities associated with sea-based systems and, thus, represent a more accurate social cost of the production of Atlantic Salmon.

Table 11.9 Atlantic Sapphire Financials

Year	Revenue (1,000 USD)	Net Earnings (1,000 USD)
2016	n.a.	(3,136)
2017	n.a.	(6,801)
2018	481	(11,399)
2019	55,40	(13,152)
2020	6,270	(55,193)
2021	16,851	(132,778)
2022	18,954	(65,006)
1st half 2023	8,058	(48,377)

Source: Atlantic Sapphire Annual Reports

Figure 11.17a Atlantic Sapphire Recent Stock Price

Source: Yahoo Finance

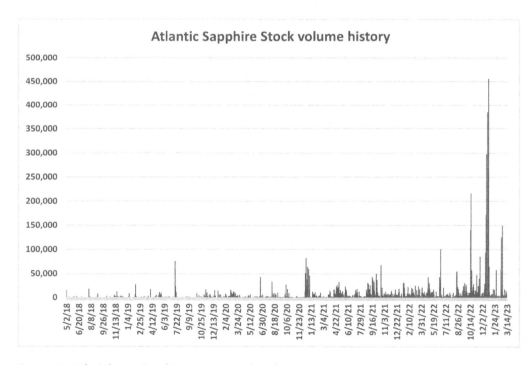

Figure 11.17b Atlantic Sapphire Recent Stock Volume

Source: Yahoo Finance

Table 11.10 LCAs of Aquacultural Systems

Aquaculture systems	ABD	GWP	HTP	MTP	ACD	EUT	CED
Net-pen	12.1	2073	639	822,000	17.9	35.3	26,900
Bag	13.9	2250	840	574,000	18	31.9	37,300
Land-based flow-through	38.1	5410	2570	3,840,000	33.3	31	132,000
Land-based recirculating	72.5	10,300	54,380	6,510,000	63.4	11.6	233,000

ABD = abiotic depletion (kg Antimony eq)
GWP = global warming potential (kg CO_2 eq)
HTP = Human toxicity potential (kg 1,4-dichlorobenzene eq)
MTP = Marine toxicity potential (kg 1,4-dichlorobenzene eq)
ACD = Acidification (kg SO_2 eq)
EUT = Eutrophication (ky PO4 eq)
CED = cumulative energy demand (MJ)

Source: Ayer 2007

A lifecycle analysis was undertaken of several aquaculture systems by Ayer (2007) and Ayer and Tyedmers (2009). The authors examined the major stages of fish output (smolt production, grow-out infrastructure, onsite fuel use, grow-out emissions, and food production) and their impact on seven environmental variables: abiotic depletion, global warming potential, human toxicity potential, marine toxicity potential, acidification, eutrophication, and cumulative energy demand. A summary of their results is presented in Table 11.10.

Like other research results, the authors identified feed production as the dominant contributor to environmental damage. The clear exception was the critical role that electricity production plays in on-land, closed systems. The authors (Ayer & Tyedmers 2009, p. 362) concluded that:

> while the use of these closed-containment systems may reduce the local ecological impacts typically associated with net-pen salmon farming, the increase in material and energy demands associated with their use may result in significantly increased contributions to several environmental impacts of global concern, including global warming, non-renewable resource depletion, and acidification. It is recommended that these unanticipated impacts be carefully considered in further assessments of the sustainability of closed-containment systems and in ongoing efforts to develop and employ these technologies on a larger scale.

Another study published by Pelletier et al. (2009, p. 8730) reported on the cumulative energy use, biotic resource use, and greenhouse gas, acidifying, and eutrophying emissions associated with producing ocean-based farmed salmon in Norway, the UK, British Columbia (Canada), and Chile. They found:

> marked differences in the nature and quantity of material/energy resource use and associated emissions per unit production across regions. This suggests significant

scope for improved environmental performance in the industry as a whole. We identify key leverage points for improving performance, most notably the critical importance of least-environmental cost feed sourcing patterns and continued improvements in feed conversion efficiency. Overall, impacts were lowest for Norwegian production in most impact categories, and highest for UK farmed salmon.

While indicative of the inherent trade-offs involved in transitioning from a marine to land-based system, the LCA did not include one critically important negative effect of marine-based, open-net systems: namely the negative impact of farmed salmon on their wild counterparts. These effects included the transmission of lice and other potential pathogens, and cross-breeding, which threatens the viability of wild salmon within their traditional ecological niche. In so far as wild salmon continue to play a critical role in natural ecosystems (Cederholm et al. 2000), especially on the Northwest coast of North America, where they are considered a keystone species contributing to the viability and survival of numerous other species (NOAA 2022), this is a vital issue in the assessment of the relative merits of open-pen and closed systems.

In sum, there are a number of innovative solutions that have emerged to address the multifaceted problems associated with current aquacultural systems (Simpson 2011; Vance 2015). These include closed containment either in the sea or on land which isolate the farmed fish from their immediate environment (*Vancouver Sun* October 20, 2018), the aforementioned increased use of herbivores, particularly in the developed countries, changes in feed to reduce their system-level resource impacts, and less intensive methods of production with lower ecological footprints. The principal criteria relevant to the assessment of these new technologies are reasonable cost, acceptable output volumes, the reduction or elimination of antibiotics for disease prophylaxis and growth stimulation, the elimination of other potentially toxic residues in the final product, the elimination of interactions with wild fish stocks, and the elimination off site-wastes. One issue in particular affects land-based systems, the presence of off-favour taste from metabolites of microorganisms found in the breeding tanks. Several approaches have been proposed or adopted to counter this negative effect: the rapid purging of the tanks with rapid water flushing known as "depuration" (Azaria & Rijn 2018). Because of several disadvantages associated with this method, alternative methods of eliminating taste problems are being explored. One such approach is an advanced oxidation process that includes photocatalysis, ultraviolet photolysis electrolysis, and ultraviolet oxidants (Kropp et al. 2022). While many of the alternatives to marine-based open net farming superficially appear costly, this represents once again a classic trade-off between private and social costs, where the level of uninternalized externalities has become ecologically and economically unacceptable.

The financial challenges of on-land recirculating systems require innovative business models. One such example has been provided by Superior Fresh, a small company in Wisconsin that runs an integrated aquaponic farm, producing both fish and leafy vegetables. In their system, wastewater from their fish tanks is treated to form a fertilizer for crop production in proximate greenhouses. The plants help purify the water before it is returned to the fish tanks, achieving a 99.9% recycling rate (Science February 9, 2023; Superior Fresh 2023). The company's recent output included 200,000 pounds of salmon and 3 million pounds of greens (Intrafish 2020a). Revenue reached 1,855 million in 2023 (Kona Equity).

A Note on Performance Measures

As in all questions related to sustainability and business, a critical element is the existence of reliable performance indicators that can compare alternative systems and policies, both spatially and temporally. A research group from the University of Victoria, BC (2010) developed a Global Aquaculture Performance Index (GAPI) based on ten variables, which measured the resulting index across marine finfish species and countries engaged in marine aquaculture. Table 11.11 categorizes the indicators into three main groupings: inputs, discharges, and biological factors. The research focuses on two types of measures: (1) the intensity of environmental impacts per unit of production, and (2) a scale variable which summarizes the overall impact of aquaculture production by species and country.

The initial results yield the highest (and least environmentally damaging) score for Chinook Salmon from New Zealand and Atlantic salmon from Chile and Norway, while the lowest scores are associated with the production of grouper in China and Indonesia.

Table 11.11 GAPI Environmental Performance Indicators

Grouping	Indicator	Indicator Description
INPUTS	Capture-based aquaculture	The extent which a system relies on the capture of wild fish for stocking farms, taking into account the sustainability of these wild fish inputs
	Ecological Energy	Amount of energy, or net primary productivity (NPP), that farmed fish divert from the ecosystem through consumption of feed ingredients
	Industrial Energy	Energy consumed in production and in the acquisition and processing of feed ingredients
	Sustainability of Feed	Amount, efficiency, and sustainability of wild fish ingredients of feed
DISCHARGES	Antibiotics	Amount of antibiotics used, weighted by a FAO/WHO measure of human and animal health risk
	Antifoulants (copper)	Estimated proportion of production using copper-based antifoulants
	Biochemical oxygen demand	Relative oxygen-depletion effect of waste contaminants (uneaten feed and feces)
	Parasiticides	Amount of parasiticides used, weighted by measures of environmental toxicity and persistence
BIOLOGICAL	Escapes	Number of escaped fish, weighted by an estimate of the per capita risk associated with escapes
	Pathogens	Number of on-farm mortalities, weighted by an estimate of wild species in the ecosystem that are susceptible to farm- derived pathogens

Source: University of Victoria (2010)

The report provides several important qualifications to this ranking which may seem to be counterintuitive. First, there are significant differences within species depending on the producing country. Second, there can be a significant divergence between the two metrics generated by GAPI: normalized vs. cumulative scores. Some country-species combinations that score highest on the normalized score fare poorly on the cumulative score due to the sheer scale of their industries. For example:

> "Chilean Atlantic salmon is the third-worst performer on a cumulative basis, despite being in the top three on a normalised scale." Similarly, while Norway "scores relatively well (72/100) per mT of production, the scale of production drops its cumulative score to 34 (UVic 2010)."

Third, a relatively high score (such as 73) must be viewed in context. This score is still "a substantial distance from the ecological target, or perfect score of 100. Thus, there is substantial room for improvement for all marine finfish, including salmon (UVic 2010, p. 17)." And fourth, since the indices are relative measures, the inclusion of additional fish may significantly affect the rankings: "While some species like salmon may lead the pack, it must be acknowledged that this pack—marine finfish—was chosen specifically for assessment because of concerns regarding wide-ranging and well-documented environmental impacts" (UVic 2010, p. 17). The complexities of interpretation of the GAPI indices are illustrative of the challenges facing scientists in unravelling the structure and dynamics of fisheries and oceans ecosystems. Nevertheless, with the availability of disaggregated scores for all species and countries, the GAPI Index may be one additional measure to help scientists and policymakers pinpoint areas where system changes can yield the most productive environmental improvements.

Summary

The outlook for global catch fisheries is not favourable in light of increasing global population, urbanization and income which will all put further pressure on food supplies, including fish. Coupled with these factors are all the direct and indirect effects of continuing climate change. Unless a concerted and radical effort is undertaken to rebuild wild fish stocks, the world must rely increasingly on aquaculture to generate sufficient fish protein to feed nations of both the developed and developing world. Under those circumstances, it is imperative that a major transformation takes place in the practice of aquaculture to reduce its reliance on wild fish and fish products for feedstock, to increase its resilience and reduce its negative ecological externalities.

A recent report (Planet Tracker 2023) summarizes the major challenges facing the aquaculture industry using the term *aquafailure*. While identifying the promise of new developments such as offshore installations, recirculating systems and lab-based cultivated seafood, the report concludes that none of these systems addresses many of the major environmental problems, the increasing opportunity costs of major feed inputs, the significant shortfall in meeting future demand, and substantial capital costs. Their proposed solution is to focus future efforts on bivalves (such as mussels, oyster and clams) and seaweed, none of which requires feed. All of these products "can even contribute to regenerating ecosystems, through the natural ecosystem services they provide like water filtering, carbon sequestration and habitat provision" (Planet Tracker 202, p. 36). The report suggests that widescale conversion to these products may encounter consumer resistance and this, in itself, may limit this approach, despite its promise to close the gap of 45.3 million tonnes in anticipated demand by 2050.

Several other reports have emphasized the magnitude of the problems facing the open-pen fishing industry. Frantz and Collins (2022, p. 75) reported that "most Mowi salmon farms are located in regions on the Seafood Watch 'Avoid' list because of heavy use of chemicals and sustainability concerns." Despite Mowi's environmental record as presented in their corporate reports, the company has faced several lawsuits for deceptive marketing and false advertising (Frantz & Collins 2022, chapter 7). The company settled one lawsuit for $1.3 million. The authors also reported that in 2018 a member of Mowi's founding family did "wish [to] be associated with what we consider an unsustainable way of farming salmon. Completely closed farms is the only way forward" (Frantz & Collins 2022: 297).

Despite these challenges, Mowi's CEO appears committed to the continuation of the company's successful profitable technological systems (Ole-Eirik Leroy, interviewed in Intrafish 2020a) despite the fact that this system may not be sustainable in the medium to long-term. As such, Mowi may face a strategic crossroads soon, forcing it to decide on one of at least four strategic options:

1 Stay the course, hoping that incremental improvements in its current harvesting systems will permit the company's continued growth and profitability.
2 Adopt a hybrid system that combines in-ocean and in-lake open-net breeding with on-land, closed systems.
3 Begin the transition to closed systems with their potentially higher costs but lower environmental externalities.
4 Explore alternative products with less environmental impact.

References

AllAfrica.com (2012) "Africa loses one million tonnes of fish yearly due to illegal fishing," October 25.

Anderson, Roy M. & Robert M. May (1979) "Population biology of infectious diseases, part 1," *Nature*, August 2, (280): 361–367.

Associated Press (2022) "Washington State ends commercial net pen aquaculture in Puget Sound," November 15.

Atlantic Sapphire (n.d.) "Get our financial reports," https://atlanticsapphire.com/investor-relations/financial-reports/.

Ayer, Nathan W. (2007) "The biophysical costs of technology: assessing the environmental Impacts of alternative Salmonid culture systems in Canada using lifecycle assessment," Masters Thesis, Dalhousie University, April.

Ayer, N. W. & P. H. Tyedmers (2009) "Assessing alternative aquaculture technologies: lifecycle assessment of salmonid culture systems in Canada," *Journal of Cleaner Production*, 17(3) 362–373.

Azaria, Snir & Jaap van Rijn (2018) "Off-flavor compounds in recirculating aquaculture systems (RAS): production and removal process," *Agricultural Engineering*, September 13.

Badiola Maddi et al. (2012) "Recirculating aquaculture systems (RAS) analysis: main issues on management and future challenges," *Aquacultural Engineering*, 51: 26–35.

Badiola, M., et al. (2018) "Energy use in recirculating aquaculture systems (RAS): A review," *Aquacultural Engineering*, March 19.

Barange, Manuel et al. (2018) "Impacts of climate change on fisheries and aquaculture," FAO Technical Paper 627.

Belhabib, Dyhia & Philppe Le Billon (2020) "Editorial: Illegal fishing as a trans-national crime," *Frontiers in Marine Science*, March 19.

Belhabib, Dyhia & Philppe Le Billon (2022) "Fish crimes in the global oceans," *Science Advances,* March 23.

Belhabib, Dyhia, et al. (2015) "A fishery tale: Namibian fisheries between 1950 and 2010," Working Paper #2015–65, Fisheries Centre, The University of British Columbia.

Bjorndal, Trond & Amalie Tusvik (2017) "Land based farming of salmon: economic analysis," Norwegian University of Science and Technology, Working paper No. 1.

Bjorndal, Trond & Amalie Tusvik (2018) "Economic analysis of alternative forms of production before farming," Society-OG Naringslifsforskning AS, Bergen, October.

Bjorndal, Trond & Amalie Tusvik (2019) "Economic analysis of land based farming of salmon," *Aquaculture Economics & Management,* September 12.

Bundy, A & L. P. Fanning (2005) "Can Atlantic cod (*Gadus morhua*) recover? Exploring trophic explanations for the non-recovery of the cod stock of the eastern Scotian Shelf, Canada," *Canadian Journal of Fisheries and Aquatic Sciences,* 62 (1474–1489).

Burge, Colleen A., et al. (2014) "Climate change influences on marine infectious diseases: implications for management and society," *Annual Review of Marine Science,* 6(249–277).

Cao, Ling, et al. (2015) "China's aquaculture and the world's wild fisheries," *Science,* January 9.

Canada, Fisheries and Oceans (2020) "Feasibility study of closed-containment options for British Columbia aquaculture industry."

CBC (2023) "Fisheries Department says it will shut 15 salmon farms off B.C.'s coast to protect wild fish," February 17.

Canadian Press (2021) "Study traces origins of virus found in B.C. salmon to fish farms in Norway," May 26.

Cawthorn, Donna-Maree, et al. (2018) "Generic names and mislabeling conceal high species diversity in global fisheries markets," *Conservation Letters,* June 22.

Cederholm, J., et al. (2000) *Pacific Salmon and Wildlife. Ecological Contexts, Relationships, and Implications for Management.* Washington State Department of Fish and Wildlife, Olympia, WA.

Chen, Jiaxin, et al. (2007) "A review of cage and pen aquaculture: China:" FAO.

Cheung, W. L., et al. (2013) "Signature of ocean warming in global fisheries catch," *Nature,* May 16.

Cheung, William W. L., et al. (2009) "Large-scale redistribution of maximum fisheries catch potential in the global ocean under climate change," *Global Change Biology,* 16(24–35).

Cheung, William W. L., et al. (2021) "Marine high temperature extremes amplify the impacts of climate change on fish and fisheries," *Science Advances,* October 1.

Christensen, V. & C. J. Walters (2004) "Ecopath with ecosim: methods, capabilities and limitations," *Ecological Modelling,* 172(2–4), pp. 109–139.

Christensen, V. & D. Pauly (1992) "Ecopath II – a software for balancing steady-state ecosystem models and calculating network characteristics," *Ecological Modeling,* 61: 169–185.

Christensen, V., C. J. Walters, D. Pauly (2000) *Ecopath with Ecosim: A User's Guide,* October 2000 Edition.

Consumer Reports (2011) "Mystery fish: the label says red snapper, the lab says baloney," December.

Daniels, Alfonso, et al. (2022) "Fishy networks: uncovering the companies and individuals behind illegal fishing globally," Financial Transparency Coalition, October.

Diaz, Patricio A., et al. (2019) "Impacts of harmful algal blooms on the aquaculture industry: Chile as a case study," *Perspectives in Phycology,* February.

Doumbouya, Alkaly, et al. (2017) "Assessing the effectiveness of monitoring control and surveillance of illegal fishing. The case of West Africa," *Frontiers in Marine Science,* March.

Dureuil, Manuel, et al. (2018 "Elevated trawling inside protected areas undermines conservation outcomes in a global fishing hot spot," *Science,* 362:1403–1407, December 21.

Fagan, Brian (2017) *Fishing: How the Sea Fed Civilization.* Yale University Press.

FAO/WHO/OIE (2007) Joint Expert Meeting on Critically Important Antimicrobials, Rome November 26–30.

Fishfarmingexpert (2021) "'All fish lost' in blaze at Atlantic Sapphire Denmark," September 16.

The Fish Site (2011) "Managing the environmental costs of aquaculture," June 30.

Food and Agriculture Organization (FAO) (n.d.) "The nutritional benefits of fish are unique," *Globefish.*

Food and Agriculture Organization (FAO) (2017) *Greenhouse gas emissions from Aquaculture.*

Food and Agriculture Organization (FAO) (2022a) *Fishery and Aquaculture Statistics 2020.*

Food and Agriculture Organization (FAO) (2022b) *The State of World Fisheries and Aquaculture: Towards Blue Transformation.*

Food and Agriculture Organization (FAO) (2022c) "Top 10 species groups in global aquaculture 2020."

Food and Agriculture Organization (FAO) (2023) *Statistical Yearbook: World Food and Agriculture 2023.*

Food and Agriculture Organization (FAO) FAO FISHSTAT www.fao.org/fishery/statistics/software/fishstat/en

Frank, Kenneth T., et al. (2005) "Trophic cascades in a formerly cod-dominated ecosystem," *Science,* June 10.

Frantz, Douglas & Catherine Collins (2022) *Salmon Wars: The Dark Underbelly of Our Favorite Fish,* Henry Holt and Company.

Gelchu, Ahmed (2006) "Growth and distribution of port-based global fishing effort with countries EEZs," doctoral thesis, University of BC.

Goldfarb, Ben (2017) "Feeling the heat: how fish are migrating from warming waters," YaleEnvironment360.

Greboval, Dominique & Gordon Munro (1998) "Overcapitalization and excess capacity in world fisheries: underlying economics and methods of control" in *Managing Fishing Capacity: Selected Papers on Underlying Concepts and Issues.* FAO Fisheries Technical Paper. No. 386.

Greenpeace (2015) *Africa's Fisheries' Paradise at a Crossroads. Investigating Chinese companies' illegal fishing practices in West Africa.*

The Guardian (2020) "Bid to grant MSC 'ecolabel' to bluefin tuna fishery raises fears for 'king of fish'," June 1.

The Guardian (2020) "'It's terrifying': Can anyone stop China's vast armada of fishing boats?" August 25.

The Guardian (2020) "Chinese fishing armada plundered waters around Galápagos, data shows," September 17.

The Guardian (2021) "Revealed: seafood fraud happening on a vast global scale," March 15.

The Guardian (2022) "Major New Zealand salmon producer shuts farms as warming waters cause mass die-offs," May 26.

Hall, S. J., et al (2011) "Blue Frontiers. Managing the environmental costs of aquaculture," The Worldfish Center, Penang, Malaysia.

Hardin, Garrett (1968) "The tragedy of the commons," *Science,*162, 1243–1248.

Henriksson, Patrik J. G., et al. (2018) "Unpacking factors influencing antimicrobial use in global aquaculture and their implication for management: A review from a systems perspective," *Sustainability Science*, 13(1105–1120).

International Development Research Centre (IDRC) (1973) *Science of the Culture of Freshwater Fish Species in China.* Ottawa, Canada, TS16e.

Intrafish (2019) "Analysis: Here's a list of high-profile land-based aquaculture failures," November 27.

Intrafish (2019) "Sea lice report," Oslo.

Intrafish (2020a) "Land-based salmon: Aquaculture's new disruptor," Oslo.

Intrafish (2020b)" World's top aquaculture producers," Oslo.

Intrafish (2020c) "Feed alternatives: The race to replace," Oslo.

Intrafish (2020d) "Over 2 million salmon escaped from Norwegian fish farms in the last decade," September 9.

Intrafish (2023) "Call for ban on netpen salmon farming in Iceland could stymie sector's expansion in the country," January 13.

Ivanovich, Catherine C., et al. (2023) "Future warming from global food consumption," *Nature Climate Change*, March 6.

Jackson, Jeremy, et al. (2001) "Historical overfishing and the recent collapse of coastal ecosystems," *Science,* July 27.

Jacquet, Jennifer L. & Daniel Pauly (2008a) "The rise of seafood awareness campaigns in an era of collapsing fisheries," *Marine Policy,* 31:308–313.

Jacquet, Jennifer L. & Daniel Pauly (2008b) "Trade secrets: renaming an mislabeling of seafood," *Marine Policy,* 32(309–318).

Jacquet, Jennifer (2009) "Fish as food in an age of globalization," doctoral thesis, University of BC

Just Economics (2021) "Dead loss: the high cost of poor farming practice and mortalities on salmon farms," February, justeconomics.co.uk

Kleisner, K., et al. (2012) "Using global catch data for inferences on the world's marine fisheries," *Fish and Fisheries*, 14(293–311).

Klinger, Dane & Rosamond Naylor (2012) "Searching for solutions in Aquaculture: Charting a sustainable course," *Annual Review of Environment and Resources*, 37(247–276).

Kona Equity (2023) "Superior fresh," konaequity.com.

Kongtorp, R. T., et al. (2014) "Pathology of heart and skeletal muscle inflammation (HSMI) in farmed Atlantic salmon *Salmo salar, Diseases of Aquatic Organisms*, June 11.

Krkosek, Martin, et al. (2007) "Declining wild salmon populations in relationship to parasites from farm salmon," *Science*, December 14.

Kropp. Ramsey, et al. (2022) "A novel advanced oxidation process (AOP) that rapidly removes geosmin and 2-methyllisoborneol (MIB) from water and significantly reduces duration times in Atlantic salmon *salmon salar* RAS aquaculture, *Agricultural Engineering*, 97 (102240).

Kurlansky, Mark (1997) *Cod: A Biography of the Fish that Changed the World*, Penguin.

Liu, Yajie, et al (2016) "Comparative economic performance and carbon footprint of two farming models for producing Atlantic salmon (*Salmo salar*): Land-based closed containment system in freshwater and open et pen in seawater," *Agricultural Engineering*, 71(1–12).

Lynam, Christopher P., et al. (2005) "Evidence for impacts by jellyfish on North Sea herring recruitment," *Marine Ecology Progress*, Vol. 298: 157–167.

Lynam, Christopher P., et al. (2006) "Jellyfish overtake fish n a heavily fished ecosystem," *Current Biology*, 16(13).

May, Robert M. & Roy M. Anderson (1979) "Population biology of infectious diseases, part II," *Nature*, August 9.

Mayer, Liza (2018) "Chan tries hand at offshore salmon farming," *Aquaculture North America*, May 7.

Mordecai, Gideon J., et al. (2021) "Aquaculture mediates global transmission of a viral pathogen to wild salmon," *Science Advances*, May 26.

Moreau, Darek T. R., et al. (2011) *Evolutionary Applications: Reproductive Performance of Alternative Male Phenotypes of Growth Hormone Transgenic Atlantic Salmon (Salmo salar)*, July 4.

Morely, James W, et al. (2018) "Projecting shifts in thermal habitat for 686 species on the North American continental shelf," *PLOS One*, May 16.

Mowi (2010–2022) *Annual Reports*.

Mowi (2022) *Salmon Farming Industry Handbook 2022*.

Myers, Ransom A. & Boris Worm (2003) "Rapid worldwide depletion of predatory fish communities," *Nature*, May 15.

Naylor, Rosamond, et al. (1998) "Nature's subsidies to shrimp and salmon farming," *Science*, October 30.

Naylor, Rosamond, et al. (2000) "Effect of aquaculture on world fish supplies," *Nature*, June 29.

Naylor, Rosamond L., et al. (2021) "A 20-year retrospective review of global aquaculture,' *Nature*, March 24.

New York Times (2008) "Salmon virus indicts Chile's fishing methods," March 27.

New York Times (2011) "Norwegians concede a role in Chilean salmon virus," July 27.

New York Times (2017) "As wild salmon decline, Norway pressures its giant fish farms," November 6.

New York Times (2017) "China's appetite pushes fisheries to the brink," April 30.

New York Times (2017) "As wild salmon decline, Norway pressures its giant fish farms," November 6.

New York Times (2018) "Climate change brought a lobster boom. Now it could cause a bust," June 21.

New York Times (2019) "Warming waters, moving fish: how climate change is reshaping Iceland," November 29.

New York Times (2023) "California salmon stocks are crashing. A fishing ban looks certain," April 4.

New York Times (2023) "The salmon on your plate has a troubling cost. These farms offer hope," October 17.

Newton, Richard W. & David C. Little (2018) "Mapping the impacts of farmed Scottish salmon from a lifecycle perspective," *International Journal of Life Cycle Assessment*, 23(1018–1029).

NOAA Fisheries (2022) "Ecosystem interactions and pacific salmon," September 7.

Nyland, Are, et al. (2019) "Wild and farmed salmon (*Salmo salar*) as reservoirs of infectious salmon anaemia virus, and the importance of horizontal- and vertical transmission," *Plos One*, April 16.

Oceana (2016) *Deceptive Dishes – Seafood Swaps Found Worldwide*.

OECD (2009) "An appraisal of the Chilean fisheries sector."

OECD-FAO (2021) *Agricultural Outlook 2021–2030*.

Owen, Brian (2022) "So long to open-net-pen salmon farms?" *Hakai Magazine*, June 2.

Park, Jaeyoon, et al. (2023) "Tracking elusive and shifting identities of the global fishing fleet, *Science Advances*, January 18.

Pauly, D., V. Christensen, & C. Walters (2000) "Ecopath, ecosim, and ecospace as tools for evaluating ecosystem impact of fisheries," *ICES Journal of Marine Science*, 57: 697.

Pauly, Daniel (2001) "Fishing down Canadian aquatic food webs," *Canadian Journal of Fisheries and Aquatic Sciences*, 58:51–62.

Pauly, Daniel (2010) *Five Easy Pieces: The Impact of Fisheries on Marine Ecosystems*, Island Press.

Pauly, Daniel (2016) "Having to science the hell out of it," *ICES Journal of Marine Science*, 73(9): 2156–2166.

Pauly, Daniel (2019) personal communication.

Pauly, Daniel & Dirk Zeller (2016) "Catch reconstructions reveal that global marine fisheries catches are higher than reported and declining," *Nature Communications*, January 19.

Pauly, Daniel & Ratana Chuenpagdee (2007) "Fisheries and coastal ecosystems: the need for integrated management," in Peter N. Nemetz (ed.) *Sustainable Resource Management, Reality or Illusion*? Edward Elgar.

Pauly, Daniel, et al. (1998) "Fishing down marine food webs," *Science*, February 6.

Pelletier, N., et al. (2009) "Not all salmon are created equal: lifecycle analysis (LCA) of global salmon farming systems," *Environmental Science & Technology*, 43, 8730–8736.

Penn, Justin L. & Curtis Deutsch (2022) "Avoiding ocean mass extinction from climate warming," *Science*, April 29.

Pew Ocean Commission (2003) *America's Living Oceans: Charting a Course for Sea Change*, May.

Pilkey, Orrin H. & Linda Pilkey-Jarvis (2007) *Useless Arithmetic: Why Environmental Scientists Can't Predict the Future*. Columbia University Press.

Pinsky, Malin L. & Alexa Fredston (2022) "A stark future for ocean life," *Science*, April 29.

Planet Tracker (2023) *Avoiding Aquafailure. Aquaculture Diversification and Regeneration Are Needed to Feed the World*.

Redi, Gregor K., et al. (2019) "Climate change and aquaculture; considering biological response and resources," *Aquaculture Environment Interactions*, November 28.

Richardson, Anthony J., et al. (2009) "The jellyfish joyride: causes, consequences and management responses to a more gelatinous future," *Trends in Ecology and Evolution*, 24(6): 312–322.

Rose, Alex (2008) *Who Killed the Grand Banks?* Wiley.

Science (2023) "Oceans away: Is raising salmon on land the next big thing in fish farming," February 9.

Seafood Source (2021) "Atlantic Sapphire suffers mass salmon mortality at its Florida RAS farm," March 24.

Simpson, Sarah (2011) "The Blue food revolution: Making aquaculture a sustainable food source," *Scientific American*, February.

Singh, Prabjeet, et al. (2011) "Polyculture: a culture practice to utilize all ecological niches of pond stems effectively," Aquafund.

Solheim, Magnus & Ola Trovatn ((2019) "The economic attractiveness of land-based salmon farming in Norway," Norwegian School of Economics, Master's Thesis, Fall.

Sommer, Ulrich, et al. (2002) "Pelagic food web configurations at different levels of nutrient richness and their implications for the ratio fish production: primary production," *Hydrobiologia*, (484) 11–20.

South China Morning Post (2018) "Chinese fish farm tests deep-sea waters with 'world's biggest' salmon cage," May 5.

Steadman, Daniel, et al. (2021) "New perspectives on an old fishing practice: Scale, context and impacts of bottom trawling," Report, Blue Ventures.

Stiles, Margot L., et al. (2011), "Bait and switch: how seafood fraud hurts our oceans, our wallets and our health," *Oceana*.

Sumaila, Ussif Rashid (2022) *Infinity Fish: Economics and the Future of Fish and Fisheries*, Academic Press

Sumaila, Ussif Rashid & Anthony T. Charles (2002) "Economic models of marine protected areas. An introduction," *Natural Resources Modeling*, 15(3).

Sumaila U. Rashid, et al. (2019) "Updated estimates and analysis of global fisheries sub asides," *Marine Policy*, 109 (103695).

Sumaila, U. R., et al. (2020) "Illicit trade in marine fish catch and its effects on ecosystems and people worldwide," *Science Advances*, February 26.

Superior Fresh (2023) "Regenerative agriculture reimagined."

Talberth, John, et al. (2006) *The Ecological Fishprint of Nations: Measuring Humanity's Impact on Marine Ecosystems*, Redefining Progress, Oakland CA.

Thorud, K. & H. O. Djupvik (1988) "Infectious anaemia in Atlantic salmon (*Salmo Salar L.*)," *Bulletin of the European Association of Fish Pathology*, 8(5) 109.

Times Colonist (2022) "Feds move to phase out open net salmon farms in B.C.," June 22, Victoria.

United Nations (2024) "The toll of illegal, unreported and unregulated fishing."

University of Victoria (UVic) (2010) "GAPI global aquaculture performance index."

Urbina, Ian (2021) "Fish farming is feeding the globe. What's the cost for locals," *The New Yorker*, March 1.

Vance, Erik (2015). "China's fish farms could save the oceans," *Scientific American* April.

Vancouver Sun (2018) "Algae bloom kills 250,000 salmon at two fish farms," June 12.

Vancouver Sun (2018) "Fish out of water: Taking aquaculture of the sea," October 20.

Vancouver Sun (2022) "Will B.C. be next to ban open-net fish farms after slew of US states halt practice?" November 23.

Veterinaerinstituttet (2018) "The health situation in Norwegian aquaculture 2017."

Veterinaerinstituttet (2021) "The health situation in Norwegian aquaculture 2020."

Walters C, Pauly D, Christensen V, & Kitchell J. F. (2000) "Representing density dependent consequences of life history strategies in aquatic ecosystems: EcoSim II," *Ecosystems*, 3:70–83.

Walters, C., V. Christensen, & D. Pauly (1997) "Structuring dynamic models of exploited ecosystems from trophic mass-balance assessments," *Reviews in Biology and Fisheries*, 7:139–272.

WatershedWatch (2024) "Fish farms kill: the long history and heavy toll salmon arms have had on fish and wildlife," March 13.

Watson, Reg & Daniel Pauly (2001) "Systematic distortions in world fisheries catch trends, *Nature*, November 29.

Welch, Heather, et al. (2022) "Hot spots of unseen fishing vessels," *Science Advances*, November 2.

World Wildlife Fund (WWF) (n.d.) "Farmed salmon." https://www.worldwildlife.org/industries/farmed-salmon

Yahoo Finance (2023) "Atlantic sapphire." https://finance.yahoo.com/quote/ASA.OL/financials/

Zeller, Dirk, et al. (2018) "Global marine fisheries discards: A synthesis of reconstructed data," *Fish & Fisheries*, 19(30–39).

Appendix Mowi Risk Categories (Mowi *Integrated Annual Report 2021*, Pages 280–287)

Risks related to the sale and supply of our products

Our results depend on salmon prices.

A reduction in the price of salmon may trigger substantial reduction in the value of our biological assets.

We may be unable to effectively hedge our exposure to short- and medium-term fluctuations in salmon prices.

Market demand for our products may decrease.

Changes in consumer preferences/lack of product innovation may have an adverse effect on our business.

Disruptions to our supply chain may impair our ability to bring our products to market.

Natural disasters, catastrophes, fire or other unexpected events could cause significant losses of operational capacity.

Risks related to governmental regulations

Governmental regulations affect our business.

Trade restrictions could have a negative impact on price in some countries.

We may face restrictions with regard to operating sites located close to protected or highly sensitive areas.

Our fish farming operations are dependent on fish farming licenses.

Antitrust and competition regulations may restrict further growth in some of the jurisdictions in which we operate.

We could be adversely affected by violations of the acceptable anti-corruption laws.

Risks related to our fish farm operations

Fish are adversely affected by sea lice, and we may incur significant costs and be exposed to regulatory actions if the challenge is not addressed.

We may be exposed to criticism and regulatory actions arising from our farming of and use of wild caught cleaner fish for sea lice control.

Our fish stocks, operations and reputation can be adversely affected by various diseases.

Our fish stocks can be depleted by environmental factors such as plankton, low oxygen levels and fluctuating seawater temperatures.

Our fish stocks are subject to risks associated with fish escapes and predation.

Intensive production may result in physical deformities, leading to downgrading and/or losses of biomass as well as to reputational harm.

Our fish stocks might be exposed to contaminants, leading to product recalls, product liability, negative publicity and governmental sanctions

Our fish may be exposed to pollutants from open seas resulting in mortality and poor end-product quality

Inclement weather could hurt our stocks negatively affect our operations and damage our facilities

Our operations are exposed to risks related to biological events or natural phenomena for which insurance coverage is expensive, limited and potentially inadequate.

Risks related to our supply of fish feed and our feed operations

Reduced availability of the main ingredients used in fish feed production could result in higher costs for fish feed.

Termination of one or more of our feed contracts at short notice could result in material additional costs.

Production issues in our own feed operations could cause us to incur material additional costs.

A reduction in the quality of our fish feed could have a materially adverse effect on our production.

Inferior or contaminated fish feed could result in product liability or other serious adverse consequences for us.

Risks related to our industry

Our facilities may be the target of sabotage by environmental organisations.

The aquaculture industry may be subject to negative media coverage.

Risks related to our business

We derive nearly all our revenues from sales of Atlantic salmon and are heavily dependent on the market for Atlantic salmon.

We rely heavily on the services of key personnel.

We are subject to risks associated with our international operations and our expansion into emerging markets.

Political instability may have a material adverse effect on our business, results of operation and financial condition.

We depend on the availability of and good relations with our employees.

We depend on a small number of contractors for key industry supplies, such as fish feed and well boats.

Some steps of the production process are outside our control.

Risks related to our financing arrangements

If we are unable to access capital, we may be unable to grow or implement our strategy as designed.

We are highly leveraged and subject to restrictions in our financing agreements that impose constraints on our operating and financing flexibility.

Fluctuations in the value of the derivatives used to hedge our exposure to salmon prices may adversely impact our operating results.

Fluctuations in foreign exchange rates may adversely impact our operating results.

We are subject to fluctuations in interest rates due to the prevalence of floating interest rates in our debt.

If our customers fail to fulfill their contractual obligations we may suffer losses.

Risks related to tax and legal matters

We are exposed to potentially adverse changes in the tax regimes of the jurisdictions in which we operate.

We may become involved in legal disputes.

Risks related to climate change

Physical related risks: the tangible effect of climate change have the potential to damage fish farming facilities, disrupt production activities and could cause us to incur significant costs.

Transitional related risks: climate change rules and regulations could increase the costs of operating our facilities or transporting our products.

Risks related to cyber security and technological innovation

We are subject to risk related to IT and cyber security

We are subject to risks related to Access Management and IT Change Management

We are subject to IT risks related to our operations and operational risk

We are subject to IT risks related to implementation of new systems and improvement projects

Risks related to our strategy – acquisitions and expansions

The construction and potential benefits of our fresh water expansion projects are subject to risks and uncertainties.

We would be adversely affected if we expanded our business through acquisitions or greenfield projects but failed to successfully integrate them or run them efficiently or retain the associated fish farming licenses.

Risks related to reporting

A failure to run an effective risk assessment process and update our internal control system accordingly, could imply that there is a risk of material mistakes in our financial figures.

Risks related to other legal matters

Developments related to antitrust investigations could have a materially adverse effect.

Failure to ensure food safety and compliance with food safety standards could result in serious adverse consequences for us.

Any failure to comply with laws and regulations in the countries in which we operate could result in serious adverse consequences for us.

12 The Search for Innovative Business Models

An Historical Case Study of Ooteel Forest Products, Ltd.

Author's Note: In contrast to the other cases in this volume that are current, this case is historical as Ooteel was recently absorbed by another private company. As such, no recent data are available. However, this case is still included here as it remains an instructive example of strategic choice.

Operations and Fundamental Challenges

Ooteel is a forestry company with private land holdings situated on the Pacific Northwest coast of North America. It had been operating a logging operation for several years whose profitability was intimately tied to variations in the market price of its timber. The company faced a major challenge. Continuation of its original business model would not guarantee future profitability, principally because of the emergence of concerns over environmental sustainability among the general public and its customers in particular. This challenge was manifested in two areas: first, the company's plans to harvest old growth trees received a major push-back from environmental nongovernmental organizations (ENGOs) and the threat of a boycott of its products if this plan were to proceed. Second, a lack of forest certification of its logging operations could threaten access to markets for some of its product. Ooteel sought the advice of consultants who generated an innovative, but potentially risky, strategy that might help the company survive. It was up to Ooteel to assess this new strategic option and determine its economic viability. The new strategic plan is described below with relevant economic data.

The Proposed Strategic Plan to be Evaluated

As presented to the management of Ooteel, the new strategic direction had four distinct components: (1) *product branding* through independent certification of responsible forest practices; (2) the launching of an *ecotourism* initiative by the company to add an additional source of revenue from the nonharvested forest; (3) *marketing of carbon credits* from nonharvested timber land that satisfies the "additionality" criterion, where the carbon comes from trees in areas that the company is not required by law to set aside; and (4) a companion proposal to *market biodiversity credits*. The challenge to management was to determine whether these strategic directions alone or in combination would be sufficient to guarantee profitability.

Operating Details

Ooteel's land holdings totalled approximately 150,000 ha and the company had been harvesting approximately 300,000 cubic meters of timber annually from approximately

DOI: 10.4324/9781003170754-15

half this area. This harvest, at a somewhat lower rate (4 cu meters per hectare) than normal because of environmental sensitivities, was composed of approximately 60% high quality cedar that lends itself to value-added remanufacturing of more expensive grade products. The remaining 40% was a mix of lower grade wood, principally hemlock with more limited opportunities for high end manufacturing. When prices for high-grade cedar are up, this proportion of the harvest is guaranteed a market and generates a reasonable profit. The challenge to the company was the uncertain market for its lower grade products. Forest certification held the promise of guaranteeing that this market will remain open and that Ooteel would have more competitive access to it than companies without an ecolabel. The four strategic initiatives are as follows:

1. ***Product branding through certification.*** While the company would prefer to receive a price premium for this lumber, premia for certified changes to logging practices vary markedly from 0–10%. What makes certification attractive even without a price premium is more competitive market access for their low-quality product. A consultant advised the company that without certification, there was a greater than 50/50 chance that this product could not be marketed, putting the corporation into a serious financial crisis. In order to receive certification, Ooteel had to change its logging practices and forest management system from clearcutting to variable retention and selective cutting. This would involve a significant increment to its operating costs. One of the principal cost differences is a shift from cable-based logging to a mix of 40% cable and 60% helicopter-based logging. The shift in forest management would also entail a reduction in annual harvest to approximately 100,000 cubic meters. An additional, though small, cost is required for certification itself, ranging from a median value of $0.27–2.40 per hectare plus $0.12–$0.49 per hectare for annual audits (Lister 2011; Cubbage & Moore 2008; Cubbage et al. 2009; Hansen et al 1998), to 2–3 cents per cubic meter in another (Gullison 2003).

2. ***Ecotourism***

   Ooteel's coastal forest operations are close to a globally popular existing tourist destination whose activities could be largely viewed as ecological in nature. The consultant's report suggested that Ooteel might be able to generate an ecotourism revenue stream from small-scale, low-capital-intensive activities such as boat tours, hiking, camping, nature walks, and wildlife viewing equal to anywhere between 5% and 10% of the gross current regional tourist revenues. This could be undertaken by itself or through strategic partnerships with existing local tourism operators.

3. ***Marketing of carbon credits***

   The company might be able to tap into the global market for carbon credits/offsets through the sequestration of carbon in the proportion of their land holdings that will be set aside as nonharvestable. It was estimated that the company could dedicate 50,000–75,000 ha for this purpose. The quantity of standing timber in this area was estimated at 600 cubic meters/ha, and the quantity of carbon sequestered was estimated at approximately 900 tons of carbon per ha.

4. ***Marketing of biodiversity credits***

   While markets for carbon credits are well along the road to development, comparable institutions for biodiversity are in their nascent stage. Part of the problem is the difficulty of developing quantifiable indicators for biodiversity. There are a great number of uncertainties at that time, but the consultants suggested that one avenue to pursue would be a per hectare payment by a corporation that is undertaking a development somewhere in North America or the world that may compromise the level of its local biodiversity. The biodiversity credits purchased from Ooteel would act as an offset. The issue is clearly one of determining the appropriate price.

There is obviously a great deal of uncertainty involved with each one of the four components, and the consultants suggested that the company might wish to hire an analyst to use a Monte Carlo analysis[1] to generate a profile of possible financial outcomes and help the management assess the corporate attitude toward risk.

Cost Projections

The consultants prepared cost projections based on an annual harvest of 100,000 cu m and these data are reproduced in Table 12.1. These cost categories are composed of the following components:

Table 12.1 Ooteel Cost Projections

Estimated costs for Ooteel Ltd.	in 2009$
Logging (Variable) costs	$/ cu m
Yarding	$49.75
Barge & Tow	$6.00
Other phase	$51.75
subtotal	$107.50
Fixed costs	
Forest Management	
Regulatory compliance & reporting	$154,000
Forestry and engineering	$547,000
Silviculture accrual	$61,000
subtotal	$762,100
SG&A	$307,600
	$/ cu m
Taxes	$17.50

1. *Yarding*: The company's former method of logging with clearcutting used cables for the retrieval of downed trees at a cost of $16.25 per cubic meter (cu m). The shift to a more sustainable method of forestry (specifically *ecoforestry*; i.e. ultra low-impact forestry) necessitated a 40% mix of cables and 60% use of helicopters, the latter costing $72 per cu m. This averages out at $49.70 per cu m.
2. *Other phase costs*: include falling, loading, hauling, sorting, booming grounds, roads, and misc. other costs.

Fixed costs:

3. *Forestry and engineering* costs are related to field, professional, and data analysis costs required to plan and execute harvesting, road building, silviculture, and protection activities.
4. *Silvicultural accrual cost* was an expected future silviculture cost equal to between $1.75–3.00 /cu m of harvest, at an assumed rate of timber harvest of 50,000–100,000 cu m/yr.
5. *SG&A* include personnel, marketing, research, accounting, legal, insurance, training, and miscellaneous others.

In addition, the company faces annual property taxes of $7.50 per hectare as well as a harvest tax of approximately $6 per cubic meter. Since Ooteel was a private landowner, it paid no stumpage fees to the government for the use of forested public lands.

Revenue Projections

While there is a fair degree of certainty concerning these cost estimates, the potential revenue side was more uncertain, especially with respect to each of the four proposed components of the new sustainability strategy. The nature and extent of this uncertainty is discussed below.

Lumber Prices

There are numerous grades of timber, each receiving a different price. Average historical prices (in 2009$) for Ooteel's mix of cedar and hemlock logs are presented in Table 12.2. Since there is every reason to assume that this price variability would continue in the future, Ooteel had to build this expected variation into its financial projections.

Ecotourism

The local region generates average tourist-related revenues of approximately $40 million, an amount that has been growing at or above the rate of inflation for some time. It is assumed that Ooteel could realize a 10–20% contribution to its bottom line from any ecotourism revenues it can capture.

Carbon Credits/Offsets

Prices tend to vary in global markets for carbon credits/offsets and Ooteel was advised by its consultants that rates run between $6–$8/ton for forest carbon but that these prices were expected to increase annually in light of rising concern over global climate change and the concomitant increase in carbon markets and trading by corporations, governments and ENGOs. Reports by the US EPA (2009, 2010) forecasted that the price of these credits would increase at or above the rate of inflation for the next several decades.

Forest carbon offsets are measured as any net reduction in forest carbon emissions on an annual basis. While conceptually simple, the calculation of these emission changes are

Table 12.2 Historical Prices for Hemlock and Cedar

Year	Cedar	Hemlock
1999	$181.62	$85.57
2000	$187.86	$83.95
2001	$172.55	$74.88
2002	$202.41	$82.10
2003	$174.58	$67.85
2004	$148.73	$68.57
2005	$115.77	$58.01
2006	$139.09	$60.04
2007	$179.31	$66.50
2008	$163.36	$55.83
2009	$113.40	$49.98
in 2009$		
per cu m		

relatively data intensive and subject to a large number of qualifications and exclusions. For simplicity, the consultants have recommended a rather conservative approach to estimation in order to give Ooteel a general idea of the relative magnitude of potential revenues should they be able to capitalize on the market for carbon. In the simplified calculation suggested by the consultants, Ooteel was required to compare the carbon emissions associated with a normal annual harvest (at a conservative 4 cubic meters per hectare per year) with no harvest from the newly dedicated land conservation area. It is important to note that not all carbon is released by harvesting. On average, the consultants estimated that fully 40% of carbon in the harvested wood remains in the product over a period of 100 years, a time span usually considered relevant for this type of carbon sequestration calculation.

Two other adjustments are required to estimate the baseline quantity of carbon credits available for offsetting. The first is a risk buffer to account for potential losses from forest fires, insect predation, and land use changes. The second is termed *economic leakage* (BC 2010) and is described as follows:

> Project activities that result in the change in the level of a service (e.g., land use of a given type, amount of wood products produced) provided from within the project boundary may result in changes in the level of those services provided outside the project area . . . due to market forces/activity shifting. Such changes, which are often referred to as "leakage," may result in changes in the amount of carbon stored in forest and/or wood product carbon pools located outside of the project boundary, but that are nonetheless affected by the project activity and that might serve to cancel out to some degree emission reductions or enhanced sequestration achieved by the project within the project boundary.

Considering these three factors, the consultant felt that the company could be credited with only a 50% reduction in carbon emissions by reducing the harvest.

Biodiversity Credits/Offsets

There is an extraordinary range of values that can be imputed for biodiversity and related ecological services from the little data that is publicly available. The consultants advising Ooteel adopted a relatively conservative approach and suggested a conservative annual value of $5 to $15 per hectare based on the experience of Costa Rica in pricing its environmental services (Castro et al 2000). There is a special opportunity to package and market a customized conservation credit product in a payment for ecoservices (PES) model (FAO 2018; Porras & Asquith 2018; WWF 2020).

Note

1 In Table 12.3 the consultant listed some of the variables that might enter such a Monte Carlo analysis. Since most of the probability distributions are unknown, it is suggested that the analyst adopt either a normal or a continuous uniform distribution. In those cases where sufficient data are available, such as price history, then a probability distribution can be used that approximates the historical data. The price of cedar and hemlock are not independent variables, since both are influenced by the state of the economy and world markets and, as such, tend to move in the same direction although hemlock prices have a lower variance than cedar. Under these circumstances, it may be appropriate to use the price of cedar as the principal price variable and determine the corresponding price of hemlock by using a probability distribution on the historical relationship between the two wood prices.

Table 12.3 Potential Variables for Ooteel Monte Carlo Analysis

Variable	Lower Bound	Upper Bound
cedar prices	$113.40	$202.41
hemlock prices as percentage of cedar prices	34%	50%
Possible branding premium from certification	0%	10%
percentage of ecotourism revenue as percentage of gross current regional tourist revenue	5%	10%
potential profit rate from eco-tourism	10%	20%
certification costs per hectare	$0.27	$2.40
auditing costs per hectare	$0.12	$0.49
current carbon offset prices ($/ton carbon)	$6.00	$8.00
possible biodiversity offset prices per hectare	$5.00	$15.00

References

British Columbia (BC) Ministry of Environment (2010) *British Columbia Forest Carbon Offset Protocol*, November 22.

Castro, Rene, et al. (2000) "The Costa Rican experience with market instruments to mitigate climate change and conserve biodiversity," *Environmental Monitoring and Assessment*, 61: 75–92.

Cubbage, Fred & Susan Moore (2008) "Impacts and costs of forest certification: A survey of SFI and FSC in North America," presentation to 2008 Sustainable Forestry Initiative Meeting, Minneapolis. MN, 23 September.

Cubbage, Fred, et al. (2009) "Costs and benefits of forest certification in the Americas." In Jeanette B. Paulding (Ed.), *Natural Resources: Management, Economic Development and Protection.* 155–183. Nova Science Pub Inc.

Food and Agriculture Organization (FAO) (2018) *Forests and Water: Valuation and Payments for Forest Ecosystem Services.*

Gullison, R. E. (2003) "Does forest certification conserve biodiversity?" *Oryx*, 37(2): 153–165.

Hanson, E., et al. (n.d.) "Understanding forest certification," IUFRO, UNECE Timber Committee, European Forestry Commission, unecefaoiufro.lsu.edu

Lister, Jane (2011) *Corporate Social Responsibility and the State: International Approaches to Forest Co-Regulation.* UBC Press.

Porras, Ina and Nigel Asquith (Eds.) (2018) *Ecosystems, Poverty Alleviation and Conditional Transfers.* IIED.

US EPA (2009) *EPA Analysis of the American Clean Energy and Security Act of 2009.* H.R. 2454 in the 111th Congress, 6/23/09.

US EPA (2010) *Supplemental EPA Analysis of the American Clean energy and Security Act of 2009.* H.R. 2454 in the 111th Congress, 1/29/2010.

WWF 2020 "Payments for ecosystem services." https://wwf.panda.org/discover/knowledge_hub/where_we_work/black_sea_basin/danube_carpathian/our_solutions/green_economy/pes/

Analytical Questions

The key questions facing the analyst are as follows:

(1) Should he/she have recommended an investment in this private company?
(2) Given that Ooteel's old business model was no longer viable, was it possible to achieve profitability by adopting one or more of the strategic initiatives suggested by the consultant?
(3) Using several of the models of a sustainable corporation described in this textbook, (e.g., Anderson, Natural Step, McDonough-Braungard), assess the extent to which the company could be described as sustainable under its new strategic direction.
(4) Would FSC certification provide Ooteel with a sustainable competitive advantage?

13 Assessing Ooteel's Strategic Options

The major strategic challenge faced by Ooteel Ltd. was that continuation of its business model would not guarantee future profitability because of a radically different business environment with the emergence of concerns over sustainability among its customers and the public. A four-pronged innovative strategy was proposed by consultants that had the potential for both sustainability and long-term profitability. If successful execution could be realized, this would represent the operationalization of Porter and van der Linde's seminal hypothesis that sustainability is the key to long-run competitive advantage. Figure 13.1 displays the goals and inherent challenges that faced the company, and

Figure 13.1 Ooteel Goals and Inherent Challenges

DOI: 10.4324/9781003170754-16

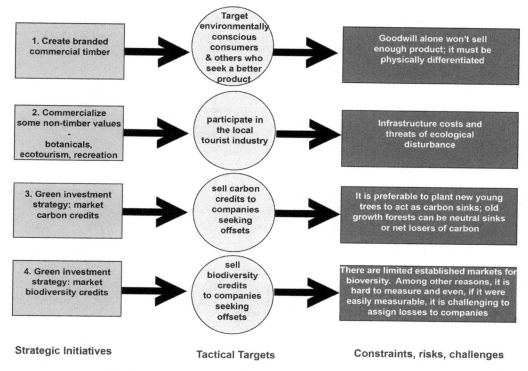

| Strategic Initiatives | Tactical Targets | Constraints, risks, challenges |

Figure 13.2 Ooteel Business Case

Figure 13.2 presents the detailed business case defined by the strategic initiatives, tactical targets, and specific constraints, risks, and challenges. It was apparent that this strategy was not without risks, and a fundamental issue was whether the company could achieve profitability through the success of any one or subset of the four initiatives, or whether the achievement of all four was necessary for success. This challenge is portrayed using a model from electrical engineering in Figure 13.3. Model A uses an "OR Gate" where satisfying any one of the independent conditions will suffice for success; while Model B uses an 'AND Gate" where all of the independent conditions are necessary for success. The following sections discuss in greater detail the opportunities and risks associated with each of the four strategic thrusts.

1. Certification

As outlined in the consultant's proposal, the intent of the certification initiative was to create branded commercial timber that could earn a price premium, gain access to new markets, or maintain existing markets that are under scrutiny from customers concerned about sustainability. A report on certification outlined its pioneering role in building a more sustainable economy (SustainAbility 2011a, p. 6). To quote:

> Certification, labeling and the standards-setting organizations . . . have made what was once invisible visible, changed societal and consumer norms, given producers access to new markets, promoted multi-stakeholder collaboration, and driven operational

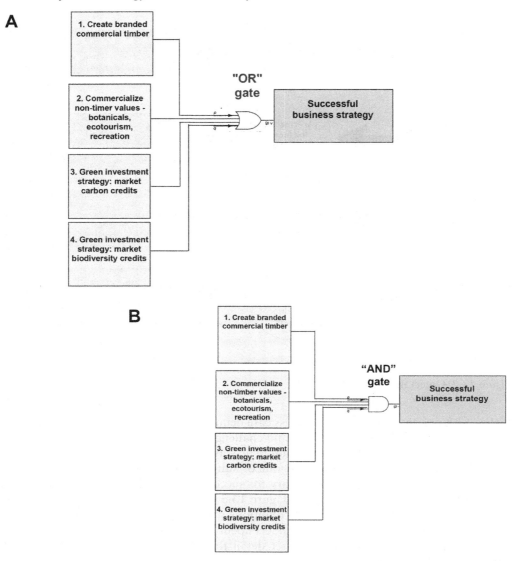

Figure 13.3a and b Electrical Engineering Analogues

changes among businesses and other large buyers. They are now in widespread use as operational tools for business to make purchasing decisions, manage supply, market and sell to B2B and B2C customers, guide employees, and respond to stakeholders and regulators.

Certification can take one of three forms: self-certification, industry certification, or third-party certification. The last of these options is the most likely to be arms-length and command the greatest credibility. The essence of certification is verification that the forest company is engaging in responsible forest practices, and this achievement is frequently accompanied by an eco-label attesting to this result. Within the last few decades, several organizations have emerged at the global level to offer forest certification services, foremost among these are the Programme for the Endorsement of Forest Certification (PEFC) and the Forest Stewardship Council (FSC). According to the UN Food and Agriculture Organization (FAO 2021), PEFC and FSC have certified 435.5 million ha as of 2020. FSC describes itself as

a nonprofit, independent and internationally recognized organization that accredits and monitors independent forest product certifiers. FSC assures consumers that certification labels are consistent and reliable, and that practices adhere to an international set of principles as well as locally developed forest management standards. . . . FSC certification is conducted by independent, credible, nongovernmental organizations. Accreditation ensures that certifiers are independent from the timber trade, that they are qualified to make accurate forest assessments, their standards are consistent with international principles, and their assessments are conducted in a reliable and consistent manner" (FSC n.d.)

If Ooteel proceeded with its reformulated forestry plan, they were virtually guaranteed FSC certification. While the company would be content with the guaranteed market access that this process offered to deliver, the prospect of a price premium enhanced the attractiveness of this option. Very little data have been assembled on the extent and magnitude of such premia, but some historical studies have suggested significant differences among markets. UNECE (2011) and others (e.g., Yuan and Eastin 2007) reported premia of 6.3% in Europe, 5.6% in Korea, 5.1% in the United States, and 1.5% in Canada.

FSC certification is based on ten principles as described in Table 13.1. It is important to note that a significant component of this certification process is performance-based as opposed to process based. This increases the likelihood that the ultimate sustainability goals will be realized.

If certification is to succeed, then the ultimate consumers of forest products must be aware of the product, be willing to accept it and, in some cases, be willing to pay the additional price premium. Since forest products are rarely sold directly to final retail consumers, the role of the intermediary is essential to the success of this process. Several home improvement chains, such as Home Depot (the largest in the United States) have chosen to stock and advertise certified timber, thereby significantly increasing the marketing of this product. Their wood purchasing policy is reproduced in Table 13.2. A poll by the American Institute of Architects showed that 91 percent of registered voters would pay a premium for a house if it was deemed to be environmentally beneficial (Germain & Penfield 2010). An additional impetus to this market has been the emergence of *green* architects and builders who are capitalizing on increased public concern about the environment and who seek LEED certification that frequently includes certified wood products. The Leadership in Energy and Environmental Design (LEED) program, administered by the US Green Building Council established a voluntary certification process for new buildings based on sustainability principles (see Appendix). It has been reported that the value of the global green building material market in 2021was $280.5 billion and could reach $523.7 billion by 2027 (imarc 2022).

Table 13.1 FSC Principles

#	Principle	Strategic Actions Required By Company
#1	Compliance with laws and FSC principles	Forest management shall respect all applicable laws of the country in which they occur, and international treaties and agreements to which the country is a signatory, and comply with all FSC Principles and Criteria.
#2	Tenure and use rights and responsibilities	Long-term tenure and use rights to the land and forest resources shall be clearly defined, documented and legally established.
#3	Aboriginal peoples' rights	The legal and customary rights of Aboriginal peoples to own, use and manage their lands, territories, and resources shall be recognized and respected.
#4	Community relations and worker's rights	Forest management operations shall maintain or enhance the long-term social and economic well being of forest workers and local communities.
#5	[Multiple] benefits from the forest	Forest management operations shall encourage the efficient use of the forest's multiple products and services to ensure economic viability and a wide range of environmental and social benefits.
#6	Environmental impact	Forest management shall conserve biological diversity and its associated values, water resources, soils, and unique and fragile ecosystems and landscapes, and, by so doing, maintain the ecological functions and the integrity of the forest.
#7	Management plan	A management plan — appropriate to the scale and intensity of the operations — shall be written, implemented, and kept up to date. The long-term objectives of management, and the means of achieving them, shall be clearly stated.
#8	Monitoring and assessment	Monitoring shall be conducted — appropriate to the scale and intensity of forest management — to assess the condition of the forest, yields of forest products, chain of custody, management activities and their social and environmental impacts.
#9	Maintenance of high conservation value forests	Management activities in high conservation value forests shall maintain or enhance the attributes which define such forests. Decisions regarding high conservation value forests shall always be considered in the context of a precautionary approach.
#10	Plantations	Plantations shall be planned and managed in accordance with Principles and Criteria 1–9, and Principle 10 and its Criteria. While plantations can provide an array of social and economic benefits, and can contribute to satisfying the world's needs for forest products, they should complement the management of, reduce pressures on, and promote the restoration and conservation of natural forests.

Source: http://www.fsc.org/1093.html

Table 13.2 Home Depot Wood Purchasing Policy

1. The Home Depot will give preference to the purchase of wood and wood products originating from certified well managed forests wherever feasible.
2. The Home Depot will eliminate the purchase of wood and wood products from endangered regions around the world.
3. The Home Depot will practice and promote the efficient and responsible use of wood and wood products.
4. The Home Depot will promote and support the development and use of alternative environmental products.
5. The Home Depot expects its vendors and their suppliers of wood and wood products to maintain compliance with laws and regulations pertaining to their operations and the products they manufacture.

Source: www.homedepot.com

Assessing the role of certification

The modern form of product certification began in the 1980s and 1990s in the forest sector (Conroy 2007), led by Collins Pine in the United States (Hansen and Punches 1998) and MacMillan Bloedel (since bought by Weyerhaeuser) in British Columbia. This phenomenon has spread to many other industries such as fisheries, finance and investment, tourism, mining, agriculture, industrial chemicals, clothing, and oil and gas. Conroy (Conroy 2007: xiii) divided the history of this phenomenon into three distinct phases:

(1) Nonprofit civil organizations create new standards for corporate social and environmental accountability, often in stakeholder negotiations with companies themselves. (2) Companies are moved to adopt these standards, either because of internal corporate culture and the new business opportunities they offer or due to NGO pressure in the form of tough market campaigns. (3) Newly created, nonprofit, standard-setting organizations implement a credible and efficient method for certifying corporate compliance with the new standards.

As might be expected with the proliferation of third-party certifiers, issues will inevitably arise with respect to cross-sectional comparability, quality control, transparency, and changing standards over time (NAS 2010). In some cases, as in fisheries, this can be the source of some controversy. Several studies have attempted to assess the state of certification, and some have identified significant shortcomings (see, for example, TerraChoice 2010; Miljoeko AB & SustainAbility 2001; SustainAbilty & Mistra 2004; SustainAbility 2011b; Lister 2011). In addition to helping consumers choose products, the rating process has been used to link executive compensation to performance, and assist asset managers in investment decision making (SustainAbility 2011b). An essential component of product certification is *chain-of-custody* (CofC) that allows the final consumer the opportunity to track the product all the way back to the original producer(s), reassuring the consumer that sustainable products and practices have been used at every stage of the supply chain. The more complex the supply chain and the more global components involved, the greater benefit of CofC despite the increased costs associated with possible product segregation and detailed tracking documentation.

The bulk of forest certification has occurred in Europe and North America, where governments and forestry companies have generally established strong programs of reforestation and forest stewardship. The degree of certification in the developing world is significantly lower (Fernholz et al. 2021). This is problematic because of the critical role of tropical forests in the global ecosystem and the large rates of deforestation in the Third World (Gustin 2021; *New York Times* March 31, 2021).

2.   Ecotourism

The essence of this second initiative is shifting from the traditional model of forestry as providing only fiber and timber to capitalizing on nontimber values such as botanicals, recreation and targeted, low-impact tourism. Each one of these aspects has the capability of generating revenue for land owners and forestry companies. These potential values are independent of the vast array of unpriced ecosystem services that flow from intact forest lands. In evaluating the potential revenue stream from these nontraditional uses of forest lands, Ooteel had to assess the market for ecotourism. The International Ecotourism Society (TIES, 2006) defines ecotourism as "responsible travel to natural areas that conserves the environment and improves the well-being of local people." This means that those who implement and participate in ecotourism activities should follow the following principles: minimize impact, build environmental and cultural awareness and respect, provide positive experiences for both visitors and hosts, provide direct financial benefits for conservation, provide financial benefits and empowerment for local people and raise sensitivity to host countries' political, environmental, and social climate.

Tourism, one of the largest sectors in the world economy, accounted for 10.4% of global GDP and employed over 334 million people, representing 10% of global employment in 2019 (WTTC). Total global tourist receipts were estimated at $1.466 trillion from 1.466 billion arrivals, a growth rate of 3.8% from 2018 to 2019 (UNWTO Barometer). The real growth in international tourism receipts was 54% over the period 2009–2019, exceeding global GDP growth of 44% over the same period (UNWTO Highlights). Of this, the ecotourism subsector had a market size of $210.4 billion in 2023 (Allied Market Research 2024) and, prior to the advent of COVID-19, was expected to grow to $333.8 billion by 2027, representing a growth rate of 14.3% (Statista 2024, Allied Market Research 2022).

3.   Marketing Carbon Credits

Various forms of carbon trading have entered the business mainstream. Ecosystem-Marketplace (2010a and b) provided an extensive analysis of forest carbon markets. Specific formal mechanisms were established under the Kyoto Protocol with the intent of reducing deforestation in the Third World, leading to the REDD (Reducing emissions from Deforestation and Degradation) initiative in 2007 at Bali (FAO et al. 2008, 2010). Paralleling this international program has been the emergence of a few regional voluntary carbon exchanges, including the now defunct Chicago Climate Exchange, other exchanges in Australia and New Zealand, and the creation of a global electronic platform for the spot trading of voluntary carbon credits, based in London and Australia (www.carbontradeexchange.com).

The fundamental principle of all these initiatives is the concept of "offsetting" where a corporation may choose to pay money to an intermediary to invest in a broad range of carbon-reducing activities where such payments are less expensive than carbon emission reduction by the corporation. In the case of forest credits, the payment may be less concerned with reducing current carbon emissions than forestalling any future release from forest harvesting by essentially paying for carbon sequestration and improved forest management. The EcosystemMarketplace report, based on a restricted dataset, suggested that the bulk of the estimated $150 million worth of global transactions were conducted in North and Latin America and more recent data found that the value of the voluntary carbon market equaled $784 million in August 2021, of which $107 million were associated with forestry and land use (Ecosystem Marketplace 2021).

Estimates of the size of this market depend on the definition and scope of the market. For example, Reuters (January 19, 2023) reported that the voluntary carbon offset market was worth $2 billion in 2021 and could grow by a factor of at least 5 by 2030 (see also the postscript below for updated estimates of key market values).

The determination of carbon credits available for an offset market is a complex process and some organizations and governments have produced detailed protocols for their calculation (WBCSD & WRI 2005; IPCC 2006; CAR 2010; BC 2011; ISO 14064-2). For example, the province of British Columbia, which contains some of the largest timber holdings in North America, produced an extensive and detailed 187-page protocol (BC 2011) that addressed such key issues as offset recognition criteria, appropriate project types, and procedures for microlevel and system-based calculations. The government identified five key offset recognition criteria: first, the project must be real (i.e., it is an identifiable project and there are sound methods available to quantify GHG emissions); second, there must be *additionality* (i.e., a reduction of GHG emissions beyond business as usual and regulatory requirements, as well as the ability to overcome economic and technical barriers); third, the undertaking is permanent (i.e., the offset has a lasting impact, measured relative to a 100-year time scale); fourth, the project is verifiable (i.e., it can be quantified, monitored and audited, and the measurement uncertainty is minimized); and fifth, there is clear ownership (i.e., of the offset attributes by the party claiming them). These are critical criteria, as some of these have been violated in the international offset market for GHG reduction under the Kyoto Protocol.

One of the most useful private sector guides to assessing and estimating forest-based carbon credits was produced by Climate Action Reserve (CAR 2010). Their extensive guide identified three categories of eligible offsets: (1) *reforestation* that "involves restoring tree cover on land that is not at optimal stocking levels and has minimal short-term (30-years) commercial opportunities," (2) *improved forest management* that "involves management activities that maintain or increase carbon stocks on forested land relative to baseline levels of carbon stocks," and (3) *avoided conversion* that "involves preventing the conversion of forestland to a non-forest land use by dedicating the land to continuous forest cover through a conservation easement or transfer to public ownership." Each of these three project types has strict eligibility criteria as described in CAR 2010 and 2022.

In essence, the principal components of a carbon offset assessment involve (a) changes in the carbon sequestration of standing timber – both decreases and accretions, (b) changes in the carbon sequestration of soil and other vegetation, and (c) carbon releases related to the process of forestry itself. Each of these categories may vary in their applicability to each of the three major offset project types as summarized in Table 13.3. The degree of carbon sequestered in forest products after harvesting is an important and complex issue. At least one study attempted to generate these values in an American context (Smith et al. 2005). There are several principal pathways of harvested forest products: to

Table 13.3 Types and Effects of Offsetting Policies

Description	Type	Gas	Reforestation	Improved Forest Management	Avoided Conversion
Primary Effect Sources, Sinks and Reservoirs					
Standing live carbon (carbon in all portions of living trees)	Reservoir / Pool	CO_2	Included	Included	Included
Shrubs and herbaceous understory carbon	Reservoir / Pool	CO_2	Included	Optional	Optional
Standing dead carbon (carbon in all portions of dead, standing trees)	Reservoir / Pool	CO_2	Included	Included	Included
Lying dead wood carbon	Reservoir / Pool	CO_2	Optional	Optional	Optional
Litter and duff carbon (carbon in dead plant material)	Reservoir / Pool	CO_2	Optional	Optional	Optional
Soil carbon	Reservoir / Pool	CO_2	Optional or included	Optional or included	Optional or included
Carbon in in-use forest products	Reservoir / Pool	CO_2	Included	Included	Included
Forest product carbon in landfills	Reservoir / Pool	CO_2	Excluded	Excluded when project harvesting exceeds baseline; inlcuded when project harvesting is below baseline	Excluded when project harvesting exceeds baseline; inlcuded when project harvesting is below baseline

(Continued)

Table 13.3 (Continued)

Description	Type	Gas	Reforestation	Improved Forest Management	Avoided Conversion
Secondary Effect Sources, Sinks, and Reservoirs					
Biological emissions from site preparation activities	Source	CO_2	Included	Included	Included
Mobile combustion emissions from site preparation activities	Source	CO_2	Included	Excluded	Excluded
		CH_4	Excluded	Excluded	Excluded
		N2O	Excluded	Excluded	Excluded
Mobile combustion emissions from ongoing project operation & maintenance	Source	CO_2	Excluded	Excluded	Excluded
		CH_4	Excluded	Excluded	Excluded
		N_2O	Excluded	Excluded	Excluded
Stationary combustion emissions from ongoing project operation & maintenance	Source	CO_2	Excluded	Excluded	Excluded
		CH4	Excluded	Excluded	Excluded
		N2O	Excluded	Excluded	Excluded
Biological emissions from clearing of forestland outside the Project area	Source	CO_2	Excluded	Excluded	Included
Biological emissions / removals from changes in harvesting on forestland outside the Project Area	Source / sink	CO_2	Included	Included/ Excluded	Excluded
Combustion emissions from production, transportation, and disposal of forest products	Source	CO_2	Excluded	Excluded	Excluded
		CH_4	Excluded	Excluded	Excluded
		N_2O	Excluded	Excluded	Excluded
Combustion emissions from production, transportation, and disposal of alternative materials to forest products	Source	CO_2	Excluded	Excluded	Excluded
		CH_4	Excluded	Excluded	Excluded
		N2O	Excluded	Excluded	Excluded
Biological emissions from decomposition of forest products	Source	CO_2	Included	Included	Included
		CH_4	Excluded	Excluded	Excluded
		N_2O	Excluded	Excluded	Excluded

Derived from CAR (2010, pp. 26–36)

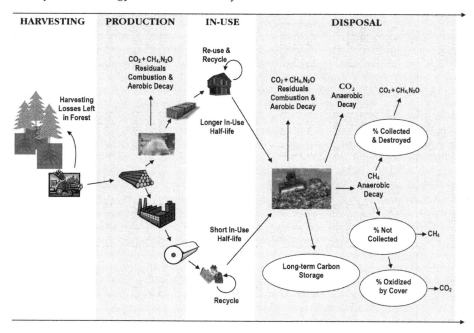

Figure 13.4 Pathways of Harvested Forest Products
Source: BC 2011

wood products, to paper products, to biofuel and disposal to landfill (see Figure 13.4). The precise estimation of these data is elusive because of the wide range of specific factors that can influence the rate of storage/loss, including type of wood, wood product, end use, location of production and use, and nature of disposal (BC 2011).

Companies contemplating forest-based carbon offsets must also address the "unavoidable risk of reversal", where human or natural induced events affect the sequestration of carbon (BC 2011). These risks include wildfire, disease or insect outbreak, wind throw from hurricane or other wind events, illegal harvesting, unplanned harvest, mining activity, or land use change.

4. Marketing of Biodiversity Credits

This fourth and final initiative proposed to Ooteel by the consultants was the most tentative, yet it held the promise of future returns as the global markets for biodiversity have continued to emerge and mature. Biodiversity is notoriously difficult to quantify, although several outstanding attempts have been made to generate quantitative measures to facilitate the development of monitoring and market making (Rio Tinto & Earthwatch 2006; GRI, 2007). Biodiversity markets have been defined as "any payment for the protection, restoration, or management of biodiversity. Just a small sample includes: biodiversity offsets, conservation easements, certified biodiversity-friendly products and services, bioprospecting, payments for biodiversity management, hunting permits, and ecotourism" (Ecosystem Marketplace 2009, p. 1).

A strong case has already been made that corporate attention to this subject is good for risk reduction and ultimately the bottom line (Earthwatch 2000 n.d.; OECD 2001, 2002, 2003, 2004; F&C 2004; IUCN 2004 and n.d.; GRI 2007; Shell Oil & IUCN 2008; SCBD 2010; UNEP 2020; MISTRA 2021). For example, Earthwatch (n.d) lists some of the major components of a business case for a corporate biodiversity-related strategy: managing risks, facilitating legal compliance with new regulations and legislation, improving reputation, attracting and retaining staff, financial benefits from cutting costs, avoiding fines and enhancing sales opportunities from green credentials, gaining and retaining investment, retaining the license to operate, securing sustainable supply chains, and demonstrating a commitment to corporate social responsibility.

Ecosystem Marktplace has produced several reports on the state of biodiversity markets (2009, 2010a, 2021) where they report that the global market size for biodiversity offsets and compensation programs was $4.88 billion in 2016, with a North American dominance (Ecosystem Marketplace 2021. The greatest volume of biodiversity-related payments and area in North America relate to US aquatic compensatory mitigation at $3.26 billion in 2016.

There have already been several major private sector initiatives undertaken to create and maintain a market in biodiversity values. For example, British-based Canopycapital has established a template for investment in ecosystem services including biodiversity (www.canopycapital.co.uk), and a major NGO-corporate collaboration has been established under the rubric of Business and Biodiversity Offsets Programme (BBOP) (forest-trends.org). Initiated by Forest Trends, Conservation International and the Wildlife Conservation Society, this organization has an advisory board from a large group of international agencies, NGOs and a diverse range of corporate sponsors such as Anglo America, Newmont, Sherritt, Alcoa, Rio Tinto and Shell Oil. The BBOP program has provided extensive documentation to assist corporations in participating in this emerging market, including a biodiversity offset cost-benefit handbook (Forest Trends 2009b), biodiversity offset design handbook (Forest Trends 2009c), biodiversity offset implementation handbook (Forest Trends 2009d), and extensive indepth case studies from the US (Forest Trends 2009e), Ghana (Forest Trends 2009g), and Madagascar (Forest Trends 2009f).

Many of these studies and initiatives appear to be concerned with companies engaging in activities which endanger biodiversity. Consequently, they fund the creation of biodiversity reserves or activities on- or offsite to compensate for this damage. The opportunities that Ooteel might, as a consequence, have been able to capitalize on were threefold: (1) offering companies who are reducing biodiversity as a result of their business activities a distant offsite opportunity to offset, (2) offering companies who are engaging in some other form of environmentally detrimental activity the opportunity to "cross offset," or (3) offering companies and other investors an opportunity to invest in biodiversity credits for other reasons (goodwill, desire to protect and preserve the environment.

As mentioned above, the development of quantifiable indicators for biodiversity remains a significant challenge to implementation. These include (OECD 2019, p. 18):

linguistic ambiguity, unnecessary complexity and redundant language . . . most of the [20] targets lack quantifiable elements, meaning there was no measurable threshold that could be met in order to judge if the target has been reached. Further . . . only two targets were composed of entirely quantifiable elements, meaning that in the vast majority of cases the measuring of target attainment is not possible. . . .

Complexity undermines the ability of countries to identify what actions need to be taken to attain the targets. Further, the use of ambiguous language can lead to divergent interpretations among Parties creating 'wiggle room', further hampering target attainment.

The Global Reporting Initiative (GRI 2016) included four topic-specific disclosures in their list of performance metrics available to participating corporations: *Disclosure 304-1* Operational sites owned, leased, managed in, or adjacent to, protected areas and areas of high biodiversity value outside protected areas; *Disclosure 304-2* Significant impacts of activities, products, and services on biodiversity; *Disclosure 304-3* Habitats protected or restored; and *Disclosure 304-4* IUCN Red List species and national conservation list species with habitats in areas affected by operations.

A problem sometimes posed by the choice of biodiversity measures is that they are either process variables or do not lend themselves to quantification and monetization for market-based transactions. One of the most exhaustive studies to address the complexities of operationalizing biodiversity-based instruments was produced by the joint efforts of Rio Tinto and the Earthwatch Institute (2006). Although conceived as an aid to mining operations, this work has implications far beyond this particular sector. The report addressed, in turn, such critical issues as biodiversity values; biodiversity risks; the advantages of going beyond species richness to include abundance, variation, and distribution; limitations in the use of nature indicators (including quality of the data, selection and evaluation, optimal conditions and scale); and a list of several potential indicators drawn from a range of international sources with critical commentary on each (see Table 13.4 where S= state of biodiversity; P = pressure; R = response indicator; a = activities; p = processes).

Table 13.4 Forty Potential Biodiversity Indicators

Guidance / Indicator	Source	Type	Comments
EN6. Location and size of land owned, leased, or managed in biodiversity-rich habitats	GRIc	P	
EN7. Description of the major impacts on biodiversity associated with activities and/or products and services in terrestrial, freshwater, and marine environments.	GRIc	PS	Means of measurement and reporting unclear
EN23. Total amount of land owned, leased, or managed for production activities or extractive use.	GRIa	P	Low linkage to biodiversity impacts
EN24. Amount of impermeable surface as a percentage of land purchased or leased.	GRIa	P	Link to biodiversity unclear
EN25. Impacts of activities and operations on protected and sensitive areas. (e.g., IUCN protected area categories 1–4, World Heritage Sites, and Biosphere Reserves).	GRIa	S	Means of measurement and reporting unclear

(Continued)

Table 13.4 (Continued)

Guidance / Indicator	Source	Type	Comments
EN26. Changes to natural habitats resulting from activities and operations and percentage of habitat protected or restored. Identify type of habitat affected and its status.	GRIa	S	Means of measurement and reporting unclear. More than one indicator
EN27. Objectives, programmes, and targets for protecting and restoring native ecosystems and species in degraded areas.	GRIa	R	Means of measurement and reporting unclear
EN28. Number of IUCN Red List species with habitats in areas affected by operations.	GRIa	S	
EN29. Business units currently operating or planning operations in or around protected or sensitive areas.	GRIa	P	
Native vegetation clearance	ICMM	S	
Aquatic habitat destruction	ICMM	S, P	
Introduced species (e.g. richness, composition, abundance, distribution)	ICMM	P	
Human inhabitancy (e.g. number of employees)	ICMM	P	Low relevance to biodiversity
Fragmentation (e.g. vegetation patch size, area occupied by roads and tracks)	ICMM	P	
Extent and condition of native vegetation (e.g. species richness, cover abundance, distribution of species/vegetation, stand-age distribution)	ICMM	S	Vague and needs to be linked to key feature's requirements
Extent and condition of terrestrial fauna habitat (e.g. density of logs, tree size density, plant species diversity)	ICMM	S/P	As above
Extent and condition of aquatic habitats (e.g. water depth, vegetation cover abundance/ composition, dissolved oxygen, invertebrate taxa composition/ abundance	ICMM	S/P	As above
Soil condition and nutrient cycling (e.g. nutrient levels, soil infiltration rate, depth of litter layer, ecosystem function analysis)	ICMM	S/P	Linkage to biodiversity features not very clear
Nutrient conditions of aquatic habitats	ICMM	P	
Significant (extinct, endangered, vulnerable, or otherwise threatened) species and communities (flora and fauna) e.g. number of species or area of communities	ICMM	S	Vague and difficult to measure

(Continued)

Table 13.4 (Continued)

Guidance / Indicator	Source	Type	Comments
Microclimate	ICMM	P	Linkage to biodiversity features not very clear
Terrestrial, marine, estuarine and wetland protected areas (e.g. hectares or funds committed to management)	GRI, ICMM	Ra	
Recovery plans (e.g. ratio of plans for significant species to number of significant species)	ICMM	Ra	Low value unless actions are reported
Pest plant and animal plans (e.g. implementation of pest management plans, area of weeds controlled)	ICMM	Ra	
Rehabilitation plans (e.g. area revegetated, number of new species recorded since implementation)	ICMM	Ra	
Extent of area by forest type relative to total forest area	MP	S	
Extent of area by forest type and by age class or successional stage	MP	S	
Extent of area by forest type in protected area categories as defined by IUCN2 or other classification systems	MP	P	
Extent of areas by forest type in protected areas defined by age class or successional stage	MP	P	
Fragmentation of forest types	MP	P/S	
The number of forest dependent species	MP	S	Vague and difficult to measure
The status (threatened, rare, vulnerable, endangered, or extinct) of forest dependent species at risk of not maintaining viable breeding populations, as determined by legislation or scientific assessment	MP	S	As above
Number of forest dependent species that occupy a small portion of their former range	MP	S	As above
Population levels of representative species from diverse habitats monitored across their range	MP	S	Need to be linked to objectives
Percent change in number of threatened species in each IUCN Red List category, number of species downlisted, and number of species that have gone extinct	CI	S	Dependent on many factors and other organizations
Percentage improvement towards achieving downlisting of each threatened species, concentrating on rates of decline, starting with Critically Endangered Species	CI	S	Difficult to measure, and dependent on many factors and organizations

Table 13.4 (Continued)

Guidance / Indicator	Source	Type	Comments
Percentage and total number of all Key Biodiversity Areas that are protected with (a) legal recognition and (b) biodiversity conservation as an official goal	CI	S	Dependent on many factors and other organizations
Percentage change in habitat cover at Key Biodiversity Areas	CI	S	Does not take into account habitat quality
Change in fragmentation statistics	CI	S	
Percentage change in suitable habitat cover for corridor-level species	CI	S	

Source: RioTinto and Earthwatch 2006, pp. 31-33

Because of the inherent complexities in arriving at defensible biodiversity indicators, Coady (2002, p. 396) argued that

> to assess the creation of biodiversity values, it makes sense to focus on the elements that sustain biodiversity such as habitat, rather than the biodiversity itself. Because biodiversity is not a thing, but a "cluster of concepts," one cannot purchase an amount of it. Managing for habitat becomes a surrogate for protecting and managing species.

Because both the markets for carbon and biodiversity are subsets of the larger concept of paying for ecosystem services (PES) this, in turn, offers the prospect for bundling both of these components in a new, more broadly focused, sustainability instrument focused on habitat management.

The adoption of a PES-based system might have been the most productive avenue for Ooteel to pursue in operationalizing this fourth element of its revised corporate strategy. For example, the government of Costa Rica compensates landowners for four main environmental services of which biodiversity is one (Porras & Chacon-Cascante 2018). Table 13.5 describes coverage of Costa Rican PES between 1997 and 2016 and Table 13.6 summarizes payment levels in 2012. This is just one example of an emerging international market in payments for such services (Wunder 2005; Wertz-Kanounnikoff 2006; Jack 2008; Katoomba Group & UNEP 2008; Kumar & Murdian 2008; FAO n.d.; WWF n.d.). Studies of this market across all sectors in 2010 (e.g., forestry, agriculture, water resources, etc.) identified over 300 programs worldwide with a value in excess of $6.5 billion (OECD 2010). Landell-Mills and Porras (2002) and the UN FAO (2007) listed five principal components of forest sector PES programs (in order of size): carbon sequestration, biodiversity conservation, watershed protection, landscape beauty, and bundled services. The payment for ecosystem services is an archetypal example of the successful application of Coase's Theorem, where a private exchange between two parties addresses an environmental issue to the satisfaction of both parties (Engel et al. 2008; Farley & Costanza 2010). Wunder et al. (2008) provided one of the most comprehensive analyses of global PES programs, their characteristics, location, design features, payments, factors affecting effectiveness, efficiency, and welfare effects. Updated examples

Table 13.5 Coverage of Costa Rica PES between 1997 and 2016

Description	Amounts
Forest protection	1,050,135 hectares (90 per cent of total area receiving PES)
Forest management	30,575 hectares
Reforestation	69,889 hectares
Natural regeneration	19,711 hectares
Totals ha by 2016	1,170,310 hectares
Total trees in agroforestry	6,824,171 trees
Number of contracts	16,498 trees
Funding allocated - cumulative 1997–2017	US$ 412.4 million (unadjusted by inflation) US$ 295.3 million (in 2017 prices)

Source: Porras & Chacon-Cascante (2018)

Table 13.6 Payment levels by modality in Costa Rica PES in 2017

Modalities	US$ (total)	US$/ha/ year
Strict forest protection (5-year contracts) General	301 US$/ha	$ 60.00
In water priority areas	376 US$/ha	$ 75.00
Reforestation		
Fast growing species (10-year contract)	1135 US$/ha	$ 113.00
Medium growth rate species (16-year contract)	1337 US$/ha	$ 84.00
Native species (16-year contract)	2005 US$/ha	$ 125.00
Natural regeneration for protection, and for timber production (5-year contracts)	193 US$/ha	$ 39.00
Sustainable forest management (5-year contracts)	235 US$/ha	$ 47.00
Agroforestry (5-year contracts) General	US$ 2/tree	$ 0.30
Coffee/ native species	US$ 2/tree	$ 0.50

Source: Porras & Chacon-Cascante (2018)

and overview of the current state of both theory and practice can be found in several sources (*Ecosystem Services* 2015; Grima et al. 2016; and IPBES 2019 and 2023).

Postscript

Although the decision faced by Ooteel occurred a decade ago, it is instructive to see the current state of the strategic target markets that the company was thinking of entering. The updated information is as follows:

- *Forest Certification*: about 13% of global forests are now ecocertified
- *Eco-tourism*: the global market is estimated at $200 billion in 2023

- *Market for carbon credits*: estimates vary but depend on the categorization. The total global offset/carbon credit market was valued at $332 billion in 2022 and is estimated to grow to $1,603 billion by 2028. A large proportion ($95 billion) of this is due to mandated trading in the European trading system (ETS), a smaller proportion of which is due to the voluntary carbon offset market, estimated at $2 billion 2021 and estimated to grow to $10–40 billion by 2030.
- *Market for biodiversity credits*: in 2017, the global biodiversity market was estimated at 91 billion.

Appendix: Leadership in Energy and Environmental Design (Leed)

LEED is a third party certification program and the nationally accepted benchmark for the design, construction and operation of high performance green buildings. Developed by the US Green Building Council in 2000 through a consensus based process, LEED serves as a tool for buildings of all types and sizes. LEED certification offers third party validation of a project's green features and verifies that the building is operating exactly the way it was designed to. LEED certification is available for all building types including new construction and major renovation; existing buildings; commercial interiors; core and shell; schools and homes. LEED systems for neighborhood development, retail and healthcare are currently pilot testing. As of May 2021, there were 38,637 LEED certifications representing over 5.9 billion gross square feet in the US (USGBC and US Census, cited by Statista). LEED is a point based system where building projects earn LEED points for satisfying specific green building criteria. Within each of the seven LEED credit categories, projects must satisfy particular prerequisites and earn points. The five categories include Sustainable Sites (SS), Water Efficiency (WE), Energy and Atmosphere (EA), Materials and Resources (MR) and Indoor Environmental Quality (IEQ). An additional category, Innovation in Design (ID), addresses sustainable building expertise as well as design measures not covered under the five environmental categories. The number of points the project earns determines the level of LEED Certification the project receives. LEED certification is available in four progressive levels according to the following scale: There are 100 base points; 6 possible Innovation in Design and 4 Regional Priority points: Certified 40–49 points, Silver 50–59 points, Gold 60–79 points, Platinum 80 points and above (Casey 2024).

References

Allied Market Research (2022) "Ecotourism market: global opportunity analysis and industry forecast, 2021–2027."

Allied Market Research (2024) "Ecotourism market size, share, competitive landscape and trend analysis report by age group, by traveler type, by sales channel: global opportunity analysis and industry forecast, 2024–2035."

Bowyer, Jim L. (2008) "The Green Movement and the forest products industry," *Forest Product Journal*, 58(7/8): 7–13.

British Columbia (BC) Ministry of Environment. (2011) *Protocol for the Creation of Forest Carbon Offsets in British Columbia*, August 12.

Canada Green Building Council (CAGBC) (2010) "Chain of custody for certified wood products within LEED Canada." http://www.cagbc.org/AM/PDF/FAQ_Certified_Wood_in_LEED_June_2010.pdf

Casey, Cillian (2024) "The LEED rating system explained," CIM Environmental Pty Ltd., February 12.

Castro, Rene, et al. (2000) "The Costa Rican experience with market instruments to mitigate climate change and conserve biodiversity," *Environmental Monitoring and Assessment*, 61:75–92.

CFI Education Inc. (2022) "Carbon credit – definition, types and trading of carbon credits."

Climate Action Reserve (CAR) (2010) *Forest Project Protocol for Board Approval*, Version 3.2 August 20.

Climate Action Reserve (CAR) (n.d.) CORSIA (Carbon Offsetting and Reduction Scheme for International Aviation). https://www.climateactionreserve.org/corsia/

Coady, Linda (2002) "Iisaak: A new economic model for conservation-based forestry in coastal old growth forests, B.C," in Peter N. Nemetz (Ed.), *Bringing Business on Board: Sustainable Development and the B-School Curriculum*. 561–576. JBA Press.

Conroy, Michael E. (2007) *Branded! How the Certification Revolution is Transforming Global Corporations.* New Society Publishers.

Conservation International (n.d.) *Monitoring Support Program: Monitoring for Conservation Planning and Management.*

Earthwatch (2000) *Case Studies in Business & Biodiversity.* http://businessandbiodiversity.org/pdf/bandbcasestudies.pdf

Earthwatch (n.d.) *Engaging Businesses with Biodiversity. Guidelines for Local Biodiversity Partnerships.* http://businessandbiodiversity.org/pdf/LBAPdocument.pdf

Earthwatch, IUCN and World Business Council for Sustainable Development (2002) *Business & Biodiversity. The Handbook for Corporate Action.*

Ecosystem Marketplace (2009) *State of Biodiversity Markets. Offset and Compensation Programs Worldwide.*

Ecosystem Marketplace (2010a) *Update. State of Biodiversity Markets. Offset and Compensation Programs Worldwide.*

Ecosystem Marketplace (2010b) *State of the Forest Carbon Markets 2009. Taking Root and Branching Out.*

Ecosystem Marketplace (2010c) *Building Bridges. State of the Voluntary Carbon Markets 2010.*

Ecosystem Marketplace (2021) "Voluntary carbon markets top $1 billion in 2021 with newly reported trades," Ecosystem Marketplace, COP26 Bulletin, November 10.

Ecosystem Marketplace (2022) *Markets in Motion – State of the Voluntary Carbon Markets 2021.*

Ecosystem Services (2015) "Biodiversity offsets as market-based instruments for ecosystem services?" 15: 1–190.

Engel, Stefanie, et al. (2008) "Designing payments for environmental services in theory and practice: an overview of the issues." *Ecological Economics* 65: 663–674.

FAO, UNDP, UNEP (2008) *UN Collaborative Programme on Reducing Emissions from Deforestation and Forest Degradation in Developing Countries (UN-REDD).* https://www.un-redd.org/sites/default/files/2021-10/UN-REDD_FrameworkDocument.pdf

FAO, UNDP, UNEP (2010) *The UN-REDD Programme Strategy 2011–2015.* https://www.un-redd.org/sites/default/files/2021-10/UNREDD_PB5_Programme%20Strategy%202010-2015.pdf

FAO (2021) *Forest Product Annual Market Review 2020–2021.* https://unece.org/sites/default/files/2021-11/2114516E_Inside_Final_web.pdf

F&C Management Ltd. (2004) *Is Biodiversity a Material Risk for Companies?* http://www.businessandbiodiversity.org/pdf/FC%20Biodiversity%20Report%20FINAL.pdf

Farley, Joshua & Robert Costanza (2010) "Payments for ecosystem service: from local to global." *Ecological Economics,* 69: 2060–2068.

Fernholz, Kathryn, et al. (2021) "Forest certification update 2021: the pace of change," Dovetail Partners, https://www.dovetailinc.org/portfoliodetail.php?id=60085a177dc07.

Forest Stewardship Council (FSC) (n.d.) "Certification," https://us.fsc.org/en-us/certification

Forest Trends, Conservation International and Wildlife Conservation Society (2009a) *Business, Biodiversity Offsets and BBOP: An Overview,* https://www.forest-trends.org/wp-content/uploads/imported/overview-phase-1-pdf.pdf

Forest Trends, Conservation International and Wildlife Conservation Society (2009b) *Biodiversity Offset Cost-Benefit Handbook,* https://www.forest-trends.org/wp-content/uploads/imported/biodiversity-offset-cost-benefit-handbook-pdf.pdf

Forest Trends, Conservation International and Wildlife Conservation Society (2009c) *Biodiversity Offset Design Handbook.* https://www.forest-trends.org/wp-content/uploads/imported/biodiversity-offset-design-handbook-pdf.pdf

Forest Trends, Conservation International and Wildlife Conservation Society (2009d) *Biodiversity Offset Implementation Handbook.* https://documents1.worldbank.org/curated/en/344901481176051661/pdf/110820-WP-BiodiversityOffsetsUserGuideFinalWebRevised-PUBLIC.pdf

Forest Trends, Conservation International and Wildlife Conservation Society (2009e) *BBOP Pilot Project Case Study. Bainbridge Island.* https://www.forest-trends.org/wp-content/uploads/bbop/bainbridge-case-study-pdf.pdf

Forest Trends, Conservation International and Wildlife Conservation Society (2009f) *BBOP Pilot Project Case Study. The Ambatovy Project.* https://ambatovy.com/en/wp-content/uploads/2023/12/BPOP-REPORT.pdf

Forest Trends, Conservation International and Wildlife Conservation Society (2009g) *BBOP Pilot Project Case Study. Akyem Gold Mining Project, Eastern Region, Ghana.* https://www. forest-trends.org/wp-content/uploads/bbop/newmont-case-study-pdf.pdf

Germain, Rene H. and Patrick C. Penfield (2010) "The potential certified wood supply chain bottleneck and its impact on leadership in energy and environmental design construction projects in New York State," *Forest Products Journal*, 80(2): 114–118.

Global Reporting Initiative (GRI) (2002) *Sustainability Reporting Guidelines.* https://www. globalreporting.org/resourcelibrary/G3.1-Guidelines-Incl-Technical-Protocol.pdf

Global Reporting Initiative (GRI) (2006/2007) *Global Reporting Initiative. Sustainability Report.*

Global Reporting Initiative (GRI) (2007) *Biodiversity: A GRI Reporting Resource.*

Global Reporting Initiative (GRI) Standards (2016) "GRI 304 – biodiversity indicators,"

Grima, Nelson, et al. (2016) "Payment for ecosystem services (pes) in Latin America: Analysing the performance of 40 case studies," *Ecosystem Services*, 17: 24–32.

Gullison, R.E. (2003) "Does forest certification conserve biodiversity?" *Oryx*, 37(2): 153–165.

Gustin, Georgina (2021) "Trees fell faster in the years since companies and governments promised to stop cutting them down," *Inside Climate News* (May 19).

Hansen, Eric & John Punches (1998) "Collins Pine: Lessons from a pioneer. Case study," Oregon State University.

Imarc (2022) *Green Buildings Materials Market: Global Industry Trends, Share, Size, Growth Opportunity and Forecast 2022–2027.*

Intergovernmental Panel on Climate Change (IPCC) (2006) "Forest land," in *Guidelines for National Greenhouse Gas Inventories, vol. 4: Agriculture, Forestry and Other Land Use.* https:// www.ipcc-nggip.iges.or.jp/public/2006gl/pdf/4_Volume4/V4_04_Ch4_Forest_Land.pdf

Intergovernmental Science-Policy Platform on Biodiversity and Ecosystem Services (IPBES) (2019) *The Global Assessment on Biodiversity and Ecosystem Services.*

International Council on Mining & Metals (ICMM) (2010) *Mining and Biodiversity. A collection of case studies – 2010 edition.*

International Council on Mining & Metals (ICMM) (n.d.) *Good Practice Guidance for Mining and Biodiversity.*

International Ecotourism Society (TIES) (2006) *TIES Global Ecotourism Fact Sheet*, September.

International Ecotourism Society (2005) *Consumer Demand and Operator Support for Socially and Environmentally Responsible Tourism.*

International Ecotourism Society (TIES) (2006) *Global Ecotourism Fact Sheet.*

International Institute for Environment and Development (IIED) (2001) "Pro-poor tourism: harnessing the world's largest industry for the world's poor," *Opinion*, May, pp. 1–8.

International Standards Organization (ISO) (2006) *ISO 14064-2 Greenhouse Gases – Part 2: Specification with Guidance at the Project Level for Quantification, Monitoring and Reporting of Greenhouse Gas Emission Reductions Or Removal Enhancements.*

Jacquet, Jennifer, et al. (2010) "Seafood stewardship in crisis," *Nature* 467(2): 28–29.

Katoomba Group, UNEP & Forest Trends (2008) *Payment for Ecosystem Services: Getting Started. A Primer.* https://wedocs.unep.org/bitstream/handle/20.500.11822/9150/payment_ecosystem. pdf?sequence=1&isAllowed=y

Kelsey, Jack B., et al. (2008) "Designing payments for ecosystem services: lessons from previous experience with incentive-based mechanisms," *PNAS* 105(28): 9465–9470.

Kumar, Pushpam and Roidan Murdian (eds.) (2008) *Payment for Ecosystem Services*, Oxford University Press.

Landell-Mills, Natasha and Ina. T. Porras (2002) *Silver Bullet or Fools' Gold? A Global Review of Markets for Forest Environmental Services and Their Impact on the Poor.* IIED.

Lister, Jane (2011) *Corporate Social Responsibility and the State: International Approaches to Forest Co-Regulation.* UBC Press.

Miljoeko A. B. & SustainAbility (2000) *Screening of Screening Companies.* Socially Responsible Investment, SRI.

National Academy of Sciences (2010) *Certifiably Sustainable? The Role of Third-Party Certification Systems.* Report of a workshop.

National Environmental Research Institute, Denmark (NERI) (1995) *Nature Indicators Survey.*

New York Times (2021) "Tropical forest destruction accelerated in 2020," March 31.

Organization for Economic Cooperation and development (OECD) (2001) *Valuation of Biodiversity Benefits: Selected Studies.*

Organization for Economic Cooperation and development (OECD) (2002) *Handbook of Biodiversity Valuation. A Guide for Policy Makers.*

Organization for Economic Cooperation and development (OECD) (2003) *Harnessing Markets for Biodiversity. Towards Conservation and Sustainable Use.*

Organization for Economic Cooperation and development (OECD) (2004) *Handbook of Market Creation for Biodiversity. Issues in Implementation.*

Organization for Economic Cooperation and development (OECD) (2010) *Paying for Biodiversity. Enhancing the Cost-effectiveness of payments for ecosystem services.*

Organization for Economic Cooperation and development (OECD) (2019) "The Post-2020 biodiversity framework: Targets, indicators and measurability implications at global and national level," November.

Porras, Ina & Adrian Chacon-Cascante (2018) "Costa Rica's payments for ecosystem services, case study module 2," International Institute for Environment and Development (IIED).

Reuters (2023) "Voluntary carbon markets set to become at least five times bigger by 2030 – Shell," January 19.

Rio Tinto & Earthwatch (2006) *A Review of Biodiversity Conservation Performance Measures.*

Secretariat of the Convention on Biological Diversity (SCBD) (2006) *Global Biodiversity Outlook 2.*

Secretariat of the Convention on Biological Diversity (SCBD) (2010) *Global Biodiversity Outlook 3.*

Shell Oil & IUNC (2008) *Building Biodiversity Business.* https://www.iucn.org/sites/default/files/import/downloads/bishop_et_al_2008.pdf

Smith, James E., et al. (2005) *Methods for Calculating Forest Ecosystem and Harvested Carbon with Standard Estimates for Forest Types of the United States,* USDA, Northeastern Research Station, General Technical Report NE-343.

Statista (2022) "LEED gross square footage certifications in USA as of 2021," US Green Building Council and US Census Bureau, March 30.

Statista (2022) "Number of LEED project certifications in USA as of 2021," US Green Building Council, March 30,.

Statista (2024) "Sustainable tourism worldwide – statistics & facts."

SustainAbility (2011a) *Signed, Sealed . . . Delivered? Behind Certifications and Beyond Limits.*

SustainAbility (2011b) *Rate the Raters, Phase Four: The Necessary Future of Ratings.* July.

SustainAbility and Mistra (2004) *Values for Money: Reviewing the Quality of SRI Research.* https://www.fondsprofessionell.at/upload/attach/86869.pdf

Swedish Foundation for Strategic Environmental Research (MISTRA) (2021) "Aligning markets with biodiversity," June.

TerraChoice (2010) *The Sins of Greenwashing.* Home and Family Edition.

United Nations Economic Commission for Europe (UNECE) (2011) *Forest Products Annual Market Review 2010–2011.*

United Nations Environment Programme (UNEP) (2020) *Beyond Business as Usual: Biodiversity Targets and Finance. Managing Biodiversity Risks Across Business Sectors,* World Conservation Monitoring Centre.

UN FAO (2007) *The State of Food and Agriculture 2007.*

UN World Tourism Organization (WTO) (2010) *World Tourism Barometer,* 8(3), October.

UN World Tourism Organization (UNWTO) (2020) *International Tourism Highlights, 2020 edition.* https://www.e-unwto.org/doi/epdf/10.18111/9789284422456

UN World Tourism Organization (UNWTO) (2021) *World Tourism Barometer, Statistical Annex,* 19(3), May.

Wertz-Kanounnikoff, Sheila (2006) "Payments for environmental services – a solution for biodiversity conservation?" *Ressources Naturelles,* 12: 1–16.

World Business Council for Sustainable Development (WBCSD) and World Resources Institute (WRI) (2005) *The GHG Protocol for Project Accounting.*

World Conservation Union (IUCN) (2004) *Biodiversity Offsets: Views, Experience, and the Business Case.*

World Resources Institute (WRI) (2005) *Ecosystems and Human Well-Being. Biodiversity Synthesis.* Millennium Ecosystem Assessment.

World Travel & Tourism Council (WTTC) (2021) *Travel & Tourism Economic Impact 2021: Global economic Impact & Trends 2021.*

Wunder, Sven (2005) *Payments for Environmental Services: Some Nuts and Bolts.* CIFOR Occasional Paper No. 42.

Wunder, Sven, et al. (2008) "Taking stock: a comparative analysis of payments for environmental services programs in developed and developing countries." *Ecological Economics*, 65: 834–852.

Yuan, Yuan & Ivan Eastin (2007) "Forest certification and its influence on the forest products industry in China." CINTRAFOR Working Paper 110.

14 Defining Sustainability and its Components

Case Study of Suncor Ltd.

Towards the far end of the corporate sustainability spectrum are firms that claim to be sustainable but there is no persuasive evidence to support these claims. Located in northern Alberta, Canada, Suncor is a leading producer of synthetic crude oil extracted from large oil sand deposits. This company and other oil sands producers have assumed particular importance because they sit on massive petroleum deposits rivalling those of Saudi Arabia, and because they offer a unique opportunity for the United States to access large supplies of oil from a friendly neighbor with minimal risk from disruption due to political, social, or military factors.

The company originally began exploiting the oil sands in the mid-1960s under the name of Great Canadian Oil Sands Ltd. Corporate profitability is directly related to global petroleum prices, so prospects for the large-scale development of the oil sands had to await the run-up in prices within the last few decades. The raw material, called bitumen, is contained in a sand matrix that has been traditionally extracted in a manner like conventional strip mining and heated with reactants to create synthetic crude. This process relies on extensive use of natural gas (approximately 750 cu ft per barrel of bitumen) to provide the fuel for this energy-intensive technology (Alberta Chamber of Resources 2004). Since most of the deposits of bitumen are inaccessible by conventional surface mining techniques, the oil sands industry has also invested large sums of capital into developing an alternative method of extraction called *in situ* mining. This recovery process can access deeper deposits by drilling holes into the underground strata and using large quantities of heated water and reagents to force the bitumen to the surface. This process is estimated to require approximately 1500 cu ft of natural gas per barrel of bitumen (Alberta Chamber of Resources 2004). The advent of higher priced oil permitted the development of the oil sands that, because of their nature, are considerably more expensive to exploit than conventional crude oil (see Appendix One for recent financial data).

In the past, Suncor has been listed in at least four sustainability indexes: the Dow Jones Sustainability Index for North America, the TD Global Sustainability Fund, the Corporate Knight's Report on Clean Capitalism, and the Fortune list of green giants. This presents an usual paradox, since the oil sands have a significant environmental impact across all receiving media: air, water, and soil (see Figure 14.1). Appendix Two presents a more comprehensive list of these emissions in several categories reported by Suncor and the Canadian National Pollutant Release Inventory (NPRI): releases to air, releases to water bodies, releases to land, on-site disposal, and off-site disposal, or transfer for disposal or recycling. Unfortunately, some of these data are inaccurate. For example, a recent scientific study (He 2024) found that much more accurate data on organic carbon emissions collected by aircraft overflights found that

DOI: 10.4324/9781003170754-17

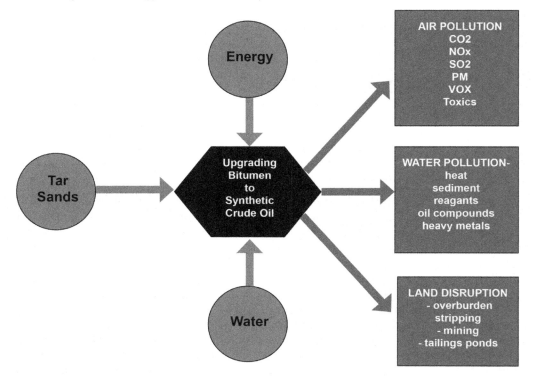

Figure 14.1 Environmental Impact of Oil Sands

these measurements exceeded those reported by the industry by over 1900–6300%. For example, NPRI data based on industry-reported output of 37,813 tonnes C in 2018 compared to the mean measured estimate of 1,585,000 tonnes C per year (range: 895,000–2,265,000) (He 2024, p. S35). These results demonstrated that the oilsands total organic carbon emissions alone were "equivalent to that from all other sources across Canada combined" (He 2024, p. 426).

In 2011, the oil sands industry began a public relations campaign to label its output as "ethical oil" to contrast it with petroleum from other nations with dubious social and political policies which impact human rights (*New York Times* Sept. 21, 2011). A major impetus for this campaign was to counter emerging concerns in both Europe and the United States about the environmental impacts of petroleum produced from the oil sands (*New York Times* December 8, 2010; Canada.com 2011). This campaign was largely abandoned after pushback even from some major supporters of oil sands development because of the incongruous nature of the claim (Finlay 2012).

The process of upgrading bitumen to synthetic crude oil has numerous environmental impacts in addition to land disturbance from the removal of boreal forest and soil overlaying the deposits. Emissions of SO_2, NO_x, and greenhouse gases, as well as water use, are greater on a per barrel basis than those associated with conventional petroleum recovery (Canada National Pollution Release Inventory 2023). In fact, the oil sands of Alberta represent one of the largest sources of carbon dioxide emissions on the planet. Estimates of direct emissions from the production process must be supplemented by estimates of the impact of open pit mining on carbon storage and sequestration by lost boreal forest and peatlands. It has been estimated that landscape changes due to currently approved surface extraction will release 11.4–47.3 million metric tons of stored carbon (equivalent to 41.8–173.4 tons of CO_2) (Rooney et al. 2012); and that tailings ponds can be a significant source of methane (CH_4), a greenhouse gas with a global warming potential (GWP) 23 times that of carbon dioxide (Alberta Auditor General 2011). Research suggests that the carbon dioxide emissions from this sector have been underestimated by almost 64% (Liggio et al. 2019). This is a significant error, given the major contribution of oil sands emissions to national GHG output.

In addition, the oil sands process produces large quantities of wastewater contaminated with toxic pollutants, which require storage in large tailings ponds for lengthy periods of time to facilitate settling and evaporation. Canada's National Pollutant Release Inventory (NPRI) – the equivalent of the American Toxic Release Inventory – lists several dozen pollutants of concern. There is continuing debate over the existence and severity of leakage from the tailings ponds (CEC 2020), as well as downwind deposition of pollutants which can influence water quality, aquatic biota, and possibly the health of aboriginals in downstream communities (Timoney & Lee 2009; Kelly et al. 2009, 2010).

Suncor is extremely sensitive to concerns over the environmental impacts of its operations and the public reaction thereto, since these impacts are a potential threat to both current and future markets for Suncor's synthetic crude as well as a possible threat to the company's social licence to operate. A large degree of negative international publicity resulted from the death of several hundred ducks which had landed on the surface of the tailings ponds of another major oil sands producer, Syncrude Ltd. (*New York Times* 2010), now owned by Suncor. Oil sands tailings ponds, some as high as 300 feet above the adjacent Athabasca River, currently cover over 170 sq km, of which Suncor accounts for approximately 40 sq km (Grant et al. 2010; see also Kunzig 2009). It has been estimated that 6 cubic meters of tailings are created for every cubic meter of bitumen recovered (Griffiths 2006).

The company's public image is enhanced by its inclusion in several sustainability indexes cited above and this inclusion appears to be based on corporate policies in several related areas. These are listed below in Table 14.1 with accompanying commentary that provides perspective on these activities under the heading "critique."

The Suncor case raises several issues that bear directly on the goal of corporate sustainability: standards for sustainability reporting, process versus performance measures, triple bottom line accounting, pollutant intensity measures versus total output, sustainability indexes, and best-in-class versus absolute measures of sustainability. Each is addressed in turn.

Sustainability Reporting

Suncor is one of many corporations that have chosen to report not only financial results but also their performance in the two other aspects of sustainability, namely environment and society. The standard procedure for so doing is to separately list results for a selection of performance indicators in each of these two major areas. In their annual reports on sustainability, Suncor has highlighted their results on such key environmental indicators as air emissions, water consumption, and land use, and social variables such as occupational injuries. These types of indicators have been developed by a wide range

Table 14.1 Suncor Sustainability Policies and Critique

Suncor's Sustainability policies	Critique
1. Use of GRI indicators	The choice of which indicators to include and publicize is at the discretion of each company. Some important environmental indicators currently not chosen by Suncor include: 302–5: reductions in energy requirements of products and services; 303–4 and 5: water discharge and consumption; 304–4: IUCN Red list species and national conservation list species with habitats in areas affected by operations; 305–6: emissions of ozone-depleting substances; 306–4: transport of hazardous waste; 308:1:new suppliers that were screened using environmental criteria; and 308–2: negative environmental impacts in the supply chain and actions taken. In general, however, while the reporting of indicators is a first step, it does not imply that a corporation is becoming any more sustainable or, in the case of Suncor, any less unsustainable. See the items below relating to land cover restoration, investment in renewables, hiring of aboriginals, GHG intensity, and water use.
2. Use of triple bottom line	As is common practice, the three accounts (financial, environmental and social) are presented separately without integration, thereby eliminating the opportunity to assess economic issues of materiality and risk (Nemetz 2013)
3. Intention to restore land cover	As of 2010, the company had achieved only a 0.2% level of restoration (Journal of Commerce 2010). The company has reported a 10% level of land reclamation in their 2018 sustainability report, however, an independent estimate places it closer to 0.1% (Pembina 2017). There is also the question of whether the original ecosystem can be replicated to any significant degree (G&M 12–03–11).
4. Investments in wind power and ethanol	As of 2010, Suncor's revenue from renewables represented only 0.1% of total revenues and capital investment in renewables was only 2.62% of total investment over the period 2002–2007. Since that time, the company has decided to scale back its renewable investments, particularly wind power, and focus on its core business of producing bitumen.
5. Use of carbon offsetting	The use of carbon offsetting has raised several major conceptual problems including concerns over the degree of additionality (Alberta Auditor General 2011).
6. Hiring local aboriginals + funding local initiatives	This must be offset against destruction of traditional hunting habitat, and concern over toxic chemicals in river water, fish and wildlife (Kelly et al. 2008 2009, Timony and Lee 2009, CBC 10–09–16) and possible links to cancer in a downstream aboriginal community (McLachlan 2014).
7. Shift to in situ recovery from surface mining	This entails much higher releases of GHG (Gosselin et al. 2001).
8. Commitment to lower GHG-intensity of production	Most of the major reductions in total GHG and GHG intensity occurred in the early years of operation and the company forecasts no significant changes over the next few years (Suncor 2018).
9. Commitment to reduce water use	The water intensity of oil sands production is approximately four times that of conventional crude oil. The company reported a drop in water consumption in 2017 after 3 consecutive years of increases. Surface water withdrawals are up however.

(Continued)

Table 14.1 (Continued)

Suncor's Sustainability policies	Critique
10. Commitment to seek replacement for natural gas in production process	It is unclear which fuel source would replace the intensive use of a high energy source to produce a lower quality energy product. At one point the idea of building nuclear reactors for the oil sands was floated and continues to receive occasion mention (CBC 19–05–21).
11. Plans to utilize carbon capture and storage	Carbon capture and storage is yet to achieve credible economic viability anywhere in the world (Greenpeace 16–07–01, Alberta Views 15–07–01, Smil 2010). See chapter 15 in this work.

of organizations – including commercial rating agencies, NGOs, standard-setting bodies, governments, international organizations, and multiple-stakeholder groups – in order to standardize the process of reporting and guarantee comparability both temporally and across companies.

One of the largest of these organizations is the Global Reporting Initiative (GRI) that issues sustainability guidelines for reporting on the economic, environmental and social dimensions of activities, products and services to a broad array of entities in addition to corporations. The choice of indicators is left to each organization and it is up to the corporation to seek third-party certification of the reported data, if so desired. This latitude allowed to each corporation can lead to the absence of key information, withheld either unintentionally or intentionally (Sridhar and Jones 2013).

In addition to the GRI, there are several other prominent agencies with promulgated guidelines or standards, including the United Nations, Organization for Economic Co-Operation and Development (OECD), AccountAbility, and the International Organization for Standardization (ISO). There are three basic types of standards (Oakley & Buckland 2004, pp. 134–135): (1) *principle-based* that set out "broad principles of behavior but do not specify how they are to be achieved or how conformity with them can be assessed," (2) *performance* standards that measure the actual achievements of the organization on the selected indicator, and (3) *process* standards that outline processes that an organization should follow in order to achieve sustainability. The conceptual difficulty of relying on process measures is that, while they may indicate good corporate intentions and activities, they fail to reflect whether the corporation has achieved any notable results with respect to sustainability. The ultimate measure in assessing a corporation's record on sustainability must be a measure of its performance.

Triple Bottom-Line Accounting

A corporation or other organizational entity that chooses to report on environmental and social effects of their operations is generally considered to have adopted triple bottom-line accounting but, clearly, the choice of standard system, number of indicators, and their level of detail, existence of temporal comparative data, and presence or absence of third-party certification all bear upon the question of validity. Perhaps the most critical conceptual difficulty with TBL accounting as currently practiced is that the three accounts – financial, environmental, and social – are standalone lists or statements that lack any form of integration. Under these circumstances, it can be difficult, if not impossible, for shareholders or other stakeholders to obtain any sense of the impact of these variables not only on the financial performance of the company, but also on the broader society, economy, and environment in which the corporation operates. This problem has been addressed by several companies that have attempted to integrate these measures into one overall statement (see, for example, the case of PUMA described in chapter 16).

Pollutant-Intensity vs. Total Pollutant Output

The ambiguous impact on the environment of reductions in pollutant-intensity has prompted many governmental regulatory agencies to abandon this type of requirement in favor of performance measures that can track total pollutant output. Pollutant-intensity reductions are a necessary but not sufficient criterion for reduced impact on the environment – the ultimate goal of any sustainability policy – because any reduction in pollution intensity can be offset by a compensating increase in product output. Changes in Suncor's GHG intensity of production and total GHG emissions are shown in Figure 14.2a, as well as historical production (Figure 14.2b). Figure 14.3 reflects the fact that *in situ* recovery is now the predominant mode of production in Alberta (Canada Energy Regulator 2021).

The challenge of producing consistent time trends of Suncor's GHG emission intensity in particular is compounded by at least three factors: (1) a change of units over time, (2) frequent retrospective revisions in these values, and (3) changes in emission categorization. In light of the last category, the time line of emission intensity in Figure 14.2 has been divided into two segments: before and after the change in the calculation of emissions.

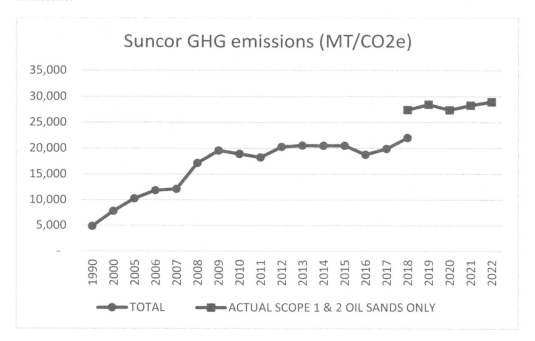

Figure 14.2a Suncor GHG Emissions – Total and Intensity

Adapted from Suncor Annual Reports

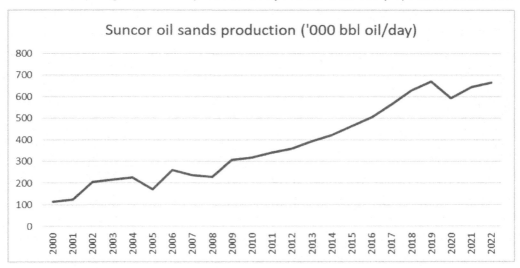

Figure 14.2b Suncor Production

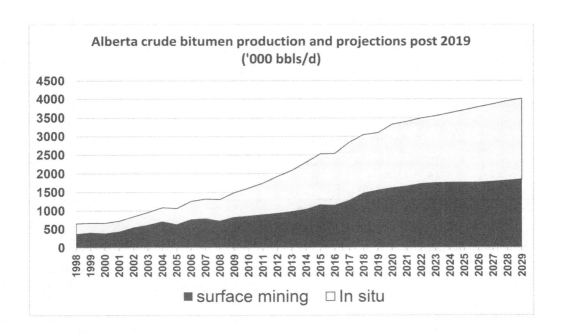

Figure 14.3 Alberta *in situ* vs. Surface Mining of Oil Sands Timeline
Source: Canada's Energy Regulator 2021

In its latest report on climate impacts, the company has listed its Scope 1 and 2 GHG emissions and categorized its potential Scope 3 emissions (see Table 14.2). Only three of these sources have been quantified although it has argued that these are the most significant.

Table 14.2 a, b Suncor Scope 1,2 and 3 Emissions

	2018	2019	2020	2021	2022
Scope 1	32.42	33.67	32.02	32.69	33.52
Scope 2	1.64	1.52	1.41	1.46	1.45
Total	*34.06*	*35.19*	*33.43*	*34.15*	*34.97*
in million tonnes of CO_2e					

Scope 3 emission estimates Location		*Category*	*Materiality*	*Data availability*	*Ability to influence*	*estimates*
UPSTREAM	1	purchased goods & services	1–10%	L	H	
	2	capital goods	1–10%	L	H	
	3	fuel & energy-related activities	1–10%	M	M	5–10 MT
	4	transportation & distribution	<1%	L	L	
	5	waste generated in operations	<1%	M	M	
	6	business travel	<1%	M	M	
	7	employee commuting	<1%	H	H	
	8	leased assets	<1%	H	M	
DOWNSTREAM	9	transportation & distribution	<1%	L	M	
	10	processing of sold products	1–10%	M	L	5–10 MT
	11	use of sold products	>50%	H	M	24–126 MT CO_2e
	12	end of life treatment of sold products	<1%	L	M	
	13	leased assets	<1%	M	L	
	14	franchises	0	M	L	
	15	investments	0	M	L	

Source: Adapted from Suncor Climate Report 2023

Suncor and Sustainability Indexes

Recently, Suncor has been listed on a least four sustainability-related indexes: FTSE4Good, Dow Jones Sustainability Index, CDP, and Progressive Aboriginal Relations (PAR). Perhaps the most prominent of these is the Dow Jones Sustainability Index (DJSI). The Index lists the criteria and weights adopted for inclusion in their sustainability index. In an earlier version of this index, the criterion of environmental reporting receives a weight of 3% and environmental performance, as measured by eco-efficiency, received a weight of 7%. Since then, the index weighted has been revised and the 2023 values are listed in Table 14.3. The central question is whether Suncor should be listed on a sustainability index. The inclusion must rest on either one of two criteria: absolute or relative performance.

If Suncor 's inclusion is based on its relative performance, then there are five alternative comparisons: all extractive and manufacturing industries, extractive industries only, the energy industry, the oil and gas sector, or the oil sands industry. Because of the

Table 14.3 DJSI Weights for Oil and Gas Sector DJSI

OGX Oil & Gas Upstream & Integrated
2023 CSA weights overview

	Weight in % of total Score	*Change from 2022*
Governance & Economic Dimension	34	0
Transparency & Reporting	2	New
Corporate Governance	9	0
Materiality	2	-1
Risk & Crisis Management	4	0
Business Ethics	8	0
Policy Influence	2	0
Supply Chain Management	3	0
Tax Strategy	2	-1
Information Security/ Cybersecurity & System Availability	2	0
Environmental Dimension	40	6
Environmental Policy & Management Systems	3	0
Emissions	7	New
Resource Efficiency & Circularity	1	New
Waste	6	New
Water	3	New
Climate Strategy	8	0
Biodiversity	4	1
Energy Mix	8	0
Social Dimension	26	-6
Labor Practice Indicators	3	0
Human Rights	4	1
Human Capital Development	3	-2
Talent Attraction & Retention	3	0
Occupational Health & Safety	7	0
Social Impacts on Communities	6	0

pollution intensity of its production process, the only category in which Suncor could achieve any relative classification of sustainability would be among the subset of oil sands companies. This essentially challenges the appellation of sustainability. The question is: If Suncor could be called sustainable, can any company in any industry satisfy this criterion? Several authors including Ray Anderson (1999), Robert (2008), and McDonough and Braungart (2002) have developed lists of absolute criteria that define a sustainable corporation. These are summarized in Table 14.4, and it can be argued that these criteria define true corporate sustainability.

In sum, Suncor has received its designation as a sustainable corporation on two propositions: first, that it has a marginally better environmental record than other oil sands companies; and second, that it has devoted some of its resources to renewable energy projects. For example, in 2010 its revenue from renewable energy was $33 million on investments of $500 million in wind power and $240 million in ethanol production (Nemetz 2013). In 2023, the company sold its wind and solar assets for $730 million (CBC May 9, 2023) although it will continue to produce 400 million liters of ethanol at its plant in St. Clair, Ontario. Currently, Suncor uses 40 million bushels of corn for ethanol production, accounting for 20% of Ontario's annual corn crop (Suncor n.d.

Table 14.4 Absolute Criteria for Corporate Sustainability

Anderson	Strongly service oriented
	Resource-efficient
	solar-driven
	Wasting nothing
	Cyclical - not linear
	Strongly connected to constituencies
Robert	no increase in concentrations of substances extracted from the earth's crust
	no systematic increase in concentrations of substances produced as a byproduct
	no systematic increasing degradation by physical means
	people not subject to conditions that systematically undermine their capacity to meet their needs
McDonough and Braungart	Waste equals food
	Use of current solar income
	respect for diversity
	Lack of product and byproduct toxicity, bioaccumulation or persistence

"Low-Carbon Intensity Fuels"). Suncor is also pursuing other renewable fuel projects using municipal waste, wood waste, agricultural excess biomass, and industrial flue gases (Suncor n.d. "Renewable Technologies"). According to its Climate Report of 2022, the company is planning to allocate 10% of its annual capital budget over the period 2022–2025 to advance their low-carbon energy initiatives (see Appendix Three for a discussion of the major conceptual issues associated with biofuels, especially ethanol made from food crops). The extent and depth of this commitment to renewables can be called into question considering a conference call by the CEO to investors on August 15, 2023 (Seeking Alpha August 15, 2023; Marketscreener.com August 15, 2023; *Vancouver Sun* August 30, 2023). In that call, the CEO told his audience that: "the company had a 'disproportionate' focus on the longer-term energy transition to low-emitting and renewable fuels. He promised a 'revised direction and tone' focused more on the immediate financial opportunities in the oilsands (CBC August 15, 2023)." Obviously, Suncor has doubled down on its commitment to its core business: bitumen extraction and processing (CBC May 12, 2023). This core business results in exceptionally high pollution of air, land and water. Appendix Four contains extracts from an early cost analysis by Trucost of Suncor's environmental impact.

In fact, the future of oil sands production hinges precariously on the future demand for and price of oil. Scenarios about the potential for an acceleration in the adoption of electric vehicles suggest that oil could be displaced by electrification in this and other sectors in the next few decades (Helm, 2017). Under these circumstances, as one of the highest cost sources of petroleum (Dale, 2015), the oil sands can be expected to face the greatest threat to their financial viability among alternative supplies of petroleum.

The Politics of Oil Sands

The future prospects for the oil sands are uncertain for at least three climate-related issues: first, the cancellation of the Keystone Pipeline intended to carry Alberta bitumen to American markets, the decision by Norwegian government and seven oil multinationals to pull out of the oil sands (Environmental Defense 2017; *Financial Post* January 12, 2021) and the decision by several major financial investors to back off funding what is perceive to be "dirty oil" (*New York Times* February 13, 2020; Funds Europe January 27, 2021; *Calgary Herald* April 27, 2023). It has been estimated that up to $13.4 billion of oilsands assets are possible candidates for sale by the international majors to domestic producers (*Vancouver Sun* July 14, 2021). Added to these factors is the difficult political and economic calculus facing the Canadian federal government considering the pledges made by Canada and other governments at President Biden's climate summit held on April 22, 2021. During the virtual meeting, Canada pledged to reduce their greenhouse gases by at least 40% by 2030 (CBC April 22, 2021). This is a particularly ambitious goal because Canada is the only G7 nation whose greenhouse gas emissions rose after the Paris climate agreement of 2015, in no small part due to the expansion of the country's oil sands deposits in Alberta. Table 14.5 lists Canada's GHG trends by key sectors over last few decades. In fact, the situation in Canada is much worse than it appears as climate change is leading to increased forest fires and insect predation in forests, turning much of the country's forests from carbon sinks into carbon sources (CBC January 28, 2019; CBC February 12, 2019; Sierra Club 2019; CCFM n.d).

The oil sands have been a cornerstone of Alberta's energy policy after the decline in conventional oil and gas reserves since their discovery in 1947 at Leduc. This commitment has continued despite the changing financial and environmental situation for fossil fuels at the global level. In fact, the Alberta government made a questionable decision to invest $1.5 billion in the Keystone pipeline at a time when it was clear that a future Democratic administration, if elected, would renew President Obama's cancellation of the project (*Calgary Herald* September 2, 2020; CTV News January 17, 2021). This is part of a larger picture of the province's budgetary philosophy. While both Norway and Alberta had established special savings funds with revenues from their energy sector, Norway adopted special measures to insulate these funds from the domestic economy to provide for future generations and avoid the "resource curse" that affects many oil and gas producers, especially in the developing world. As of 2023, Norway's Sovereign Wealth Fund amounted to $1.4 trillion (Reuters August 16, 2023) compared with a GDP of $482.2 billion, while Alberta's was only $18.4 billion in February 2022 (CBC February 17, 2022) compared with a GPP of $335.6 billion. Alberta's budgetary approach buffers the gap between low taxes (including low royalties, no sales tax, and low income

Table 14.5 Canada GHG trends (megatonnes)

	1990	1995	2000	2005	2016	2017	2018	2019	2020	2021
National GHG total	589	639	719	732	705	712	725	724	659	670
Oil and Gas	100	125	153	168	191	194	202	201	183	189
Electricity	95	98	129	118	74	73	63	62	54	52
Transport	118	127	142	157	162	165	169	170	143	150
Heavy industry	99	102	97	89	78	77	80	79	74	77
Buildings	72	78	84	85	85	88	92	93	89	87
Agriculture	49	57	61	64	66	67	69	69	70	69
Waste and others	54	52	53	52	48	49	50	50	46	47
Oil Sands	15	20	26	35	69	76	81	83	81	85
Forest Land	-200	-190	-180	-140	-140	-140	-130	-140	-130	-130

Source: Canada's National Greenhouse Gas Inventory (1990–2021)

taxes) and relatively high-spending levels funded by oil and gas revenues. To quote one recent article on Alberta's fiscal philosophy (CBC February 17, 2022):

> Initially, Alberta paid 30 per cent of its oil royalties into the fund. But, in 1987, the province stopped transferring money into it, except for some payments between 2005 and 2007. The problem, according to Allan Warrack, a former Progressive Conservative cabinet minister who helped create the fund, is that when successive Alberta governments have faced tough economic times, they avoided diversifying revenues or increasing taxes. Instead, it's politically easier to dip into the fund, he said in an interview with Radio- Canada in 2019. Since Alberta's nest egg was created by Premier Peter Lougheed in 1976, governments have used the fund and its investment income to pay for nearly $45-billion worth of programs, services and infrastructure — including building the Kananaskis Country Golf Course in the Rocky Mountains, west of Calgary. "A lot of the money was wasted with foolish projects," Warrack said. . . . We have very healthy oil and natural gas prices right now," said Keith Brownsey, a political science professor at Mount Royal University in Calgary. "We should be saving it for the next generation," he said. Alberta will continue riding the highs and lows of commodity prices and struggle to build up its trust fund in earnest until it introduces a sales tax, said Brownsey. "No government seems willing to do that, to take the hard road and to stabilize Alberta finances. And that's where we end up," he said. "We are subject to the boom and bust cycle with oil prices. It's a mess.

It appears that the Albertan government has made the strategic decision to make an unqualified commitment to the oil sands, what may eventually become a sunset industry. The wisdom of this decision remains to be seen but, at a minimum, it has created a serious fiscal situation for the provincial government faced with significant pushback over the ecological consequences of oil sands production and potential volatility of petroleum prices in the future. While a significant amount of funding has been devoted to renewable energy projects in Alberta, the government recently instituted a moratorium on new wind and solar projects, further solidifying the role of oil sands in its energy portfolio (Global News August 7, 2023).

In a renewed effort to rebrand the industry and maintain its social licence to operate in the face of increased global pressure to reduce GHGs, the five largest oil sands producers, including Suncor, announced an alliance in June 2021 to achieve net zero output of carbon dioxide from their operations by 2050 using carbon capture and storage (CCS) (Suncor June 9, 2021). This initiative entails several controversial components. First, if this initiative is accepted by the federal government, it guarantees the right of the industry to continue operating for three more decades despite its dominant contributions to Canada's GHG emissions. Second, it calls for the government to make major financial contributions to the project at a time when the government needs to spend its scarce resources on more immediate, effective and less expensive initiatives to restructure the economy to meet its Paris GHG commitments. Third, the technology is extremely costly and has several inherent environmental risks associated with it (see chapter 2). Fourth, even when companies announce that CCS is in place, provision must be made for third party verification. A recent report found that Shell Oil had sold millions of carbon credits for carbon emitted by their oil sands operation despite the fact that this carbon was never captured (CBC May 9 2024). And finally, even if the stated goals were to be achieved, net zero output of GHG from the production process accounts for at most

20–30% of total lifecycle emissions and does not address the problem of the residual 70–80% of emissions associated with the downstream combustion of the fuel itself (Canadian Energy Centre 2020).

Risk Factors

Under law, companies filing with regulatory agencies, such as the US Securities and Exchange Commission, must include potential risk factors, In doing so, corporations err on the side of caution, although some of the risk identified may be small or virtually nonexistent. However, a company does not want to be in the position if one or more of these factors materialize and they have both been previously identified. Under those circumstance, the corporation could be accused of withholding material facts and be subject to criminal prosecution and/or subject to civil fines. With this in mind, Suncor has listed a long list of potential risk factors under several generic headings (Suncor AR 2022): volatility of commodity prices; carbon risk; greenhouse gas emissions and targets; environmental compliance; market access; major operational incidents (safety, environment, and reliability); government/regulatory policy; digital and cybersecurity; competition; portfolio development and execution; technology risk; cumulative impact and pace of change; skills; resource shortage and reliance on key personnel; labour relations; joint arrangement risk; financial risks; E&P reserves replacement; uncertainty affecting reserves estimates; third-party service providers; foreign operations; security and terrorist threats; land claims and indigenous consultation; litigation risk; and control environment and insurance coverage.

From the perspective of this book, climate change poses the greatest, and potentially existential risk to the viability of Suncor over time. As such, Appendix Five presents several extracts of details from the climate-related risks outlined by the company.

Case Questions

1. In your view, should Suncor be included in sustainability indexes?
2. In what sense is Suncor sustainable by the standard definition of the term?
3. Is Suncor's decision to abandon renewable wind and solar projects and concentrate on oil sands production, with some investment in biofuels, a viable strategy in the short-term, medium term, or long term? If not, what options does it have?
4. What are the major concerns about the net energy contribution of biofuels? Do these apply to Suncor's current commitments?
5. Did the original investment in renewables represent a fundamental change in their business model or did it serve some other purpose?
6. How significant are the risk factors that the company identified in its submission to regulatory agencies?
7. Compare Suncor's Scope 3 coverage with Interface. Is this difference significant?

References

Alberta Auditor General of Alberta (2011) *Report of the Auditor General of Alberta*, Edmonton, November.

Alberta Chamber of Resources (2004) *Oil Sands Technology Roadmap. Unlocking the Potential*, Edmonton, January 30.

Anderson, Ray (1999) *Mid-Course Correction: Toward a Sustainable Enterprise: The Interface Model*. Peregrinzilla Press.

British Petroleum (BP) (2023) *Statistical Review of World Energy 2023*.

Calgary Herald (2020) "Alberta burned for billions in energy investment gambles," September 2.

Calgary Herald (2023) "Totalenergies exits canadian oilsands, selling stakes to Suncor for $5.5 billion," April 27.

Canada, Government of (2012) *National Pollutant Release Inventory* (NPRI), https://www.canada.ca/en/services/environment/pollution-waste-management/national-pollutant-release-inventory.html

Canada Energy Regulator (2021) "Canada's energy futures 2021 fact sheet: Oil sands https://www.cer-rec.gc.ca/en/data-analysis/canada-energy-future/2021oilsands/index.html

Canadian Energy Centre (2020) "Evaluating the Canadian oil and gas sector's GHG emissions intensity record," August 11.

CBC (2019) "B.C. forests contribute 'handle' carbon emissions that dwarf official numbers," January 28.

CBC (2019) "Canada's forests actually emit more carbon than they absorb – despite what you have heard on Facebook," February 12.

CBC (2020) "Alberta's heritage savings trust fund hits lowest value in eight years," July 13.

CBC (2021) "Trudeau pledges to slash greenhouse gas emissions by at least 49% by 2030," April 22.

CBC (2022) "How Alberta can learn from some first nations on how to save oil money," February 17.

CBC (2023) "New Suncor energy CEO Rich Kruger focussed on cost-cutting," May 9.

CBC (2023) "Climate effort at Suncor may take a backseat under new CEO," May 12.

CBC (2023) "Suncor has been too focused on energy transition, must get back to fundamentals: CEO," August 15.

CBC (2024) "Shell sold millions of carbon credits for carbon that was never captured, report finds," May 9.

Canadian Council of Forest Ministers (CCFM) (n.d.) "Forests: A stabilizing force for the climate."

Commission for Environmental Cooperation (CEC) (2020) *Alberta Tailings Ponds II. Factual Record Regarding Submission ESM-17-001*, North American Environmental Law and Policy, 36.

CTV (2021) "Alberta 'big loser' on Keystone XL: NDP says Kenney made a bad investment," January 17.

Dale, Spencer (2015) "BP, economics of oil." Society of Business Economists Annual Conference, London, October 13.

Environmental Defense (2017) "Seven oil multinationals that are pulling out of canada's tar sands," March 14.

Financial Post (2021) "Norwegian oil company to quit Alberta, focus on offshore activities in Atlantic Canada," January 12.

Findlay, Martha Hall (2012) "Please stop calling it 'ethical oil'," *Globe and Mail*, April 20.

Funds Europe (2021) "Blackrock vows to divest from climate change laggards," January 27.

Global News (2023) "Why did Alberta pause new wind and solar projects? Premier says feds,"

Grant, Jennifer, et al. (2010) *Northern Lifeblood. Empowering Northern Leaders to Protect the Mackenzie River Basin from Oil sands Risks*. Pembina Institute.

Griffiths, Mary (2006) "Water use in the oil patch: the motivation for innovation," PTAC – Water Innovation in the Oil Patch Conference (June 21), Pembina Institute.

He, Megan, et al. (2024) "Total organic carbon measurements reveal major gaps in petrochemical emissions reporting," *Science*, January 26.

Helm, Dieter (2017) *Burn Out: The Endgame for Fossil Fuels*. Yale University Press.

Kelly, Erin N., et al. (2009) "Oil sands development contributes polycyclic aromatic compounds to the Athabasca River and its tributaries," *PNAS*, 106(52): 22346–22351.

Kelly, Erin N., et al. (2010) "Oil sands development contributes elements toxic at low concentrations to the Athabasca River and its tributaries," *PNAS* 107(37): 16178–16182.

Kunzig, Robert (2009) "The Canadian oil boom," *National Geographic,* March.

Liggio, John, et al. (2019) "Measured Canadian oil sands CO_2 emissions are higher than estimates made using internationally recommended methods," *Nature Communications*, April.

MarketScreener (2023) "Suncor has been too focused on energy transition, must get back to fundamentals: CEO," August 15, 2023.

McDonough, William & Michael Braungart (2002) *Cradle to Cradle: Remaking the Way We Make Things*. North Point Press.

http://ngm.nationalgeographic.com/2009/03/Canadian-oil-sands/kunzig-text

New York Times (2010) "Alberta's tar sands and the dead duck trial," March 10.

New York Times (2010) "Backers rev up oil sands campaign," December 8.

New York Times (2011) "An oil ad vexes the Saudis," September 25.

New York Times (2020) "Global financial giants swear off funding an especially dirty fuel, February 13.

Oakley, Ros & Ian Buckland (2004) "What if business as usual won't work?" in Adrian Henriques & Julie Richardson (Eds.) *The Triple Bottom Line. Does it all add up?* 131–141. London: Earthscan.

Pimental, David and Tad W. Patzek (2005) "Ethanol production using corn, switchgrass, and wood; biodiesel production using soybean and sunflower," *Natural Resources Research*, March.

Robert, Karl-Henrik (2008) *The Natural Step Story. Seeding a Quiet Revolution.* New Society Publishers.

Rooney, Rebecca C., et al. (2012) "Oil sands mining and reclamation cause massive loss of peatland and stored carbon," *PNAS*, March 27.

Seeking Alpha (2023) "Suncor Energy Inc. (SU) Q2 2023 earnings call transcript," August 15.

Sierra Club of BC (2019) "Hidden, ignored and growing: B.C.'s forest carbon emissions," January.

Sovereign Wealth Fund Institute (SWFI) "Top 95 largest sovereign wealth fund rankings by total assets."

Sridhar, Kaushik and Grant Jones (2013) "The three fundamental criticisms of the triple bottom line approach: an empirical study to link sustainability reports in companies based in the Asia-Pacific Region and TBL shortcomings," *Asian Journal of Business Ethics*, 2: 91–111.

Suncor (n.d.) "Renewable technologies."

Suncor (n.d.) "Low-carbon intensity fuels."

Suncor (2021) Press release. "Canada's largest oil sands producers announce unprecedented alliance to achieve net zero greenhouse gas emissions," June 9.

Suncor (2023) *Annual Report 2022.*

Suncor (2023) *Report on Sustainability.*

Suncor (2023) *Climate Report.*

Sustainablebrands.com (2018) "Shaw industries achieves carbon neutrality in its commercial carpe manufacturing operations."

Timoney, Kevin P. & Peter Lee (2009) "Does the Alberta tar sands industry pollute?: Scientific evidence," *The Open Conservation Biology Journal*, 3: 65–81.

Trucost (2012) "Suncor Energy Inc. Trucost Company briefing," September 7.

Vancouver Sun (2021) ""$13.4B of oilsands assets seen as candidates for sale," July 14.

Vancouver Sun (2023) "Suncor pledge alarms minister," August 30, 2023.

Appendix One: Some Recent Suncor Financial Data

Table 14.6 Suncor P&L

For the years ended December 31 ($ millions)	*2022*	*2021*
Revenues and Other Income		
Operating revenues, net of royalties	58 336	39 132
Other income (loss)	131	(31)
	58 467	39 101
Expenses		
Purchases of crude oil and products	20 775	13 791
Operating, selling and general	12 807	11 366
Transportation and distribution	1 671	1 479
Depreciation, depletion, amortization and impairment	8 786	5 850
Exploration	56	47
Loss (gain) on disposal of assets	45	(257)
Financing expenses	2 011	1 255
	46 151	33 531
Earnings before Income Taxes	12 316	5 570
Income Tax Expense (Recovery)		
Current	4 229	1 395
Deferred	(990)	56
	3 239	1 451
Net Earnings	9 077	4 119
Other Comprehensive Income		
Items That May be Subsequently Reclassified to Earnings:		
Foreign currency translation adjustment	160	(63)
Items That Will Not be Reclassified to Earnings:		
Actuarial gain on employee retirement benefit plans, net of income taxes	838	856
Other Comprehensive Income	998	793
Total Comprehensive Income	10 075	4 912
Per Common Share (dollars)		
Net earnings - basic	6.54	2.77
Net earnings - diluted	6.53	2.77
Cash dividends	1.88	1.05

Source: Suncor Annual Report (2022)

Table 14.7 Suncor Balance Sheet

	December 31	*December 31*
($ millions)	*2022*	*2021*
Assets		
Current assets		
Cash and cash equivalents	1 980	2 205
Accounts receivable	6 068	4 534
Inventories	5 058	4 110
Income taxes receivable	244	128
Assets held for sale	1 186	—
Total current assets	14 536	10 977
Property, plant and equipment, net	62 654	65 546
Exploration and evaluation	1 995	2 226
Other assets	1 766	1 307
Goodwill and other intangible assets	3 586	3 523
Deferred income taxes	81	160
Total assets	84 618	83 739

(Continued)

Table 14.7 (Continued)

($ millions)	December 31 2022	December 31 2021
Liabilities and Shareholders' Equity		
Current liabilities		
Short-term debt	2 807	1 284
Current portion of long-term debt	—	231
Current portion of long-term lease liabilities	317	310
Accounts payable and accrued liabilities	8 167	6 503
Current portion of provisions	564	779
Income taxes payable	484	1 292
Liabilities associated with assets held for sale	530	—
Total current liabilities	12 869	10 399
Long-term debt	9 800	13 989
Long-term lease liabilities	2 695	2 540
Other long-term liabilities	1 642	2 180
Provisions	9 800	8 776
Deferred income taxes	8 445	9 241
Equity	39 367	36 614
Total liabilities and shareholders' equity	84 618	83 739

Source: Suncor Annual Report (2022)

Table 14.8 Suncor Cash Flows

For the years ended December 31 ($ millions)	2022	2021
Operating Activities		
Net earnings	9 077	4 119
Adjustments for:		
Depreciation, depletion, amortization and impairment	8 786	5 850
Deferred income tax (recovery) expense	(990)	56
Accretion	316	304
Unrealized foreign exchange loss (gain) on U.S. dollar denominated debt	729	(113)
Change in fair value of financial instruments and trading inventory	(38)	(13)
Loss (gain) on disposal of assets	45	(257)
Loss on extinguishment of long-term debt	32	80
Share-based compensation	328	205
Settlement of decommissioning and restoration liabilities	(314)	(263)
Other	130	289
(Increase) decrease in non-cash working capital	(2 421)	1 507
Cash flow provided by operating activities	15 680	11 764
Investing Activities		
Capital and exploration expenditures	(4 987)	(4 555)
Capital expenditures on assets held for sale	(133)	—
Proceeds from disposal of assets	315	335
Other investments and acquisitions	(36)	(28)
Decrease in non-cash working capital	52	271
Cash flow used in investing activities	(4 789)	(3 977)
Financing Activities		
Net increase (decrease) in short-term debt	1 473	(2 256)
Repayment of long-term debt	(5 128)	(2 451)
Issuance of long-term debt	—	1 423

(Continued)

Table 14.8 (Continued)

For the years ended December 31 ($ millions)	2022	2021
Lease liability payments	(329)	(325)
Issuance of common shares under share option plans	496	8
Repurchase of common shares	(5 135)	(2 304)
Distributions relating to non-controlling interest	(9)	(9)
Dividends paid on common shares	(2 596)	(1 550)
Cash flow used in financing activities	(11 228)	(7 464)
(Decrease) Increase in Cash and Cash Equivalents	(337)	323
Effect of foreign exchange on cash and cash equivalents	112	(3)
Cash and cash equivalents at beginning of year	2 205	1 885
Cash and Cash Equivalents at End of Year	1 980	2 205
Supplementary Cash Flow Information		
Interest paid	973	980
Income taxes paid (received)	4 737	(532)

Source: Suncor Annual Report (2022)

Appendix Two: Some Environmental Data Suncor

Table 14.9 Suncor Environmental Data

Part One

	UNITS	2018	2022
Fresh water withdrawal	million cubic meters	126.6	110.53
Freshwater consumption	million cubic meters	86.6	66.4
total fluid tailings volumes	million cubic meters	905	983
annual treated tailings volumes	million cubic meters	42	31
land disturbed	cumulative hectares	45232	48726
land reclaimed	cumulative hectares	7619	9189
SO_2 emissions	000 tonnes	0.07 [2019]	0.06
NO_x emissions	000 tonnes	59.49	62.38
VOC emissions	000 tonnes	32.23	45.83
PM10 emissions	000 tonnes	5.39 [2019]	5.33
H_2S emissions	000 tonnes	52.38	50.23
total waste generated	000 tonnes	2637	3066
hazardous waste generated	000 tonnes	985	1113
total active footprint	cumulative hectares	63224	68553

Part Two - Water Releases Reported By NPRI 2022

Naphthenic acid fraction compounds (and their salts)	3.33 tonnes
Manganese (and its compounds)	1.55 tonnes
Ammonia (total)	0.81 tonnes
Nickel (and its compounds)	0.46 tonnes
Vanadium (and its compounds)	0.28 tonnes
Phosphorus (total)	0.23 tonnes
Zinc (and its compounds)	0.03 tonnes
Chromium (and its compounds)	0.01 tonnes
Copper (and its compounds)	0.01 tonnes
Selenium (and its compounds)	19.93 kg
Arsenic (and its compounds)	6.44 kg
Cobalt (and its compounds)	5.32 kg
Lead (and its compounds)	1.86 kg
Quinoline	0.22 kg
Acenaphthene	0.09 kg
Thallium (and its compounds)	0.09 kg
Phenanthrene	0.08 kg
Acenaphthylene	0.07 kg
Benzo[e]pyrene	0.07 kg
Cadmium (and its compounds)	0.05 kg
Fluorene	0.05 kg
Perylene	0.05 kg
Benz[a]anthracene	0.03 kg
Benzo[ghi]perylene	0.03 kg
Benzo[k]fluoranthene	0.03 kg
Chrysene	0.03 kg
Fluoranthene	0.03 kg
Indeno[1,2,3-cd]pyrene	0.03 kg
Pyrene	0.03 kg
Dibenz[a,h]anthracene	0.02 kg
Mercury (and its compounds)	0.01 kg

(Continued)

Table 14.9 (Continued)

Part Three Air Emissions Reported By NPRI 2022

Total particulate matter	29,572.74 tonnes
Volatile Organic Compounds (Total)	24,811.61 tonnes
Sulphur dioxide	11,666.73 tonnes
Nitrogen oxides (expressed as NO_2)	9,879.05 tonnes
PM10	8,511.41 tonnes
Carbon monoxide	4,728.84 tonnes
PM2.5	2,107.83 tonnes
Xylene (all isomers)	777.12 tonnes
n-Hexane	727.76 tonnes
Toluene	603.08 tonnes
Propylene	222.96 tonnes
Ethylene	208.2 tonnes
1,2,4-Trimethylbenzene	192.2 tonnes
Sulphuric acid	182.63 tonnes
Cyclohexane	171.49 tonnes
Ethylbenzene	146.04 tonnes
Ammonia (total)	125.47 tonnes
Total reduced sulphur (expressed as H2S)	54.68 tonnes
Benzene	53.69 tonnes
Methyl ethyl ketone	51.62 tonnes
Carbonyl sulphide	39.39 tonnes
Styrene	32.37 tonnes
Formaldehyde	19.4 tonnes
Hydrogen sulphide	19.36 tonnes
Copper (and its compounds)	17.64 tonnes
Methanol	17.33 tonnes
p-Dichlorobenzene	10.2 tonnes
Naphthalene	8.42 tonnes
Isopropyl alcohol	6.61 tonnes
Vanadium (and its compounds)	4.32 tonnes
Nickel (and its compounds)	0.93 tonnes
Zinc (and its compounds)	0.88 tonnes
Phosphorus (total)	0.85 tonnes
Manganese (and its compounds)	0.19 tonnes
Chromium (and its compounds)	0.13 tonnes
Silver (and its compounds)	0.05 tonnes
Selenium (and its compounds)	114.49 kg
Arsenic (and its compounds)	73.28 kg
Lead (and its compounds)	66.34 kg
Phenanthrene	37.19 kg
Fluorene	33.69 kg
Acenaphthene	28.91 kg
Acenaphthylene	25.81 kg
Fluoranthene	13.7 kg
Pyrene	12.33 kg
Benzo[k]fluoranthene	11.75 kg
Chrysene	8.18 kg
Benz[a]anthracene	6.1 kg
Benzo[ghi]perylene	5.9 kg
Cadmium (and its compounds)	3.76 kg
Benzo[b]fluoranthene	3.43 kg
Indeno[1,2,3-cd]pyrene	1.9 kg

(*Continued*)

Table 14.9 (Continued)

Part Three Air Emissions Reported By NPRI 2022	
Dibenz[a,h]anthracene	1.65 kg
Benzo[a]pyrene	1.14 kg
Mercury (and its compounds)	0.53 kg
Benzo[e]pyrene	0.24 kg
Perylene	0.06 kg
Quinoline	0.01 kg

Source: Suncor Report on Sustainability (2023)

Appendix Three: Conceptual Problems with Biofuel Production

Production of Ethanol from Food Crops

While renewable energy sources appear more environmentally benign and cost-competitive when market distortions, such as subsidies and externalities are accounted for, there is one prominent case where the opposite is true. After adjustments for net energy output (Pimental & Patzek 2005; Patzek & Pimental 2005) and total system impacts on greenhouse gas production (Fargione et al. 2008; Searchinger et al. 2008; Grafton et al. 2014), it appears that most government initiatives for the production of ethanol as a transportation fuel have been counterproductive. This experience with biofuels provides a cautionary tale about the necessity for a systematic study of all environmental, social, and economic ramifications of any new energy technology, even renewables.

Biofuel production has been rising steadily in the last few decades, but both production and consumption are currently dominated by the United States and Brazil, although significant production is occurring in China, Europe, and India, largely because of government support policies through subsidies or mandated production (OECD 2008). Figure 14.4 shows biofuel production by major country in 2022 (BP 2022), and Figure 14.5 displays the rapid run-up in US production of ethanol over the last several decades (US EIA 2023). The OECD and FAO have estimated that by 2027, China will become the world's third largest producer (OECD-FAO 2018). It has been reported that in 2011, 98% of Thailand's cassava chips were destined for biofuel production in China (*New York Times*, April 6, 2011). Prices for cassava doubled in the preceding three-year period as demand increased fourfold. The OECD (2019: 39) predicted that:

> Global use of ethanol is expected to grow around 18% or an additional 21 bln L by 2028 with greater use expected mostly in China (+5.4 bln L). In 2017, the Chinese government announced the goal of a 10% ethanol blending share for 2020, which is expected to be filled through domestic production coming from domestic maize and imported cassava.

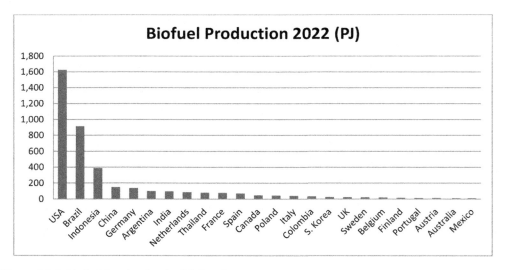

Figure 14.4 Biofuel Production by Major Country

Source: BP Statistical Review of World Energy 2023

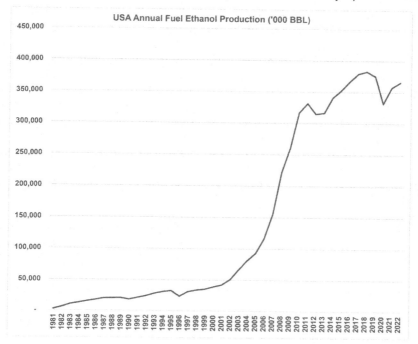

Figure 14.5 US Ethanol Production History
Source: US EIA 2023

Biofuels currently take two forms: ethanol, largely derived from grain and sugar cane, and biodiesel derived from vegetable oils. The rationale to produce biofuels is beguilingly simple. These are supposed to be carbon-neutral since the emissions of carbon dioxide during their combustion in the automotive sector, for example, are offset by carbon take-up during plant growth. In fact, concern has been raised that "waste cooking oil" imported from East Asia as a biofuel feedstock in the EU may not indeed be waste and therefore may contribute to deforestation and the loss of animal feed (CE Delft 2020; Transport & Environment 2021; BBC April 21, 2021). Equally important, the World Bank concluded in 2008 that the large increase in biofuels production in the US and the EU was the most important driver of rising global food prices over the period 2002–2008, imposing an increasing burden on the poor in developing countries. This and other purported benefits of biofuel production and use raise several major conceptual problems. A cautionary tale is provided by US experience with the production of ethanol.

American Ethanol Production

Over the past few decades, the United States has implemented several major policy initiatives to introduce alternative fuels into the domestic gasoline supply using a combination of tax subsidies and minimum production mandates (*New York Times* November 30, 2015). Foremost among these fuels is *gasohol*, a blend of gasoline and plant-based ethanol. Within the United States, four major normative rationales have been advanced for this policy: to reduce greenhouse gas emissions, to reduce dependence on foreign oil supplies (now somewhat moot in light of recent advances in oil extraction from nonconventional sources), to reduce air pollution in cities, and to provide additional income to the farm sector. In the US the feedstock of choice has been corn; in Canada, wheat and, in Brazil, sugarcane. The production of ethanol is an energy-intensive process that involves the distillation of fermented sugars to achieve a water-free alcohol suitable for blending with conventional gasoline. To grasp the chemical and economic significance of this process, it is necessary to understand the concept of net energy analysis (NEA).

NEA focuses on the relationship between energy required to produce an energy product and the energy available for use after the production process. The crucial characteristic of this analysis is that it is conducted at the system level (i.e., it includes inputs at all relevant stages of the production process). Included are not only energy used in the production of the final energy product, but also energy used in the production of the capital goods employed in the recovery or production of the energy product. The net energy ratio is defined as:

(the energy output from the fuel produced) / (the energy input required to extract the energy plus the energy embodied in the capital equipment required to extract the energy).

Note that this is a variant of Hall's (2017) energy return on investment (EROI) whose calculation is:

(energy output – energy input)/ (energy input).

Net energy ratios have been calculated for a broad range of energy products and Figure 14.6 summarizes the results of one early comprehensive study conducted by the Canadian government (Winstanley et al. 1977). As evident from these data, domestic and conventional natural gas have the highest ratio. What is noteworthy, however, are the values for gasohol, which range from a high of 1.8 to a low of 0.8. Put simply, a ratio less than 1.0 means that more energy is required to produce the product than is available for consumption. This ratio has not changed over the past few decades. In other words, ethanol in North America has no positive net energy balance if produced by standard agricultural production techniques and conventional distillation technology. There may be a modest net positive energy balance only if: (1) energy-conserving farm practices are developed, (2) energy-conserving industrial technology is used, and (3) crop residues are used to back out conventional fuels, such as oil used in distillation, the most energy-intensive part of the production process. However, from a systems perspective, the use of crop residues deprives a field of nutrients, necessitating the increasing application of fertilizers that are themselves energy-intensive. Based on extensive research undertaken by Pimental and Patzek (2005), it is possible to conduct a precise net energy analysis of ethanol produced in the United States. Figure 14.7 summarizes the results of their analysis. DeCicco et al. (2016) report that additional carbon uptake by crops offsets only 37% of biofuel-related biogenic CO_2 emissions. These results suggest a net increase, rather than decrease in GHGs based on a systems analysis which includes displacement effects and land-use changes.

The inability of corn-based ethanol to achieve a positive net energy balance has prompted researchers to consider other agricultural and nonagricultural feedstocks (Table 14.10). While some may hold promise with further development in the technology of conversion, this remains a work in progress.

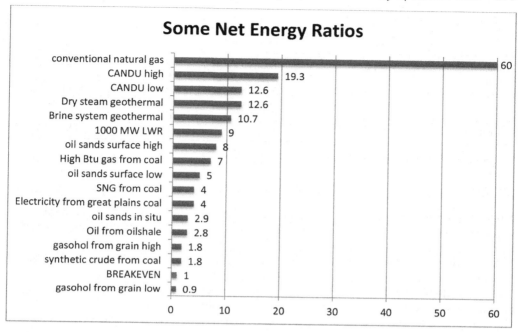

Figure 14.6 Net Energy Ratios

Source: Winstanley et al. 1977

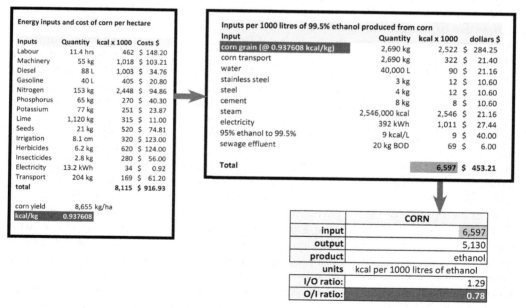

Figure 14.7 Net Energy Analysis of US Ethanol

Adapted from Pimental and Patzek 2005

Table 14.10 Alternative Biofuel Sources

	Corn	Switchgrass	Wood Cellulose	Soybeans	Sunflower
input	6,597	7,455	8,061	11,878	19,599
output	5,139	5,130	5,130	9,000	9,000
product	ethanol	ethanol	ethanol	biodiesel	biodiesel
units		kcal per 100 liters of ethanol		kcal per 100 liters of biodiesel	
I/O ratio	1.28	1.45	1.57	1.32	2.18
O/I ratio	0.78	0.69	0.64	0.76	0.46

Adapted from Pimental & Patzek (2005)

A Gasohol Scorecard

Under the *normative theory of government*, the principal reason for government intervention in the economy is to correct market failure where markets fail to achieve efficient resource allocation. One example includes prices that do not reflect social costs. The US federal government has charged no sales tax on ethanol, thereby creating a large de facto subsidy for its production and use in gasohol.

The product is gaining acceptance by the consumer because it is price-competitive at the pump. One should be circumspect about this policy because of at least one red flag: the fact that a massive de facto subsidy has been required to keep this product viable. While the government has backed off a direct financial subsidy, the same result has been achieved by government mandates that require the production of a given amount of ethanol every year.

The question arises as what are prices at the pump (i.e., the market price) not telling us? Net energy balances tell us that this entire venture does not make any sense from the perspective of energy analysis. We are putting in more energy than we are getting out. Net energy analysis confirms the suspicion that if the federal government was not heavily subsidizing or mandating its production, ethanol would be a dead duck. Why is the government following a policy that seems so ill-advised? This requires the application of the *positive theory of government*, which attempts to explain why government behaviour may deviate from the normative model. Of the four posited reasons for promoting the use of gasohol, only the environmental reduction of some air pollutants (excluding GHG) seems plausible, although weak. We can hypothesize about the US government's motives: (1) they originally wanted to appear to be tackling the problem of foreign oil dependence; (2) they want to appear to be tackling the problem of urban air pollution, although there may be better ways of achieving this end; (3) they want to appear to be tackling the issue of global warming; (4) the government is ignorant of the systems implications of their policy: or (5) the government may be responding to special interest groups.

The relevant US special interest groups in gasohol policy include corn farmers who represent a powerful lobby in the United States. Promoting the use of gasohol increases the demand for their products and raises the prices they receive for their grain. This is an indirect and less obvious way of subsidizing this sector of the economy. The USDA has reported that as much as 45% of the American corn crop was devoted to the production of ethanol in 2019. A similar economic rationale relating to farm-based interest groups may explain continued European support for ethanol-blended gasoline. Within the US, there has a strong lobbying effort by the American agribusiness giant, ADM (Archer Daniells Midland) Ltd. that has controlled between 60–75% of US ethanol production.

In the 1992 US federal election and subsequent elections, ADM has made significant monetary contributions to both the Republicans and the Democrats in order to maintain tax policies favourable to the continued production of ethanol and use of gasohol. In sum, the widespread support for ethanol production, at least in the United States, represents a victory of political power over economics and sustainable agriculture and transportation. According to one research study published in 2015 (Manhattan Institute for Policy Research), the Renewable Fuel Standard that mandates the blending of ethanol into gasoline has cost American motorists more than $10 billion per year in extra fuel costs. In essence this is a massive rent (i.e., nonproductive) transfer from the driving public to special interests such as farmers, distillers and marketers who profit from its production. The American federal government has recently reaffirmed its commitment to the use of ethanol as a vehicle to maintain farm incomes for what may be primarily political reasons (*New York Times* October 4 & 7, 2019).

Other Countries and Issues

The only country where ethanol-based automotive fuel is being widely used and appears to have a positive net energy balance is Brazil that uses sugarcane as a feedstock. A systems analysis would suggest, however, that there are notable externalities associated with the its production in Brazil, including rampant forest destruction in the Amazon with the loss of biodiversity and other forest ecosystem services, degradation or loss of soils, water contamination or depletion, and lower levels of food security for indigenous tribes and other Brazilians (Goldemberg et al. 2008; *The Guardian* August 17, 2007, July 2 & 3, 2019).

There are several broader issues to be addressed in the production of ethanol fuels: (1) the question of net greenhouse gas production and (2) the system-wide impacts on the agricultural sector, both domestic and foreign. Because there is usually no net energy output, there is rarely a net reduction in greenhouse gas production (*New York Times* September 14, 2011). Even if there is some net reduction in GHG emissions from the ethanol production process per se, there is another issue: more greenhouse gases are being produced by the net conversion of forests and grasslands to produce ethanol producing crops (Searchinger et al. 2008, 2015) (see Tables 14.11). Using a worldwide agricultural model to estimate emissions from land use change, the authors found that corn-based ethanol, instead of producing a 20% savings, nearly doubles greenhouse emissions over 30 years and increases greenhouse gases for 167 years. Fargione et al. (2008) refer to a "biofuel carbon debt," where rainforests, peatlands, savannahs, and grasslands are converted to biofuel production, leading to the release of 17 to 420 times more CO_2 than the annual GHG reductions that biofuels provide through the displacement of fossil fuels.

With respect to system-wide impacts on other components of the agricultural sector, crops grown for ethanol production are replacing food crops, thereby limiting their supply and driving up food prices. This can have a significant impact on consumer prices for commodities that use corn as a component (Figure 14.8). Corn is a major component of numerous products, especially the food we eat, both directly as an additive and indirectly as a major feed source for livestock (see Tables 14.12 and 14.13). Rosegrant and Msangi (2014) ascribe the reduction in the availability of calories and increase in malnutrition to the negative effects of food price increases in the developing world. In many such countries, the effects can be devastating. For example, the average Mexican has relied on tortillas made of corn to provide 40% of their protein. The resulting increase in corn prices has created a major problem in that country (*New York Times* January 19, 2007).

Table 14.11 GHG from Ethanol Production from Forests and Grasslands (grams of GHG CO2e per MJ of energy in fuel)

Source of fuel	Making feedstock	Refining fuel	Net land-use effects		Land-use change	Total GHGs	% change in net GHGs versus gasoline
			Vehicle operation (burning fuel)	Feedstock carbon uptake from atmosphere			
Gasoline	4	15	72	0	0	92	
Corn ethanol	24	40	71	-62		74 without feedstock credit	-20% without feedstock credit
Corn ethanol plus land use change	24	40	71	-62	104	177	93%
Biomaas ethanol	10	9	71	-62		27	-70%
Biomass ethanol plus land use change	10	9	71	-62	111	138	50%

Source: Searchinger et al. 2008 (reproduced with permission)

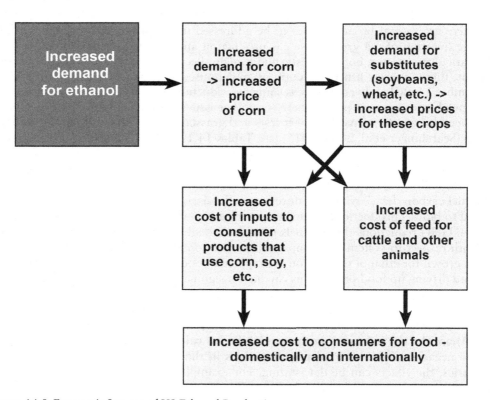

Figure 14.8 Economic Impact of US Ethanol Production

Table 14.12 Non-Food Products that Use Corn

Adhesives (glues, pastes, mucilages, gums, ETC.)	Ink for stamping prices in stores
Aluminum	Insecticides
Antibiotics (penicillin)	Insulation, fibreglass
Asbestos insulation	Latex paint
Aspirin	Leather tanning
Automobiles (everything on wheels)	Livestock feed
Batteries, dry cell	Paper board, (corrugating, laminating, cardboard)
C.M.A. (calcium magnesium acetate)	Paper manufacturing
Coatings on wood, paper & metal	Paper plates & Cups
Colour carrier in paper & textile, printing	Pharmaceuticals
Cosmetics	Powders
Cough syrups	Rugs, carpets
Crayon and chalk	Shaving cream & lotions
cylinder heads	Shoe polish
Degradable plastics	Soaps and cleaners
Dessert powders	spark plugs
Dextrose (intravenous solutions, icing sugar)	Stamps
Disposable diapers	Starch & glucose
Dyes	Starched clothing
Envelopes	synthetic rubber finishes
ethanol - fuel & windshield washer fluid	Talcums
Ethyl and butyl alcohol	Textiles
Explosives - firecrackers	tires
Finished leather	Toothpaste
Fuel ethanol	Wallpaper
Gypsum wallboard	

Table 14.13 Food Containing Corn

Alcohol	Gum
Ale/Beer	Hominy Grits
Baby food	Ice Cream
Bacon	Infant Formula
Baking Mixes	Instant coffee & tea
Baking Powders	James, jellies and preserves
Batters for frying	Jams
Beer	Jellies
Beverages (sweetened)	Ketchup
Bleached White Flour	Licorice
Breads & Pastries	Malted products
Breakfast cereals	Margarine
Cakes	Margarine
Candies	Mayonnaise
Canned vegetables	Meats (bologna, sausage)
Carbonated beverages	Mustard, prepared
Catsup	Oleo
Cheese spreads	Peanut Butter
Chewing gum	Peanut butter
Chocolate products	Popcorn
Cookies	Potato chips
Corn chips	Powdered Sugar
Corn Flakes	Preserves

(*Continued*)

Table 14.13 (Continued)

Corn meal	Puddings
Cream Pies	Salad dressings
Edible oil	Salas Dressings
Flour & grits	Soft drinks
Fritos	Soups Soybean Milks
Frostings	Syrup
Frozen foods	Syrups
Fructose	Tacos, tortillas
Fruit (canned)	Tortillas
Fruit Drinks	Vinegar, Distilled
Gelatin Capsules	Vitamins
Gelatin Desserts	Wheat bread
Graham Crackers	Whiskey
Gravies	Wine
Grits	Yogurts

Appendix Four: Excerpts from Trucost's Environmental Assessment of Suncor (2012 only)

Table 14.14 Estimates of Suncor's Direct Environmental Damage

Emission/Resource	Quantity	External Cost (CAD m)
CO_2 to air (tonnes)	18,516,000	$656
River Abstraction (cubic metres)	152,460,000	$77
Sum of VOCs to air (tonnes)	37,600	$60
SO_2 to air (tonnes)	43,900	$59
NO_x to air (tonnes)	43,200	$27
Particulates to air (tonnes)	2,090	$26
Methane to air (tonnes)	28,200	$25
Hazardous waste (tonnes)	132,000	$11
Nitrous Oxide to air (tonnes)	933	$9.85
Landfill (nonhazardous) (tonnes)	67,100	$3.15
TOTAL		$965

Source: Trucost (2012)

Table 14.15 Estimates of Suncor's Supply Chain Environmental Damage

Emission/Resource	Quantity	External Cost (CAD m)
CO_2 to air (tonnes)	10,943,608	$388
Water Consumption (cubic metres)	197,378,679	$99
Sum of VOCs to air (tonnes)	30,005	$48
Methane to air (tonnes)	52,252	$46
Particulates to air (tonnes)	3,376	$42
SO_2 to air (tonnes)	30,616	$41
Open Cast coal (tonnes)	573,093	$17
NO_x to air (tonnes)	19,476	$12
Deep mined coal (tonnes)	373,365	$11
Nuclear waste to land (tonnes)	2.49	$9.96
TOTAL		$769

Source: Trucost (2012)

Table 14.16 Trucost's Issue Assessment for Suncor

Category	Environmental Damage Cost Exposure
GHG	High
Other emissions	High
Water abstraction	High
VOCs	High
General Waste	Low
Natural Resources	Low
Heavy Metals	Very Low

Source: Trucost (2012)

Appendix Five: Excerpts from Suncor's Declared Climate-Related Risks

Carbon Risk

Existing and future laws and regulations in support of a transition to low-carbon energy and climate change action may impose significant constraints on fossil fuel development. Concerns over climate change, fossil fuel extraction, GHG emissions, and water and land-use practices could lead governments to enact additional or more stringent laws and regulations applicable to Suncor and other companies in the energy industry in general, and in the oil sands industry in particular. These risks to the oil sands industry can be offset over time through the commercialization and implementation of low-carbon technologies (e.g., carbon capture, utilization and sequestration) and by increasing growth in low-carbon energies such as hydrogen, renewable fuels and power.

Changes to environmental regulations, including regulations relating to climate change, could impact the demand for the company's products or could require increased capital expenditures, operating expenses, abandonment and reclamation obligations, and distribution costs. These potential added costs may not be recoverable in the marketplace and may result in some current operations or growth projects becoming less profitable or uneconomic. . . . In addition, legislation or policies that limit the purchase of production from the oil sands may be adopted in domestic and/or foreign jurisdictions, which, in turn, may limit the world market for Suncor's upstream production and reduce the prices the company receives for its petroleum products, and could result in delayed development, stranded assets or the company being unable to further develop its hydrocarbon resources. The complexity, breadth and velocity of changes in GHG emissions regulations make it difficult to predict the potential impact to Suncor.

Suncor continues to monitor international and domestic efforts to address climate change. While GHG regulations and targets will continue to become more stringent, and while Suncor continues its efforts to reduce its GHG emissions, the absolute operational GHG emissions of the company may rise as a result of growth, mergers and acquisition activities. . . . There is also a risk that Suncor could face litigation initiated by third parties relating to climate change, including litigation pertaining to GHG emissions, the production, sale, or promotion of fossil fuels and petroleum products, and/or disclosure. For example, the Board of County Commissioners of Boulder County, the Board of County Commissioners of San Miguel County and the City of Boulder, all of Colorado, have brought an action against Suncor and certain of its subsidiaries seeking, among other things, compensation for impacts they allege with respect to climate change. In addition, the mechanics of implementation and enforcement of the Oil Sands Emissions Limit Act and the federal government's stated intention to cap and reduce emissions from the oil and gas sector by setting five-year targets to achieve net zero by 2050 are currently under review and it is not yet possible to predict the impact on Suncor. However, such impact could be material.

These developments and future developments could adversely impact the demand for Suncor's products, the ability of Suncor to maintain and grow its production and reserves, and Suncor's reputation, and could have a material adverse effect on Suncor's business, financial condition, reserves and results of operations.

Financial Risks

Access to Capital

This ability is dependent on, among other factors, commodity prices, the overall state of the capital markets, and financial institutions and investor appetite for investments in the energy industry generally, and the company's securities in particular. In addition, some stakeholders may compare companies based on climate-related performance that can be impacted by

numerous factors and perceptions. The company's ability to access capital may also be adversely affected in the event that financial institutions, investors, rating agencies and/or lenders adopt more restrictive decarbonization policies.

15 Volkswagen

A Case Study in Corporate Malfeasance and Recovery

Volkswagen was originally founded in 1937 by the Nazi government of Germany to provide a "family car" for the country's citizenry, but the actual production of cars did not begin until 1945 because the first factories had been devoted to producing war materiel. From an initial production of approximately 2000 cars, the company has steadily grown, reaching a high of 11 million motor vehicles in 2018 before falling to 8.7 million in 2022 The bulk of this production is composed of passenger cars (see Figure 15.1). This growth was marked by a progression of purchases and mergers, including Auto Union 1965; Audi 1969; SEAT 1986; Skoda 1991; Bentley, Lamborghini and Bugatti 1998; Scania 2008; MAN 2011; and Porsche and Ducati 2012 (Ewing 2018). Volkswagen

Figure 15.1 VW Production History

Source: VW Annual Reports

DOI: 10.4324/9781003170754-18

has grown to be among the top two vehicle producers in the world, along with Toyota (see Figure 15.2). While the company has markets throughout the world, the peak of its Chinese sales in 2019 accounted for 39.4% of VW's total sales, representing their largest single market. Table 15.1 shows the changes in units sold and market share by destination over the period 2019–2023. Of note is the loss of almost one million units in China over that period. While Volkswagen established itself as that country's largest single supplier since entering the Chinese market in 1985 (see Table 15.2), this dominance is being threatened by the emergence of Chinese auto makers.

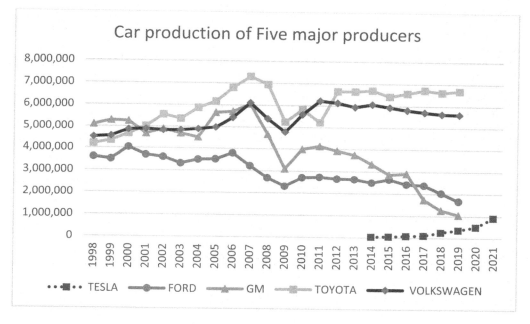

Figure 15.2 VW's Position in Global Car Production

Sources: Wards, WSJ, BACKLINK

Table 15.1 VW's Global Sales by Region

	2020	percentage	2023	percentage
Europe/Other Markets	3,779,778	41.5%	3,953,397	44.4%
Western Europe	2,848,861	31.3%	3,141,434	35.3%
of which: Germany	1,065,811	11.7%	1,141,418	12.8%
France	222,522	2.4%	263,643	3.0%
United Kingdom	409,064	4.5%	489,088	5.5%
Italy	239,167	2.6%	269,479	3.0%
Spain	213,700	2.3%	232,483	2.6%
Central and Eastern Europe	652,813	7.2%	474,357	5.3%
of which: Czech Republic	112,589	1.2%	123,471	1.4%

(Continued)

Table 15.1 (Continued)

	2020	*percentage*	2023	*percentage*
Russia	221,811	2.4%	3,504	0.0%
Poland	126,883	1.4%	140,518	1.6%
Other Markets	278,104	3.1%	337,606	3.8%
of which: Turkey	121,129	1.3%	166,001	1.9%
South Africa	64,693	0.7%	69,150	0.8%
North America	784,299	8.6%	899,652	10.1%
of which: USA	574,822	6.3%	639,622	7.2%
Canada	83,531	0.9%	110,019	1.2%
Mexico	125,946	1.4%	159,011	1.8%
South America	440,326	4.8%	465,842	5.2%
of which: Brazil	336,773	3.7%	356,682	4.0%
Argentina	57555	0.6%	57,931	0.7%
Asia-Pacific	4,110,782	45.1%	3,582,447	40.2%
of which: China	3,844,679	42.2%	3,233,933	36.3%
India	28,423	0.3%	101,553	1.1%
Japan	66,935	0.7%	65,635	0.7%
Worldwide	9,115,185	100.0%	8,901,338	100.0%

Source: VW Annual Report (2000, p.106)

Table 15.2 VW's Competitors in China

	Model	2019	*Share*	*cumulative*
1	Volkswagen	3,100,498	14.60%	14.6%
2	Honda	1,553,086	7.30%	21.9%
3	Toyota	1,409,198	6.60%	28.5%
4	Geely	1,220,832	5.70%	34.2%
5	Nissan	1,174,030	5.50%	39.7%
6	Buick	871,506	4.10%	43.8%
7	Changan	787,878	3.70%	47.5%
8	Haval	769,454	3.60%	51.1%
9	Hyundai	685,738	3.20%	54.3%
10	Audi	620,001	2.90%	57.2%
11	Baojun	604,204	2.80%	60.0%
12	Mercedes-Benz	595,486	2.80%	62.8%
13	BMW	544,500	2.60%	65.4%
14	Chevrolet	516,087	2.40%	67.8%
15	BYD	451,246	2.10%	69.9%
16	Chery	451,139	2.10%	72.0%
17	SAIC Roewe	426,128	2.00%	74.0%
18	GAC	388,364	1.80%	75.8%
19	Dongfeng	377,349	1.80%	77.6%
20	Wuling	374,878	1.80%	79.4%
21	BAIC	286,343	1.30%	80.7%
22	Kia	283,307	1.30%	82.0%
23	Skoda	278,378	1.30%	83.3%
24	SAIC MG	269,751	1.30%	84.6%
25	Ford	232,555	1.10%	85.7%
26	Mazda	224,977	1.10%	86.8%
27	FAW	222,188	1.00%	87.8%
28	Cadillac	212,506	1.00%	88.8%

Source: Ward's Automotive Yearbook

A mainstay of Volkswagen's vehicle fleet have been engines powered by diesel fuel, representing 49% of sales in 2015, 39% in 2917, and 43% in 2018. There are certain inherent advantages of diesel over gasoline powered cars: diesel engines are more powerful as they deliver more torque; are more fuel efficient, since the fuel contains up to 15% more energy than gasoline; are simpler to maintain; and, perhaps most important in a world experiencing climate change, they emit less carbon dioxide. However, there are several drawbacks: they emit more particulates than gasoline powered engines (HHS 2021). Several of the particulates such as hydrocarbons, aldehydes, and PAH are known or suspected carcinogens (Carex n.d.; Krivoshto et al. 2008; EPA 2022).

Equally important is the elevated level of nitrogen oxide (NOx) emissions resulting from higher compression ratios and higher combustion temperatures than gasoline powered cars. Nitrogen dioxide is one of a group of highly reactive gases (US 2022), a precursor for ozone and acid rain, and a known health hazard for humans, leading to respiratory tract irritation and asthma (US EPA 2002). This problem posed by NOx emissions led to a major strategic blunder by the management of Volkswagen, known as "Dieselgate."

Building on its dominant share of both the Chinese and European markets in the 1980s, Volkswagen was intent on becoming the world's largest car manufacturer. The principal gap in this plan was Volkswagen's relatively minor role in the US market, which at that time was the largest market for automobiles in the world. The company had entered the American market in 1949 when it shipped its first "Type 1" (better known as the "Beetle") to an individual in New York City (*Los Angeles Times* January 31, 2014). This vehicle caught on quickly and sales grew rapidly until reaching their peak of 570,000 vehicles in 1970, capturing approximately 7% of the American market. Sales soon fell off in the face of increasing competition from low cost imports from Asia. By 1987, Volkswagen's US sales had shrunk to 130,641 vehicles, representing only 1.3% of the US market (Wards MVF&F 1987, BTS 2018).

Volkswagen was determined to reverse this decline and decided to build several new models that would appeal to American tastes. These cars would be powered by a new, fuel-efficient diesel engine, following the company's successful marketing of diesel power cars in the European market. The challenge facing the company was engineering the car to meet the more stringent American standards for the emissions of nitrogen dioxides. Not only were US standards tighter that their European counterparts, the US had a more rigorous system of enforcement. A major push in this direction came from regulators in California, the largest car market within the United States, which was intent on addressing the problem of automobile-related air pollution in that state. Figure 15.3 shows a comparison of American and European standards for NOx. The US had established standards for this pollutant as early as 1972 and had subsequently tightened these standards in several increments over the following decades. In contrast, the European Union had only promulgated standards for the combination of hydrocarbons and NOx in 1992 and for NOx by itself in 2000. It is noteworthy, that American standards for NOx are still more stringent that their European counterparts to date.

After several unsuccessful attempts to produce an engine that would meet these standards without sacrificing performance, it became apparent to the company that an alternative approach would be required. This is when the company made the fateful decision to circumvent American regulations by introducing a "defeat device" that would fool regulators and the American public into believing that their cars were meeting the more rigorous US standards. This deception was based on the fact that regulatory approval of

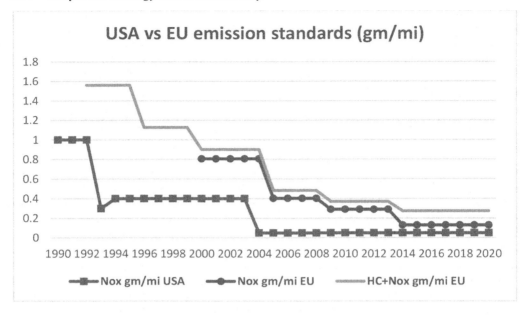

Figure 15.3 US vs. European Standards for NOx

Source: US EPA

emission limits were enforced by static tests of car performance (i.e., cars tested in laboratories rather than in real-world driving conditions). While the latter would provide a more accurate test of actual emissions, at the time this type of testing was not available in the US. As such, the defeat device created by Volkswagen and its affiliate Audi was designed to control emissions only when software determined that the car was undergoing a laboratory test (see Figure 15.4).

This software was installed in 482,000 cars shipped to the United States following 2008. For several years it avoided detection. At the global level, the number of cars outfitted with this device numbered more than 11 million (*New York Times* July 19, 2016). In 2011 Volkswagen began a "clean diesel" advertising campaign in the US (Ewing 2018) to portray the cars as even more environmentally friendly that Toyota's hybrid Prius. The Prius had been introduced into the US market in 2000 and its sales had grown steadily, until by 2007 its sales in the US were 82% of Volkswagen's.

Volkswagen's situation changed dramatically with the publication of a report by Thompson et al. (2014) from the University of West Virginia's (UWV) Department of Mechanical & Aerospace Engineering, which had been commissioned by the International Council on Clean Transportation (ICCT) to design and conduct on-road testing of light-duty diesel vehicles in the United States using a portable emissions measurement systems (PEMS). As Thompson et al (2014, p. 1) state the ICCT request had been prompted by an earlier study from Europe on exhaust from light-duty diesel vehicles using a PEMS. This report (Weiss et al. 2011) found that "average NOx emissions of diesel vehicles (0.93 ± 0.39 g/km), including Euro 5 diesel vehicles (0.62 ± 0.19 g/km), substantially exceed respective Euro 3–5 emission limits. The observed deviations range from a factor of 4–7 for average NOx emissions over entire test routes up to a factor of 14 for NOx emissions of individual averaging windows" (Weiss et al. 2011: iii).

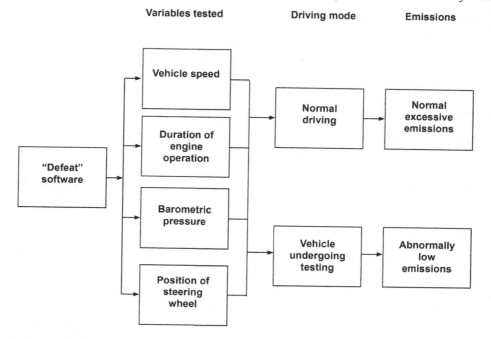

Figure 15.4 VW and Audi System for Hiding Emissions

The UVW scientists tested three vehicles with two different treatment technologies designed to reduce NOx emissions: one lean-NOx trap (LNT) and two urea-based selective catalytic reduction (SCR) systems. Weiss et all (2011, p. ii) found that:

> Real-world NOx emissions were found to exceed the US-EPA Tier2-Bin5 (at full useful life) standard by a factor of 15 to 35 for the LNT-equipped vehicle, by a factor of 5 to 20 for one and at or below the standard for the second urea-SCR fitted vehicle.

While the UWV report was silent on the names of the cars tested, they were a 2013 M+BMW SUV, a 2012 VW Jetta and a VW 2012 Passat (Ewing 2018, p. 169).

Once the result of the UWV study were released, the US EPA (2015a) issued a notice of violation of the Clean Air Act to Volkswagen (VW), Audi AG, and VW Group of America. The notice read in part (US EPA 2015a, pp. 1–2):

> The United States Environmental Protection Agency (EPA) has investigated and continues to investigate Volkswagen AG, Audi AG, and Volkswagen Group of America (collectively, VW) for compliance with the Clean Air Act (CAA), 42 USC. 7401–767lq, and its implementing regulations. As detailed in this Notice of Violation (NOV), the EPA has determined that VW manufactured and installed defeat devices in certain model year 2009 through 2015 diesel light-duty vehicles equipped with 2.0 liter engines. These defeat devices bypass, defeat, or render inoperative elements of the vehicles' emission control system that exist to comply with CAA emission standards. Therefore, VW violated section 203(a)(3)(B) of the CAA, 42 USC.7522(a)(3)(B). Additionally, the EPA has determined that, due to the existence of the defeat devices in these vehicles, these vehicles

do not conform in all material respects to the vehicle specifications described in the applications for the certificates of conformity that purportedly cover them. Therefore, VW also violated section 203(a)(l) of the CAA, 42 USC. 7522(a)(I), by selling, offering for sale, introducing into commerce, delivering for introduction into commerce, or importing these vehicles, or for causing any of the foregoing acts.

A second EPA notice to Volkswagen was issued on November 2, 2015 (US EPA 2015b) (see also US EPA October 18, 2021 for a summary of the case.)

A subsequent study by Hou et al. (2016, p.1) on the health and economic effects of these emission exceedances concluded that:

the total extra NOx emitted over one year of operation would result in 5 to 50 premature deaths, 687 to 17,526 work days with restricted activity, and economic costs of $43,479,189 to $423,268,502, based on various assumptions regarding emission scenarios and risks.

The findings by the US EPA and California Air Resources Board (2015) ultimately resulted in a range of civil complaints, consumer lawsuits, and criminal charges against senior management of Volkswagen. These actions included nearly identical lawsuits filed by the Attorneys-General of New York, Massachusetts, and Maryland for violating their environmental laws (Reuters July 19, 2016). Ultimately, the total cost to Volkswagen approximated $21 billion, composed of $14.7 civil settlements; a $4.3 billion dollar fine after the company agreed to plead guilty to conspiring the defraud the US government and violate the Clean Air Act; and a further $1.3 billion agreement to reimburse owners of Audi, Porsche, and Volkswagen vehicles not covered by the earlier settlement (FTC March 29, 2016; Ewing 2018; FTC July 27, 2020; US EPA September 14, 2023r). The behavior of Volkswagen was less than exemplary as senior management continued to blame lower management for the fraud despite strong evidence that they were aware of the strategy and actively promoting it (*New York Times* July 19, 2016). Ewing (2018, p. 261) concluded that this cases "vividly shows how a dysfunctional corporate culture can threaten the existence of even the mightiest corporations".

The civil and criminal actions against the corporation had an immediate and substantial, although surprisingly somewhat transitory economic impact on Volkswagen. Figure 15.5 shows operating results over the period 2010–2023, and Figure 15.6 portrays stock price and trading volume over the period 2006–2021. The results of the legal proceedings against Volkswagen led to a spike in trading volume on September 22–23, 2015 and a 15% loss in stock price. The year 2015 was marked by a billion Euro loss in profit and the company's profitability did not recover fully until 2017. As of 2024, the impact of the initial fraud has not disappeared as the trial of the former Volkswagen CEO over the diesel scandal started in September 2024 (AP March 15, 2024).

Parenthetically, it is interesting to note two other price and volume anomalies in the data. The first on October 28, 2008, was a virtual doubling of stock price ascribed to short sellers rushing to cover their positions after being caught by surprise when Porsche increased its holdings in Volkswagen to 75%. While the stock closed at $109.75, it had reached a high of $1258 during the day (*New York Times* October 28, 2008). The second anomaly occurred on March 16–22, 2021, with a spike in volume attributed to Volkswagen's announced intent to solidify its commitment to electric vehicles (*New York Times* March 15, 2021).

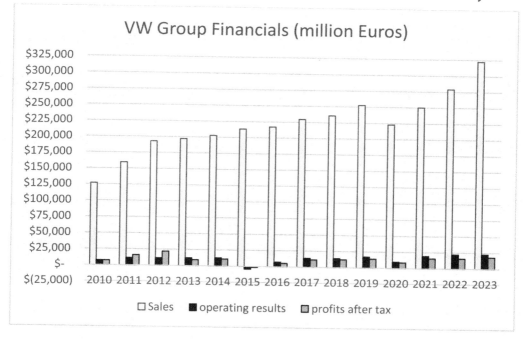

Figure 15.5 VW Financials 2010–2023

Source: VW Annual Reports

Figure 15.6a VW Stock Price 2006–2022

Source: Yahoo Finance

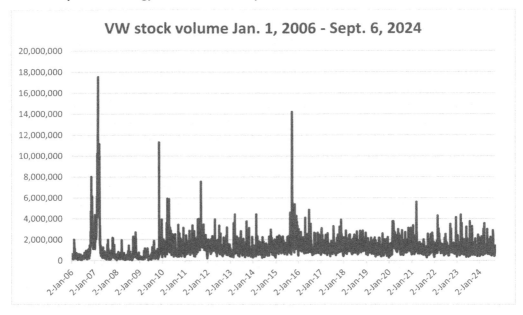

Figure 15.6b VW Stock Trading Volume 2006–2022

Source: Yahoo Finance

Figure 15.7 displays Volkswagen's sales in the US over the period 1987–2020. After the debacle of the defeat mechanism, Volkswagen ceased selling diesel powered cars in the US and sales consequently dropped. The company's share of the shrinking American market had dropped from its high in 2001 and 2002 of 5.1% to 4.0% in 2020.

As an aside, it is interesting to understand the historical and current regulatory approaches of the European Union as distinct from the United States. The EU has traditionally taken a much less strict approach to controlling NOx emissions from diesel cars as their lower emissions of carbon dioxide than automobiles powered with gasoline have been one major component of the EU's focus on reducing overall emissions of greenhouse gases (Klier & Linn 2106). This tolerance for NOx emissions even included the acceptance of emissions in excess of established standards. To quote a study by the European Parliament (2017):

> US federal emissions standards are broadly more ambitious for key local air quality pollutants, particularly NOx, than EU standards. A key difference is that the US applies a single set of standards to petrol and diesel vehicles, while the EU allows higher levels of air quality pollutants to diesel vehicles. In addition, California, and a number of other states that chose to adopt California's rules, apply emissions standards that are more ambitious than federal standards.

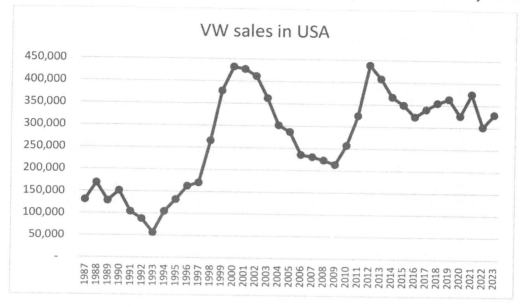

Figure 15.7 VW Sales in the US 1987–2023

Source: VW Annual Reports

In fact, the EU has a much more tolerant approach to defeat devices as well. To quote the same study cited above:

> The definitions of defeat device in the US and the EU legislation are fundamentally similar, with a similar range of allowed exemptions. The key difference lies in implementation. In the EU, manufacturers are not obliged to seek prior approval for their reliance on exemptions for defeat devices, or even to identify any such devices when applying for type approval. In the US, manufacturers are required to provide full details of any auxiliary emissions control devices to the EPA. And while in the EU there has been no clarification of how the definition of defeat devices should be implemented, the EPA has provided manufacturers and evaluators with a range of advisory circulars providing further interpretative detail.

Volkswagen, nevertheless, continues to produce large numbers of cars power by diesel fuel for Europe and the international market. In 2017, 39% of its global sales were diesel and this percentage rose to 43% in 2018 (CNN January 30, 2019 and *Green Car Reports* March 20, 2019).

Financial data for Volkswagen are presented in Tables 15.3a, 15.3b, and 15.3c. Despite the company's dominant position in the global car market and remarkable recovery of the market for diesel engines, the company is facing several major changes in the strategic landscape that entail both major opportunities and risks: the continuing development of the Chinese market, the global transition to electric vehicles, the promise of autonomous vehicles, and the changing nature of personal transportation.

Table 15.3a VW Group Income Statement 2022–2023

VOLKSWAGEN GROUP – ANNUAL REPORT 2023
INCOME STATEMENT OF THE VOLKSWAGEN GROUP

€ million	2023	2022[1]
Sales revenue	322,284	279,050
Cost of sales	−261,262	−226,866
Gross result	61,022	52,184
Distribution expenses	−21,340	−19,840
Administrative expenses	−12,724	−11,655
Other operating income	15,152	19,234
Other operating expenses	−19,534	−17,813
Operating result	22,576	22,109
Share of the result of equity-accounted investments	2,291	2,403
Interest income	2,658	1,325
Interest expenses	−3,592	−408
Other financial result	−739	−3,359
Financial result	618	**−40**
Earnings before tax	23,194	22,070
Income tax income/expense	−5,266	−6,217
Current	−6,791	−5,263
Deferred	1,526	−954
Earnings after tax	17,928	15,852
of which attributable to		
Noncontrolling interests	1,329	395
Volkswagen AG hybrid capital investors	586	576
Volkswagen AG shareholders	16,013	14,881
Basic/diluted earnings per ordinary share in €	31.92	29.66
Basic/diluted earnings per preferred share in €	31.98	29.72

1 Prior-year figures adjusted (see disclosures on IFRS 17 in the "Effects of new and amended IFRSs" section).

Source: VW Annual Report (2022)

Table 15.3b VW Group Balance Sheet

VOLKSWAGEN GROUP – ANNUAL REPORT 2023
BALANCE SHEET OF THE VOLKSWAGEN GROUP

€ million	Dec. 31, 2023	Dec. 31, 2022[1]
Assets		
Noncurrent assets		
Intangible assets	89,109	83,241
Property, plant and equipment	66,880	63,890
Lease assets	64,094	59,380
Investment property	632	610

(*Continued*)

Table 15.3b (Continued)

€ million	Dec. 31, 2023	Dec. 31, 2022[1]
Equity-accounted investments	12,239	12,668
Other equity investments	4,431	3,489
Financial services receivables	94,474	86,944
Other financial assets	11,757	13,832
Other receivables	2,702	2,477
Tax receivables	437	394
Deferred tax assets	13,940	12,929
	360,694	339,853
Current assets		
Inventories	53,601	52,274
Trade receivables	21,849	18,534
Financial services receivables	66,381	61,549
Other financial assets	16,953	15,148
Other receivables	8,799	7,813
Tax receivables	1,649	1,732
Marketable securities and time deposits	26,772	37,206
Cash and cash equivalents	43,449	29,172
Assets held for sale	190	733
	239,644	224,159
Total assets	600,338	564,013
Equity and liabilities		
Equity		
Subscribed capital	1,283	1,283
Capital reserve	14,551	14,551
Retained earnings	147,830	137,272
Other reserves	−3,125	−1,851
Equity attributable to Volkswagen AG hybrid capital investors	15,155	14,121
Equity attributable to Volkswagen AG shareholders and hybrid capital investors	175,694	165,376
Noncontrolling interests	14,218	12,952
	189,912	178,328
Noncurrent liabilities		
Financial liabilities	122,323	121,737
Other financial liabilities	6,968	8,188
Other liabilities	9,885	9,144
Deferred tax liabilities	9,781	10,736
Provisions for pensions	29,672	27,553
Provisions for taxes	4,287	4,320
Other provisions	21,636	21,283
	204,552	202,961
Current liabilities		
Financial liabilities	110,476	83,448
Trade payables	30,901	28,738
Tax payables	556	726
Other financial liabilities	14,022	19,807
Other liabilities	24,345	22,665
Provisions for taxes	1,663	2,586
Other provisions	23,881	24,596
Liabilities associated with assets held for sale	31	158
	205,874	182,723
Total equity and liabilities	600,338	564,013

1 Prior-year figures adjusted (see disclosures on IFRS 17 in the "Effects of new and amended IFRSs" section).

Source: VW Annual Report (2022)

Table 15.3c VW Group Cash Flow Statement

CASH FLOW STATEMENT BY DIVISION

€ million	Volkswagen Group		Automotive[1]		Financial Services	
	2023	2022[2]	2023	2022[2]	2023	2022[2]
Cash and cash equivalents at beginning of period	**29,738**	**39,123**	**23,042**	**24,899**	**6,695**	**14,224**
Earnings before tax	23,194	22,070	19,419	16,474	3,775	5,595
Income taxes paid	−7,716	−4,416	−6,328	−3,562	−1,389	−854
Depreciation and amortization expense[3]	28,282	30,670	17,729	20,854	10,552	9,816
Change in pension provisions	262	898	251	857	11	41
Share of the result of equity-accounted investments	271	568	244	639	27	−71
Other non-cash income/expense and reclassifications[4]	4,161	−509	4,474	−2,086	−313	1,577
Gross cash flow	**48,453**	**49,280**	**35,789**	**33,177**	**12,665**	**16,104**
Change in working capital	**−29,097**	**−20,784**	**2,062**	**−3,312**	**−31,160**	**−17,472**
Change in inventories	−2,071	−8,385	−651	−8,262	−1,419	−123
Change in receivables	−4,361	−3,065	−1,250	−526	−3,111	−2,539
Change in liabilities	5,272	8,713	3,179	8,179	2,094	535
Change in other provisions	358	−3,042	236	−2,950	123	−92
Change in lease assets (excluding depreciation)	−14,964	−8,711	558	406	−15,522	−9,117
Change in financial services receivables	−13,332	−6,294	−8	−158	−13,324	−6,136
Cash flows from operating activities	**19,356**	**28,496**	**37,851**	**29,865**	**−18,495**	**−1,369**
Cash flows from investing activities attributable to operating activities	**−28,031**	**−25,454**	**−27,153**	**−25,058**	**−878**	**−396**
of which: investments in property, plant and equipment, investment property and intangible assets, excluding capitalized development costs (capex)	−14,653	−12,948	−14,371	−12,731	−282	−217
capitalized development costs	−11,142	−9,723	−11,142	−9,723	–	–
acquisition and disposal of equity investments	−2,738	−3,219	−2,115	−2,997	−622	−222

(*Continued*)

Table 15.3c (Continued)

€ million	Volkswagen Group		Automotive[1]		Financial Services	
	2023	2022[2]	2023	2022[2]	2023	2022[2]
Net cash flow[5]	**−8,675**	**3,042**	**10,698**	**4,807**	**−19,373**	**−1,765**
Change in investments in securities and time deposits, as well as in loans	8,219	−16,368	9,512	−15,052	−1,293	−1,316
Cash flows from investing activities	**−19,812**	**−41,822**	**−17,641**	**−40,110**	**−2,171**	**−1,712**
Cash flows from financing activities	**16,008**	**4,225**	**−12,927**	**8,621**	**28,934**	**−4,396**
of which: capital transactions with noncontrolling interests	−8	16,198	−8	16,198	–	–
capital contributions/ capital redemptions	1,003	−235	−2,919	−235	3,922	0
Effect of exchange rate changes on cash and cash equivalents	−1,765	−285	−1,620	−233	−145	−52
Change of loss allowance within cash and cash equivalents	−2	1	−2	1	0	0
Net change in cash and cash equivalents	**13,785**	**−9,385**	**5,661**	**−1,856**	**8,124**	**−7,529**
Cash and cash equivalents at Dec. 31[6]	**43,522**	**29,738**	**28,704**	**23,042**	**14,819**	**6,695**
Securities and time deposits, as well as loans	41,858	49,771	20,994	30,891	20,864	18,880
Gross liquidity	**85,380**	**79,509**	**49,698**	**53,934**	**35,683**	**25,575**
Total third-party borrowings	−232,813	−205,312	−9,409	−10,919	−223,404	−194,393
Net liquidity at Dec. 31[7]	**−147,433**	**−125,803**	**40,289**	**43,015**	**−187,722**	**−168,818**

1 Including allocation of consolidation adjustments between the Automotive and Financial Services divisions.
2 Prior-year figures adjusted (see disclosures on IFRS 17).
3 Net of impairment reversals.
4 These relate mainly to the fair value measurement of financial instruments and the reclassification of gains/ losses on disposal of noncurrent assets and equity investments to investing activities.
5 Net cash flow: cash flows from operating activities, net of cash flows from investing activities attributable to operating activities (investing activities excluding change in investments in securities, time deposits and loans).
6 Cash and cash equivalents comprise cash at banks, checks, cash-in-hand and call deposits.
7 The total of cash, cash equivalents, securities and time deposits, as well as loans to affiliates and joint ventures net of third-party borrowings (noncurrent and current financial liabilities).

Source: VW Annual Report (2022)

The Chinese Automobile Market

As illustrated in Figure 15.8, Volkswagen's major markets remain in Europe and China. Volkswagen had the foresight to enter the Chinese market in 1991 and captured 44% of the rather small market at that time by selling 34,913 cars. While Volkswagen continued to increase its sales in China in partnership with Chinese manufacturers, the percentage share had declined to 24% in the much larger domestic Chinese market by 2020 (Wards various years). Table 15.4 lists all the manufacturers of automobiles in China as of 2020, giving a sense of the competition that Volkswagen faces despite its recent preeminent position in this market.

Figure 15.8 VW's Major Markets

Source: VW Annual Reports

Table 15.4 China Vehicle Production by Manufacturer, 2020

	Total
Cars	
FAW Volkswagen	*1,468,581*
Shanghai VW	*927,170*
Dongfeng Nissan	837,387
Shanghai GM	836,223

(*Continued*)

Table 15.4 (Continued)

Cars	Total
Geely	689,413
Guangzhou Toyota	614,837
FAW Toyota	538,992
Shanghai AIC	483,892
Guangzhou Honda	441,151
Beijing Benz	365,752
Brilliance BMW	351,934
Dongfeng Honda	349,509
Beijing Hyundai	307,463
Changan	245,916
Shanghai GM Wuling	232,085
FAW	194,711
BYD	161,684
Chery	153,512
Tesla	152,957
Dongfeng Kia	122,735
Chana Ford	113,744
Nanjing	94,026
Chana Mazda	85,660
Guangzhou AC	69,126
Volvo	67,795
Great Wall	57,266
Dongfeng	46,984
JAC	35,382
Dongfeng PSA	33,748
BAIC	23,887
Chana Suzuki	15,294
Leapmotor	11,199
Brilliance China	4,183
JMC	3,388
Young Man	2,712
China National	2,087
Southeast	1,431
Honda	1,326
Other	1,274
Haima Zhengzhou	931
Qoros	700
Changhe	530
Dongfeng Renault	476
Zotye	400
Chana PSA	10
Guangzhou Fiat	1
Lifan	1
Total Cars	**10,149,465**

Source: Ward's Automotive Yearbook

The Chinese market has become an indispensable component of the strategy of Volkswagen and most major global producers. Figure 15.9 show the change in relative shares of the three largest national markets over the past decade (Multiple). China has clearly

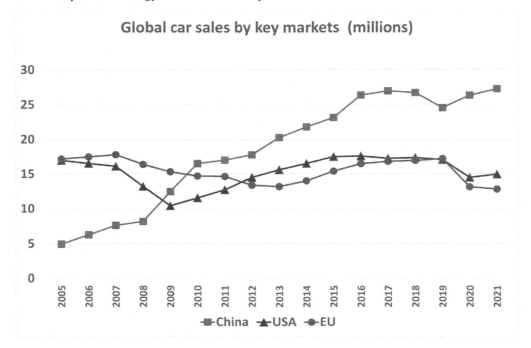

Figure 15.9 Relative Share of National Markets for Cars Over the Past Decade

Source: Wards multiple years

emerged as the world's largest buyer of automobiles, propelled by the growth and increasing prosperity of its middle class. The Chinese auto sector is still in its developmental stage with over four dozen individual companies and joint ventures with annual vehicle production ranging from a low of 2 units (Guangzhou Fiat) to over 2.7 million (joint ventures FAW Volkswagen and Shanghai VW) (Wards 2021).

Figure 15.10 tracks the remarkable emergence of China as the world's largest producer of motor vehicles and Figure 15.11 displays the equally rapid rise in domestic registrations. This extraordinary increase over a relatively short time span has created significant problems with congestion, and particularly urban air pollution, in cities that are already heavily polluted from industrial process and coal combustion. Chinese cities have 10 places in the top 24 congested cities in the world (TomTom 2017) and 30 places among the top 100 cities with air pollution measured by the annual average concentration of PM10 (WHO, 2019).

While China's national average annual increases in the number of automobiles have ranged as high as 36%, these increases have been matched or exceeded in many of the country's regions. These increases are clearly unsustainable and have recently been the subject of new research and policy initiatives by the central government. However, as of 2016, only two regions in China, Beijing and Tianjin, had been able to reduce recent growth rates to 1% and 0%, respectively, through a bundle of aggressive policy measures. These new policy responses could not have come any sooner in light of the ecological implications of business-as-usual. Table 15.5 indicates the current number of cars registered in China compared to the number of additional cars required if automotive density were to equal Japan, the US, or the world. Table 15.6 repeats this exercise for

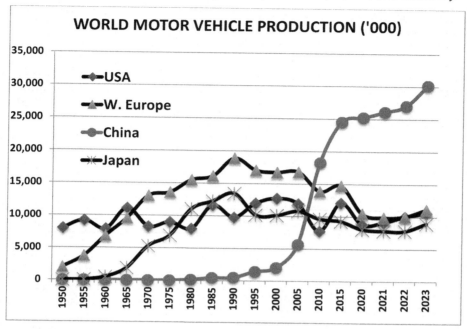

Figure 15.10 China's MV Production vs. Competitors

Source: Wards and OICA

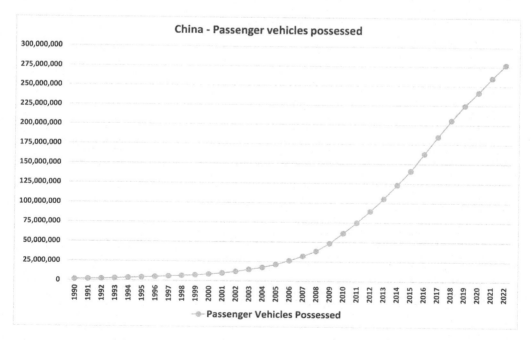

Figure 15.11 China's Domestic Registration of Cars

Source: China Statistical Yearbooks

Beijing, Shanghai, and Chongqing if they were to aspire to New York City's automotive density. Estimates of increased greenhouse gas emissions under a business-as-usual scenario in China have been calculated by Huo et al. (2012a, 2012b):

Road transport in China would create 410–520 million metric tons (MMT) of oil-equivalent oil demand (three to four times the current level), 28–36 billion GJ of WTW [*wheel-to-wheel or lifecycle analysis*] energy demand and 1900–2300 MMT of CO_2-equivalent of WTW GHG emissions by 2050.

(Huo et al. 2012b, pp. 37)

Table 15.5 Chinese Car Registration Scenarios

China projections based on persons per car

Country		*2016*	
	# registered cars	*persons/car*	*total population*
China	165,600,000	8.3	1,378,665,000
Japan	61,873,000	2.1	126,994,511
USA	123,552,650	2.6	323,127,513
WORLD	973,352,643	7.2	7,008,810,000
Total cars in China if equal to car density in			
Japan	656,507,143		
USA	530,255,769		
World	191,481,250		
Increment for China			
Japan	490,907,143		
USA	364,655,769		
World	25,881,250		
Ratio to present			
Japan	296%		
USA	220%		
World	16%		

Table 15.6 Chinese Urban Car Registration Scenarios

Three Chinese cities: projections based on persons per car

City	*urban area pop*	*#cars in 2015*	*People per car*
Los Angeles	11,901,050	6,433,000	1.85
New York City	18,106,430	7,771,000	2.33
San Francisco	2,989,610	1,769,000	1.69
Beijing	21,500,000	4,290,390	5.01
Shanghai	24,500,000	2,082,200	11.77
Chongqing	18,384,000	2,118,200	8.68

(Continued)

Table 15.6 (Continued)

City	urban area pop	#cars in 2015	People per car
ADDITIONAL CARS TO EQUAL NEW YORK CITY CAR DENSITY			
	total	*net new*	
Beijing	9,227,468	4,937,078	
Shanghai	10,515,021	8,432,821	
Chongqing	7,890,129	5,771,929	

The immensity of the challenge is exacerbated by the shift among Chinese buyers towards SUVs that now dominate market growth in this sector (McKinsey & Company 2017). These projections clearly depend on the penetration of electric cars into the Chinese market, an important goal of the central government (Liang et al. 2019). Three central issues include material requirements to meet the rapidly increasing demand for automobiles, whether ICE or EV, the source of energy used to power the electric vehicle sector, and the continued problem of non-GHG externalities.

It would not be an overstatement to say that China's automotive sector hangs like the sword of Damocles over the global automotive industry. While most of China's current domestic production is destined for the national market, China's traditional manufacturing cost advantage poses a monumental threat to the continued dominance of the current major producers in Europe, North America, Japan, and Korea. Figure 15.12

Figure 15.12 International Comparison of Auto Industry Wages

Source: Wards 2022 and Statista

compares hourly wage rates in the auto industry among major producing countries in 2015. Because of China's increasing wealth, wage rates across many industries have risen in the last few years, prompting many manufacturers of labor-intensive, low-value-added products to move their production to South or Southeast Asia. However, China's determination to become a major player in the international automotive sector suggests that the production base will likely remain in China, supplemented with outsourcing of some components.

China's pronounced cost advantage vis-à-vis the developed countries is clearly necessary but not sufficient, however, to capture a significant share of global markets. The missing ingredient is technology. China has made a policy of attracting technology transfer not only through joint production agreements and purchase, such as the acquisition of Volvo in 2010, one of the global leaders of automotive technology, but also through the recruiting of foreign talent. The Chinese track record in building technological competence has already been demonstrated in such areas as high-speed computing, and solar and wind power. Their intentions to achieve similar preeminence in commercial airline production and automobiles (both internal combustion and electric) are credible in light of the fact that China has recently graduated 4.7 million students in Science, Technology, Engineering, and Mathematics (STEM) in contrast to 568,000 in the USA and 195,000 in Japan (WEF 2016). In addition, over the period 2010 to 2020, the share of international patents changed markedly: US from 15% to 10%, Japan 35% to 15%, Europe 12% to 8%, but China grew from 6% to 49% (NSB 2022; see also UNESCO 2017). From 2008 to 2018, China also leapfrogged the US in the number of international scientific publications, jumping from 249,049 to 528,263, while the US only increased from 393,979 to 422,808 (NSF 2020). All these factors are part of a concerted and powerful Chinese effort, labeled "Made in China 2035," designed to achieve global dominance in a broad range of high value-added, advanced technologies (*New York Times* November 1&7, 2017; *South China Morning Post* September 24, 2020).

Foreign car manufacturers have certainly got this message and already have a significant presence in the domestic Chinese market. Some of these companies are using the Chinese manufacturing environment as an export platform back into the global market, further jeopardizing the economic viability of their own national domestic manufacturing operations. Equally threatening to foreign manufactures who are currently producing through joint ventures in China is a recent assessment of McKinsey & Co. (2017, p. 3) that "local brands have begun to exhibit real competitiveness based on vehicle designs and quality levels" and are increasing their share of the domestic market. McKinsey & Co. conclude that "the increasing competence of local brands constitutes an urgent warning to Western OEMs that opportunities to earn 'easy money' in China may be gone forever."

While China has increased its exports within recent years to approximately three-quarters of a million vehicles, its principal market is Asia, followed to a lesser extent by Europe. Except for Volvo, Chinese manufactures have made no direct impact on the American market. However, several US car companies have already started to ship Chinese-made cars back to the United States under the brand names of Ford Focus, Cadillac CT6 Plug-in hybrid, and Buick Envision.

All these factors suggest that the current reliance on the Chinese market by Volkswagen and other major Western automobile manufactures may have a limited lifespan. Volkswagen alludes to the potential risks associated with the Chinese market in a section of their

Annual Report of 2023 devoted to risk. In 2019 Volkswagen added a risk matrix to their annual report, focussing on seven categories of risks: (1) risks from the macroeconomy, markets and sales; (2) research and development risks; (3) operational risks; (4) environmental and social risks; (5) legal risk; (6) financial risks; and (7) risk from mergers &

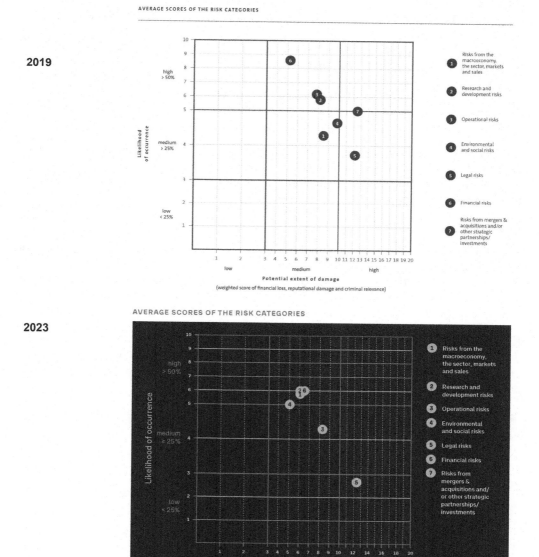

Figure 15.13 VW's Assessment of Future Risks

Source: VW Annual Reports 2019 and 2023

acquisitions and/or other strategic partnerships/investments. Figure 15.13 compares the matrices of 2019 and 2023. To quote from theVolkswagen 2023 annual report:

- Western Europe, especially Germany, and China are our main sales markets. A drop in demand in these regions due to the economic climate would have a particularly strong impact on the Company's earnings including financial services. We counter this risk with a clear, customer-oriented and innovative product and pricing policy (p. 229).
- To defend our strong market position in China over the long term, we are continuously expanding our product range to include models that have been specially developed for this market. We are increasingly forging partnerships and further extending our production capacity in this growing market (p. 231).
- Due to changes in the competitive environment, especially in China, there is also the risk of losing market share (p. 234).

Considering the fundamental medium to long-term uncertainty associated with the Chinese market, other strategic initiatives are required to complement or replace this reliance. Foremost among these is the emergence of electric vehicles as a potential solution to greenhouse gas emissions in the transportation sector.

Electric Vehicles

Since diesel-powered vehicles cannot play a substantial role in reducing global greenhouse gas emissions, many governments have turned to electric cars as a major solution to this problem. While the transportation sector contributes 14% of global GHG emissions (US EPA 2021), this ratio is significantly higher in countries with a large transportation sector. By way of illustration, Figures 15.14 and 15.15 display estimates of the breakdown

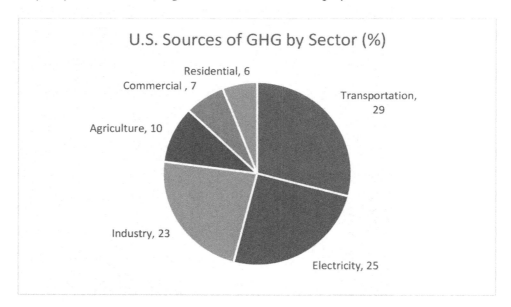

Figure 15.14 US GHG Emissions by Sector
Source: US EPA

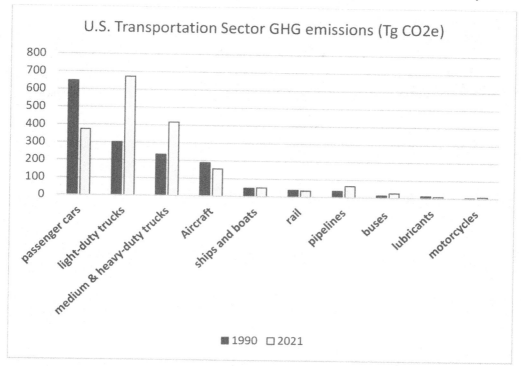

Figure 15.15 US GHG Emissions in the Transportation Sector 1990 & 2021
Source: US EPA

of sources of GHG by sector in the US, as well as a breakdown within the transportation sector itself (US EPA 2018, 2021). SUVs are included in the category of light-duty trucks, along with pickup trucks, vans, and minivans.

At the COP26 Conference in November 2021, 32 countries made the following commitment: "We have agreed that our shared aim is to make zero emission vehicles the new normal by making them accessible, affordable, and sustainable in all regions by 2030" (UN COP26 2021). This declaration was also signed by several major automobile manufacturers: Ford, GM, Mercedes-Benz, Jaguar, Land Rover, and Volvo (Electrek November 10, 2021; *New York Times* January 28, March 22, & April 23, 2021). To further this goal, several countries have already enacted mandates for the sale of EVs within the next several decades, led by Norway in 2025 (see Figure 15.16) (Inside EVs October 10, 2016; *The Guardian* July 6, 2017; BBC July 26, 2017; IEA 2020 & ICCT 2020). While the US did not sign the declaration, the Biden administration has budgeted $174 billion to encourage the adoption of EVs (*New York Times* March 31, 2021). The estimated relative contribution of car manufacturers to GHG production is related to the volume and mix of their automotive production and these data have been provided by Greenpeace in their 2019 study entitled "Crashing the Climate: How the Car Industry is Driving the Climate Crisis" (see Table 15.7)

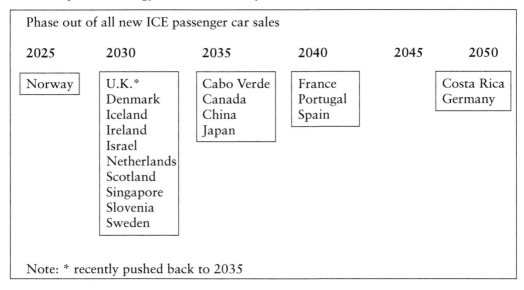

Figure 15.16 National Mandates for EV Sales

Table 15.7 Car Manufacturer GHG Emissions

	Million Vehicles Sold	GHG Emissions Per Vehicle in Tons	Average Lifetime GHG Emissions In Million Tons
VW Group	10.8	53.8	582
Renault-Nissan Alliance	10.3	55.7	577
Toyota	10.4	53.8	562
General Motors	8.6	61.3	530
Hyundai-Kia	7.4	54	401
Ford Motor Corp	5.6	61.4	346
F.C.A	4.8	63.1	305
Honda	5.2	54.1	283
PSA Group (incl Opel)	4.1	49.2	201
Suzuki	3.3	49.6	164
Daimler AG	2.7	58.7	161
BMW AG	2.5	54.4	136

Source: Greenpeace (2019)

In view of the dramatic shift in the regulatory environment over the next few decades, Volkswagen, along with most major automobile manufactures have made major capital investments in the production of electric vehicles and their components, especially batteries. For example, Wards (2021) cites the following recent undertakings by Volkswagen:

- Volkswagen will acquire a 26% stake in battery manufacturer Gotion High-Tech for $1.2 billion, becoming the company's largest shareholder
- Ford and VW say they plan to make up to 8 million medium pickup trucks and commercial vans as part of an alliance announced in January 2019 to build electric vehicles as well as develop self-driving technology
- Volkswagen of America's Chattanooga, TN complex was being expanded to accommodate production of EV battery cells and battery packs, with VW investing $800 million to build EVs at the Tennessee facility
- VW announced plans to convert plants in Emden and Hanover, Germany, to electric vehicle production as part of an $86 billion investment to ramp up development of EVs and self-driving cars

The company is entering a highly competitive environment for electric cars. Figures 15.17 and 15.18 portrays the global market share of EVs in total automotive production and of EV production by major markets over the last decade. Table 15.8 lists recent levels of EV production by the five leading global car companies and their EV markets, and Figure 15.19 displays the Boston Consulting Groups' (2020) predictions for the automotive market over the next decade. In 2019, the company announced a goal of launching 75 EVs and 60 hybrids by 2029 (Motor1.com November 16, 2019). In 2023, Volkswagen produced 394,000 electric vehicles as well as 256,500 plugin hybrids.

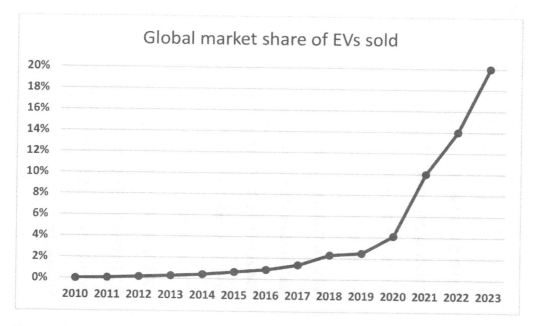

Figure 15.17   Global Share of EVs Sold 2010–2023
Source: IEA 2021a

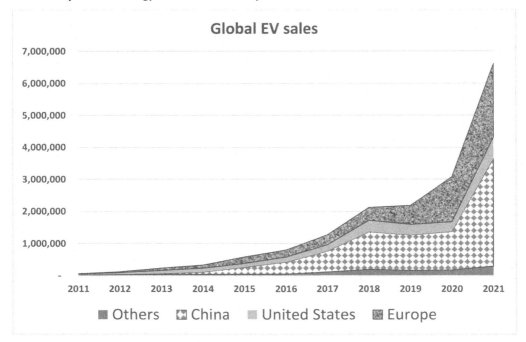

Figure 15.18 EV Production by Major Market
Source: EVvolumes.com

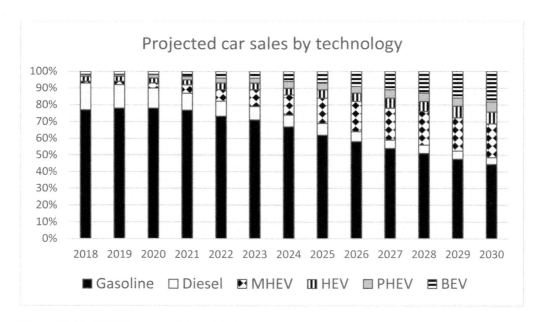

Figure 15.19 BCG Forecast of Auto Market

Table 15.8 EV Production by Leading Car Companies

	World	*Europe*	*China*	*USA*	*Other*
Tesla	936	170	321	352	93
VW Group	763	549	154	44	15
BYD	598	1	595	0	2
GM	517	0	486	25	6
Stellantis	385	324	14	42	5

Source: IEA (2021a) Electric cars end off supply challenges to more than double global sales, January 30, thousands of vehicles

The central question is not only to what extent the production of electric cars is ecologically sustainable, but also whether it will lead to sustainable corporate strategy for Volkswagen and other major global producers. To answer this question, it is necessary to understand the nature of electric vehicles, both their advantages and disadvantages.

Bloomberg (April 12, 2019 & December 16, 2020) has forecasted that battery-electric vehicles will be cheaper than ICEs in 2025 and more than half of all global light duty vehicle sales will be electric vehicles by 2040. This prediction of cost parity has been reaffirmed by the investment bank, UBS (2020) that expects the total cost gap with conventional cars will fully close by 2024. The sales of EVs have been accelerating as sales increased by 43% globally in 2020 and some analysts feel that the adoption of these vehicles are near a tipping point (IEA 2021a; *New York Times* September 20, 2020; *The Guardian* January 22, 2021). While China and the US have the largest number of EVs currently in operation (IEA 2021a), Norway became the first country in the world where the sales of EVs outstripped all other types of propulsion (*The Guardian* January 5, 2021). Nevertheless, it appears that China may achieve major dominance in the global production of EVs because of government policy, the development of technological expertise and its dominant position in lithium-ion battery production (Ward's 2019; McKinsey 2020; *New York Times* January 29, 44 and 6, September 22, & December 22, 2021).

There are three principal variants of EVs: gasoline-electric hybrids (plugin or on-board generated) and pure plugin EVs. From the point of view of addressing climate change, only the pure electric vehicle satisfies the criterion of eliminating fossil fuel as a direct fuel. The International Energy Agency (2020) has estimated that given the right circumstances, the stock of EVs could reach as high as 140–245 million by 2030. Bloomberg's estimates for 2040 (2018) suggest as many as 600 million by 2040.

While a conceptually appealing answer to the dilemma posed by the rapidly surging dissemination of ICEs, there are several critical issues concerning electric vehicles:

1. The familiar "chicken and egg" problem where the widespread adoption of EVs requires extensive infrastructure (principally charging stations), but the incentive for building such stations is influenced by the number of EVs on the road. The adoption rate will also be constrained by a fleet turnover problem as new ICE vehicles sold today could last one or two decades before trade-ins or disposal (*New York Times* January 29 & March 13, 2021). Tesla already has a global network of 30,000 fast-charging stations and has had plans to triple the size of this network over the next two years. These goals may be in jeopardy in light of recent equivocation by their CEO, Elon Musk. To overtake Tesla's leads in this market, Volkswagen, plans

to increase its network of chargers to 45,000 by 2025 with 18,00 in Europe, 17,00 in China, and 10,000 in North America (Reuters November 17, 2021). It is not unreasonable to expect that as national mandates become effective, there will be a rapid rise in the number of charging stations funded by government and the business sector (*New York Times* March 2, 2021 & February 10, 2022). In fact, this may present an opportunity for the major corporate suppliers of gasoline for vehicle markets to broaden their industrial strategy by capitalizing on their in-place, service station real estate by modifying these installations to include recharging power for electric vehicles. This is one small example of a potential reorientation of major fossil-fuel companies to a more viable long-term strategy by becoming suppliers of energy as opposed to a sole focus on oil and natural gas. Several examples of relatively small steps in this direction are already evident. For example, Shell Oil has decided to add a significant component of renewable energy to its portfolio of products (Shell Strategic Report 2020; *New York Times* September 16, 2021). In addition, BP has joined the French oil company, Total, in spending 879 million pounds to purchase options to build offshore wind farms in the United Kingdom. It has been estimated that the budget of this project, once developed, could total tens of billions of dollars. The company has also paid $1.1 billion dollars for a 50% share in an offshore wind facility off the US east coast (*New York Times* February 8, 2021). Included in the proposed new energy portfolio are plans to invest heavily in solar power (Bloomberg September 16, 2020).

2. Critical questions concerning battery capacity and miles between charges as well as charging times (*New York Times* May 4, 2021a). Nevertheless, Toshiba has announced that it is developing a sold-state battery with fast charging capability that can reduce recharge times to as low as 6 minutes, while researchers at PennState have developed technology for a 10-minute recharge making it comparable to refueling times for internal combustion cars (Toshiba 2017, Messer 2019). This challenge has become a central focus of the auto industry with the prospect of major technological advances in the near to medium-term future (Crabtree 2019; Pomerantseva et al. 2019; Yang et al. 2019). The Ford Motor Company has predicted that the successful development of a solid-state battery could increase battery energy density by at least 25–30%, leading to a comparable increase in driving range with the same size battery (*US News & World Reports* May 5, 2021). In December 2021, Volkswagen announced that it has entered into three strategic partnerships in the area of battery research and production (Volkswagen News December 8, 2021).

3. While EVs are generally found to have a lower environmental impact than ICEs (Patterson et al. 2011; ICCT 2019; Knobloch et al. 2020; *New York Times* January 15, and March 2, 2021) there are some concerns; for example, the absence of any major reductions in total material use and weight. Hawkins et al. (2012, p. 53) conducted a comparative lifecycle assessment (LCA) of materials content of a standard ICE and EV and concluded that:

EVS exhibit the potential for significant increases in human toxicity, freshwater eco-toxicity, freshwater eutrophication, and meta depletion impacts, largely emanating from the vehicle supply chain. Results are sensitive to assumption regarding electricity source, use phase energy consumption, vehicle lifetime, and battery replacement schedules.

These conclusions have been reaffirmed by a major study by the consulting firm, Arthur D Little (Brennan and Barber 2016). A study by McKinsey (May 2018a, 2018b) anticipates increased demand and price rises for commodities currently essential to EV technology, such as cobalt and lithium (*New York Times* May 6, 2021). However, the future development and rollout of solid-state batteries may reduce and change the nature of material requirements (Bloomberg, 2018). Building, repairing, recycling and disposal of EV-related material will pose new challenges that have to be addressed (Harper et al. 2019; *New York Times* March 31, 2021) as well as the geopolitical, ethical, and environmental issues of sourcing of exotic metals and conflict minerals (*New York Times* May 6, 2021, IEA 2021b). The downside of the extensive adoption of batteries is the problem of disposal and Morse (2021) reports that there is a concerted push to develop better recycling methods. However, the upside is that the average battery cell composition of several of these metals and materials is projected to decrease within the next decade (Transport & Environment 2021). An additional challenge is highlighted by Melin et al. (2021) who call for clear global standards for battery regulation to avoid investment distortions, material leakage and investment slowdown. One of the most important developments has been ongoing research on sodium-ion batteries that have the advantage of faster charging speeds, increased durability, longer overall life spans, and considerably lower environmental and health effects from production and use. While they store less energy than lithium-ion batteries, they, along with other emerging battery technologies, such as Zinc-ion, may ultimately pose a threat to the dominant role of the lithium-ion industry. To Volkswagen's credit, they have realized the potential of sodium-ion batteries and have backed a new Chinese EV brand called Yiwei that has just produced the first EV powered by this technology (Stenzel 2024). Other interested players include the Chinese powerhouse BYD Auto.

4. Two British reports (Eyre & Killip 2019; CCC 2019a, 2019b) have identified another potential problem with the widescale adoption of electric vehicles. Since electric vehicles are cheaper to run than ICE's, the net result might be an increase, rather than decrease, in vehicle use, reflecting a typical downward sloping demand curve.

5. The potential risk of fire associated with batteries in electric vehicles. *The Washington Post* (August 4, 2021) recently reported on a fire in a Tesla car parked overnight in a resident's garage. To quote:

Automakers including General Motors, Audi and Hyundai have recalled electric vehicles over fire risks in recent years and have warned of the associated dangers. Chevrolet last year advised owners not to charge their vehicles overnight or keep their fully charged vehicles in garages. It recalled more than 60,000 of its Bolt electric vehicles over concerns about the cars spontaneously combusting while parked with full batteries or charging, after reports of five fires without prior impact damage. The company issued another recall last month covering the same vehicles after two reports of battery fires in repaired vehicles.

This issue may be resolved with development of new, cheaper and less dangerous batteries made of easily available materials such as zinc, the subject of ongoing research (Service 2021). There is a clear need for governments and the automobile industry to intensify their research on battery safety, replacement and repair. In one extraordinary incident in Vancouver in 2023, the "battery cover plate on the bottom of a car was scratched and showed a small deformation, which indicated the battery had suffered an impact" (*Vancouver Sun* December 21, 2023). "Damage to the battery voided the vehicle's warranty and the $60,000 replacement cost was more than a new car was worth, so [the insurance company] wrote off and scrapped the nearly new automobile (*Vancouver Sun* December 21, 2023)."

6. The most important issue is the source of electricity supply used to power EVs. From the point of view of greenhouse gases, the wide-scale adoption of EVs may replace the multitude of individual cars generating GHGs by fewer but much larger individual sources of GHGs from centralized power plants. This is critically dependent on the fuel used (i.e., fossil vs. nonfossil) to generate the electricity and this, in turn, will vary markedly by geographic location. Assuming, for the sake of argument, that countries were somehow able to convert all their existing automotive stock to electric power, then the question arises as to how much additional national power capacity would be required (*New York Times* May 13, 2021). One research study concluded that a shift to EVs may have little overall system-wide effect on GHGs if the national grid is dominated by coal-fired generation (Wilson 2013), although other researchers are less pessimistic about the net impact on total emissions (Knobloch et al. 2020).

Clearly, the current mix of fuel sources is less important than the nature of new sources brought on line at the margin. As a case in point, China has made it national policy to lead the world in the introduction of renewables-sourced power. Despite this fact, however, the country is still adding coal-based capacity at a significant rate in order to meet rapidly expanding demand. McKinsey (2018b) has estimated that if half the cars on the roads in the US were EVs, daily natural gas demand for new generating capacity would increase by more than 20%. Electric vehicles would have to be charged largely off peak in order to avoid creating peaking problems in electricity demand, requiring significant more generating capacity. As far as the US is concerned, a hopeful sign is that much of the recent incremental additions to generating capacity have been renewable (US EIA 2018, 2019a, 2019b), suggesting that the increased adoption of electric vehicles in the U.S may not make a major contribution to greenhouse gases. In fact, green power accounted for more than 50% of global net additional electricity capacity as early as 2015 (*The Guardian* October 25, 2016).

Another potential game-changing breakthrough has been the introduction of an electric version of Ford's iconic and bestselling F-150 truck (*New York Times* May 19, 2021). The potentially widespread appeal of the F150 Lightning holds the promise of moving the acceptance of EV's into the mainstream of the US automotive market, attracting buyers who might have been indifferent or hostile to the use of electric automobiles (*New York Times* February 8, 2021). However, the sales of this vehicle have recently dropped off after concerns emerged about its loss of range in cold weather (*New York Times* February 7, 2024).

In sum, the net contribution to the amelioration of climate change by the widespread adoption of electric vehicles remains an open question at the moment, pending major new advances in battery and related technologies. Even if such obstacles were to be overcome, many of the negative effects of automobile use, such as material use, pollution from tire, brake and road wear, congestion, the need for supporting road infrastructure and accidents would remain unaddressed (e.g., Maddison et al. 1996). Nevertheless, there are already signs that urban mobility modes and design are being reimagined and some public policies with respect to permitted automotive density and street use are being adjusted in light of the emergence of electric vehicles (Statista July 19, 2019; Sengupta and Popovich 2019; Manjoo 2020; *The Daily Telegraph* June 26, 2020; *New York Times*, March 3 and May 27, 2021, CNN February 9, 2021).

While it appears that the electric car will emerge as the principal form of personal transportation in the next few decades, the question remains as to the range of strategic options available to Volkswagen. The company clearly intends to become a world leader in the production of electric vehicles. In this regard Volkswagen is an industry leader with investments in EVs and batteries in excess of $110 billion (*New York Times* March 15 2021; Reuters November 10, 2021). While major Chinese producers are listed with much lower levels of planned investments, a question remains as to the accuracy of these estimates in light of the Chinese government's extensive economic and political support of all facets of the industry, including its supply chains.

What threats and opportunities face Volkswagen in pursuing this strategy? Two issues in particular appear salient: the future of the Chinese automotive market and the future of personal transportation itself, which includes autonomous vehicles and what has been termed the *Internet of Motion*. In attempt to build on its track record as global leader in ICE-powered automobiles, both globally and in China, Volkswagen clearly intends to make China a continuing major focus of its EV marketing. As the world's fastest growing and largest market for automobiles, China presents an irresistible opportunity for western manufacturers that have already established manufacturing plants, either under their own name or in joint ventures with Chinese companies. By way of example, "GM and Volkswagen both sell more cars through joint ventures in China than in their home markets" (*New York Times* January 29, 2021). To quote Volkswagen's (2021) Annual Report (p. 46):

> China remained the largest single market for Volkswagen in 2020. In the Chinese market, the Group offers more than 160 imported and locally produced models. . . . The Volkswagen Group remained the clear number one with Chinese customers with a market share of 19.3%. . . . The new energy vehicle (NEV) segment was the fastest growing segment in China in 2020. . . . In spite of the Covid-19 pandemic, Volkswagen continued to put all its energies into the strategic direction of e-mobility in China in 2020. The seven new NEV models increased the Groups' portfolio to 22 electrified models in China. . . . With a 26% stake, Volkswagen (China) Investment Co. Ltd. wants to become the largest shareholder in Gotion High-Tech Co., Ltd. and thus the first international automotive manufacturer to directly invest in a Chinese battery supplier.

There are several challenges to the strategic success of the Western producers' plans. China clearly intends to become a world leader in EV production with a target of 8 million cars by 2028 (see Figure 15.20). The market for these cars will be supported by government policy that has mandated that most cars sold in China must be electric by 2035 (*New York Times* January 29, 2021). The EV market in China is in a rapid state of flux, with the both domestic and foreign companies vying for leadership. Table 15.9 lists the top 10 selling EVs, both pure electric (BEV) and plugin hybrids (PHEV), in China for the period 2017–2021 (CPCAuto 2023), while Table 15.10 provides a more detailed picture of the major EV producers in the country in 2020 (SupChina December 2021).

Beyond the issue of automotive competitiveness, lies the broader significance of Chinese industrial and technological policy (UNCTAD July 2020; EastAsia Forum

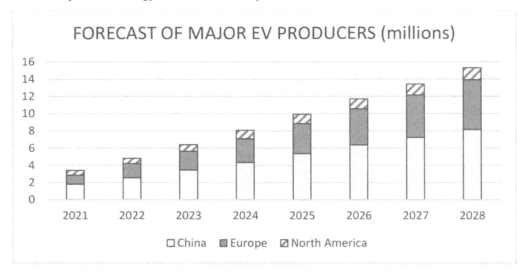

Figure 15.20   Forecast of EV Production by Region
Source: New York Times September 22, 2021

November 27, 2020; EPC April 21, 2021; Brookings January 6, 2022). China already has already achieved world-class status, if not leadership, in several areas of technological development and application: solar photovoltaics, wind power, military equipment, high-speed rail, ultra-high voltage transmission and supercomputing (for example, McKinsey 2020, Techradarpro 2021). It is not unreasonable to expect that China's ambitions extend to the transportation sector including advanced automotive design and production (*New York Times* May 4, 2021b).

> Chinese companies dominate the world's production of electric motors. China has even gained control of much of the world's production of key raw materials needed for electric cars, including lithium, cobalt and minerals known as rare earth metals . . . China is also moving quickly to commercialize large numbers of self-driving cars [and] is also trying to take the lead on how cars connect to the internet through its planned nationwide deployment of 5G mobile communications" (*New York Times* January 29, 2021).

The Chinese government's active participation in the development of its ambitious industrial strategy has affected the automobile sector in general, and the EV industry in particular. To quote one assessment (Protocol January 24, 2022):

> The Chinese EV industry's stunning 2021 performance didn't come out of nowhere: Favorable policies supporting this industry started over a decade ago. From 2010 to 2016, the central government subsidized almost every electric or hybrid vehicle purchase by as much as $10,000; the subsidy amount dwindled after 2016, and many cars, from hybrid vehicles to small-sized ones, were eliminated from the qualified categories. But the heavy subsidies spurred the growth of the "new force," as well as the world's largest battery supplier: CATL.

Table 15.9 Top Ten Bev Producers in China 2017–2021

CPCA.com

BEV rankings

	BEV (2017/1-11)		BEV (2018/1-12)		BEV (2019/1-12)		BEV (2020/1-12)		BEV (2021/1-12)	
	Producer	Units	Producer	Units	Producer	Units	Producer	Units	Producer	Units
1	BAIC BJEV	60,891	BAIC BJEV	######	BYD AUTO	######	SGMW (SAIC-GM-WULING)	######	SGMW (SAIC-GM-WULING)	423,171
2	ZHIDOU Electric Vehicle	25,669	BYD AUTO	93,829	BAIC BJEV	86,339	TESLA (CHINA)	######	TESLA (CHINA)	322,020
3	BYD AUTO	24,590	CHERY AUTO	62,440	GEELY AUTO	49,658	BYD AUTO	######	BYD AUTO	296,663
4	JAC MOTORS	23,884	JAC MOTORS	50,408	TESLA (IMPORT)	49,156	GAC AION	63,306	GWM(GREAT WALL MOTOR)	133,510
5	ZOTYE AUTO	20,067	JIANGLING MOTORS	45,429	SGMW (SAIC-GM-WULING)	48,950	GWM(GREAT WALL MOTOR)	54,070	GAC AION	122,681
6	CHERY AUTO	19,565	GEELY AUTO	40,288	GWM(GREAT WALL MOTOR)	35,886	BAIC BJEV	47,781	CHANGAN AUTO	100,075
7	JIANGLING MOTORS	19,111	SAIC MOTOR	32,325	JAC MOTORS	30,139	NIO	43,369	XIAOPENG	96,641
8	CHANGAN AUTO	16,332	ZOTYE AUTO	31,357	SAIC MOTOR	29,547	CHERY NEW ENERGY	39,615	NIO	90,886
9	TESLA	15,078	SAIC-GM	24,984	CHANGAN AUTO	29,169	CHANGAN AUTO	27,743	CHERY NEW ENERGY	85,720
10	GEELY AUTO	15,025	CHANGAN AUTO	20,199	GAC AION	27,751	SAIC MOTOR	27,601	SAIC PASSENGER VEHICLE	84,555
TOTALS		######		######		######		######		######
% OF TOTAL MARKET		84%		76%		71%		77%		74%

PHEV rankings

	PHEV (2017/1-11)		PHEV (2018/1-12)		PHEV (2019/1-12)		PHEV (2020/1-12)		PHEV (2021/1-12)	
	Producer	Units	Producer	Units	Producer	Units	Producer	Units	Producer	Units
1	BYD AUTO	38,351	BYD AUTO	######	BYD AUTO	######	BYD AUTO	42,084	BYD AUTO	229,198
2	SAIC MOTOR	24,777	SAIC MOTOR	59,940	BMW BRILLIANCE AUTO	54,250	LEADING IDEAL (LI)	33,457	LEADING IDEAL (LI)	91,310
3	GAC MOTOR	2,120	BMW BRILLIANCE AUTO	21,910	SAIC MOTOR	31,176	BMW BRILLIANCE AUTO	27,742	SAIC PASSENGER VEHICLE	29,807
4	PORSCHE	1,835	GEELY AUTO	12,416	SAIC VOLKSWAGEN	30,695	SAIC VOLKSWAGEN	24,206	BMW BRILLIANCE AUTO	24,946
5	BMW BRILLIANCE AUTO	1,549	GAC MOTOR	10,209	GEELY AUTO	29,434	SAIC MOTOR	23,553	FAW-VOLKSWAGEN	24,852
6	SAIC-GM	1,388	BMW	3,927	FAW-TOYOTA	15,538	FAW-VOLKSWAGEN	16,676	SAIC VOLKSWAGEN	23,905
7	GEELY AUTO	951	SAIC-GM	3,631	GAC TOYOTA	7,992	GEELY AUTO	8,697	GEELY AUTO	18,270
8	CHERY AUTO	429	GWM(GREAT WALL MOTOR)	2,947	DYK(DONGFENG YUEDA KIA)	7,115	FAW-TOYOTA	7,133	SAIC GM	13,221
9	VOLVO ASIA PACIFIC	325	FAW-VOLKSWAGEN	2,725	GAC AION	5,648	GAC TOYOTA	4,822	DONGFENG-HONDA	11,037
10	Volkswagen	282	GAC MITSUBISHI	2,384	CHANGAN AUTO	3,871	PORSCHE	4,819	PORSCHE (IMPORT)	9,542
TOTAL		72,007		######		######		######		476,088
% OF TOTAL MARKET		99%		95%		91%		88%		87%

Table 15.10 China EV Production

2020 data	Units shipped	Revenue in China (billions)	# models	# factories	# employees	Primary industry	EV-related affiliates
1. Tesla	500,000	$ 6.60	4	4	70,757	EVs, batteries	Contemporary Amperex Technology
2. BYD	130,970	$ 23.40	5	13	229,154	Misc	Toyota, Didi, FAW
3. SAIC Motor	n.a.	$ 113.00	n.a	n.a	147,738	ICEs	Wuling, VW, Zhiji, Alibaba
4. SAIC Volkswagen	n.a.	n.a	3	1	96,974	Evs	SAIC, VW, Audi
5. SAIC-GM-Wuling	n.a.	$ 533.53	3	12	147,738	Evs	SAIC, GM, Wuling
6. NIO	43,728	$ 2.50	5	1	7,000	Evs	Tencent, Baidu
7. Xpeng	27,041	$ 895.70	3	1	3,676	Evs	Alibaba, JD, Xiaomi
8. Li Auto	14,464	$ 1.45	1	1	2,628	plug-in hybrids	Meituan, ByteDance
9. WM Motor	22,495	$ 0.01	3	1	2,500	Evs	Baidu, Tencent, SAIC
10. Geely	n.a.	$ 0.85	5	2		ICEs, Evs	Baidu, London Taxi Co., JD.com
11. Byton	n.a.	n.a.	2	1		Evs	Tencent, Foxconn, FAW, Nanjing Zhixing
12. Enovate	n.a.	n.a.	2	1		Evs	
13. Zhiji (SAIC-Alibaba)	n.a.	n.a.	2	1		Evs	SAIC, Alibaba
14. Xiaomi	n.a.	$ 37.63	n.a	n.a	22,074	consumer electronics & hardware	Xpeng
15. Dongfeng Motor	n.a.	$ 128.00	3	1	136,550	ICEs, military vehcles, autoparts	Renault-Nissan, CATL, Tencent
16. Chang'an Automobile	n.a.	$ 9.90	12	n.a.	80,000	ICEs, vans and trucks	Baidu, Huawei, CATL
17. Guangzhou Automobile	6,876	$ 9.10	7	2	93,854	ICEs, commercial & sports vehicles, autoparts	SAIC, Huawei, CATL
18. Chery Automobile	n.a.	$ 5.60	10	2	16,721	ICEs, commerical vehicles, autoparts	
19. FAW Group	550,869	$ 89.20	3	1	6,891	ICEs, buses, trucks, auto parts	BYD

(Continued)

Table 15.10 (Continued)

2020 data	Units shipped	Revenue in China (billions)	# models	# factories	# employees	Primary industry	EV-related affiliates
20. FAW-Volkswagen Automobile	n.a.	$ 89.20	9	5	100,000	ICEs, buses, trucks, auto parts	FAW, Volkswagen, Audi
21. Evergrande	n.a.	$ 0.11	6	3		Evs	Tencent
22. BAIC Motor	n.a.	$ 1.80	20	3	20,720	ICEs	Huawei, Didi, Daimler, BJEV, CATL, Baidu
23. Zotye	145,000	$ 0.21	5	5	2,143	ICEs and Evs	Tech New Group, Bak Power
24. Aiways	2,500	$ 0.06	3	1	1,600	Evs	Tencent, Didi Chuxing, Jianling Motors Group, Changan Automobile
25. Great Wall Motors	38,865	$ 16.52	6	4	63,174	vehicles	BMW, Xiaomi
26. Human Horizons	n.a.	n.a.	4	1	1,000	Evs, AI	DYK, Qualcomm, JOYNEXT, Questel, Meridican Auto, Microsft China, Bosch Group, State Grid, China Southern Power Grid, TELD
27. Singulato Motors	n.a.	n.a.	2	1	140	Evs	Toyota, BAIC
28. Hozon Auto	16,439	$ 0.30	3	2	837	Evs	Harmony Auto, CATL, Qihoo 360
29. Brilliance Auto	n.a.	$ 0.60	6	2	5,610	Vehicles	BMW
30. Avatr Technology	n.a.	n.a.	1	1	n.a.	Evs	Chang'an Automobile, CATL, Huawei, NIO

Source: Sup China (2021)

In light of the direction of China's policy, it is by no means certain that western automotive producers can maintain a significant presence in the Chinese market over the long-term. In fact, traditional western dominance of the international market for automobiles may also be at risk because of the aforementioned combination of Chinese policy, financial support of industry, relatively low labour costs, planned additions to production capacity, and the large number of highly trained personnel in science, technology, and engineering (see for example, *Forbes* January 9, 2021). Recent data suggest that China's share of the electric car market is accelerating with sales of 86,000 battery electric cars in Europe, representing 8.25% of the European EV market (*The Guardian* September 4, 2023). Two companies dominate global EV sales. Estimated sales in the first half of 2023 were 1,191,405 for BYD (a company backed by Warren Buffet), Tesla with 888,879 and Volkswagen in fifth place with 209,852 (Statista September 5, 2023). A recent *New York Times* (September 6, 2023) article reporting on the Munich Auto show, described the Chinese car industry as a "battery-powered juggernaut." One recent opinion piece in the *New York Times* (Meyer 2024) was entitled "China's Electric Vehicles are going to hit Detroit like a Wrecking Ball." The author focussed on the extraordinary growth of BYD that is building factories in South America, Asia and Europe. Adding to this concern is the prospect of Chinese-made EVs selling for under $11,000, significantly less than their American counterparts (*New York Times* February 29, 2024).

The Chinese approach represents a classic strategic realignment where an industry shifts from a focus on a soon-to-be obsolete technology (ICE) and leapfrogs into cutting edge technology (EVs) to gain advantage over its rivals. This strategy seems to be paying off handsomely and presents a major challenge for Western automobile manufacturers. In fact, the Chinese automobile industry has adopted a dual strategy. While focussing on the goal of global dominance in EVs, it must adjust to the change in taste in its own domestic market where consumers now prefer EVs to ICEs. As such, the industry has been left with unused factory capacity to build about 15 million ICESs per year. Capitalizing on their cost advantage, the industry is now "flooding the world" with low-cost ICEs (*New York Times* September 6, 2023). As a consequence, China is now the global leader in global automobile exports.

In view of the extraordinary changes taking place within the automotive sector, Volkswagen is adopting a multifaced strategy by expanding its research and development efforts into the area of autonomous vehicles and the redefinition of individual mobility to include mobility services, such as Mobility-as-a-Service and Transport-as-a-Service (Volkswagen Annual Report 2021, p. 38).

To quote from Volkswagen's 2020 Annual Report (2021):

- The automotive industry is facing a process of transformation with far-reaching changes. Electric drives, connected vehicles and autonomous driving are associated with both opportunities and risks for our sales. In particular, more rapidly evolving customer requirements, swift implementation of legislative initiatives and the market entry of new competitors from outside the industry will require changed products at a faster pace of innovation and adjustments to business models. There is uncertainty regarding the widespread use of electric vehicles and the availability of the necessary charging infrastructure (p. 181).
- Data is the new driving force of prosperity for economies. Its usage strengthens customer orientation and provides safer and more convenient mobility. Digital upgrades and additional services relating to the entire vehicle are creating new areas of business

that we are developing. Particularly in fully connected traffic, data will become the basis for autonomous driving, thus redefining individual mobility. This is why we are planning to invest €27 billion, representing about one-fifth of the Group's total capex expenditure, in digitalization over the next five years (p. 7).

- With electric drives, digital connectivity and autonomous driving, we want to make the automobile cleaner, quieter, more intelligent and safer (p. 85).

Autonomous Vehicles

While the emergence of the electric car as a viable alternative to the traditional fossil-fueled vehicle is, in many ways, a landmark development, it is by no means revolutionary, as electric-powered vehicles were in production and use in the early nineteenth century. In contrast, the development of the self-driving car could revolutionize not only the private and commercial vehicle sectors, but also drastically change the economic, social, and political context in which this new technology will exist. Arbib and Seba (2017, p. 6) feel that "we are on the cusp of one of the fastest, deepest, most consequential disruptions of transportation in history."

At the present, there are several variants of the autonomous vehicle (AV) technology, some operational, others in development. Mervis (2017) listed five levels describing the degree of automotive self-driving and current status: (1) accelerates, brakes *or* steers (present fleet); (2) accelerates, brakes *and* steers (now in testing); (3) assumes full control within narrow parameters, such as when driving on the freeway, but not during merges or exits (might never be deployed); (4) everything, only under certain conditions, such as specific locations, speed, weather, and time of day (where the industry wants to be); and (5) *everything*, meaning goes everywhere, any time, and under all conditions (somewhere in the next half-century). As Mervis observes, only level five represents a true AV vehicle (see also US EIA 2017).

While some of the benefits of this new technology remain speculative at this time, there are several purported benefits that have received wide scale publicity: (1) AV's will reduce congestion by removing cars from the road, reducing air pollution; (2) AVs could help create more public space because they would eliminate the need for parking structures; and (3) AVs will be shared, meaning fewer cars on the road, thereby also promising significant reduction in greenhouse gas emissions (Arieff 2017). Additional benefits might include the ultimate reduction in urban sprawl, fewer traffic accidents, injuries and deaths, and more free time for the pursuit of work or leisure.

Because of the recent introduction and testing of AVs (Mervis 2017; Calthorpe & Walters 2017), there is little empirical evidence to support any of these promised benefits at this time. The general tenor of these assumed positive effects follows a long history of promised benefits accompanying the introduction of any new technology with little consideration of possible short-term and long-term costs or disadvantages (*New York Times* May 24, 2021). In many respects, the automobile is the archetypal example of revenge theory (i.e., the law of unintended consequences [Tenner 1996]). Despite all its manifest benefits, the private vehicle has created enormous negative externalities, not the least of which is its significant contribution to global warming and the concomitant threat to human civilization. While the self-driving vehicle promises to alleviate many of these externalities, there is little evidence at this point to support this optimistic conclusion. In fact, several researchers have hypothesized that the AV may worsen, rather than alleviate, the problems that we so desperately need to address.

In the short run, there are several critical technological challenges that must be addressed: resolution of intersensor conflict, interpretation and response to roadworks and other animate and inanimate obstacles, unusual weather conditions, and interactions with human driven vehicles (*The Guardian* July 5, 2016). The complex nature of human-automated machine interaction has been illustrated in the context of air travel by a US FAA report (2013, p. 26) that found:

> "Automation behavior is unexpected or unexplained" . . . was present in about 46% of the accident reports, 60% of major incident reports, and 38% of ASRS incidents. The general issue "Understanding of automation is inadequate" was present in about 34% of the accident reports, 30% of the major incident reports, and 5% of the ASRS [Aviation Safety Reporting System] incidents. Also included in this set is the issue "Automation is too complex" because complex systems are often difficult to understand.

While automotive automation differs in many respects from aviation, the generic issue of how humans respond to automated systems transcends specific technologies (Schiff 2015). New issues will also have to be addressed such as the increased potential for motion sickness (Sivak & Schoettle 2015), liability (Popper 2017), and hacking and security threats (Lu 2017; *New York Times* March 18, 2021).

There are several serious concerns raised in the research literature about the utopian vision of an AV future. Sivak and Schoettle (Sept 2016) anticipated no significant increase in occupant productivity despite promises to this effect. Arieff (2017) argued that AVs will not reduce congestion and that given the American love for their cars, few will be willing to give them up for car sharing. Walker (2018) used a simulation model to predict that not only will congestion not be reduced, but also that vehicle miles will increase despite a potential decrease in the total vehicle fleet. But perhaps the most serious prediction was generated by the US National Renewable Energy Laboratory (NREL 2013) that concluded that under one scenario, total fuel demand by light-duty vehicles could increase by as much as 217%, thereby leading to a worsening of global warming rather than its alleviation.

One tantalizing promise of the new technology is the reduction in the enormous human cost of road accidents in the form of injuries and fatalities. The number of both fatal and nonfatal injuries could increase significantly in the next decade as the adoption of automobiles continues to spread, especially in the developing world. The associated economic costs are enormous, estimated at $518 billion USD and representing as much as 3–5% of GDP (CDC 2016, WHO 2021). Clearly any new technology, such as autonomous automobiles, which promises to drastically reduce these numbers would be a benefit if successful. This is clearly a goal yet to be achieved in light of a few recent fatalities and related incidents and safety concerns with *AVs* (*New York Times*, December 7, 2020, March 25, June 29, July 5, & August 16, 2021; CNN April 19, 2021; BBC February 18, 2022; *New York Times* November 15, 2023).

Captain Sully Sullenberger, pilot of the airplane that made a dramatic landing on the Hudson River in 2009, had the following comment about new technology in the form of increased automation (Wachter 2015):

> When automation became possible in aviation, people thought, 'We can eliminate human error by automating everything.' We've learned that automation does not eliminate errors. Rather, it changes the nature of the errors that are made. And it makes possible new kinds of errors.

A more general articulation of this phenomenon was proposed by Charles Perrow in his 1984 book entitled *Normal Accidents: Living with High-Risk Technologies*. While much has been made of the inevitable role of human error, Perrow's central thesis is that accidents are inevitable — that is, they are "normal" — in modern complex technologies and cannot be engineered out.

Perrow's theory concentrates on the properties of systems themselves, rather than on the errors that owners, designers and operators make in running them. In other words, he seeks a more basic explanation for accidents than operator error, faulty design or equipment, inadequately trained personnel, or the fact that the system is claimed to be too big, underfinanced, or mismanaged. In fact, some accidents can be ascribed to safety systems themselves.

Technology is, in theory, value neutral. However, its implementation raises philosophical challenges, and requires ethical judgments. Yuval Noah Harari, author of the imaginative and controversial book on the future of humankind, *Homo Deus: A Brief History of Tomorrow* (2017), illustrates this problem with a modern interpretation of the classic philosophical problem of the runaway tram car (Greene et al. 2001). He offers the following scenario: an automated automobile finds itself in the situation where it is about to run over five pedestrians unless it engages in extreme evasive action, in this case driving over a cliff and killing the occupant of the automated car. Clearly, the software in the car must make a determination of that course of action is preferable. The algorithm that makes this decision must be the result of a deep and challenging ethical thought process by the computer programmers who create the algorithm. In a somewhat tongue-in-cheek resolution to this problem, Harari suggests that we could let the market determine the answer. Toyota, for example, could design two variants of its cars: a Toyota Altruist and a Toyota Egotist. The car buyer could choose which model to buy. The former would save the five pedestrians at the expense of the car occupant; the latter would do the opposite (Harari 2018). Clearly the larger implications of moving to automated cars is not as simple as it may appear.

In a recent paper in *Nature* (Awad et al. 2018, p. 63), an international group of academics reported on an innovative research project that attempted to determine public perceptions of appropriate ethical guidelines for automated vehicles, noting:

> Never in the history of humanity have we allowed a machine to autonomously decide who should live and who should die, in a fraction of a second, without real-time supervision. We are going to cross that bridge any time now, and it will not happen in a distant theatre of military operations; it will happen in that most mundane aspect of our lives, everyday transportation.

One particularly distinguishing feature of this research was the use of the web to gather opinions from several million people in over 200 countries. The survey focused on nine specific trade-offs, by asking for preferences for sparing: (1) humans vs. pets; (2) passengers vs. pedestrians; (3) more vs. fewer lives; (4) men vs. women; (5) the young vs. the elderly; (6) pedestrians who cross legally vs. those who jaywalk; (7) the fit vs. the less fit; (8) those with higher vs. lower social status; and (9) preference for staying on course or swerving.

The analysis was conducted at four different levels: global preferences, individual variation, cultural clusters, and country-level predictors. In general, the strongest preferences were observed for sparing: (1) humans over animals, (2) more lives rather than fewer, and (3) young lives. There were strong cultural variations, but "the fact that broad regions of the world displayed relative agreement suggests that our journey to consensual machine ethics is not doomed from the start" (Awad et al. 2018, p. 63).

Despite this relatively optimistic assessment, and the utopian vision of the future dominated by autonomous vehicles, they cannot be relied upon to solve the increasing threat of global warming. Society must look elsewhere for real solutions. We must be cautious about the age-old temptation to assume that new technology will solve the problems generated by past technology. Car-based solutions are probably not the answer to car-based problems of this magnitude.

In sum, the era of driverless cars has yet to arrive (*New York Times* May 12, 2020; *The Guardian* January 3, 2021). Part of the problem is the mixed attitudes by potential users. A report by the Boston Consulting Group (Lang et al. 2016) found that while many individuals welcomed the introduction of AVs, many were also concerned about safety, specifically ten factors for hesitation were identified in the survey:

- I do not feel safe if the car is driving itself (50%)
- I want to be in control at all times (45%)
- I do not want the car to make any mistakes (43%)
- Driving is a pleasure for me (30%)
- I don't know enough about self-driving technology (27%)
- I like a vehicle to be proven and tested for some rime (27%)
- I wouldn't trust being in mixed traffic with a self-driving car (26%)
- I am not willing to pay extra for self-driving functionalities (25%)
- I am concerned that the car could be hacked (23%)
- I fear that the car could break down (20%)

IOT et al. (2023) have summarized the issues and prospects for self-driving cars:

> The autonomous vehicle market is predicted to grow from $19.5 billion in 2021 to $74.4 billion by 2027. However, there are concerns about the safety of autonomous vehicles and the potential loss of driving jobs. Experts believe that while automation will change the role of drivers, they will still have important tasks such as passenger safety, assistance, and customer service. As technology advances, the role of human drivers may evolve to focus more on supervision and service. Overall, there will still be a role for drivers in the age of self-driving cars, but it will require adaptability and ongoing education.

Considering the risks and opportunities identified by Volkswagen with respect to both EVs and AVs, there is an additional strategic role for Volkswagen in other components of a mixed transportation strategy, namely something called the Internet of Motion.

The Internet of Motion

Tom Standage, deputy editor of *The Economist*, in his recent work, *A Brief History of Motion* (2021), provides an insightful overview of transportation from 3500 BCE to modern times. In contemplating the future, he asks: "What will be the dominant mode of urban transport in the postcar era? Will it be buses, trains, taxis, ride hailing, car clubs, bike sharing, or scooters? The answer is yes— to all of the above." He visualizes an Internet of Motion made feasible by the advent of the smartphone, which would provide individuals with a menu of options – single or combined – for moving from point A to point B. Under this model, mobility is a service, potentially replacing or supplementing individual ownership of the means of transit. This concept is redolent of Ray Anderson's reconceptualization of business outlined in chapter 10 of this volume where Interface is in essence selling the service rather than the product per se.

The emergence of this phenomenon will force a major reorientation of strategy among the world's major automotive manufacturers. In fact, such a strategic adjustment is already underway. Standage (2021, p. 212) observes that:

> Given that such programs explicitly aim to provide an alternative to car ownership, it may seem odd that car makers are also moving into the field. After all, a future in which different modes of transport can seamlessly be combined will involve fewer cars and less private ownership. But carmakers hope to provide vehicles (and later autonomous vehicles) for ride- hailing and car-sharing fleets. In some cases they are also dabbling with providing mobility services themselves . . . Carmakers claim that the new model provides an opportunity for them to shift from selling cars into the potentially more profitable business of selling rides. Total car sales each year add up to around \$2 trillion; but the personal transport market, which includes vehicles, services, and software, is worth more like \$10 trillion, according to industry estimates.
>
> The stage is therefore set for a brutal fight between carmakers, ride- hailing giants, and mobility start- ups in the coming years, as the emphasis shifts from car ownership to mobility services.

It is clearly this prospective future that Volkswagen has already advanced as part of their strategy for commercial vehicle with *mobility-as-a-service* and *transport-as-a-service* (VW AR 2020 p. 38). The company has been considering melding their AV production with an hourly or monthly subscription for the service (*Driving* June 12, 2021).

A version of Standage's vision has already been introduced in several cities in Europe and Tokyo under the rubric MaaS (mobility as a service) and a version has been proposed for Pittsburgh and a new suburb outside Phoenix. The results have been mixed because of the difficulties of assembling all mobility providers under one umbrella, the advent of COVID-19, and the difficulty of coaxing people out of their private automobiles (*New York Times* December 15, 2021). Yet, this may indeed be the wave of the future as governments, companies, and the general public become more sensitive to the necessity of greening transportation systems (UITP 2019).

Peter Norton, a professor in the Department of Engineering and Society at the University of Virginia, adopts a similar and broader view of options available to the public in pursuit of mobility. In his recent book, *Autonorama: The Illusory Promise of High-Tech Driving* (2021), Norton focuses on the misplaced promise of AVs, citing an eighty-year history of unfulfilled promises. In his view, the automobile industry has succeeded in narrowing the perceived range of options to a choice between the status quo of car dependency and the futuristic promise of high-tech car dependency. To Norton (2021, p. 223), this is a blind alley as "applied to complex systems, high-tech innovations never just solve problems – they change problems, disrupting balances and introducing new problems." Norton specifically criticizes the industry and many policymakers who describe the public's love of driving as a rationale for continuing down the path of car dependency. To Norton, this narrow choice set reflects the elimination from consideration of a broad of range of mobility alternatives that are cheaper, more efficient, safer, and currently available. While other jurisdictions, such as the Netherlands, have a multimodal solution to mobility in place, the range of choices in the United States, for example, has been narrowed by past actions of the automobile industry (e.g., the purchase and elimination of urban tram lines), and government decisions to expand the highway system and redesign urban spaces to accommodate automobiles: "Since the 1930s, US transportation policy— local, state and national— has prioritized the least efficient mode at the expense of all others" (Norton 2021, p. 201). To Norton, the view that AVs are the inevitable future "interprets the loss of choices as a choice, and driving in the absence of good choices as a preference to drive," (p. 200). He states: "Whenever alternatives to driving have been attractive possibilities, people have taken advantage of them, to the benefit of not just the individual but also the community" (p. 235).

A Sobering Reassessment of Volkswagen's Current Position

In July of 2023, Thomas Schaefer, Volkswagen's CEO, gave an extraordinary talk to 2000 senior managers. Using the phrase "The Roof Is on Fire," Schaefer described the predicament that the company was facing in making the transition from ICEs to EVs over the next few decades. His comments were followed by the chief financial officer who stated that "our vehicle business is unwell" (Wards August 10, 2023). There are several interrelated problems facing Volkswagen:

1. Production costs are too high compared to competitors (see Figure 15.12).
2. While the company has hired 3,000 engineers in China to solidify their position in the Chinese market (*New York Times* December 12, 2023), the company is losing sales in China in both ICE and EV segments, due not only to significantly lower prices, but also increasing Chinese technological advances and consumer preferences.
3. Potentially lower productivity than its principal global competitor, Toyota. One report states that in 2015 VW employed 600,000 people to produce 10 million cars, while Toyota employed 340,000 to produce just under 9 million cars. While suggestive of a major productivity difference, the author states that interpretation of the data must be tempered by the potential role of outsourcing that could affect these numbers (Baudin n.d.).
4. Massive capital requirements to redesign and retool for the EV market. Estimates of these costs run as high as $193 billion (*New York Times* March 14, 2023), twice the size of the company's cash reserves (Wards).
5. The transition is made more difficult by the continuing capital requirements to service the ICE market considering increasingly stringent emission and safety regulations. Timing is clearly critical, as the company must be prepared for the emerging EV market while not getting ahead the preferences of their customer base. Wards (August 10, 2023) reports that "in the coming months, VW will begin sales of the electric-powered ID.7 sedan in Europe. It also plans to unveil new-generation ICE Tiguan and Passat models."
7. While the company is planning a mix of pure EVs and plugin hybrids, it is instructive to note that Toyota's strategy differs significantly. The company is currently focusing more of its efforts on hybrids and hydrogen powered cars in the belief that in the near to medium term, these options make more sense from an environmental, logistical, and cost perspective (Gilboy 2023). This may be a risky strategy as the

European Union will ban all cars with an internal combustion engine in 2035. Toyota has already lost market share in the US and its sales in China have fallen. Nevertheless, the company feels its pace of introduction of EVs will be sufficient to retain its market dominance (*New York Times* September 7, 2023). In the near-term future, Toyota's strategy appears to be paying off as the market for EVs is slowing down over concerns about price and driving range (*New York Times* January 19, 2024; Reuters February 6, 2024; The Auto Journal February 27, 2024; *New York Times* March 9, 2024).

Concluding Comments

With the prospect of two billion motor vehicles on the planet within the next few decades, coupled with the remaining multifaceted and unresolved problems, even with the widespread adoption of EVs, it appears that the transport sector has little prospect of becoming sustainable in the immediate to medium-term future. In its latest Automotive Environment Guide, Greenpeace (2023, pp. 2–3) has a somewhat somber assessment of the shift to electric vehicles:

- Despite rapid growth in EVs, ICE vehicles continue to dominate the global automotive market.
- Traditional automakers are losing the race when it comes to zero emission vehicles (ZEV) sales.
- Global ZEV sales are on the rise, but progress has been uneven.
- Traditional automakers have failed to substantially increase ZEV sales outside China and Europe.
- Automakers' existing decarbonisation targets are insufficient to limit the global average temperature increase to 1.5°C.
- Sports utility vehicle (SUV) sales continue to grow at an alarming rate, representing a major climate threat due to the high energy consumption of these vehicles.
- Investment in renewable energy charging by the world's biggest automakers is inadequate.
- Automakers have neglected the critical role that supply chains and materials play in decarbonisation.

Three critical questions emerge from this analysis: (1) Can mass transit or the Internet of Motion succeed in replacing the widespread use of automobiles? (2) Is it possible to reduce total distance traveled by encouraging densification to locate individuals closer to their place of work? (3) Can we foresee a future where work-related travel is eliminated through such mechanisms as telecommuting? Already a part of business practice, and further promoted by the recent pandemic, telecommuting is the modern re-creation of the disseminated artisan workshops of the pre-Industrial Revolution era. At a minimum, it is essential that future urban planning tightly integrates transportation options with urban form issues such as zoning and building design. In the long run, it appears clear that we must totally reconceptualize the concept of the city— the location of work, residence, and leisure.

In sum, the complex and rapidly evolving environment in which Volkswagen and other major automobile producers operate presents a major challenge to companies to design strategies that are imaginative, resilient, and ultimately sustainable not only for the corporation but also for society in general.

References

Associated Press (AP) (2024) "Trial of former Volkswagen CO Winterkorn over diesel scandal set to start in September," March 15.

Arbib, James & Tony Seba (2017) "Rethinking transportation 2020–2030," *RethinkX*.

Arieff, Allison (2017) "Automated vehicles can't save cities," *New York Times*, February 27.

The Auto Journal (2024) "Why hybrids are winning the electrified vehicle wars," *Good Car Bad Car*, February 27.

Awad, Edmond, et al. (2018) "The moral machine experiment," *Nature*, November 1.

Baudin, Michel (n.d.) "Cost per employee and productivity at Volkswagen versus Toyota," Michel Baudin's Blog, https://michelbaudin.com/2015/11/03/cars-per-employee-and-productivity-at-volkswagen-versus-toyota/

BBC (2017) "New diesel and petrol vehicles to be banned from 2040 in UK," July 26.

BBC (2021) "China's biggest brand to launch rival to Tesla," March 24.

BBC (2021) "Ford announces $11.4 bn investment in electric vehicle plants," September 28.

BBC (2022) "Tesla investigated over 'phantom braking' problem," February 18.

Bloomberg (2019) "Electric vehicle battery shrinks and so does the total cost," April 12.

Bloomberg New Energy Finance (2018) "Long-term electric vehicle outlook 2018," May 21.

Bloomberg News (2020) "Electric cars closing in on gas guzzlers as battery costs plunge," December 16.

Boston Consulting Group (BCG) (2020) "Who will drive electric cars to the tipping point?" January.

Brennan, John W. & Timothy R. Barber (2016) "Battery electric vehicles vs. internal combustion engine vehicles," Arthur D. Little, November.

California Air Resources Board (CARB) (2015) "The Report on diesel exhaust," July 21.

California Air Resources Board (CARB) (2015) "EPA, California notify Volkswagen of Clean Air Act violation," September 18.

Calthorpe, Peter & Jerry Walters (2017) "Autonomous vehicles: hype and potential," *Urban Land*, March 1.

Carex Canada (n.d.) "Diesel engine exhaust profile."

Centers for Disease Control (CDC) (2016) "Road traffic injuries and deaths—a global problem," October 23.

China (multiple years) *China Statistical Yearbook*.

CNBC (2021) "China EV/ Tesla Xpeng Nio BYD are best-selling electric cars in 2021," October 14.

CNN (2019) "Volkswagen nearly killed diesel cars. now it says they're back," January 30.

CNN (2021) "New 'future city' to rise in southwest China," February 9.

CNN (2021) "Ford is investing $1 billion in Germany as it goes electric in Europe," February 17.

CNN (2021) "Police say no one was in driver's seat in fatal Tesla crash," April 19.

Committee on Climate Change (CCC) (2019a). "Net-zero: The UK's contribution to stopping global warming," May.

Committee on Climate Change (CCC) (2019b) *Net-Zero: Technical Report*, May.

CPCAauto (2023). Translated from Chinese by Dr. Jane Pan.

Crabtree, George (2019) "The coming electric vehicle transformation," *Science*, October 25.

Cronin, Audrey Kurth (2019) *Power to the People*, Oxford University Press.

CTV News (2017) "China maintains reign over world supercomputer rankings/ survey," November 14.

Daily Telegraph (2020) "Beijing steals a march as its smart metropolis is west's forbidden city," June 26.

Driving (2021) "VW considers hourly subscriptions on EVs for autonomous driving," June 12.

EastAsiaForum (2020) "How China's 'technological independence' strategy will transform its economy," November 27.

EHSO.com (2022) "The development and chronology of automobile emissions reduction efforts in the United States," January 20.

Electrek (2021) "Countries and automakers agree to go all-electric by 2040 in weak new goal set at COP26," November 10.

European Parliament (2017) "Comparing EU and US car emissions legislation," February.

European Policy Centre (EPC) (2021) "China's grand industrial strategy and what it means for Europe," April 21.

Ewing, Jack (2018) *Faster, Higher, Farther: How One of the World's Largest Automakers Committed a Massive and Stunning Fraud*, W.W. Norton & Co.

Eyre, Nick & Gavin Killip (Eds.) (2019) "Shifting the focus: energy demand in a net-zero carbon UK," Centre for Research into Energy Demand solutions, July 5.

Forbes (2021) "Chinese EV invasion! The electric car to look out for in 2021," January 9.

Gilboy, James (2023) "Toyota is right: We need more Hy drib cars and fewer EVs Here's why," *The Drive*, July 6.

Good Car Bad Car (2024) "Reliability & purchase decisions: How Toyota is leading the industry," February.

Green Car Report (2019) "VW sold twice as many diesels in 2018 as in 2017," March 20.

Greene, Joshua D., et al. (2001) "An fMRI Investigation of emotional engagement in moral judgment," *Science*, September 14.

Greenpeace (2019) *Crashing the Climate: How the Car Industry is Driving the Climate Crisis*, September.

Greenpeace (2023) *Automobile Environmental Guide: A Comprehensive Analysis of Decarbonisation Efforts by Global Automakers*.

The Guardian (2016) "Why self-driving cars aren't safe yet/ rain, roadworks and other obstacles," July 5.

The Guardian (2016) "Renewables made up half of net electricity capacity added last year," October 25.

The Guardian (2017) "France to ban sales of petrol and diesel cars by 2040," July 6.

The Guardian (2021) "'Peak Hype': Why the driverless car revolution has stalled," January 3.

The Guardian (2021) "Electric cars rise to record 54% market share in Norway," January 5.

The Guardian (2021) Electric vehicles close to 'tipping point' of mass adoption, January 22.

The Guardian (2023) "China's share of Europe's electric car market accelerates as UK leads sales, "September 4.

Harari, Yuval Noah (2017) *Homo Deus. A Brief History of Tomorrow*, Signal.

Harari, Yuval Noah (2018) Interview on *Ideas in the Afternoon*, CBC, May 7.

Harper, Gavin, et al. (2019) "Recycling lithium-ion batteries from electric vehicles," *Nature*, November 6.

Hawkins, Troy R., et al. (2012) "Comparative environmental life cycle assessment of conventional and electric vehicles," *Journal of Industrial Ecology*, 17(1).

Holdway, Aaron R., et al. 2010) "Indirect emissions from electric vehicles – emissions from electricity generation," *Energy & Environmental Science*, September 22.

Hou, Lifang, et al. (2016) "Public Health Impact and Economic costs of Volkswagen's Lack of Compliance with the United States' Emission Standards," *International Journal of Environmental Research and Public Health*, September 8.

Huo, Hong, et al. (2012a) "Projection of energy use and greenhouse gas emissions by motor vehicles in China: policy options and impacts," *Energy Policy*, 43:37–48.

Huo, Hong, et al. (2012b) "Vehicle-use intensity in China: current status and future trend," *Energy Policy*, 43:6–16.

The Independent (2017) "China to ban petrol and diesel cars, state media reports," September 10.

Inside EVs (2016) "Germany moves to ban ice vehicle sales by 2030, electric-only from 2030 on," October 10.

International Council on Clean Transportation (ICCT) (2019) "Fuel economy in major car markets: technology and policy drivers 2005–2017," March 2, Working Paper 19.

International Association of Public Transport (UITP) (2019) "Mobility as a service," April.

International Council on Clean Transportation (ICCT) (2020) "Growing momentum: Global overview of government targets for phasing out sales of new internal combustion engine vehicles," November 11.

International Energy Agency (IEA) (2021a) *Global EV Outlook 2021. Accelerating Ambitions Despite the Pandemic*, June 18.

International Energy Agency (IEA) (2021b) *The Role of Critical Minerals in Clean Energy Transitions*.

International Energy Agency (2022) "Electric Cars Fend Off Supply Challenges to More than Double Global Sales," January 30.

IOT World Today, WardsAuto & WardsIntelligence (2023) *The IOT Transportation Yearbook. What the 2023 News Headlines Mean for Connected, Autonomous Vehicles in 2023 & Beyond.*

Jigang, Wei (2020) *China's Industrial Policy. Evolution and Experience*, UNCTAD, July.

Klier, Thomas & Joshua Linn (2016) "Comparing US and EU approaches to regulating automotive emissions and fuel economy," Resources for the Future, April.

Knobloch, Florian, et al. (2020) "Net emissions reductions from electric cars and heat pumps in 59 world regions over time," *Nature Sustainability*, March.

Krivoshto, Irina N., et al. (2008) "The toxicity of diesel exhaust. Implications for primary care," *Journal of the American Board of Family Medicine*, January.

Lang, Nikolaus, et al. (2016) "Self-driving vehicles, robo-taxis, and the urban mobility revolution," Boston Consulting Group, July 21.

Liang, Xinyu, et al. (2019) "Air quality and health benefits from fleet electrification in China," *Nature Sustainability*, October.

Los Angeles Times (2014) "First Volkswagen arrived in a US showroom 65 years ago," January 31.

Lu, Yiren (2017) "The blind spot of A.I. cars," *New York Times Magazine*, November 7.

Maddison, David, et al. (1996) *The True Costs of Road Transport*, Blueprint 5, Earthscan, London.

Manjoo, Farhad (2020) "I've seen a future without cars, and it's amazing," *New York Times*, July 9.

McKinsey & Co. (2017) "Riding China's huge, high-flying car market," October.

McKinsey & Company (2018a) "Electric vehicles' resource implications on energy, raw materials, land," May.

McKinsey & Company (2018b) "Three surprising resource implications from the rise of electric vehicles," May.

McKinsey & Company (2020) "How to drive winning battery-electric-vehicle design: lessons from benchmarking ten Chinese models," June.

Melin, Hans Eric, et al. (2021) "Global implications of the EU battery regulation," *Science*, July 23.

Mervis, Jeffrey (2017) "Not so fast," *Science*, December 20.

Messer, Andrea Elyse (2019) "In and out with 10-minute electric vehicle recharge," PennState, College of Engineering, Mechanical Engineering, October 30.

Meyer, Robinson (2024) "China's electric vehicles are going to hit Detroit like a wrecking ball," *New York Times*, February 27.

Mobility Pricing Independent Commission (MPIC) (2018) *Metro Vancouver Mobility Study*, May.

Morse, Ian (2021) "A dead battery dilemma," *Science*, May 21, Vol 372, Issue 6544, pp. 780–783.

Motor1.com (2019) "VW Groups vows to launch 75 EVs, 60 hybrids by 2029," November 16.

Motor1.com (2021) "Global plugin car sales June 2021: Record of over 580,000," August 3.

National Renewable Energy Laboratory (NREL) (2013) "Autonomous vehicles have a wide range of possible energy impacts," July 16.

New York Post (2021) "New Yorkers wade through underground lakes as subway stations flood," July 8.

New York Times (2008) "Panicked traders take VW shares on a wild ride," October 29.

New York Times (2016) "Volkswagen scandal reaches all the way to the top, lawsuits say," July 19.

New York Times (2017) "How Volkswagen's 'defeat devices' worked," March 16.

New York Times (2017) "China hastens the world toward an electric-car future," October 9.

New York Times (2017) "Where the STEM jobs are (and where they aren't)," November 1.

New York Times (2017) "China's technology ambitions could upset the global trade order," November 7.

New York Times (2019) "Mapping US auto emissions", October 10.

New York Times (2020) "This was supposed to be the year driverless cars went mainstream," May 12.

New York Times (2020) "The age of electric cars is dawning ahead of schedule," September 20.

New York Times (2020) "Uber is giving self-driving car project to a start-up," December 7.

New York Times (2021) "Electric cars are better for the planet – and often your budget, too," January 15.

New York Times (2021) "G.M. will sell only zero-emission vehicles by 2035," January 28.

New York Times (2021) "G.M. wants to make electric cars. China dominates the market," January 29.

New York Times (2021) "Oil giants win offshore wind leases in Britain," February 8.

New York Times (2021) "Electric cars are coming, and fast. Is the nation's grid up to it?" March 2.

New York Times (2021) "How green are electric vehicles?" March 2.

New York Times (2021) "Volvo plans to sell only electric cars by 2030," March 2.

New York Times (2021) "The city where cars are not welcome," March 3.

New York Times (2021) "Electric cars are coming. How long until they rule the road?" March 13.

New York Times (2021) "Volkswagen aims to use its size to head off Tesla," March 15.

New York Times (2021) "Carmakers strive to stay ahead of hackers," March 18.

New York Times (2021) "Tesla's autopilot technology faces fresh scrutiny," March 25.

New York Times (2021) "Biden's push for electric cars/ $174 billion, 10 years and a bit of luck," March 31.

New York Times (2021) "Three electric S.U.V.s with Tesla in their sights," April 23.

New York Times (2021a) "The auto industry bets its future on batteries," May 4.

New York Times (2021b) "As cars go electric, China builds a big lead in factories," May 4.

New York Times (2021) "Lithium mining projects may not be green friendly," May 6.

New York Times (2021) "Electric cars are coming, and fast. is the nations' grid up to it?" May 13.

New York Times (2021) "Ford's electric F-150 pickup aims to be the Model T of E.V.s," May 19.

New York Times (2021) "The costly pursuit of self-driving cars continues on. and on. and on," May 24.

New York Times (2021) "Can removing highways fix America's cites?" May 27.

New York Times (2021) "Crashes involving teal autopilot and other driver-assistance systems get new scrutiny," June 29.

New York Times (2021) "Tesla says autopilot makes its cars safer, crash victims say it kills," July 5.

New York Times (2021) "Tesla autopilot faces US inquiry after series of crashes," August 16.

New York Times (2021) "Shell gets greener, even as climate advocates say, 'Go faster'," September 16.

New York Times (2021) "China is set to rule electric car production," September 22.

New York Times (2021) "China's popular electric vehicles have put European automakers on notice," October 31.

New York Times (2021) "Is an all-encompassing mobility app making a comeback?" December 15.

New York Times (2021) "How China's CATL became the top electric car battery maker," December 22.

New York Times (2022) "Why this could be a critical year for electric cars," February 8.

New York Times (2022) "Biden administration outlines plan to build more E.V. chargers," February 10.

New York Times (2023) "Volkswagen will invest $193 billion in electric cars and software," March 14.

New York Times (2023) "Chinese Cars star at Munich auto show, underscoring German economic woes," September 6.

New York Times (2023) "China is flooding the world with cars," September 6.

New York Times (2023) "Toyota, a hybrid pioneer, struggles to master electric vehicles," September 7.

New York Times (2023) "Tesla recalls autopilot software in 2 million vehicles," November 15.

New York Times (2023) "Why Volkswagen is building a team of 3,000 engineers in China, December 12.

New York Times (2024) "Hybrid cars enjoy a renaissance as all-electric sales slow," January 19.

New York Times (2024) "How Ford's F-150 Lightning, once in hot demand, lost its luster, February 7.

New York Times (2024) "Biden Calls Chinese Electric Vehicle a Security Threat," February 29.

New York Times (2024) "Toyota's hybrid-first strategy is delivering big profits," March 9.

Patterson, Jane, et al. (2011) "Preparing for a life cycle CO_2 measure," www.Ricardo.com, May 20.

Perrow, Charles (1999) *Normal Accidents: Living with High-Risk Technologies*, 2nd edition, Princeton University Press.

Pomertantseva, Ekaterina, et al. (2019) "Energy storage. The future enabled by nanomaterials," *Science*, Nov. 22.

Popper, Nathaniel (2017) "The liability conundrum," *New York Times Magazine*, November 7.

Protocol (2022) "Why China is outselling the US in EVs 5 to 1," January 24.

Reuters (2016) "Three US states sue Volkswagen, say executives covered up diesel cheating," July 19.

Reuters (2021) "Global carmakers now target $515 billion for EVs, batteries," November 10.

Reuters (2021) "Volkswagen powers up the grid to take on Tesla," November 17.

Reuters (2024) "Toyota hikes annual profit forecast after Q3 beats expectations, February 6.

Schiff, Capt. Brian (2015) "Automation dependency," *Lift Magazine*, Spring.

Sengupta, Somini & Nadja Popovich (2019) "Cities worldwide are reimagining their relationship with cars," *New York Times*, November 14.

Service, Robert F. (2021) "Zinc aims to beat lithium batteries at storing energy," *Science*, May 28.

Shell (2021) *Strategic Report 2021*. https://reports.shell.com/annual-report/2021/

Sivak, Michael & Brandon Schoettle (2015) "Motion sickness in self-driving vehicles," April, University of Michigan, Transportation Research Institute.

Sivak, Michael & Brandon Schoettle (2016) "Would self-driving cars increase occupant productivity?" September, University of Michigan, Transportation Research Institute.

South China Morning Post (2020) "China unveils 'strategic emerging industries' plan in fresh push to get away from US technologies," September 24.

Standage, Tom (2021) *A Brief History of Motion, From Wheel, to the Car, to What Comes Next*, Bloomsbury, New York.

Statista (2019) "Mobility Berlin: Get around sustainably," July 19.

Statista (2023) "Average cost of a mechanic labor hour in China in 2020, by type of provider," March 23.

Statista (2023) "BYD and Tesla dominate global EV sales," September 5.

Stenzel, Wes (2024) "New automaker backed by Volkswagen debuts first EV with novel battery: 'An entirely new battery chemistry'," autosyahoo.com, February 27.

Sup China (2021) "All the electric car companies in China — a guide to the 46 top players in the Chinese EV industry," December 1.

Techradarpro (2021) "China may be secretly sitting on the two most powerful supercomputers in the world.," October 27.

Tenner, Edward (1996) *Why Things Bite Back. Technology, and the Revenge of Unintended Consequences*, Vintage Books.

Thompson, Gregory J. (2014) "In-use emissions testing of light-duty diesel vehicles in the United States," West Virginia University Center for Automotive Fuels, Engines & Emissions, May 15.

TomTom.com (2017) "Traffic congestion index full ranking."

Toshiba (2017) News Release. "Toshiba develops next-generation lithium-ion battery with new anode material," October 3.

Transport & Environment (2021) "Key transport trends in Q1 2021," March 30.

US News & World Report (2021) "Ford is betting that solid-state batteries will cut EV costs," May 5.

UBS Investment Bank (2020) "Q-Series: Tearing down the heart of an electric cap lap 2: cost parity a closer reality?" July 17.

UITP (2019) *Mobility as a Service*, International Association of Public Transport, April.

UNESCO (2017) *Cracking the Code: Girls' and Women's Education in Science, Technology, Engineering and Mathematics (STEM)*.

United Nations (2021) "Zero emission vehicles transition council: 2022 Action Plan," COP26, November.

US Bureau of Labor Statistics (2023) "Foreign labor statistics."

US Bureau of Transportation Statistics (BTS) (2018) *Transportation Statistics Annual Report 2018*.

US Congressional Research Service (CRS) (2014) "US and EU motor vehicle standards: Issues for Transatlantic trade negotiations," February 18.

US Department of Health and Human Services (HHS) (2021) "Diesel exhaust particulates," *Report on Carcinogens*, National Toxicology Program, December 21.

US Energy Information Administration (EIA) (2017) *Study of the Potential Energy Consumption Impacts of Connected and Automated Vehicles*, March.

US Energy Information Administration (EIA) (2018) "Today in energy – natural gas and renewables make up most of 2018 electric capacity additions," May 7.

US Energy Information Administration (EIA) (2019a) *Electric Power Monthly*, May.

US Energy Information Administration (EIA) (2019b) *Short-Term Energy Outlook*, January.

US Environmental Protection Agency (EPA) (2002) *Health Assessment Document for Diesel Engine Exhaust*, May.

US Environmental Protection Agency (EPA) (2015a) "Notice of violation of Clean Air Act to Volkswagen," September 18.

US Environmental Protection Agency (EPA) (2015b) "EPA, California notify Volkswagen of additional Clean Air Act violations," News release from headquarters. Enforcement and Compliance Assurance (OECA), November 2, updated April 18, 2016.

US Environmental Protection Agency (EPA) (2016) *Integrated Science Assessment (ISA) for Nitrogen Oxide Health Criteria*, January 28.

US Environmental Protection Agency (EPA) (2017) "Global greenhouse gas emissions data."

US Environmental Protection Agency (EPA) (2018a) "Greenhouse gas emissions from a typical passenger vehicle."

US Environmental Protection Agency (EPA) (2018b) "Global greenhouse gas emissions data."

US Environmental Protection Agency (EPA) (2021) "Sources of greenhouse gas emissions in US," July 27.

US Environmental Protection Agency (EPA) (2021) "Learn about Volkswagen violations" October 18.

US Environmental Protection Agency (EPA) (2021) "Fast facts: US transportation sector greenhouse gas emissions 1990–2019," December.

US Environmental Protection Agency (EPA) (2021) "Sources of greenhouse gas emissions."

US Environmental Protection Agency (EPA) (2021) "Fast Facts on transportation greenhouse gas emissions," December 16.

US Environmental Protection Agency (EPA) (2022) "Learn about Volkswagen violations."

US Federal Aviation Administration (FAA) (2013) *Operational Use of Flight Path Management Systems*, PARC report.

US Federal Trade Commission (FTC) (2016) "FTC charges Volkswagen deceived consumers with its 'clean diesel' campaign," March 29.

US Federal Trade Commission (FTC) (2020) "In final court summary, FTC reports Volkswagen repaid more than $9.5 billion to car buyers who were deceived by 'clean diesel' ad campaign," July 27.

US National Science Board (NSB) (2022) *The State of U.S Science & Engineering 2022.*

US National Science Foundation (2020) "Science & engineering indicators. publications, outputs US trends and international comparisons."

Vancouver Sun (2023) "ICBC scraps 2022 electric car after owners faced with a $60,000 bill to replace damaged battery," December 21.

Volkswagen (2021) "Volkswagen enters into strategic partnerships for the industrialization of battery technology," December 8.

Volkswagen (2019) *Annual Report.*

Volkswagen (2023) *Annual Report.*

Wachter, Bob (2015) "My interview with Capt. Sully Sullenberger: On Aviation, Medicine, and Technology," The Official Blog of the Society of Hospital Medicine, February 23, https://blog.hospital-medicine.org/my-interview-with-capt-sully-sullenberger-on-aviation-medicine-and-technology/

Walker, Joan (2018) "The traffic jam of robots: Implications of autonomous vehicles on trip-making," Automated Vehicle Symposium 2016, University of California, Berkeley, July 9–12.

Wards (MVF&F) (1987) *Motor Vehicle Facts & Figures.*

Wards (2019) *China's New Energy Vehicle Future.*

Wards (2021) "Volkswagen AG," *World Motor Vehicle Data*: 18.

Wards (2022) "Labor costs in the automotive industry: For select countries," *World Motor Vehicle Data.*

Wards Auto (2023) "Volkswagen CEO Schaefer to managers: 'The roof is on fire'," August 10.

The Washington Post (2021) "Tesla Model S garage fire follows pattern prompting warnings for other EVs," August 4.

Weinstein, Emily (2022) "Beijing's 're-innovation' strategy is key element of US-China competition," Brookings, January 6.

Weiss, Martin, et al. (2011) *Analyzing On-Road Light-Duty Vehicles with Portable Emission Monitoring Systems (PEMS)*, European Commission, Institute for Energy, Report: EUR 24697.

Wilson, Lindsay (2013) "Shades of green: Electric cars carbon emissions around the globe, ShrinkThatFootprint.com," February.

Winston, Clifford (2013). "On the performance of the US Transportation System: Caution ahead," *Journal of Economic Literature*, 51(3) 773–824.
World Economic Forum (WEF) (2016) *The Human Capital Report*.
World Economic Forum (WEF) (2019) "China's lead in the global solar race – at a glance," June 19.
World Health Organization (WHO) (2019) *Ambient Air Pollution Database*.
World Health Organization (WHO) (2021) "Road traffic injuries," June 21.
Yang, Xiao-Guang, et al. (2019) "Asymmetric temperature modulation for extreme fast charging of lithium-ion batteries," *Joule*, Dec. 10.

Analytical Questions:

1. Considering the opportunities and risks associated with the marked changes to the nature and economic and political environment of the global automotive market (especially, the less hospitable environment for diesel engines and the emerging markets for electric cars, automated vehicles, and the Internet of Motion), how should Volkswagen prioritize its strategic options?
2. In particular, how should Volkswagen view the role of the medium and long-term capabilities and potential threat of the Chinese automobile industry (especially its production and marketing), both in China and globally?
3. On September 2, 2024, the *New York Times* ran an article entitled: "Volkswagen, Seeking to Cut Costs, Considers German Plant Closures." It read in part:

   Volkswagen warned on Monday that it would consider closing factories in Germany for the first time in its 87-year history and end a decades-old guarantee of job security for workers, as it faces profitability problems amid increasing pressure from Asian competitors.

   "In the current situation, even plant closures at vehicle production and component sites can no longer be ruled out without swift countermeasures," the company said. "The situation is extremely tense and cannot be resolved through simple cost-cutting measures."

   "The company — and the VW brand — are in a very dangerous situation," said Ferdinand Dudenhöffer, director of the Center for Automotive Research in Gelsenkirchen, Germany.

   In light of this information, how would you assess the strategic direction and options facing the company?

16 Five Short Cases

Patagonia, H&M, Walmart, Ford, Fossil Fuel Companies

H&M

The fashion industry has one of the largest environmental impacts in the world with over 100 billion units sold in 2015 and the negative impacts of this output are projected to dramatically increase by 2050 (MacArthur Foundation 2017; Niinimaki et al. 2020). A Swedish multinational clothing retailer company, H&M is the second-largest global clothing retailer with annual sales in 2020 of $22.25 billion USD (H&M 2022). In 2017, the company introduced a new sustainability strategy partly in response to negative publicity about two of the foundational elements of sustainability: environment and social factors. In 2010 it was revealed that the corporation was disposing of excess clothing in New York City (*New York Times* Jan. 5, 2010). Garments had been rendered unfit to wear by slashing with box cutters or razors. Just three years later, a disastrous fire in a Bangladesh sweatshop killed over 1,100 workers (*New York Times* April 21, 2018).

Although H&M was not directly involved in this factory, it was a general wakeup call for the clothing industry. In its launch of its 2017 comprehensive sustainability strategy, H&M articulated three principal goals: (1) to provide good and fair opportunities for workers, (2) to transform their production process to become 100% circular and climate positive. This entails "the continued quest for more recycled and sustainably source materials, improved design, production processes and product lifespans, (H&M n.d., p. 1), " and (3) to further develop customer engagement around sustainability. This involves a clear commitment to the Higg Index developed by The Sustainable Apparel Coalition.

> The Higg Index is a suite of tools that enables brands, retailers, and facilities of all sizes — at every stage in their sustainability journey — to accurately measure and score a company or product's sustainability performance. The Higg Index delivers a holistic overview that empowers businesses to make meaningful improvements that protect the well-being of factory workers, local communities, and the environment.
>
> (Apparel Coalition n.d.)

While H&M has received its fair share of criticism for its business practices relating to sustainability, it is only one company in a fashion industry that has experienced the same

DOI: 10.4324/9781003170754-19

challenges. The United Nations Economic Commission for Europe (UNECE, 2018: 1) has stated that the fashion industry is an "environmental and social emergency":

> The fashion industry is responsible for producing twenty per cent of global wastewater and ten per cent of global carbon emissions – more than the emissions of all international flights and maritime shipping combined. Cotton farming is responsible for 24 per cent of insecticides and 11 per cent of pesticides despite using only 3 per cent of the world's arable land. In addition, the textiles industry has been identified in recent years as a major contributor to plastic pollution in the world's oceans. It was estimated that around half a million tonnes of plastic microfibers shed during the washing of plastic-based textiles such as polyester, nylon, or acrylic end up in the ocean every year. In addition to the negative environmental impacts, fashion is also linked to dangerous working conditions due to unsafe processes and hazardous substances used in production.

A recent major research report into the environmental impact of the Global Apparel and Footwear Industries (Quantis 2018: 3) provides a detailed breakdown of these impacts at all stages of the production process, focussing on the contribution to greenhouse gas release. The lifecycle analysis finds that "the apparel industry alone represents 6.7% of global GHG emissions . . . [and] more than 50% of emissions come from three stages: dyeing & finishing, yarn preparation and fiber production."

In response to the environmental and social challenges facing the industry and H&M particularly, the company's 2017, 2019 and 2022 sustainability reports provided detailed historical data, as well as future goals for two of its main strategic thrusts: 100% circular and renewable production, and fairness and equity in the labour market. These goals along with recent and target results are reproduced in Table 16.1. In general, for the fashion industry to achieve their sustainability goals, they may require a reassessment of the performance of their supply chain, especially in the developing world where the bulk of clothing is now manufactured.

There is a major threat to the attainment of corporate sustainability in this industry. H&M, along with Zara, have been pioneers in the field of *fast fashion*. This production and marketing philosophy is based on the large-scale production of relatively low-value goods with a very short fashion cycle, sometimes numbering only several weeks. The net result of this approach is the *de facto* encouragement of consumer overconsumption in constant pursuit of rapidly changing fashion. The concomitant high levels of production lead in turn to a markedly increased and negative impact on the environment and working conditions (Cline 2012; Hobson 2013; Taplin 2014a, 2014b; *Forbes* July 26, 2017; *The Independent* January 8, 2018). Symptomatic of this problem is a report in the *New York Times* (March 27, 2018) that H&M was facing a $4.3 billion pile of unsold clothing.

Despite its attempt to burnish it image after the reports of damaging perfectly usable clothing in 2010, it was revealed that the company provided 15 tonnes of discarded products to a power plant in a small Swedish city in 2017 (*New York Times* March 27, 2018). The *Times* report suggested that the destruction of unsold consumer goods was endemic to the industry citing several prominent companies' practices: Burberry destroyed more than 90 million GBP worth of goods over the past five years; the Swiss watch maker, Richemont, destroyed more than $400 million GBP worth of watches in two recent years;

Table 16.1 H&M Sustainability Achievements and Goals

Category	Goal 2025	Goal 2030	Actual 2022
CLIMATE			
absolute scopes 1,2 & 3 GHG		reduce by 56% from 2019 baseline	8% reduction in scope 1&2 emissions and 7% reduction in scope 3 emissions from 2019 baseline
MATERIALS AND RESOURCES			
% of our materials in commercial goods to be either recycled or other more sustainably sourced materials		100%	84%
% of our materials in commercial goods to be certified recycled	30%		23%
PACKAGING			
% of packaging from recycled material or other more sustainably sourced materials		100%	85%
% reduction in plastic packaging (baseline 2018)	25%		44%
WATER			
% reduction in absolute freshwater use (Baseline 2022)	10%	30%	38% (relative to 2017 baseline)

Source: H&M Group. Annual and sustainability Report (2022)

Nike slashed unwanted running shoes before disposal; and Urban Outfitters poured green paint on unsold Toms shoes.

The bottom line is that despite the laudable efforts at improving their sustainability indicators, there is a fundamental incompatibility of H&M's business model with the goal of sustainability, a problem face by all other players in the both the fast and slow fashion marketplace. The Council for Textile Recycling (n.d.: 3) reported that the amount of post-consumer textile waste (PCTW) was estimated to grow from 25.6 billion pounds in 2009 to 35.4 billion pounds in 2019: "Between 1999 and 2009 the volume of PCTW generated grew by 40%, while the diversion rate only increased by 2%." An iconic example of this phenomenon was a recent report (Grist 2024) of a burning mound of discarded fabric estimated at 11,000 to 59,000 tons in Chile's Atacama Desert. Similar massive waste dumps of discarded clothing can be found in several Africa countries, such as Ghana and Kenya (Besser (2021; *The Guardian* June 5, 2023).

In a report released in December 2023, the NGO Stand.earth (Kitchin & Zhang 2023) ranked 43 major fashion companies on their degree of success in phasing out fossil fuels. Interesting enough, H&M ranked first with an overall letter grade of B-, meaning that the other 42 companies turned in poorer performances. Pumas was third with C+, Patagonia eighth with C, and Walmart 24th with a D. These rankings changed, however, when the component subrankings were considered: (1) climate commitments and transparency, (2) renewable energy and energy-efficient manufacturing, (3) renewable energy advocacy, (4) low-carbon and longer lasting materials, and (5) greener shipping. The principal conclusions of the report were:

- Greenhouse gas emissions continued to rise on average compared to pre-pandemic levels
- Most brands showed a lack of willingness to publicly disclose salient supply chain information
- Brands have been slow to cut out fossil fuel derived fibres such as virgin polyester
- By failing to act in an urgent and equitable manner to decarbonise, major fashion brands are not meeting their climate responsibilities
- Robust policy and legal measures enforced by multilateral bodies and governments are required to ensure a rapid and just energy transition from fossil fuels and toward renewable energy use

Of particular importance was the need to focus on energy consumption and consequent GHG emissions in the supply chain, as several of the supplier countries such as Bangladesh, China, India, and Vietnam have sustained significant increased use of coal in electricity production. Patagonia has reported that 97% of their emissions are generated by their supply chain (Patagonia 2019).

Of the 43 companies studied by Stand.earth (Kitchin and Zhang 2023), nine did not report their emissions, 13 reported a decrease in their emissions, with one experiencing a reduction of 44%, and 21 reported increases ranging as high as 412%. Of the companies discussed in this volume, the emission changes were as follows: H&M up 7.04%, Puma down 22.43%, Walmart up 31.61%, and Patagonia not disclosed, although they reported their total emissions in 2019.

Patagonia

Along with Interface Carpets, Patagonia, the outdoor clothing company, is one of the few companies that has demonstrated a deep, company-wide philosophical commitment to the principle of sustainability based on the passionate beliefs of its founder, Yvon Chouinard. Again, in parallel with Interface, Patagonia has achieved a solid financial record where sustainability provides its differentiation strategy and consequent competitive advantage. First and foremost, the company clearly recognizes the challenges it faces (Patagonia, 2018, pp. 1–2):

> Our work has always begun first by acknowledging that Patagonia is part of the problem. We make products using fossil fuels, built in factories that use water and other resources, create waste and emit carbon into the air. We ship our products around the world in boxes and plastic bags. We consume electricity—some generated using renewable resources and some not—at our corporate offices, distribution centers and stores. We drive cars and ride on airplanes. As individuals, we consume products of all shapes and sizes—probably more than we need. Knowing we are part of the problem, we must also recognize that climate change—as a deadly condition of infinite human actions—is not an issue we can tackle outright. That's why we try to stay focused on specific things Patagonia

can do to reduce, neutralize, or even reverse the root causes of climate change. We believe in extending our mission to cause no unnecessary harm to every area where Patagonia has influence. That way, as Patagonia grows in size, our efforts to meet the challenge of our mission can be amplified exponentially.

Specific actions include measuring and tracking the carbon footprint of their global operations, using renewable energy wherever possible, improving existing buildings rather than constructing new ones for their retail operations, using monetary incentives to encourage their employees to drive less, using sustainable paper, developing a program to help manage the chemicals and environmental impacts in their global supply chain, and relying wherever possible on natural fibers (e.g., hemp, organic cotton, Tencel [Lyocell], and Yulex) to supplement their use of recycled nylon, polyester, cotton wool, and down fibers. (Patagonia 2018) (see Figure 16.1).

As indicated in its online statements of philosophy, Patagonia is not only committed to transforming the company into a truly sustainable enterprise, it has also actively promoted similar initiatives in its own industry by helping to fund the Sustainable Apparel Coalition, an alliance of thirty companies from the clothing and footwear industries; has helped to fund likeminded charities and grassroots organizations by donating one percent of its annual sales; and has backed a fund called *$20 Million and Change* which assists startup companies with demonstrable environmental benefits.

Figure 16.1 Patagonia T-Shirt

To achieve all of these multifaceted goals, Patagonia has registered as a *B Corporation*, a new approach to business that focuses less on maximizing shareholder returns, and more on achieving social and environmental goals (B Lab 2023). While there are now over 1,200 companies worldwide with B-corporation status, this strategic reorientation does not obviate the longstanding legal requirement of first duty to shareholders. Patagonia is able to skirt this legal requirement because of its status as a privately held corporation. The status of this strategy remains unclear for public companies, despite the fact that a small number of such entities (such as the Brazilian toiletries company, Natura) have announced this type of strategic change. It has been reported that Unilever is giving serious consideration to become a BCorporation as well, and their subsidiary, Ben and Jerry's, has already moved in this direction. What makes this move possible, however, is that Ben and Jerry's is a wholly-owned entity within the panoply of Unilever companies (FastCompany 2012; Unilever 2019).

In essence, Patagonia's approach stands in stark contrast to the business model used by H&M and Zara. Patagonia's mantra is "reduce, repair, reuse and recycle," which focuses on durable long-lasting products, and encourages their customers to return their old Patagonia wear to the store for a credit, after which the company will repair or recycle these goods. The corporate approach is summed up in the words of the late environmentalist David Brower: "There is no business on a dead planet." (Dilley 2014).

And yet, it is one of the underlying themes of this book that the achievement of sustainability is more elusive than once thought and this is no more apparent than in the corporate sector. Within the last decades, numerous research studies have identified a new and consequential environmental problem associated, in part, with the production and use of synthetic fibers (e.g., Napper and Thompson 2016), the output of which has risen dramatically within the last several decades (*Textile World* Feb 3, 2015). Vast quantities of microplastics, of which microfibers are a part, have been released into the environment and threaten the ocean-based food chain. The effects are at least twofold: first, filter-feeders such as oysters and mussels incorporate these fibers into their tissue, and this tissue progresses up the food chain to human consumers; and, second, synthetic fibers tended to absorb chemicals, many of which are toxic and/or carcinogenic, and these also move up the food chain (Cox et al. 2019; Mishra et al. 2019).

Recent estimates suggest that the US may be releasing as much as 64,000 pounds of tiny synthetic clothing fibers into the water every day (Insider 2016). This is of particular relevance to Patagonia in light of their significant production and sale of fleece jackets with the potential to release large quantities of microfibers during washing. To their credit, this unexpected result of the widespread use of synthetic fibers prompted the company to commission a study of the quantities released by their products (Hartline et al. 2016). The results were astonishing, suggesting that a single fleece jacket sheds as many as 250,000 synthetic fibers (*The Guardian* Feb 12, 2017). Cognizant of this problem, Patagonia has been devoting considerable resources to address and reduce this problem. Nevertheless, it is symptomatic of the general dichotomy between early benefits and delayed costs of new technologies. Given the projected increase in the production of polyester (see Figure 16.2), the fibre and clothing industries now face a major challenge in addressing the environmental consequences of is use.

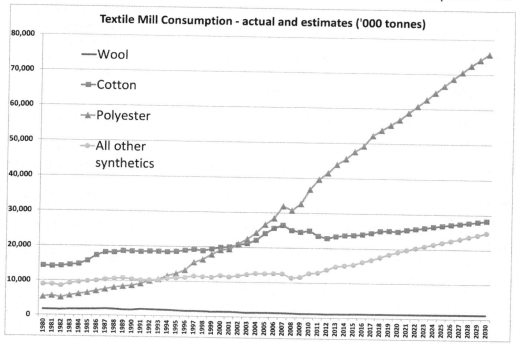

Figure 16.2 Textile Mill Consumption – Actual and Estimates
Source: PCI Wood Mackenzie, Fibres Global Supply Demand Report 2017

A recent interview with Patagonia's CEO, Ryan Gellert outlined the unique challenges facing the company in their steps to address the major sustainability issues they face (*The Guardian* March 12, 2023):

On the surface, all appears to be business as usual. But over the last six months, Patagonia has been wrestling with an existential dilemma that has long obsessed the company: can the group sincerely fight the climate crisis as a for-profit apparel company? "If you're serious about [the climate crisis] and this is your business, you've got to develop a level of comfort with contradiction," said the chief executive, Ryan Gellert, sitting in his wood-paneled office. "The idea of ultimately running a regenerative business, that is the biggest idea that we're capable of, and we're a long, long way from realizing that." The company made a big step toward realizing that big idea last September when Yvon Chouinard, the rock climber turned founder of Patagonia, announced that his family will reshape the way it controls the privately held company. Under the new structure, 2% of the shares and all decision-making authority has been transferred to a family trust, giving the Chouinards continuing control over corporate decisions and the mission. The rest – 98% of the stock, worth about $100m a year in dividends – will go to a new nonprofit, the Holdfast Collective, focused on climate activism, including political advocacy. Patagonia will soon have three core activist segments. As it has since 1985, the company still donates 1% of its revenue to community-oriented, grassroots environmental groups through small grants, worth up to $15,000. The creation of the Holdfast Collective introduced a second activist arm, a nonprofit that will funnel larger grants and donations in the millions. Then in April, the company will formally launch a third activist unit, Home Planet Fund, a nonprofit that will fundraise and funnel money to those fighting climate change in isolated and fragile regions, with particular attention to Indigenous communities.

With this monumental challenge facing the fashion industry, several niche companies have seized the initiative and adopted radically new business models. One of these is Tonle, with production based in Cambodia. Ninety percent of the company's raw materials are discards from major companies in the fashion industry, composed of cut waste, quality control failure, overstock and dead stock (Tonle 2018). Coupled with the use of natural dyes and inks, and recycled packaging, the company has drastically reduced the ecological footprint of clothing production. The increasing production of garments in Cambodia has not been without major environmental challenges, however. The French environmental organization, Geres (n.d.) reports that the industry is the country's largest contributor to GHG, largely through the destruction of old growth forests as an energy source.

In March 2024, France's lower house of parliament voted to levy an environmental surcharge and advertising ban on low-cost, fast fashion, although approval is also required from the French Senate. Despite the outcome of this measure, this is the first formal governmental recognition of this major global pollution issue and may represent the beginning of a new trend to alter the path of this industry strategy (*The Guardian* March 15, 2024).

Walmart

Walmart, the world's largest company, with 2.1 million employees and revenue in FY2023 of $611 billion, (Walmart 2023) is a much more complex example of the paradoxical juxtaposition of a clearly articulated sustainability policy and the underlying business model.

On October 24, 2005, Lee Scott, Walmart's Chief Executive Officer, delivered his "Twenty First Century Leadership Lecture "(Scott 2005), billed as a major reorientation of its strategy toward sustainability. Scott (2005: 4) began his speech by moulding Hurricane Katrina into a metaphor for the crisis that is facing our physical and business environment:

> We should view the environment as Katrina in slow motion. Environmental loss threatens our health and the health of the natural systems we depend on. The challenges include: increasing greenhouse gases that are contributing to climatic change and weather-related disasters; increasing air pollution which is leading to more asthma and other respiratory diseases in our communities; water pollution which is increasing while safe fresh water supplies are shrinking; water-borne diseases causes millions of death each year, mostly among children; destruction of critical habitat, causing unprecedented threat to the diversity of life, the natural world and us. And that's just to name a few. As one of the largest companies in the world, with an expanding global presence, environmental problems are OUR problems. The supply of natural products (fish, food, water) can only be sustained if the ecosystems

that provide them are sustained and protected. There are not two worlds out there, a Walmart world and some other world.

Scott then enunciated Walmart's environmental goals and outlined the intimate relationship between environmental stewardship and good business practice. The principal goals were: (1) to be supplied 100 percent by renewable energy; (2) to create zero waste; and (3) to sell products that sustain resources and the environment. Scott (2005: 5) stated that:

> These goals are both ambitious and aspirational, and I'm not sure how to achieve them. . . . at least not yet. This obviously will take some time. But we do know the way. There is a simple rule about the environment. If there is waste or pollution, someone along the line pays for it.

Walmart's CEO then presented specific examples in four environmentally-related areas to illustrate the nature and magnitude of the potential savings: trucking, store design, and operation, waste generation, and product design and sourcing. To assist the multitude of firms in their supply chain coordinate their activities with Walmart's sustainability programs, Walmart (no date) has published an extensive *Supplier Sustainability Assessment* manual. This document first asks each supplier to answer fifteen basic questions in the four areas of energy and climate, material efficiency, nature and resources, and people and community; scores these responses depending on the level of performance; explains some of the benefits from improving their performance scores in each of the four areas; and finally, lists a group of tools and resources that suppliers can use to improve their performance.

Several years have passed since the declaration of new goals for Walmart and the company is now under different leadership. In 2023, the corporation published data on its progress so far, which is summarized in Table 16.2. Whether its lofty goals will be attainable in the near to midterm future remains an open question, but the contents and import of Scott's talk are remarkable.

Table 16.2 Walmart Sustainability Highlights

- >750 Million MT CO2e reduced or avoided by suppliers since 2017
- Annual GHG emissions from Scope 1&2 reduced from 19.92 MMT CO2e in CY2015 to 13.99 MMT CO2e in CY 2021
- 23.2% reduction in combined Scope 1 & 2 emissions vs. 2015 baseline through 2020
- >2 million acres of land conserved through Acres for America since 2005
- 63% of global private brand packaging is recyclable, reusable, or industrially compostable, a 5% increase over FY2022
- >400 suppliers set goals and/or reported progress on responsible recruitment through Walmart's Supplier Leadership Program on People
- Achieved at least 95% "more sustainable" certification for several commodities, including fresh and frozen seafood, bananas, coffee and tea
- Increased percentage of electricity supplied by renewable source to 46% (through 2021)
- Diverted 78% of operational waste globally, including 89% in Canada, 80% in Mexico, and 78% in the U.S.
- Reduced food waste 12% (vs.2016 baseline); diverted >900 M lbs. of food waste to composting, animal feed, anaerobic digestion, and biochemical processing; and donated >750M lbs. of food globally

Adapted from Walmart (2023)

Walmart's Unique Role in the Diffusion of Sustainability Technology and Policy

There is a clear role for government in facilitating the diffusion of sustainable technology, policy, and practices throughout the economy by providing a level playing field that allows these initiatives to compete freely with existing alternative technologies and strategies. Prime examples of this approach can be found in renewable energy sources and demand-side management. However, an equally important phenomenon is the diffusion of sustainability within the corporate sector itself. Figure 3.4 presented several models of diffusion that may be applied to the challenge of moving the industrial system closer to the goal of sustainability. *Model A* represents horizontal diffusion; *Model B* vertical diffusion up the supply chain, and *Model C* vertical diffusion down the supply chain.

Walmart provides a particularly cogent example of Model C (vertical diffusion, down the supply chain). Bearing in mind that if Walmart were a country it "would be the twentieth largest in the world," the corporation has an extraordinary capacity to leverage the nature of global business practices, but no company has had such a polarizing effect on public discourse in the United States. While its social impacts on small business, urban cores and labor have been a lightning rod for criticism, its massive presence in the American economy entails less visible but extraordinary impacts on material throughput and energy use throughout its supply chain. Because of its virtually unique role, Walmart can dramatically change the face of commerce not only in the US, but also globally.

So, if Walmart can achieve its stated sustainability goals and induce similar responses among its many international suppliers, where is the problem? In two thought-provoking books entitled *Eco-Business. A Big Brand Takeover of Sustainability*, (Dauvergne & Lister 2013) and *Will Big Business Destroy Our Planet?* (Dauvergne 2018) the authors articulate the nature of the paradox. Big business is engaging in what the authors call *eco-business*, which is labelled "sustainability" by corporations but is more about corporate sustaining the corporation than the environment. The principal driver is increased efficiencies and more secure markets, which guarantee larger sales and profitability. Dauvergne and Lister (2013: 36) argue that:

> recent brand company efforts through their global supply chains are achieving environmental gains in product design and production. Yet, these advances are also fundamentally limited. Total environmental impacts of consumption are increasing as brand companies leverage corporate sustainability for competitive advantage, business growth, and increased sales. Big brand sustainability, while important, will not on its own resolve the problems of global environmental change.

This raises a rather paradoxical question: Considering all the steps that Walmart has taken to advance sustainability, is its overall business model ultimately compatible with sustainability?

The Ford Motor Company

Few companies have displayed the deep philosophical commitment to sustainability demonstrated by Interface, which has not only sought to revolutionize its business model by transforming its technology, but also to fundamentally change the nature of the market in which it operates. Most other firms which have sought to move closer to a sustainable business model have done so opportunistically. This is not a bad thing *per se*, as it embodies Porter and van der Linde's message that the combination of sustainability and profitability are not only possible, but also advantageous. The critical ingredient in this type of corporate transformation from one business model to another is the existence of a favorable environment marked by either changes in consumer tastes, regulatory pressures, or some combination of changes in the relative prices of inputs and outputs.

A perfect example of this is the remarkable success of the Ford Motor Company, which escaped the bankruptcy that afflicted its main American competitors. After the crude oil price shock of the 1970s and the emergence of Japanese imports of small automobiles as a major threat to business-as-usual, Ford made the historic decision to cast itself as a green company by focusing on smaller and more fuel-efficient cars. But the environment changed: consumer tastes moved toward larger, less fuel-efficient SUVs. This was facilitated by the absence of any significant increasing trend in real gasoline prices, higher profit margins on SUVs and a shift in the nature of the service economy that promotes greater self-reliance. Ford recently announced its imminent departure from the American passenger car market, with the exception of the Mustang, in order to focus on building more trucks, SUVs, and crossovers NBC (2018) "Ford to Stop Making all Passenger Cars Except the Mustang," April 26. Figure 16.3 explains the motivation: passenger car sales have been steadily declining while Ford's SUV sales now exceed those of its passenger cars. Reinforcing this decision is the low to negative profit margins on most of the company's standard automotive products and the much higher profit margin on SUVs (*New York Times* May 24, 2018). While the decision was clearly motivated to generate higher profit levels in the short to medium term, this strategy could be counterproductive in the future if gasoline prices increase (*New York Times* May 1, 2018).

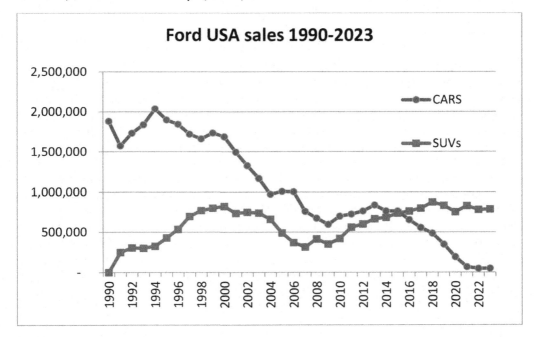

Figure 16.3 Ford's Sales by Car Type

Source: Wards multiple years

In 2021, Ford undertook a major strategic reorientation in one of its markets by announcing its intention to phase out gasoline-powered cars in Europe by 2030 (*New York Times* February 17, 2021). However, the *Times* reported that Ford would continue to sell commercial vehicles with gasoline or diesel engines in Europe "for years to come." This shift in focus, albeit in one of Ford's smaller markets, reflects major changes in the industry with several other major players, including GM, Volvo, and Volkswagen, signalling their intention to convert their production to electric vehicles. This move can only be reinforced by the announcement of the Biden administration to actively promote the adoption of electric vehicles in the United States (*New York Times* March 31, 2021). The recent history of industry strategy and government response unambiguously demonstrates the necessity of a systemwide economic and political environment that is supportive of corporate sustainability initiatives and provides an opportunity for profitability and sustainable competitive advantage.

Fossil Fuel Companies

While changes in the economic environment can induce corporations to scale back or abandon their commitment to sustainability, these changes can be a double-edged sword. There have been recent changes in the relative price of alternative fuels and warnings from the investment community about the effect of climate change on "stranded assets" (i.e., fossil fuels that cannot be extracted without further accelerating climate change) in the oil and coal sector (Ansar et al. 2013; Oxford 2013, 2014, 2015; Carbon Tracker 2020a). These developments will ultimately force major producers to make major changes in their business models. This is already happening in the coal sector where several companies have filed for bankruptcy or are facing serious financial problems (*New York Times* April 13, 2016; Carbon Tracker 2018).

The oil sector, however, remains relatively resistant to these considerations now considering the continued global reliance on liquid fuels. Several reports on companies in the energy and utility sectors (Brulle 2018; *HuffPost* December 24, 2019; Forbes March 25, 2019; *New York Times* November 11, 2020) found that they have actively engaged in lobbying and election spending to forestall both the federal and state governments from enacting clean energy standards, improving energy efficiency and closing fossil fuel tax loopholes. This involves both direct funding as well as indirect initiatives through financial support to selected nonprofits groups and what is called "astroturf" activity (see, for example, *The Guardian* March 8, 2024).

Two companies, ExxonMobil and Shell Oil, are prime examples of this phenomenon. Both have consistently denied the existence of global warming and, in the case of both Mobil and Exxon, have funded a campaign of misinformation reminiscent of the tobacco industry in its long fight against the regulation of cigarettes (Michaels 2008; Oreskes & Conway 2010; Brulle 2014; Banerjee et al. 2015; Otto 2016). It has been reported that BP has also participated in the funding of anticlimate lobby groups despite their public posture in support of sustainability (*HuffPost* September 28, 2020). It is particularly noteworthy that corporate documents (*Inside Climate News* 2015; Supran & Oreskes 2017; Franta 2018; *The Guardian* June 12, 2019; *HuffPost* December 3, 2019) have revealed that both ExxonMobil and Shell have known for a considerable time that human-induced climate change does in fact exist and poses a threat to their ultimate survival. It is ironic that this behavior is perfectly rational from a purely private perspective of profit maximization in the short- to medium-term, as fossil fuel firms attempt to perpetuate a business model that has been so profitable in the past. The problem is that such private pursuit of profit represents a classic case of market failure, reflecting a serious disconnection between private and social costs and benefits, through the generation of massive negative externalities.

This attempt to shape public perception and government policy has been accompanied, at least in the case of ExxonMobil, by a conscious effort to deceive current and potential investors. In October of 2018, the New York State's Attorney initiated an ultimately unsuccessful lawsuit against the company, claiming that Exxon engaged in a longstanding fraudulent scheme to deceive investors and the investment community about the risks posed to its business by climate change regulation (Reuters October 24, 2018; *New York Times* December 10, 2019). The Appendix includes excerpts from New York State's case against ExxonMobil, a case the state ultimately lost (*New York Times* December 10, 2019).

A recent report (Influence Map 2019) has calculated that the five largest publicly traded oil and gas companies (ExxonMobil, Shell, Chevron, BP, and Total) "have invested over \$1Bn of shareholder funds in the three years following the Paris Agreement on misleading climate-related branding and lobbying." This involves "carefully devised campaigns of positive messaging combined with negative policy lobbying on climate change" (Influence Map 2019, p. 2) with the tactical use of social media such as Facebook and Instagram (see also *Huff Post* February 25, 2021; *The Guardian* February 26, 2024).

Recent statements by the fossil fuel industry purporting to support the concept of sustainability lack credibility given recent reports (Carbon Tracker 2019; *New York Times* September 23, 2019; Wang et al. 2019) that no major oil company has invested to support the Paris goals of keeping global temperature rise below 2 degrees. In fact, the industry has just approved \$50 billion worth of major projects that "undermine climate targets and risk shareholder returns." (see, for example, SEI et al. 2023). At risk is the continued vitality of the fossil fuel industry with stranded assets in excess of one trillion dollars (Caldecott et al. 2014, 2015; Jakob & Hilaire 2015; McGlade & Ekins, 2015; IRENA 2017). It has recently been revealed that ExxonMobil lobbyists were quoted as saying that the company's support for a carbon tax as a key component of climate action was a public relations ploy (*The Guardian* June 30, 2021; *New York Times*, June 30, 2021). This is a damning indictment of a major energy multinational but certainly in keeping with the company's longstanding record of secretly funding initiatives to counter governmental efforts to combat climate change.

The Significance of Energy Megaprojects – Both Conventional and Nonconventional

As stated, despite public policy pronouncements from the fossil fuel sector concerning a reorientation of strategy toward sustainability, the actions of many of these energy giants appear inconsistent with these stated objectives (see, for example, Bloomberg October 5, 2020). The principal manifestation of this apparent paradox is the continued planning and development of major fossil fuel megaprojects mentioned above. A 2020 report by the International Energy Agency found that "investment by oil and gas companies outside their core business areas has been less than1% of total capital expenditures (IEA 2020: 7)." A 2019 study by the NGO, Global Witness, reported on planned capital expenditures on new oil and gas development over the period

2020–2029. Figure 16.4 summarizes these planned expenditures by major company. The report reached three critical conclusions:

- Any production from new oil and gas fields, beyond those already in production or development, is incompatible with limiting warming to 1.5°C
- All the $4.9 trillion forecast capex in new oil and gas fields is incompatible with limiting warming to 1.5°C
- 9% of oil and 6% of gas production forecast from existing fields is incompatible with limiting warming to 1.5°C

Since the publication of this report, some of these projects, especially for Liquified Natural Gas (LNG), have been rescheduled in light of climate concerns, pandemic delays, and the recent state of energy markets (Global Energy Monitor 2020; Reuters 2020). But in light of projected increases in global energy demand, there remains a strong incentive for major fossil fuel producers to stay the course. This is especially the case for ExxonMobil, which has made the decision to focus on megaprojects at the expense of reducing carbon emissions (*The Economist* February 9, 2019; Nasdaq 2019; Bloomberg October 5, 2020; *New York Times* September 22, 2020). As the Bloomberg report observes: "The largest US oil producer has never made a commitment to lower oil and gas output or set a date by which it will become carbon neutral. Exxon has also never publicly disclosed its forecasts for its own emissions." Whether this major strategic decision will stand remains to be seen, as there are already signs of tangible costs to this strategy. The company has been dropped from the Dow after nearly a century (CBS News August 25, 2020) and the NGO, Carbon Tracker (2020a), has concluded that chasing growth has destroyed shareholder value in the company.

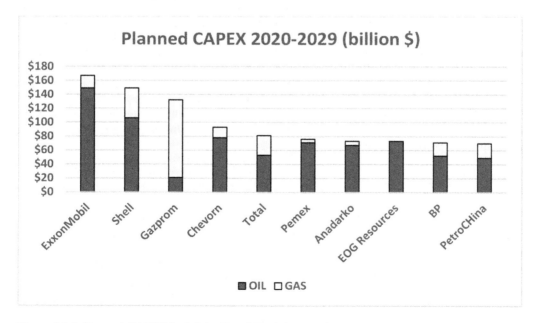

Figure 16.4 Planned CAPEX by Major Fossil Fuel Companies
Source: Global Witness 2019

Two other major fossil fuel companies have publicly announced a different strategic direction from ExxonMobil. Both Royal Dutch Shell and BP have undertaken to move toward more sustainable corporate strategy. In a press release on February 11, 2021, Shell announced that it was accelerating its "drive for net-zero emissions with a customer-first strategy," expanding on its commitment to become a net-zero carbon company by 2050 (*The Guardian* April 16, 2020; Shell 2021) although skepticism has been voiced over whether this goal is attainable in the stated time frame (BBC May 12, 2020). As part of this strategy, Shell has recently bought Ubitricity, one of biggest vehicle charging networks in Europe (*The Week* January 30, 2021).

Royal Dutch Shell has invested several billion dollars to develop a clean energy business but has fallen at least $3 billion short of its announced target of $6 billion over the past 3 years (*The Guardian* January 3, 2020). This figure pales in comparison to its announced plans to invest a further $149 billion in oil and gas development over the period 2020–2029 (see Figure 16.4 and *New York Times* February 11, 2021). Perhaps the most critical commentary on Shell's original plans was presented by George Monbiot (2019) when he observed that:

> Shell's "cash engines", according to its annual report, are oil and gas. There is no sign that it plans to turn the engines off. Its "growth priorities" are chemical production and deep water oil extraction. It does list low-carbon energy among its "emerging opportunities" in future decades, but says it will develop them alongside fracking and liquefied fossil gas technologies. In the future, the company says, it will "sell more natural gas". But as an analysis by Oil Change International explains, "there is no room for new fossil fuel development – gas included – within the Paris agreement goals". Even existing gas and oil extraction is enough to push us past 1.5C of global heating. Shell is a company committed for the long term to fossil fuel production.

BP has also announced its intention to become net-zero by 2050 (BP February 12, 2020; *The Guardian* February 12, 2020).

While admirable in their stated goals, there are several qualifications required interpreting the effectiveness of these undertakings. BP, for example, went down this route once before over a decade ago. Under the leadership of Lord John Brown from 1995–2007, the company attempted to rebrand itself as "Beyond Petroleum" by planning a major transition to renewable energy. This policy was reversed, however, by his successor, Tony Hayward, who reestablished the company focus on petroleum. Jonathan Watts, writing in *The Guardian* (Watts 2020), has provided a detailed critique of BP's recently announced plans by noting that:

> there is nothing in the statement to suggest that BP will move away from previous plans to increase oil and gas production by 20% over the next 10 years. . . . There are no concrete details here about scaling down production of fossil fuels or scaling up renewables. This will raise concerns that the company thinks it can just plant trees or use other offsets to make up for ever greater petrochemical production. This would not be enough to stabilize the climate.

Other analysts have also expressed concern over the difficulty in achieving the company's announced targets (Reuters August 9, 2020). BP has joined the French oil company,

Total, however, in spending 879 million pounds to purchase options to build offshore wind farms in the United Kingdom. It has been estimated that the total budget of this project, once developed, could total tens of billions of dollars. The company has also paid $1.1 billion dollars for a fifty percent share in an offshore wind facility off the US east coast. (*New York Times* February 8, 2021). Included in the proposed new energy portfolio are plans to invest heavily in solar power (Bloomberg September 16, 2020).

Coupled with outsized environmental impacts of continued funding of energy megaprojects by the major fossil fuel companies is their concomitant depressing effect on the development of renewable energy sources. The large capital investments involved in megaprojects and their long lifespan displaces renewable energy projects and technologies necessary to achieve global climate goals. It has been reported that the energy industry is planning to construct 235 gas-fired power stations in the United States at a cost of over $100 billion (*New York Times* Nov. 12, 2020). It is remarkable that many such projects are being planned by industry with the tangible risk that the resources may have to be left in the ground as renewable energy technology evolves in an attempt to keep global temperature rise below the IPCC's 1.5-degree benchmark. Under these circumstances, the entire fossil fuel industry faces shut-ins and stranded assets and must ultimately undergo profound and sweeping structural realignment (McKinsey 2021). What is equally remarkable is that funding for these projects continues to be provided by major international banks and some western governments, such as France (CTV News November 15 2020). While most western banks tend to focus on oil and natural gas projects, several major Chinese, Japanese, and American banks are funding the continued development of coal projects in countries still heavily dependent on this fuel as a major source of electricity and/or export earnings. In their annual fossil fuel finance report, the Rainforest Alliance and partners (RAN et al. 2020) provide a detailed list of 35 international banks and their investments of $2.7 trillion in the four years following the Paris Accord. Included in this listed was financing directed at oil sands, Arctic oil and gas, offshore oil and gas, fracked oil and gas, liquified natural gas, coal mining, and coal power.

To retard this trend toward greater fossil fuel production, particularly in the coal sector, the G7 nations agreed in June 2021 to stop international funding of any coal-fired power stations that lacked technology for carbon capture and storage, although there was no agreement on a specific end date for the use of coal (*New York Times* June 14, 2021). It has been reported that the G7 ministers were heavily influenced by a recent report on pathways to net zero from the International Energy Agency (IEA 202: 21), which concludes that "Beyond projects already committed as of 2021, there are no new oil and gas fields approved for development in our pathway, and no new coal mines or mine extensions are required." However, China was not included in the agreement about coal by the major western industrialized countries and, since China consumes more than half the world's coal, the potential impact of this agreement remains to be seen.

The year 2020 was a watershed for fossil fuel companies as many, such as Shell, Exxon, Chevron, and BP, downgraded their assets by $87 billion in nine months (Reuters June 30, 2020; *The Guardian* August 14, 2020) and lost billions of dollars resulting from the negative impact of the COVID pandemic on energy prices as a result of the declining demand for gasoline, diesel and jet fuel (*New York Times* December 10, 2020; February 2, 2021). This raised expectations that a major strategic realignment might occur in the fossil fuel industry away from their traditional reliance on oil and natural gas. BP did take the unprecedented step of writing-off $17.5 billion in assets not only from the effect of COVD-19 but also because of recognition of potentially stranded assets in the future (*Oil Change International* June 16, 2020). It has also been reported that oil and gas companies in North American and Europe wrote down roughly $145 billion in the first three quarters of 2020 (*Wall Street Journal* December 27, 2020). The steep drop in global CO_2 emissions which accompanied this decline in energy demand also suggested that the fossil fuel industry, and the world, might be on a new path to a more sustainable energy future. Unfortunately, the International Energy Agency reported on March 2, 2021a that global emissions of carbon dioxide have rebounded sharply (IEA 2021a), suggesting that "we are returning to carbon-intensive business-as-usual." (see also *The Guardian* July 16, 2023).

On balance, it is easy to understand why a corporation would be reluctant to abandon a business model that has proved to be so remunerative for decades. However, it is difficult to imagine a starker example of the divergence between private and social costs and benefits than is provided by the business decision to continue down the same path, potentially increasing even further the emissions of greenhouse gases and resulting global warming. The problem is compounded by the existence of corporate incentive structures that "trap companies in a loop of fossil growth" (Carbon Tracker, 2020a, 2020c, 2020b). As Kenner and Heede (2021: 9) observe in their study of the role of compensation in BP, Chevron, ExxonMobil, and Shell:

> what the executives and directors share in common is a desire to maintain demand for oil and gas, and to defend their company's social license to operate. They are paid to run fossil fuel supply chains - with large greenhouse gas emissions.

Several recent events may change the current path of fossil fuel development, even if at a relatively slow pace. In May and June 2021, three climate activists were elected to the board of ExxonMobil, much to the surprise of management (*New York Times*, June 2, 2021). To quote the *Times* (May 26, 2021):

> The success of the campaign, led by a tiny hedge fund against the nation's largest oil company, could force the energy industry to confront climate change and embolden Wall Street investment firms that are prioritizing the issue. Analysts could not recall another time that Exxon management had lost a vote against company-picked directors.

The *Times* also described the unusual confluence of events which led to this outcome (*New York Times* June 9, 2021):

> an activist investor successfully waged a battle to install three directors on the board of Exxon with the goal of pushing the energy giant to reduce its carbon footprint. The investor, a hedge fund called Engine No. 1, was virtually unknown before the fight. The tiny firm wouldn't have had a chance were it not for an unusual twist: the support of some of Exxon's biggest institutional investors. BlackRock, Vanguard and State Street voted against Exxon's leadership and gave Engine No. 1 powerful support. These huge investment companies rarely side with activists on such issues.

Nevertheless, another article by the *New York Times* (May 27, 2021) presented a some-what more somber appraisal of the potential consequences:

> But it is not clear if the activists can deliver on their dual goals – reducing the emissions that are warming the planet and lifting the profits and stock price of Exxon. The potential tensions between those objectives could doom the investor effort to transform the company and the oil industry. Getting Exxon, a behemoth company with $265 billion in revenue in 2019 and oil and gas fields around the world, to switch to cleaner energy will be a yearslong and difficult process. It is unlikely to produce quick returns and could sap profits for a while as the company spends a small fortune to retool itself. And the biggest investment firms, which lent critical support to the activists and control a lot of Exxon's stock, may be too timid to keep the pressure on company executives and board members who are determined to resist big changes.

Perhaps, more significant was the decision of a Dutch court ordering Royal Dutch Shell to cut its carbon dioxide emissions by 45% by 2030 from 2019 levels (*The Guardian* May 26, 2021; CNN May 26, 2021). This ruling was preceded by a shareholder rebellion at Shell over the credibility of its plans to reduce GHGs led by Britain's biggest fund manager, Legal & General Investment Management (*The Guardian* May 24, 2021). It is hoped that the shareholder-led activism and the court decision may set a precedent influencing the behaviour of other major polluters.

Adding further impetus to this reorientation of corporate strategic direction has been the recent decision of 17 major British insurance companies to support the transition to a less carbon-intensive economy by "expanding insurance coverage for projects such as off-shore windfarms, and partnering with governments to provide better disaster protection cover in countries facing serious risks like extreme weather caused by global heating" (*The Guardian* June 24, 2021). Foremost among these companies is Lloyd's, the world's biggest insurance market, which decided in late 2020 to quit fossil fuel insurance by 2030 (*The Guardian* December 17, 2020). This shift in attitudes in the financial community was also reflected in a recent letter signed by 450 major investors, managing more than $41 trillion in assets, calling on governments to set more ambitious emission reduction targets focusing on decarbonizing pollution -intensive industry and implementing mandatory climate risk disclosure requirements (CNN June 10, 2021).

References

Ansar, Atif, et al. (2013) *Stranded Assets and the Fossil Fuel Divestment Campaign: Report*, Smith School of Enterprise and the Environment, Oxford University

Apparel Coalition (n.d.) "The Higg index," https://cascale.org/resources/publications/summary-report-higg-index-tools-analysis-and-compliance-initiatives/?page&publication=summary-report-higg-index-tools-analysis-and-compliance-initiatives&post_type=publication

Banerjee, Neela, et al. (2015) *Exxon: The Road Not Taken*, Inside Climate News.

BBC (2020) "Climate change – Study pours cold water on oil company net zero claims," May 11.

B Lab (2018) "Patagonia and B Corp Community co-create a new model of capitalism," September 6, https://usca.bcorporation.net/zbtcz9z23zpatagonia-and-b-corp-community-co-create-a-new-model-of-capitalism/

Besser, Linton (2021) "Dead white man's clothes," ABC News, August 11.

Bloomberg (2020) "BP's clean energy push starts with five-year dash on solar, wind," September 16.

Bloomberg (2020) "Exxon's plan for surging carbon emission revealed in leaked documents," October 5.

Bloomberg (2020) "Exxon's plan for surging carbon emissions revealed in leaked documents," October 5.

BP (2020) "BP sets ambition for net zero by 2050, fundamentally changing organisation to deliver," February 12.

Brulle, Robert J. (2014) "Institutionalizing delay: foundation funding and the creation of U.S. climate change counter-movement organizations," *Climate Change*, 122:681–694.

Brulle, Robert J. (2018) "The climate lobby – a sectoral analysis of lobbying spending on climate change in the USA, 2000 to 2016," *Climate Change*, July 19.

Caldecott, Ben, et al. (2014) "Stranded assets and scenarios," Discussion Paper, School of Enterprise and the Environment, Oxford University, January.

Caldecott, Ben, et al. (2015) *Stranded Assets and Subcritical Coal – The Risk to Investors and Companies, School of Enterprise and the Environment*, Oxford University, March.

Carbon Tracker (2018) Press release. "42% of global coal power plants run at a loss, finds world-first study."

Carbon Tracker (2019*) Breaking the Habit.*

Carbon Tracker (2020a) *Fanning the Flames*, March.

Carbon Tracker (2020b) *Fault-Lines: How Diverging Oil and Gas Company Strategies Link to Stranded Asset Risk*, October.

Carbon Tracker (2020c) *Groundhog Pay*, December

Carbon Tracker (2020d) *How the Mighty are Fallen*, October.

CBS News (2020) "Exxon Mobil dropped from the Dow after nearly a century," August 25.

Cline, Elizabeth (2012) *Over-Dressed: The Shockingly High Cost of Cheap Fashion*, Portfolio.

CNN (2021) "Court orders Shell to slash CO_2 emissions in landmark climate ruling," May 26.

CNN (2021) "Investors holding $41 trillion demand action on climate – now," June 10.

Council for Textile Recycling (n.d.) "The facts about textile waste."

Cox, Kieran D., et al. (2019) "Human consumption of microplastics," *ES&T*, June 5.

CTV (2020) Public money guarantees 'risky' fossil fuel projects: experts," November 15

Dauvergne, Peter (2018) *Will Big Business Destroy Our Planet?* Polity Press.

Dauvergne, Peter & Jane Lister (2012) "Big brand sustainability: governance prospects and environmental limits," *Global Environmental Change*, 22: 36–45.

Dauvergne, Peter & Jane Lister (2013) *Eco-Business: A Big Brand Takeover of Sustainability*. MIT Press.

Ditz, Daryl, et al. (Eds.) (1995) *Green Ledgers: Case Studies in Corporate Environmental Accounting*, World Resources Institute, Washington, D.C.

The Economist (2019) "Bigger oil," February 9.

Emblemsvag, Jan & Bert Bras (2001) *Activity-Based Cost and Environmental Management*, Springer.

FastCompany (2012) "When Unilever bought Ben & Jerry's: A story of CEO adaptability," August 14.

Forbes (2017) "Fast fashion is a disaster for women and the environment," July 26.

Forbes (2019) "Oil and gas giants spend millions lobbying to block climate change policies," March 25.

Franta, Benjamin (2018) "Letter. Early oil industry knowledge of CO_2 and global warming," *Nature Climate Change*, December 18.

Geres.eu (n.d.) "Fueling the low carbon development of Cambodian manufacturing industries."

Global Energy Monitor (2020*) Gas Bubble: Tracking Global LNG Infrastructure.*

Global Witness (2019) *Overexposed: How the IPCC's 1.5C Report Demonstrates the Risk of Overinvestment in Oil And Gas*, April 23.

Grist (2024) "Burn after wearing," January 4.

The Guardian (2017) "Microfibers are polluting our food chain. This laundry bag can stop that," February 12.

The Guardian (2019) "Revealed: Mobil sought to fight environmental regulation, documents say," June 12.

The Guardian (2020) "Royal Dutch Shell may fail to reach green energy targets," January 3.

The Guardian (2020) 'BP's statement on reaching net zero by 2050 – what it says and what it means,' February.

The Guardian (2020) "Shell Unveils plans to become net-zero carbon company by 2050," April 16.

The Guardian (2020) "Seven top oil firms downgrade assets by $87bn in nine months", August 14.

The Guardian (2020) "Lloyd's market to quit fossil fuel insurance by 2030," December 17.

The Guardian (2021) "Court orders Royal Dutch Shell to cut carbon emissions by 45% by 2030," May 26.

The Guardian (2021) "Influential investor joins shareholder rebellion over shell's climate plan," May 24.

The Guardian (2021) "Top insurers join Prince Charles to fight climate crisis," June 24.

The Guardian (2021) "ExxonMobil lobbyist filmed saying oil giant's support for carbon tax a PR ploy," June 30.

The Guardian (2023) "We've lost the right to be pessimistic': Patagonia treads a fine line tackling climate change as a for-profit company," March 12.

The Guardian (2023) "'It's like a death pit': Ghana became fast fashion's dumping ground," June 5.

The Guardian (2023) "Big oil quietly walks back on climate pledges as global heat records tumble," July 16.

The Guardian (2024) "'A Trojan horse of legitimacy': Shell launches a 'climate tech' advertising jobs in oil and gas," February 26.

The Guardian (2024) "Oil industry has sought to block state backing for green tech since 1960s," March 8.

The Guardian (2024) "France's lower house votes to limit 'excesses' of fast fashion with environmental surcharge," March 15.

H&M (2017, 2019 and 2022) *Sustainability Performance Report*.

H&M (2020) *Annual Report*.

H&M (n.d.) "Interview with Anna Gedda, Head of Sustainability," https://hmgroup.com/our-stories/interview-with-anna-gedda/

Hartline, Niko L., et al. (2016) "Microfiber masses recovered from conventional machine washing of new or aged," *ES&T*, September 30.

Hobson, John (2013) "To die for? The health and safety of fast fashion," *Occupational Medicine*, June 63(5):317–9

Huff Post (2019) "28 Years Ago, Big Oil Predicted It Would Take A High Price On Carbon To Stop Warming," December 3.

Huff Post (2019) "Fossil Fuel Giants Claim To Support Climate Science, Yet Still Fund Denial," December 24.

Huff Post (2020) "Revealed/ BP And Shell Back Anti-Climate Lobby Groups Despite Pledges," September 28.

Huff Post (2021) "Despite its pledges, Shell funded Anti-climate lobbying last year," February 25.

Humes, Edward (2011) *Force of Nature. The Unlikely Story of Walmart's Green Revolution*, New York: Harper Business.

The Independent (2018) "The environmental costs of fast fashion," January 8.

Influence Map (2019) *Big Oil's real agenda on climate change*.

InsideClimate News (2015) "Exxon's own research confirmed fossil fuels' role in global warming decades ago," September 16.

Insider (2016) "The US may be releasing over 64,000 pounds of tiny synthetic clothing fibers int the water every day," November 1.

International Energy Agency (IEA) (2020) "The Oil and Gas Industry in Energy Transitions. Insights from IEA analysis."

International Energy Agency (IEA) (2021a) "After steep drop in early 2020, global carbon dioxide emissions have rebounded strongly," March 2.

International Energy Agency (IEA) (2021b) *Net Zero by 2050. A Roadmap for the Global Energy Sector*.

International Renewable Energy Agency (IRENA) (2017) *Stranded Assets. How the energy transition affects the value of energy reserves, buildings and capital stock*, July.

Jakob, Michael & Jerome Hilaire (2015) *Nature*, "Unburnable fossil-fuel reserves," January 8.

Kaplan, Robert & Steven Anderson (2007) *Time-driven activity-based costing*, Harvard Business Review Press.

Kenner, Dario & Richard Heede ((2021) "White knights or horsemen of the apocalypse? Prospects for Big Oil to align emissions with a 1.5C pathway," *Energy Research & Social Science*, April 15.

Kitchin, Rachel & Xixi Zhang (2023) *Fossil-Free Fashion Scorecard 2023*, Stand.earth.

McGlade, Christophe & Paul Ekins (2015) "The geographical distribution of fossil fuels unused when limiting global warming to 2C," *Nature*, January 8.

McKinsey (2021) "Global oil outlook to 2040," February.

Michaels, David (2008) *Doubt is Their Product: How Industry's Assault on Science Threatens Your Health*, Oxford University Press.

Mishra, Sunandr, et al. (2019) "Marine microfiber pollution – a review on present status and future challenges," *Marine Pollution Bulletin*, 140, 188–197.

Monbiot, George (2019) "Shell is not a green saviour. It's a planetary death machine," *The Guardian*, June 26.

Napper, Imogen E. & Thompson (2016) "Release of synthetic microplastic fibres from domestic washing machines: effects of fabric type and washing conditions," *Marine Pollution Bulletin*, November.

Nasdaq (2019) "Exxon aims to sell $25 billion of assets to focus on megaprojects – sources," November 21.

NBC (2018) "Ford to Stop Making All Passenger Cars Except the Mustang," April 26.

Nemetz, Peter N. & Marilyn Hankey (1984) *Economic Incentives for Energy Conservation*. New York: John Wiley & Sons.

New York Times (2010) "Clothes discarded by H & M in Manhattan are first destroyed," January 5.

New York Times (2010) "A clothing clearance where more than just the price has been slashed," January 5.

New York Times (2016) "Peabody energy, a coal giant, seeks bankruptcy protection," April 13.

New York Times (2018) "'Mustang means freedom': Why Ford is saving an American icon," May 24.

New York Times (2018) "H&M, a fashion giant, has a problem/ $4.3 billion in unsold clothes," March 27.

New York Times (2018) "Opinion: Why is a 'green' car company pivoting back to S.U.V.'s? May 1.

New York Times (2018) 'The real cost of cheap shirts," April 21.

New York Times (2018) H&M, a fashion giant, has a problem: $43 billion in unsold clothes," March 27.

New York Times (2019) "New York loses climate change fraud case against Exxon Mobil," December 10.

New York Times (2020) "'Is Exxon a survivor?': The oil giant is at a crossroads," December 10.

New York Times (2020) "How one firm drove influence campaigns nationwide for Big Oil," November 11.

New York Times (2020) "US and European oil giants go different ways on climate change," September 22.

New York Times, (2020) "When will electricity companies finally quit natural gas?" November 12.

New York Times (2021) "After a bruising year, the oil industry confronts a diminished future," February 2.

New York Times (2021) "Oil giants win offshore wind leases in Britain," February 8.

New York Times (2021) "Ford says it will phase out gasoline-powered vehicles in Europe," February 17.

New York Times (2021) "Biden's push for electric cars – $174 billion, 10 years and a bit of luck," March 31.

New York Times (2021) "Climate activists defeat Exxon in push for clean energy," May 26.

New York Times (2021) "Activists crashed Exxon's Board, but forcing change will be hard," May 27.

New York Times (2021) "Exxon board to get a third activist pushing cleaner energy," June 2.

New York Times (2021) "Exxon's board defeat signals the rise of social-good activists," June 9.

New York Times (2021) "G7 nations take aggressive climate action, but hold back on coal," June 14.

New York Times (2021) "In video, Exxon lobbyist describes efforts to undercut climate action," June 30.

Niinimaki, Kirsi, et al. (2020) "The environmental price of fast fashion," *Nature Reviews. Earth & Environment*, April 7.

Oil Change International (2020) "'Historic moment' as BP writes-off billions of reserves as stranded assets," June 16.

Oreskes, Naomi & Erik M. Conway (2010) *Merchants of Doubt: How A Handful of Scientists Obscured the Truth on Issues from Tobacco Smoke to Global Warming*, Bloomsbury Publishing.

Otto, Shawn (2016) *The War on Science: Who's Waging It, Why It Matters, What We Can Do about It*. Milkweed Editions.

Oxford Smith School of Enterprise and the Environment (2013) "Stranded assets and the fossil fuel divestment campaign: what does divestment mean for the valuation of fossil fuel assets?" Stranded Assets Programme, October.

Oxford Smith School of Enterprise and the Environment (2014) "Stranded assets and scenarios," Discussion Paper, Stranded Assets Programme.

Oxford Smith School of Enterprise and the Environment (2015) "Stranded assets and subcritical coal. The risk to companies and investors," Stranded Assets Programme, March.

Dilley, Maura (2014) "Patagonia 's new, decentralized approach to sustainability management," Triple Pundit, November 23.

Patagonia (2018) "Our business and climate change," patagonia.com

Patagonia (2019) "How we're reducing our carbon footprint," September 18.

PCI Wood Mackenzie (2017) *Fibre Global Supply Demand Report 2017*.

Quantis (2018) "Guiding insights for the fashion industry."

Rainforest Action Network, et al. (RAN) (2020) *Banking on Climate Change: Fossil Fuel Finance Report 2020*.

Reuters (2018) "New York sues Exxon for misleading investors on climate change risk," October 24.

Reuters (2020) "BP's green energy targets will be tough to meet," August 9.

Reuters (2020) "Shell to cut asset values by up to $22 billion after coronavirus hit," June 30.

Reuters (2020) "Global LNG projects jeopardized by climate concerns, pandemic delays – report," July 6.

Royal Dutch Shell (2021) "Shell accelerated drive for net-zero emissions with customer-first strategy," February 11.

Sarkis, Joseph (2010) *Greening the Supply Chain Eco-Efficiency*, Springer.

Scott, Lee (2005) "Twenty First Century Leadership," October 24, http://walmartwatch.com/wp-content/blogs.dir/2/files/pdf/21st_Century_Leadership.pdf

Stockholm Environment Institute (SEI), et al. (2023) *Phasing Down or Phasing Up?: Production Gap Report 2023*.

Supran, G. & N. Oreskes 2017 "Assessing ExxonMobil's Climate Change Communications 1977–2014," *Environmental Research Letters*, 12(084019).

Taplin, Ian M. (2014a) 'Global commodity chains and Fast Fashion: How the apparel industry continues to re-invent itself'," *Competition and Change*, 18/3: 246–64.

Taplin, Ian M. (2014b) 'Who is to blame? A re-examination of Fast Fashion after the 2013 factory disaster in Bangladesh," *Critical Perspectives on International Business*, 10/1–2: 72–83.

Textile World (2015) "Man-made fibers continue to grow," February 3.

Tonle (2018) "What is fast fashion, and why is it a problem?" Tonle.com.

UNECE (2018) "Fashion is an environmental and social emergency, but can also drive progress towards the Sustainable Development Goals."

Unilever (2019) "Ben & Jerry's: joy for the belly and soul since 1978." (Unileverusa.com)

Walmart (2016) *Global Responsibility Report*. https://s201.q4cdn.com/262069030/files/doc_financials/2016/ar/WMT_2016GRR.pdf

Walmart (2023) "Environmental, social and governance highlights, FY 2023."

Walmart (n.d.) "Supplier sustainability assessment – full packet."

Wall Street Journal (2020) "2020 was one of the worst-ever years for oil write-downs," December 27.

Wang, Pei, et al. (2019) 'Estimate of the social cost of carbon: a review based on meta-analysis," *Journal of Cleaner Production*, February 1.

Wards (multiple years) *Motor Vehicle Facts and Figures*, Ward's Communications.

Watts, Jonathan (2020) "BP's statement on reaching net zero by 2050 – what it says and what it means," *The Guardian*, February 12.

The Week (2021) "Shell/Ubitricity: charging ahead," January 30.

Appendix Excerpts from New York State's Lawsuit against ExxonMobil (October 2018)

Nature of the Action

1. This case seeks redress for a longstanding fraudulent scheme by Exxon, one of the world's largest oil and gas companies, to deceive investors and the investment community, including equity research analysts and underwriters of debt securities (together, "investors"), concerning the company's management of the risks posed to its business by climate change regulation. Exxon provided false and misleading assurances that it is effectively managing the economic risks posed to its business by the increasingly stringent policies and regulations that it expects governments to adopt to address climate change. Instead of managing those risks in the manner it represented to investors, Exxon employed internal practices that were inconsistent with its representations, were undisclosed to investors, and exposed the company to greater risk from climate change regulation than investors were led to believe.

2. For years, and continuing through the present, Exxon has claimed that, although it expects governments to impose increasingly stringent climate change regulations, its oil and gas reserves and other long-term assets face little if any risk of becoming stranded (i.e., too costly to develop or operate) due to those regulations, and reassured investors that it would be able to profitably exploit those assets well into the future. In particular, to simulate the impact of future climate change regulations, Exxon has claimed that, since 2007, it has rigorously and consistently applied an escalating proxy cost of carbon dioxide (CO_2) and other greenhouse gases (together, "GHGs") to its business, including in its investment decisions, business planning, company oil and gas reserves and resource base assessments, evaluations of whether long-term assets are impaired (i.e., have net present value lower than book value), and estimates of future demand for oil and gas.

3. Exxon's proxy cost representations were materially false and misleading because it did not apply the proxy cost it represented to investors. This was especially true of investments with high GHG emissions, where applying the publicly represented proxy cost would have had a particularly significant negative impact on the company's economic and financial projections and assessments.

7. Exxon misled investors by presenting a deceptive analysis that concluded that the company faced little risk associated with a "two degree scenario," in which the production and consumption of fossil fuels is severely curtailed in order to limit the increase in global temperature to below two degrees Celsius compared to pre-industrial levels. Exxon's analysis of the costs associated with a two degree scenario was based on assumptions it knew to be unreasonable and unsupported by the sources upon which it purported to rely.

8. Exxon's fraud was sanctioned at the highest levels of the company.

11. When confronted with the negative impact to its economic and financial assessments that would result from applying proxy costs in a manner consistent with the company's representations to investors, Exxon's management directed the company's planners to adopt what an employee called an "alternate methodology." . . . By applying this "alternate methodology," Exxon avoided the "large write-downs" it would have incurred had it abided by its stated risk management practices, and failed to take into account "massive GHG costs" resulting from expected climate change regulation.

12. For example, Exxon's decision not to apply the publicly represented proxy costs in connection with fourteen oil sands projects in Alberta, Canada resulted in the understatement of those costs in the company's cash flow projections by approximately $30 billion CAD (Canadian dollars), or more than $25 billion USD (US dollars). For one of these projects, an investment at Kearl, a 2015 economic forecast shows that the company understated projected undiscounted costs of GHG emissions by as much as 94% – approximately $14 billion CAD ($11 billion USD) – by applying lower costs to GHG emissions than those publicly represented.

13. Exxon's decision not to apply the publicly represented proxy costs in its company oil and gas reserves assessments enabled the company to avoid "large write-downs" in reserves that it would have had to take had it abided by its public representations. For example, at Cold Lake, an oil sands asset in Alberta, the company's own planners noted that applying a proxy cost consistent with Exxon's public representations would shorten the asset's projected economic life by 28 years and reduce company reserves by more than 300 million barrels of oil equivalent – representing billions of dollars in lost revenues. When presented with these facts, Exxon management instructed the planners to apply a lower cost projection based on existing regulations, contrary to the company's public representations.

19. Through its fraudulent scheme, Exxon in effect erected a Potemkin village to create the illusion that it had fully considered the risks of future climate change regulation and had factored those risks into its business operations. In reality, Exxon knew that its representations were not supported by the facts and were contrary to its internal business practices. As a result of Exxon's fraud, the company was exposed to far greater risk from climate change regulations than investors were led to believe.

20. Indeed, rather than protecting against the risk of future climate change regulation by reducing investment in GHG-intensive assets, Exxon expanded its investments in such assets. Between 2008 and 2016, the percentage of Exxon's oil and gas development and production (i.e., upstream) projects in GHG-intensive heavy oil and oil sands increased from less than 20% to more than 30% in oil-equivalent barrels. This increased the GHG intensity of the company's upstream operations and, in turn, increased the company's exposure to future climate change regulation.

21. The State brings this action to enforce General Business Law § 352 et seq. (securities fraud) and Executive Law § 63(12) (persistent fraud or illegality), and for common law fraud.

Part 4
Special Topics

17 Internalizing Sustainability into Corporate Strategy

A fundamental prerequisite to internalizing sustainability into corporate strategy is to transform relevant ecological and social data into a form both recognizable to and usable by senior corporate decisionmakers. As discussed in chapter 14, Triple Bottom Line (TBL) accounting became the gold standard of sustainability reporting, allowing stakeholders the ability to gauge the degree of corporate success in achieving the elusive goal of sustainability – at least in theory. It has recently been supplemented, if not superceded, by the emergence of ESG reporting as discussed in chapter 2. The challenge is to transform the standalone reporting of environmental and social indicators into monetary values that can be compared with or ultimately unified with a corporation's financial statements. This is a formidable task, as there are several major conceptual complexities of monetizing just a few key environmental values, excluding a number of critical ecosystem services and social values (Nemetz 2022). This chapter describes some recent advances in this endeavor and promise of future progress.

In a pathbreaking article published in the *American Economic Review*, Muller et al. (2011) developed a theoretical framework for incorporating air pollution externalities into systems of national accounts. The research developed monetized industry-level estimates of environmental damages based on emissions of the six criteria pollutants (SO_2, NOx, VOC, NH_3, PM2.5, and PM10) then compared these results with the corresponding value added of 820 US industries. Not surprisingly, the industries with the largest gross external damages (GED) included coal-fired electric power generation (with a GED of $53.4 billion) followed by crop production, livestock production, and highway, street, and bridge construction. What is surprising, however, is that fact that seven industries had air pollution damages that exceed their value added. These industries were: solid waste combustion and incineration (with a GED/VA ratio of 6.72), petroleum-fired electric powered generation (5.13), sewage treatment facilities (4.69), coal-fired electric power generation (2.20), and dimension stone mining and quarrying (1.89). The authors cautioned the reader about the correct interpretation of these values. First, these damages were confined to air pollution; second, they did not address possible offsetting benefits (such as water pollution control from sewage treatment); and, third and perhaps most important, they did not suggest that the American economy would be better off without these industries. What the data did demonstrate, however, is that the level of pollution control in these industries was far below the social optimum (and, as such, the price of the product did not reflect the marginal cost of pollution). This critique even applies to the pollution reduction already achieved by the cap-and-trade system currently in place to address SO_2 and NOx emissions from US power plants.

DOI: 10.4324/9781003170754-21

At least two important conclusions emerge from this analysis. First, it is a confirmation of the central tenet of environmental economics that "getting the price right" is an essential prerequisite to achieve the socially optimal level of pollution control. Second is a realization that some form of environmental accounting is absolutely critical to bringing environmental and ecological values into both public sector and corporate strategic decision making. In recognition of this critical emerging issue, there has been a proliferation of textbooks on the subject. For example: Schaltegger and Burritt (2000), Bennett et al. (2003), Rikhardsson et al. (2005), Pahuja (2009), Baldarelli et al. (2018), Babbington et al. (2014, 2023).

Without a clear economic signal, society runs the very large risk of proceeding down the path of paying lip service to environmental issues but not addressing them in an efficient, effective, and comprehensive manner. This type of challenge applies equally to social values, and that is the subject of chapter 19.

This chapter borrows a fundamental distinction from the accounting literature to frame the discussion: the difference between financial and managerial accounting. The former is designed to signal critical corporate financial information to a company's many external stakeholders such as shareholders, suppliers, purchasers, insurance companies, banks, government regulatory agencies, and the general public. In contrast, the latter is designed to provide senior management with all the information required to make reasoned and efficient decisions concerning products manufactured and marketed, financing, logistics, and resource allocation in general. The next sections discuss these two sustainability-related accounting issues from both an external and internal perspective, bearing in mind that some signals are designed for both types of stakeholders.

Signalling External Stakeholders

As stated above, the critical challenge to assessing the performance of a firm with respect to sustainability is to align its private costs and benefits with their social costs and benefits. This is achieved through a process of monetization, albeit imperfect and incomplete, which takes the three distinct accounts of triple bottom line and/or ESG accounting and achieves some form of synthesis. Only then is it possible to determine whether a company or product is adding to or detracting from social value. Matthews and Lave (2003) provided a cogent rationale for this consolidation:

> If a company calculated its costs on the basis of social costs, it would see where it was imposing large costs on society and perhaps where it is likely to be regulated in the future. Using social costs would show the firm where corporate citizenship could contribute the most to environmental quality. Having social costs substantially greater than private costs indicates a possible problem.

The first question that comes to mind is why a company would choose to report data relating to sustainability. As chapter 2 demonstrated, virtually all the top companies in the US Fortune 500 have chosen to do just that. Figure 17.1, drawn from the work of Schaltegger and Wagner (2006), summarizes the most important factors that drive the decision to report. Figure 17.2 identifies the major external and internal stakeholders and to what propose this information is ultimately put. Several companies have attempted the consolidation of TBL, although this approach generally focuses on monetizing environmental values to the exclusion of more intractable social values. In the rest of this chapter several methodologies are described and examples are provided. It should be noted that some of these companies undertook this type of analysis as an experiment and have since moved on to ESG reporting, instead. This does not detract from the value of the methodologies per se. One company, described in this chapter, Puma, introduced its innovative methodology in 2011 and has continued to develop and use it to today.

Environmental Financial Statements

Table 17.1 which reproduces the last *Environmental Financial Statement* from Baxter Health (2012) reproduces not only direct environmental costs but also environmental income, savings, and cost avoidance. While not directly incorporated into the corporate profit and loss statement, the monetization of these values could easily permit this consolidation. Unfortunately, the company ceased producing these data in the following years and has focussed instead on the reporting, without monetization, of GHG emissions, energy use, waste management, and air pollution.

Table 17.1 Example of an Environmental Financial Statement

Environmental Costs (dollars in millions)	2011
Basic Program	
Corporate Environmental – General and Shared Business Unit Costs[2]	$2.1
Auditor and Attorney Fees	0.3
Energy Professionals and Energy Reduction Programs	1.2
Corporate Environmental – Information Technology	0.3
Business Unit/Regional/Facility Environmental Professionals and Programs	11.3
Pollution Controls – Operation and Maintenance	3.9
Pollution Controls – Depreciation	2.4
Basic Program Total	**$21.5**

Remediation, Waste and Other Response (proactive environmental action will minimize these costs)

Attorney Fees for Cleanup Claims and Notices of Violation	$0.2
Settlements of Government Claims	0.0
Waste Disposal	8.0
Carbon Offsets[3]	0.2
Environmental Fees for Packaging[4]	0.9
Environmental Fees for Electronic Goods and Batteries	0.1
Remediation/Cleanup – On-site	0.2
Remediation/Cleanup – Off-site	0.4
Remediation, Waste and Other Response Total	**$10.0**
Total Environmental Costs	**$31.5**

Environmental Income, Savings and Cost Avoidance (dollars in millions; see Detail on Income,

From Initiatives in Stated Year	
Regulated Waste Disposal	$0.3
Regulated Materials[5]	(0.6)
Non-hazardous Waste Disposal	(0.6)
Non-hazardous Materials[5]	(8.5)
Recycling (income)	5.1

(Continued)

Table 17.1 (Continued)

Environmental Income, Savings and Cost Avoidance *(dollars in millions; see Detail on Income,*

Energy Conservation	1.2
Water Conservation	(0.2)
From Initiatives in Stated Year Total[6]	$(3.3)
As a Percentage of Basic Program Costs	-15%
Cost Avoidance from Initiatives Started in the Six Years Prior to and Realized in Stated Year[6,7]	$39.3
Total Environmental Income, Savings and Cost Avoidance in Stated Year	$36.0

Detail on Income, Savings and Cost Avoidance from 2011 Activities *(dollars in millions)*

	Income and Savings
Regulated Waste Disposal Cost Reduction	$(0.2)
Regulated Waste Materials Cost Reduction	(1.5)
Non-hazardous Waste Disposal Cost Reduction	(0.6)
Non-hazardous Waste Materials Cost Reduction	(10.6)
Recycling Income	5.1
Energy Consumption Cost Reduction	(11.5)
Water Consumption Cost Reduction	(1.7)
Total	$(21.0)

Cost Avoidance Detail From Efforts Initiated in the Six Years Prior to Report

	2011
Regulated Waste Disposal	$0.8
Regulated Waste Materials	(2.0)
Non-hazardous Waste Disposal	1.5
Non-hazardous Waste Materials	4.6
Energy Consumption	29.9
Water Consumption	4.5
Total	$39.3

Derived from Howes (2004, p. 105)

For example, in its latest report (Baxter Health Corporate Responsibility Report 2022b) lists their GHG emissions from corporate operations in 2022 of 615,000 metric tons of CO_2e. When the scope of the analysis is broadened to include all 3 scopes, the total amount of CO_2 dramatically increases to 6,794,000 metric tons. It is possible to perform a back-of-the-envelope estimate of the environmental damage associated with these discharges. The challenge is to determine the cost of carbon that reflects these damages.

There are several candidate values for the cost of carbon that can act as a surrogate measure of these damages, including: carbon taxes, market value of carbon in cap-and-trade systems, and US EPA estimates of the social cost of carbon. The problem with using carbon taxes is that they vary markedly by country and are influenced by local political and economic conditions. For example, they range from the lowest in Ukraine with $0.82 per ton of carbon to the highest in Switzerland at $130.81 (Tax Foundation 2023). British Columbia, one of the first jurisdictions in North America to implement a

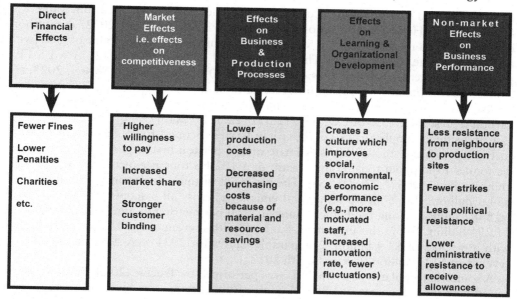

Figure 17.1 Important Factors Driving Corporations to Report on Sustainability

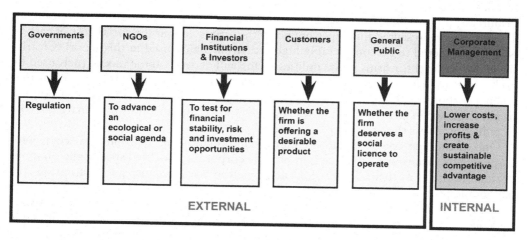

Figure 17.2 Major External and Internal Stakeholders

carbon tax has a current rate of $65 per tonne of CO_2e (Carbon Tax Center 2023). Cap and trade values tend to vary markedly over time depending on the number of extant permits and changing demand. In August 2023, California had a carbon price of $36.34 per metric ton (Bloomberg August 3, 2023), while a recent market value for permits in the European Union's Emissions Trading System (ETS) was 85.48 Euros per metric ton of carbon in September 2023 (Statista 2023). It may be more useful to use an estimate of the social cost of carbon established by the US EPA through an extensive process of consultation and review among economists and other experts. In 2022, this value was $51 per tCO_2. However, in a scholarly analysis by Rennert et al. (2022) the authors concluded that a more appropriate value may be as high as $185 per tonne of CO_2 (with a potential range of $44-$413). This was followed in November 2022, by a US EPA proposal to increase their previous estimate to $190 (Asdourian and Wessel, 2023; see also US EPA September 2022). In interpreting these divergent estimates, it is important to distinguish between the cost of CO_2 and carbon by itself. On an atomic weight basis, carbon represents 27.3% of CO_2 [i.e., $12.011/(12.011+(2x15.999))$].

Conducting a simple analysis of the cost of Baxter's Scope 1 CO_2 emissions of 615,000 metric tonnes using the US EPA's estimate of $51 per ton first requires converting metric tonnes to imperial tons. Using a ratio of 1.102 US tons per metric tonne yields an emission figure of 677,730 US tons. The net result of this calculation is a total value of $34.6 million. If one includes the total emissions across all 3 scopes, the value would be $382 million. Using the higher figure of $190 per metric ton would yield a value of $1.291 billion. To put this in context, Baxter Health's revenues in 2022 were $15 billion with a net loss of $2.4 billion. Comparable figures for 2021 were $1.3 net income on revenue of $12.8 billion (Baxter Health 2022a).

A somewhat similar type of analysis was performed by Trucost (2009) that attempted to estimate the percentage of EBITDA at risk from carbon costs by major sector. Using a price of $28.24 per metric ton, the report concluded that "carbon costs could almost halve their combined earnings" (Trucost 2009: 3). Clearly, the burden of these costs will vary by sector depending on their carbon intensity. The highest exposure was the utilities sector at almost 120% of EBITDA, followed by oil & gas (almost 100%), basic resources (about 95%), food and beverages (about 70%), and chemicals (about 30%). These values represented the upper bound of the estimates, but the social cost of carbon is now considered to be considerably higher than the figure used in this report. Clearly, the exposure level for firms in the utilities sector will depend on the mix of fuels used by each company. However, it is important to remember that economic theory tells us that when a corporation faces an external price for carbon either in the form of a carbon tax or market price in a cap-and-trade system, it will lower its emissions if its marginal cost of reduction is less than the price of carbon.

One of the first companies to attempt a consolidation of environmental costs with corporate financials was Interface Europe. The corporation focused specifically on monetizing the effects of their air emissions and opted to use avoidance and restoration cost methodology in order to simplify their calculations. Table 17.2 identifies the specific air pollutants and the valuation approach adopted for each, and Table 17.3 displays the consolidated results (Howes 2000). After deducting sustainability costs attributable to corporate air pollution emissions, operating income decreased from 17 million to 15.752 million UK pounds, an adjustment of approximately 7%. This latter figure was deemed a first pass estimate of environmentally sustainable profits. This experimental approach by Interface to reporting the degree of corporate sustainability has since been replaced with an emphasis on a list of sustainability metrics as well the lifecycle footprint of products and GHG emissions, as detailed in chapter 10, which Interface now feels presents a more accurate and comprehensive picture of their impacts and achievements (personal correspondence, November 2023). On their website, Interface originally chose to brand their approach to sustainability as "Mission Zero" but has since been replaced by a policy called "Climate Take Back" (see chapter 10).

Table 17.2 Identification of Air Pollutants and Valuation Methodology

Target	Approach	Details
Electricity consumption	premium of green electricity production over current rates	1 p per kWh on top of 4 p per kWh current rates
CO_2	Sequestering cost in forests - from current market price for warrants	5.45 UK pounds per tonne
NOx from manufacturing processes	end-of-pipe treatment costs	14,000 UK pounds per tonne
VOC from manufacturing processes	end-of-pipe treatment costs	7,200 UK Pounds per tonne
NOx and VOC from ground transport	cost of switching to LPG cars - note that while CO_2 is similar for LPG and gasoline-powered cars, NOx is reduced 40% and HC are reduced between 40 and 95%	1500 UK pounds per vehicle plus total annual fuel savings of 18,000 UK pounds
SO_2 from manufacturing processes	end-of-pipe treatment costs (thermal incineration, scrubbing)	2,400 UK pounds per tonne
PM (particulates)	electrostatic precipitators	2,800 UK pounds per tonne

Derived from Howes (2000)

Table 17.3 Interface Europe External Costs

Emissions	Tonnes	Units	Unit Cost	Totals
Natural Gas consumption of 26 million kWh equivalent				
CO_2	4,761	6	£28,566	
NOx	4	14,000	£56,000	
SO_2	4	2,400	£9,600	
Total				£94,166
Electricity consumption of 17 million kWh				
CO_2	7,537	n.a.		
NOx	20	n.a.		
SO_2	43	n.a.		
Total (avoidance)				£170,000
Direct Production emissionss				
NOx	3	n.a.		
SO_2	0	n.a.		
VO_c	17	n.a.		
CO	4	n.a.		
Total (avoidance)				£350,000
Transport distribution of 4.645 million kms				
CO_2	3,079	6	£18,474	
NOx	34	14,000	£476,000	
VO_c	1	7,200	£7,200	
CO	9	40	£360	
PM	2	2,800	£5,600	
Total Haulage/Distribution				£507,634

(Continued)

Table 17.3 (Continued)

Emissions	Tonnes	Units	Unit Cost	Totals
Transport (company cars) of 8.875 million kms				
CO_2	2,026	6	£12,156	
NOx (50 percent of 2)	1	14,000	£14,000	
VO_C	low	7,200		
PM	low	2,800		
LPG Net Conversion costs			£265,000	
LPG Annual Fuel Savings			-£283,000	
Net			-£18,000	
Total Cars				£22,000
Air travel of 6.397 million kms				
CO_2	1,215	6	£7,290	
NOx	4	14,000	£56,000	
Total air travel				£63,290
Rounding				£41,000
Total Sustainability Cost				£1,248,090
Operating Income per the financial Accounts				£17,000,000
Environmentally sustainable profits				£15,751,910

Howes (2000, p. 234 [reproduced with permission of Edward Elgar Ltd])

Table 17.4 displays the approach to consolidation adopted by Wessex Water Services (2004) in the United Kingdom. The adjustment for environmental costs was approximately 6%, similar in magnitude to initial estimates by Interface. In a recent report entitled *Sustainability Indicators and Accounting 2017–2018*, Wessex Water stated that:

> Since 2002 we have produced accounts that enable a wider view of our sustainability. Firstly, they provide a monetary assessment of environmental effects that are not typically dealt with through investment or some other payment. Secondly, they summarise our expenditure on items relevant to sustainability in its broader sense.

Their net operating emissions for 2017–2018 were 122,000 tonnes CO_2e, a decrease of 15,000 tonnes from the previous year. In their conclusion to the report, they stated that "the monetary cost of our greenhouse gas emissions using shadow prices, based on guidance from the Department for Energy and Climate Change, would be £0.5m [GBP] using traded carbon values and £8.0m [GBP] using nontraded carbon values." To place this in context. Wessex Water achieved a profit of 122.8m GBP on revenue of 540.6m GBP (Wessex Water 2018a).

Even though Wessex Water no longer produces this type of report, they have currently published an innovative report describing their "Sustainable Finance Framework" (2022). In this report, they lay out their strategy to achieve net zero carbon by 2030 with an array of policy options from most preferable (avoiding emissions) to least preferable (buying offsets). They have divided their route map into three groups: business-as-usual, readily available options, and innovative technology (see Figure 17.15). Also presented is a matrix that displays the linkages (both direct and indirect) between 14 outcome measures and the 17 UN Sustainable Development Goals. The rationale for their framework is described as follow:

> The Sustainable Finance Framework aligns our purpose and our business plan commitments to our financing ambitions through the use of targeted financing. We intend to finance key projects and assets that are fundamental to our purpose and which will deliver tangible environmental and social benefits on an individual and/ or combined basis, in addition to achieving global targets formalised by the Paris Agreement on Climate Change, and contributing to the United Nations' Sustainable Development Goals more broadly. . . . Under this Framework, the Wessex Water Group may issue green, social and/or sustainability debt instruments (individually or together, a "Sustainable Financing Instrument(s)") to support our environmental and social objectives, including but not limited to: green, social and/or sustainability bonds; green, social and/or sustainability private placements; and green and/or social loans.
>
> (Wessex Water 2018b, pp. 15–16)

A critical question facing a corporation that decides to signal its degree of sustainability to its stakeholders is to what degree this signaling is successful. There is empirical evidence to suggest that signals from third party sources, such as the US Toxic Release Inventory, can have an impact on stock prices (see Nemetz 2022), and that some opinion polls suggest that consumers are more willing to buy products deemed to be green (Fashion Network 2023).

Very little research has been conducted, however, to determine whether consumer perceptions accurately reflect corporate achievements. An initial test of this hypothesis was conducted by a Canadian research organization (MapChange 2008). The stated goal of the experiment was to clarify:

> how committed Canada's top brands are to the environment. And, how committed consumers think they are. In the world of branding, what is real is only what is perceived to be real. What a brand does, good or bad, only affects its value if those actions change consumer opinion.

The somewhat surprising results of this study are portrayed in Figure 17.3. If consumers had a correct perception of corporate sustainability performance, then one would expect to see the brands occupying only the lower left and upper right quadrants. In fact, a sizable number of corporations, many of which are multinationals with high brand recognition, appear to have a negative perception despite their reported high scores on sustainability.

While a promising attempt to address the question of the effectiveness of corporate communication of sustainability performance, the study raises several questions concerning the analytical methodology employed. While consumer attitudes were derived from a consumer attitude survey, the degree of corporate sustainability, against which consumer attitudes were compared, was based on four criteria: (1) *disclosure* (16%): a measure of the availability and readability of current information related to a company's environmental impact and programs; (2) *support* (18%): a measure of the amount of support a company provides for sustainability programs internally and within their

Table 17.4 Example Consolidation of Environmental Costs and Savings

Environmental cost component	Consumption	Emissions (gas)	Emissions (tonnes)	Target level (tonnes)	Difference (tonnes)	Cost / tonne to avoid impact (UK pounds sterling)	Impact cost 2000/2001 ('000 UK pounds sterling)
Fossil fuel grid electricity	181.2m kWh	CO_2	77,922	36,074	41,848	£5.50	-£230
		NOx	217	132	85	£14,000	-£1,190
		SOx	453	400	53	£2,400	-£127
Natural gas	19m kWh	CO_2	3,612	1,577	2,035	£5.50	-£11
Diesel oil	8.9m kWh	CO_2	2,247	616	1,631	£5.50	-£9
Methane		CO_2	63,963	28,753	35,210	£5.50	-£194
Vehicles		CO_2	6,999	2,176	4,823	£5.50	-£27
		Other	58	144	n.a.	n.a.	
Abstraction	Meeting Defra guidance onlow flow rivers at "priority 2" sites						-£1,850
Contaminated land	An estimated cost for dealing with land used for sewage disposal. The value is based on the current market cost for remediation						-£120
Environmental impact cost							-£3,758
Profit after tax							£63,300
Environmentally sustainable profit							£59,542

Source: Wessex Water (2004)

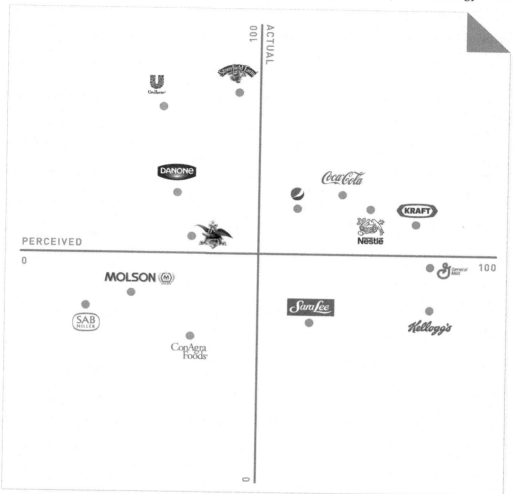

Figure 17.3 Matrix of Consumer Perceptions vs. Reality

Source: Change 2010, reproduced with permission

community; (3) *planning* (20%): a measure of the presence, validity and magnitude of a company's sustainability goals and initiatives; and (4) *performance* (46%): a measure of achievement in lessening environmental impact and achieving stated goals. With these measures, General Motors appeared to have had a better record of sustainability than Toyota. This somewhat counterintuitive conclusion may be the result of the experimental design that relied exclusively on self-reported corporate data rather than third-party certification. Correcting for this deficiency poses several challenges with respect to the availability of relevant information, but this alternative path offers the opportunity to revisit this question with a more powerful dataset. As of 2022, Change Adverting had not updated this analysis, but the principles of distorted consumer perceptions undoubtedly still hold, especially in the era of social media.

Signalling Management

In an insightful study from the World Resources Institute, Ditz et al. (1995) addressed the fundamental challenges that continue to face senior management in internalizing environmental costs into corporate decision-making. The basic thesis of their book was that the lack of recognition of the true magnitude and location of all environmental costs can cripple a firm and prevent it from making intelligent resource allocation decisions – either avoiding unnecessary costs or capitalizing on hidden revenue opportunities. The authors identified four major environment-related questions faced by senior corporate management: (1) What are their environmental costs? (2) How large are these costs? (3) Where do these costs arise within the organization? and (4) How can these costs be better managed? Most importantly, lack of information about these costs can foreclose important strategic opportunities for corporations.

Ditz et al. described how most corporate attention to environmental accounting has been generally concentrated on financial accounting, particularly on the significant liabilities arising from the remediation of contaminated property. However, pollution abatement and control represent only a portion of a firm's environmentally driven costs. Environmental costs associated with other activities can be much greater. For example, a company's choice of raw materials, manufacturing processes and product design can profoundly affect these costs. There are pathologies of traditional accounting practices in the face of environmental factors. Even to this day, many companies have no conception of the extent and location of environmental costs borne by the firm. Products with *relatively lower environmental costs* will subsidize those with higher environmental costs, and products with *relatively higher environmental costs* may appear profitable but impose significant environmental costs on other parts of the business, and such costs are not attributed to their original source. The result is a major distortion in the process of profit maximization through inefficient resource allocation decisions at the margin. Certain products or processes may be encouraged/discouraged based on such incorrect price signals within the corporation.

To illustrate their hypothesis, Ditz et al. cited the example of a small privately owned company in the Pacific Northwest that has served the global market for stained glass products. As anyone can attest who has visited some of the grand cathedrals in Europe, among the most visually striking components are stained glass windows with orange and red coloring. Artists have long relied on cadmium-based pigments to create these colors, yet cadmium and its compounds are exceedingly toxic, creating significant issues of hazardous solid waste and air emissions. Although ruby-red glass, which relies on cadmium-based pigments, generates more hazardous wastes than other colors, the company had allocated environmental costs equally across all its different glass products, and had not charged a premium for ruby-red glass. The company was paying approximately $3,500 per ton (about $32,500 a year) to dispose of its hazardous waste. The net result of the traditional accounting practice used by the company was that ruby-red glass appeared profitable while it was actually making a loss.

EMIS, EMS and EFS

The solution to the dilemma facing the manufacturer of stained glass is the creation of an *Environmental Management Information System (EMIS)* – that is, in turn, part of a much broader corporate *Environmental Management System (EMS)* that is defined as "organizational structure, responsibilities, practices, processes and resources for developing, implementing, achieving, reviewing and maintaining environmental policy" (Sheldon & Yoxon, 2002). To Thompson (2002: 20), the central purpose of an EMS is:

> to improve environmental performance by: setting goals and objectives (policy); identifying, obtaining, and organizing the people, skills, and knowledge, technology, finances, and other resources necessary to achieve the goals and objectives; identifying and assessing options for reaching the goals; assessing risks and priorities; implementing the selected set of options; auditing performance for necessary adjustments by providing feedback to the system; and applying the environmental management tools as required.

EMS procedures have been codified in ISO 14001 and have been extensively described in numerous works directed at middle and upper management (Sheldon & Yoxon 2002; Tinsley & Pillai 2012; Marguglio 2019; Haider 2019; Ashrafi et al. 2021). Some of the tools that form an integral part of an EMS are described in detail in this textbook. A critical component of an Environmental Management System is the *Environmental Financial Statement (EFS)* that allocates costs in a manner that allows a company to identify the location of its costs and opportunities for savings. Howes (2004) lists some of the basic components of a model EFS (see Table 17.5). To Matthews and Lave (2003), "a *reasonable* MIS tabulates current environmental costs and likely future liabilities and traces them to the material, product, and process generating them, allowing decision-makers to assess their current status." In contrast, "a *good* MIS would give decision-makers information about how environmental costs and liabilities would change if there were a change in materials, design, or process." At that time it was estimated that environmental costs could account for as much as 20% of total costs for some companies, depending on their products, production processes, and waste generation (Ditz et al. 1995; Henriques & Richardson 2004).

A recent study by Greenstone et al. (2023) of 15,000 public companies globally found average carbon damages equaling roughly 44% of firms' operating profits using a carbon price of $190 per ton of CO_2e. These estimated varied widely both within and across industries. For example, globally/(USA) corporate carbon damages as a share of profits in the energy sector are 382.9% (237.7%) for the 90th percentile firm and just 48% (4.5%) for the 10th percentile firm in the sector (Greenstone et al. (2023: 839).

An example of a good EMIS is presented in Table 17.6 that identified both environmental costs and offsetting environmental savings resulting from the identification and remediation of environmental costs by the Dartford and Gravesham Hospital in Kent, England (Howes 2003). Their most recent document addressing issues of sustainability (entitled *Dartford & Gravesham NHS Trust Green Plan 2021–2026*) provides a detailed discussion of their policy goals, action plan, path to net zero, and achievements so far. Trend data provide show corporate carbon emissions from energy down 22% from 2013 and down 9% for water use over the same period. The original EMIS was produced by a third party (Howes 2003) and there does not appear to be an updated version of the EMIS since that time, but the methodology continues to be relevant.

Some Methodologies for Cost Allocation

The critical issue is one of cost allocation, and there are several promising methodologies for recognizing and/or incorporating environmental costs into conventional

Table 17.5 Basic Components of an EFS

Environmental Costs

Costs of Basic Program
Environmental services (percentage of)
Environmental/energy coordinators, etc.
Business unit environmental programmes and initiatives (including personnel costs, professional
  fees, etc.) Waste minimization and pollution prevention - operations and maintenance
Waste minimization and pollution prevention - capital costs

Total costs of basic program

Remediation, waste and other cots
Fines and prosecutions
Waste disposal costs
Environmental taxes - e.g., landfill, climate levy
Remediation/clean-up costs
Other costs, etc.
Total remediation, waste and other costs

Total environmental Costs

Environmental Savings
Income, savings and cost avoidance from report year
Reduced insurance from avoidance of hazardous materials
Reduced landfill tax and other waste disposal costs
Energy conservation savings
Water conservation savings
Reduced packaging savings
Income from sale of recovered and recycled materials
Other savings, etc.

Total environmental savings
As a percentage of environmental costs

Summary of savings
Savings in report year
Savings brought forward from initiatives in prior years

Total income, savings and cost avoidance

Source: Derived from Howes 2004, p. 105

Table 17.6 Example EMIS

Environmental Costs	UK Pounds
Payroll and Labour costs	
Apportionment of technical service manager's and others' time	60,000
Other costs?	x
Costs of basic programme	60,000
Remediation, waste and other costs	
Waste disposal costs	250,000
Tree protection - metal fencing	7,500
Environmental taxes paid - landfill tax, other costs, etc.	x

(Continued)

Table 17.6 (Continued)

Environmental Costs	UK Pounds
Total remediation, waste and other costs	257,500
Total environmental costs	317,500
Environmental Savings	
Income, savings and cost avoidance	
Ground stabilization - net savings building materials avoided	111,500
Re-use of excavated material on-site - fuel costs avoided	-
Avoided landfill charges/waste disposal costs	50,000
Construction of drainage swale - avoided drainage infrastructure costs	20,000
Reduced landfill tax and other waste disposal costs	x
Income from sale of recovered and recycled materials	
Other savings, etc.	x
Total environmental savings	181,500
Savings as a percentage of environmental costs	57%

Source: Howes, 2003, p. 12, reproduced with permission of Chartered Institute of Management Accountants

Table 17.7 Reasons Why Environmental Costs and Performance are Relevant

(1) Many environmental costs can be significantly reduced or eliminated as a result of business decisions, ranging from operational and housekeeping changes, to investment in "greener" process technology, to redesign of processes/products. Many environmental costs (e.g., wasted raw materials) may provide no added value to a process, system, or product.

(2) Environmental costs (and, thus, potential cost savings) may be obscured in overhead accounts or otherwise overlooked.

(3) Many companies have discovered that environmental costs can be offset by generating revenues through sale of waste by-products or transferable pollution allowances, or licensing of clean technologies, for example.

(4) Better management of environmental costs can result in improved environmental performance and significant benefits to human health as well as business success.

(5) Understanding the environmental costs and performance of processes and products can promote more accurate costing and pricing of products and can aid companies in the design of more environmentally preferable processes, products, and services for the future.

(6) Competitive advantage with customers can result from processes, products, and services that can be demonstrated to be environmentally preferable.

(7) Accounting for environmental costs and performance can support a company's development and operation of an overall environmental management system. Such a system will soon be a necessity for companies engaged in international trade due to pending international consensus standard ISO 14001, developed by the International Organization for Standardization.

Source: US EPA 1995, pp. 1–2

financial analysis (see, for example, the discussion of full cost accounting in Blokdyk 2021a). These methodologies include, inter alia: activity-based costing (ABC); environmental profit and loss accounts (EP&L); genuine wealth accounting (GWA); sustainable balanced scorecard (SBC); and ratio-based financial models for sustainability. Each is briefly described below.

Table 17.7 summarizes seven reasons provided by the US EPA (1995) why environmental costs and performance are worthy of corporate attention. As indicated earlier, the first challenge is to identify all the types of environmentally related costs associated with corporate operations. Table 17.8 provides a listing of these costs identified by the US EPA under four general rubrics: conventional, potentially hidden, contingent, and image/relationship costs.

Table 17.8 Examples of Environmental Costs Incurred by Firms

Potentially Hidden Costs

Regulatory	*Upfront*	*Voluntary (Beyond Compliance)*
Notification	Site studies	Community relations/outreach
Reporting	Site preparation	Monitoring/testing
Monitoring/testing	Permitting	Training
Studies/modeling	R&D	Audits
Remediation	Engineering and procurement	Qualifying suppliers
		Reports (e.g., annual environmental reports)
Recordkeeping	Installation	Insurance
Plans	**Conventional Costs**	Planning
Training	Capital equipment	Feasibility studies
Inspections	Materials	Remediation
Manifesting	Labor	Recycling
Labeling	Supplies	Environmental studies
Preparedness	Utilities	R & D
Protective equipment	Structures	Habitat and wetland protection
Medical surveillance	Salvage value	Landscaping
Environmental		Other environmental projects
insurance	**Back-End**	Financial support to environmental groups and/or researchers
Financial assurance	Closure/	
Pollution control	decommissioning	
Spill response	Disposal of inventory	
Stormwater management	Post-closure care	
Waste management Taxes/fees	Site survey	

	Contingent Costs	
Future compliance costs	Remediation	Legal expenses
Penalties/fines	Property damage	Natural resource damages
Response to future releases	Personal injury damage	Economic loss damages

	Image and Relationship Costs	
Corporate image	Relationship with Professional staff	Relationship with lenders
Relationship with customers	Relationship with workers	Relationship with host communities
Relationships with investors Relationship with Insurers	Relationship with suppliers	Relationship with regulators

US EPA (1995, p. 9)

Activity-Based Costing

An important methodology to address the complex issue of cost allocation is material-flow-oriented, activity-based costing (ABC). There have been numerous books written on this methodology. See for example: Glad (2002), Leitner (2005), Kaplan and Anderson (2007), Zeuner (2008), Khurana (2015), Blokdyk (2021a, 2021b, and 2022) (see also chapter 5 for a discussion of mass and material balance calculations). In an early study, Schaltegger and Muller (1998) outlined the three-step allocation process in ABC, using as an example a production process that relied on an incinerator for waste disposal (see Figure 17.4): first, allocation from joint environmental cost centers (e.g., an incinerator) to *responsible* cost centers (i.e., production centers); second, from

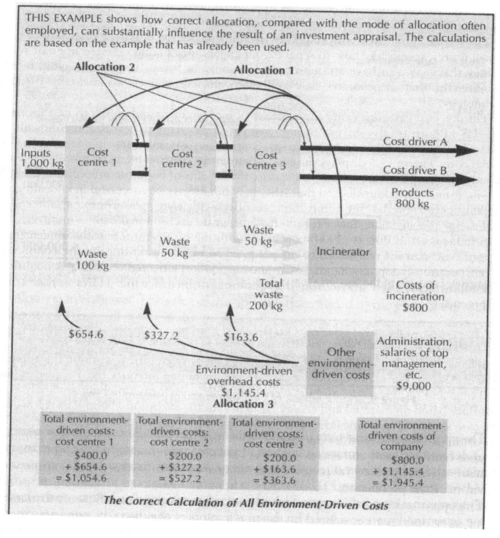

Figure 17.4 Example ABC

Source: Schaltegger and Muller 1998, reproduced wit permission

responsible cost centers to final cost objects (i.e., units of final products); and third, the allocation of other environmentally induced (i.e., indirect) costs to both cost centers and cost objects.

While conceptually simple, ABC encounters several practical complexities. The first is the choice of allocation keys that are critical to the analysis. Schaltegger and Muller identified four common keys: the volume of throughput (materials, emissions, and waste treated); the toxicity of emissions and waste treated; the environmental impact added (volume multiplied by the impact per unit of volume of the emissions treated); and the induced costs associated with treating different kinds of throughput (materials and emissions treated). There is no clear best alternative; the choice is situation dependent. Some authors felt, however, that a commonly used metric – namely, direct labor hours –can distort corporate decisions concerning the appropriate mix of factor inputs (Burritt 1998) and should be avoided in instances with environmental impacts.

The second complexity with respect to the implementation of ABC is related to capital expenditures, specifically how to separate out expenditures undertaken to upgrade technology that may also have an improved environmental effect designed to avoid future liabilities or that incorporates new and more efficient and environmentally friendly technology.

Thirdly, cost categories vary in their ease of measurement and ability to be allocated. The US EPA arrays five environmental cost categories from easiest to most difficult to measure: conventional costs, hidden costs, contingent costs, relationship/image costs, and social costs. Figure 17.5 displays the US EPA's four-tier cost and financial protocol recommended for corporations seeking to measure the benefits of pollution prevention (US EPA 1989). It must be acknowledged that ABC may not always be successful in allocating all relevant costs, and that the companion use of eco-efficiency measures (see chapter 3) is still useful as a signaling device for internal corporate decision making.

Schaltegger and Burritt (2000) concluded with the observation that the implementation of ABC and the realization of the potential costs and profit impacts are contingent on corporations adopting material-flow and energy-flow oriented ecological accounting. The following example drawn from the operations of Interface Inc. addresses both types of practices.

ABC Case Study: Interface Inc.

Emblemsvag and Bras (2001) published a comprehensive empirical work on the application of ABC in four major corporate case studies, including Interface Inc. Because of limited time and resources, the authors were only able to perform a preliminary analysis of Interface based on material and energy efficiency, to the exclusion of cost data. However, the case study yielded some insightful results that aided the corporation in its own analysis of the sustainability of its operations. The authors were able to track the complex flow of both materials and energy across six facilities, ten product lines, and forty-nine distinct activities. Table 17.9 presents their summary estimates of resource consumption based on 1997 product and process data. The most remarkable conclusion from this analysis was that over 91% of attributable energy consumption and 97% of attributable waste generation was associated with *material usage in production* (i.e., purchased inputs whose environmental impact is outside the boundaries of Interface's production operations). On reflection, however, this is not completely surprising as one important factor is Interface's reliance on synthetic fabrics that are highly energy intensive with respect to

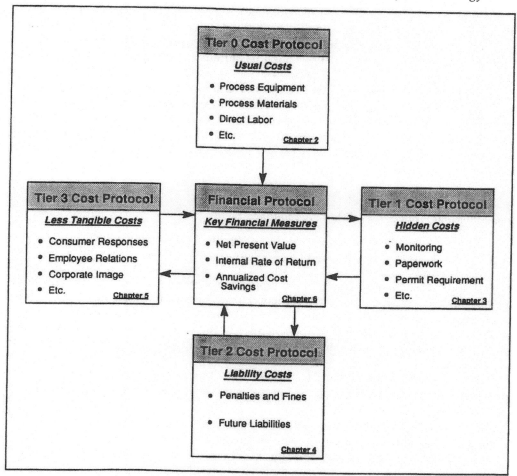

Figure 17.5 US EPA's Four-Tier Cost and Financial Protocol

Table 17.9 Interface's Summary Estimation of Resource Consumption

Resource Category	Energy consumption (MJ/year)	Waste Generation [pWU/year]
Depreciation and Maintenance	2,567,020	1,786
Buildings	344,008,015	700,917
Freight within Troup County	915,212	3,837
Material Usage in Production	3,637,859,399	23,827,025
Total	3,985,349,646	24,533,565

Source: Emblemsvag & Bras (2001, p. 214 [reproduced with permission])

production and embodied energy (see chapter 10). It is important to note, however, that the USA EPA's Toxic Release Inventory data on environmental releases from Interface's operations have shown significant plant-level improvements since the TRI commenced data gathering in 1987 (US EPA TRI n.d.).

In light of the important role of Interface's supply chain in the company's overall environmental impact, the challenge is to identify what technology and policy levers are available to the corporation in their goal of moving towards sustainability. Emblemsvag and Bras offered three possible initiatives: first, asking their suppliers to generate information on the embodied energy of their products (this is now an essential part of corporate attempts to identify and measure their Scope 3 emissions); second, shifting corporate purchasing decisions toward material with lower embodied energy; and third, increasing the role of recycling in order to reduce reliance on eternal supplies of raw materials. As outlined in chapter 10, Interface has made this a major component of their sustainability strategy as they attempt to close the loop in the manufacturing process.

Environmental Profit & Loss (EP&L) Accounting

The critical importance of the supply chain in the overall environmental impact of corporate operations has been graphically demonstrated by the development of a new methodology announced in 2011 by the German sportswear giant, Puma, the third largest sportswear manufacturer in the world. Developed in collaboration with PriceWaterhouseCoopers and the environmental research group, Trucost, Puma created and published what they termed an *Environmental Profit and Loss (EP&L)* statement in 2011. This analysis attempted to monetize all the company's major environmental and social impacts not only in the company itself but also throughout its extensive supply chain.

The results demonstrated that 94% of Puma's environmental costs were attributable to the production of raw materials in its supply chain. The PWC consultant observed that:

> fundamentally, this analysis is about risk management for the environment, and for business, because you cannot separate the two. . . . This is a first for a company to measure and value the impact of its business in this way and gives PUMA a unique and challenging insight into their supply chain. It's a game–changing development for businesses to integrate environmental issues into their current business model like this, because it provides a basis for embedding their reliance on ecosystem services into business strategy.
>
> (PUMA & PPR May 16, 2011)

The total environmental impact measured in the first phase of the multistage analysis yielded a figure of 145 million Euros. To place this in the context of total corporate operations, Puma had profits in 2010 of 202.2 million Euros on sales of 2,706.4 million Euros. It was proposed that the following phase would attempt the more conceptually challenging task of estimating the impact of social factors such as fair wages, safety and working conditions. Finally, the creation of an integrated profit-and-loss analogue that includes environmental, social and economic components requires the measurement of any offsetting benefits related to the creation of jobs, tax contributions, philanthropic initiatives, and other value-adding elements.

Puma focused initially on five environmental impacts: water use, GHGs, land use, air pollution, and waste. Three categorizations were used: (1) principal product lines,

(2) global markets by region, and (3) tiers in the supply chain. Puma core operations include offices, warehouses, stores, and logistics: Tier 1 is the manufacturing of corporate products; Tier 2 represents outsourced processes and inputs such as energy supply, embroiders, printers, and outsole production; Tier 3 is the processing of raw materials, such as leather tanneries, chemical industry and oil refining; and Tier 4 is raw material production, such as cotton cultivation and harvesting, natural rubber production, oil drilling, and cattle ranching for leather that represents the largest contribution to land-use impacts. The company also reported that the single most important contributor to air pollution was ammonia emissions from animal waste and fertilizers used in agricultural processes.

The development of this innovative methodology allowed Puma to structure its operations in a more sustainable manner and measure its degree of success on each of the component initiatives. A critical part of this reorientation of its business model and corporate strategy would clearly require extensive collaboration with suppliers (PUMA & May 16, 2011, p. 4):

> PUMA and PPR Home (its parent company) will look to play a catalytic role in raising awareness that the current business model is outdated and needs decisive reforms, forging partnerships and collaborations to explore new and innovative ways to differentially attribute the responsibilities and equitably share the costs of these, while building capacity at suppliers' factories and developing new materials and products. PUMA and PPR HOME are sharing the results of the EP&L with other industry players and corporations to leverage adopting a new business model that takes the costs of using natural resources within business operations into account. This analysis will also help to better assess the relative environmental impacts of sourcing from different countries and regions. Down the line it will allow PUMA to improve supply chain management and reduce supply chain risks.

In 2021, Puma (PUMA 2023) revised their EP&L methodology to reflect the fact that:

> many savings made by our Tier 1 and Tier 2 suppliers had not been captured by the EP&L methodology and for some of our major materials used, such as Better Cotton, no specific EP&L emission factors have been developed. . . . However we are still in the process of fully aligning our EP&L methodology for Tiers 3 and 4 with internal and external standards.

Table 17.10 lists Puma's ES&L results over the period of 2013–2022 and Table 17.11 is a summary table of PUMA's 2022 results by Tier and pollutant source. It clearly demonstrates that emissions from Tier 3 and 4 dominate the total impact This is consistent with most industry results where Tier 1 (and frequently Tier 2) capture only a fraction of a company's environmental impact. Puma also provides a breakdown of Scope 3 CO_2e emissions from selected value chain activities, including purchased goods and services, fuel and energy-related activities, upstream transportation and distribution, and business travel.

In summary, Puma's annual sustainability reports provide one of the most exhaustive analyses of sustainability data among major corporations and sets a benchmark for other companies to follow. Table 17.12 summarizes their sustainability targets and performance in 2022.

Table 17.10 Puma ES&L Time Series (million Euros)

	ES&L	Revenue	EBT
2013	432	2985.3	53.7
2014	421	2972.0	121.8
2015	441	3387.4	85.0
2016	457	3626.7	118.9
2017	511	4135.9	231.2
2018	585	4648.3	313.4
2019	711	5502.2	417.6
2020	441	5234.4	162.3
2021	530	6805.4	505.3
2022	549	8465.1	551.7

Data provided by PUMA

Table 17.11 Puma's ES&L Results for 2022 by Tier and Pollutant Source

PERCENTAGE

		Tier 0	Tier 1	Tier 2	Tier 3	Tier 4
	%	Own operations	Product manufacturing	Component manufacturing	Raw material processing	Raw material production
Air Pollution	8%	0.03%	0.79%	1.58%	4.82%	0.82%
GHG emissions	28%	2.04%	3.22%	4.38%	14.44%	4.16%
Land use	26%	0.00%	0.07%	0.03%	1.25%	24.44%
Water pollution	21%	0.03%	0.62%	1.18%	2.94%	16.66%
Water Use	14%	0.08%	0.11%	0.28%	4.53%	8.98%
Waste	2%	0.04%	0.91%	0.97%	0.34%	0.23%
TOTAL		2%	6%	8%	28%	55%

Data provided by PUMA

Genuine Wealth Accounting

Once a corporation has adopted a more comprehensive approach to reporting such as the Triple Bottom Line or ESG, there are several possible additional steps that may be useful in helping the company realize greater long-term sustainability and profitability. One of these is the adoption of a corporate *Genuine Wealth Model* (GWM) that is an outgrowth of the development of a sustainability index for public sector entities, such as cities (Anielski 2007). The GWM can incorporate physical, qualitative, and monetary conditions of five critical capital assets (i.e., financial, human, social, built, and natural) into the daily operation of an organization. To quote Anielski (2007: 155):

> such accounts inform directors, shareholders and communities about the effective rate of return to investment in all five capital assets and analyze the efficiency and effectiveness of total capital management. This includes evaluating the integrity or coordination of capital for sustained flows of benefits as well as the annual depreciation or depletion rate of capital.

Table 17.12 Puma's Sustainability Targets and Performance in 2022

Target Area	Targets For 2025	Performance 2022	Status
Human Rights	Target 1: Train 100,000 direct and indirect staff members on women's empowerment	168,037 factory workers and 2,077 PUMA employees trained	achieved
	Target 2: Map subcontractors and Tier 2 suppliers for human rights risks	Tier 2 mapping completed and 48 Tier 1 subcontractors mapped	on track
	Target 3: 25,000 hours of global community engagement per year	43,000 hours	achieved
Health and Safety	Target 1: Zero fatal accidents (PUMA and suppliers)	Zero fatal accidents at Puma, and Two fatal accidents at suppliers	in progress
	Target 2: Reduce accident rate to 0.5 (PUMA and suppliers)	0.3 injury rate at PUMA suppliers and 0.45 at PUMA	in progress
	Target 3: Building safety policy operational in all high-risk countries	ACCORD Bangladesh: Progress rate 91%, Signed ACCORD Pakistan, building safety assessments in 13 factories in Indonesia, India and Pakistan	on track
Chemicals	Target 1: Ensure 100% of PUMA products are safe to use	No product recall from the market	achieved
	Target 2: Maintain RSL compliance rate above 90% (target changed since 2020)	RSL compliance rate of 98.5%	achieved
	Target 3: Reduce organic solvent usage to under 10 gr/pair	VOC index at 13.2 g/pair	in progress
Water and Air	Target 1: 90% compliance with ZDHC Wastewater Guidelines	Conventional parameters: 98%; restricted chemicals 99%; heavy metals 99%	achieved
	Target 2: 90% compliance with ZDHC Air Emissions Guidelines	Our core Tier 1 and Tier 2 follow local regulations	in progress
	Target 3: 15% water reduction per pair or piece based on 2020 baseline	Textile: -5%; leather -17%; apparel -17%; footwear -36%	on track
Climate	Target 1: Align PUMA's climate target with 1.5 degrees global warming scenario	Applied to SBTi to approve new absolute GHG emission reduction: Scope 1 and 2 by 90%, Scope 3 by 33% in 2030	Scope 1&2 achieved; Scope 3 in progress
	Target 2: 100% renewable electricity for PUMA entities	100% renewable electricity used for PUMA entities (including RECs)	achieved
	Target 3: 25% renewable energy for core suppliers	11% for Tier 1 (finished goods); 10.8% for Tier 2 (Materials); 10.8% for Tier 2 (materials) (including RECs)	on track

(Continued)

Table 17.12 (Continued)

Target Area	Targets For 2025	Performance 2022	Status
Plastics and the Oceans	Target 1: Eliminate plastic bags from owned and operated PUMA stores	48% reduction compared to 2021 (189 tons), 99 tons in 2022, no more plastic bags used starting 1st January 2023	achieved
	Target 2: Support scientific research on microfibers	12 shedding tests conducted	on track
	Target 3: Research biodegradable plastics options for products	Launched RE:SUEDE as a test for biodegradability	in progress
Circularity	Target 1: Establish takeback schemes in all major markets	Hong Kong takeback scheme ongoing since 2019; US takeback ongoing (footwear) Germany (HQ), Manchester City, AC Milan, Borussia Dortmund and Olympique de Marseille rolled out, Australia rolled out	in progress
	Target 2: reduce production waste to landfills by at least 50% compared to 2020	-45% waste to landfill per footware pair; +1% waste to landfill per apparel piece	in progress
	Target 3: develop recycled material options for cotton, leather and rubber	recycled cotton and leather used in PUMA ReGen collection recycled rubber used	achieved
Products	Target 1: Procure 100% cotton, polyester, leather and down from certified sources	99.8% cotton; 70.4% polyester; 100% leather; 100% down	on track
	Target 2: Increase recycled polyester use to 75% (apparel & accessories)	51.5% recycled polyester for apparel and accessories	on track
	Target 3: 90% of apparel and accessories classified as more sustainable	79% apparel volume; 46% accessories volume	on track
	90% of all footwear contains at least one more sustainable component	61% footwear volume	on track
Fair Income	Target 1: Fair-wage assessments for the top five sourcing countries	4 out of 5 (Bangladesh, Cambodia, Indonesia, Vietnam)	on track
	Target 2: Effective and democratically elected worker representatives at all core suppliers .	48% of core Tier 1 factories covered	in progress
	Target 3: Ensure bank transfer payments for all core suppliers	99.3% core Tier 1 and Tier 2 suppliers use digital payment; 99.7% of workers are paid digitally in core factories	on track
Biodiversity	Target 1: Support setting up a biodiversity SBT	Sponsored a landscape analysis report	in progress
	Target 2: Procure 100% cotton, leather, and viscose from certified sources	99.8% cotton, 100% leather, 97.2% viscose, 100% down feathers	on track
	Target 3: Zero use of exotic skins or hides	New Animal Welfare Policy published	achieved

Source: PUMA (2023)

Figure 17.6 presents a conceptual diagram that illustrates the components of each form of capital. Operationalizing this concept requires the companion development of a quantitative sustainable performance index for the firm, as illustrated in Figure 17.7. As the author states, the advantage of this integrated model is that it shows the delicate balance required to achieve genuine sustainability. The challenge in implementation is developing

Financial Assets
· Current financial assets: cash, accounts receivable, inventories
· Capital assets

Financial Liabilities
· Debt (short and long-term borrowings)
· Accounts payable

Shareholders' Equity
· Preferred securities
· Share capital
· Retained earnings

· People (employees, contractors, suppliers)
· Intellectual capital: educational attainment, knowledge, skills
· Employment rate
· Labor participation rates
· Full-time, permanaent job rate
· Benefits including work-place interventions
· Creativity and entrepreneurship
· Capabilities
· Motivation

· Productivity
· Happiness (self-rated)
· Time use balance (work, family, leisure, community)
· Health (disease, diet, overall health)
· Physical well-being (fitness)
· Mental well-being
· Spiritual well-being
· Addictions (drugs, alcohol, gambling)
· Workplace safety
· Training and professional development
· Personal self-development

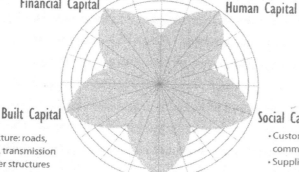

Financial Capital

Human Capital

Built Capital

· Infrastructure: roads, pipelines, transmission lines, other structures
· Buildings
· Machinery and equipment
· Technology
· Patents
· Brands
· Intellectual property (ideas, innovations)
· Management processes
· Production processes
· Databases

Natural Capital

· Environmental goods and services
· Natural resources (stocks and flows): land, minerals, oil, gas, coal, forests (trees), fish and wildlife, water, air, carbon sinks
· Ecosystem integrity
· Energy (by type, source, and end-use)

Social Capital

· Customer relationships (value, loyalty and commitment by customers)
· Supplier relationships (value and commitment by suppliers)
· Reputation
· Workplace relational capital: employee interrelationships, workplace climate (e.g., stress, excitement, joy), social cohesion (teams and team spirit), workplace climate (happiness with work)
· Equity (incomes, age-sex distribution, women in management)
· Employee family quality of life
· Networks
· Friendships amongst workplace colleagues
· Membership in professional associations, clubs, and other organizations
· Social events with colleagues
· Family outings with workplace colleagues
· Financial investment/giving/donations to the community

Figure 17.6 Genuine Wealth Account Attributes

Source: Anielski 2007, p. 157 reproduced with permission

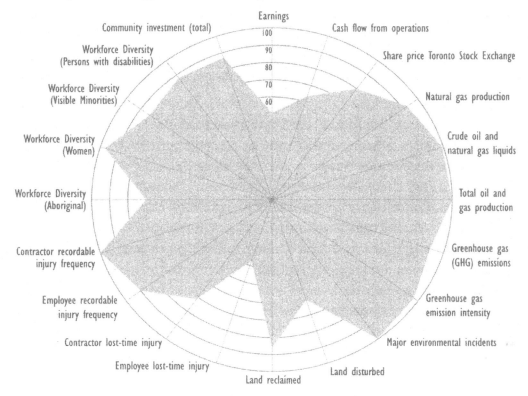

Figure 17.7 GWA Index Illustration

Source: Anielski 2007, p. 157, reproduced with permission

common standards for measurement and reporting to allow both temporal intracorporate tracking, as well as cross-firm and industry comparisons. In 2021, Anielski published a follow-up work that broadened the concept of Genuine Wealth to "help communities and nations become more flourishing and happier places to live." Even though the model is a work-in-progress, there is no reason why an organization could not adopt some variant as a first step to a more comprehensive analysis.

Sustainable Balanced Scorecard

The concept of the *Balanced Scorecard* was first introduced into the popular business literature by Kaplan and Norton in the *Harvard Business Review* in 1992 and was followed by numerous additional works on the subject by the authors (Kaplan 2002; Kaplan & Norton, 1993, 1995, 2001, 2004, 2007). Now widely used by corporations, nonprofits and governments (see Balanced Scorecard Institute website), this instrument was originally designed to provide managers with a structured series of interlinked indicators that could provide an organization with a comprehensive understanding of its performance. The Balanced Scorecard Institute reported in 2023 that over 9,000 people worldwide have been certified in Balanced Scorecard. Bernard Marr & Co. (2021) reported that:

> About half of major companies in the US, Europe and Asia are using Balanced Scorecard Approaches. The exact figures vary slightly but the Gartner Group

suggests that over 50% of large US firms had adopted the BSC by the end of 2000. A study by Bain & Co finds that about 44% of organisations in North America use the Balanced Scorecard and a study in Germany, Switzerland, and Austria finds that 26% of firms use Balanced Scorecards. The widest use of the Balanced Scorecard approach can be found in the US, the UK, Northern Europe and Japan.

In their original articulation of this concept, Kaplan and Norton (1995: 1) developed sets or parameters designed to address four specific questions:

First, how do customers see your company? Find out by measuring lead times, quality, performance and service, and costs. Second, what must your company excel at? Determine the processes and competencies that are most critical, and specify measures, such as cycle time, quality, employee skills, and productivity, to track them. Third, can your company continue to improve and create value? Monitor your ability to launch new products, create more value for customers, and improve operating efficiencies. Fourth, how has your company done by its shareholders? Measure cash flow, quarterly sales growth, operating income by division, and increased market share by segment and return on equity. The balanced scorecard lets executives see whether they have improved in one area at the expense of another.

The questions were presented in four linked tables (financial, customer, internal business process and learning and growth) that enunciated organizational goals and their related performance measures (Kaplan and Norton 2007). Figure 17.8 and Figure 17.9 depict a generic balanced scorecard and an example using a hypothetical privately held energy company (Rohm et al. 2013). The Scorecard has been used to aid strategic management,

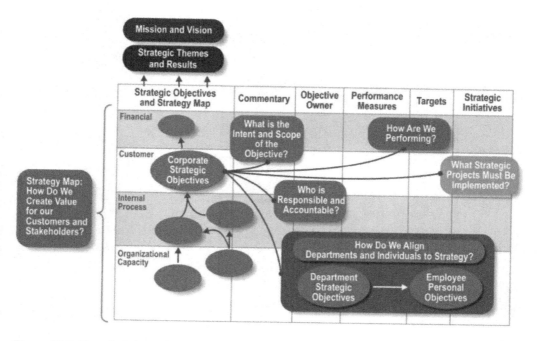

Figure 17.8 Generic Balanced Scorecard

Source: Rohm et al. 2023, reproduced with permission

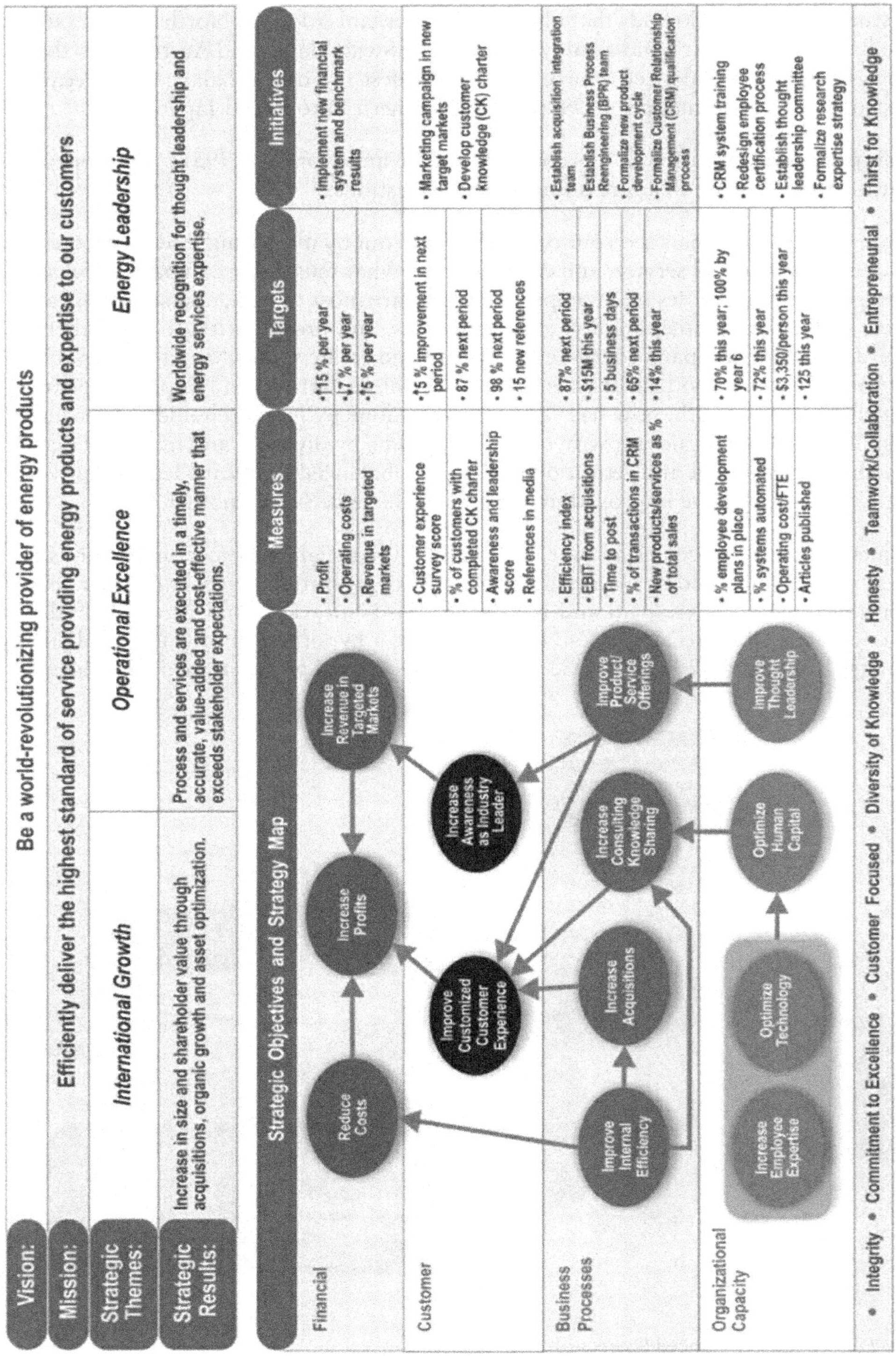

Vision: Be a world-revolutionizing provider of energy products

Mission: Efficiently deliver the highest standard of service providing energy products and expertise to our customers

Strategic Themes: International Growth | Operational Excellence | Energy Leadership

Strategic Results:
- International Growth: Increase in size and shareholder value through acquisitions, organic growth and asset optimization.
- Operational Excellence: Process and services are executed in a timely, accurate, value-added and cost-effective manner that exceeds stakeholder expectations.
- Energy Leadership: Worldwide recognition for thought leadership and energy services expertise.

Strategic Objectives and Strategy Map	Measures	Targets	Initiatives
Financial Reduce Costs; Increase Profits; Increase Revenue in Targeted Markets	• Profit • Operating costs • Revenue in targeted markets	• 15 % per year • 7 % per year • 5 % per year	• Implement new financial system and benchmark results
Customer Improve Customized Customer Experience; Increase Awareness as Industry Leader; Improve Product/Service Offerings; Improve Thought Leadership	• Customer experience survey score • % of customers with completed CK charter • Awareness and leadership score • References in media	• 5 % improvement in next period • 87 % next period • 98 % next period • 15 new references	• Marketing campaign in new target markets • Develop customer knowledge (CK) charter
Business Processes Improve Internal Efficiency; Increase Acquisitions; Increase Consulting Knowledge Sharing; Optimize Human Capital	• Efficiency index • EBIT from acquisitions • Time to post • % of transactions in CRM • New products/services as % of total sales	• 87% next period • $15M this year • 5 business days • 65% next period • 14% this year	• Establish acquisition integration team • Establish Business Process Reengineering (BPR) team • Formalize new product development cycle • Formalize Customer Relationship Management (CRM) qualification process
Organizational Capacity Increase Employee Expertise; Optimize Technology	• % employee development plans in place • % systems automated • Operating cost/FTE • Articles published	• 70% this year; 100% by year 6 • 72% this year • $3,350/person this year • 125 this year	• CRM system training • Redesign employee certification process • Establish thought leadership committee • Formalize research expertise strategy

• Integrity • Commitment to Excellence • Customer Focused • Diversity of Knowledge • Honesty • Teamwork/Collaboration • Entrepreneurial • Thirst for Knowledge

Figure 17.9 Example Balanced Scorecard

Source: Rohm et al. 2023, reproduced with permission

inform decision making and reporting of results, and to drive organizational performance by influencing the actions and behaviour of managers and individuals and the way they are appraised. The more recent extensive study of the balanced scorecard cited above was cowritten by Howard Rohm (president and cofounder of the Balanced Scorecard Institute) and entitled: *The Institute Way. Simplify Strategic Planning & Management with the Balanced Scorecard* (2013).

A balanced scorecard has several critical characteristics (Schaltegger & Burritt 2000):

it measures a set of performance indicators, specifies goals and measures goals in similar terms, removes the focus on a single short-term measure of financial results, and provides physical as well as financial measures of performance. Furthermore, it provides a strategic action process with the following four steps: formulation and implementation of vision and strategy, communicating and linking, business planning, and strategic feedback and learning.

In a book published after their original *Harvard Business Review* article, Kaplan and Norton (2001) acknowledged that while the original purpose of the scorecard was to solve a measurement problem associated with the inability of traditional financial metrics to measure the value-creating activities from an organization's intangible assets, this was being supplanted by the emerging use of the Scorecard to guide the implementation of new corporate strategies (see also Cobbold & Lawrie 2002). As is inevitable with an analytical tool with such a large uptake, there is a continual process of evolution. Cobbold and Lawrie described three distinct generations of Balanced Scorecards, beginning with the original conceptualization of Kaplan and Norton. The authors describe four key components of subsequent manifestations of this management tool: (1) a destination statement that describes what the organization is likely to look like at an agreed future date; (2) an articulation of strategic objectives; (3) a Strategic Linkage Model that incorporates four zones or "perspectives" relating to financial and market characteristics, external relationships, activities and processes, and organization and culture; and, finally, (4) measures and initiatives designed to support management's ability to monitor progress towards goal achievement.

Clearly, an instrument with this track record offers a potential opportunity in sustainability. Table 17.13 illustrates how Epstein (2008) adapted the Balanced Scorecard for explicit use by organizations interested in the impact of strategies, policies, products and procedures on social and environmental responsibilities, competitive advantage and financial viability. Epstein also stated that a corporation may choose to add a fifth dimension to this analysis that includes social and environmental performance indicators linked with the other four components shown in Table 17.13.

Figge et al. (2002) presented a hypothetical case study of a textile company to illustrate how a *Sustainability Balanced Scorecard* can aid in the incorporation of environmental and social factors into high-level corporate strategy. Borrowing from Kaplan and Norton (2001), Figge et al. used the concept of a *Balanced Scorecard Strategy Map* (see also Kaplan & Norton 2004) to create a hierarchical network of cause-and-effect chains for all relevant economic, environmental and social issues facing their hypothetical firm (see Figure 17.10). Once this initial step has been completed, it is possible to proceed to the Balanced Scorecard process of defining indicators targets and measures. The usefulness of this methodology was illustrated with reference to a hypothetical company producing textiles (Figge et al., p. 26) that wishes to increase its return on

Table 17.13 Epstein's Adaptation of the Balanced Scorecard

Financial Dimension	Stakeholder Dimension
• Percent of sales revenues from "green" products • Recycling revenues • Energy costs • Fines and penalties for pollution	• Sustainabiliy awards • Funds donated for community support • Number of community complaints • Employee satisfaction
Internal business process dimension	*Learning and growth dimension*
• Percent of suppliers certified • Volume of hazardous waste • Packaging volume • Number of community complaints • Cost of minoritty business purchases • Number of product recalls	• Diversity of workforce and management • Number of volunteer hours • Cost of employee benefits • Percent of employees trained in sustainability

Source: Epstein 2008, p. 138. Reprinted with permission of the publisher. From Making Sustainability Work,

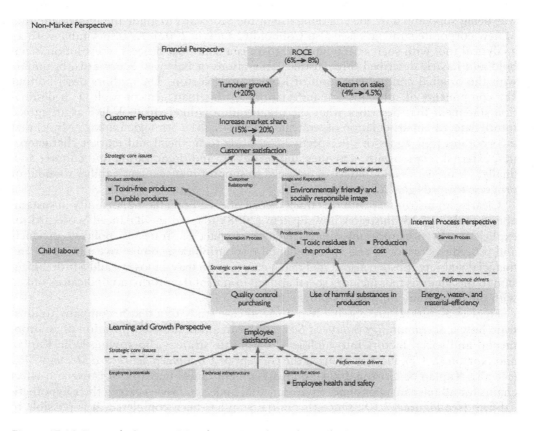

Figure 17.10 Example Strategy Map for a Hypothetical Textile Company

Source: Figge et al. 2002, p. 25, reproduced wit permission

capital from 6% to 8%. To achieve this goal, the company wants to increase its sales margin from 4% to 4.5% and boost its turnover by 20% by increasing its market share from 15% to 20%. The company proposes reaching these goals by adopting several initiatives that will increase customer demand and improve its environmental and social image: (1) a shift to less toxic inputs and more durable products; (2) ensuring that no child labor is involved in the supplier chain; (3) increasing efficiency in the use of energy, water and material; and (4) adopting measures to increase employee motivation and satisfaction. These four goals continue to resonate today in discussions of corporate initiatives toward sustainability. The strategy map in Figure 17.10 illustrates this integration of environmental and social issues in the Sustainability Balanced Scorecard as conventional success factors so that nonmarket issues become part of a mainstream management system.

Ratio-Based Financial Models for Sustainability

Chousa and Castro (2006) developed *a Model of Financial Analysis of Sustainability* based on the Dupont system of ratio analysis (see, for example, Baltova 2023) to integrate sustainability considerations into traditional financial models. The distinguishing characteristic of their model was the inclusion of specific ratios that reflect the relationship between physical measures of pollution and more conventional financial values, such as sales. Figure 17.11 was used by the authors to demonstrate the value of this hybrid and integrated approach. The authors contrasted two alternative approaches: first a focus on the sales/fixed assets ratio and its role in corporate profitability. The relevant path is denoted by the shaded ratios in the area demarcated by the large box with a dashed-line perimeter. To quote (Chousa & Castro, p. 138):

From a traditional perspective, when the value of this ratio is high, it is believed to reflect the efficient use of the capital invested in the company's site and the likely reduction of the financial leverage of the company's capital structure (owing to the improved ROA, which would lead to higher profit that would allow the reduction of total liabilities).

In contrast, the authors posit that the company may be delaying capital expenditures on necessary pollution control equipment. Conventional financial analysis would not reflect the potentially detrimental impact such a decision might have on long-run profitability by negatively affecting competiveness or exposing the corporation to environmental liability and governmental regulatory action. The inclusion of all of the shaded ratios outside the dashed-line box allow the analyst to track the cascading effect of the decision to avoid pollution control expenditures all the way through to ROA, ROE, and profitability. To quote:

The analysis of ratios such as sales/waste value, cost of emissions/sales, environmental fines/sales, etc. can add valuable information to the financial ratio analysis. Although a high sales/fixed assets ratio may be signaling an improved ROA and ROE, other ratios may be signaling the opposite. A high cost of emissions/sales ratio and/or a high environmental fines/sales ratio will limit profit generation and a low sales/waste value ratio will reduce the sales/current assets ratio, this compensating for the high value initially found for the sales/fixed assets ratio (Chousa & Castro, p. 142).

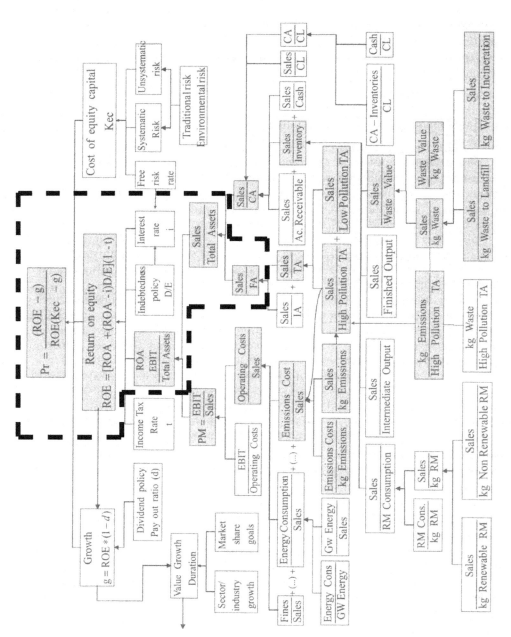

Figure 17.11 Expanded Financial Analysis with Environmental Factors Influencing Profitability

Source: Chousa and Castro 2006, pp. 140–141, reproduced with permission.

Two Other Methodologies of Note

Sustainable Value

Figge and Hahn (2005) developed an interesting valuation methodology to calculate the sustainable value creation of companies and their cost of *sustainability capital*. The essence of the analysis, based on the concept of opportunity cost, measures to what degree any corporation's resources could be used elsewhere in a national economy with a lower environmental impact. The methodology was illustrated by a case study of British Petroleum (BP) laid out in Tables 17.14 and 15.15. In the first step, as illustrated in Table 17.14, relative financial and pollutant emission data were presented for both the UK national economy and BP. BP's *net value added* was defined as "the value created within a company after depreciation. It excluded any value that has been created by suppliers or that will be created by customers." BP's *nonfinancial assets* "were estimated by subtracting all financial assets (e.g., securities) from BP's total assets (Figge & Hahn, p. 53)."

Table 17.14 BP Sample Financial and Pollutant Emission Data

BP	Amount	Units	UK	Amount	Units	Ratios
Net value added	15,563	UK pounds	Net domestic product	884,718	million UK pounds	1.76%
nonfinancial assets	69,885	million UK pounds	total net wealth	4,375,200	million UK pounds	1.60%
CO_2	73,420,000	tons	CO_2	572,500,000	tons	12.82%
CH_4	367,201	tons	CH_4	2,195,238	tons	16.73%
SO_2	224,541	tons	SO_2	1,125,000	tons	19.96%
NOx	266,133	tons	NOx	1,680,000	tons	15.84%
CO	124,584	tons	CO	3,966,500	tons	3.14%
Work accidents	83	number	Work accidents	132,696	number	0.06%
PM10	16,666	tons	PM10	178,000	tons	9.36%

Derived from Figge and Hahn (2005, p. 53, Tables 1 & 2 [reproduced with permission of the authors])

Table 17.15 Example Sustainable Value Calculation

Type of Capital	BP's return on capital [Mio UK pounds / unit]	UK return on capital [i.e. the opportunity cost] [Mio UK pounds / unit]	Difference in returns on capital [Mio UK pounds / unit]	BP's absolute amounts [from Table 25–12]	Value created [Million UK Pounds]
Economic capital	0.2227	0.2022	0.0205	69,885	1,433
CO_2	0.0002	0.0015	-0.0013	73,420,000	-95,446
CH_4	0.0424	0.4030	-0.3606	367,201	-132,413
SO_2	0.0693	0.7864	-0.7171	224,541	-161,018
NOx	0.0585	0.5266	-0.4681	266,133	-124,577
CO	0.1249	0.2230	-0.0981	124,584	-12,222
Work accdents	187.506	6.6673	180.8387	83	15,010
PM10	0.9338	4.9703	-4.0365	16,666	-67,272
				total	-576,506
				sustainable value	-72,063

Derived from Figge and Hahn (2005 [reproduced with permission of the authors])

The second step, as illustrated in Table 17.15, involved the creation of two critical ratios: (1) a return on *sustainability capital* for BP calculated by relating BP's estimated value added to all eight forms of *capital* listed in the table. While a pollutant would not normally be considered a form of capital, there is a logic to its use here. For example, a pollutant could be linked to a form of capital in the sense that there is corresponding natural ecosystem capital used to receive, assimilate, disperse or otherwise respond to the emission of this particular pollutant. (2) A similar ratio for the UK calculated the cost of capital based on the economy as a whole. The difference between the BP and UK ratios was multiplied by BP's performance data to estimate the sustainability value created by BP. The underlying rationale for this analysis was that "BP covered its cost of sustainability capital if and only if it used its different forms of capital more efficiently than the British economy (Figge & Hahn 2005, p. 53)."

The authors' calculations yielded a net sustainability deficit for BP of 72,373 million UK pounds, calculated as the quotient of the total value created (578,984 million UK pounds) divided by 8 (i.e. the number of types of capital under consideration) in order to avoid double counting. This implied that "had the resource been allocated to the British economy on average rather than to BP, an additional 72,373 million UK pounds more value would have been created (Figge & Hahn 2005, p. 54)." Only two of the resources (economic capital and work accidents) make a positive contribution to the company's sustainable value; the other resources create a negative sustainability value. While this conclusion is readily apparent from the "ratio" column in Table 17.16, the additional analysis conducted by the authors facilitates the allocation of monetary value to the sustainability measures. In the third and final step, the authors calculated a measure of BP's *sustainability efficiency*. The ratio was defined as: (net value added)/(cost of sustainability capital). The resulting value is 0.177 derived from the ratio: (15.563 million UK pounds)/ (72,373 + 15.563 million UK pounds). The author's conclusion was that "BP earns only 17.7 pence per UK pound of opportunity cost of sustainability capital. Consequently, its sustainability efficiency is below unity. BP thus falls short of covering its cost of sustainability capital."

This analysis raises at least two interesting issues: first, the choice of the benchmark and, second, the avenues available for remedying negative sustainable value.

The use of a national economy as a benchmark is potentially problematic as it implies that all those companies with higher efficiency levels than the national economic average are somehow *sustainable*, and that all those companies with lower efficiency levels are *nonsustainable*. This approach does not address the question of whether any country's national average values are necessarily sustainable with respect to any recognizable criteria. The authors recognize this potential dilemma and suggest possible alternative benchmarks including the efficiencies of other economic entities "such as national economies, regions, industry sectors, or companies other than the one under examination. On the other hand, one could also use performance targets such as emission reduction targets to form the benchmark efficiencies (Figge & Hahn 2005, p. 53)."

The second, and related, issue is the question of what type of signals this analysis generates for ameliorating poor sustainability performance. In this respect the analysis of Figge and Hahn is not inconsistent with standard environmental economic theory. A company might be able to improve its efficiency rating by raising the price for its products and thereby lowering their demand. This would move the company closer to the optimal social output for its product. In general, while providing information of this sort for external stakeholders is exceedingly useful, providing signals for management is

Schedule A   Costs of social risks

Risk	Benefit	Cost types	Costs	Likelihood	Expected value
Civil unrest surrounding site	$	• Costs of engaging employers skilled in negotiating with protesters • Cost of engaging extra security personnel *Reputation-related:* • Cost of hiring community relations manager • Cost of managing activist NGO relations	$ .... $ .... $ .... $	.... %	$ ....
Prostitution near site	$	• Costs of implementing health education for workers to teach about sexually transmitted diseases (to avoid costs related to HIV infection)	$	.... %	$ ....
Child labor	$	*Reputation-related:* • Costs of reputation damage • Cost of managing boycotts when information reaches activist consumers • Cost of NGO relations manager	$ .... $ .... $	.... %	$ ....
Infringement of indigenous lands	$	• Costs of litigation in international courts • Cost of remunerating population • Cost of work stoppages due to local strike, reputation damage, community protests, work stoppages *Reputation-related:* • Cost of hiring community relations manager • Cost of managing activist NGO relations	$ .... $ .... $ .... $ .... $	.... %	$ ....
Reputation costs, including lost sales and profits					$ ....
NPV					$ ....

Figures 17.12a and 17.12b Costing Social Risks for a Hypothetical Mining Company in a Developing Country

Source: Epstein 2008, reproduced with permission

Schedule B   Costs of political risks

Risk	Benefit	Cost types	Costs	Likelihood	Expected value
Changes in legislation that change the rules of the game	$	• Lost revenues • Increased taxes and tariffs	$ .... $	.... %	$ ....
Forced contract negotiation with host government	$	• Lost profits • Lost investment	$ .... $	.... %	$ ....
Armed insurrection	$	• Cost of hiring private security • Cost of training local police/military to prevent human rights abuses (if required to use these forces by contract)	$ .... $	.... %	$ ....
Associated reputation risk	$	• Costs of incentive packages to attract workers to location • Cost of protests, etc. due to potential linkages with human rights abuses	$ .... $	.... %	$ ....
Endemic corruption	$	• Costs of payoffs and bribes • Costs of potential lawsuits for that activity	$ .... $	.... %	$ ....
Targeted criminal activity	$	• Costs of protecting personnel, including extra security, reinforcing security at private homes, providing security training to employees and families • Costs of attracting workers, including increased pay, time off, and hardship bonuses • Costs of increased security to protect facility • Costs of potential work stoppages	$ .... $ .... $ .... $	.... %	$ ....
Terrorism	$	• Costs of reinforcing infrastructure • Costs of hiring additional security personnel • Costs of rebuilding	$ .... $ .... $	.... %	$ ....
Reputation costs, including lost sales and profits					$ ....
NPV					$ ....

Figures 17.12a and 17.12b (Continued)

at least as important – if not more so - for the simple reason that without such internal signals, a company cannot determine the appropriate path to sustainability.

Social and political risk analysis

The focus of the discussion so far has been on how to incorporate environmental risk into corporate decision making traditionally reliant on convention financial metrics. In many cases, however, corporate risk may extend into both the social and political realms, and it is these additional risks that Epstein (2008) addressed in his book *Making Sustainability Work*. (See also Bekefi & Epstein 2006, 2011). The example Epstein used is a mining company operating in the Third World, although the general structure of this analysis could easily be expanded to cover corporate operations in the developed world where there are different types of social and political risk. Figures 17.12a and 12b illustrate the calculations that a corporation might employ to generate expected values that could then be incorporated directly into traditional ROI calculations. It should be noted however, that the use of the simple expected value for each of these risks, which implies risk neutrality, may have to be modified in light of two factors: (1) management's attitude toward risk, especially its degree of risk tolerance or risk aversion (see for example MacCrimmon & Wehrung 1986), and (2) the possibility of *fat tail* phenomena, which are low probability events that could threaten the survival of the corporation (Taleb 2007; Weitzman 2009).

Measuring sociopolitical risk has become even more relevant today in a world marked by regional conflicts. A recent comprehensive analysis of the topic has been undertaken by Marolla and others in an edited volume by Engemann (2023).

Summary Observations

The above examples are merely some of numerous efforts to incorporate sustainability considerations into high-level corporate decision making. One organization in particular that has been raising corporate awareness to the long-term benefits of sustainability has been the World Business Council on Sustainable Development, a collaborative research and information-disseminating association of over 200 major global corporations that is based in Geneva, Switzerland. Much of the published work of the WBCSD is composed of case studies and analytical documents that address key issue in corporate sustainability and help to develop new tools for managerial decision making. Foremost among these tools is the creation of *sustainable business decision frameworks* that clearly demonstrate how a focus on sustainability issues can create intangible strategic benefits and improve environmental and social performance, leading to both increased enterprise and external stakeholder value (WBCSD 2017). Joseph Fiksel (2003; Fiksel et al. 2002) detailed the multifaceted benefits in Figure 17.13 from expanding the purview of corporate strategy from the three traditional financially related cells in the top left of the table (i.e., financial results such as EBITDA of interest to shareholders and investors, business results, and personal income of concern to managers, and the personal income of employees) to the 24 other cells that address environmental and social issues that benefit not just the enterprise directly, but also all the indirect benefits accruing to the corporation through the broad range of stakeholders.

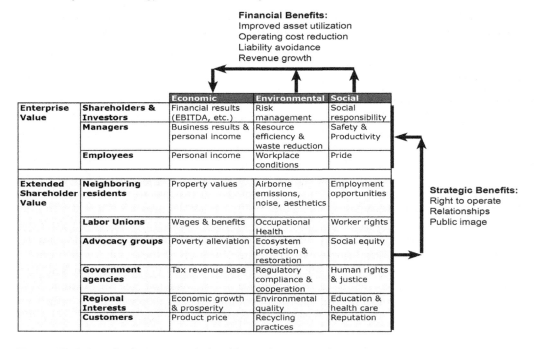

Financial Benefits:
Improved asset utilization
Operating cost reduction
Liability avoidance
Revenue growth

		Economic	Environmental	Social
Enterprise Value	**Shareholders & Investors**	Financial results (EBITDA, etc.)	Risk management	Social responsibility
	Managers	Business results & personal income	Resource efficiency & waste reduction	Safety & Productivity
	Employees	Personal income	Workplace conditions	Pride
Extended Shareholder Value	**Neighboring residents**	Property values	Airborne emissions, noise, aesthetics	Employment opportunities
	Labor Unions	Wages & benefits	Occupational Health	Worker rights
	Advocacy groups	Poverty alleviation	Ecosystem protection & restoration	Social equity
	Government agencies	Tax revenue base	Regulatory compliance & cooperation	Human rights & justice
	Regional Interests	Economic growth & prosperity	Environmental quality	Education & health care
	Customers	Product price	Recycling practices	Reputation

Strategic Benefits:
Right to operate
Relationships
Public image

Figure 17.13 Benefits from Expanded Analysis of Sustainability Issues

Source: Fiksel 2003, p. 23, reproduced with permission

A Final Reflection on Triple Bottom Line Reporting and the Integration of Sustainability Accounts

Hahn et al. (2010) wrote a provocative and still relevant article that challenged the common view of corporate sustainability. It was their contention that the literature was dominated by what they termed a "win-win paradigm," where corporate sustainability is achieved through the simultaneous attainment of all three legs of the sustainability "stool": economic, environmental, and social. It was the authors' hypothesis that the complexity of sustainability issues makes this an exceedingly rare accomplishment, and fundamental trade-offs characterize this domain as they do in all other avenues of human endeavor. In many cases, corporate achievement of one aspect of sustainability may come at the expense of another. It was their view that the sole pursuit of all three forms of sustainability, without the realization of the inherent trade-offs, will foreclose many viable and productive options. A central conclusion of this thesis was that corporations can make a significant contribution to sustainability at the societal level by excelling in just one or two forms of sustainability, be they economic, environmental, or social (Hahn et al. 2010: 219):

> corporate sustainability based on the win–win logic will be restricted to conflict-free solutions with little ambition to fundamentally change core business practices for the sake of sustainable development. . . . By following the win–win paradigm sustainability issues are ultimately judged through the lens of profit maximization rather than being treated as ends in themselves."

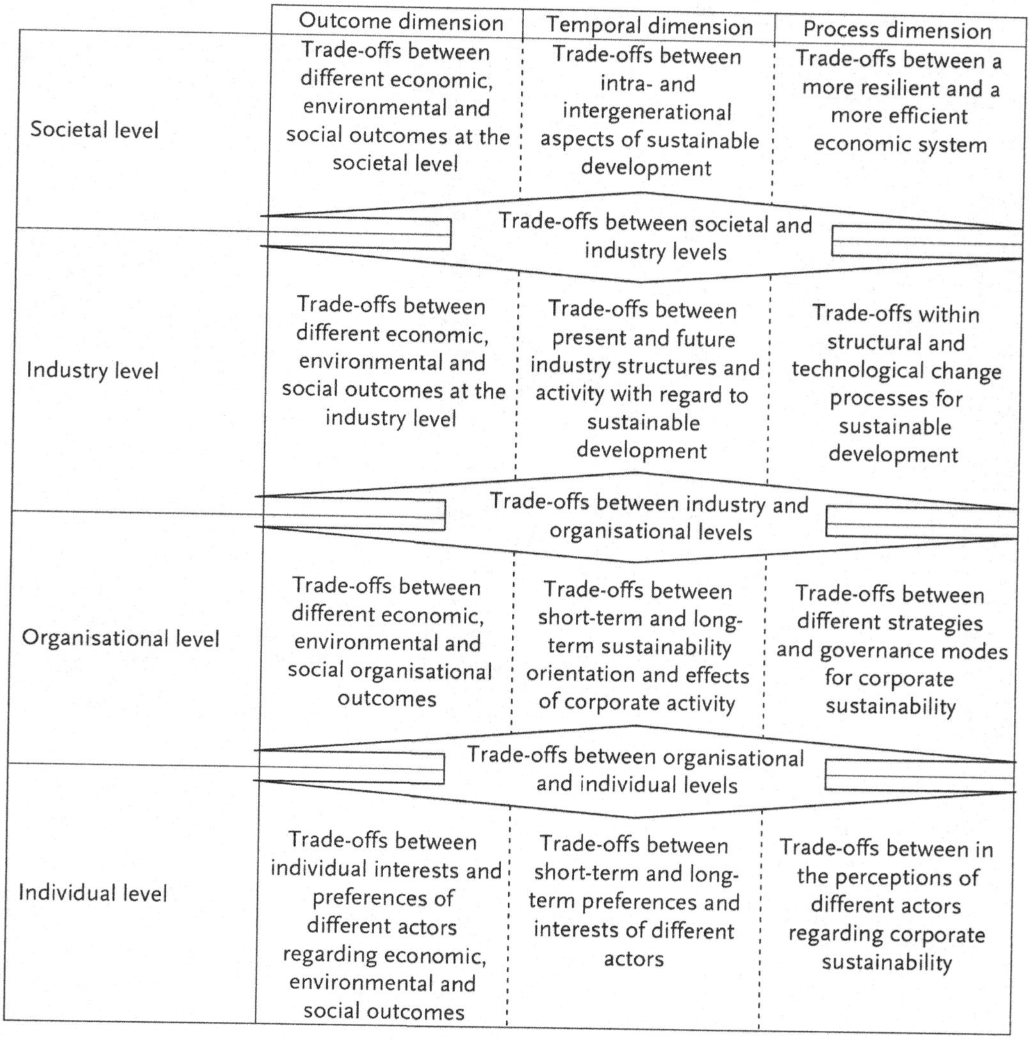

	Outcome dimension	Temporal dimension	Process dimension
Societal level	Trade-offs between different economic, environmental and social outcomes at the societal level	Trade-offs between intra- and intergenerational aspects of sustainable development	Trade-offs between a more resilient and a more efficient economic system
	Trade-offs between societal and industry levels		
Industry level	Trade-offs between different economic, environmental and social outcomes at the industry level	Trade-offs between present and future industry structures and activity with regard to sustainable development	Trade-offs within structural and technological change processes for sustainable development
	Trade-offs between industry and organisational levels		
Organisational level	Trade-offs between different economic, environmental and social organisational outcomes	Trade-offs between short-term and long-term sustainability orientation and effects of corporate activity	Trade-offs between different strategies and governance modes for corporate sustainability
	Trade-offs between organisational and individual levels		
Individual level	Trade-offs between individual interests and preferences of different actors regarding economic, environmental and social outcomes	Trade-offs between short-term and long-term preferences and interests of different actors	Trade-offs between in the perceptions of different actors regarding corporate sustainability

Figure 17.14 Analytical Framework for Trade-Offs in Corporate Sustainability

Source: Hahn et al. 2016, p. 223, reproduced with permission

In Figure 17.14, Hahn et al. presented a model that laid out the multifaceted nature of trade-offs faced in the pursuit of sustainability. These tradeoffs can occur at four levels (individual, organizational, industry, and societal), and in three dimensions (outcome, temporal, and process). Some of these include the trade-off between efficiency and resilience (Nemetz 2022), and the tradeoff between current and future generations. Hahn et al. were convinced that "truly proactive corporate sustainability strategies are those strategies that do not shy away from taking into account conflicts, but rather accept trade-offs for the sake of substantial sustainability gains at the societal level" (p. 226).

Appendix: Wessex Water's Route Map Options

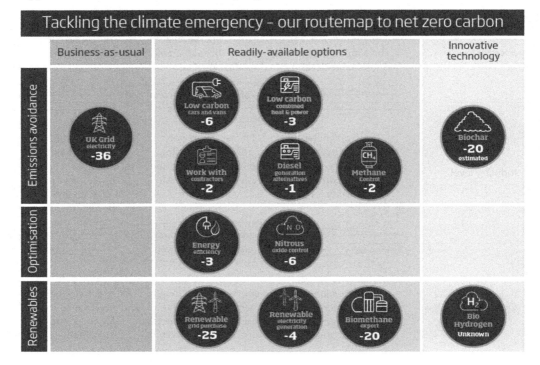

Figure 17.15 Wessex Water's Route Map to Net Zero

Reproduced with permission

References

Anielski, Mark (2007) *The Economics of Happiness: Building Genuine Wealth.* New Society Publishers.

Anielski, Mark (2021) *An Economy of Well-Being: Common-Sense Tools for Building Genuine Wealth and Happiness.* New Society Publishers.

Asdourian, Elijah & David Wessel (2023) "What is the social cost of carbon," Brookings Institute, March 14.

Ashrafi, Parisa, et al. (2021) *Environmental Management System.* Academic Publishing.

Baldarelli, Maria-Gabriella, et al. (2018) *Environmental Accounting and Reporting: Theory and Practice.* Springer.

Baltova, Antoniya (2023) "DuPont analysis – a pyramid of ratios," Knowledge Hub, Financial Analysis, June 2.

Baxter Health (2012) *Environmental Financial Statement.*

Baxter Health (2022a) *Annual Report.*

Baxter Health (2022b) *Corporate Responsibility Report.*

Bebbington, Jan, et al. (2014) *Sustainability Accounting and Accountability.* Routledge.

Bebbington, Jan, et al. (2023) *Routledge Handbook of Environmental Accounting.* Routledge.

Bekefi, Tamara & Marc J. Epstein (2006) *Integrating Social and Political Risk into Management Decision-Making,* Management Accounting Guideline, CMA Canada, AICPA.

Bekefi, Tamara & Marc J. Epstein (2011) "Integrating social and political risk into ROI calculation," *Environmental Quality Management,* Spring, pp. 11–23.

Bernard Marr & Co. (2021) "Balanced scorecard: how many companies use this tool?," https://bernardmarr.com/balanced-scorecard-how-many-companies-use-this-tool/

Blokdyk, Gerardus (2021a) *Activity Based Costing: Complete Self-assessment Guide.* 5STARCooks.

Blokdyk, Gerardus (2021b) *Activity-Based Costing*. 5STARCooks.

Blokdyk, Gerardus (2021c) *Full Cost Accounting: A Complete Guide*. 5STARCooks.

Blokdyk, Gerardus (2022) *Activity-Based Costing: ABC Standard Requirements*. SSTARCooks.

Bloomberg NEF (2023) "California carbon price hits a peak as supply cuts loom," August 3.

Burritt, Roger L. (1998) "Cost allocation," in Martin Bennett & Peter James (Eds.) *The Green Bottom Line: Environmental Accounting for Management – Current Practices and Future Trends*, pp. 152–161. Greenleaf.

Carbon Tax Center (2023) *Carbon Tax Center: Pricing Carbon Efficiently and Equitably*, pp. 152–161.

Chousa, Juan Pineiro & Noelia Romero Castro (2006) "A model of financial analysis at the service of sustainability," in Stefan Schaltegger & Marcus Wagner (Eds.) (2006) *Managing the Business Case for Sustainability: The integration of Social, Environmental and Economic Performance*. Routledge.

Cobbold, I. & Gavin Lawrie (2002) "The development of the balanced scorecard as a strategic management tool," 2GC Conference Paper, presented at PMA Conference. Boston, MA.

Dartford & Graveshan NHS Trust (2023) *Green Plan 2021–2026*.

Ditz, Daryl, et al. (Eds.) (1995) *Green Ledgers: Case Studies in Corporate Environmental Accounting*. World Resources Institute.

Emblemsvag, Jan & Bert Bras (2001) *Activity-Based Cost and Environmental Management: A Different Approach to the ISO 14000 Compliance*. Springer.

Engemann, Kurt J. (Ed.) (2023) *Developments in Managing and Exploiting Risk, Volume 4: Socio-Political Risks Management: Assessing and Managing Global Insecurity: Strategic Management and Policy Decisions*. De Gruyter.

Epstein, Marc J. (2008) *Making Sustainability Work. Best Practices in Managing and Measuring Corporate Social, Environmental, and Economic Impacts,* Greenleaf Publishing and Berrett-Koehler Publishers.

Fashion Network (2023) "69% US consumers willing to pay more for sustainable products," March 31.

Figge, Frank, et al. (2002) "The sustainability balanced scorecard – theory and application of a tool for value-based sustainability management," paper presented at the Greening of Industry Network Conference, Gothenburg.

Figge, Frank & Tobias Hahn (2005) "The cost of sustainability capital and the creation of sustainable value by companies," *Journal of Industrial Ecology*, 9(4): 47–58.

Fiksel, D., et al. (2002) *Toward a Sustainable Cement Industry,* Sub-study 3, Business Case Development, Battelle Report to the World Business Council for Sustainable Development. Geneva.

Fiksel, Joseph (2003) "Revealing the value of sustainable development," *Corporate Strategy Today*, June: 28–36.

Glad, Ernest (2002) *Activity-Based Costing*, Juta & Co. Ltd.

Global Environmental Management Initiative (GEMI) (1994) *Finding Cost-Effective Pollution Prevention Initiatives: Incorporating Environmental Costs into Business Decision Making A Primer*.

Greenstone, Michael, et al. (2023) "Mandatory disclosure would reveal corporate carbon damages," *Science*, August 25.

Hahn, Tobias, et al. (2010) "Trade-offs in corporate sustainability: you can't have your cake and eat it," *Business Strategy and the Environment*, 19: 217–229.

Haider, Syed (2019) *Environmental Management System ISO 14001: 2004: Handbook of Transition*. CRC Press.

Henriques, Adrian & Julie Richardson (eds.) (2004) *The Triple Bottom Line: Does It All Add Up?* Earthscan.

Howes, Rupert (2000) "Corporate environmental accounting: accounting for environmentally sustainable profits," in Sandrine Simon & John Proops (Eds.), *Greening the Accounts*. 223–245. Edward Elgar.

Howes, Rupert (2003) *Environmental Cost Accounting: An Introduction and Practical Guide, London:* Chartered Institute of Management Accountants (CIMA Research)

Howes Rupert (2004) "Environmental cost accounting: coming of age? tracking organizational performance towards environmental sustainability," in Adrian Henriques & Julie Richardson (Eds.), *The Triple Bottom Line. Does It All Add Up?* 99–112. Earthscan.

International Standards Organization (ISO) (2023) "ISO 14001 and related standards," Environmental Management.

Kaplan, Robert S. (2002) "The balanced scorecard and nonprofit organizations," *On Balance.* November–December.

Kaplan, Robert S. & Steven R. Anderson (2007) *Time-Driven Activity-Based Costing: A Simpler and More Powerful Path to Higher Profits.* Harvard Business School Press.

Kaplan, Robert S. & David P. Norton (1992) "The balanced scorecard: measures that drive performance," *Harvard Business Review,* January–February: 71–90.

Kaplan, Robert S. & David P. Norton (1993) "Putting the balanced scorecard to work," *Harvard Business Review,* September–October, 134–147.

Kaplan, Robert S. & David P. Norton (1995) "The balanced scorecard. measures that drive performance," *Harvard Business Review,* July–August.

Kaplan, Robert S. & David P. Norton (2001) *The Strategy-Focused Organization: How Balanced Scorecard Companies Thrive in the New Business Environment.* Harvard Business School Press.

Kaplan, Robert S. & David P. Norton (2004) *Strategy Maps: Converting Intangible Assets in Tangible Outcomes.* Harvard Business School Press.

Kaplan, Robert S. & David P. Norton (2007) "Using the balanced scorecard as a strategic management system," *Harvard Business Review,* July–August: 150–161.

Khurana, Kanwaljeet (2015) *Activity Based Costing: Basic Concepts and Application.* KAPP Edge Solutions.

Kuhre, W. Lee (1995) *ISO 14001 Certification: Environmental Management Systems.*

Leitner, Andreas (2005) *Activity Based Costing.* GRIN Vertag.

MacCrimmon, Kenneth R. & Donald A. Wehrung (1986) *Taking Risks: The Management of Uncertainty.* Free Press.

MapChange (2008) *Change 2008. A Sustainability Brand Map Study.*

Marguglio, B. (2019) *Environmental Management Systems.* CRC Press.

Marolla, Cesar (2023) "The dynamics of global risks: sociopolitical risks in strategic management and policy decisions," in Kurt J. Engemann (Ed.), *Developments in Managing and Exploiting Risk, Volume 4: Socio-Political Risks Management: Assessing and Managing Global Insecurity: Strategic Management and Policy Decisions.* 3–18. Berlin. De Gruyter.

Marr, Bernard & Co. (2022) "Balanced scorecard: how many companies use this tool?"

Matthews, H. Scott & Lester B. Lave (2003) "Using input-output analysis for corporate benchmarking," *Benchmarking: An International Journal,* 10(2): 152–167.

Muller, Nicholas Z., et al. (2011) "Environmental accounting for pollution in the United States economy," *American Economic Review,* 101(5): 1649–1675.

Nemetz, Peter N. (2022) *The Economics and Business of Sustainability.* Routledge.

Pahuja, Shuchi (2009) *Environmental Accounting and Reporting. Theory, Law and Empirical Evidence.* New Century Publications.

PUMA & PPR (2011) Joint Press Release, Munich/London, May 16.

PUMA (2023) "Environmental key performance data."

Rennert, Kevin, et al. (2022) "Comprehensive evidence implies a higher social cost of CO_2," *Nature,* October 27.

Rikhardsson, Pall M., et al. (2005) *Implementing Environmental Management Accounting: Status and Challenges.* Springer.

Rohm, Howard, et al. (2023) *The Institute Way: Simplify Strategic Planning & Management with the Balanced Scorecard,* The Institute Press.

Schaltegger, Stefan & Roger Burritt (2000) *Contemporary Environmental Accounting. Issues, Concepts and Practice.* Greenleaf.

Schaltegger, Stefan & Kasper Muller (1998) "Calculating the true profitability of pollution prevention," in Martin Bennett & Peter James (Eds.), *The Green Bottom Line. Environmental Accounting for Management: Current Practices and Future Trends.* 86–99. Greenleaf.

Schaltlegger, Stefan & Marcus Wagner (Eds.) (2006) *Managing the Business Case for Sustainability. The Integration of Social, Environmental and Economic Performance.* Greenleaf.

Sheldon, Christopher & Mark Yoxon (2002) *Environmental Management Systems, A Step-by-Step Guide to Implementation & Maintenance.* Earthscan.

Statista (2023) *European Union Emissions Trading System – Statistics & Facts.*

Taleb, Nassim Nicholas (2007) *The Black Swan: The Impact of the Highly Improbable.* Random House.

Tax Foundation (2023) "Carbon taxes in Europe," September 5.

Thompson, Dixon (2002) *Tools for Environmental Management. A Practical Introduction and Guide.* New Society Publishers.

Tinsley, Stephen & Ilona Pillai (2012) *Environmental Management System: Understanding Organizational Drivers and Barriers.* Routledge.

Trucost (2009) *Carbon Risks and Opportunities in the S&P 500.* IRRC Institute.

US EPA (1989) *Pollution Prevention Benefits Manual. Volume I: The Manual. Phase II*, October.

US EPA (1995) *An Introduction to Environmental Accounting as a Business Management Tool: Key Concepts and Terms.*

US EPA (2022) "Report on the social cost of greenhouse gases: Estimates incorporating recent scientific advances."

US EPA TRI website (www.epa.gov/tri/)

Weitzman, Martin (2009) "On modeling and interpreting the economics of catastrophe," *Review of Economic and Statistics*, 91(1): 1–19.

Wessex Water Services Limited (2004) "Wessex Water environmental accounts," Bath UK.

Wessex Water (2018a) "Annual report and accounts 2007–2018."

Wessex Water Services Limited (2018b) *Sustainability Indicators and Accounting 2017–2018*, Bath UK.

Wessex Water (2022) *Wessex Water's Sustainable Finance Framework*, September.

World Business Council for Sustainable Development (WBCSD) (2017), "Integrating strategic sustainability into business decision-making," Geneva, https://docs.wbcsd.org/2017/10/Integrating_Strategic_Sustainability.pdf

Zeuner, Patrick (2008) *Activity-Based Costing: Introducing Process Thinking into Cost Management.* GRIN Vertag.

Analytical Questions

1. Using a public company, apply any one of the metrics outlined in this chapter to reassess the sustainability of the corporate enterprise in question.
2. If possible, apply more than one metric and determine if the results are comparable.

18 Reforming the Financial System

There is an emerging consensus that the financial sector has a central role in moving the broader corporate sector towards a truly sustainable path (see Appendix). Several major initiatives undertaken by international financial regulatory bodies have been outlined in chapter 2. While incremental in nature, they have the capacity to induce major shifts in corporate reporting and strategy in the near future. Beyond these measures, however, it is useful to step back and ask what other broader reforms might be worthwhile in an evolving financial marketplace. Two examples in particular come to mind in this regard: the first by Professor Rebecca Henderson of the Harvard Business School, and the second by Mark Carney, former Governor of the Bank of Canada and Bank of England.

Professor Henderson is one of several academics re-examining the role of our modern capitalist system in the current climate crisis. In her most recent work (2021) entitled *Reimaging Capitalism in a World on Fire*, she concludes that the current form of our capitalist system is "broken" and the single-minded pursuit of profit has led to climate change, inequality and hatred, polarization, and distrust. This is an extremely powerful critique, but the author sees a potential solution in the form of a reimagined model of business that maintains the central role of business in our society but focuses on a realignment of corporate values to include social goals. The book is replete with case studies of companies that have already made the effort to seriously reorient their corporate strategy in a more socially effective manner. A fundamental component of her prescription is a concomitant "rewiring" of our global and financial system. The author advances the concept of enlightened industry self-regulation but one that is coordinated with government, the entity ultimately responsible for society's wellbeing (Henderson 2021: 203):

> We need governments to provide either the economic incentives that will move firms to action, or the regulations that will force everyone to do the right thing. Business, in its own interest, must take the lead. Without good government and free politics, the free market will not survive.

What distinguishes this proposal from the traditional laissez-faire model of self-regulation is the coordination with government and the role of leading companies in inducing others to adopt a broader interpretation of their mission through a combination of targeted purchasing and investment decisions. This is a more expanded version of the Walmart model (see chapter 16), where the company uses its role as a de facto *private regulator* to induce its suppliers to adopt more sustainable means of production.

In fact, some of what Henderson is espousing is already underway. Numerous banks, investment houses, insurance companies, and pension funds are now increasingly sensitive

DOI: 10.4324/9781003170754-22

to climate risk in investment decisions, and this is having a direct impact on corporate decision making. Examples abound:

- The emergence of green and clean energy and innovation indexes (CNN April 23, 2021, Clean Edge March 2023.
- Pension funds dropping fossil fuel stocks (*New York Times* December 9, 2020).
- An investment house's decision to overhaul their investment strategy to incorporate climate risk (RFF 2020) and another's decision to cease funding of oil projects.
- Research that has identified increased profitability from divestment (IEEFA, Blackrock)
- Several reports from national and international agencies, universities, and research institutes highlighting the need for revised risk analysis considering climate change (US CFTC 2020; NGFS 2020; IIPP 2020; NGFS 2020; Harvard Law School n.d.; Ceres 2020).
- The decision by the US Federal Reserve to join a network of global financial regulators focussed on the systems risks of climate change and their management (*New York Times* December 15, 2020).
- Several major reports by international agencies identifying the gains from climate-related investment and renewable energy (IEA 2017; OECD 2017).
- An initiative by at least one western government to require banks to disclose their climate risk
- Funds, such as mutual funds and ETFs, that focus on environmental, social, and governance principles (ESG Funds) have gained popularity with investors over time (SEC 2023).
- The United Securities and Exchange Commission is enhancing its focus on climate-related disclosure in public company filings. The Commission in 2010 provided guidance to public companies regarding existing disclosure requirements, as they apply to climate change matters. As part of its enhanced focus in this area, the staff will review the extent to which public companies address the topics identified in the 2010 guidance, assess compliance with disclosure obligations under the federal securities laws, engage with public companies on these issues, and absorb critical lessons on how the market is currently managing climate-related risks (SEC 2023).

It can be argued that the solution to the existential threat of climate change is ultimately political rather than relying on the development of radically new technology. Several authoritative studies have already concluded that the necessary technology already exists in partnership with natural climate solutions to address the social, economic, and ecological effects of climate change (Allwood et al. 2019; Princeton University 2021; WEF 2021). This does not mean that the necessary changes will come easily. The Princeton report describes the six crucial pillars necessary to support the transition to net-zero. These include: (1) end-use energy efficiency and electrification; (2) clean energy in the form of wind and solar generation with transmission and firm power; (3) bioenergy and other zero-carbon fuels and feedstocks; (4) carbon dioxide capture, utilization, and storage; (5) reduced non-CO_2 emissions; and (6) enhanced land sinks. *The New York Times* (December 15, 2020) also illustrated the nature of the challenge by providing at least six examples of what must be done:

- In 2020, energy companies proposed to install 42 gigawatts of new wind turbines and solar panels, smashing records. But that annual pace would need to nearly double over the next decade, and then keep soaring, transforming the landscapes in states like Florida or Missouri.

- The capacity of the nation's electric grid would have to expand roughly 60% by 2030 to handle vast amounts of wind and solar power, which would mean thousands of miles of new power lines crisscrossing the country.
- Car dealerships would look radically different. Today, electric-vehicle models are just 5.8% of new sales in the US By 2030, at least 50% of new cars sold would need to be battery-powered, with that share rising thereafter. In contrast, Norway, a leader adopter of EVs has achieved a level of 80% of new sales.
- Most homes today are heated by natural gas or oil. But in the next ten years, nearly one-quarter would need to be warmed with efficient electric heat pumps, double today's numbers.
- Virtually all the 225 remaining US coal-burning power plants would have to shut down by 2030.
- Today, there are no cement plants that bury their emissions underground, and there are no facilities sustainably producing hydrogen, a clean-burning fuel. By the mid-2020s, several such plants would need to be operating to prepare for wider deployment.

Only government in a leading role, in concert with business, can act effectively using a combination of economic incentives and regulation to address this historic challenge. But to achieve this goal, most governments around the world would have to significantly up their game as current national proposals to curtail emissions fall significantly short of what is required to achieve a meaningful impact on climate change (SEI et al. 2019). Failing that, it has been estimated that climate change could cut the world economy by as much as $23 trillion in 2050 (SwissRe 2021). One major emitter, India, has already labelled the achievement of net-zero targets as "pie in the sky," stating that poor nations want to continue using fossil fuels and the rich countries "can't stop it" (BBC March 31, 2021).

Reengineering Global Financial Systems

Perhaps the most definitive and authoritative assessment of the need to reengineer the financial systems has been provided by Mark Carney, the former governor of the Bank of Canada and Bank of England in his 2021 book, *Value(s) Building a Better World for All*.

Carney identifies two type of climate-change related risks: the physical/ecological and the transition risks. Carney (2021: 278) transition risks arise:

> As a result of the adjustment towards a lower carbon economy. Changes in policies, technologies and physical risk will prompt reassessment of the value of a large range of assets, as the costs and opportunities of the transition become apparent. The longer meaningful adjustment is delayed, the more transition risks will increase.

Carney (2021: 300) describes effort to address climate change as a "struggle between urgency and complacency." The urgency flows from three interrelated phenomena: (1) the urgency of carbon budgets that could be consumed within a decade, (2) the urgency of the sixth mass extinction, and (3) the urgency to reorient the financial system to finance the tens of trillions of dollars of investment needed over the next three decades for the transition to a sustainable economy.

Several other reports have also suggested financial needs in the trillions of dollars. The United Nations Environment Programme's report on the *State of Finance for Nature* (UNEP 2021) concluded that there is a $4.1 trillion financing gap in nature by 2050 (including climate change, biodiversity, and land degradation targets), and the International Renewable Energy Agency (IRENA 2021: 28) concluded that "USD 131 trillion will need to flow into an energy system over the period to 2050 that prioritises technology avenues compatible with a 1.5C Pathway."

Carney is reasonably optimistic that humanity can rise to the challenges, but solving the climate crisis requires three technologies: engineering, political, and financial: "All our within our grasp." The required *engineering* entails three priorities: building a zero-carbon economy by greening the generation of electricity, decarbonizing transportation, and reducing emissions. The *political* aspect requires setting the right goals, and a major step in this direction has been taken with the creation of the UN's Sustainable Development Goals (UN 2023).

The principal focus of Carney's work is his emphasis on the creation of a financial technology to ensure that every financial decision takes climate change into account. This requires "a new sustainable *financial* system to fund private sector innovation, amplify the effectiveness of government climate polices and accelerate the transition" (Carney 2021, p. 317). He envisages three fundamental building blocks:

- *Reporting*: disclosure of climate-related financial impacts must become comprehensive
- *Risk*: climate risk management needs to be transformed
- *Returns*: investing for net-zero world must go mainstream.

Table 18.1 summarizes the key components of these building blocks.

Carney's final plea is for global climate equity where a new sustainable financial system helps emerging developing economies in at least there ways (pp. 329–330): (1) by financing investments in sustainable infrastructure; (2) comprehensive reporting by companies in advanced economies of their scope 1, 2 and 3 emissions will encourage them to minimize climate risks and maximize opportunities across their supply chains since

Table 18.1 Carney's Three Fundamental Building Blocks

REPORTING

Disclosure of governance, strategy and risk management

Consistent and comparable metrics applicable across all sectors, as well as specific metrics for themost carbon-intense sectors

Use of scenario analysis so as to consider dynamically the potential impact of the risks and opportunities of the transition to a low-carbon economy on strategy and financial planning

RISKS

Disclosures need to go beyond the static to the strategic (that is, what their plans are for their emissions tomorrow and the associated financial impact.)

Climate stress tests that differ from normal stress tests. These stress tests will include outcomes as well as more traditional macro and financial impacts aspects. Specifically they need to assess physical and transition risk together - because businesses and our economies will face both.

RETURNS

Emerging best-practice transition plans include:

defining a net-zero objective in terms of scope 1, 2 and 3

outlining clear short-term milestones and metrics that senior management uses to monitor progress and gauge success

board level governance

embedding metrics in executive compensation.

Source: Carney (2021)

developing countries are where most scope 3 emissions are generated or outsourced; and (3) the transition to net zero will require new market structures that could substantially increase capital flows to developing and emerging economies.

Addendum: A Brief Overview of Green Finance

Given the finance sector's pervasive presence throughout the economic system all the way from government, through the business sector, civil sector and ultimately to the individual household and consumer, there is an extraordinary opportunity for the development of new custom-tailored instruments to further the cause of sustainability. There are at least five general categories of such instruments that are either in the nascent stage or are already well developed: green bonds, green loans, green equity, green microfinance, and green insurance (Muciri 2023). Brief descriptions of each category are provided below:

Green Bonds

In a study of green bonds in the developing world, The World Bank (2023) concluded that:

> Developing countries are increasingly raising money for climate action by issuing green and sustainability bonds. Colombia, Egypt, India, and Indonesia are among 19 emerging-market countries funding renewable energy and mass transit from the proceeds of green bonds. The World Bank assists countries that want to issue their own green and sustainability bonds to finance sustainable development.

By their estimates as of January 2023, over $2.5 trillion had been raised globally to support green and sustainable projects.

In another study S&P Global (2023, Table 1) reported on the type and size of green, social, sustainable and sustainability-linked bonds (GSSSB) in 2023: Green bonds $309.81 billion, Social bonds $95.49 billion, Sustainability bonds $87.05 billion, Sustainability-linked bonds $33.07 billion and transition bonds $1.08 billion, for a total of $526.50 billion.

Green Loans

The World Bank (2021) reported on the state of green loans in both the developing and developed world. The Bank differentiates between green loans and green bonds as follows:

> A green loan is similar to a green bond in that it raises capital for green eligible projects. However, a green loan is based on a loan that is typically smaller than a bond and done in a private operation. A green bond usually has a bigger volume, may have higher transaction costs, and could be listed on an exchange or privately placed. Green loans and green bonds also follow different but consistent principles: The Green Loan Principles and the Green Bond Principles (GBP) of the International Capital Market Association (ICMA). Both instruments specify that 100% of the proceeds should be used only for green eligible activities.

Estimates of outstanding green loans are $33 billion with developing countries accounting for only 5% currently.

Green Equity

Recourse et al. (2022) have reported on the current state of green equity and the challenges it faces in tackling climate change. While their estimates of sustainable investments are as high as $35.3 trillion, they caution that the broad definition frequently used in classification of this type of investment allows of the inclusion of investment in fossil fuel companies under certain circumstances. This echoes the discussion in chapter 16 of the contested claims of several fossil fuel companies that they are pursuing sustainability.

Green Microfinance

Allet and Hudon (2013: 395) described the characteristics of Microfinance Institutions involved in environmental managements. Based on a study of 160 global microfinance institutions, they concluded that:

> larger MFIs and MFIs registered as banks tend to perform better in environmental policy and environmental risk assessment. Furthermore, more mature MFIs tend to have better environmental performances, in particular in providing green microcredit and environmental non-financial services. On the other hand, financial performance is not significantly related to environmental performance, suggesting that 'green' MFIs are not more or less profitable than other microfinance institutions.

Green Insurance

> Green insurance is a type of insurance that not only covers people in case of injury or damage, but also contributes to protecting our environment. It is also known as eco-friendly insurance or sustainable insurance. Green insurance can take various forms, such as: 1. Offering discounts or incentives for customers who adopt green practices, such as driving electric vehicles, installing solar panels, using energy-efficient appliances etc. 2. Providing coverage for environmental damages or liabilities, such as pollution, contamination, clean-up costs etc. 3. Supporting green initiatives or projects, such as renewable energy sources, carbon offsetting programs, conservation efforts etc. Green insurance can benefit both customers and insurers by reducing risks, saving costs, enhancing reputation and promoting social responsibility (Fiscal Comparisons 2023).

Fiscal Comparisons lists some major types of environmental insurance for green business: pollution liability, environmental impairment liability, green building, renewable energy, sustainable agriculture, carbon credit, and water damage. The report lists the benefits of this type of insurance, as well as the challenges or drawbacks.

Summary

There are several estimates of the size of the global sustainable finance market. For example, Precedence Research (2023) estimates it at $4,562.85 billion in 2022 with an expected value of $29.11 trillion by 2032. A similar forecast was produced by Spherical Insights (2024), which anticipates the global green finance market size to exceed $28.71 trillion by 2033. The most optimistic assessment is from FMI (2023), which expects the sustainable finance market to exceed $37 trillion by 2034. Clearly, these values represent a significant step towards sustainability within financial markets, bearing in mind of course, that much can happen in a volatile global geopolitical environment before then that could shift these figures either up or down slightly or significantly.

On a final note, the *New York Times* (February 18, 2024) recently reported on an innovative and controversial proposal to convert natural asset value to financial capital through the creation of *natural asset companies* that would "put a market price on improving ecosystems rather than destroying them." The proposal went as far as the SEC that was considering a proposal from the NYSE to list these companies on the exchange. (see IDB 2021, SEC 2023, Intrinsic 2024). However, the proposal was rejected after serious objections raised by a variety of interest groups. It is ironic that this proposal received so much negative feedback considering the existence of somewhat similar existing mechanisms such as carbon and biodiversity credits, payment for ecosystem services, and purchases of private lands by nature conservancies.

Appendix One: Views on the Financial Sector and Sustainability

Battiston, Stefano (2017) "A climate stress test of the financial system," *Major Climate Change*, April.

Battiston, Stefano, et al. (2016) Complexity theory and financial regulation," Science, February 19.

Bloomberg (2019) "Green finance is now $31 trillion and growing," June 6.

Buchner, Barbara, et al. (2019) "Global landscape of climate finance," Climate Policy Initiative, November.

Carbon, Tracker (2011) "Unburnable carbon: Are the world financial markets carrying a carbon bubble?"

Carney, Mark, et al. (2019) "The financial sector must be at the heart of tackling climate change," *The Guardian*, April 17.

CERES (2020) "Addressing climate as a systemic risk, a call to action for US financial regulators," June.

Energy transition Accelerator Financing Platform (ETAF) (2020) "A multi-stakeholder climate finance solution."

Financial Stability Oversight Council (FSOC) (2021) *Report on climate related financial risk*.

Future Market Insights Inc. (FMI) "Sustainable finance market outlook for 2024 to 2034," December.

Glasgow Financial Alliance for Net Zero (GFANZ) (2023) *Progress Report*.

GreenBiz (2023) "Global decarbonization and the critical role of financial institutions," August.

GreenFin Weekly (2023) "Sustainable finance needs better climate policy," August 9.

Kenward, Katie (2020) "Managing nature related financial risks: a precautionary policy approach for central banks and financial supervisors," UCL Institute for Innovation and Public Purpose. Working paper WP 2020–09.

Kruger, Joseph (2017) "Climate-related financial disclosure: the new convergence of finance, policy, and science," Resources for the Future (RFF)

Lander, Brad (2022) "Investors deserve to know the climate risk, their assets face," guest essay, *New York Times*, June 15.

MarketWatch (2020) "Why Blackrock's Larry Fink warns climate change is on the edge of reshaping finance," January 14.

New York Times (2021) "US warns climate poses 'emerging threat' to financial system," October 21.

NGFS (2020) "NGFS promotes environmental risk analysis in financial industry."

O'Neill, Rebecca and Suzanne Volkman (2019), "The art of alignment, sustainability and financial transparency," Sustainability Transparency Network.

Precedence Research (2023) "Sustainable Finance Market."

Rainforest Action Network, et al. (2020) *Banking on climate change, fossil fuel financial report*.

Ramani, Veena, et al. (2020) "Addressing climate as a systemic risk: a call to action for financial regulators,", 2020 Harvard Law School Forum on Corporate Governance, June 28.

Recourse, et al. (2022). Putting People and Planet at the heart of green equity," April.

Roubini, Nouriel & Reza Bundy (2023) "What green finance need to speed the global transition to a net zero economy," September 20, *The Guardian*.

Spherical Insights (2024) "Global green finance market size to exceed USD 28.71 trillion by 2033, CAGR of 4.18%."

The Global Compact (2017) "Who cares wins, connecting financial markets to a changing world," World Bank.

The Globe and Mail (2022) "The climate fight is getting harder. Can Mark Carney keep his Green finance push on track?" April 23.

The Globe and Mail (2023) "New federal rules call for financial institutions to bolster climate disclosure, risk management," March 7.

United Nations (2021) Climate action. "Biggest financial players back net zero," April.

United Nations (2021) Climate Change "New financial alliance for net zero emissions launches," April.

US Commodity Futures Trading Commission (2020) "Managing climate risk in the US financial system. Report of the climate related market risk subcommittee market risk advisory committee of US commodity futures trading commission.

Wagner, Gernot (2022) "Climate risk is financial risk," editorial, *Science*, June 9.

WWF & Allianz (2009) "Major tipping points in the earth's climate system and consequences for the insurance sector."

References

Allet, Marion & Marck Hudon (2013) "Green microfinance: characteristics of microfinance institutions involved in environmental management," *Journal of Business Ethics*, November 12.
BBC (2021) "Climate change: net zero targets are 'pie in the sky,'" March 31.
BlackRock (n.d.) "Investment and fiduciary analysis for potential fossil fuel divestment, phase 1, survey of divestments of fossil fuel reserve owners and identification of securities issued by fossil fuel reserve owners," Report Draft.
Carney, Mark (2021) *Value(s) Building a Better World for All*. Penguin Random House.
Ceres (2020) *Addressing Climate as a Systemic Risk: A Call to Action for US Financial Regulators*, June.
Clean Edge (2022) "Q4 2022: Index review & top trends.
Clean Edge (2023) "Nasdaq clean edge green energy index (CELS)," March.
CNN (2021) "The world is waking up to the climate crisis. Just look at Wall Street," April 23.
Fiscal Comparisons (2023) "What is green insurance? 15 things you should know."
Harvard Law School Forum on Corporate Governance (2020) "Addressing climate as a systemic risk: a call to action for financial regulators," June 28.
Henderson, Rebecca (2021) *Reimagining Capitalism in a World On Fire*. Hachette Book Group.
Iabd.org (IDB) (2021) "NYSE and intrinsic exchange group announce a new asset class to power a sustainable future," September 14.
Institute for Energy Economics & Financial Analysis (IEEFA) (2021) "Major investment advisors Blackrock and Meketa provide a fiduciary path through the energy transition."
International Energy Agency (IEA) (2023) *Credible Pathways to 1.5C. Four Pillars for Action in the 2020s*.
Intrinsic Exchange Group (2024) "How NACs work."
Muciri, Njeri (2023) "Investing in a greener future: exploring different types of green finance instruments," *Behavioural Science*, March 14.
New York Times (2020) "New York's $226 billion pension fund is dropping fossil fuel stocks," December 9.
New York Times (2020) "To cut emissions to zero, us needs to make big changes in next 10 years," December 15.
New York Times (2020). "Fed joins climate network, to applause from the left," December 15.
New York Times (2024) "Nature has value. Could we literally invest in it?" February 18.
Network for Greening the Financial System (NGFS) (2020) "Overview of environmental risk analysis by financial institutions," September.
OECD (2017) *Investing in Climate, Investing in Growth*.

Princeton University (2021) *Net-Zero America. Potential Pathways, Infrastructure, And Impacts.*

Resources For the Future (RFF) (2020) "Lessons from COVID-19 on air pollution, managing climate risk in investments, and more," May 15.

S&P Global Ratings (2023) "Global sustainability bonds 2023 issuance to exceed $900 billion," September 14.

Stockholm Environment Institute (SEI), et al. (2019) *The Production Gap Report: The Discrepancy Between Countries' Planned Fossil Fuel Production and Global Production Levels Consistent with Limiting Warming to 1.5C or 2C.*

SwissRe Institute (2021) *The Economics of Climate Change – No Action Not an Option*, April.

United Nations (2023) *The Sustainable Development Goals. Special edition.*

United Nations Environment Programme (UNEP) (2021) *State of Finance for Nature.*

US Commodity Futures Trading Commission (CFTC) (2020) *Managing Climate Risk in the US Financial System.* Report of the Climate-Related Market Risk Subcommittee, Market Risk Advisory Committee of the US Commodity Futures Trading Commission.

will increase through 2050," September 30.

US Securities and Exchange Commission (SEC) (2023) Release No. 34-98665; File No. SR-NYSE-2023-09, "Self-regulatory organizations; New York Stock Exchange llc: Notice of filing of proposed rule change to amend the NYSE listed company manual to adopt listing standards for natural asset companies."

US Securities and Exchange Commission (SEC) (2021) "SEC Division of Examinations Announces 2021 Examination Priorities. Enhanced Focus on Climate-Related Risks."

US Securities and Exchange Commission (SEC) (2023) Letter to US SEC from Wildlife Conservation Society re SR-NYSE-2023-09, "Notice of Filing of proposed rule change to amend NYSE Listed Company Manual to adopt listing standards for Natural Asset Companies," October 25.

Wallwood, J. M., et al. (2019) *Absolute Zero: Delivering the UK's Climate Change Commitment with Incremental Changes Today's Technology.* UK FIRES.

World Bank (2021) "What you need to know about green loans," October 4.

World Bank (2023) "From India to Indonesia, green bonds help countries move toward sustainability," april 10.

World Economic Forum (WEF) (2021) *Consultation: Nature and Net Zero*, January.

19 Social Enterprise and the Social Return on Investment

It has been the principal thrust of this textbook that a truly sustainable economy can be achieved only when both traditional as well as green investors can agree on processes and products that are both profitable and sustainable (see Figure 19.1). This does not mean, however, that there is no room for investment opportunities that appeal largely to green investors. In fact, the emergence of the phenomenon of social entrepreneurship signals the viability of this option. The social enterprise (SE) is a broad and somewhat amorphous category, as it includes not only traditional nonprofits, but also organizations that can be profitable but have as their principal, if not exclusive, focus the advancement of social and environmental objectives. Any profits that might be generated are reinvested in order to advance the particular social goals of the organization. Another way of viewing the strategic functioning of this type of entity is to see it as maximizing the achievement of social goals with a non-negative profit constraint. This chapter first provides a brief review of the state of social enterprise in the United Kingdom, United States, Southeast Asia the European Union, and part of the developing world before summarizing some of the more common metrics for measuring the success and impact of social enterprise.

		Sustainable Investor	
		YES	**NO**
Traditional Investor	**YES**	**Sustainable Enterprise Economy**	Traditional for-profit enterprise
	NO	Social enterprise	

Figure 19.1 Ideal Business Sustainability Investment Model

DOI: 10.4324/9781003170754-23

One of the principal challenges in studying social enterprise is the varied definitional boundaries (see for example, Mair et al. 2006). Dacin et al. (2010) surveyed the literature and concluded that the definitions focus on four key factors: "the characteristics of individual social entrepreneurs, their operating sector, the processes and resources used by social entrepreneurs, and the primary mission and outcomes associated with the social entrepreneur." They believe that "the definition that holds the most potential for building a unique understanding of social entrepreneurship and developing actionable implications is one that focuses on the social value creation mission and outcomes, both positive and negative, of undertakings aimed at creating social value." In Table 19.1, the authors outline the principle distinctions between social and three other forms of entrepreneurship. Young (2001) summarized the juxtaposition between the organizational identities of social enterprises and the legal forms they may take in Table 19.2.

In a comprehensive review of Social Enterprises in 29 countries in the EU, Borzaga et al. (2020) define SEs in an ESG framework (see Table 19.3)

One of the most famous social enterprises was the Grameen Bank established by Professor Muhammed Yunus in 1976 to provide small loans to impoverished people in Bangladesh. Yunus subsequently was awarded the Nobel Peace Prize for his work.[1] The critical characteristic of these loans was the absence of required collateral (Yunus 2003, 2008, 2010). This venture has been extraordinarily successful and has over 9 million subscribers, mainly women, allowing many of them to start their own businesses (Grameen Bank Annual Report 2020). This concept of microcredit has now reached many parts of the developing world.

Before considering country-specific data, it is useful to distinguish between nonprofits and social enterprises. A short description of the principal differences and similarities is provided below (Insight Global Education n.d.):

How are they different?

The fundamental difference between nonprofits and social enterprises is the source of funding. Non-profits rely on public funding through donations. Social enterprises are businesses; they generate their own profit to keep themselves running. Social enterprises also have a product or service that they sell to a consumer base that helps them in some way; whereas non-profits operate more directly with the social issue through areas like advocacy, direct aid, food relief, and empowerment.

How are they the same?

Non-profit organizations and social enterprises are often grouped together – and for good reason. They both are efforts by organized groups of people to work towards the betterment of some social issue. Within both these types of organizations, the cause is the focus of their actions. Non-profits and social enterprises both have a social cause that drives the heart of what they do. Though social enterprises generate revenue, all profits go back into the business. So, while they do create a profit, they operate like a nonprofit by directing all funds towards the social, economic, or environmental cause. It is also possible for nonprofits to operate social entrepreneurial initiatives, like the Girl Scouts or Goodwill. The line between non-profit organizations and social enterprises are often blurred, and the differences between the two are both quite clear and yet frustratingly nuanced.

Table 19.1 Types of Entrepreneurs

	Conventional	Institutional	Cultural	Social
Definition	An agent who enables or enacts a vision based on new ideas in order to create successful innovations	An agent who can mobilize resources to influence or change institutional rules, in order to support or destroy an existing institution, or to establish a new one	An agent who identifies an opportunity and acts upon it in order to create social, cultural, or economic value	An actor who apples business principles to solving social problems
Wealth distribution	Shareholder	Shareholder and/or stakeholder	Shareholder and/or stakeholder	Shareholder and/or stakeholder
Predominant organizational form	Profit	Profit	Nonprofit or profit	Nonprofit or profit
Primary goal (or motives)	Economic	Institutional reform/ development	Cultural diffusion/ enlightenment	Social change/well-being
Product	Create and/or distribute consumer product or service	Establish legitimacy	Establish new norms and values	Promotes ideology/social change
Tensions	Growth versus survival	Resistance to change (isomorphism versus competitive advantage?)	Commercialization versus culture (authenticity)	Economic sustainability versus social mission
Examples	Business service providers Software developers Tourism companies	Edison Kodak Apple	Museums Folk art festivals Symphony orchestras	Aravind Eye Clinic Greyston Bakery Rugmark

Source: Dacin et al. (2010) Reproduced with permission

Table 19.2 Legal Forms of SEs

Identity / Legal Form	Nonprofit	For-Profit
Corporate Philanthropy	major nonprofits competing for market share who find it useful to help other charities as part of corporate strategy	business corporations whose philanthropy is part of a business strategy to enhance profits
Social Purpose Organization	nonprofits that undertake commercial activities to generate funds and support social goals	businesses whose owners are focussed on social goals and where the for-profit form is more comfortable or practical
Hybrid	nonprofits whose leaders seek both income and social benefits	businesses whose owners sacrifice some profits to achieve social goals

Source: Young (2001)

Table 19.3 EU Definition of SEs

Main dimension	General definition	Minimum requirements
Entrepreneurial/ economic dimension[2]	**Stable and continuous production of goods and services** >Revenues are generated mainly from both the direct sale of goods and services to private users or members and public contracts. **(At least partial) use of production factors functioning in the monetary economy (paid labour, capital, assets)** > Although relying on both volunteers (especially in the start-up phase) and non-commercial resources, to become sustainable, SEs normally also use production factors that typically function in the monetary economy.	SEs must be market-oriented (incidence of trading should be ideally above 25%).
Social dimension	**The aim pursued is explicitly social. The product supplied/ activities run have a social/ general interest connotation** >The types of services offered or activities run can vary significantly from place to place, depending on unmet needs arising at the local level or in some cases even in a global context.	Primacy of social aim must be clearly established by national legislations, the statutes of SEs or other relevant documents.

(*Continued*)

Table 19.3 (Continued)

Main dimension	General definition	Minimum requirements
Inclusive governance-ownership dimension	**Inclusive and participatory governance model** >All concerned stakeholders are involved, regardless of the legal form. >The profit distribution constraint (especially on assets) guarantees that the enterprise's social purpose is safeguarded.	The governance and/or organisational structure of SEs must ensure that the interests of all concerned stakeholders are duly represented in decisionmaking processes.

Source: Borzaga et al. (2020, Appendix 2, p. 158)

Social Enterprise in the United Kingdom

Social Enterprise UK (2023) has estimated that there are more than 100,000 social enterprises in the UK, creating 2 million jobs and contributing 60 billion GBP to GDP. The EU (Borzaga et al. 2020) has a somewhat more conservative estimate at 30,753 SEs with 35,357 employees. The British banking corporation, NatWest, periodically hosts social business award ceremonies in eight categories (ImpactFest 2020; GSG 2021): environmental champion, growth champion, impact management champion, trailblazing newcomers, social investment award, leadership award, resilience award, and storyteller award. NatWest (2020), has produced a *SE100 Health & Fitness Report* that reports on the results of survey questions posed to members of the SE community in the UK. Of particular interest were the responses to two specific questions: the first was the identification of barriers and enablers. The survey results found that 34% of respondents stated the lack of cash flow was the main barrier to growth and 44% felt threatened by staffing issues. On the other hand, 50% identified "motivated staff" as the key enabler for growth, 51% felt that word of mouth was best for business, and 85% stated that resilience needs a "great team culture." Clearly, good leadership is essential and 46% stated the necessity of a clear vision, 66% emphasized the need to get the right people, and 40% found that leaders having served 10+ years providing continuity for the enterprise.

Social Enterprise in the United States

Because of the fuzzy definitional borders of social enterprise it can be difficult to get a sense of its role in a national economy. The *New York Times* reported on October 12, 2011 on the emergence of hybrid companies, defined as those putting social goals ahead of profit, and the legal challenges these organizations may face at the state level. Corporate law jurisdiction rests at the state rather than the federal level, and most state legislation has enshrined the traditional view that shareholder interests (i.e. profitability must be paramount). Despite this fact, numerous states such as California amended their laws to allow three variants that facilitate social enterprise (*New York Times* 2011):

LC3 – a specialized form of limited liability corporation with a primary purpose intended to take investments from foundations.

Benefit [B] Corporation: a corporation that emphasizes social impact over profitability. Social and environmental goals must conform to statutory definitions, and directors must consider the impact of corporate decisions on the community and the environment as well as shareholders. [see "The Emergence of the B Corps" below]

Flexible purpose corporation: a corporation with a stated social purpose. Directors are required to keep its social purpose in mind when considering how to maximize shareholder value. Annual reports of social impact and planned future expenditures to achieve that impact are required.

Van den Hoek et al. (2023) provide a current compilation of social enterprise forms in the US and their availability by state (see Table 19.4).

Up until 2021, there had been no comprehensive study of the number and type of Social Enterprises in the US. In that year, Georgetown University's McDonough School of Business published a report entitled *Jobs for All: Employment Social Enterprise and Economic Mobility in the United States.* While the report focussed on social enterprises that addressed employment-related challenges for six groups (people with disabilities, youth, formerly incarcerated, immigrants and refugees, veterans, and low-income persons), the research group participated in a national survey that generated the first reasonable estimates of the number of SEs in the US. Their summary findings are reproduced in Table 19.5. Another smaller study of SEs in the US (Crunchbase 2023) that focussed

Table 19.4 Social Enterprise Forms in the US

General form	Specific form	Available in:
LLC	LLC	IL, LA, ME, MI, RI, UT, VT, WY
	BLLC	DE, MD, OR, PA, UT
Corporation	Benefit Corporation	41 states + DC
	Social Purpose Corporation	CA, TX, FL, WA
Limited Partnership	Statutory Public Benefit Limited Partnership	DE

Source: Van den Hoek et al. (2023)

Table 19.5 Scale and Scope of SEs in the US

	Categories of SEs	Number
Socially responsible companies	Organizations registered as limited liability companies (LLCs) with socially responsible programs or social enterprise branches	887,574
Enterprising nonprofits	Organizations registered as 501(c)3 legal status, with programs or branches earning commercial income	314,744
SEs with hybrid legal status	Low-profit limited liability companies (L3Cs)	1,651
	Benefit Corporations	1,605
	B Corps (certified by B Lab) [an extension of the concept of a benefit corporation. While B Corps are certified by B Lab, benefit companies are legal entities recognized by the government (Green Economy Law 2023)]	2,933
	Benefit limited liability companies (BLLCs)	2,112
	Co-operatives	64,017
	TOTAL	**1,274,636**

Source: Georgetown University (2021)

on 741 companies identified five investor types: acceleration, venture capital, incubator, entrepreneurship program, and university program; and the top funding types: seed, grant, venture - series unknown, pre-seed, and nonequity assistance. An earlier study from 2020 (The Annie E. Casey Foundation) estimated that employment-related SEs in the US market generated over $1 billion and employed 56,000 people. These latter data are probably serious underestimates considering the more recent comprehensive Georgetown University findings.

Despite the large number of SEs in the US, there remain several challenges facing social enterprises in the country. Abramson and Billings (2019) have identified at least six such challenges: ill-fitting legal forms, obstacles to effective governance, problems in evaluating impact, weak supportive networks, difficulties in raising funding, and management tensions.

The European Union

The EU has conducted the most comprehensive and detailed study of its social enterprises in a 2020 report entitled: *Social Enterprises and the Ecosystems in Europe. Comparative Synthesis Report* (Borzaga et al.). The report covered:

(i) the historical background and conditions of the emergence of social enterprises; (ii) the evolution of the concept and the existing national policy and legal framework for social enterprise; (iii) the scale and characteristics of social enterprise activity; (iv) networks and mutual support mechanisms; (v) research, education and skills development; and (vi) the resources available to social enterprises. The study also provided insights on the factors constraining the development of social enterprise, a reflection on the debate currently at play in national contexts, and an overview of possible developmental trends.

Table 19.6 provides estimates of the number of social enterprises in European countries, Table 19.7 lists the legal status and legal forms adopted in Europe, and Table 19.8

Table 19.6 Estimated Number of SEs by European Country

Country	#SEs	#SEs per million inhabitants	# Employees
Albania	379	132	2,000–2,500
Austria	approx. 1,535	approx. 174	n.a.
Belgium	18,004	1,530	572,914
Bulgaria	approx. 3,700	approx. 525	26,000
Croatia	526	128	n.a.
Cyprus	190	22	n.a.
Czech Republic	373	356	n.a.
Denmark	411	71	n.a.
Estonia	121	92	1,603
Finland	1,181	214	approx. 52,500
France	approx. 96,603	1,414	>1,187,249
Germany	77,459	936	n.a.
Greece	1,148	107	n.a.
Hungary	15,855	1,621	72,642

(Continued)

Table 19.6 (Continued)

Country	#SEs	#SEs per million inhabitants	# Employees
Iceland	258	740	1,488
Ireland	3,376	699	>25,000
Italy	102,461	1,694	894,800
Latvia	approx. 200	approx. 103	n.a.
Lithuania	3,476	1,237	n.a.
Luxembourg	928	1,546	n.a.
Malta	31–62	65–130	24,055
Montenegro	150	241	n.a.
Netherlands	5,000–6,000	290–350	<500
North Macedonia	551	266	65,000–80,000
Norway	250	47	n.a.
Poland	29,535	768	n.a.
Portugal	7,938	771	428,734
Romania	617	323	145,734
Serbia	411	59	17,117
Slvakia	3,737	687	4,273
Slovenia	1,393	674	15063
Spain	9,680	208	>91,500
Sweeden	qpprox. 3,000	approx. 296	n.a.
Turkey	1,776	22	n.a.
UK	30,753	464	353357

Source: Borzaga et al. (2020, Table 14, pp. 106–107)

Table 19.7 Legal Status and Legal Forms for SEs

Type of SE	Description	Legal form/ status exclusively for SE	Countries
Institutionalized SE	Through a legal form designed specifically for SEs with a broad focus (different fields of activity of general interest)	YES	Belgium, France, Germany, Greece, Italy, Latvia, Spain, UK
Institutionalized SE	Through a legal form designed specifically for SEs with a specific focus on work integration	YES	Czech Republic, Greece, Hugary, Poland, Portugal
Institutionalized SE	Through a WISE (work integration social enterprise) status	YES	Albania, Austria, Belgium, Bulgaria, Croatia, Finland, France, Germany, Lithuania, Luxembourg, Poland, Romania, Serbia, Slovakia, Slovenia, Spain

(Continued)

Table 19.7 (Continued)

Type of SE	Description	Legal form/ status exclusively for SE	Countries
Organization with a public benefit status	Status that related to a tax-privileged organisation that exists for public benefit	NO	Albania, Austria, Bulgaria, Czech Republic, Estonia, Finland, France, Germany, Hungary, Latvia, Malta, Netherlands, Poland, Romania, Sweden, Turkey (non-exhaustve list)
de facto SE	Organisation that fulfils the criteria set by the EU operational definition of SE, but uses a legal form not specfic to social enterprises (e.g. association, cooperative, conventional enterprise)	NO	all countries

Source: Borzaga et al. (2020, Table 15, p. 109)

Table 19.8 Drivers and Trends of SEs in Europe

Type of Welfare system	Main drivers boosting SE development
Poor supply of welfare services by public providers and, traditionally, gaps in welfare delivery and strong civic engagement	Bottom-up experimentation by groups of citizens of new services; Consolidation of SEs thanks to public policies that have regularised social service delivery
Extensive public supply of social services, increasingly contracted out to private providers	Privatisation of social services; bottom-up dynamics
Extensive public and non-profit welfare structures, covering the majority of the needs of the population	Public support system designed to support work integration; bottom-up emergence of SEs to address new needs
Welfare systems that have undergone drastic reforms, weak associative and cooperative tradition (particularly central, Eastern, and Southeast/Southeastern European countries, e.g. the Balkans)	Public policies (start-up grants) specificallyl tailored to supprt WISES; initiatives with philanthropic background and donor's programmes

Source: Borzaga et al. (2020, Table 6, p. 46)

summarizes drivers and trends of SEs. Major support measures for starting up social enterprises include grants and subsides from public authorities and European funds, grants and other support from private stakeholders, foundations and second level organizations, and private and public support for incubators and business innovation centers.

In addition, there are four major categories of fiscal benefits grants to SEs, including corporate tax exemption on retained profits, value-added tax exemption or reduced rates, social insurance costs reduced or covered by subsides, and tax reductions granted to private and/or institutional donors.

The EC report (p. 135) observes that:

> social enterprises have gained stronger visibility and have grown in number since 2014. Their relevance is, moreover, likely to increase further over the coming decades, given the pressing challenges faced by European countries. Positive changes are particularly impressive in countries where the degree of development of social enterprise was rather poor in 2014. However, without further legitimisation, adequate support to scale up and consolidate (also through tax breaks), proper capacity building and access to financial resources tailored to their peculiar needs, social enterprises will remain vulnerable. The vulnerability of social enterprises is to a certain extent connected to the fragmented debate and conceptual confusion that revolves around their role in contemporary societies. Moreover, vulnerability results from the strong dependency of social enterprises upon national and local policies.

The report also observes that the domains of relevance are broadening to address many of the emerging problems facing the European Union including demographic changes, in- and out-migration, regional development, and marginalization of remote communities and groups. The increasing presence of SE's is also related to a shift in priorities and policy responsibility, although some critics fear that the development of SEs may serve as an excuse for government agencies to withdraw from their traditional role of providing public services.

The report also details some of the many challenges facing the development and strength of social enterprises in Europe. First, "the capacity of social enterprises to self-organise and set up networks has proved crucial for social enterprise expansion and the success of both nascent and existing social enterprises (p.141)." Second, there is still a need for increased awareness and knowledge about the sector in the general public. Third, there is a need for legislation that establishes clear definitions for what constitutes a SE so that the terminology cannot be misappropriated by conventional enterprises. Fourth, fragmentation of the sector may interfere with their ability to organize as a group to lobby for more favourable policies. Fifth, in many countries there is still an absence of a comprehensive support programme for the creation of new SEs. Sixth, many SEs are not investor-ready. In this respect there is a need for an array of financing options such as grants, loans and consulting modules tailored to the need of SEs. Several possible additional avenues of financing include equity crowdfunding and financial support from venue philanthropy. Seventh, in many European countries, there is little systematic data collection on SEs. The results is that it is more difficult for policymakers and other stakeholders to make informed decisions to support the sector. Eighth, there is

> lack of internal capacities as one of the main barriers to social enterprise development. While social enterprises that developed from community groups tend to lack business and investment skills and have poor capacities for developing financial plans or promoting their products and services on the market, on the other end of the spectrum, social enterprises coming from the business sector tend to neglect social aspects.

While some of these challenges may apply to some or all of the European countries, there is reason to believe that other national or subnational SEs may face many of the same obstacles.

Southeast Asia

A collaborative effort by the British Council, UN ESCAP, Social Enterprise UK and HSBC published a report on the state of social enterprise in South East Asia in 2021. They estimated that there may be between one half to 1 million social enterprises across the region while acknowledging the difficulty of generating a comprehensive and accurate estimate. Most major sectors of the economy have participants that are SEs, including the arts, agriculture, culture, heritage, education, food, health and manufacturing. Estimates by country are as follows: Indonesia 342,000, the Philippines 164,473, Thailand 115,000, Malaysia 20,749, Singapore 6,000 and Hong Kong 4,000. The SEs receive significant support from national governments including specialist units or offices, legislation, incentives and awards. The SEs in the region generally take one of five legal forms: sole trader, partnership, private company, charitable organization/NGO, and other.

Other Developing Nations

Within the last several decades there has been a literal explosion of social enterprise across the globe. In each country, various manifestations of this phenomenon have emerged in response to perceived needs, particularly widespread poverty, often flowing from the absence of a strong market environment, legal system, or effectively functioning government. Among the most noteworthy of these developing nations are: India (2,000,000 SEs), Pakistan (448,000), Bangladesh (150,000), Ethiopia (55,000), Sudan (55,000), Kenya (40,000), Ghana (26,100), and Sri Lanka (10,000).

Global Diversity in Social Enterprise

While the United States and the United Kingdom and several countries in Western Europe have been leaders in the development of the theory and practice of social enterprise, there are both similarities and differences in their approach to this organizational phenomenon. Authors such as Kerlin (2009) and Defourny and Kim (2011) have identified three spheres of influence on social enterprise: the market, the state, and civil society.[2] Not surprising, the strong market ethic combined with a common suspicion of big government in the United States has bred a social enterprise model embedded in both civil society and the market. In contrast, the tradition of government intervention in Europe coupled with a somewhat less enthusiastic embrace of the free market has dictated that social enterprise in the UK and on the Continent tends to be a product of civil society and the state (see also Defourny & Nyssens 2010). Borzaga et al. (2020) make a similar observation when they conclude that:

> Rather than deriving from business models as it does in the United States, in Europe and bordering countries social enterprise stems mainly from organisational models and values that have strong roots in European societies, including solidarity,

self-help, participation, and inclusive and sustainable growth. As such, the social enterprise mainly results from a collective dynamic, and it is a collective entrepreneurial model (p. 148).

The more formalized and structured approach to social enterprise in Europe led to the creation of a research network in 1996 called "The Emergence of Social Enterprise in Europe" (EMES) that conceptualized an "ideal type" social enterprise with several distinctive characteristics (OECD n.d.; Defourny & Nyssens 2008, Kerlin 2006). They are directly engaged in the production and/or sale of goods and services; are voluntarily created and managed by groups of citizens; enjoy a high degree of autonomy; are dependent on the efforts of their members for their financial viability; face a significant level of economic risk; rely on a minimum number of paid workers; are the result of an initiative by citizens involving people belonging to a community or to a group that shares a certain need or aim; are characterized by decision-making power not based on capital ownership; are participatory in nature; avoid profit maximizing behaviour, as they involve a limited distribution of profit; and pursue an explicit aim to benefit the community or a specific group of people.

The Emergence of the B Corp

An unusual and innovative form of social enterprise that has emerged in recent years is the B Corp. Meagher (2023a) summarizes the distinction between a SE and B Corp:

> B Corps undergo a certification process conducted by B Lab, which evaluates their overall impact and governance. On the other hand, social enterprise is a concept describing a business' mission and purpose. It is not a legal structure or certification."

Certification is provided by B Lab, which requires the following actions to achieve certification (B Lab 2023):

> a company must: Demonstrate high social and environmental performance by achieving a B Impact Assessment score of 80 or above and passing our risk review. Multinational corporations must also meet baseline requirement standards. Make a legal commitment by changing their corporate governance structure to be accountable to all stakeholders, not just shareholders, and achieve benefit corporation status if available in their jurisdiction. Exhibit transparency by allowing information about their performance measured against B Lab's standards to be publicly available on their B Corp profile on B Lab's website.

Meagher (2023b) describes the governance requirements to become certified as a B Corp using Australia as an example:

1. *Eligibility*: Be a registered Australian business and demonstrate a commitment to social and environmental responsibility.
2. *Complete the B Impact Assessment (BIA)*: B Corps undergo a rigorous assessment process called the B Impact Assessment. This questionnaire evaluates the organisation's

policies, contributions, and metrics to determine their positive impact on the community. A minimum score of 80 is required to achieve B Corp certification.

3. *Verify the assessment*: Provide supporting documents, pay the one-off verification fee, and have an independent analyst review your assessment.
4. *Meet legal requirements*: B Corps must incorporate clauses within their governing documents (such as the company constitution or trust deed) that reflect their commitment to a triple bottom line approach — balancing social, environmental, and financial objectives.
5. *Sign the B Corp Declaration of Interdependence*: Embrace values and principles guiding B Corps.
6. *Pay certification fees*: Submission, verification, and annual certification fees based on revenue.

Currently, there are 7,200 companies registered with B Lab employing 645,620 workers in 93 countries (B Lab 2023). According to *Forbes* magazine (May 11, 2022), Natura was the first public company to become a B Corp and is now the world's largest. Table 19.9 lists the top 20 countries with the most certified B Corps (Gallizzi 2022). An exhaustive list of global countries is provided by ZenBusiness (2021). The sector with the highest number of B Corps is the food & drink industry (12.4% of all B Corp companies), followed by the IT software and services sector (7%), management and financial consulting (6.2%), and marketing and communication services (5.9%) (ZenBusiness 2021). Several well-known companies are B Corps, including Ben and Jerry's, Nespresso, Moodle, TOMS, and Warby Parker (Gallizzi 2022; Nestle 2022).

Table 19.9 Top 20 Countries with the Most Certified B Corps

Country	# Of B Corps
USA	1418
UK	590
Canada	323
Australia	296
Brazil	181
Chile	136
France	151
Italy	134
The Netherlands	126
Argentina	119
Spain	88
Colombia	60
Mexico	53
Switzerland	52
New Zeland	49
Germany	41
Denmark	38
Taiwan	33
Peru	28
China	27

Source: Gallizzi (2022)

A Note on the emergence of Base of the Pyramid Commerce

As described further in chapter 21, a significant proportion of social enterprise in the Third World is focused on the alleviation of poverty. Paralleling this phenomenon in the last two decades has been the emergence of a for-profit business model that has developed to capitalize on a heretofore unrecognized market opportunity of large proportions by selling goods and services to the poorest members of the global population who have largely subsisted outside the global capitalist market. Termed Base-of-the-Pyramid [BoP], this population grouping has been estimated to number approximately 4 billion people (i.e., a majority of the human population) (Prahalad & Hart 2002; Prahalad 2009). According to London and Hart (2011), however, this marketing concept is seriously flawed as it focuses on "finding a fortune at the base of the pyramid" through the mass merchandising of low-cost goods with potentially detrimental environmental impacts. At its worst, this marketing phenomenon can be exploitative and spur rampant consumerism among the poor. An example of this perverse result is the takeover of microcredit by large banks focused principally on the pursuit of profit as opposed to Yunus's original goal of poverty alleviation (*New York Times* April 13, 2010).

London and Hart make the case for a fundamental transformation in the BoP model, arguing strongly for a transition from "fortune finding" to "fortune creating" through business *with* four billion by co-creating new business models and technological solutions. As the authors state: "the most effective BoP strategies can actually build capacity and generate income among the poor, not simply extract wealth in the form of increased consumer spending" (London & Hart 2011: 7). These strategies would not only succeed in raising the standard of living of the bottom four billion, but also attempt to do so in an environmentally sustainable manner (see also London 2009; Hart 2010).

Metrics for Measuring the Impact of Social Enterprise

With the emergence of the social enterprise as a major player in sustainability, there is a pressing need to generate metrics that can be used to evaluate not only the attractiveness of such ventures for potential investors, but also to measure both temporally and across enterprises the impact of the broad range of initiatives undertaken. In many cases the transference of conventional financial measures is inappropriate or insufficient to measure the unique characteristics of these ventures. Table 19.10 presents nine alternative approaches to measuring the performance of social enterprise (Social Capital Partners and Vancity Community Foundation n.d). Of these metrics, the one most conceptually similar to conventional for-profit analysis is the social return on investment (SROI). Several comprehensive guides have been produced on this subject, most notably "SROI Methodology" by the Roberts Enterprise Development Fund (REDF) in San Francisco (2001), and an updated "Guide to Social Return on Investment" from the British Government in cooperation with several NGOs (2012).

REDF (2001) developed six key SRPI stages and accompanying quantitative metrics to help inform investors on the degree of value creation from their philanthropic investments in

Table 19.10 Alternative Approaches to Measuring Performance of SEs

Approach	What it Measures	Key Aspects	Who Promotes	Further Information
Outcome measurement	Short, medium & long-term benefits of programs/services	Logic model that can be modified to the enterprise situation	United Way of America	www.national.unitedway.org/outcomes/
Program measurement and management	The difference between planned goals and actual achievements	Logic model and goal-setting process to help identify improvement needs	Seedco	www.seedco.org
Benchmarking	Compares processes used by one enterprise with one or more others	Involves building partnerships with other businesses to look at efficiencies	Used in industries, usually with large-scale production processes	www.benchmarkingnetwork.com
Balanced scorecard	Creates an information feedback loop to ensure that internal processes align with the mission as seen by external stakeholders	Sets goals according to the enterprise mission, then tracks progress on internal and external indicators	The Balanced Scorecard Institute	www.balancedscorecard.org
Sustainable livelihoods framework	Client assets and constraints and progress related to their ability to realize a sustainable livelihood	Interviews individuals and tracks over time to improve program design and outcomes	Department for International Development (UK)	www.livelihoods.org;www.ekonomos.com
Triple Bottom Line	Identifies overall impact in three areas: social, environmental, financial	Separates and identifies intentional and unintentional effects of enterprise	Frequently used in private sector	www.bsdglobal.com

(Continued)

Table 19.10 (Continued)

Approach	What it Measures	Key Aspects	Who Promotes	Further Information
NESsT	Assesses impact in four areas: financial impact; financial sustainability; social impact; and organizational sustainability	Looks at organizational impact of enterprise in addition to business and social impact	Non-profit Enterprise and self Sustainability team	www.nesst.org
Social Return on Investment (SROI)	Calculates the net benefit of a financial investment in monetary terms	Translates social benefits into monetary terms to compare investment in the enterprise to resulting social benefit	Roberts Enterprise Development Fund (San Francisco)	www.blendedvalue. org;www.redf.org
Social Capital Partners	Combines sustainable livelihoods and SROI approach	Uses sustainable livelihoods framework to set baseline indicators, then uses SROI analysis to translate the social impact into monetary terms	Social Capital Partners (Toronto)	www.socialcapitalpartners. ca, For an example, go to the "ideas" section of the site and check out the ICR report cards

Source: Social Capital Partners and Vancity Community Foundation (n.d. [reproduced with permission of the authors])

social enterprises. These metrics are divided into two general categories (measures of value and indices of return), as illustrated in Tables 19.11 and 19.12. As explained by REDF:

> These first three metrics measure what a social purpose enterprise is 'returning' to the community. The next three metrics compare these returns against the philanthropic investments required to generate them. This comparison of returns generated to investments required is articulated in the Index of Return. The Index of Return (Index) is a ratio used to determine impact of an investment. It compares an investment to the value created by the investment. The resulting number shows whether the investment lost, maintained, or created value. An Index of one means that all investors will receive their required rate of return. An Index greater than one shows that excess value is generated. If the Index is less than one, value is lost. However, it is important to remember that the SROI metrics only measure monetizable value. Social Purpose Enterprises create value that is not captured by these measures. An Index of Return less than one does not necessarily imply a poor investment.

The British Government guide was also designed to give detailed, hands-on instructions to stakeholders in social enterprises on how to construct and interpret measures of social value from social enterprises. The manual outlines six stages in SROI analysis: (1) establishing scope and identifying key stakeholders, (2) mapping anticipated or realized outcomes, (3) finding evidence of outcome occurrence and valuing them, (4) establishing impacts, (5) calculating the SROI, and (6) verifying and reporting the results and embedding processes that produce the desired outcomes. The underlying principles of analysis are similar in kind to standard financial analysis but require their adaptation to situations where outcome measures may be somewhat more difficult to measure and monetize. Key outcomes

Table 19.11 Measures of Value

Type of Value `Created	Metric	Definitions
Economic	Enterprise value	Present value of excess cash generated by enterprise's business operations (excluding social operating epenses and subsidies)
Socio-economic	Social purpose value	Present value of projected social savings and new tax revenue generated by employees of social purpose enterprises less social operating expenses
Socio-economic	Blended value	Enterprise value + social purpose value - long-term det
Social	n.a.	n.a.

Source: REDF (2001, p. 7)

Table 19.12 Indices of Return

Enterprise Index of Return	= Enterprise Value / Present Value of Investment to Date
Social Purpose Index of Return	= Social Purpose Value / Present Value of Investment to Date
Blended Index of Return	= Blended Value / Present Value of Investment to Date

Source: REDF (2001, p. 9)

are identified for all major stakeholders and then appropriate indicators for each outcome are also identified. The final step is determining possible financial proxies that accurately capture and reflect the underlying processes.

There are several complexities in this analysis, as adjustments must be made to reflect four important factors: (1) *deadweight* (the amount of outcome that would have occurred without the social enterprise); (2) *displacement* (any net losses elsewhere that might offset the gains from the activities of the social enterprise); (3) *attribution* (separating out the effect of other organizations and people on the final outcomes); and (4) *predicting or tracking the effect of the program over time* that may decline due to reduced effort or external factors.

Finally, the monetized results can be presented in one or more of several formats: net present value, SROI or payback period. Wherever a stream of future costs and benefits must be included, it is recommended that a social rate of discount be applied somewhere in the range of 3.0–3.5%. A real-life example of the approach to calculating a SROI is presented in the following section.

Case study: MillRace IT

MillRace IT was a social enterprise with two related goals: to increase the employability of disabled people, and to reduce the flow of electronic equipment to landfills (UK Cabinet Office 2009; Nicholls et al. n.d.). It was incorporated in 2000 and dissolved in 2020. It accomplished these tasks by employing and training people with mental health problems to repair and refurbish old computers and peripheral electronic equipment. It was intended that some of these employees would eventually move into the normal work stream; others may remain working at MillRace, thereby reducing their risk of falling back into their former state of reliance on state support. Table 19.13 identifies the key variables in the analysis: relevant stakeholders, financial and other inputs, principal outputs, indicators, and impacts. Figure 19.2 maps the process of analysis in the derivation of net impact, and Table 19.14 provides monetized estimates of total social benefits. The final step in this analytical process is calculation of the SROI, as illustrated in Figure 19.3, the results of that are reported in Table 19.15.

Table 19.13 MillRace Indicator Map Stakeholders - Based on NEF (n.d., p. 32)

Stakeholder	Input	Outputs	Outcome Indicators	Impact
Participants	Number of participants	(1) Number of tonnes of computers recycled AND (2) Length of time in programme	(1) Length of time in recovery AND (2) change in medical costs AND (3) change in income	Deadweight: Number of computers that would have been recycled anyway Displacement: Assumed nil given nature of participant population

(Continued)

Table 19.13 (Continued)

Stakeholder	Input	Outputs	Outcome Indicators	Impact
Government	Funding	(1) Number of trained participants AND (2) Number of tonnes of computers recycled	(1) Number who obtain jobs AND (2) Number who extend recover AND (3) Number of decrease use of the local health care system	Deadweight: Number of computers that would have been recycled anyway Displacement: Assumed nil given nature of participant population

Table 19.14 MillRace IT SROI Model - Based on NEF (n.d., p. 40)

Indicator	Value (UK pounds)
Benefits to participants	
Employee wages (for some participants)	£13,500
Less welfare benefits lost (weighted average)	-£6,900
Less increase in tax contribution	-£1,600
Less increase in National Insurance	-£500
Net benefit per participant that moves on to full-time employment	£4,500
Number of participants that move on to full time employment per annum	3
Total benefits to participants	£13,500
Benefits to local government	
Cost to send one tonne of waste to landfill	£39
Number of tonnes recycled per annum	50
Net savings to local government	£1,950
Benefits to national government (per employee)	
Welfare benefits saved (weighted average)	£6,900
Number of participants that no longer require welfare benefits per annum	3
Net savings in welfare benefit expenditure	£20,700
Savings in the cost of mental health provision	£20,500
Number of participants who do not require intensive care	4
Total health care savings	£82,000
Net benefit to national government	£102,700
Combined net benefit	
Payback period (in months)	1
Aggregate annual benefits	£118,150
Less deadweight from computer recycling (118,150–1950)	£116,200
Less attribution	75%
MillRace IT share of outcome	£87,150

Table 19.15 MillRace IT SROI Results

Case study: MillRace IT
SROI

The returns are calculated annually due to the nature of Social Firms, in that their 'output' is the ongoing training and support for disabled people. Therefore, no benefits are projected forward. Therefore, the calculations that we do in this instance for SROI are simply:

$$SROI = \frac{\text{Net benefits}}{\text{Net investment}}$$

Therefore, to determine the SROI we complete the following calculation:

$$SROI = \frac{£10,325}{£10,325}$$

SROI generated by MillRace IT

	Total value created	MillRace IT share	Investment	SROI	MillRace IT share
Aggregate benefits	£107,825	£78,288	£10,325	10.44	7.58
Less deadweight	£105,875	£76,825	£10,325	10.25	7.44

Source: NEF (n.d., p. 51)

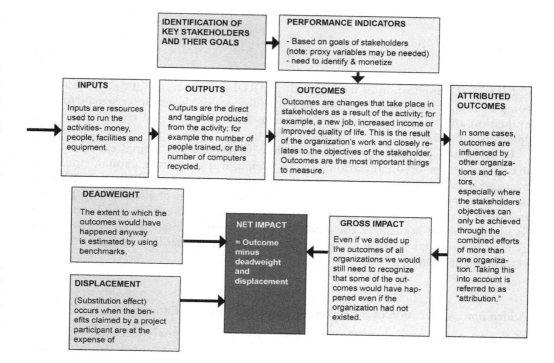

Figure 19.2 Mapping the SROI Process

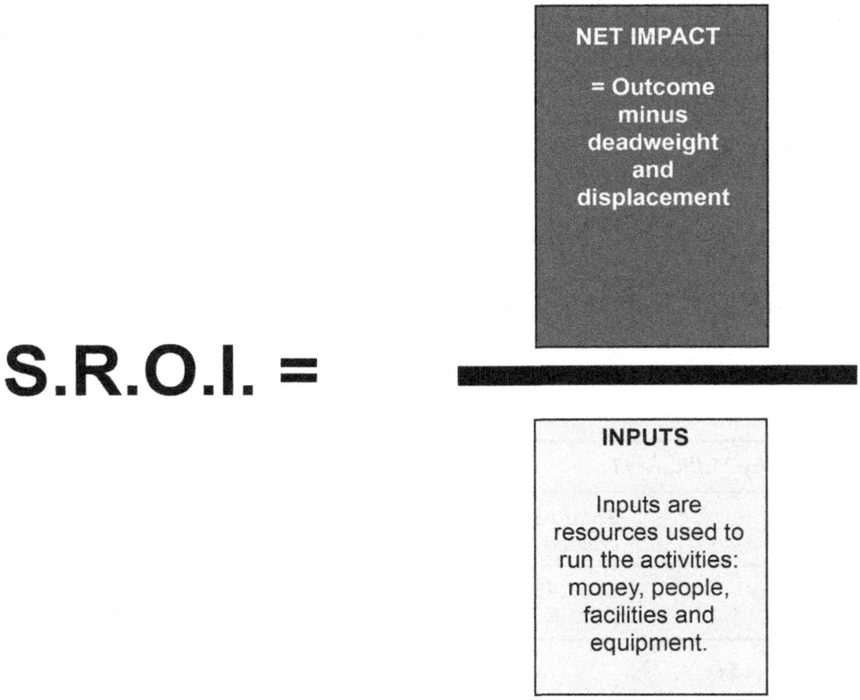

S.R.O.I. =

NET IMPACT

= Outcome
minus
deadweight
and
displacement

─────────────────

INPUTS

Inputs are
resources used to
run the activities:
money, people,
facilities and
equipment.

Figure 19.3 SROI Derivation

Clearly, the application of metrics such as SROI and others will be somewhat more complex in a Third World environment in the absence of clear market signals to aid in evaluation and the frequent inability to gauge the full extent and reach of any social enterprise program.

In summary, the past several decades have witnessed the formal emergence of a major new form of organization linking philanthropy, venture capital, and entrepreneurial talent to the goals of social and environmental amelioration. With this development has come the need to generate useful measures of social return and such measures have been forthcoming. Further work is required even in the United States to measure more accurately the total extent and impact of social enterprise as well as modify the legal framework of organizational law to facilitate the growth of this sustainable industry.

Addendum: Application of the Balanced Scorecard to Social Enterprise

Figure 19.4 (Rohm et al. 2023) illustrates how a powerful analytical tool, such as the Balanced Scorecard (see chapter 17) for developing organizational strategy can be

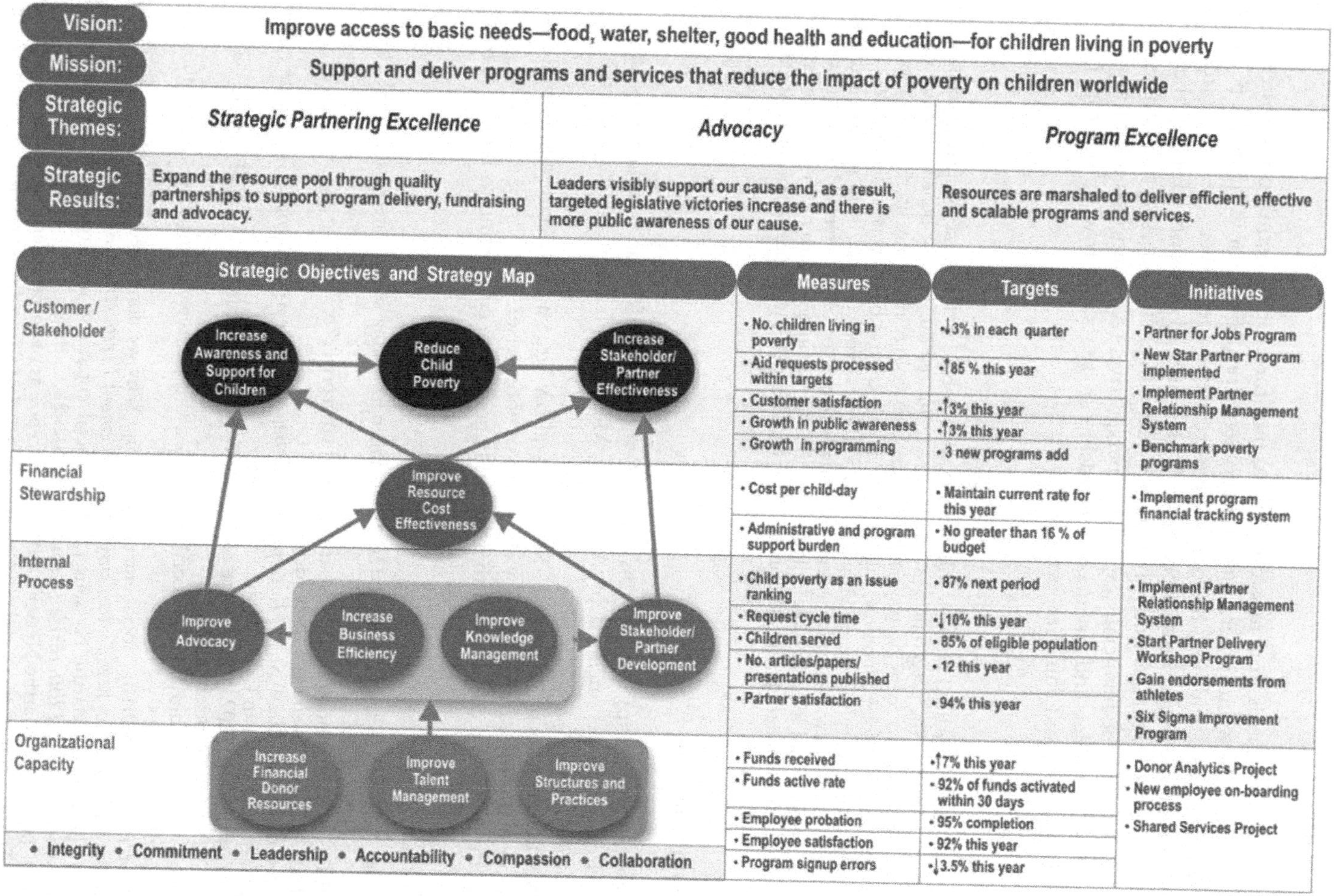

Vision: Improve access to basic needs—food, water, shelter, good health and education—for children living in poverty

Mission: Support and deliver programs and services that reduce the impact of poverty on children worldwide

Strategic Themes:

Strategic Partnering Excellence	Advocacy	Program Excellence

Strategic Results:

Expand the resource pool through quality partnerships to support program delivery, fundraising and advocacy.	Leaders visibly support our cause and, as a result, targeted legislative victories increase and there is more public awareness of our cause.	Resources are marshaled to deliver efficient, effective and scalable programs and services.

Strategic Objectives and Strategy Map

	Measures	Targets	Initiatives
Customer / Stakeholder	• No. children living in poverty • Aid requests processed within targets • Customer satisfaction • Growth in public awareness • Growth in programming	• ↓3% in each quarter • ↑85 % this year • ↑3% this year • ↑3% this year • 3 new programs add	• Partner for Jobs Program • New Star Partner Program implemented • Implement Partner Relationship Management System • Benchmark poverty programs
Financial Stewardship	• Cost per child-day • Administrative and program support burden	• Maintain current rate for this year • No greater than 16 % of budget	• Implement program financial tracking system
Internal Process	• Child poverty as an issue ranking • Request cycle time • Children served • No. articles/papers/presentations published • Partner satisfaction	• 87% next period • ↓10% this year • 85% of eligible population • 12 this year • 94% this year	• Implement Partner Relationship Management System • Start Partner Delivery Workshop Program • Gain endorsements from athletes • Six Sigma Improvement Program
Organizational Capacity	• Funds received • Funds active rate • Employee probation • Employee satisfaction • Program signup errors	• ↑7% this year • 92% of funds activated within 30 days • 95% completion • 92% this year • ↓3.5% this year	• Donor Analytics Project • New employee on-boarding process • Shared Services Project

Strategic objectives (strategy map nodes): Increase Stakeholder/Partner Effectiveness; Reduce Child Poverty; Increase Awareness and Support for Children; Improve Stakeholder/Partner Development; Improve Resource Cost Effectiveness; Improve Knowledge Management; Increase Business Efficiency; Improve Advocacy; Improve Structures and Practices; Improve Talent Management; Increase Financial Donor Resources

• Integrity • Commitment • Leadership • Accountability • Compassion • Collaboration

Figure 19.4 Example Balanced Scorecard for a Not-for-Profit Organization

Source: Rohm et al. 2023, reproduced with permission

used in a social enterprise devoted to alleviating child poverty. As Rohm et al. (2023, pp. 46–47) state:

> Developing scorecards for mission driven, not-for-profit organizations differs with regard to how customers and stakeholders are defined, how financial performance is viewed and how the perspectives relate to each other. . . . Scorecards for mission-driven organizations put mission first, instead of vision, to reflect their focus. The constituent/customer and stakeholder satisfaction perspective is listed first, followed by the financial/stewardship perspective. (A variation is to put both customer/stakeholder and financial/stewardship in the same row at the top to emphasize shared and equal importance).

Notes

1 Under the terms of Alfred Nobel's will of 1895, the Nobel Prize was established to recognize "those who, during the preceding year, shall have conferred the greatest benefit on mankind." Nobel's intent was to focus on physics, chemistry, physiology-medicine, literature and peace, although an award for Economics, funded by Sweden's central bank, was added in 1968.
2 The term civil society has been defined as "as a 'third sector,' distinct from government and business." In this view, civil society refers essentially to the so-called 'intermediary institutions' such as professional associations, religious groups, labor unions, citizen advocacy organizations, that give voice to various sectors of society and enrich public participation in democracies (Civicus 2003).

Discussion Questions

1. To what extent do any of the forms of social enterprise satisfy the criteria for a sustainable organization enunciated by Anderson, McDonough-Braungart or Robert? (see Table 14.4)
2. How scalable is social enterprise? Specifically, how large a contribution toward a sustainable economy can be made by this form of enterprise?
3. Can you think of a corporation that would benefit from converting to B Corp status?

References

Abramson, Alan J. & Kara C. Billings (2019) "Challenges facing social enterprises in the United States," Nonprofit Policy Forum.
Annie F. Casey Foundation (2020) "What is a social enterprise?"
B Lab (2023) "Make business a force for good."
Borzaga, Carlo, et al. (2020) *Social Enterprises and their Ecosystems in Europe: Comparative Synthesis Report*. European Commission.
British Council, et al. (2021) "The state of social enterprise in South East Asia," February.
Civicus (2003) "Civil society index."
Crunchbase (2023) "United States social companies," https://www.crunchbase.com/hub/united-states-social-companies
Dacin, Peter A., et al. (2010) "Social entrepreneurship: Why we don't need a new theory and how we move forward from here," *Academy of Management Perspectives*, August.
Defourny, Jacques & Marthe Nyssens (2008) "Social enterprise in Europe: Recent trends and developments," *Social Enterprise Journal*, 4(3): 202–28.
Defourny, Jacques & Marthe Nyssens (2010) "Conceptions of social enterprise in Europe and the United States: Convergences and divergences," *Journal of Social Entrepreneurship*, 1(1): 32–53.

Defourny, Jacques & ShinYang Kim (2011) "Emerging models of social enterprise in Eastern Asia: A cross-country analysis," *Social Enterprise Journal*, 7(1): 86–111.

Forbes (2022) "How the world's largest B Corp Natura (Owner of Body Shop, Avon and Aesop) uses purpose to drive performance and wellbeing," May 11.

Gallizzi, Ben (2022) "The most popular eco-friendly businesses in the world, according to Google," https://www.uswitch.com/gas-electricity/most-popular-bcorps/

Georgetown University McDonough School of Business (2021) *Jobs for All: Employment Social Enterprise and Economic Mobility in the United States*, Washington D.C.

Global Impact Summit (GIS) (2021) "Top 100 social enterprises in UK revealed: Natwest SE100 2020," National Westminster Bank, London UK.

Grameen Bank (2020) *Annual Report*.

Green Economy Law (2023) "Social enterprises, B Corps, benefit companies, ESG," https://www.greeneconomylaw.com/social-enterprises-b-corps-benefit-esg

Hart, Stuart L. (2010) *Capitalism at the Crossroads: Next Generation Business Strategies for a Post-Crisis World*, Prentice Hall.

ImpactFest (2020) "Finalists revealed: NatWest SE100 Social Business Awards 2020," https://www.pioneerspost.com/news-views/20200221/finalists-revealed-natwest-se100-social-business-awards-2020

Insight Global Education (n.d.) "Non-profits vs. social enterprises: What's the difference?," https://blog.insightglobaleducation.com/non-profits-vs-social-enterprises-whats-the-difference

Kerlin, Janelle A. (2006) "Social enterprise in the United States and Europe: Understanding and learning from differences," *Voluntas*, 17: 247–263.

Kerlin, Janelle A. (Ed.) (2009) *Social Enterprise: A Global Comparison*, UPNE.

London, Ted (2009) "Making better investments at the base of the pyramid," *Harvard Business Review*, pp. 106–113.

London, Ted & Stuart L. Hart (2011) *Next Generation Business Strategies for the Base of the Pyramid. New Approaches for Building Mutual Value*, FT Press.

Mair, Johanna, et al. (Eds.) (2006) *Social Entrepreneurship*, Palgrave Macmillan.

Meagher, Brinley (2023a) "What are the differences between a social enterprise and a B Corp," LegalVision, August 31.

Meagher, Brinley (2023b) "A guide to getting B Corp certified," LegalVision, August 31.

NatWest (2020) "SE100 health & fitness report," National Westminster Bank, UK.

Nestle (2022) "Nespresso achieve B Corp certification," April 26.

New York Times (2010) "Banks making big profits from tiny loans," April 13.

New York Times (2011) "A quest for hybrid companies that profit but can tap charity," October 12.

Nicholls, Jeremy, et al. (n.d.) *Measuring Real Value: A DIY Guide to Social Return on Investment*. New Economic Foundation (NEF)

Prahalad, C. K. (2009) *The Fortune at the Bottom of the Pyramid. Eradicating Poverty Through Profits*, Wharton School Publications.

Prahalad, C. K. & Stuart L. Hart (2002) "The fortune at the bottom of the pyramid," *Strategy + Business*, January (26): 54–67.

Roberts Enterprise Development Fund (REDF) (2001) *SROI Methodology: Analyzing the Value of Social Purpose Enterprise within a Social Return on Investment Framework*.

Rohm, Howard, et al. (2023) *The Institute Way: Simplify Strategic Planning & Management with the Balanced Scorecard*. The Institute Press.

Salamon, Lester M., et al. (2004) *Global Civil Society: Dimensions of the Nonprofit Sector*, vol. 2, Kumarian Press.

Social Enterprise UK (2023) "Social enterprises are businesses with a social or environmental purpose."

UK Cabinet Office. Office of the Third Sector (2009) *A Guide to Social Return on Investment*.

UK Cabinet Office. Office of the Third Sector (2012) *A Guide to Social Return on Investment – Updated*.

Van den Hoek, Elise, et al. (2023) "The state of social enterprise and the law 2022–2023," New York University Law.

Young, Dennis R. (2001) "Social enterprise in the United States: Alternate identities and forms," EMES Conference. Trento, Italy. 131–135. Springer.

Yunus, Mohammad (2003) *Banker to the Poor: Micro-Lending and the Battle against World Poverty*. Public Affairs.

Yunus, Mohammad (2008) *Creating a World Without Poverty: Social Business and the Future of Capitalism*. Public Affairs.

Yunus, Mohammad (2010) *Building Social Business. The New Kind of Capitalism that Serves Humanity's Most Pressing Needs*. Public Affairs.

ZenBusiness (2021) "Business with benefits: the world's most valuable B Corp companies mapped," https://www.zenbusiness.com/blog/most-valuable-b-corps/

20 Corporate Culture and Leadership

As outlined in this textbook, the successful transition from traditional corporate management to sustainability requires a number of critical prerequisites: first, a change of worldview that recognizes the economy as a subset of our ecological system; second, a method for monetizing the nonpriced externalities of human industrial activity; third, an accounting system that allows the integration of social and environmental accounts with traditional financial statements; and, finally, a cultural shift in attitudes and behaviour, not only among the general public as citizens and consumers, but also as a fundamental change in the culture of the corporate entity.

Eccles et al. (2011, 2014) examined the impact of corporate culture on corporate behavior and performance by studying 180 companies over an eighteen-year period. They found that *high sustainability* firms (defined as those who voluntarily adopted environmental and social policies many years ago) significantly outperformed their *low sustainability* competitors on both stock market and standard accounting measures. Eccles et al. (2011: 2) posited that:

> these policies reflect the underlying culture of the organization, a culture of sustainability, where environmental and social performances, in addition to financial performance, are important, but also forge a stronger culture by making explicit the values and beliefs that underlie the mission of the organization.

In contrast to social enterprise where both management and employees have usually self-selected into the organization and fully subscribe to its social and environmental goals, there is a major challenge to introducing the principles of sustainability into a conventional business entity, as management culture is embedded in a system of economic organization – the corporation – that has been one of the most resilient and productive inventions of modern society. While it has been posited that the successful integration of social and environmental values into corporate profit and loss statements will go a long way toward shifting corporate culture, the question remains as to whether this is sufficient in and by itself. If recent examples of corporations realizing that "waste is lost profit" have heightened awareness of issues of sustainability at the upper levels of corporate management, several questions might be legitimately asked: Why only now? Why were not these obvious opportunities to increase profits not realized before?

As Porter and van der Linde (1995) stressed, the traditional corporate mindset viewed environmental concerns solely as cost centers. Some of this has changed with increasing

DOI: 10.4324/9781003170754-24

public and governmental influence on corporate decision making but, clearly, this process of transition is incomplete. It is here that the issue of corporate culture assumes importance. As Hoffman (2001: 21) observed, "The essence of how environmentalism changes the corporate enterprise lies not primarily in its technical adjustments but more important, in its structural, strategic and cultural transformation."

Corporate culture has been characterized as the mind and soul of a company, and many corporations have well-established cultural identities. ExxonMobil, for example, gained notoriety for funding antienvironmental groups and initiatives (*The Guardian* 2006; UCS 2007; Michaels 2008; Hoggan 2009; McKibben 2010; Oreskes & Conway 2010: Otto 2016; Brulle 2018), while other companies such as Shell and BP have adopted the language of sustainability in their public persona despite debate over the seriousness of their commitment to the principle in an industry characterized by massive negative externalities from the production and consumption of energy (Greenpeace n.d.; Magner 2011). Nevertheless, there are many other companies that have established positive records with respect to environmental issues.

Table 20.1 lists the top companies in Newsweek's 2023 survey of most green companies in the United States. It is interesting to note that the top firms in this list differ significantly from those of Business Insider and Barron's in Table 2.3. The difference is undoubtedly due to the application of different criteria. How do companies earn such reputations? There is a consensus among most scholars of organizational behavior that the role of the Chief Executive Officer is critical in forming and maintaining corporate culture. One need only think of such visionary CEOs as Apple's Steven Jobs, Interface's Ray Anderson, IBM's Tom Watson Jr., Polaroid's Edwin Land, Chrysler's Lee Iacocca, Microsoft's Bill Gates, Berkshire Hathaway's Warren Buffett, Amazon's Jeff Bezos, and GE's Jack Welch and Jeff Immelt to understand the central role of such key individuals in the lifeblood of their corporations. The influence of the CEO is particularly important when that person is the organizational founder. Hillestad et al. (2010: 442) characterized the founder's role as a *cultural architect* "crafting and energizing organizational culture in the early years of an organization."

When leadership changes, corporate culture can be significantly impacted and, again, this is especially critical when the leader is the founder who has retired, died, or been replaced. There are several possible outcomes. On the one hand, a new leader may carry on the corporate traditions established by his/her predecessor, supplementing them with a new set of values that are gradually absorbed by the organization (Jackofsky et al. 1988: 39) or, on the other hand, may consciously or unconsciously

Table 20.1 Newsweek's Greenest Companies

1	AAON
2	Abbott Laboratories
3	AbbVie
4	Accenture
5	Activision Blizzard
6	Acuity Brands
7	Adobe
8	Advanced Micro Devices
9	AECOM
10	Affiliated Managers

Source: Newsweek (2023)

alter the culture and performance of the organization for better or for worse. In a study of public sector organizations, Boyne et al. (2011) found that succession has a positive effect where prior performance is low and the opposite effect when it is high.

Succession can lead to dramatic change, as aptly illustrated by the changing leadership of British Petroleum (BP). For example, the company experienced a dramatic change in strategic direction when Tony Hayward replaced Lord John Browne as CEO in 2007 and moved the corporation away from its emerging interest in renewable energy sources, (characterized by the slogan "Beyond Petroleum") back toward a primary focus on petroleum. Hayward's philosophy of corporate governance and behaviour became apparent in the US in the wake of the massive oil spill from BP's Deepwater Horizon oil rig in the Gulf of Mexico on April 20, 2010. This event led to his departure in that same year.

Hayward was followed by Robert Dudley who changed corporate strategy once again by investing almost $1 billion in low carbon energy sources, such as solar power. Dudley was followed by Bernard Looney in 2020, and in 2023 by Murray Auchincloss, the company's CFO, who assumed the role of CEO as an interim measure. Both Looney and Auchincloss reaffirmed the company's commitment to a goal of net zero by 2050.

The central and critical role of the CEO in corporate affairs does not necessarily mean that the CEO has an unfettered ability to change corporate culture. Gagliardi (1986) identified two polar views on this subject: one that postulates a limited scope for action; the other suggesting that there are numerous direct and indirect levers of influence at the command of an organizational leader. It is possible to posit at least four factors that may constrain the role of a CEO in molding corporate culture: (1) organizational complexity, (2) organizational inertia, 3) organizational entropy, and (4) organizational myopia.

Organizational Complexity

One of the seminal works in organizational theory was published in 1971 by Graham Allison. Focusing on the events of the Cuban Missile Crisis of 1962, Allison developed several conceptual models that transcended the traditional view of government policy as being a unified and rationale approach to critical issues of public policy. In essence, Allison opened the black box of organizational strategy and focused on the existence of both competing suborganizational units or groups and individuals within an organization.

An interesting and modern example of this complexity is the recent emergence of an environmental ethic at the highest level of the Chinese central government. Realizing that environmental despoliation poses a significant threat to continued economic growth and prosperity, Beijing has put in place a large array of new legislation and regulations intended to reduce air and water pollution, soil contamination, and excessive reliance on fossil fuels. China has encountered serious challenges to the achievement of these ambitious goals for many reasons, some of which are due to the competing goals of regional actors, such as provincial and urban governments and local businesses that are focused principally on social stability and direct economic outcomes (Economy 2004, 2005). Yet, while China has been a world leader in the installation of renewable power (IRENA 2023), the nation's insatiable demand for power has led to continued heavy investment in coal (IEA 2022, *New York Times* July 20, 2023).

Howard-Grenville (2008: 46) adopted a somewhat similar conceptual approach to Allison by attempting to deconstruct corporate decision making with respect to environmental issues:

> If we treat the organization as a "black box" and regard external factors, including regulation, scientific information, public pressure, new technology, and competitive and economic forces, as the primary drivers of environmental practice (Porter and van der Linde, 1995), we cannot necessarily understand why organizations respond to some environmental issues rather than others and why organizations facing similar issues show a range of responses.

Howard-Grenville (2008: 50) focused her attention on the existence of competing subcultures with asymmetrical power and influence:

> Organizational cultures are rarely monolithic, however, and subcultural differentiation may be more the norm than the exception. Indeed, researchers have found that subcultures form around occupational groupings, organizational roles, hierarchical levels, and functional or professional identifications. Subcultures can also emerge around shared understandings of tasks, mission, and authority structures. Some have even shown that subcultures cut across organizations or exist at the level of industries.

In a companion work, Howard-Grenville et al. (2008) identified five specific factors that contribute to problem solving within a corporation and its strategies for action: managerial incentives, organizational culture, organizational identity, organizational self-monitoring, and personal commitment and affiliations (see Table 20.2). Synthesizing the work of other scholars in the field, the authors distinguished between *organizational culture*, which is embedded in the everyday actions that people take throughout the company and influences how things are done, and *organizational identity* that refers to "an overarching sense among members of what the organization stands for and where it intends to go (p. 82)."

Table 20.2 Organizational Factors Contributing to Problem Setting and Strategies for Action

Factor	Definition	Sources of Evidence
Managerial incentives	Opportunities (or lack thereof) for managerial initiatives and actions, stemming from the structure, rules, and routines of the organization and the informal patterns of influence and control	Formal reporting structure; patterns of information flow; approval procedures; compensation schemes
Organizational culture	System of meanings and norms that shape daily action and interactions within a company; i.e. "the way things are done"	Tacit norms of behavior; observed, repeated patterns of interaction; rules revealed through actions that breach them

(Continued)

Table 20.2 (Continued)

Factor	Definition	Sources of Evidence
Organizational identity	Members' perceptions of what is central, enduring and distinctive about their company; i.e. "what kind of company we are"	Member's statements of what the organization "is about"; reflections of what is threatened when outsiders are critical of the organization
Organizational self-monitoring	Choices about how an organization portrays its actions to outsiders, in response to its impressions of those outsiders and the value it places on adhering to socially appropriate portrayals	Public portrayals through media, web site, and commercial outreach; number, variety, and scope of partnerships or associations with external groups
Personal commitment and affiliations	Individual members' profession experiences, education and training, and personal interests and values that influence their awareness of and perspectives on environmental issues	Professional backgrounds; memberships in other business or environmental organizations; stated values

Source: Howard-Grenville et al. (2008, p. 80 [reproduced with permission of Law & Policy])

Organizational Inertia

Over a period, successful corporations develop standard operating procedures and cultural norms. When new leadership attempts to change the philosophical direction of a corporation, a type of organizational inertia can pose a significant barrier to change. As Gagliardi (1986: 119) stated, "the more deeply rooted and diffuse these values are, the more tenacious and unalterable is the culture." Bartunek and Moch (1987) outlined several types of organizational development interventions and their increasing degrees of complexity. The analysis was cast in terms of changes to "schemata," defined as organizing frameworks that guide cognitions, interpretations or ways of understanding events. Bartunek & Moch (1987: 486) distinguished among three orders of schematic change:

> *First order change*: the tacit reinforcement of present understandings; *second-order change*: the conscious modification of present schemata in a particular direction; and *third-order change*: the training of organizational members to be aware of their present schemata and thereby more able to change these schemata as they see fit.

The apparent ease with which Tony Hayward was able to redirect the strategic initiatives of Lord John Browne in BP, may ironically reinforce the concept of organizational inertia. It could be posited that Browne had not succeeded in dramatically altering the culture of a long-established and successful multinational energy company and that Hayward had only reinforced the pre-existing culture. And yet, as described above, after Haywards' departure, the strategic direction of the firm changed back to Browne's initiatives, which would now be called sustainability. The question remains whether this was, in fact, a substantial or superficial change in strategy. Criticisms have been leveled against the company for engaging in greenwashing (see Table 2.5) and its continued investment in fossil fuels (see Figure 16.4) (Influence Map 2019; *The Guardian* February 12, 2020; *Huff Post* September 28, 2020; CleanTechnico 2023).

On balance, It is easy to understand why a corporation would be reluctant to abandon a business model that has proved to be so remunerative for decades. However, it is difficult to imagine a starker example of the divergence between private and social costs and benefits than is provided by the business decision to continue down the same path, potentially increasing even further the emissions of greenhouse gases and resulting global warming. The problem is compounded by the existence of corporate incentive structures that "trap companies in a loop of fossil growth" (Grant and Coffin 2020, Coffin and Grant 2020). As Kenner and Heede (2021: 9) observe in their study of the role of compensation in BP, Chevron, ExxonMobil and Shell:

> what the executives and directors share in common is a desire to maintain demand for oil and gas, and to defend their company's social license to operate. They are paid to run fossil fuel supply chains - with large greenhouse gas emissions.

Organizational Entropy

Chapter 10 introduced the theory of *strategic decay* where corporations face the risk of loss of competitive advantage through changes in their external environment and/or a loss of exceptionalism through a type of regression to the mean in internal strategies and processes due to loss of zeal or innovation, internal political and personal distractions, acceptance of the status quo, increase in bureaucratic red tape and rule-driven decision-making systems. The remedy to this problem is a process of rejuvenation and reinforcement of corporate goals and direct and indirect systems of influence and control within the organization.

Organizational Myopia

In a conversation with the author, Richard Haskayne, former president and chairman of several major Canadian petroleum companies including Hudson's Bay Oil and Gas Company, Home Oil Company, Interprovincial Pipeline Company, Nova Corporation, and TransCanada Pipelines, remarked that the planning horizon in his industry was far too short for the benefit of the corporation and society. This cogent observation seems even more relevant today in light of the temporal effects of climate change. This limited attention to the longer term implications of corporate strategy imposes an unnecessary constraint not only on the CEO but all of senior management and their support staff. A prime example of this problem is the aforementioned intention of the fossil fuel to double down on the production of fossil fuel in a time when large capital investments in such technology could place serious limits on strategic flexibility in an increasingly uncertain future and lead to substantial stranded assets in excess of $1 trillion (Ansar 2013; Caldecott et al. 2015; McGlade and Ekins, 2015; Jakob and Hilaire 2015; IRENA 2017; Grant and Coffin 2020). It is McKinsey's view (2021) that this discretionary strategy adopted in the light of continued climate change will force the entire fossil fuel to ultimately undergo profound and sweeping structural realignment.

The problem of limited planning horizons has been manifested by the practice of American corporations, for example, to fixate on quarterly profits at the potential expense of longer term corporate profitability or even survival. This restricted time horizon is not the only model for corporate strategic decision making as there is a long tradition among

Asian corporations to adopt a longer term view when formulation and implementing strategy (Witt & Redding 2014; Liao et al. 2021). In fact, Liao et al. (2021) of the Boston Consulting Group have identified at least four other characteristics of successful Asian executives in addition to their long-term perspective. These include:

- Institutionalizing the owner's mindset where the CEOs may use financial incentives and other tactics to get managers and employees to think as they do. This has been termed "delegating to the edge."
- Adopting a strong people orientation where the business will make an investment in developing the skills and personally encouraging the people they hire, and senior management may actively participate in the hiring process.
- Effectively navigating their ecosystems, which can include governments, NGOs, labor unions, suppliers, and distributors. This can mean, for example, taking into consideration issue facing suppliers and distributors even when it is not in their financial interest to do so.
- Demonstrating a fierce agility and an ability to survive and thrive in a rapidly growing economy where experience may not always be the best guide.

There are clear contextual differences between the environment facing Asian and Western businesses. Some of the unique characteristics of the Asian environment include a history of colonialism, the significant presence of the state in the economy, the prevalence of family-owned and operated businesses, and social norms and societal bonds that may stress consensus and communal decision making over strong individualism.

Having said this, however, the distinction between Asian and Western business philosophy and practice may not be as pronounced as it once was. As Adena Friedman, President and CEO of Nasdaq, has said: "sustainability requires the ability to prioritize long-term social and environmental benefits that may not be realized for decades to come (Friedman 2022).

The Recent Literature

Within the last two decades, numerous books have been published on the essence of corporate leadership in general and sustainable leadership in particular. Some notable examples include: Bertels et al. 2010, 2015; Avery and Bergsteiner 2011; Dewar et al. 2022; and Murphy 2022.

Dewar, Keller and Malhotra, all senior partners in McKinsey & Company, undertook the task, based on intensive interviews with 67 CEOs of the world's most successful companies, of distilling the mindsets that distinguish the best leaders from the rest. One of their most interesting observations is that many of the practices that predominate in modern business have ancient roots. They cite a Chinese text entitled *Officials of Chou*, written at in 1100 BCE. Rindova and Starbuck (1997: 155) cited these specific rules of good management proposed by King Ching:

Personal qualities: To be lazy and indifferent undermines your management. Let carefulness and economy be sincere virtues, and do not show them hypocritically. If you practice them sincerely, your minds will be at ease and you will daily become more admirable. If you practice them hypocritically, your minds will be stressful and you will daily become more tiresome.

Self-improvement: Study history in order to perform your offices well; such study will make your arts of management free from error. Without study, you stand facing a wall and your management of affairs will run into trouble.

Effects of goals on behavior: High achievement comes from high aims, and higher positions come only through diligence. Extinguish all selfish aims and the people will have confidence in you and obey gladly.

Effects of rewards on behavior: With high rank, pride comes unnoticed, and with high pay, extravagance comes unseen. In the enjoyment of favored positions, think of risk and be ever cautious. Those who act without such caution find themselves amid what they should have feared.

Decisions and actions: By means of bold decisions you can avoid future difficulties. To build up uncertainty undermines your plans. Be careful about the commands you issue, for once issued, they must be put into effect and not retracted.

Conformity to rules: Follow the statutes of our kingdom, and do not use artful language to introduce discretion into your offices.

Promoting subordinates: Push forward the worthy and make room for the able, and harmony will prevail among your subordinates. When they are not harmonious, the government becomes a tangled confusion. If those whom you promote show ability in their offices, the ability is yours as well. If you promote the unqualified, you are unequal to your responsibility.

Dewar et al. distinguish between six key responsibilities of the CEO (setting the direction, aligning the organization, mobilizing through leaders, engaging the board, connecting with stakeholders, and managing personal effectiveness). These responsibilities describe the job but do not capture the mindset that the CEO adopts and the actions they take. The mindsets identified by Dewar et al. fall into six categories.

1. having a bold vision,
2. "treating the soft stuff as the hard stuff,' where the soft stuff is the corporate culture and its employees
3. solving for the team's psychology by focusing on how these members work together
4. helping directors help the business by embracing the board as a valuable and trusted source of expertise
5. starting with *why* by putting yourself in the shoes of your stakeholders and asking oneself what they are trying to do. [fn.1]
6. doing what only the CEO can do, as they are ultimately responsible for direction setting, despite the useful input they receive from their team.

This type of analysis set the groundwork for research on how to apply best leadership practices to the challenge of sustainability.

Over the last decade, Bertels and colleagues at Simon Fraser University have produced, under the rubric of the *Embedding Project*, an extensive library of resources for embedding sustainability into corporate practice. This library focusses on seven distinct areas: systems, strategy, governance, value chains, culture, change agents, and storytelling. To quote from the website:

The Embedding Framework was first developed in 2010 by Dr. Stephanie Bertels from a Systematic Review conducted for the Network for Business Sustainability

(NBS) to bring together the best available knowledge on how to embed sustainability in business. The original framework was enthusiastically received by the business community. Firms requested more information and sought direct guidance on how to implement the framework. In response, NBS launched an Embedding Sustainability Working Group, led by Dr. Bertels and South African researcher, Jess Schulschenk, which brought together 16 companies from across North America, Europe and Africa over a period of three years to refine the framework into a diagnostic tool to assess a company's maturity. The original 'embedding wheel' framework outlined a portfolio of 60 business practices that help companies embed sustainability.

The most recent version of the Resource Wheel focusing on 40 practices is reproduced in Figure 20.1. Under the heading of corporate culture, the authors have provided four comprehensive documents: *Embedding Sustainability in Organization Culture* (Bertels 2010), *Embedding Sustainability Self-Assessment* (Bertels et a. 2014), *An Introduction to the Embedding Framework* (Bertels & Schulschenk 2015), and *EDI Leading Practice. A Guide for Companies* (Dekker et al. 2024).

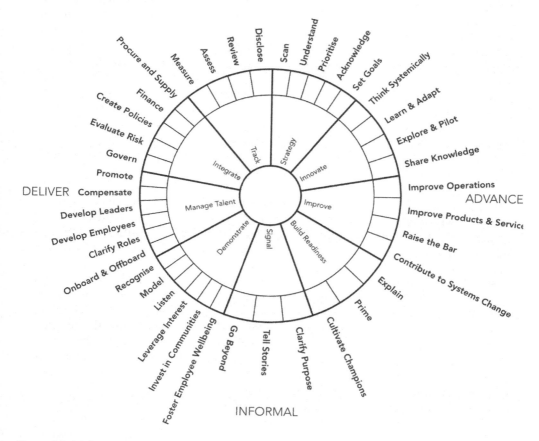

Figure 20.1 The Resource Wheel

Source: Bertels 2024, reproduced with permission

Avery and Bergsteiner (2011) have adopted a highly imaginative approach to distinguish sustainable from nonsustainable leadership. The metaphor they use is the contrast between honeybees and locusts. The former "collaborate and generate value for themselves and their communities and their environment. Others serve their own self-interests. They consume whatever lies in their paths like locusts" (Avery & Bergsteiner 2011: XI). The authors developed a list of 23 leadership practices and "facilitate outcomes that go beyond what is commonly referred to as the triple bottom line." These practices are divided into three groupings: foundation practices (14), higher-level practices (6), and key performance drivers (3) (see Figure 20.2). Their unique contribution is to identify how "honeybee" leadership (sophisticated, stakeholder, social sharing) differs on each one of these 23 elements from "locust leadership (tough, ruthless, asocial, profit-at-any cost) (see Table 20.3). The authors complete their analysis by highlighting which performance outcomes (financial performance, shareholder value, customer satisfaction, and brand and reputation) are directly supported by the 27 honeybee practices. It is particularly interesting to note that financial performance is the one area that benefits most by the honeybee practices (25/27); these positive effects are closely followed by brand and reputation (19/27), customer satisfaction (15/27), and finally shareholder value (14/27).

More recently, Clarke Murphy (2022) is the author of a work on sustainable leadership and coauthor of a report with the United National Global Compact (UNGC), which represents the meeting of the minds of Murphy and Lise Kingo, former CEO and president of UNGC. The UNGC Report, entitled *Leadership for a Decade of Action*, summarizes the authors' conclusions concerning the attributes of sustainable leadership (Murphy 2022: 15):

A Sustainable Mindset - The purpose-driven belief that business is not a commercial activity divorced from the wider societal and environmental context in which it operates. To be successful in the long term, leaders must innovate and manage across commercial, societal and environmental outcomes.

This mindset is coupled with four specific competencies:

Multilevel Systems Thinking - Sustainable leaders go beyond a deep understanding of their own organizational system and incorporate the interplay with the larger business, societal and environmental systems around them. Critically they cut through that complexity to drive targeted decisions and actions that turn sustainability into a competitive advantage.

Stakeholder Inclusion - Sustainable leaders do not manage stakeholders — they include them. They actively seek to understand a wide range of points of view in order to drive decision-making with all those stakeholders in mind and where possible, actively involve those stakeholders in actioning the decisions and sharing the benefits.

Disruptive Innovation -Sustainable leaders possess the courage to challenge traditional approaches — they ask why it cannot be done differently. They cut through bureaucracy to drive the breakthrough innovation that is needed to find novel solutions that do away with a trade-off between profitability and sustainability.

Long-term activation -Sustainable leaders do not simply have an orientation towards the long term, they set audacious goals and drive concerted action and investments in the pursuit of them. To do this requires a great deal of courage to stay the course in the face of setbacks and to make decisions that may be unpopular with some short-term oriented stakeholders.

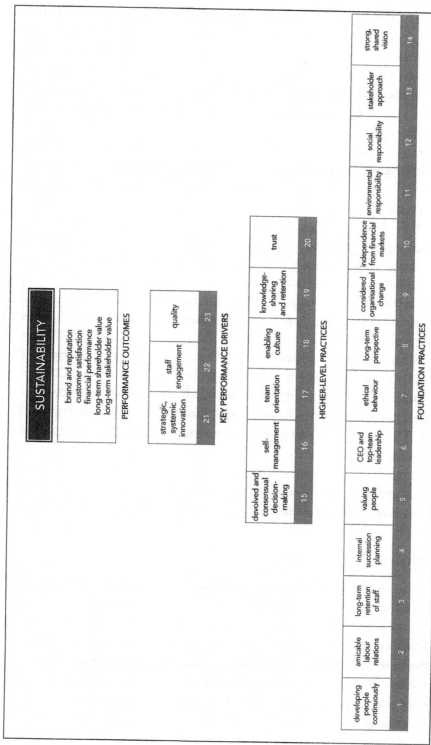

Figure 20.2 The Sustainable Leadership Pyramid

Source: Avery and Bergsteiner 2011, reproduced with permission

Table 20.3 Avery and Bergsteiner List of Sustainable Leadership Elements

	Honeybee Philosophy	Locust Philosophy
FOUNDATION PRACTICES		
1 Developing people	develops everyone continuously	develops people selectively
2 Labour relations	seeks cooperation	acts antagonistically
3 Retaining staff	values long tenure at all levels	accepts high staff turnover
4 Succession planning	promotes from within wherever possible	appoints from outside wherever possible
5 Valuing staff	is concerned about employees' welfare	treats people as interchangeable and a cost
6 CEO and top team	CEO works as a top team member or speaker	CEO is decision-maker, hero
7 Ethical behaviour	doing 'the right thing' as an explicit core value	ambivalent, negotiable, an assessable risk
8 Long- or short-term perspective	prefers the long term over the short term	short-term profits and growth prevail
9 Organisational change	change is an evolving and considered process	change is fast adjustment, volatile, can be ad hoc
10 Financial markets orientation	seeks maximum independence from others	follows its masters' will, often slavishly
11 Responsibility for environment	protects the environment	is prepared to exploit the environment
12 Social responsibility (CSR)	values people and the community	exploits people and the community
13 Stakeholder consideration	everyone matters	only shareholders matter
14 Vision's role in the business	shared view of future is essential strategic tool	the future does not necessarily drive the business
HIGHER-LEVEL PRACTICES		
15 Decision-making	is consensual and devolved	is primarily manager-centred
16 Self-management	staff are mostly self-managing	managers manage
17 Team orientation	teams are extensive and empowered	teams are limited and manager-centred
18 Culture	fosters an enabling, widely shared culture	culture is weak except for a focus on short-term results that may or may not be shared
19 Knowledge-sharing and retention	spreads throughout the organisation	limits knowledge to a few 'gatekeepers'
20 Trust	high trust through relationships and goodwill	control and monitoring compensate for low trust
KEY PERFORMANCE DRIVERS		
21 Innovation	strong, systemic, strategic innovation evident at all levels	innovation is limited and selective; buys in expertise
22 Staff engagement	values emotionally committed staff and the resulting commitment	financial rewards suffice as motivators, no emotional commitment expected
23 Quality	is embedded in the culture	is a matter of control

Source: Avery & Bergsteiner (2011, Table 2-1, pp. 36–37 [reproduced with permission of the authors])

While much of these attributes will seem familiar to a student of corporate management, what makes Murphy's contribution to the literature of sustainable leadership is the inclusion in his book (2022) of 84 sustainable leadership takeaways spread over 11 chapters of analysis and first-hand empirical data. The book concludes with ten recommendations for current CEOs and board members thinking about their legacy, and six lessons for next-generation leaders aspiring to become a CEO focussed on the twin goals of profitability and sustainability.

Several brief examples follow that illustrate the interacting roles of complexity, inertia, entropy, and short-termism in both corporate success and failure.

Case Studies

In a book entitled *When Good Companies Do Bad Things*, Schwartz and Gibb (1999) studied companies who had run afoul of government regulation and public perception in the environment and other high visibility public policy arenas. Among these were Royal Dutch Shell, Unocal, Texaco, Union Carbide, and Tor Chemicals. The reasons for these problems were, according to the authors: (1) failing to create a culture that tolerates dissent or one in which planning processes are encouraged to take nonfinancial risks seriously; (2) focusing exclusively on financial measures of performance; (3) discouraging employees from thinking about their work as whole people, from using their moral and social intelligence as well as their business intelligence; (4) talking to the same circle of people and information sources all the time and avoiding people or organizations who disagree with or criticize them; (5) letting their commitment to a particular project or product overwhelm all other considerations – financial, ethical, or social; and (6) senior managers considering ethical or social issues as matters for somebody else to resolve (Schwartz & Gibb 1999: 177–178). The authors concluded that companies are more vulnerable to these types of problems if they have not examined their operations *from a long-term perspective in a social context.*

In light of these challenges, what levers are available to a company and its CEO in particular to rectify these problems? First, the leader must be a visionary, able to communicate and motivate others; second, systems for influencing corporate culture must be designed to induce buy-in at all levels of the corporation, among all subcultural groups and individuals; and third, these messages must be reinforced through a process of continued monitoring, feedback and renewal. A ten-point list of recommended elements to embed sustainability was assembled by a team of advisors to HRH The Prince of Wales and published as *The Prince's Accounting for Sustainability Project* (2007). These elements are: (1) board and senior management commitment; (2) understanding and analyzing the key sustainability drivers for the organization; (3) integrating the key sustainability drivers into the organization's strategy; (4) ensuring that sustainability is the responsibility of everyone in the organization (and not just of a specific department); (5) breaking down sustainability targets and objectives for the organization as a whole into targets and objectives that are meaningful for individual subsidiaries, divisions and departments; (6) processes that enable sustainability issues to be taken into account clearly and consistently in day-to-day decision-making; (7) extensive and effective sustainability training; (8) including sustainability targets and objectives in performance appraisal; (9) champions to promote sustainability and celebrate success; and (10) monitoring and reporting sustainability performance.

An outstanding example of this integrated approach to inculcating the ideals of sustainability throughout an organization is Ray Anderson's Interface Carpets (Anderson et al. 2010) (see chapter10). The guiding principles of Anderson et al. (2010: 96) are based on the realization that:

Vital to the transition of the economy is the very institution that serves as its primary engine: business and industry. To lead this shift, business must delve much deeper than just the array of eco or clean technologies that are in vogue, to the core beliefs that drive actions. While a few visionary companies have been founded on the principles of sustainability, most businesses will require radical change.

Anderson and his coauthors described five development phases of change at their company in pursuit of this goal: *awakening* (defining the vision); *cocooning* (creating the road map that included goals, timelines, resource allocation and metrics); *metamorphosis* (aligning the organization); *emergence* (ongoing integration); and *engagement* (a continuing effort to influence others).

Several important initiatives have been undertaken by Interface and other companies in a broad range of endeavors to maintain the momentum of sustainability and reverse any tendency toward corporate entropy. These include regular training and feedback session for employees, flattened hierarchical organizational structures, shortened lines of intrafirm communication, and regular internal peer review of major staffing and strategic decisions. By way of example, Sun Microsystems instituted a system where any employee could email the CEO at any time and expect to receive a timely reply (William Raduchel, personal communication, 2024). Mayo Clinic has maintained its reputation as a world leader in the delivery of health care through continuous committee peer-based quality control, participative and collaborative management, and publication of performance metrics on both its intranet and internet that have been used as benchmarks for other healthcare delivery organizations (Berry & Seltman 2008; Heskett 2011). Central to this effort is the Mayo Clinic *Model of Care* that codifies its values, culture, and expectations in a document given to all employees and available on the web as a twenty-one-page publication (*Middle East Health* September 27, 2023). [fn. 2]

Many major corporations now have mission statements that attempt to elucidate and communicate their underlying philosophy of business. Such an exercise is not without risks however, as companies must beware of situations where their behaviour is inconsistent with their cultivated public image. One of the most prominent of such statements is Johnson & Johnson's *Credo*, directed to both internal and external stakeholders that outlines their responsibility to doctors, nurses and patients, employees, the communities in which they live and work, and shareholders. Over the years, Johnson & Johnson has achieved an unsurpassed level of recognition as one of the country's most respected brands (Reputation Institute, 2011). Despite this achievement, Johnson & Johnson has been bedeviled with a series of controversies and lawsuits over the last two decades concerning some of its practices, drugs and medical devices (*New York Times* January 17, 2010).

The Harvard Business School teaches future executives the gold standard in brand crisis management. . . . The template is based on Johnson & Johnson's conduct in 1982, when several people died after taking tainted Tylenol pills. The company's reaction to the crisis is widely regarded as exemplary. But last week, Johnson & Johnson appeared to abandon its own template, stunning a few business school professors. Its conduct also drew harsh criticism from federal officials.

The event that prompted this strongly negative reaction was the recall of several well-know, over-the-counter medicines such as Benadryl, Motrin, Rolaids, Simply Sleep, St. Joseph Aspirin, and Tylenol by McNeil Consumer Healthcare, a division of Johnson & Johnson. This precipitated a warning letter from the FDA after an internal agency study found a twenty-month delay in the recall after initial consumer complaints about tainted products. Just two days earlier, the *New York Times* (January 15, 2010) had reported that Johnson & Johnson was the subject of a complaint filed by the Office of the US attorney in Boston, accusing the company of paying kickbacks to nursing homes for prescribing some of its pharmaceutical problems.

In his autobiography, Richard Haskayne (2007: 274) observes that "the best definition of the word 'culture' that I've heard is that is how people behave when nobody is watching." A leading proponent of ethics in business, Haskayne continues (2007: 274):

> A study of 365 enterprises in 30 countries found that 89% have corporate-values statements and more of the most financially successful companies singled out the qualities of honesty, openness, and commitment to employees. But while such statements are all well and good, it's useful to know the Enron had its own code of ethics, sixty-two pages long, with a forward by Ken Lay as chairman, who wrote, "Enron's reputation finally depends on its people, on you and me. Let's keep that reputation high." Another classic example to illustrate that strategy is one thing, execution another.

In fairness to Johnson & Johnson, there is no reason to believe that the *Credo* had been rendered totally inoperative by this pattern of recent behaviour. What is more likely to have been the cause is the confluence of at least two of the three factors described above: the existence of an entropic process where the company in several notable circumstances allowed the principles to be compromised by the short-term pursuit of profitability by subunits and subcultures with different goals to the exclusion of its philosophical mandate. Unfortunately, this pathology of corporate behaviour had not been remedied by 2012, as the company was engulfed in another public image fiasco over knowingly distributing defective hip implants (*New York Times* February 21, 2012).

In 2015, the *HuffPost* published an article entitled: "America's most admired Lawbreaker" (Brill 2015) that focussed on J&J's promotion of its highly profitable drug, Respirdal, for children with emotional problems despite the FDA's order not to market it to children. While the J&J example lies outside the area of sustainability, it exemplifies the challenges that corporations may face in attempting to convey to the general public the relationship between their culture and the achievement of society's goals. In a tongue-in-cheek study by Don Watson (2003), entitled *Death Sentences*, the author described how corporate mission statements may act to misinform rather than education the public. The epitome of such misinformation is one corporate mission statement that reads, in part: "At CACI we take pride in our commitment to quality service and best value for our clients, individual opportunity and respect for each other, integrity and excellence in our work, and distinction and the competitive edge in our work" (Watson 2003: 75). The problem with this mission statement is that CACI was one of the private contractors at the infamous Abu Ghraib prison near Baghdad.

The clearest manifestation of this type of organizational pathology in sustainability involves the process of greenwashing (see, for example, Greer & Bruno 1997; Greenpeace n.d.; and chapter 2). One of the most exhaustive early studies of this phenomenon was published by TerraChoice in 2007. The company conducted a survey of 1,108 consumer products bought in six national big box retail chains in North America. Their conclusion was that "all but one made claims that are demonstrably false or that risk misleading intended audiences (p.1)." Their findings, as reported in several reports, were that greenwashing is pervasive and can have significant consequences (Terrachoice 2007, p. 1; see also Terrachoice 2010).

- Well-intentioned consumers may be misled into purchases that do not deliver on their environmental promise. This means both that the individual consumer has been misled and that the potential environmental benefit of his or her purchase has been squandered.
- Competitive pressure from illegitimate environmental claims takes market share away from products that offer more legitimate benefits, thus slowing the penetration of real environmental innovation in the marketplace.
- Greenwashing may create cynicism and doubt about all environmental claims. . . . This would eliminate a significant market-based, financial incentive for green product innovation and leave committed environmental advocates with government regulations as the most likely alternative.

Among the most controversial recent claims relating to sustainability are associated with "ethical oil from the oil sands" (see chapter 14), "clean coal" (Richmond 2014, ASA August 20, 2014) and other fossil fuels from carbon capture and storage (see chapter 2). One of the most important enunciated changes in corporate culture with respect to sustainability, that of Wal-Mart, the world's largest retailer, is detailed in chapter 16.

Corporate Leadership and Culture in the Age of ESG

As described in chapter 2, one of the most important developments in the state of corporate sustainability has been the emergence of an international regulatory focus on ESG and the resulting readjustment of corporate reporting and strategy to accommodate new government regulations as well as expectations of the financial community and the general public. An important part of this reorientation is the need for corporations to expand their estimates of their carbon footprint by determining the contributions of their supply chain, commonly referred to Scope 3 emissions. Accompanying this new focus on the environmental impacts of their suppliers is an increased focus on suppliers' labour practices especially in the developing world – a topic that is always guaranteed to generate extensive press coverage. The import of this new environment goes beyond mere adherence to government regulation and sensitivity to the responses and requirements of the financial community. It forces the corporation to revisit its corporate strategic focus, corporate culture and leadership models. Fortunately, the consulting industry has stepped up and made numerous recommendations to help their clients make this adjustment. On balance, this change represents a subtle shift in corporate policies and practices already in place to deal with broader issues of sustainability.

In 2022, the Diligent Institute in partnership with SpencerStuart surveyed almost 600 corporate directors to determine how they are addressing ESG, adjusting to address

ESG topics and increasing their overall board competency around ESG (Ciccarelli et al. 2022: 4). They found that:

> Seventy-one percent of corporate boards are incorporating environmental, social and governance (ESG) objectives and goals into overall company strategy, with 85% taking action to increase fluency on ESG. . . . The survey finds that a plurality of boards (43%) are placing primary oversight of ESG at the full board level. Meanwhile 30% house ESG oversight within the Nominating and Governance committee and 15% within the ESG/Sustainability committee, indicating that they may become a more common element of the board committee structure in the future (Diligent 2022: 1–2).

Two graphics in particular presented critical survey findings for both American and overseas companies: (1) how boards are incorporating ESG goals and metrics, and (2) methods used to increase Board ESG fluency (see Appendix Two; Table 20.4; Table 20.5).

In 2021, the Harvard Law School Forum on Corporate Governance produced a report on the next generation of ESG leadership (Harrison et al. 2021: 1–2):

> the next-generation ESG leaders will look quite different from earlier archetypes. . . . These leaders are predominantly female, overwhelmingly hired from outside of the company versus being promoted into the role, and bring cross-functional business experience to the position.

These *ESG 2.0* leaders have four primary responsibilities:

1. Create a best-in-class enterprise-wide ESG policy and framework
2. Integrate ESG policy across the organization, ensuring a consistency of messaging and execution throughout each individual business line/investment strategy
3. Serve as the "face of the franchise" both internally and externally, articulating to investors how ESG permeates all levels of the organization and is embedded into each business line/investment strategy
4. Engage with external partners (portfolio companies, operating partners, supply chain) to help them create more sustainable business strategies for their own organizations.

ESG issues will continue to grow in importance, requiring increased literacy in the topic not only among senior management but also at the board level. Helm (2023) of PracticalESG.com provides ten tips for how ESG leadership can support company boards as they address these complex issues. Helm recognizes that boards typically lack members with ESG expertise, frequently do not know what ESG issues their companies face, and may not think ESG issues are important, but it is boards that ultimately make important ESG decisions for the company (Helm 2023: 3–4).

Helm's advice is: (1) present the best data possible, (2) be flexible by considering "What if?" scenarios to address unanticipated changes or requests, (3) communicate in terms the board can understand, (4) help directors understand the multifaceted views of different stakeholders, (5) be careful about the quality of risk data presented, (6) explain clearly the company's ESG targets and goals, (7) be conservative with respect to ESG-related opportunities, (8) exercise caution with respect to consumer survey data, (9) present ESG from both the company's and industry's perspective, and (10) be clear, concise, and brief.

At the center of all this discussion lies the nature of corporate culture and how deeply it has been absorbed at all levels of the company – from the production line and/or front-line workers to senior management and the board of directors. This is no easy task as it involves clear and realistic thinking shorn of spin, clear articulation, constant monitoring and feedback – and last, but not least, deeply committed leadership.

Notes

1 As a parenthetical note, this lesson emerged as one of the reasons the world avoided annihilation during the Cuban Missile Crisis of October 1962. As described by Robert Kennedy in his book entitled *Thirteen Days: A Memoir of the Cuban Missile Crisis* (1973). Both President John F. Kennedy and his brother Robert determined to put themselves in the shoes of the Russian Leader, Nikita Khrushchev, to understand his motivation in creating the crisis and to determine what actions would allow Khrushchev to save face and deescalate. In retrospect, this is considered the closest we all came to World War Three.
2 vol10.cases.som.yale.edu; history.Mayoclinic.org

Study Questions

1. Can you think of recent examples where corporate culture was instrumental in the success or failure of a strategic direction?
2. Using your knowledge of statistical theory, how would you evaluate studies where the outstanding qualities of corporations, their leaders, and their strategy was based on the experience of the most successful companies?
   HINT: you may wish to consult Rosenzweig (2014)

References

Advertising Standards Authority (ASA) (2014) "ASA adjudication on peabody energy corporation," August 20.

Allison, Graham (1971) *Essence of Decision: Explaining the Cuban Missile Crisis*. Little Brown.

Anderson, Ray, et al. (2010) "Changing business cultures from within," Worldwatch Institute, State of the World 2010. Transforming Cultures. From Consumerism to Sustainability, pp. 96–102.

Ansar, Atif, et al. (2013) *Stranded Assets and the Fossil Fuel Divestment Campaign: Report, Smith School Of Enterprise And The Environment*. Oxford University.

Avery, Gayle C. & Harald Bergsteiner (2011) *Sustainable Leadership: Honeybee and Locust Approaches*. Routledge.

Bartunek, Jean M. & Michael K. Moch (1987) "First-order, second-order and third-order change and organization development interventions: A cognitive approach," *The Journal of Applied Behavioral Science*, 23: 483–500.

Berry, Leonard L. & Kent D. Seltman (2008) *Management Lessons from Mayo Clinic. Inside One of the World's Most Admired Service Organizations*. McGraw Hill.

Bertels, Stephanie, et al. (2010) *Embedding Sustainability in Organizational Culture. A Systematic Review of the Body of Knowledge*. Network for Business Sustainability, Simon Fraser University.

Bertels, Stephanie (2015) *Embedding Sustainability Self-Assessment Resource*. Embedding Project, (embeddingproject.org).

Bertels, Stephanie & J. Schulschenk (2015) *An Introduction to the Embedding Framework*. Embedding Project, (embeddingproject.org).

Boyne, George A., et al. (2011) "Leadership succession and organizational success: When do new chief executive make a difference?" *Public Money & Management*, September, pp. 39–346.

Brill, Steven (2015) "America's most admired lawbreaker," *HuffPost*, September 15.

Brulle, Robert J. (2018) "The climate lobby a sectoral analysis of lobbying spending on climate change in the usa 2000 to 2016," *Climate Change*, 149: 289–303.

Caldecott, Ben et a. (2015) *Stranded Assets and Subcritical Coal – The Risk to Investors and Companies, School of Enterprise and the Environment.* Oxford University.

Ciccarelli, Kira, et al. (2022) "Sustainability in the spotlight: board oversight and strategy," *Diligent Institute and SpencerStuart*, May.

Clean Technico (2023) "More BP greenwashing for 2023, less tangible progress toward clean energy."

Coffin, Mike & Andrew Grant (2020) *Fanning the Flames, Carbon Tracker*, March.

Dekker, Rachel, et al. (2024) *EDI Leading Practices: A Guide for Companies.* Embedding Project, https://embeddingproject.org/pub/resources/EP-EDI-Leading-Practices.pdf

Dewar, Carolyn, et al. (2022) *CEO Excellence: The Six Mindsets That Distinguish the Best Leaders from The Rest.* Scribner.

Diligent Institute (2022) "New report from spencer stuart and diligent finds 71% of boards are incorporating esg into their company strategy, with 85% taking action to increase fluency on esg."

Eccles, Robert G., et al. (2011) "The impact of a corporate culture of sustainability on corporate behavior and performance," Working Paper 12–035, Harvard Business School, November 4.

Eccles, Robert G., et al. (2014) "The impact of corporate sustainability on organizational processes and performance," *Management Science*, 60(11).

Economy, Elizabeth C. (2004) *The River Runs Black: The Environmental Challenge to China's Future.* Cornell University Press.

Economy, Elizabeth C. (2005) "Environmental enforcement in china," in Kristen A. Day (Ed.) *China's Environment and the Challenge of Sustainable Development.* 102–120. Routledge.

Friedman, Adena T. (2022) "Foreword," in Clarke Murphy (Ed.), *Sustainable Leadership: Lessons of Vision, Courage, and Grit From The CEOs Who Dared to Build A Better World.* Wiley.

Gagliardi, Pasqaule (1986) "The creation and change of organizational cultures: A conceptual framework," *Organization Studies*, 7: 117–134.

Grant, Andrew & Mike Coffin (2020) *Fault-Lines: How Diverging Oil and Gas Company Strategies Link to Stranded Asset Risk*, Carbon Tracker, October.

Greenpeace (n.d.) *The Greenpeace Book of Greenwash.*

Greer, Jed & Kenny Bruno (1997) *Greenwash: The Reality Behind Corporate Environmentalism*, Rowman & Littlefield.

The Guardian (2006) "Royal society tells Exxon: Stop funding climate change denial," September 20.

The Guardian (2020) "BP's statement on reaching net zero by 2050 – What it says and what it means," February 12.

Harrison, Kurt B., et al. (2021) "ESG 2.0 – The next generation of leadership," *Harvard Law School Forum on Corporate Governance.*

Haskayne, Dick (with Paul Grescoe) (2007) *Northern Tigers: Building Ethical Canadian Corporate Champions.* Key Porter Books.

Helm, Lawrence (2023) "10 Tips for how ESG leadership and staff can support company boards," PracticalESG.com.

Heskett, James (2011) *The Culture Cycle: How to Shape the Unseen Force That Transforms Performance.* Pearson FT Press.

Hillestad, Tore, et al. (2010) "Innovative corporate social responsibility: The founder's role in creating a trustworthy brand through 'green innovation,'" *Journal of Product & Brand Management*, 19(6): 440–451.

Hoffman, Andre J. (2001) *From Heresy to Dogma: An Institutional History of Corporate Environmentalism.* Stanford Business Books.

Hoggan, James (2009) *Climate Cover-Up: The Crusade to Deny Global Warming.* Greystone Books.

Howard-Grenville, Jennifer (2008) "Inside the 'black box,'" *Organization & Environment*, 19(1): 46–73.

Howard-Grenville, Jennifer, et al. (2008) "Constructing the license to operate: internal factors and their influence on corporate environmental decisions," *Law & Policy*, 30(1): 73–107.

Huff Post (2020) "Revealed: BP and Shell back anti-climate lobby groups despite pledges," September 28.

International Energy Agency (IEA) (2022) *Coal 2022: Analysis and Forecast to 2025.*

Influence Map (2019) "Big oil's real agenda on climate change: how the oil majors have spent $1bn since paris on narrative capture and lobbying on climate," March.

International Renewable Energy Agency (IRENA) (2023) *Renewable Energy Statistics 2023*.

International Renewable Energy Agency (IRENA) (2017) *Stranded Assets: How the Energy Transition Affects the Value of Energy Reserves, Buildings and Capital Stock*, July.

Jackofsky, Ellen F., et al. (1988) "Cultural values and the CEO: Alluring companions?" *The Academy of Management Executive* II(1): 39–49.

Jakob, Michael & Jerome Hilaire (2015) "Unburnable Fossil-Fuel Reserves." *Nature*, January 8, pp. 150–152.

Kennedy, Robert F. (1973) *Thirteen Days: A Memoir of the Cuban Missile Crisis*. W. W. Norton & Co.

Kenner, Dorio & Richard Heede (2021) "White knights, or horsemen of the apocalypse? prospects for Big Oil to align emissions with a 1.5c pathway," *Energy Research & Social Science*, September.

Liao, Carol, et al. (2021) "What top-performing Asian leaders do differently," Boston Consulting Group, June 15.

Magner, Mike (2011) *Poisoned Legacy: The Human Cost of BP's Rise to Power*, St. Martin's.

Mayo Clinic (2014) "Mayo Clinic model of care," https://history.mayoclinic.org/toolkit/mayo-clinic-model-of-care/

McKibben, Bill (2010) *Eaarth. Making a Life on a Tough New Planet*. Knopf.

McGlade, Christophe & Paul Ekins (2015) "The geographical distribution of fossil fuels unused when limiting global warming to 2c," *Nature*, January 8.

McKinsey (2021) "Global oil outlook to 2040," February.

Michaels, David (2008) *Doubt Is Their Product: How Industry's Assault on Science Threatens Your Health*, Oxford University Press.

Middle East Health (2023) "Best US hospital has unique model of care," September 27.

Murphy, Clarke (2022) *Sustainable Leadership: Lessons of Vision, Courage, and Grit from The CEOs Who Dared To Build A Better World*. Wiley.

New York Times (2010) "In recall, a role model stumbles," January 17.

New York Times (2010) "Johnson & Johnson accused of drug kickbacks," January 15.

New York Times (2012) "Hip maker discussed failures," February 21.

New York Times (2023) "Why heat waves are deepening China's addiction Coal," July 20.

Newsweek (2023) "America's greenest companies 2024."

Oreskes, Naomi & Erik M. Conway (2010) *Merchants of Doubt*. Bloomsbury.

Otto, Shawn (2016) *The War on Science: Who's Waging It, Why It Matters, What We Can Do About It*. Milkweed.

Porter, Michael & Claas van der Linde (1995) "Green and competitive: ending the stalemate," *Harvard Business Review*, September/October: 120–134.

Prince of Wales (2007) *The Prince's Accounting for Sustainability Project*. www.accountingforsustainability.org/

Reputation Institute (2011) *2011 Forbes Reputation Institute US RepTrak Pulse Study*. Top-Line Summary.

Richmond, Ben (2014) "'Clean coal' was rule false advertising by UK regulators," *Motherboard*.

Rindova, Violina P. & William H. Starbuck (1997) "Ancient Chinese theories of control," *Journal of Management Inquiry*, June.

Rosenzweig, Phil (2014) *The Halo Effect . . . and the Eight Other Business Delusions That Deceive Managers*. Free Press.

Schwartz, Peter & Blair Gibb (1999) *When Good Companies Do Bad Things: Responsibility and Risk in an Age of Globalization*. Wiley.

TerraChoice (2007) *The Six Sins of Greenwashing*.

TerraChoice (2010) *The Sins of Greenwashing*.

Union of Concerned Scientists (UCS) (2007) *Smoke, Mirrors & Hot Air: How ExxonMobil Uses Big Tobacco's Tactics to Manufacture Uncertainty on Climate Science*, January.

United Nations Global Compact & Russell Reynolds Associates (2020) "Leadership for the decade of action: a United Nations Global Compact-Russell Reynolds Associates study of the characteristics of sustainable business leaders."

Watson, Don (2003) *Death Sentences: How Cliches, Weasel Words, And Management-Speak Are Strangling Public Language*. Gotham.

Witt, Michael A. & Gordon Redding (Eds.) (2014). *The Oxford Handbook of Asian Business Systems*. Oxford.

World Economic Forum (2023a) "100 business leaders call for transformative policies at cop28 to accelerate decarbonization," https://www.weforum.org/press/2023/10/100-business-leaders-call-for-transformative-policies-at-cop28-to-accelerate-decarbonization/

World Economic Forum (2023b) "Alliance of CEO climate leaders share open letter to world leaders for COP28," October 24, https://www.weforum.org/agenda/2023/10/alliance-of-ceo-climate-leaders-open-letter-cop28/

Appendix Two: Diligent's Survey Results

Table 20.4 How Boards are Incorporating ESG Goals and Metrics Diligent Institute (2022)

Strategic plan	16%
Integrated risk management plan	11%
Director appointments	11%
Executive Compensation	10%
Executive team evaluations	9%
Employee onboarding and training	8%
Board evaluations	7%
Employee recruitment	7%
Director onboarding and training	7%
Executive recruitment	7%
M&A opportunities	5%
None	2%
Other	0.4%
Registering as a B Corp	0.2%
	100%

Source: Diligent Institute

Table 20.5 Methods to Increase Board ESG Fluency Diligent Institute (2022)

Bringing in outside consultants	24%
Getting training for the board and/or sending directors to training programs	21%
Conducting an ESG-specific board-effectiveness review to identify current gaps	16%
Conducting scenario planning around various ESH risks	15%
looking to appint new directors with ESG experience	12%
None	8%
Other	3%

Source: Diligent Institute

21 Afterword

Chapter 19 introduced the concept of the base of the pyramid (BoP) (Prahalad and Hart 2002, Hammond et al. 2007, London et al. 2011). This is one component in a model that utilizes the pyramid analogy to characterize the multiple layers of global economic activity. Sitting astride the pyramid are the approximately 1.6 billion citizens in the developed nations with their extensive purchasing power; at the very bottom are the lowest income countries with 1.25 billion or so individuals who subsist on meager daily earnings. Sandwiched between these two groups are two other groups with progressively higher incomes (UN HDI 2021/2022) (see Table 21.1).[1] Two entirely different models of sustainability emerge from the two extremes of this pyramid, and each is briefly summarized in turn.

The Top of the Pyramid

This is the market predominantly serviced by the large multinationals and their vast networks of suppliers. Wal-Mart is a pre-eminent example of this model. With an extraordinary capacity to leverage the nature of global business practices, perhaps no company has had such a polarizing effect on public discourse in the United States. While its social impacts on small business, urban cores and labor have been a lightning rod for criticism, its massive presence in the American economy entails less visible but extraordinary impacts on material throughput and energy use throughout its supply chain. As discussed earlier in this textbook (see chapter 16), because of its virtually unique role, Wal-Mart has the ability to dramatically change the face of commerce not only in the US, but also globally.

Table 21.1 Global Income Groupings

Category	# Countries	Total Population	Average Per Capita Income in Gross National Income Per Capita (2017 Ppp$) – total by group weighted by income	Range of Per Capita Income by Country
Very high human development	66	1.644 billion	$43,752	$14,664-$146,830
High human development	49	2.775 billion	$15,167	$5,308-$25,831
Medium human development	43	2.290 billion	$6,353	$2,482-$16,198
Low human development	32	1.248 billion	$3,009	$732-$5,025

Source: UN HDI (2021/2022)

DOI: 10.4324/9781003170754-25

The bottom of the pyramid

In 2010, Stuart L. Hart published the third edition of a work entitled *Capitalism at the Crossroads*, a distillation of over a decade of analysis and empirical research devoted to the creation of a new model of sustainable business anchored in at the bottom of the pyramid. He argued that the centralized solutions used by corporations targeting the market at the top of the pyramid cannot provide global sustainable solutions due to a wide array of factors. These include the environmental impact of most First World products, consumer inertia in the face of familiar and entrenched products (*the inertia of affluence*), established corporate culture, prices that do not reflect social cost, the vested interests of producers, and the inability of top-of-the-pyramid products to meet the needs of the bottom half of humanity. He cites the strategic reorientation of General Electric (Immelt et al. 2009), in calling for "reverse innovation" – the development of "disruptive technologies" or low-cost innovative products specifically designed for the Third World, which can be successfully migrated up to the developed world.

Hart maintains that the distributed business model that is inherent in this approach can produce more sustainable or "green" products at reasonable cost while raising the standard of living of the poorest members of the global community. Cited examples of corporations that have successfully implemented at least part of this model include Honda, Toyota, Sony, Galanz, Grameen Bank and Grameen Telecom, and Philips (Hart 2010). Hart speaks of a *Great Convergence* that seeks to "fuel growth through the incubation and rapid commercialization of distributed green technologies from the bottom-up." Several other authors have stressed the extraordinary opportunities of recognizing the potential market at the base of the pyramid that can encompass countries with both medium and low economic development.

The fundamental question is whether either one of these two divergent approaches or the variants of smaller scale sustainable enterprise described in chapter 19 represent an economic model that can meet the aspirations of all global citizens for a higher quality of life, while simultaneously reducing the massive throughput of energy and material that threaten to destroy the ecological and social fabric that sustains global civilization. Or, if none of these paths is the right one, is there some other nascent business model yet to emerge that satisfies the rigorous criteria of sustainability established by Anderson, McDonough-Braungart, and Robert that can meet this most extraordinary of challenges?

Final thoughts

It has been a dominant theme of this volume that sustainability can be achieved only with the whole-scale participation of the business sector – the engine of economic prosperity. To some authors, such as Anderson, McDonough, and Braungart, nothing short of a new industrial revolution will suffice. While sustainability brings with it challenges and threats to the established order, it also brings extraordinary opportunities not only for longrun corporate profitability but also for a more stable social, political, and physical environment. Figure 21.1 summarizes the dual nature of the challenge facing business, as epitomized by the ancient Chinese phrase for "crisis" composed of two characters: the first represents "danger" but the second represents "opportunity." To date, we have witnessed the adoption of numerous incremental steps towards sustainability by many mainstream businesses, as well as the emergence of social enterprise dedicated to the advancement of sustainable goals. What is ultimately required is the adoption of fundamental principles of sustainable strategy, process and products across *all* sectors of the global economy and *all* types and sizes of enterprises. This goal still remains a distant hope.

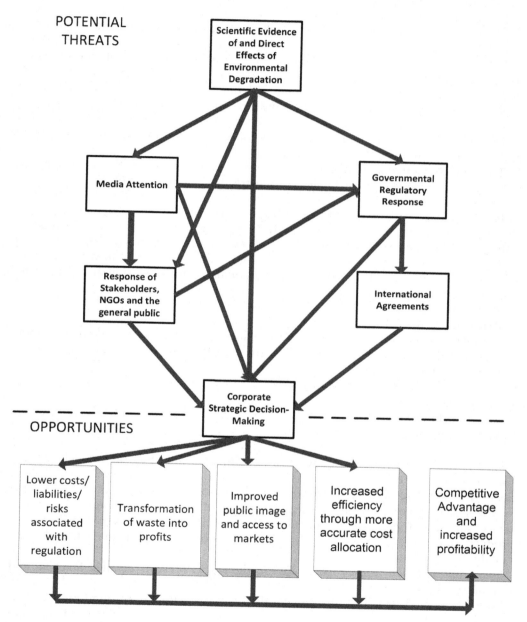

Figure 21.1 Dual Nature of Challenges Facing Business

While it is difficult to be optimistic considering the cascade of portentous scientific studies referenced in chapter 1, there is some potentially promising news. It is quite clear that the world will need to transition away from fossil fuels as soon as possible. This is proving to be an extraordinary challenge, considering the fossil fuel industry doubling down on fossil fuel production. The prospect of an electrified future relaying on renewable energy has seemed to be an elusive goal being outpaced by increasing demand for fossil fuels.

In November 2023, over one hundred member companies in the Alliance of CEO Climate Leaders, representing $1 trillion in global assets, wrote a letter to the attendees of the COP28 summit in Dubai arguing that the corporate sector "must commit to 100% decarbonized power systems by 2035 for richer economies, and help developing countries financially so they could ditch fossil fuels by 2040 at the latest" (Reuters October 24, 2023). The letter made four specific recommendations: (1) massively scale up investment in renewable energy and power networks and streamline permitting and regulatory processes, (2) lead by example on public procurement practices, (3) turbocharge nature- and technology-based carbon removals, and (4) simplify and harmonize climate disclosure and measuring standards (WEF October 24, 2023).

The list includes major companies from a broad range of sectors with the notable, and not surprising, exception of the fossil fuel industry. The complete list of the signatories is provided in the Appendix.

Is this goal even possible? Until recently, it was considered extremely unlikely if not impossible. However, a recent report by Tesla has suggested that this transition is not only possible but at a faster pace than currently contemplated. Entitled *Master Plan Part 3* (Tesla 2023), the report lays out an extraordinarily detailed path to the replacement of the fossil economy with electricity. The report summaries its conclusion in seven points:

- Storage required: 240 TWh
- Renewable power: 30TW
- Manufacturing investment required: $10 trillion. (To put this in perspective, the report estimates the projected twenty-year investment in fossil fuels at the 2022 investment rate would be $14 trillion).
- Energy required: ½ current production
- Land area required: 0.21%
- 2020 World GDP: 10%
- Insurmountable Resource Challenges: 0

The radical transformation of the world economy would rely on six technologies: solar, onshore and offshore wind, hydropower, nuclear power, and geothermal energy. Six critical steps are outlined in the report to achieve this goal: (1) repower the existing grid with renewables; (2) switch to electric vehicles; (3) switch to heat pumps in residential, business, and industry; (4) electrify high temperature heat delivery and hydrogen production; (5) use sustainable fuel for planes and boats; and (6) manufacture the sustainable energy economy.

As ambitious each of these steps appear, the report presents detailed financial and technological information and data on how each could be achieved.

What is now clear is that the coming decades may witness profound and dislocative global ecological and economic changes driven by accelerating climate change and increased resource and energy throughputs. Under the circumstances it is imperative that emerging business leaders understand the fundamental risks and opportunities associated with sustainability. Underlying this all is the broader necessity across all sectors of society of adopting a worldview that totally reconceptualizes the relationship between humanity and the environment. Human history has been largely based on the explicit view of human dominion over the environment with unlimited access to global resources. While some traditional civilizations managed to survive on the interest produced by natural capital from such sources as forests, soils, fisheries, and the assimilative capacity of the environment, the modern world now consumes this natural capital and considers it income. No sensible businessperson would consider liquidating their corporate capital and folding it into their income statement. Even for those few who have recognized this paradox, the inertia of affluence has given them a false sense of security and permitted the continued tolerance of this practice.

As outlined in Figure 1.3 the economy is embedded in the natural ecosystem and cannot function without it. Recognition of this fundamental principle is the essence of Ecological Economics, a discipline steadily gaining more credence, although still not universally accepted.

It has been the goal of these three volumes to outline explicitly what the problems are that we face collectively and explore what business, government, and society can do to rectify them. Nothing less than the survival of our civilization as we know it is at stake.

Note

1 Note that the classification of countries differs between the World Bank and United Nations. The World Bank (2023) lists the following average per capita income by category: $721 (low income), $2,517 (lower middle income), $10,530 (upper middle income), and $51,087 (high income).

References

Hammond, Allen L., et al. (2007) *The Next 4 Billion: Market Size and Business Strategy at the Base of the Pyramid*. World Bank Group.

Hart, Stuart L. (2010) *Capitalism at the Crossroads: Next Generation Business Strategies for a Post-Crisis World*. Third Edition. FT Press.

Immelt, Jeffrey R., et al. (2009) "How GE is disrupting itself," Harvard Business Review, October: 56–65.

London, Ted & Stuart L. Hart (2011) *Next Generation Business Strategies for the Base of the Pyramid: New Approached for Building Mutual Value*. Pearson FT Press.

Prahalad, C. K. & Stuart L. Hart (2002) "The fortune at the bottom of the pyramid," *Strategy + Business*, 26: 54–67.

Reuters (2023) "Nestle, Volvo among 130 companies urging COP28 agreement to ditch fossil fuels," October 23.

Tesla (2023) *Master Plan Part 3*. https://www.tesla.com/ns_videos/Tesla-Master-Plan-Part-3.pdf

United Nations (2022) *Human Development Report 2021/2022*.

World Bank (2023) "GNI per capita, Atlas Method (current US$)". https://data.worldbank.org/indicator/NY.GNP.PCAP.CD?year_high_desc=true

World Economic Forum (WEF) (2023) "Alliance of CEO climate leaders share open letter to world leaders for COP 28," October 24.

Appendix: Signatory Companies to Letter to COP28, November 2023

A.P. Moller-Maersk
ABB
Accenture
Arçelik
Arup
AstraZeneca
AVEVA
AXA
Bain & Company
Banco Santander
BASF SE
Bayer AG
BBVA

Bloomberg
Boston Consulting Group
Capgemini
Carlsberg Group
CEMEX

Coca-Cola HBC AG
Dalmia Cement (Bharat) Limited

Danfoss A/S
Dell Technologies
Deloitte
Dentsu Group Inc.
Deutsche Bank AG
Deutsche Post DHL Group
Drax
dsm-firmenich
Ecolab
Edge
EDP
Enel
ENGIE3
Envision
EQT
Ericsson

EY
3 Flex
GEA Group
Grundfos
Heineken NV
Henkel
Henry Schein Inc.
Hewlett Packard Enterprise
Hitachi, Ltd.
Holcim
HP Inc.
Iberdrola
Inditex

nfosys Limited
ndorama Ventures
ING
Ingka Group
JLL

Johnson Controls
Kearney

LG Chem
LGT
Mahindra Group
Majid Al Futtaim
ManpowerGroup Inc.
McKinsey & Company
Microsoft
Mott MacDonald Ltd
Naturgy
Nestlé
Newmont
NN Group
Novo Nordisk
Novozymes
Ørsted

Palo Alto Networks
PensionDanmark
PepsiCo
PwC
ReNew
Roland Berger GmbH
Royal Philips
Salesforce
SAP SE
Scania
Schneider Electric
Siemens AG
Siemens Gamesa Renewable
  Energy
Solvay
Sony Group Corporation
Standard Chartered Bank
Suntory Holdings
Swiss Reinsurance Company
  Ltd
Sysco
Takeda Pharmaceutical
  Company
Teck
Telenor
Trane Technologies
Tyson Foods Inc.
Umicore
Unilever
Vestas Wind Systems
Volvo Cars
Volvo Group
Wipro Limited
Workday
Xylem
Yara International
ZF Group
Zurich Insurance Group

Index

Note: Page numbers in *italics* indicate a figure and page numbers in **bold** indicate a table on the corresponding page.

Printed in the United States
by Baker & Taylor Publisher Services